Excel 97

Carole Tobias
Instructor, Microcomputing
Forsyth Technical Community College
Winston-Salem, NC

Glencoe
McGraw-Hill

New York, New York   Columbus, Ohio   Woodland Hills, California   Peoria, Illinois

This program has been prepared with the assistance of Gleason Group, Inc., Norwalk, CT.

Editorial Director: Pamela Ross

Developmental Editors: Thomas Cain, Michele Ruschhaupt

Copy Editor: Beth Conover

Composition: PDS Associates, Creative Ink, Inc., Gaskill Publishing Services

Screens were captured using Pizazz 5 for Windows from Application Techniques, Inc., Pepperell, MA.

Glencoe/McGraw-Hill

A Division of The ***McGraw-Hill*** *Companies*

Excel 97: A Professional Approach
Student Edition
ISBN 0-02-803322-1

Excel 97: A Comprehensive Approach
Student Edition
ISBN 0-02-803354-X

Excel 97: A Professional Approach
Annotated Instructor's Edition
ISBN 0-02-803326-4

Excel 97: A Comprehensive Edition
Annotated Teacher's Edition
ISBN 0-02-803356-6

Copyright © 1998 by The McGraw-Hill Companies, Inc. All rights reserved. Printed in the United States of America. Except as permitted under the United States copyright Act of 1976, no part of this publication may be reproduced or distributed in any form or by any means, or stored in a data base or retrieval system, without the prior written permission of the publisher.

5 6 7 8 9 10 027/043 01 00 99

Microsoft, Microsoft Excel, MS, MS-DOS, and Windows are either registered trademarks or trademarks of Microsoft Corporation in the United States and/or other countries.

PostScript is a registered trademark of Adobe Systems, Inc.

Contents

UNIT 3

Changing the Appearance of a Worksheet

UNIT 4

Formula and Template Construction 287

*Available in *Excel 97: A Professional Approach*

Preface

Excel 97 has been written to help you master Microsoft Excel for Windows. The text is designed to take you step-by-step through the features in Excel that you are likely to use in both your personal and business life.

Case Study

Learning about the features of Excel is one thing, but applying what you've learned is another. That's why a *Case Study* runs throughout the text. It offers you the opportunity to learn Excel within a realistic business context. Take the time to read the Case Study about Kearny-Sansome Accounting, Inc., a fictional business set in San Francisco. All of the worksheets for this course will deal with the clients of Kearny-Sansome.

Organization of the Text

The text includes seven *units*. Each unit is divided into smaller *lessons*. There are 21 lessons, each building on previously learned procedures. This building block approach, together with the Case Study and the features listed below, enables you to maximize your learning process.

Features of the Text

- *Objectives* are listed for each lesson
- The *estimated time* required to complete the lesson is stated
- Within a lesson, each *heading* corresponds to an objective
- *Exercises* that walk you through all procedures in a lesson are titled for easy reference
- *Key terms* are italicized and defined as they are encountered
- Extensive *graphics* display screen contents
- *Toolbar buttons* and *keyboard keys* are shown in the text when they are used
- *Large toolbar buttons in the margins* provide easy-to-see references
- Lessons contain important *Notes* and useful *Tips*
- A *Command Summary* lists the commands learned in the lesson
- *Using Help* introduces you to a Help topic related to the content of a lesson
- *Concepts Review* includes True/False, Short Answer, and Critical Thinking questions to focus on lesson content
- *Skills Review* provides skill reinforcement for each lesson
- *Lesson Applications* ask you to apply your skills in a more challenging way
- *Unit Applications* give you the opportunity to use all of the skills you learned throughout the unit

- ☑ The last application in each Unit Application asks you to create your own worksheet, developing your ability to create worksheets "from scratch."
- ☑ Appendices
- ☑ Glossary
- ☑ Index

Conventions Used in the Text

This text uses a number of conventions to help you learn the program and save your work.

- Text that you are asked to key either in **boldface** or as a separate figure.
- Filenames appear in **boldface**.
- You will be asked to save each file with your initials, followed by the exercise name. For example, an exercise may end with the instruction: "Save the workbook as *[your initials]***5-12.xls**."
- Menu letters you can key to activate a command are shown as they appear on screen, with the letter underlined (example: "Choose Print from the File menu."). Dialog box options are also shown this way (example: "Click Replace in the Find dialog box.").

If You Are Unfamiliar with Windows

If you're unfamiliar with Windows, you'll want to work through *Appendix A: "Windows Tutorial"* before beginning Lesson 1. You may also need to review *Appendix B: "Using the Mouse"* and *Appendix C: "Using Menus and Dialog Boxes"* if you've never used a mouse or Windows before.

Screen Differences

As you read about and practice each concept, illustrations of the screens have been provided to help you follow the instructions. Don't worry if your screen has a somewhat different appearance than the screen illustration. These differences result from variations in system and computer configurations.

Acknowledgments

We would like to thank the many reviewers of this text, and those students and teachers who have used this book in the past, for their valuable assistance. We would particularly like to thank the following reviewers: Susan Olson, Northwest Technical College, East Grand Forks, MN; and Jo Ann Weatherwax, Saddleback College, Mission Viejo, CA.

Installation Checklist

You'll need Microsoft Excel 97 to work through this textbook. Excel needs to be installed on an IBM or IBM-compatible microcomputer's hard drive (or on a network). To properly install Excel, refer to the manual that came with the program. The following checklist will help you evaluate the requirements for installing Excel.

Hardware

- ☑ Personal computer with a 486 or higher processor
- ☑ Hard drive
- ☑ 3.5-inch high-density disk drive or CD-ROM player
- ☑ Minimum of 8 MB of RAM
- ☑ Available hard disk space
- ☑ VGA or higher-resolution video monitor
- ☑ Printer (laser or ink-jet recommended)
- ☑ Mouse

Software

- ☑ Excel 97 for Windows or Microsoft Office 97 (3.5-inch disks or CD-ROM)
- ☑ Windows 95

What's Installed with Excel 97

The following table lists components installed during a "Typical" installation and others available when you perform a "Custom" installation. The table also indicates where you can find these components in both the Excel 97 and Office 97 Setup programs.

To add a component:

1. Load the CD-ROM or the "Setup" floppy disk originally used in the installation.
2. Click the Windows Start button, click Settings, and click Control Panel.
3. Double-click the Add/Remove Programs icon.
4. On the Install/Uninstall tab, click Add/Remove or Install, whichever is available.
5. Follow the Setup instructions. Click the item listed in the Options list in Setup. If you need to see more options for an item you've selected, click the Change Option button.

Component	Installed with Typical?	Office Setup Option	Excel Setup Option
Microsoft Excel Program Files	Yes	Microsoft Excel	Microsoft Excel Program Files
Help for Microsoft Excel	Yes	Microsoft Excel; Help and Sample Files	Help and Sample Files
Sample Files	Yes	Microsoft Excel; Help and Sample Files	Help and Sample Files
Microsoft Map	No	Microsoft Excel; Microsoft Map	Microsoft Map
Expense Report Template	No	Microsoft Excel; Spreadsheet Templates	Spreadsheet Templates
Invoice Template	Yes	Microsoft Excel; Spreadsheet Templates	Spreadsheet Templates
Purchase Order Template	No	Microsoft Excel; Spreadsheet Templates	Spreadsheet Templates
AccessLinks	No	Microsoft Excel; Add-ins	Add-ins
Analysis ToolPak	Yes	Microsoft Excel; Add-ins	Add-ins
AutoSave	Yes	Microsoft Excel; Add-ins	Add-ins
File Conversion Wizard	No	Microsoft Excel; Add-ins	Add-ins
Lookup Wizard	Yes	Microsoft Excel; Add-ins	Add-ins
Report Manager	No	Microsoft Excel; Add-ins	Add-ins
Conditional Sum Wizard	Yes	Microsoft Excel; Add-ins	Add-ins
Solver	No	Microsoft Excel; Add-ins	Add-ins
Template Wizard with Data Tracking	No	Microsoft Excel; Add-ins	Add-ins
Web Page Authoring (HTML) (Microsoft Excel Internet Assistant and Web Form Wizard)	No	Web Page Authoring (HTML)	Add-ins; Web Form Wizard and Add-ins; Internet Assistant Wizard
Bookshelf Basics	Yes	Bookshelf Basics	Not available
Microsoft Access Driver	Yes in Office; no in Excel Setup	Data Access; Database Drivers	Data Access; Database Drivers
Microsoft Excel Driver	Yes in Office; no in Excel Setup	Data Access; Database Drivers	Data Access; Database Drivers
Text Driver	Yes in Office; no in Excel Setup	Data Access; Database Drivers	Data Access; Database Drivers
Microsoft Query	No	Data Access; Microsoft Query	Data Access; Microsoft Query
Graphics filters (Office: 18 filters; Microsoft Excel: 8 filters)	Some in Office; no in Excel Setup	Converters and Filters; Graphics Filters	Converters and Filters; Graphics Filters
Microsoft Binder Program Files	Yes	Microsoft Binder	Not available
Office Assistant	Yes	Office Tools	Office Assistant
Spelling Checker	Yes	Office Tools	Tools
Organizational Chart	Yes	Office Tools	Not available
Popular Clipart	Yes	Office Tools	Not available
Clip Gallery	Yes	Office Tools	Not available
Find Fast	Yes	Office Tools	Tools
Microsoft TrueType fonts (six fonts)	Yes	Office Tools; Microsoft TrueType fonts	Not available
Find All Word Forms	Yes	Office Tools	Not available

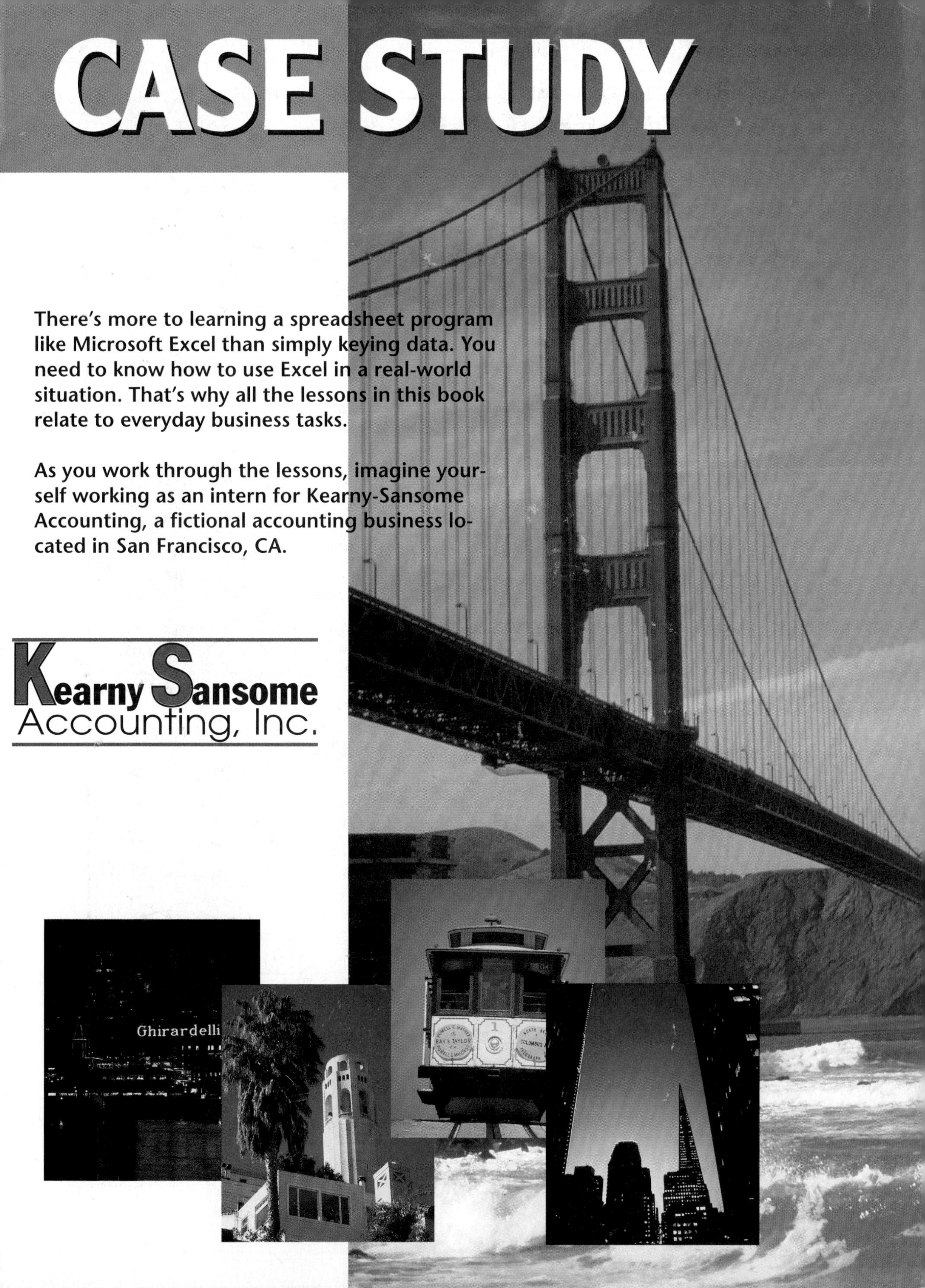

CASE STUDY

There's more to learning a spreadsheet program like Microsoft Excel than simply keying data. You need to know how to use Excel in a real-world situation. That's why all the lessons in this book relate to everyday business tasks.

As you work through the lessons, imagine yourself working as an intern for Kearny-Sansome Accounting, a fictional accounting business located in San Francisco, CA.

CASE STUDY

Kearny-Sansome Accounting, Inc.

240 Montgomery St., San Francisco, CA 94101
(415)555-2000

Kearny-Sansome Accounting, Inc. was formed in 1908 by a group of San Francisco businesspeople to provide accounting services to small San Francisco businesses trying to recover from the earthquake of 1906. The company has grown over the years, but still focuses on smaller businesses. Located in San Francisco's busy Financial District, Kearny-Sansome has clients from all across the nation, although the majority of clients are still from California. The company provides accounting, data processing, and consulting assistance to its clients.

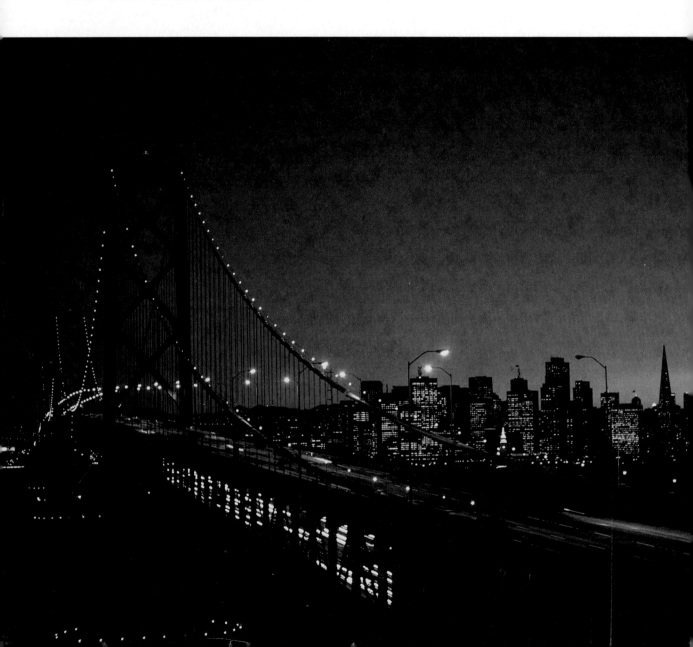

Working As an Intern

You'll be working as an intern at Kearny-Sansome. This involves working with one client for a few weeks, then working with another client for a few weeks, and so on. Kearny-Sansome feels that it's important for new employees to gain experience working with a variety of clients before they begin working on their own.

Kearny-Sansome expects that any incoming employee will have a solid foundation of skills.*

Basic Skills
Reading, writing, arithmetic/mathematics, listening, and speaking

Thinking Skills
Creative thinking, decision making, problem solving, being able to visualize problems and solutions, knowing how to learn, and reasoning

Personal Qualities
Responsibility, self-esteem, sociability, self-management, and integrity/honesty

In addition, Kearny-Sansome believes that the five competencies identified below are the keys to job-performance.

Keys to Successful Job-Performance*

1. Resources: Identifies, organizes, plans, and allocates resources

A. *Time*—Selects goal-relevant activities, ranks them, allocates time, and prepares and follows schedules

B. *Money*—Uses or prepares budgets, makes forecasts, keeps record, and makes adjustments to meet objectives

C. *Material and Facilities*—Acquires, stores, allocates, and uses materials or space efficiently

D. *Human Resources*—Assesses skills and distributes work accordingly, evaluates performance and provides feedback

2. Interpersonal: Works with others

A. *Participates as a Member of a Team*—Contributes to the group effort

B. *Teaches Others New Skills*

C. *Serves Clients/Customers*—Works to satisfy customers' expectations

D. *Exercises Leadership*—Communicates ideas to justify a position, persuades and convinces others, responsibly challenges existing procedures and policies

E. *Negotiates*—Works toward agreements involving exchanges of resources, resolves differing interests

F. *Works with Diversity*—Works well with men and women from diverse backgrounds

3. Information: Acquires and uses information

A. *Acquires and Evaluates Information*

B. *Organizes and Maintains Information*

C. *Interprets and Communicates Information*

D. *Uses Computers to Process Information*

4. Systems: Understands complex relationships

A. *Understands Systems*—knows how social, organizational, and technological systems work and operates effectively with them

B. *Monitors and Corrects Performance*—Distinguishes trends, predicts impacts on system operations, diagnoses systems' performance and corrects malfunctions

C. *Improves or Designs Systems*—Suggests modifications to existing systems and develops new or alternative systems to improve performance

5. Technology: Works with a variety of technologies

A. *Selects Technology*—Chooses procedures, tools or equipment including computers and related technologies

B. *Applies Technology to Task*—Understands overall intent and proper procedures for setup and operation of equipment

C. *Maintains and Troubleshoots Equipment*—Prevents, identifies, or solves problems with equipment, including computers and other technologies

* These skills and competencies were identified by the Secretary of Labor and the Secretary's Commission on Achieving Necessary Skills (SCANS). They are included in the report *What Work Requires of Schools: A SCANS Report for America 2000*, published in June, 1991, by the U.S. Department of Labor.

CASE STUDY

Your Clients During the Intern Period

During your intern period at Kearny-Sansome, you will be working with seven clients.

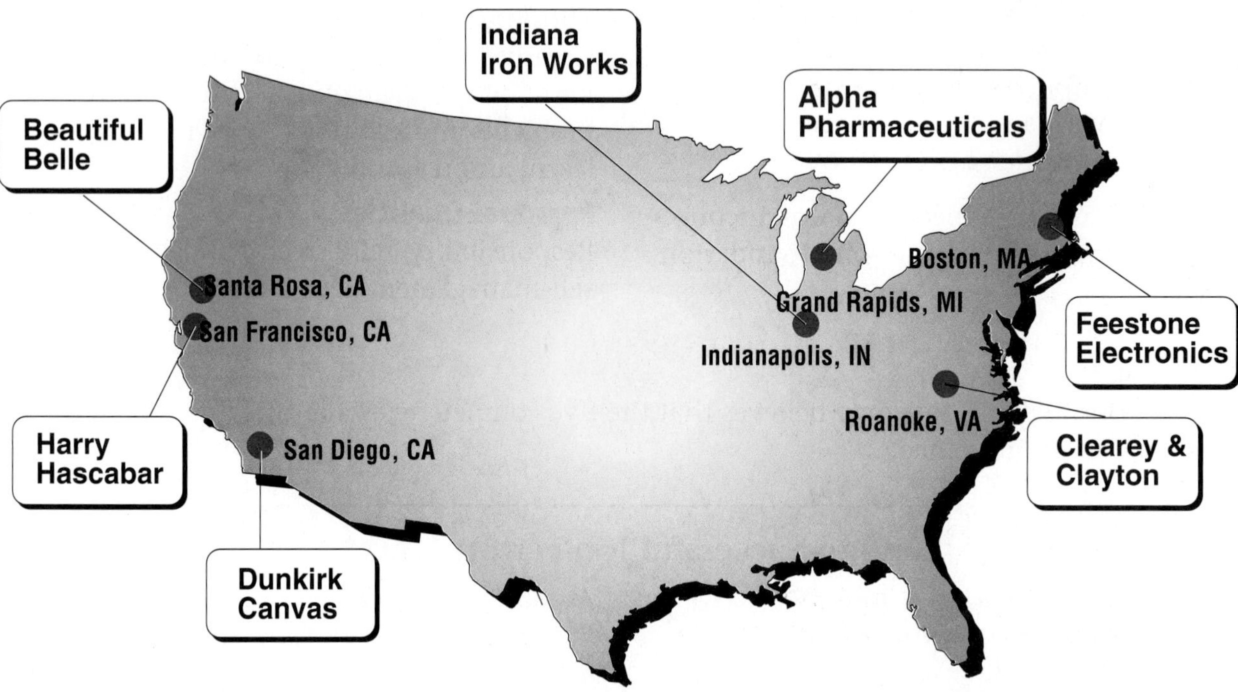

ALPHA Pharmaceuticals

Alpha Pharmaceuticals

145 Bostwick Ave., NE
Grand Rapids, MI 49503
(616)555-4698

Alpha Pharmaceuticals manufactures generic over-the-counter drugs, such as ibuprofen, acetaminophen, and aspirin, for large grocery and drug-store chains. You'll be helping Alpha Pharmaceuticals study historical data about pain relievers. Alpha's president, Mark Latzko, thinks that people are switching from aspirin to ibuprofen. Your worksheets will indicate if he's right.

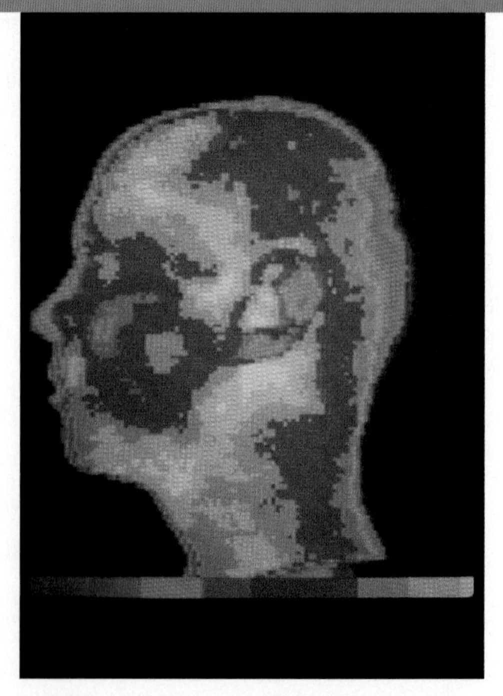

Beautiful
BelleCompany

Beautiful Belle Company

103 Professional Center Drive
Santa Rosa, CA 95403
(707)555-2398

The Beautiful Belle Company manufactures a moderately priced line of cosmetics. The company is currently promoting a product called "Sun Soft," a natural, hypo-allergenic lotion that has refined almond and sesame oils as main ingredients. Renata Santo, the Southwest regional sales manager, is test marketing Sun Soft in the Phoenix area. You'll be developing worksheets that track Sun Soft's sales performance against a competing product.

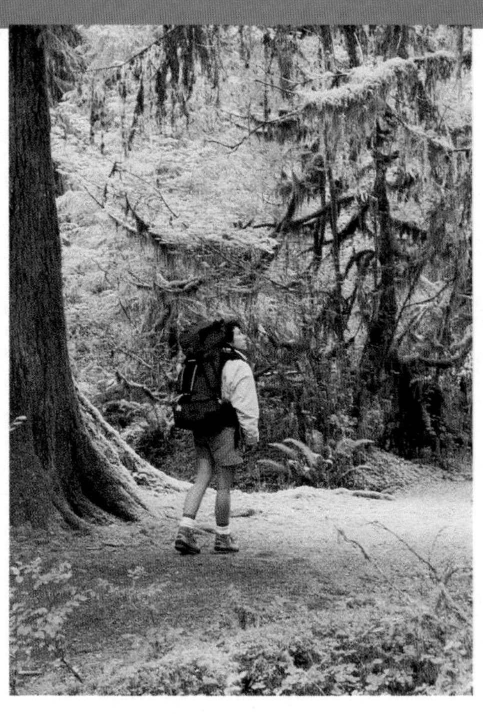

Clearey & Clayton

411 Fort Belknap Dr.
Roanoke, VA 24038
(703)555-0371

Clearey & Clayton got its start by producing scaled-down backpacks and camping gear for small people and children. They now produce camping gear such as backpacks, tents, and kayaks for people of all sizes. You'll be helping Bettina Clearey and John Clayton develop a promotional product list and an order blank for a mail-order catalog.

Dunkirk Canvas Company

7270 Mesa Drive
San Diego, CA 9211
(619)555-8954

Dunkirk Canvas Company used to make sails for boats. While they continue to make sails today, their fastest growing business is producing made-to-order canvas boat covers. In fact, the boat cover business has become so big, that the company now finds that it sometimes needs to use independent contractors to make some of their sails. You'll be helping Frank Bouchard and Mickey Finnegan computerize their business records and track independent contractors.

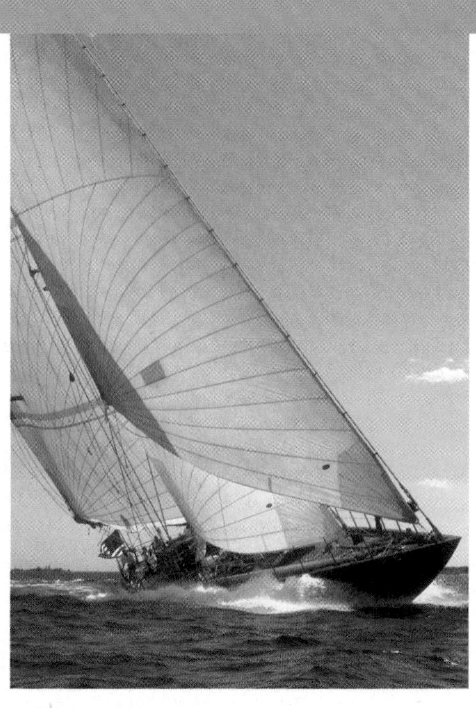

Feestone Electronics

17 New Rutherford Ave.
Boston, MA 02129
(617)555-8700

Feestone Electronics is a nationwide distributor of business machines, such as cellular phones, fax machines, and copy machines. Each of its four regional offices writes its own invoices and keeps track of its own sales and inventory. They provide data to the central office each quarter. You'll be helping Craig Herman, the company's bookkeeper, put together a system that will use e-mail to consolidate data from all the regional offices in one worksheet.

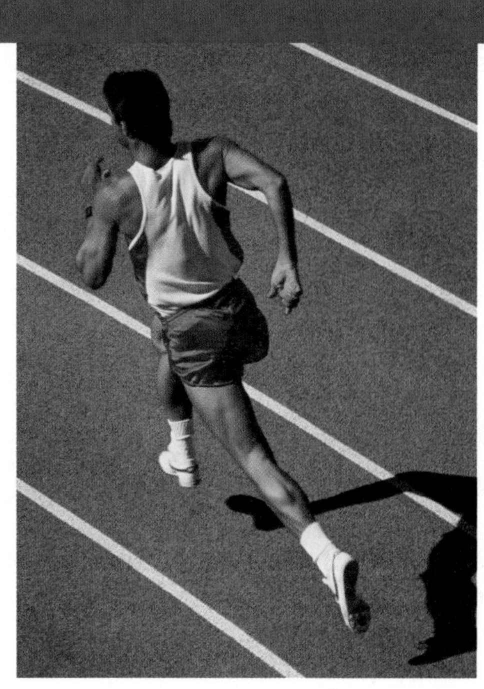

Harry Hascabar's Hand-Crafted Leather Goods

25529 Taylor St.
San Francisco, CA 94194
(415)555-5895

Harry Hascabar has five shops in San Francisco that sell leather goods such as briefcases, shoes, and handbags. But Harry's first love is running. He's been making special running shoes for long-distance runners for over a decade—and now he wants to start a new company that will sell his shoes and other products for runners. You'll be helping Harry Hascabar create worksheets that present his unique experimental data in attractive charts.

Indiana Iron Works

45 W. 26th St.
Indianapolis, IN 46206
(317)555-4510

Indiana Iron Works is an iron and steel foundry started in 1854 (as "Indiana Horseshoes"). Today, the company specializes in producing beautiful decorative iron work, much of it based on the intricate iron work of the early Renaissance. Over the years, Indiana Iron Works has also acquired quite a bit of property that it now is interested in selling. You'll be helping Dexter Peabody IV, the president of the company, create a customer database, as well as a database of the property holdings of the company.

CASE STUDY

Preview

As you learn Microsoft Excel, you'll be producing professional worksheets, charts, and maps for the clients of Kearny-Sansome Accounting. You'll learn all of the important Excel features, from keying data and creating simple worksheets, to using functions, creating charts and maps, and using Excel's database features. By "working" as an intern at Kearny-Sansome Accounting, you'll gain experience that you can apply to a real-world business.

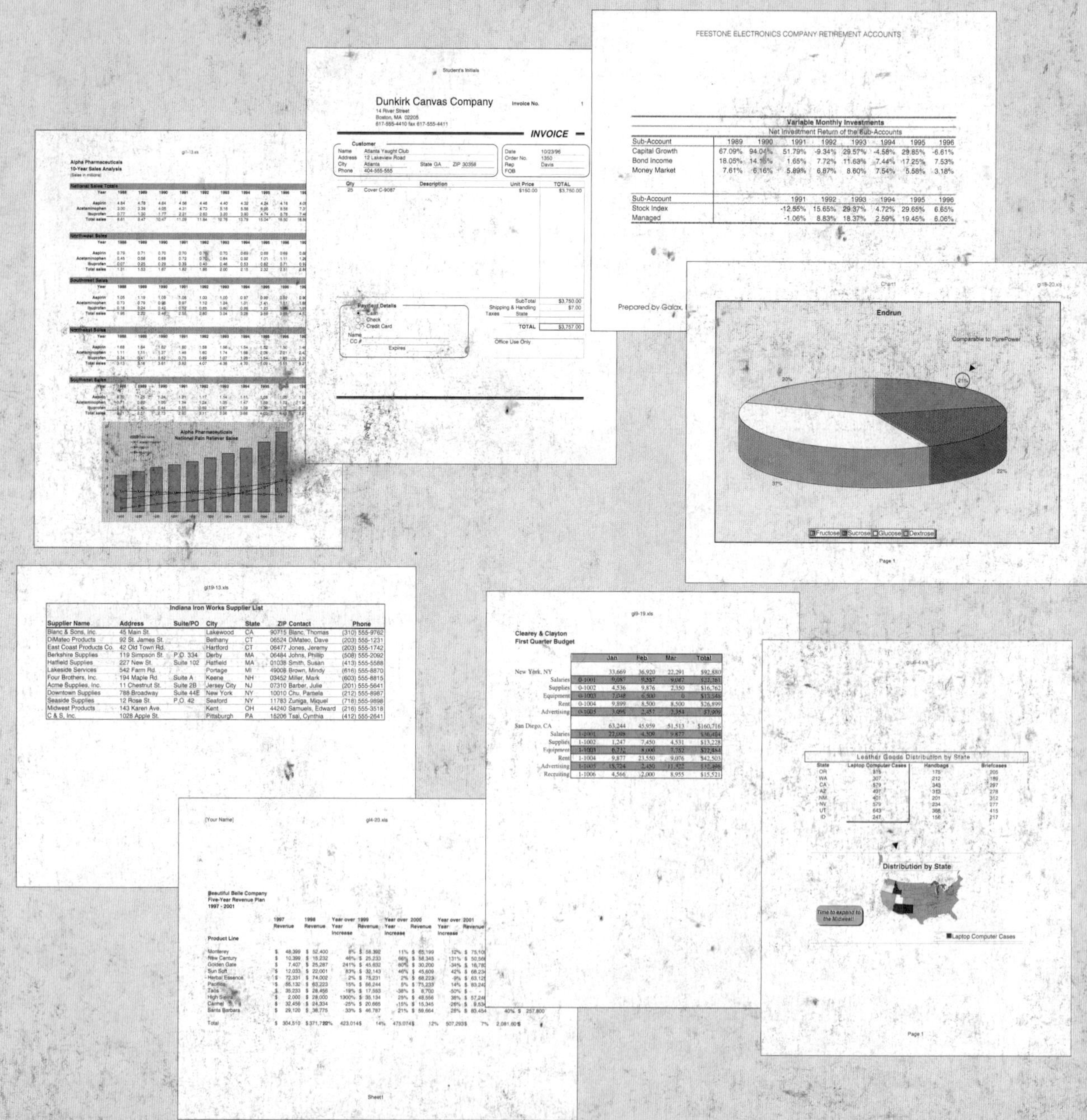

UNIT

1

Basic Skills

LESSON 1	What Is Excel?
LESSON 2	Creating a Simple Worksheet
LESSON 3	Enhancing a Simple Worksheet

Alpha Pharmaceuticals

ALPHA Pharmaceuticals

Drug Company Banks on Growing Pains

Alpha Pharmaceuticals manufactures generic over-the-counter drugs, such as ibuprofen and aspirin, for large grocery and drug-store chains. Because demographic studies are showing that the average age of the general population is trending upward, and since older people tend to have more minor aches and pains than younger people, Alpha anticipates that the pain-reliever business will grow steadily into the 21st century.

Alpha's president, Mark Latzko, has asked his market-research team to study the company's historical data to confirm his belief that people are switching from aspirin to ibuprofen as the pain reliever of choice.

Jean Brody, who heads up the market-research team, has requested the following information to fulfill Mark's request:

- ✔ A detailed worksheet showing sales of aspirin, acetaminophen, and ibuprofen for the past ten years in each of the four national sales regions, with a chart illustrating trends. **(Lesson 1)**
- ✔ A summary sheet showing Alpha's sales of each product for the last four years and projected sales for the current year. **(Lesson 2)**
- ✔ An attractively styled worksheet showing the five-year sales analyses developed in Lesson 2. **(Lesson 3)**

What Is Excel?

OBJECTIVES

After completing this lesson, you will be able to:

1. **Start Excel.**
2. **Change the active cell.**
3. **Navigate between worksheets.**
4. **Open and close workbooks.**
5. **Navigate within a worksheet.**
6. **Key data in a worksheet.**
7. **Save a workbook.**
8. **Print a worksheet and close Excel.**

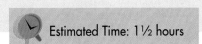

Estimated Time: 1½ hours

Microsoft Excel is an electronic workbook that gives you the ability to perform business and scientific calculations effortlessly. It provides powerful charting, database management, and macro programming capabilities. Although Excel is powerful, it's very intuitive and easy to use. Once you learn a few basics, you'll become a productive Excel user very quickly.

Starting Excel

There are several ways to start Excel, depending on your system setup and personal preferences. For example, you can use the Start button on the Windows

FIGURE 1-1
Shortcut icon to start Excel

taskbar, the Microsoft Office Shortcut Bar, or Windows Explorer. If you have an Excel shortcut on your desktop, you can double-click it to start Excel.

NOTE: Windows provides many ways to start applications. If you have problems, ask your instructor for help.

EXERCISE  1-1 Start Excel

1. Turn on your computer. Windows loads.
2. Click the Start button on the Windows taskbar and point to Programs.

FIGURE 1-2
Starting Excel from the Windows taskbar

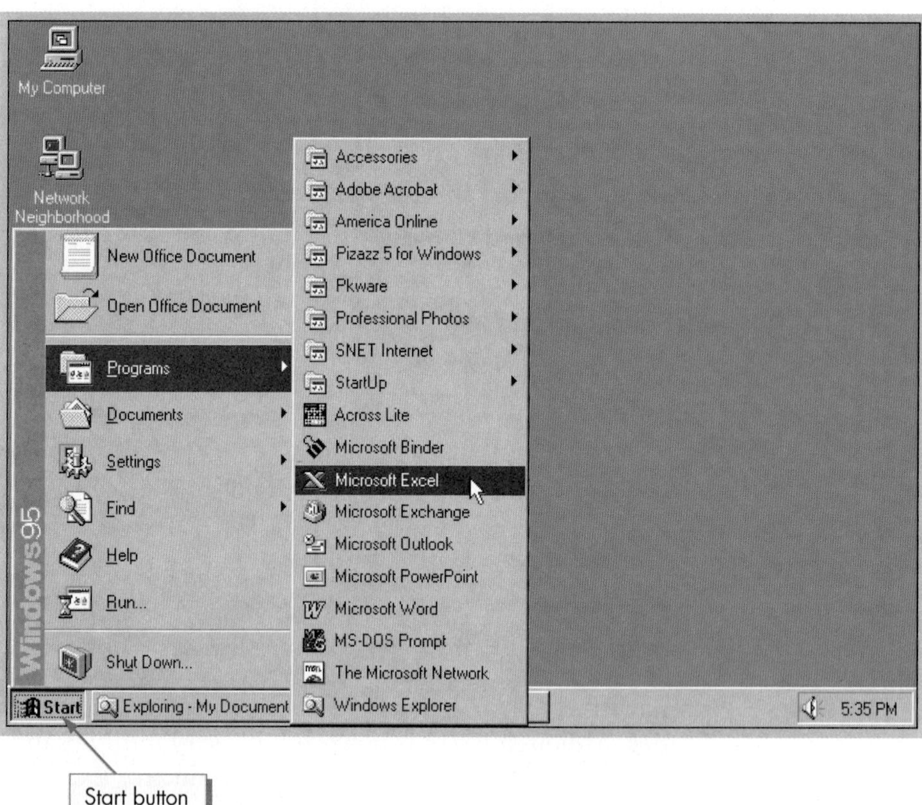

3. Click Microsoft Excel. If you do not see Microsoft Excel listed, you may have to point first to the program group that contains Excel (such as Microsoft Office). The program is loaded in a few seconds and the Excel window appears.

FIGURE 1-3
The Excel window

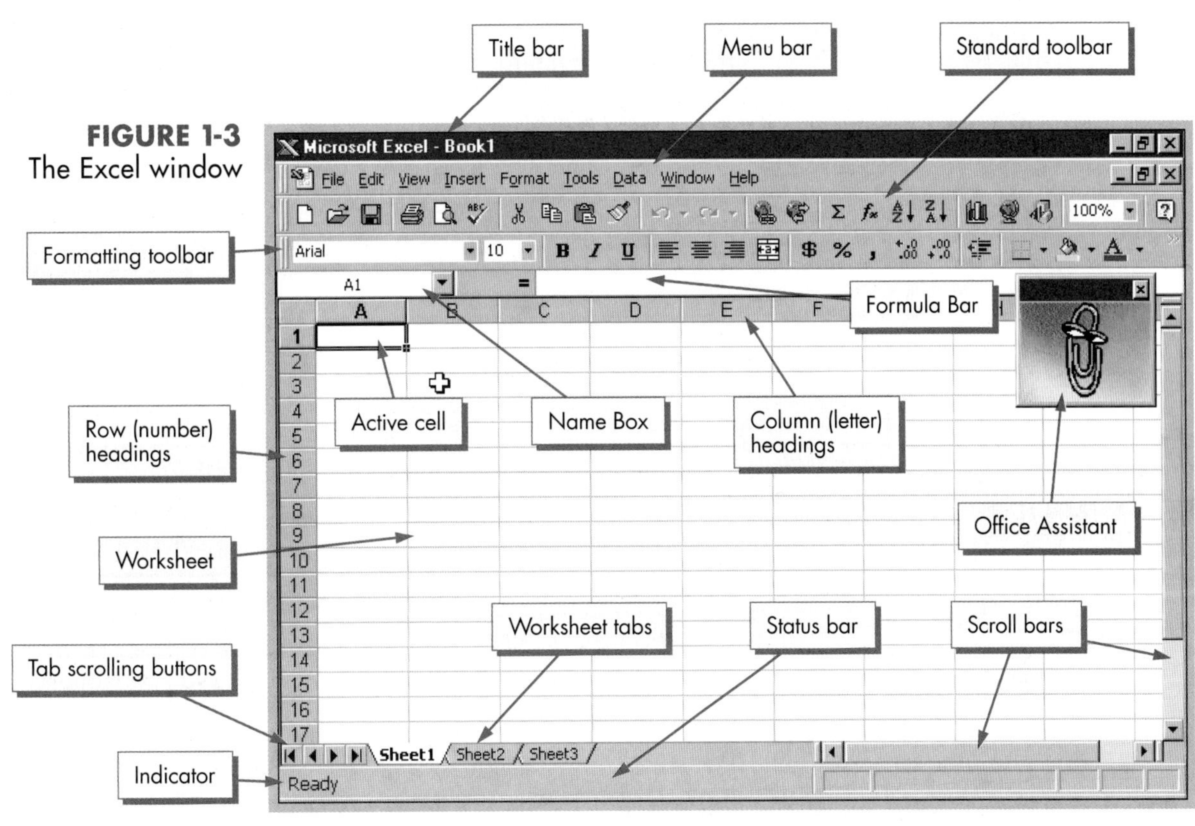

TABLE 1-1 Parts of the Excel Screen

PART OF SCREEN	PURPOSE
Title bar	Displays the name of the workbook. The opening Excel window is always called "Book1."
Menu bar	Contains the menus that you use to perform various tasks. You can open menus using the mouse or the keyboard.
Toolbars	Contain buttons you click to initiate commands. Each button is represented by an icon. Excel opens with the Standard and Formatting toolbars displayed.
Office Assistant	Provides tips as you work and suggests Help topics related to the work you're doing.
Name Box	Indicates where data being keyed or edited will appear on the worksheet.
Formula Bar	Displays formulas used in the worksheet.

continues

TABLE 1-1 **Parts of the Excel Screen** ***continued***

PART OF SCREEN	PURPOSE
Worksheet	Area where you enter and work with data.
Column headings	Columns on the worksheet. Columns are labeled with letters.
Row headings	Rows on the worksheet. Rows are labeled with numbers.
Scroll bars	Used with the mouse to move right or left and up or down within the worksheet.
Tab Scroll buttons	Used to scroll between sheet tabs.
Worksheet tabs	Used to move from one worksheet to another.
Status bar	Displays information about a selected command or an operation in progress.
Indicators	Displays modes of operation, such as NUM when the number keypad is on.
Active cell	Cell that is current—that is, ready to receive information.

EXERCISE 1-2 Identify Toolbar Buttons

Some parts of the Excel window, such as toolbar buttons, are identified for you when you point to them with the mouse.

1. Position the pointer over the New icon on the Standard toolbar. You click this button to open a new workbook. The icon appears as a button when you point to it and a *ScreenTip* (a box with the button name) appears below the button.

NOTE: Some toolbar icons are light gray, which indicates they are not currently available. Even if an icon is gray, you can identify it by positioning the mouse pointer over it.

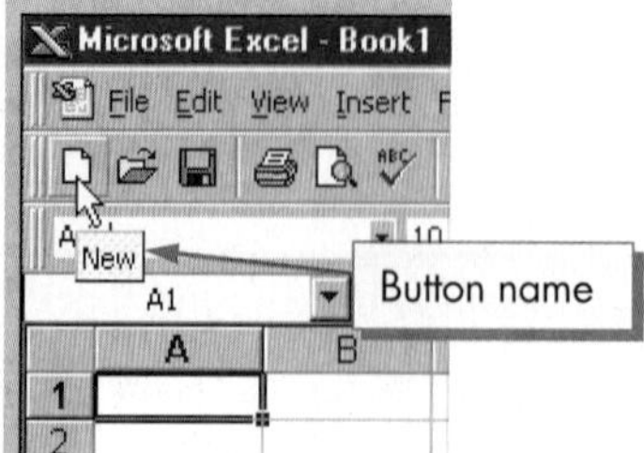

FIGURE 1-4 Identifying a toolbar button

2. Position the pointer over the Office Assistant button on the Standard toolbar. Click the button to display the Office Assistant's balloon. Notice that when you click (or "press") a button, it briefly becomes darker.

TIP: Use the Office Assistant to discover quicker, easier ways to work. When you display the Office Assistant, it provides Help topics and tips that can simplify and speed your tasks.

3. Click [?] again. The Office Assistant balloon is hidden.
4. Move the pointer to the Close button [x] in the Office Assistant box and click the left mouse button. This turns off the Office Assistant. Leave it off unless your instructor directs you to turn it on.
5. Point to other toolbar buttons to identify them.

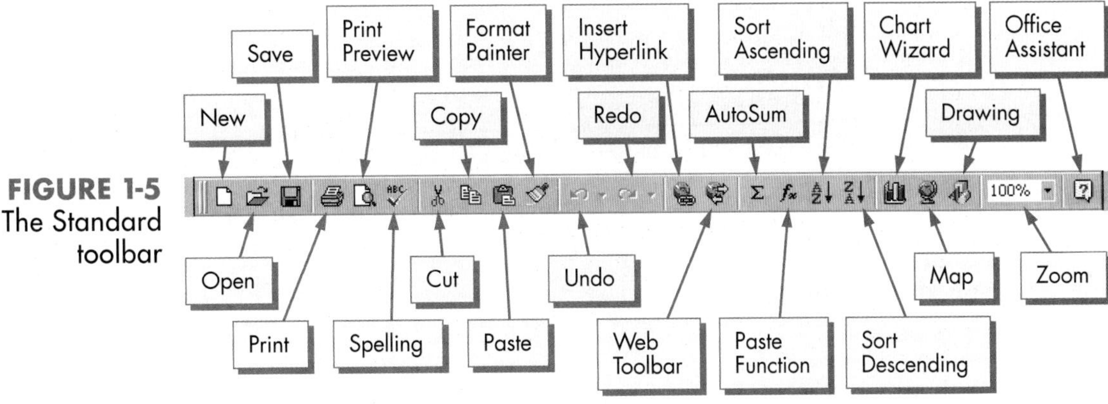

FIGURE 1-5 The Standard toolbar

EXERCISE 1-3 Identify Menus and Menu Buttons

1. Move the pointer to File on the menu bar. Click the left mouse button to open the menu. See Figure 1-6 on the next page.

TIP: The menu shows which commands have corresponding toolbar buttons and keyboard shortcuts. Notice that you can save a worksheet by choosing Save from the File menu, by clicking the Save button on the Standard toolbar, or by pressing Ctrl+S.

2. Without clicking the mouse button, move the pointer to highlight one of the File menu options.
3. With the menu open and without clicking the mouse button, move the pointer to Edit on the menu bar. This opens the Edit menu.
4. Click Edit to close the menu.
5. Click View to open the View menu. Without clicking the mouse button, move the pointer to the Toolbars menu option.The right-pointing arrow indicates a submenu that shows which toolbars are currently displayed.

FIGURE 1-6
Displaying menu options

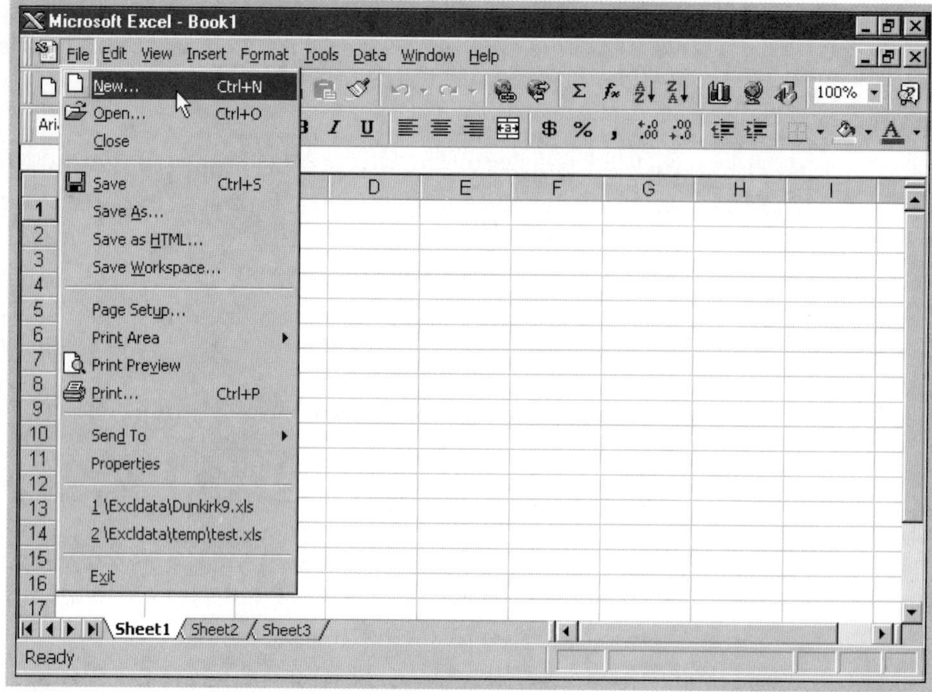

NOTE: You can open a menu using the keyboard. Press Alt and the underlined letter on the menu. For example, press Alt+F to open the File menu. Press Esc twice to exit the menu.

Changing the Active Cell

When you start Excel, a blank *workbook* named "Book1" appears, ready for you to create a new worksheet. The workbook contains three *worksheets* that you can visualize as pages bound in a notebook. You can add or remove worksheets from the workbook. A workbook can contain from 1 to 255 worksheets.

Each worksheet contains a grid that defines a series of rows and columns. A worksheet can use as many as 65,536 rows and 256 columns to store data. Rows are numbered. Columns are labeled A through Z, then AA through AZ, and so forth, up to column IV.

The intersection of a row and a column forms a rectangle called a *cell*. Each cell in a worksheet has a unique *cell address* that is determined by the column and row in which it is located. A cell address always indicates the column letter followed by the row number (for example, A1, C25, or AF14).

The cell that is current—that is, ready to receive information—is called the *active cell*. The active cell has a heavy border and its address is displayed in the Name Box.

EXERCISE 1-4 Change the Active Cell

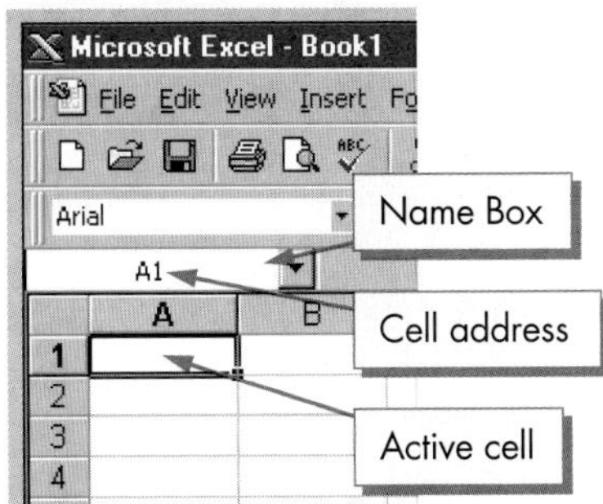

FIGURE 1-7
The Name Box shows the address of the active cell.

1. Press the Down Arrow key [↓] twice. Notice that the active cell changes.
2. Hold down the Ctrl key [Ctrl] and press the Home key [Home]. Cell A1 becomes active. You can tell it's active because a heavy border surrounds it. The Name Box displays the address of the active cell.

NOTE: Whenever keyboard combinations (such as [Ctrl]+[Delete]) are indicated, hold down the first key while you press the second key. Release the second key and then release the first key. An example of the entire sequence is: Hold down [Ctrl], press [Home], release [Home], release [Ctrl]. With practice, you'll find it natural to execute this sequence.

3. Press [↓] three times and press the Right Arrow key [→] five times. F4 is now the active cell.

Navigating Between Worksheets

To move between worksheets in a workbook, you can use:

- keyboard commands
- worksheet tabs, which also allow you to move to a specific worksheet in a workbook

EXERCISE 1-5 Navigate Between Worksheets

1. Press [Ctrl]+[PgDn]. The next worksheet appears in the window. The worksheet tab for Sheet2 is highlighted. The active cell is A1. See Figure 1-8 on the next page.
2. Press [Ctrl]+[PgUp] to return to Sheet1.
3. Click the worksheet tab for Sheet3. Worksheet 3 appears in the window.
4. Click the worksheet tab for Sheet1 to return to worksheet 1.

FIGURE 1-8
The worksheet tab for worksheet 2 is highlighted.

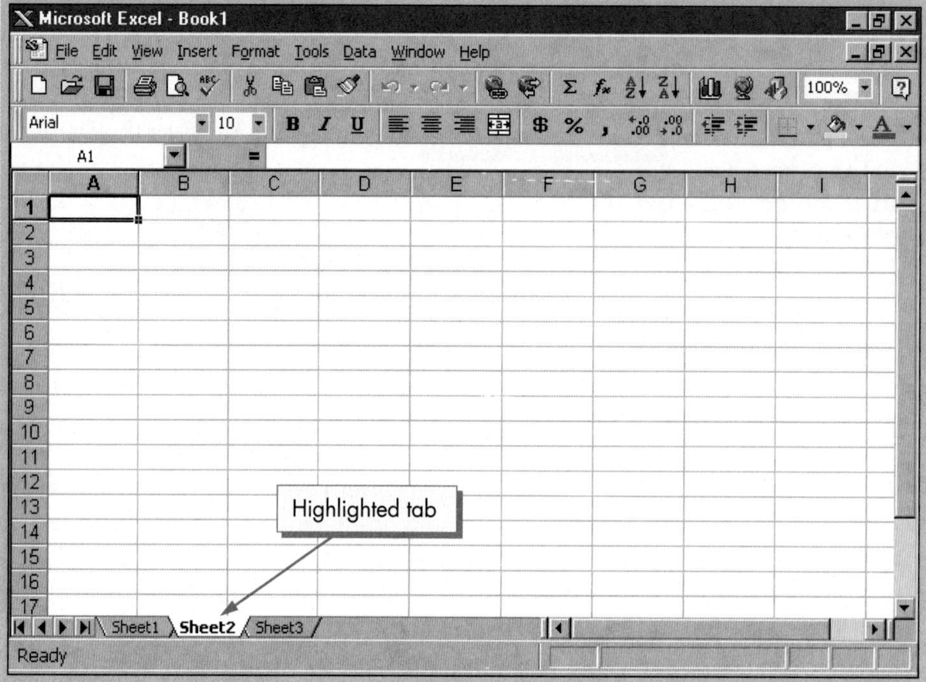

FIGURE 1-9
Tab scrolling buttons

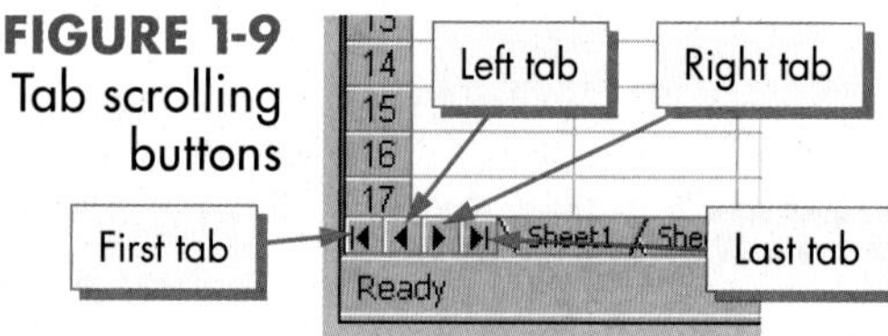

NOTE: You can use the tab scrolling buttons to scroll between sheet tabs if all tabs are not visible on the screen. For example, the First Tab button and the Last Tab button display the first and last tabs in the workbook. Note that the tab scrolling buttons only scroll the tabs. To open a worksheet, you must click the worksheet tab.

TABLE 1-2 Keyboard Commands for Navigating Between Worksheets

KEYSTROKE	ACTION
Ctrl + PgDn	Move to the next worksheet in the workbook.
Ctrl + PgUp	Move to the previous worksheet in the workbook.

Closing and Opening Workbooks

In the following exercises, you look at a workbook containing a 10-year sales analysis for Alpha Pharmaceuticals as you learn basic Excel skills. The worksheet is fairly large, showing historical data for Alpha's four sales regions and each of its products: aspirin, acetaminophen, and ibuprofen.

To open an existing workbook that's stored on a hard disk or floppy disk, you can:

- Choose Open from the File menu.
- Click the Open button on the Standard toolbar.

In the next exercise, you use the Open button.

EXERCISE 1-6 Close and Open Workbooks

Before you open Alpha's workbook, you close "Book1," the workbook you were just examining. Normally, you would save the file before you close it, but since you didn't key any data in "Book1," it isn't worth saving. (You learn how to save a file later in this lesson.)

1. Choose Close from the File menu.

NOTE: If no workbook is open, the workbook window is gray. You can open an existing workbook or start a new one.

2. Click on the Standard toolbar. The Open dialog box appears.

FIGURE 1-10 The Open dialog box

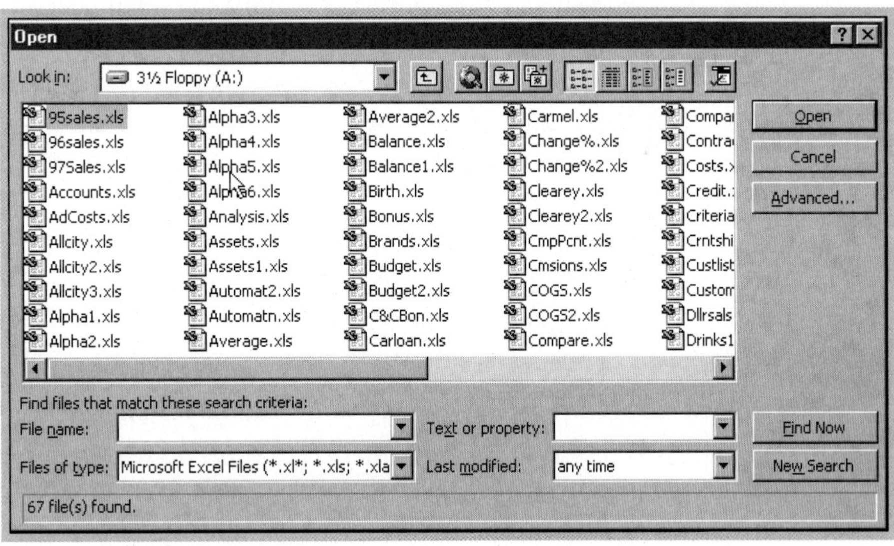

3. Double-click the file **Alpha1.xls** (you could also click it and then click the Open button). Excel opens the Alpha Pharmaceuticals worksheet.

NOTE: You may have to change the folder or the drive to locate the file. Follow your instructor's directions to find the files that you open in this lesson and in future lessons.

The Alpha Pharmaceuticals worksheet is formatted using shading, varying column widths, and several type sizes and number formats. These features are easy to use and will be discussed in later lessons.

Navigating Within a Worksheet

You can move to any location in the worksheet by pressing the Arrow keys, but you can move to distant cells quickly using the scroll bar and keyboard commands.

Notice that "Alpha Pharmaceuticals" appears in both the Formula Bar and the active cell. The cell address A1 appears in the Name Box.

EXERCISE  1-7 Navigate Within a Worksheet Using Keyboard Commands

1. Press the Down Arrow key ↓ four times. "National Sales Totals" appears in the Formula Bar and the cell address A5 appears in the Name Box.
2. Using ↓ and the Right Arrow key →, move to cell C8. A formula that adds data in cells C17, C25, C34, and C43 appears in the Formula Bar. The formula result, 4.78, appears in the active cell.
3. Press Home. The active cell moves to column A in the current row.
4. Press the PgDn key PgDn to move down one window.

NOTE: The actual rows or columns that are visible vary from screen to screen, depending on the screen's size and settings.

5. Press the PgUp key PgUp to move up to the original rows.
6. Press the Alt key Alt+PgDn to move one window to the right.
7. Press Alt+PgUp to move back to the original columns.
8. Press Ctrl+↓ four times. Cell A17 is now the active cell. Each time you press Ctrl+↓, the active cell jumps to the edge of a group of cells containing data.
9. Press Ctrl+↑ three times. Cell A11 is now active.
10. Press Ctrl+→ once. The active cell jumps to cell K11, the last column in the table that starts at cell A5.
11. Press Ctrl+→ again. Column IV, the very last column in the worksheet, is displayed.

12. Press Ctrl+↓. Row 65536, the last row in the worksheet, appears. Move up or across the worksheet to get an idea of its huge size.
13. Press Ctrl+Home. Pressing this key combination always brings you back to cell A1.
14. Press Ctrl+End. The active cell moves to the cell in the last row in the last column that contains data or formatting instructions.

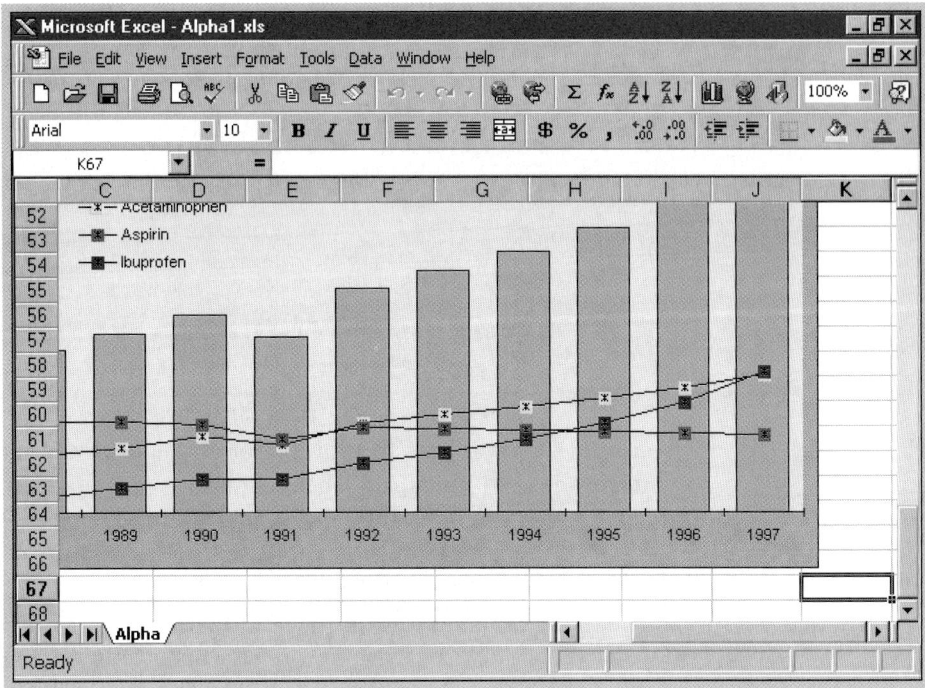

FIGURE 1-11 Cell K67 is now active.

NOTE: A chart showing Alpha Pharmaceuticals' sales figures appears at the bottom of the worksheet. The numbers contained in the worksheet are used to create the chart. You learn more about using worksheets to generate charts in later lessons.

TABLE 1-3 Keyboard Commands for Navigating Within a Worksheet

KEYSTROKE	ACTION
Arrow keys	Move one cell in the direction of the arrow.
Ctrl+Arrow keys	Move to the edge of a group of cells containing data.
Home	Move to the beginning of the row.

continues

TABLE 1-3 Keyboard Commands for Navigating Within a Worksheet *continued*

KEYSTROKE	ACTION
Ctrl + Home	Move to the beginning of the worksheet (cell A1).
Ctrl + End	Move to the lower right corner of the worksheet.
PgDn	Move down one window.
PgUp	Move up one window.
Alt + PgDn	Move right one window.
Alt + PgUp	Move left one window.
Ctrl + Backspace	Move to the active cell.

EXERCISE 1-8 Navigate Within a Worksheet Using Scroll Bars

You use the scroll bars to move through a worksheet using the mouse. When you use the scroll bars, the active cell does not move. You must click a cell to make it active.

1. Press Ctrl + Home to move back to cell A1.
2. Click the down arrow on the scroll bar five times. The active cell scrolls out of view. The cell in the top left corner of the worksheet is A6. Notice that the Name Box still displays A1. See Figure 1-12 on the next page.
3. Click cell A6 to make it active. Remember that scrolling in a worksheet doesn't change the active cell. You must click a cell to make it active.
4. Click the up arrow on the scroll bar until you can see cell A1 again. Cell A6 is still the active cell. This is indicated by the Name Box.
5. Click the right arrow on the horizontal scroll bar six times to move to the right in the worksheet.
6. Drag the scroll box back to the left arrow. Excel displays the column names that you pass over as you move to the left. Column A again becomes visible.

TIP: To "drag" the scroll box, move the pointer to the box, hold down the left mouse button, and move the mouse.

7. On the vertical scroll bar, click between the scroll box and the down arrow. Excel moves down the worksheet one window (13 or more rows, depending on the size of your screen).

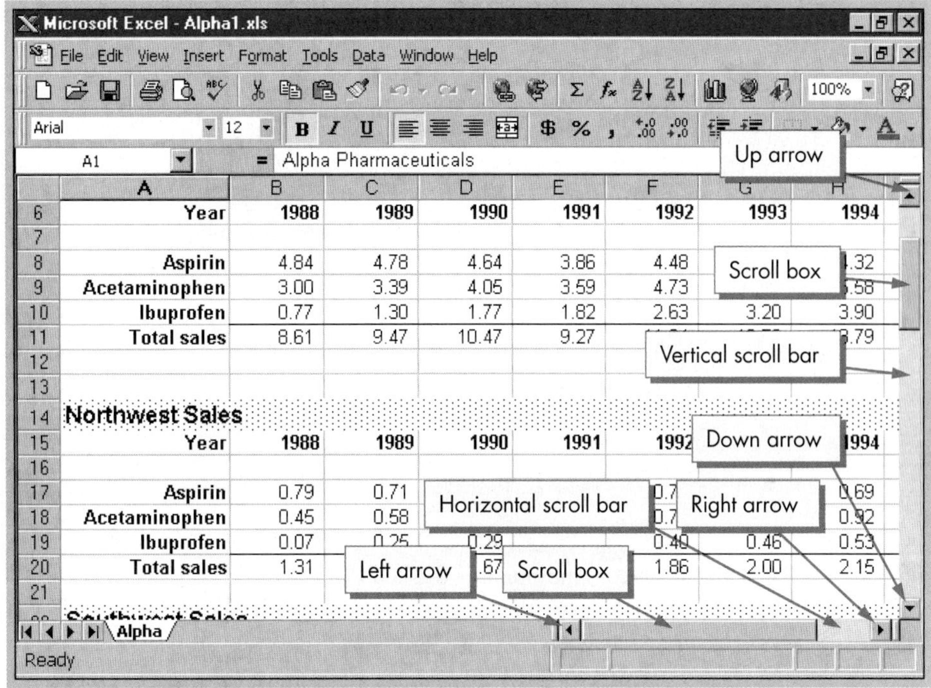

FIGURE 1-12
Scroll bars

8. Click between the scroll box and the up arrow to move up one window in the worksheet.

9. In steps 4 through 8, cell A6 remained the active cell. Change the active cell back to cell A1.

TABLE 1-4 **Navigating with Scroll Bars**

ACTION	RESULT
Click up or down scroll arrow once	Scroll up or down one row.
Click left or right scroll arrow once	Scroll left or right one column.
Click between scroll arrow and scroll box	Scroll up, down, left, or right one window (at least 9 columns or 13 rows).
Drag scroll box	Scroll a variable amount, depending on the distance you drag the scroll box.

EXERCISE 1-9 Use the Go To Command

You use the Go To command on the Edit menu to move to a specific cell address quickly.

1. Choose Go To from the Edit menu. The Go To dialog box appears.

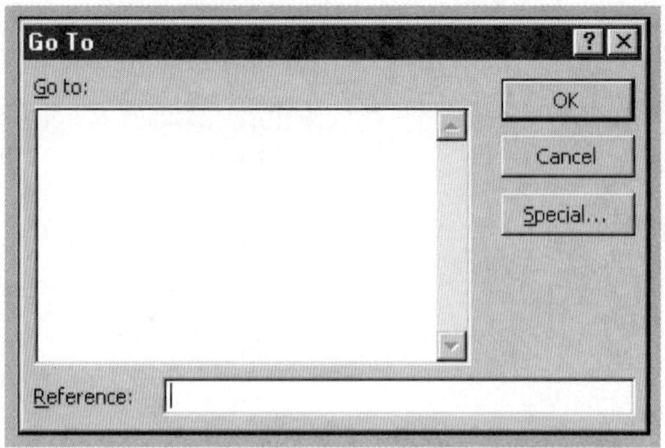

FIGURE 1-13 The Go To dialog box

NOTE: If you do not see the Go To command, move the cursor to the bottom of the menu and point to the triangle. The rest of the menu will be visible.

2. Key **J17** in the Reference text box and click OK (or press Enter). The dialog box closes and cell J17 becomes the active cell.

NOTE: Cell J17 displays the number 0.69, but the Formula Bar displays the number 0.6869. The two differ because the number format for this cell is set for two decimal places. You learn about number formatting in Lesson 3.

3. Press F5, the shortcut key for the Go To command.
4. Key **BX94** and press Enter. The active cell moves to column BX, row 94.
5. Press Ctrl+Home to return to cell A1.

TIP: Go To maintains a list of the cells you moved to. You can select a cell from this list.

Keying Data in a Worksheet

In the following exercises you key data in the worksheet for Alpha Pharmaceuticals.

EXERCISE 1-10 Key Data in a Worksheet

1. Click cell E17 to make it active.
2. Key **0.7023**. Notice that the Cancel box and the Enter box appear in the Formula Bar, indicating the Formula Bar is active.

TIP: If you make a mistake while keying data, press the Backspace key Backspace to delete the error.

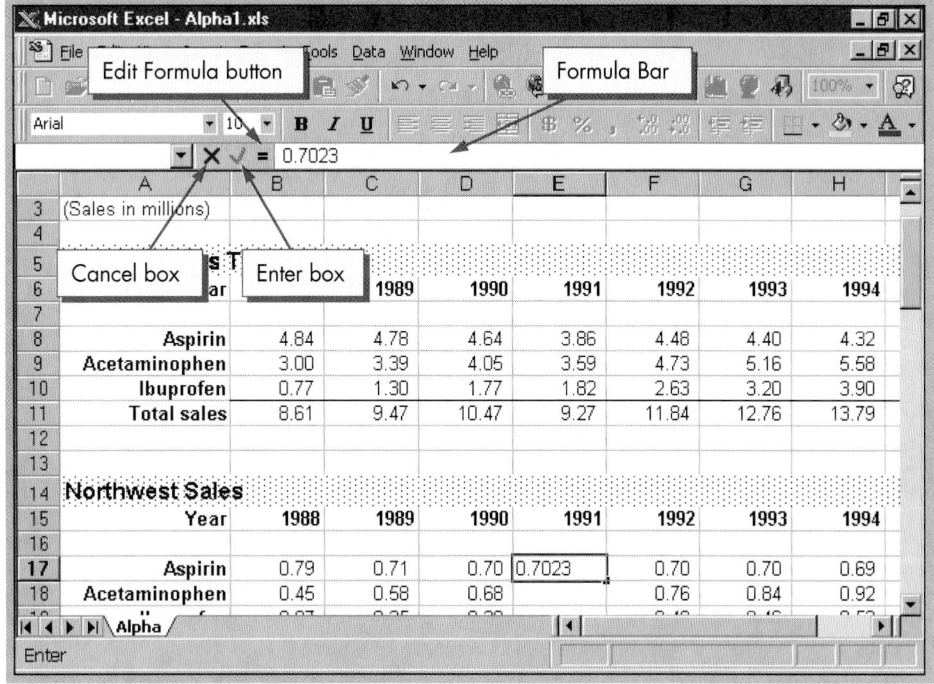

FIGURE 1-14 The Formula Bar becomes active when you key data.

3. Press Enter. The numeric value 0.70 appears in cell E17 and cell E18 becomes active. Notice that the Formula Bar is no longer active because you haven't yet keyed data in this cell.
4. Key **0.7193** in cell E18 and press ↓. The value 0.72 appears in cell E18 and cell E19 becomes active. You can complete a cell entry by pressing Enter or an Arrow key. Notice the change in cell E20.
5. Key **3.941** in cell E19 and press Enter. Cell E20 reflects the new total.

EXERCISE 1-11 Change Data in a Worksheet

To change data in a worksheet, you move to the cell that contains the incorrect data, key the correct data, and press Enter or an Arrow key. The new data replaces the old data.

1. Press ↑ to move to cell E19.
2. Key **0.3941** and press Enter. The new total is 1.82.
3. Press Ctrl+Home to move to cell A1.

Saving a Workbook

In Excel, workbooks are saved as files. When you create a new workbook or make changes to an existing one, you must save the workbook to make your changes permanent. Until you save your changes, they can be lost if you have a power failure or hardware problem.

The first step in saving a workbook for future use is to give it a *filename*. In Windows, filenames can be up to 255 characters and generally end with a period and a three-character extension. Filename extensions are used to distinguish between different types of files. For example, Excel workbooks have the extension .xls and Word documents have the extension .doc.

Throughout the exercises in this book, filenames consist of three parts:

- *[Your initials],* which may be your initials or the identifier your instructor asks you to use, such as **rst**
- The number of the exercise, such as **4-1**
- The **.xls** extension that Excel uses automatically for workbooks

An example of a filename is: **rst4-1.xls**

Before you save a new workbook, decide where you want to save it. Excel saves workbooks in the current drive and folder unless you specify otherwise. For example, to save a workbook to a floppy disk, you need to change the drive to a: or b:, whichever is appropriate for your computer.

NOTE: Your instructor will advise you on the proper drive and folder to use in this course.

When you work with an existing file, such as the current file **Alpha1.xls**, choosing the Save command (or clicking the Save button on the Standard toolbar) replaces the file on the disk with the one you are working with. After you save the workbook, the old version of the file no longer exists; the new version contains all the changes you made.

When you give an existing workbook a new name using the Save As command, the original workbook remains on the disk unchanged and a second workbook is saved with the new name.

EXERCISE 1-12 Name and Save a Workbook

1. Click File to open the File menu and choose Save As. The Save As dialog box appears.

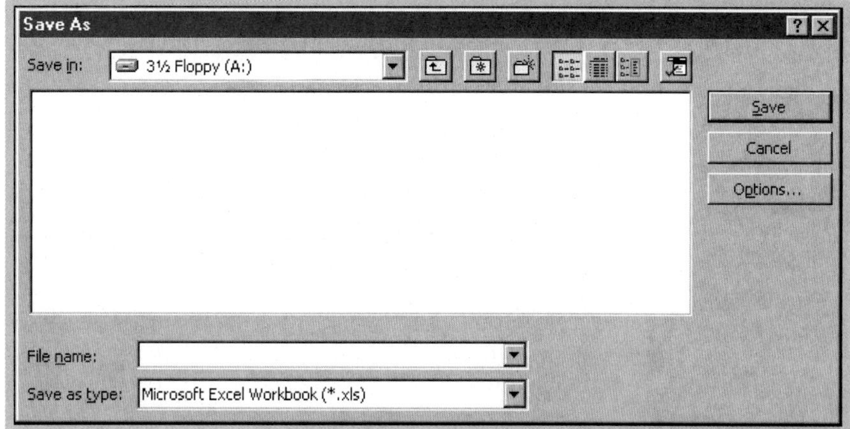

FIGURE 1-15 The Save As dialog box

2. In the File name text box, key *[your initials]***1-12.** (You don't have to key the .xls extension. Excel applies the extension automatically. However, in this book we show the .xls extension.)

NOTE: When naming files you can use any combination of uppercase and lowercase letters. Filenames can be up to 255 characters and can include spaces. For example, a file can be named "Alpha Business Plan.xls."

3. If necessary, change the drive to your data disk by clicking the down arrow in the Save in drop-down list and choosing the appropriate drive. Make sure a formatted disk is inserted in the drive.
4. Click Save. Your workbook is named and saved for future use.

Printing a Worksheet and Closing Excel

Once you create a worksheet, it's easy to print it. You can use any of these methods:

- Click the Print button on the Standard toolbar.
- Choose Print from the File menu.
- Press Ctrl+P.

The menu and keyboard methods open the Print dialog box, where you can choose different printing options. Pressing sends the worksheet directly to the printer using Excel's default settings. Note that all three methods print the active worksheet, not the entire workbook.

EXERCISE 1-13 Print a Worksheet

1. Choose Print from the File menu to open the Print dialog box. The dialog box displays Excel's default settings and shows your designated printer.

FIGURE 1-16
Print dialog box

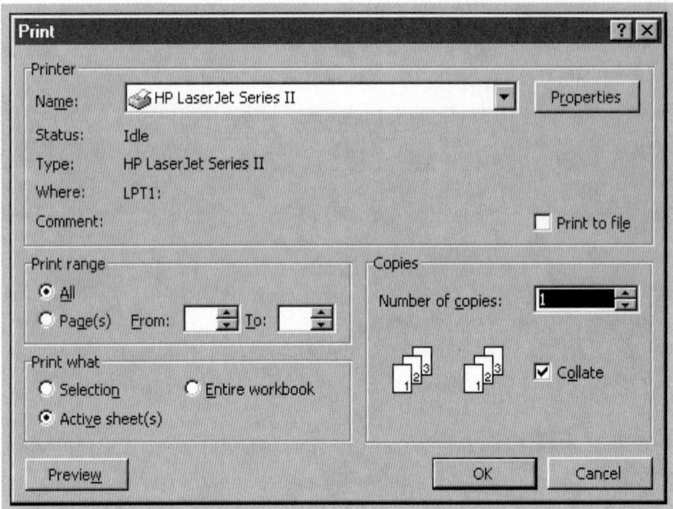

2. Click OK or press Enter to accept the settings. A printer icon appears on the taskbar as the worksheet is sent to the printer.

TIP: To print all worksheets in the workbook, click the Entire Workbook option in the Print dialog box.

EXERCISE 1-14 Close a Workbook and Exit Excel

After you finish working with a workbook and save it, you can close it and open another workbook or you can exit Excel.

There are four ways to close a workbook or to exit Excel. You can use:

FIGURE 1-17
Close buttons

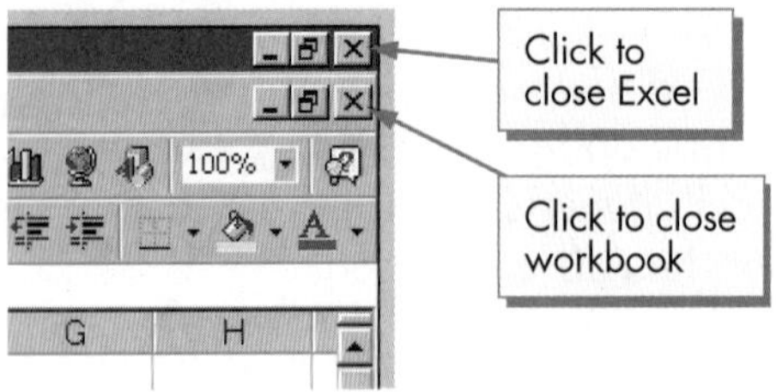

- the File menu. You already learned how to close a workbook using Close. To exit Excel, choose Exit.
- the Close button ☒ in the upper right corner of the window.
- keyboard shortcuts. Ctrl+W closes a workbook and Alt+F4 exits Excel.

1. Double-click the Workbook Control icon to close the workbook.
2. Click the Close button ☒ in the upper right corner of the window to close Excel and display the Windows desktop.

COMMAND SUMMARY

FEATURE	BUTTON	MENU	KEYBOARD
Go to a specified address		Edit, Go To	F5
Close current workbook		File, Close	Ctrl+W
Exit Excel		File, Exit	Alt+F4

USING HELP

The Office Assistant is your guide to Excel on-line Help. The Office Assistant provides tips based on the kind of work you're doing and directs you to relevant Help topics. It may also amuse you with its animated movements. If you find it annoying, you can hide it or choose another character.

Get acquainted with the Office Assistant

1. Start Excel, if necessary.
2. If the Office Assistant is not displayed, click the Office Assistant button on the Standard toolbar.
3. Click the Office Assistant figure. A balloon appears with the question "What would you like to do?"

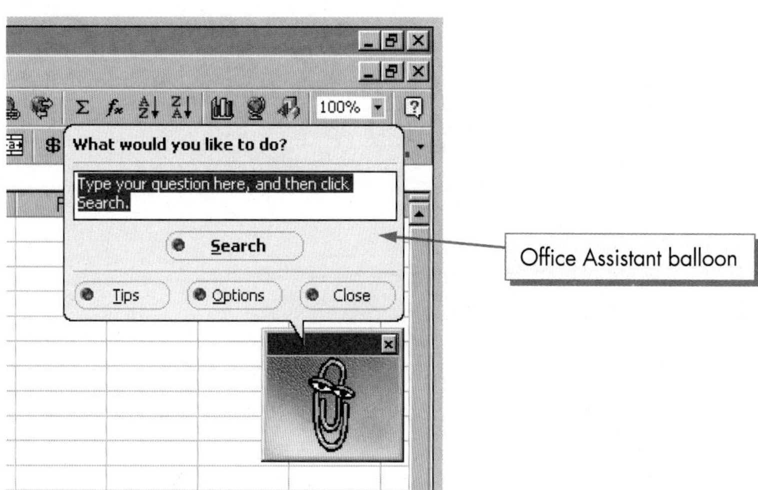

FIGURE 1-18
Using Office Assistant

4. Key **How do I use Office Assistant?** In the text box and click Search. The Office Assistant locates Help topics related to your question.
5. Review the displayed topics and click "See more" to display additional topics.
6. Click the topic "Ways to get assistance while you work." A Microsoft Excel Help window with the same topic name is displayed. This window provides a general overview of Help.
7. Click the topic Office Assistant to display a descriptive box. Review the description and then click the box to close it. Click the topic Office Assistant Tips and review the description.
8. Explore other topics in the "Ways to get assistance while you work" Help window, and then click the window's Close button ☒ to close Help.

Concepts Review

TRUE/FALSE QUESTIONS

Each of the following questions is either true or false. Indicate your choice by circling either T or F.

T F *1.* There is only one way to start Excel.

T F *2.* The Standard toolbar indicates the location of data being keyed in the active cell.

T F *3.* A workbook can contain up to 255 worksheets.

T F *4.* PgDn moves the screen down one page.

T F *5.* Columns are numbered and rows are labeled with letters.

T F *6.* The address of the active cell is displayed in the Name Box.

T F *7.* Scrolling with the scroll bar doesn't change the active cell.

T F *8.* Moving to a cell using the Go To dialog box doesn't change the active cell.

SHORT ANSWER QUESTIONS

Write the correct answer in the space provided.

1. What is the name of the area on the screen that displays information about a selected command or an operation in progress?

____

2. What is the name of the rectangle formed by the intersection of a row and a column?

____

3. What is the name of the area within a worksheet that is current, or ready to receive information?

____

4. Which keyboard command moves you to the beginning of a row?

____

5. Which keyboard command moves to the beginning of a worksheet?

____

6. What command allows you to move to a specific cell address quickly?

____

7. When do the Cancel and Enter boxes appear on the Formula Bar?

____

8. Which filename extension is used for Excel workbooks?

____

CRITICAL THINKING

Answer these questions on a separate piece of paper. There are no right or wrong answers. Support your answer with examples from your own experience, if possible.

1. What advantages would a spreadsheet program like Excel offer for a business compared with a noncomputerized pencil and paper spreadsheet? What advantages for an individual?
2. Excel allows great flexibility when naming files. Many businesses and individuals establish their own rules for naming files. What kinds of rules would you recommend for naming files in a business? For personal use?

Skills Review

EXERCISE 1-15

Start Excel, change the active cell, navigate between worksheets, and close the workbook without saving it.

1. Start Excel, if necessary, by following these steps:
   a. Click the Start button [Start] on the Windows taskbar.
   b. Point to Programs and point to Microsoft Excel (you may need to point first to the program group that contains Microsoft Excel) and click it.
2. Use the Arrow keys to change the active cell to AB15 by following these steps:
   a. Press the Down Arrow key [↓] until the active cell is A15.

b. Press the Right Arrow key → until the active cell is AB15.

3. Change to worksheet 3 by pressing Ctrl+PgDn twice.
4. Make D5 the active cell.
5. Use the mouse to make worksheet 1 the current worksheet by following these steps:

   a. Move the pointer over the Sheet1 tab.

   b. Click the worksheet tab for Sheet1.
6. Change the active cell to A1 by pressing Ctrl+Home.
7. Close the workbook by choosing Close from the File menu. (You won't save this workbook.)

EXERCISE 1-16

Open a file and use keyboard commands to navigate within the worksheet.

1. Open the file **Alpha1.xls** by following these steps:

   a. Click [Open] on the Standard toolbar.

   b. Double-click the file **Alpha1.xls**.
2. Use ↓ and → to move to cell K19.
3. Return to cell A1 by pressing Ctrl+Home.
4. Press the PgDn key PgDn three times to move down three windows.
5. Press the PgUp key PgUp twice to move up two windows.
6. Press Alt+PgDn once to move one window to the right.
7. Press Alt+PgUp once to move one window to the left.
8. Press ↓ once.
9. Press Ctrl+→ to move to the last column in this group of cells.
10. Press Ctrl+↓ to move to the last row in this group of cells.
11. Press Ctrl+End to move to the last cell in the last row that contains data or formatting instructions.
12. Press Ctrl+↑. The active cell jumps to the edge of the previous group of cells containing data.
13. Press Ctrl+↑ two more times. K41 becomes the active cell.
14. Return to cell A1.
15. Close the workbook without saving it.

EXERCISE 1-17

Open a file, use the scroll bars and the Go To Command to navigate within the worksheet, key data, and save, print, and close the worksheet.

1. Open the file **Alpha1.xls**.
2. Make cell A1 active (if it isn't already).
3. Click the down arrow on the vertical scroll bar seven times to scroll down seven rows.
4. Click the right arrow on the horizontal scroll bar eight times to scroll eight columns to the right.
5. Drag the scroll box on the horizontal scroll bar to the left so the first column becomes visible again.
6. On the vertical scroll bar, click between the scroll box and the down arrow to move down one window.
7. Use the Go To command by performing the following steps:
   - *a.* Choose Go To from the Edit menu.
   - *b.* Key **E17** in the Reference text box and click OK.
8. Key **0.59** and press Enter.
9. Key **0.55** in cell E18, press ↓, key **0.78** in cell E19, and press Enter.
10. Save the file by following these steps:
    - *a.* Choose Save As from the File menu.
    - *b.* In the File name text box, key *[your initials]***1-17.xls**
    - *c.* If necessary, change the drive to your data disk by clicking the down arrow in the Save in drop-down list and choosing the appropriate drive.
    - *d.* Click Save.
11. Print your worksheet by following these steps:
    - *a.* Choose Print from the File menu.
    - *b.* Click OK.
12. Close the workbook and close Excel by following these steps:
    - *a.* Choose Close from the File menu to close the workbook.
    - *b.* Click the Close button ☒ in the upper right corner of the window to close Excel.

EXERCISE 1-18

Start Excel, open an existing file, change data, and print and save the workbook.

1. Start Excel.
2. Open the file **Alpha3.xls**.
3. Change the data as shown in Figure 1-19 by following these steps:
   a. Make the cell containing data you want to change active.
   b. Key the new data.
   c. Move to another cell or press Enter.

FIGURE 1-19

Salesperson	Qtr 1	Qtr 2	Qtr 3	Qtr 4	Total	% of Total	
Robert Johnson	*65.3*	*62.7*	*58.6*	*52.9*			
Ewald Rhiner	61.0	65.5	70.1	75.3	271.9	10.0%	
~~Ruth Seuratadot~~	~~81.7~~	~~60.7~~	~~54.0~~	~~47.3~~	243.7	9.0%	
Buster Manatee	50.8	56.1	57.5	58.5	222.9	8.2%	
Jose Garcia	75.2	77.9	72.4	73.8	299.3	11.0%	
Colleen Masterhouse	65.3	70.9	54.6	74.5	265.3	9.8%	These will change automatically
Anthony Chen	88.5	74.6	66.4	68.9	298.4	11.0%	
Elouise Swift	66.7	73.9	64.7	69.9	275.2	10.1%	
~~Lloyd Polaski~~	~~87.5~~	~~42.3~~	~~57.6~~	~~50.3~~	237.7	8.7%	
Murray Diamond	61.0	65.8	74.6	74.2	275.6	10.1%	
Barbara Bloomberg	70.0	87.7	82.3	90.2	330.2	12.1%	
Richard Daniels	*53.1*	*51.1*	*56.7*	*72.8*			

4. Save the workbook as *[your initials]***1-18.xls** on your data disk.
5. Click the Print button on the Standard toolbar to print the worksheet.
6. Close the workbook and exit Excel.

Lesson Applications

EXERCISE 1-19

Start Excel, open an existing file, change the active cell, enter data, use the Save As command, print and close the workbook, and exit Excel.

1. Start Excel.
2. Open the file **Alpha1.xls.**
3. Make cell B17 active.
4. Change the data in cell B17 to 0.6314.
5. Change the data in cell B18 to 0.5563.
6. Add the following data for "Northwest Sales" in 1991:

Aspirin	**0.7233**
Acetaminophen	**0.7036**
Ibuprofen	**0.3179**

7. Save the workbook as *[your initials]***1-19.xls** on your data disk.
8. Print the worksheet.
9. Close the workbook and exit Excel.

EXERCISE 1-20

Open a file, change data, and save, print, and close the workbook.

1. Open Excel. Open the file **Alpha4.xls**.
2. Use the Go To command to move to the following cells and change the data as shown:

Cell	*Change Data to:*
K10	**6.8431**
D18	**0.6219**
J19	**0.6891**
B25	**1.0618**
K27	**2.0662**
G34	**1.4817**
C36	**0.3993**
K43	**1.4216**
D45	**0.5225**

3. Save the workbook as *[your initials]***1-20.xls** on your data disk.
4. Print the worksheet.
5. Close the workbook.

EXERCISE 1-21

Open a file, navigate in the spreadsheet, enter data, and save, print, and close the workbook.

1. Open the file **Alpha2.xls**.
2. Go to cell B10 on the Northwest worksheet.
3. Key the following data in cells B10, C10, and D10:
   0.074
   0.071
   0.036
4. Go to cell B7 on the Southeast worksheet.
5. Key the following data in cells B7, C7, and D7:
   0.135
   0.097
   0.037
6. Save the workbook as *[your initials]***1-21.xls** on your data disk.
7. Print all the worksheets and close the workbook.

TIP: To print all the worksheets in a workbook, click Entire Workbook in the Print dialog box.

EXERCISE 1-22

Open a file, navigate in the spreadsheet, enter data, and save, print, and close the workbook.

Because the sales volume in Alpha Pharmaceuticals' Northwest region is significantly lower than the other regions, the company president requested detailed figures for each salesperson. Complete the worksheet containing the sales data by entering the second- and fourth-quarter numbers shown in Figure 1-20 (on the next page).

FIGURE 1-20

Salesperson	Qtr 2	Qtr 4
Ewald Rhiner	66.4	54.6
Ruth Seuratadot	82.2	86.0
Buster Manatee	73.8	74.1
Jose Garcia	50.3	81.6
Colleen Masterhouse	57.7	74.6
Anthony Chen	81.2	69.7
Elouise Swift	45.9	60.7
Lloyd Polaski	71.0	67.0
Murray Diamond	65.3	70.6
Barbara Bloomberg	79.8	52.4

1. Open the file **Alpha5.xls**.
2. Move to cell C8 and key **66.4** (Ewald Rhiner's second-quarter sales).
3. Press Enter to enter the data and move down one cell.

TIP: When entering data in more than one column, it's usually easier to press Enter and move down the column than to use the arrow keys to move across a row, especially if you are moving more than one cell.

4. Continue keying the second-quarter data. When you finish entering it, enter the fourth-quarter data.
5. When you finish entering the data, verify that the total figure in cell F19 is 2726.87. If it isn't, check the figures you keyed and correct them where necessary.
6. Save the workbook as *[your initials]***1-22.xls** on your data disk.
7. Print the worksheet and close the workbook.

EXERCISE 1-23

Open a file, key data in four worksheets within one workbook, and save, print, and close the workbook.

Alpha Pharmaceuticals' sales force is divided into four regions. Annual company sales are shown in a workbook that consists of four worksheets—one worksheet for each region. Some adjustments are needed in the Annual Sales figures for each region.

1. Open the file **Alpha6.xls**.
2. Add the following data for "May" to Sheet2:

Aspirin	**0.074**
Acetaminophen	**0.070**
Ibuprofen	**0.042**

3. Add the following data for "February" to Sheet3:

Aspirin	**0.126**
Acetaminophen	**0.080**
Ibuprofen	**0.030**

4. Change the amounts for "Ibuprofen" on Sheet4 as shown below:

October	**0.201**
November	**0.210**
December	**0.212**

5. Change the amounts for "September" on Sheet1 as shown below:

Aspirin	**0.132**
Acetaminophen	**0.202**
Ibuprofen	**0.207**

6. Save the workbook as *[your initials]***1-23.xls** on your data disk.
7. Print the entire workbook. Then close the workbook and close Excel.

Creating a Simple Worksheet

OBJECTIVES

After completing this lesson, you will be able to:

1. **Enter and edit data in a worksheet.**
2. **Use Pick From List and AutoComplete to enter labels.**
3. **Enter data in selected cells.**
4. **Construct basic formulas.**
5. **Use the SUM function.**
6. **Use AutoCalculate.**

Estimated Time: 1½ hours

In Lesson 1, you opened an existing worksheet, examined its contents, and keyed some data. In this lesson, you create a simple worksheet from scratch, containing text, numerical values, and formulas.

Entering Labels and Values in a Worksheet

Excel recognizes text and numbers automatically and formats them differently. For example:

- An entry that begins with a number or mathematical sign is recognized as a value. Values are aligned at the right margin of the cell by default and are included in calculations.

- An entry that contains a letter is recognized automatically as a *label*. Labels are aligned at the left of the cell and are excluded from calculations. You can format a number as a label if you begin the entry with an apostrophe ('). The number is then excluded from calculations.

When you key data, the information appears in both the Formula Bar and the active cell. Before you complete the entry, you can use the Backspace key [Backspace] to edit the text or the Escape key [Esc] to start over. To complete the entry, you can use one of several mouse or keyboard methods.

TABLE 2-1 Methods for Completing an Entry

ACTION	RESULT
Click another cell	Completes the entry and makes the selected cell active.
Click [✓]	Completes the entry. The current cell remains active.
Press [Enter]	Completes the entry and the cell below becomes active.
Press [Tab]	Completes the entry and the cell to the right becomes active.
Press an Arrow key	Completes the entry and the cell above, below, to the right, or to the left becomes active.

EXERCISE 2-1 Enter Labels and Values in a Worksheet

1. Start Excel. The workbook Book1 appears and cell A1 on Sheet1 becomes the active cell.
2. Key **Sales Analysis** in cell A1. (Do not press the Enter key [Enter] yet.) Notice that the status bar indicates you are in Enter mode. The text appears in both the Formula Bar and the active cell. Notice also that the Enter box and Cancel box appear on the Formula Bar in Enter mode. (See Figure 2-1 on the next page.)
3. To delete three of the characters you entered, press the Backspace key [Backspace] three times.

4. Key **sis** to complete the word "Analysis" and click the Enter box [✓] in the Formula Bar. A1 remains the active cell. Notice that the mode returns to *Ready* upon completion of the entry. The text appears in cell A1 and overlaps cell B1.

FIGURE 2-1
Text appears in the Formula Bar in Enter mode.

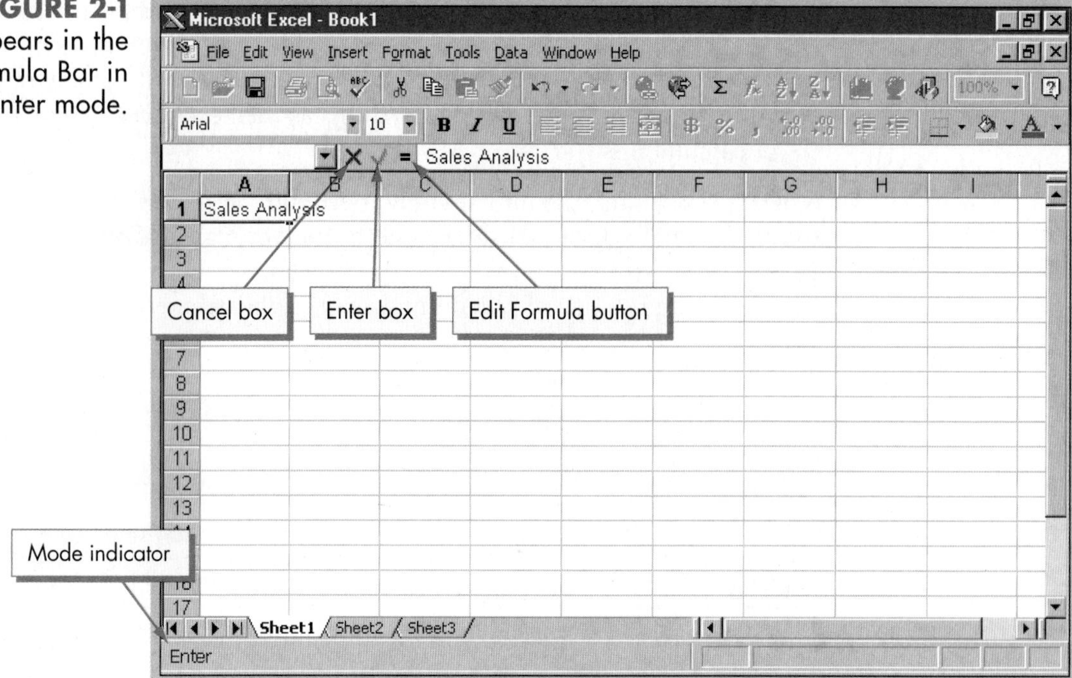

5. Key **Alpha Pharmaceuticals** and press Enter. The new text replaces "Sales Analysis" in cell A1 and cell A2 becomes the active cell. You can change the contents of the active cell by keying a new label or value.
6. In cell A2, key **Regional Sales** and press Enter to complete the cell entry. Cell A3 becomes the active cell. Whenever you press Enter, the active cell moves down one row.
7. In cell A3, key **Sales in $ millions** and press Enter.
8. Press ↑ and key **1994**. Do not press Enter. Cell A3 now contains "1994," but it should contain "Sales in $ millions."
9. Press the Escape key Esc. The original cell contents is restored.

TIP: If you overwrite a cell by mistake, do not press Enter. Press Esc or click the Cancel box ☒ on the Formula Bar to restore the cell's previous contents.

10. Move to cell B7. Key **'1994** and press the Tab key Tab. Note that an apostrophe precedes the "1994" portion of the entry. The apostrophe tells Excel this entry is a label, not a value. Observe that the apostrophe is not displayed in the cell, but it does appear in the Formula Bar. Pressing Tab activates the cell to the right and C7 is now the active cell.
11. Key **'1995** in cell C7 and press Tab. The year is entered as a label and cell D7 becomes the active cell.

12. Key the remaining text as shown in Figure 2-2, entering all years as labels.

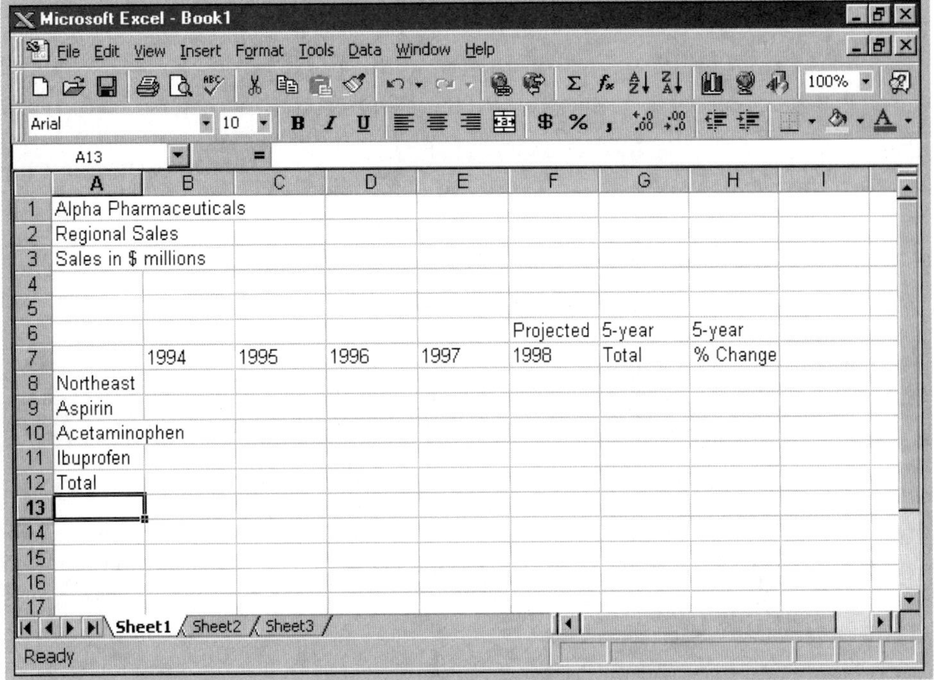

FIGURE 2-2
The Alpha Pharmaceuticals worksheet layout

13. Widen column A to accommodate the column entry "Acetaminophen." To do this, click anywhere in column A, choose Column from the Format menu, and select Width. Key **13** in the text box and click OK. (If the column is still not wide enough to accommodate the label, repeat the command, keying a larger value in the text box.)

14. Save the workbook as *[your initials]***2-1.xls.**

NOTE: The text at the top of the worksheet is the worksheet title. Typically, this text is entered in column A and aligned across the entire worksheet. Aligning text and changing column width is explained in more detail in Lesson 8: "Formatting Text and Numbers."

EXERCISE 2-2 Clear the Contents of a Cell

If you key incorrect data into a cell, you can clear the cell's contents. Simply make the cell active and press the Delete key Delete. Another way to clear a cell is to use the Clear option on the Edit menu and then choose Contents.

FIGURE 2-3
Edit menu, Clear cascading menu

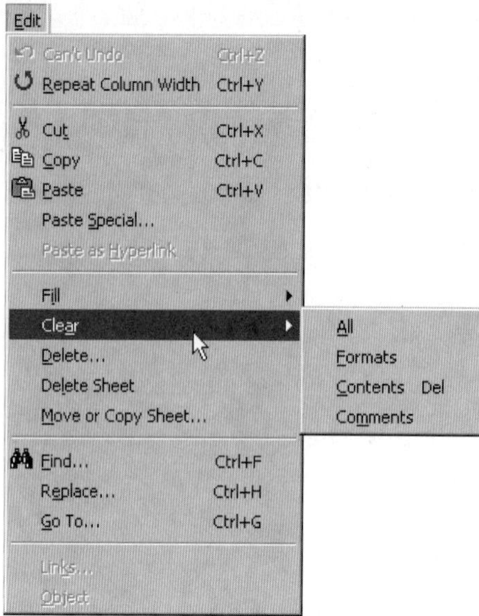

1. In the current workbook, move to cell A8, which contains "Northeast."
2. Choose Clear from the Edit menu. A cascading menu appears.
3. Choose Contents to clear cell A8.
4. Key **Southeast** in cell A8 and press Enter.
5. Press ↑ to reactivate cell A8 and press Delete to clear the cell.
6. Key **Northeast** in cell A8 and press Enter.

NOTE: You can also use the Clear cascading menu to clear formats and notes. Formats, such as bold or italic, are discussed in Lesson 3: "Enhancing a Simple Worksheet." Notes, which explain cell contents and appear as hidden text, are used in Lesson 11: "Advanced Formulas."

EXERCISE 2-3 Edit the Contents of a Cell

If a cell contains a long or complicated entry, you might want to edit the contents rather than rekey the entire entry.

To change to Edit mode you can:

- Double-click the cell.
- Click the cell to make it active and click the Formula Bar.
- Press F2.

1. Double-click cell A3. You are now in Edit mode, as indicated on the status bar. Notice that the pointer changes from a white cross to an I-beam and you can position the insertion point (the flashing vertical bar) to edit text.
2. Click the I-beam between "in" and "$" to position the insertion point.
3. Press ← and → several times. The insertion point moves to the left or right, one character at a time.

4. Press Home. The insertion point moves to the left of "Sales." In Edit mode, keys such as Home and End operate within the cell, rather than within the entire worksheet as they do in Ready mode.
5. Press Delete nine times to delete "Sales in."
6. Key **(** (open parenthesis), and press End to move to the right of the text.
7. Key **)** (close parenthesis), and press Enter to complete the entry and exit Edit mode. Cell A3 now contains "($ millions)."

TABLE 2-2 **Keystrokes in Edit Mode**

KEYSTROKE	RESULT
Enter	Completes the entry and returns to Ready mode.
Esc	Restores the previous cell contents and returns to Ready mode.
← or →	Moves the insertion point left or right by one character.
Home	Moves to the beginning of the cell contents.
End	Moves to the end of the cell contents.
Delete	Deletes one character to the right of the insertion point.
Ctrl + Delete	Deletes text to the end of the line.
Backspace	Deletes one character to the left of the insertion point, or deletes selected text.
Ctrl + ← or Ctrl + →	Moves left or right by one word.

Using Pick From List and AutoComplete

Labels for rows are usually keyed in a single column and often are repeated. For instance, if your worksheet shows sales for three products in four regions, the product names appear four times, once in each region.

Excel provides two features that make it easier to enter labels:

- Pick From List
- AutoComplete

Both features use information you already entered in consecutive cells of a column.

EXERCISE 2-4 Use the Pick From List and AutoComplete Features

1. In cell A13, key **Southeast** and press Enter.
2. Right-click cell A14 (position the mouse pointer in cell A14 and click the right button). The shortcut menu appears.

FIGURE 2-4
Shortcut menu

3. Choose Pick From List from the shortcut menu. The list contains the labels that you already keyed in consecutive cells A8 through A13.
4. Click "Aspirin" in the list. Excel automatically inserts this row label in cell A14.
5. Right-click cell A15, choose Pick From List, and click "Acetaminophen" from the list. Excel inserts this label in the active cell.

A14

	A	B
3	($ millions)	
4		
5		
6		
7		1994
8	Northeast	
9	Aspirin	
10	Acetaminophen	
11	Ibuprofen	
12	Total	
13	Southeast	
14		

Acetaminophen
Aspirin
Ibuprofen
Northeast
Southeast
Total

FIGURE 2-5
Using the Pick From List feature

6. Move to cell A16 and key **I**. The AutoComplete feature highlights "buprofen" as a choice to complete the entry. AutoComplete chooses an item from Pick From List when you key the first letters of that item. Because "Ibuprofen" is the only item that begins with an "I," you needed to key only one letter in this case.
7. Press Enter to accept "Ibuprofen."
8. Key **As** in cell A17, but do not press Enter. AutoComplete suggests "Aspirin."
9. Press Esc to start over and key **T**. AutoComplete suggests "Total." Press Enter to complete the entry.
10. Complete the labels in column A as shown in Figure 2-7 (on the next page). Key text for the new entries. Use AutoComplete or the Pick From List feature to insert items that you already keyed.

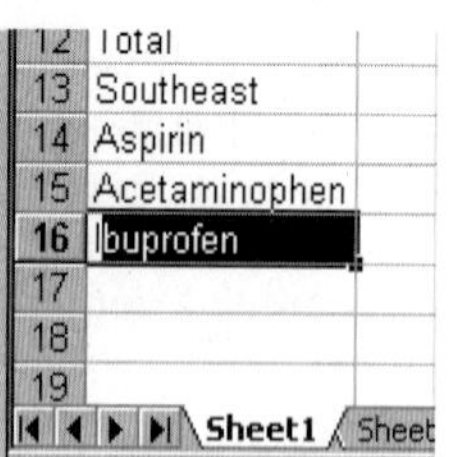

FIGURE 2-6
AutoComplete suggests an item from Pick From List.

NOTE: Excel provides data entry assistance for values with the Validate Data feature, which is described in Lesson 4: "Designing and Printing a Worksheet."

FIGURE 2-7

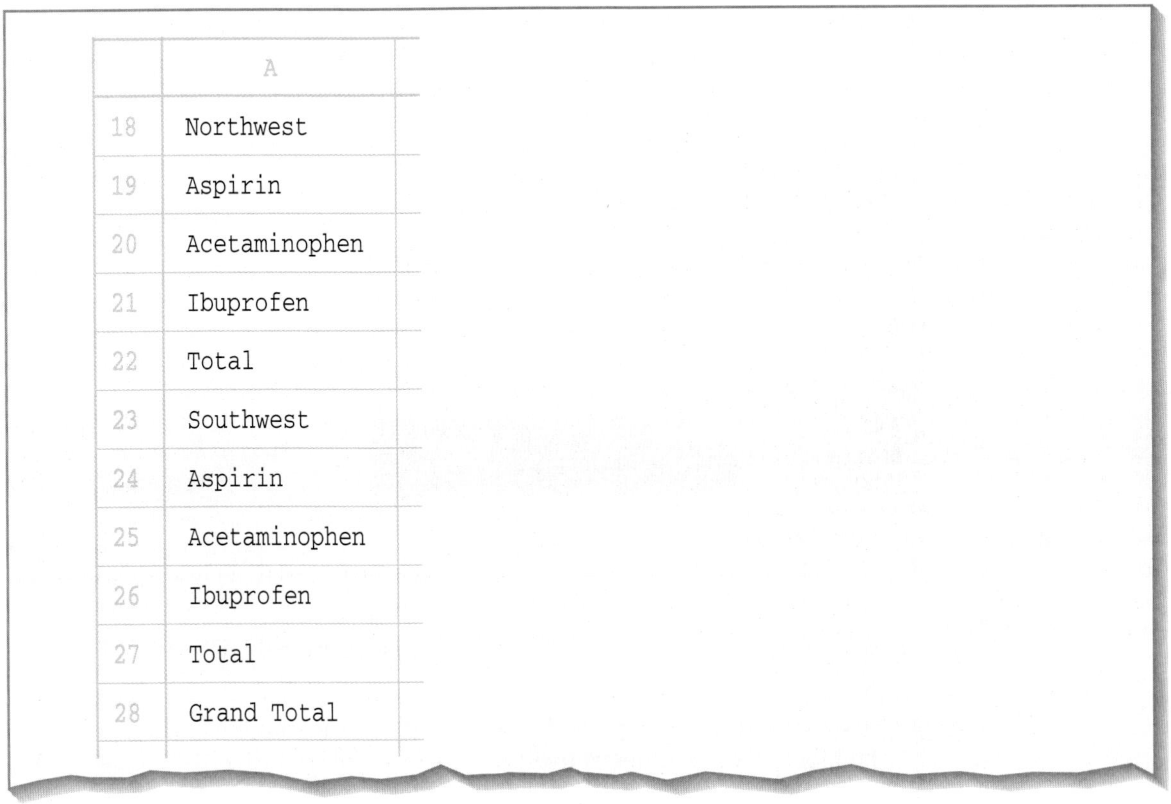

	A
18	Northwest
19	Aspirin
20	Acetaminophen
21	Ibuprofen
22	Total
23	Southwest
24	Aspirin
25	Acetaminophen
26	Ibuprofen
27	Total
28	Grand Total

Entering Data in Selected Cells

In many cases, you may find it convenient to work with a group of selected cells. You can select groups of cells as either blocks or ranges. A *block* is a group of cells that are next to one another. A *range* is any group of selected cells.

Excel provides three methods of selecting cells. You can use the:

- Keyboard
- Mouse
- Name Box

EXERCISE 2-5 Select a Block of Cells Using the Keyboard

When you make a cell active, you have actually selected it. To extend the selection using the keyboard, press Shift in combination with the navigation keys.

1. Make cell B9 active.
2. Hold down Shift and press → three times. A dark border surrounds the selected cells, B9 through E9. The first cell in the selection, B9, which is also the active cell, appears white. Cells C9 through E9 are highlighted.
3. Press ↓ twice and release the Shift key. The selected block now extends from B9 through E11.

FIGURE 2-8
Selected block of cells

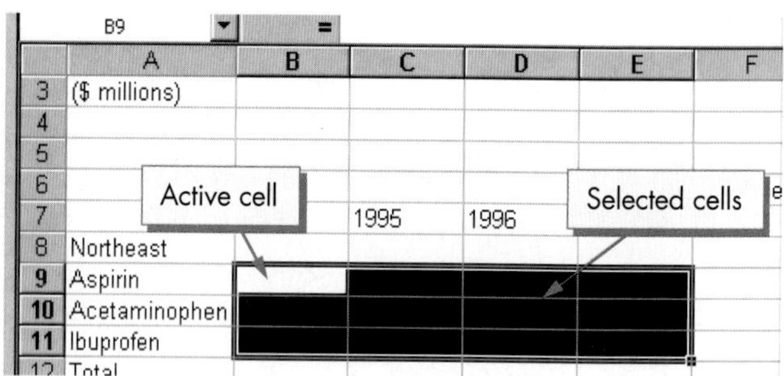

4. Key **1.112** and press Enter. The value appears in cell B9 and B10 becomes active.
5. Key **1.465** and press Enter. The value appears in cell B10 and B11 becomes active.
6. Key **1.085** and press Enter. The value appears in cell B11. The next cell in the block, C9, becomes active.

NOTE: Entering data in selected cells can be a very efficient technique, as Enter or Tab moves only within the selection.

7. Key the remaining data for the selected block as shown in Figure 2-9.

FIGURE 2-9

	A	B	C	D	E
9	Aspirin	1.112	1.082	1.053	1.024
10	Acetaminophen	1.465	1.592	1.73	1.94
11	Ibuprofen	1.085	1.36	1.704	2.225

8. Press ↓. The block is deselected.
9. Select cell F11 (make it active), hold down Shift, and press Home. The selection extends from F11 through A11.
10. Press Shift+Ctrl+Home. The selection extends from F11 through A1.

11. Press Shift+↓. The selection shrinks by one row.

12. Press any arrow key to deselect the block.

TABLE 2-3 Navigation Key Combinations

SELECTION KEY COMBINATION	ACTION
Shift+Arrow key	Extend the selection one cell in the direction indicated by the Arrow key.
Shift+PgUp or Shift+PgDn	Extend the selection one window up or down.
Shift+Ctrl+Home	Extend the selection to the beginning of the worksheet.
Shift+Home	Extend the selection to the beginning of the row.
Shift+Ctrl+End	Extend the selection to the end of the data in the worksheet.
Shift+Ctrl+Arrow key	Extend the selection to the edge of a block of data in the direction indicated by the Arrow key.
Ctrl+Spacebar	Select an entire column.
Shift+Spacebar	Select an entire row.
Ctrl+A or Ctrl+Shift+Spacebar	Select an entire worksheet.

EXERCISE 2-6 Select Cells Using the Mouse

Excel provides several ways to select cells using the mouse:

- Click a column heading letter to select an entire column or click a row heading number to select an entire row.
- Click the Select All button to select the entire worksheet.
- Drag across adjacent cells to select a block.
- Hold down Shift and click a cell to select a block beginning with the active cell and ending at the new location.
- Add a non-adjacent block of cells to a selection by holding down Ctrl and dragging across the additional cells.

1. Click cell B14, hold down the mouse button, and then drag the pointer diagonally to cell E16.

2. Release the mouse button. Cells B14 through E16 are selected and B14 becomes the active cell.
3. Click any cell to deselect the block.

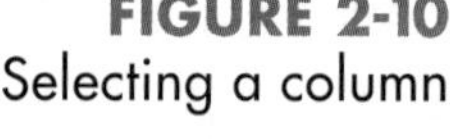

FIGURE 2-10
Selecting a column

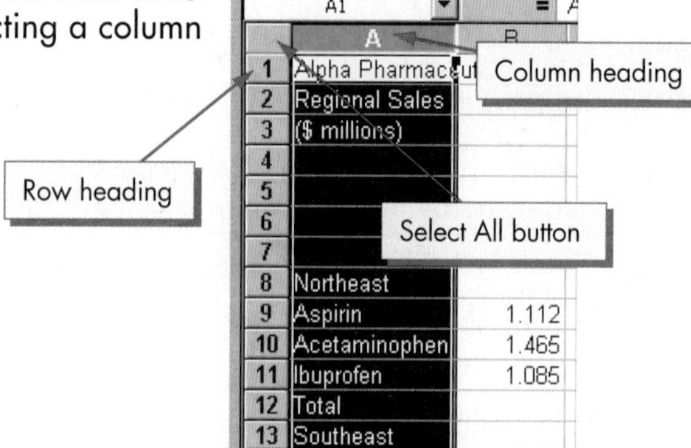

4. Click column heading A to select the entire column.
5. Click anywhere in the worksheet to deselect the column. Click row heading 1 to select the entire row.
6. Click the Select All button (left of column heading A) to select the entire worksheet. (See Figure 2-10 for the location of the Select All button.)
7. Click cell B7 (containing "1994"), hold down Shift, and click cell E7. Cells B7 through E7 are selected.
8. Press Delete to clear the cells. The block is still selected and B7 becomes the active cell.
9. Rekey **1994**, **1995**, **1996**, and **1997** in cells B7, C7, D7, and E7, respectively, pressing Tab between each entry. Remember to enter the years as labels by beginning each entry with an apostrophe.

TIP: Tab moves the active cell to the right. Shift+Tab moves the active cell to the left.

10. Press ↓ once to deselect the block of cells.
11. Drag from cell B14 to E16 to select this block.
12. Click the down arrow in the vertical scroll bar to display row 28 of the worksheet. Hold down Ctrl and drag from B19 to E21. A second block is added to the range.
13. Hold down Ctrl and drag from B24 to E26. A third block is added to the range.
14. Hold down Ctrl and click B14 to make it the active cell. See Figure 2-11 on the next page.
15. Key **1** and press Enter to enter the value in the cell. Press Enter again. B15 becomes the active cell.
16. Press Enter repeatedly to move through the range. Notice that the active cell moves from the end of one block to the beginning of the next block and from the end of the range to the beginning of the range.

TIP: Enter moves the active cell down. Shift+Enter moves the active cell up.

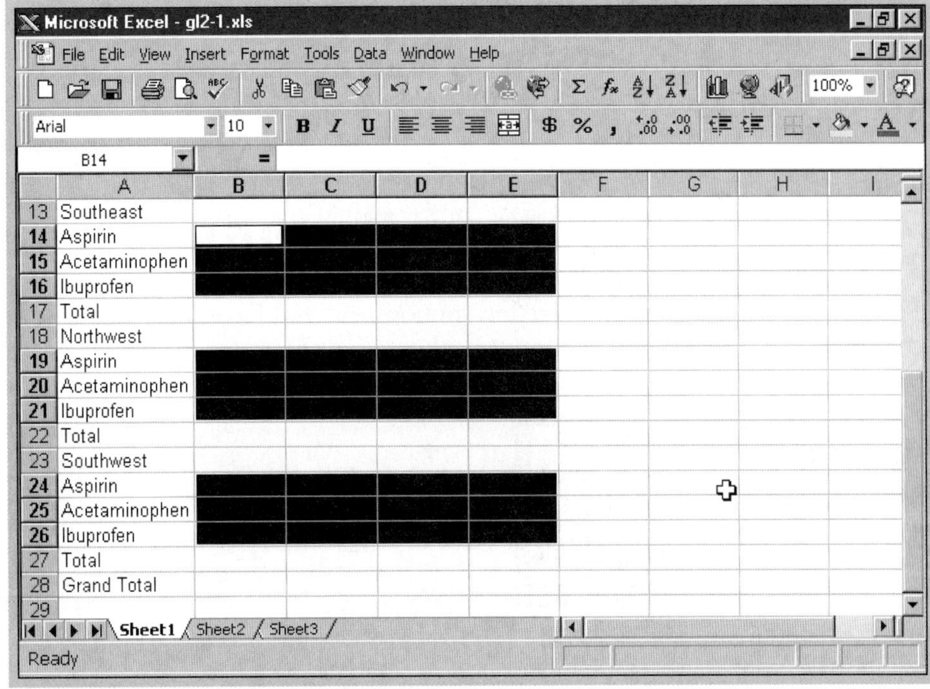

FIGURE 2-11 Selected range of non-adjacent blocks

17. Press Delete to clear the range contents.

18. Click anywhere in the worksheet to deselect the range.

NOTE: If you're using the Microsoft IntelliPoint Mouse (and IntelliPoint software is installed), additional navigating options are available in Excel. For example, you can roll the wheel forward and backward instead of using the vertical scroll bars; hold down the wheel and drag in any direction to pan the document; or hold Ctrl as you roll the wheel to change the magnification.

EXERCISE 2-7 Select Cells Using the Name Box

You can select a range of cells by keying the first and last cells separated by a colon in the Name Box. For example, you can enter C9:E10 to select the block including cells C9, C10, D9, D10, E9, and E10.

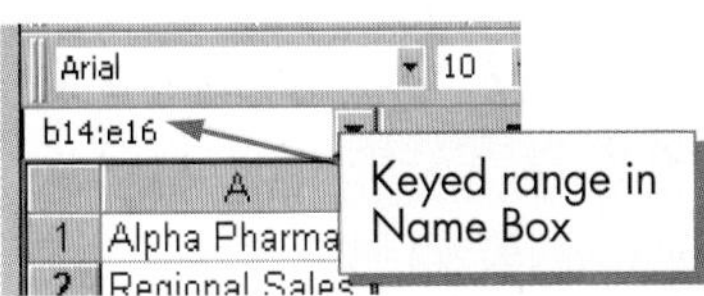

FIGURE 2-12 Using the Name Box to select cells

1. Click in the Name Box and key **b14:e16**. (Cell references are not case-sensitive, so you can key lowercase letters.)

2. Press Enter. The cells in the specified range are selected.
3. Click any cell to deselect the block.
4. Save the worksheet as *[your initials]***2-7.xls**.

Constructing Basic Formulas

Formulas are instructions that tell Excel how to perform calculations. Formulas can contain mathematical operators, values, cell references, cell ranges, and functions. Excel performs the operations indicated in the formula in a specific order.

TABLE 2-4 Commonly Used Mathematical Operators

OPERATOR	PRECEDENCE	DESCRIPTION
^	1st	Exponentiate
*	2nd	Multiply
/	2nd	Divide
+	3rd	Add
-	3rd	Subtract
( )		Used to control the order of mathematical operations

NOTE: The exponentiation operator (^) raises a value to a power. The expression 2^3 means "two to the third power," or 2^3, or 2x2x2.

Excel's *order of precedence* defines the order in which it performs formula operations. In a formula, Excel performs exponentiation operations first, multiplication and division next, and addition and subtraction last. Operations with equal precedence are performed from left to right. You can use parentheses () to override the order of precedence. Excel performs operations inside parentheses first. You can also "nest" expressions—that is, put parenthetical expressions within parentheses. The innermost operations are handled first. The following figure shows how parentheses change the order of precedence for operations.

FIGURE 2-13 These two formulas include the same numbers and operators, but parentheses change the order of operations.

$$1 + 2 * 3 - 1 = 1 + 6 - 1 = 6$$

(2nd: 1 + 2; 1st: 2 * 3; 3rd: - 1)

$$((1 + 2) * 3) - 1 = ((3) * 3) - 1 = 9 - 1 = 8$$

(1st: 1 + 2; 2nd: * 3; 3rd: - 1)

You can create formulas using the keyboard or by entering a combination of keystrokes and mouse clicks. As you key a formula, it appears in both the active cell and the Formula Bar. When you complete the entry, the result of the calculation appears in the active cell, but the Formula Bar displays the formula. Excel formulas begin with = (an equal sign). Because cell references in a formula are not case-sensitive, you can enter them in either uppercase or lowercase.

TABLE 2-5 Typical Excel Formulas

FORMULA	ACTION
=245+374	Adds the values 245 and 374.
=F4+F5	Adds the values in cells F4 and F5.
=c3+b3-d5	Adds the values in cells C3 and B3 and subtracts the value in cell D5 from the result.
=(A3+B3)/C9	Adds the values in cells A3 and B3 and divides the result by the value in cell C9.
=F5*1.02	Multiplies the contents of cell F5 by 1.02 (or 102%).
=F5*C10	Multiplies the contents of cell F5 by the contents of cell C10.

EXERCISE 2-8 Key an Addition Formula

1. In the current workbook, select and clear the contents of cells A13 through A28.
2. Move to cell B12,which should display the total of 1994 sales.
3. Key **=B9+B10+B11** and press Enter. The result, "3.662," appears in cell B12.
4. Press ↑ to make B12 the active cell. The formula is displayed in the Formula Bar.

EXERCISE 2-9 Build an Addition Formula with the Mouse

You can enter a cell reference in a formula by clicking the cell with the mouse. While building a formula, clicking another cell switches the worksheet into Point mode. If you click the wrong cell or make another error, just press Backspace to delete the incorrect characters. You can then continue building the formula.

1. Move to cell C12 and click the Edit Formula button. Excel changes to Edit mode, opens the Formula Bar, and enters an equal sign to start the formula. (You can also key the equal sign to start the formula.)

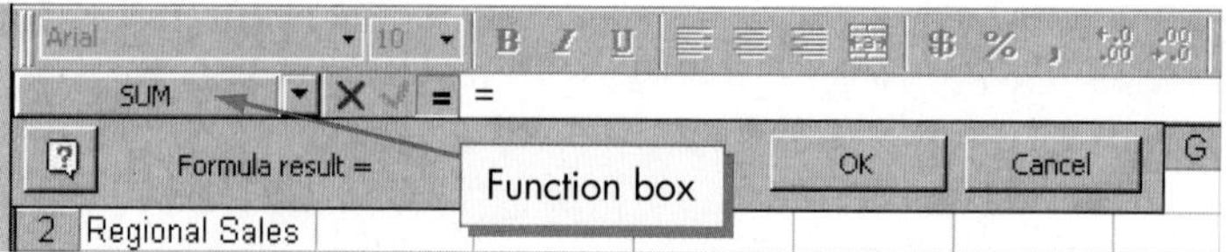

FIGURE 2-14 Formula Bar opens when the Edit Formula button is clicked.

2. Click cell C9. Excel changes to Point mode and a moving dashed border surrounds cell C9. Notice that "=C9" appears in both the active cell and the Formula Bar.
3. Key **+** (the plus sign). The plus sign is added to the formula and the moving border disappears. Excel changes to Edit mode.
4. Click cell C10 and key **+** (the plus sign). The formula "=C9+C10+" appears.
5. Click cell C11 and then press Enter, click the Enter box on the Formula Bar, or click OK on the Formula Bar. The result, "4.034," appears in cell C12.

EXERCISE 2-10 Build Multiplication Formulas

Alpha Pharmaceuticals' sales figures are available for the years 1994 through 1997, but a projection must be calculated for 1998. The company is predicting that aspirin sales will decrease by 5% in 1998 and acetaminophen and ibuprofen sales will increase by 2% and 3%, respectively.

1. In cell F9, key **=** (the equal sign) or click and click cell E9. (You can drag the Formula Bar out of the way if you need to see the column headings.)
2. Key * (the multiplication operator), key **.95**, and press Enter.

3. Press [↑] to return to cell F9. The formula "=E9*0.95" appears in the Formula Bar and "0.9728" appears in cell F9. This formula is equivalent to "=E9-E9*0.05" or "5 percent less than E9."
4. Move to cell F10, key **=E10*1.02**, and press [Enter]. The result, "1.9788," appears in cell F10. The formula "=E10*1.02" is equivalent to the formula "=E10+E10*0.02."
5. Move to cell F11, key the formula **=E11*1.03,** and press [Enter]. The result "2.29175" appears.

EXERCISE 2-11 Calculate a Percentage Change

The Alpha Pharmaceuticals worksheet needs calculations to determine the percentage change in each product over the five-year sales period. The general formula for a percentage change is (new-old)/old*100. The subtraction must be performed before division. The resulting decimal must be multiplied by 100 to convert it to a percentage.

1. Move to cell H9 and key **=(**
2. Click cell F9 and key **-** (the minus sign).
3. Click cell B9 and key **)**
4. Key **/** (the forward slash, which is the division operator).
5. Click cell B9, key * (the asterisk), key **100**, and press [Enter].
6. Move back to cell H9. The formula "=(F9-B9)/B9*100" appears in the Formula Bar and the result "-12.518" appears in cell H9.
7. In cell H10, enter the formula **=(F10-B10)/B10*100**.
8. In cell H11, enter the formula **=(F11-B11)/B11*100**. The result shows that ibuprofen sales more than doubled over the five-year period, increasing 111.2212 percent.

FIGURE 2-15 Calculating percentage changes

H11 = =(F11-B11)/B11*100

	A	B	C	D	E	F	G	H	I
5									
6						Projected	5-year	5-year	
7		1994	1995	1996	1997	1998	Total	% Change	
8	Northeast								
9	Aspirin	1.112	1.082	1.053	1.024	0.9728		-12.518	
10	Acetaminophen	1.465	1.592	1.73	1.94	1.9788		35.07167	
11	Ibuprofen	1.085	1.36	1.704	2.225	2.29175		111.2212	
12	Total	3.662	4.034						
13									
14									
15									
16									

Using the SUM Function

Keying individual cell references is a reasonable way to add two or three cells. It is not practical for adding a long column or row of values, however. Excel's SUM function greatly simplifies the process of adding many values.

In general, a function is constructed with an equal sign and the function name followed by a set of parentheses, with one or more cell references or values within the parentheses.

FIGURE 2-16 Structure of a SUM formula

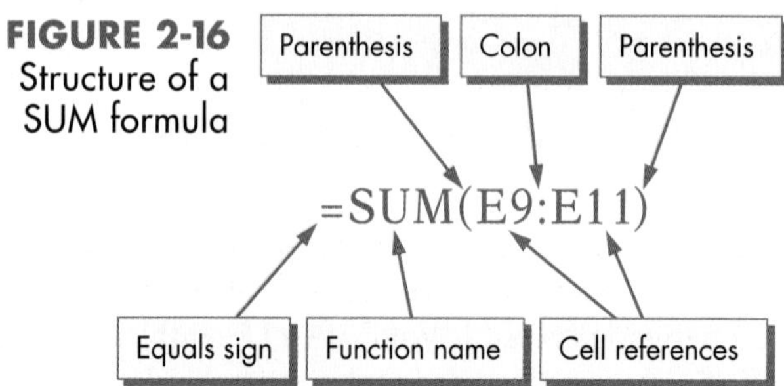

In a SUM formula, the cell references can consist of a single cell or a block of cells. Excel refers to these references as a range. Technically, a range is any group of cells specified to be acted upon by a command. To identify a range, key the cell references for two diagonally opposite corners of a group of cells, separated by a colon.

TABLE 2-6 Examples of Ranges

RANGE	DEFINES
C4:C4	A single cell
B5:B10	A range of cells in column B
D3:G3	A range of cells in row 3
C5:F12	A rectangular range of cells in columns C through F, rows 5 through 12

EXERCISE 2-12 Key a SUM Formula

1. Move to cell D12.
2. Key **=SUM(D9:D11)** and press Enter. The formula adds the contents of cells D9 through D11. The result, "4.487," appears in cell D12.

NOTE: Like cell references, function names are not case-sensitive, so you can key them in lowercase letters.

EXERCISE 2-13 Enter a SUM Formula Using the Arrow Keys

1. Move to cell E12.
2. Key **=SUM(**
3. Press ↑. A moving border surrounds cell E11 and "=SUM(E11" appears in the Formula Bar.
4. Key **:** (the colon) or **.** (the period) to anchor the border. The formula "=SUM(E11:E11" appears in the Formula Bar.
5. Press ↑ twice. The border extends the range from cell E9 through cell E11.
6. Press Enter to complete the formula. Excel inserts the closing parenthesis for you automatically. The completed formula is "=SUM(E9:E11)" and the result is 5.189. In this case, you defined the cell range from the bottom to the top. Excel can add cell contents in either direction.

EXERCISE 2-14 Use the Mouse to Enter a SUM Formula

You can also create SUM formulas using the mouse to drag across cells instead of using the Arrow keys. You can also use the buttons on the Formula Bar to build a SUM formula.

1. In cell G9, key **=SUM(**
2. Using the mouse, click cell B9.
3. Drag across the row from cell B9 to cell F9 and release the mouse button. A moving border surrounds the selected range and the formula "=SUM(B9:F9" appears in the Formula Bar.
4. Click ✓ on the Formula Bar, or press Enter. The formula is completed and the result, "5.2438," appears in cell G9.
5. Move to cell F12.
6. Click =. An equal sign is entered in the cell to start the formula.
7. Click the Function box on the Formula Bar. The SUM function and a suggested range are displayed in the Formula Bar and the Formula Palette pop-up window is displayed under the Formula Bar. (See Figure 2-17 on the next page.)
8. Click OK. The formula is completed and the result, "5.24355," appears in cell F12.

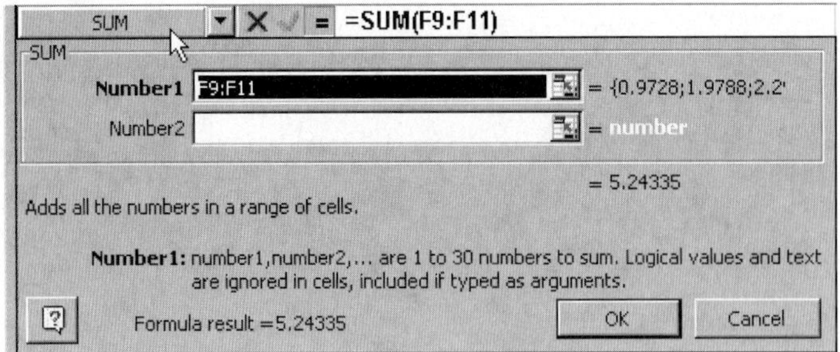

FIGURE 2-17 Formula Palette pop-up window

EXERCISE 2-15 Use the AutoSum Button to Enter a SUM Formula

The AutoSum button Σ is a shortcut for entering the SUM formula, similar to the Function box. It enters **=SUM(** and suggests a range to total. At the bottom of a column of values, AutoSum totals the column. At the right of a row of values, AutoSum totals the row.

1. Move to cell G10.
2. Click the AutoSum button Σ on the Standard toolbar. The formula "=SUM(B10:F10)" appears in the Formula Bar and a moving border surrounds the cells B10 through F10 on the worksheet.
3. Click the Enter box ✓ on the Formula Bar or press Enter. The result, "8.7058," appears in cell G10.
4. With cell G11 selected, double-click Σ. The SUM formula is entered with the result "13.9496." Notice that the formula range is G9:G10 (for the column) rather than B11:F11 (for the row). The AutoSum feature automatically adds column numbers above a cell before adding row numbers to the left of the cell. Because two values appeared above cell G11, Excel assumed a column SUM formula.
5. To correct the range, click Σ again. Notice the moving border surrounds the incorrect range.
6. Drag across cells B11 to F11 and press Enter. The correct result, "8.66575," appears in cell G11.
7. Enter a SUM formula in cell G12, using any method. Check that the formulas contain the correct ranges. (See Figure 2-18 on the next page.)
8. Save the workbook as *[your initials]***2-15.xls**.
9. Print the worksheet.

FIGURE 2-18
Completed worksheet

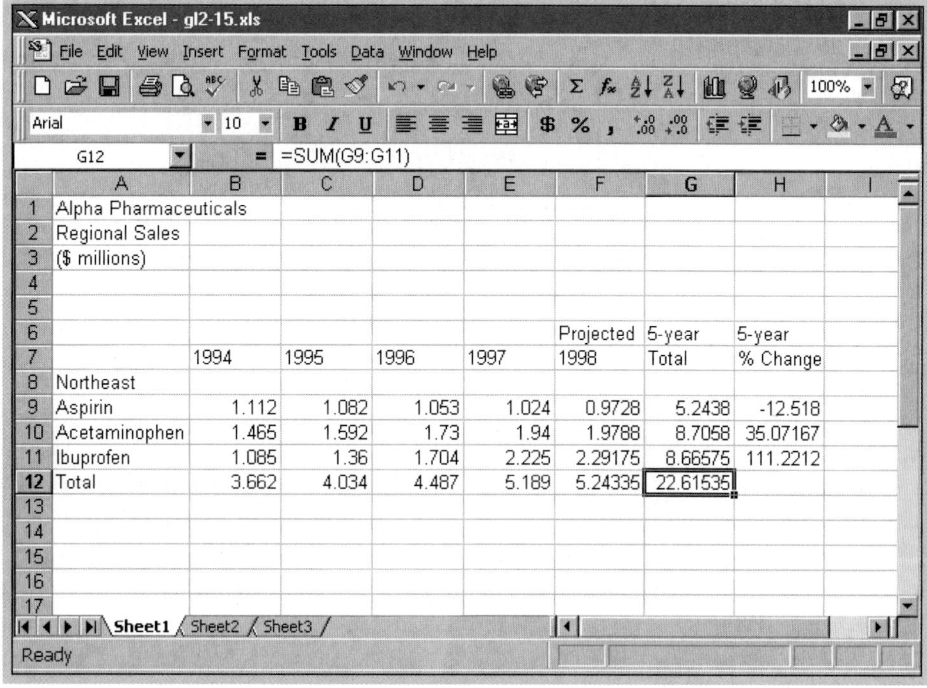

	A	B	C	D	E	F	G	H
1	Alpha Pharmaceuticals							
2	Regional Sales							
3	($ millions)							
4								
5								
6						Projected	5-year	5-year
7		1994	1995	1996	1997	1998	Total	% Change
8	Northeast							
9	Aspirin	1.112	1.082	1.053	1.024	0.9728	5.2438	-12.518
10	Acetaminophen	1.465	1.592	1.73	1.94	1.9788	8.7058	35.07167
11	Ibuprofen	1.085	1.36	1.704	2.225	2.29175	8.66575	111.2212
12	Total	3.662	4.034	4.487	5.189	5.24335	22.61535	
13								
14								
15								
16								
17								

Using AutoCalculate

Excel includes an easy-to-use calculator that is built into the program. You can use this calculator, which is called AutoCalculate, to perform simple calculations without entering a formula. For example, if you select a range of cells, AutoCalculate displays the sum of the cells in the status bar.

EXERCISE 2-16 Use AutoCalculate to Find a Sum

1. Select cells D12 and E12, which contain the total sales for the years 1996 and 1997. At the bottom of the screen, the right portion of the status bar should display "Sum=9.676."
2. Right-click the status bar to display the AutoCalculate menu. Notice the various function names.
3. Choose Sum from the menu, if necessary.
4. Select another range of cells. Notice the sum displayed on the status bar.

FIGURE 2-19 Using AutoCalculate

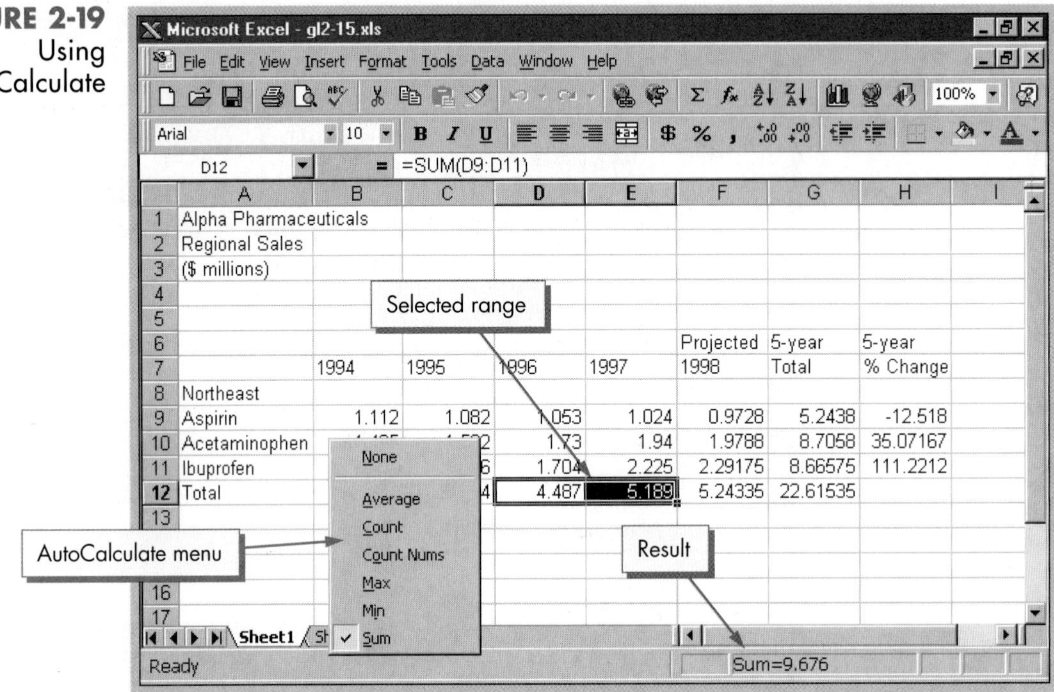

5. Close the workbook without saving it.

COMMAND SUMMARY

FEATURE	BUTTON	MENU	KEYBOARD
Delete cell contents		Edit, Clear, Contents	Delete
Cancel current entry	✕		Esc
Enter	✓		Enter
Edit Formula	=		
AutoSum	Σ		Alt+=

USING HELP

The previous lesson introduced you to the Office Assistant and showed you how to display ScreenTips to identify onscreen items. You can also display a ScreenTip that describes an item. Descriptive ScreenTips are available for menu commands, dialog box options, and parts of the Excel screen.

Display descriptive ScreenTips:

1. Open a new workbook.

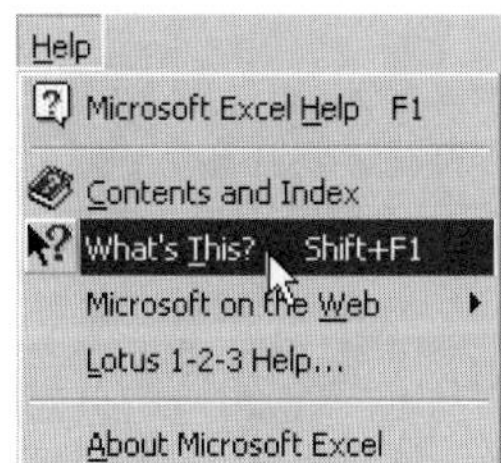

FIGURE 2-20
Help menu

2. Click Help to open the Help menu. Click the menu item What's This? Notice that you can also press Shift+F1. The pointer now has a question mark attached to it.
3. Click the tab scrolling buttons. Review the description and click it to close it.
4. Press Shift+F1 to display the question mark pointer again. Choose Save As from the File menu. Review the description of this command and click to close it.

5. Choose Properties from the File menu and display the Summary tab, if necessary. Click the question mark button [?] to display the question mark pointer. Click Subject (the word or the blank text box), review the description, and close it. In a dialog box, you can repeat this process for as many descriptions as you want.
6. Close the dialog box and close the workbook without saving it.

Concepts Review

TRUE/FALSE QUESTIONS

Each of the following statements is either true or false. Indicate your choice by circling either T or F.

T F *1*. The Delete key has the same effect as choosing Clear from the Edit menu and then choosing Contents.

T F *2*. If a cell containing a formula is included in another formula, the value of the first formula is included in the calculation.

T F *3*. In Excel, formulas begin with an asterisk (*).

T F *4*. You can use parentheses () in a formula to control the order of mathematical operations.

T F *5*. The formula **=SUM(A6:D6)** adds the cells in row 6, from column A to column D.

T F *6*. In formulas, function names must be entered in uppercase letters only.

T F *7*. You can use the AutoSum button to enter a SUM formula.

T F *8*. You can use the SUM function to add the contents of both columns and rows.

SHORT ANSWER QUESTIONS

Write the correct answer in the space provided.

1. Which mode must be displayed in the Status Bar before you begin keying information into a worksheet?

____

2. When you key information into a cell, where else does the information appear on the screen?

____

3. In Edit mode, which key moves to the first character in the Formula Bar?

____

4. Which mathematical operation is indicated by an asterisk (*)?

____

5. Which mathematical operations are given last priority in the order of precedence?

____

6. Which function adds columns and rows?

____

7. What is the result given by the following formula =(10-4)/2?

____

8. What is the result given by the following formula =10-4/2?

____

CRITICAL THINKING

Answer these questions on a separate piece of paper. There are no right or wrong answers. Support your answers with examples from your own experience, if possible.

1. Your boss asks you to proofread a complex worksheet and its printed sources of data. How might AutoCalculate help you verify that data were entered accurately?
2. Last month's sales report worksheet lists products in rows and sales representatives in columns. Your boss asks you to update this report with new data. How can you select cells to speed your work? If your data came from the sales reports of individual sales representatives, would you press Enter or Tab after each entry? Why?

Skills Review

EXERCISE 2-17

Enter data, edit data, and enter labels using the Pick From List and AutoComplete features.

1. Click [New] to start a new workbook.
2. Key **Alpha Pharmaceuticals** in cell A1 and press Enter.
3. Key **1997 Sales - Northeast Region** in cell A2 and press Enter.
4. Key **(in thousands)** in cell A3 and press Enter.

5. Key **Region** in cell B5 and press Enter.
6. Label columns for regional data by following these steps:
   a. In cell B6, key **NE** and press Tab.
   b. In cell C6, key **SE** and press Tab.
   c. In cell D6, key **NW** and press Tab.
   d. In cell E6, key **SW** and click ✓ on the Formula Bar.
7. In cells A7 through A11, key the labels as shown in Figure 2-21.

FIGURE 2-21

	A
7	Q1
8	Aspirin
9	Acetaminophen
10	Ibuprofen
11	Subtotal

8. In cell A12, enter **Q2** (for "second quarter").
9. In cell A13, use the Pick From List feature by following these steps:
   a. Right-click in cell A13 to display the shortcut menu.
   b. Choose Pick From List.
   c. Click "Aspirin" in the list.
10. Use AutoComplete to complete the labels for the second quarter by following these steps:
    a. In cell A14, key **Ac** and press Enter to enter "Acetaminophen."
    b. In cell A15, key **I** and press Enter to enter "Ibuprofen."
    c. In cell A16, key **S** and press Enter to enter "Subtotal."
11. To fit the 13-character row label "Acetaminophen," click any cell in column A and choose Column from the Format menu. Choose Width, key **13**, and click OK.
12. Edit cell A2 to read "1997 Sales" by following these steps:
    a. Double-click cell A2 to switch to Edit mode.
    b. Click the I-beam in the text to the right of "Sales" to position the insertion point.

c. Press Shift + End to select the text to the end of the line.

d. Press Delete.

e. Click ✓ or press Enter.

13. Enter the data as shown in Figure 2-22.

FIGURE 2-22

	A	B	C	D	E
6		NE	SE	NW	SW
7	Q1				
8	Aspirin	250	175	150	200
9	Acetaminophen	500	485	390	450
10	Ibuprofen	600	500	480	510
11	Subtotal				
12	Q2				
13	Aspirin	240	180	160	210
14	Acetaminophen	520	470	400	460
15	Ibuprofen	610	640	490	520
16	Subtotal				

14. Clear the word "Subtotal" from cells A11 and A16 by selecting each cell and pressing Delete.

15. Save the workbook as *[your initials]***2-17.xls**.

16. Print the worksheet and close the workbook.

EXERCISE 2-18

Select cells, enter data in selected cells, and construct basic formulas.

1. Start a new workbook.

2. Create a heading for the worksheet by keying **Alpha Pharmaceuticals** in cell A1 and **Quality Control Payroll** in cell A2.

3. Create column headings by keying the following text in cells A4 through D4, pressing Tab to move across columns:

   Name Salary Years Bonus

4. Practice selecting cell ranges by following these steps:
   a. Click column heading B to select that column.
   b. Click row heading 4 to select that row.
   c. Drag from cell A6 to cell A13 to select the range A6:A13.
   d. Click cell A6, hold down Shift, and click cell C13 to select the range A6:C13.
   e. Hold down Ctrl and drag across the range D6:D13 to add it to the selection.
   f. Click anywhere to deselect the block.

5. Select a cell range and then enter data for eight employees by following these steps:
   a. Select the range A6:C13.
   b. Enter the data shown in Figure 2-23, pressing Enter to move down each column. Begin with the name "Berenson."

FIGURE 2-23

	A	B	C
6	Berenson	28,000	2
7	Alvarez	33,000	6
8	Czerny	42,000	5
9	Teij	54,100	11
10	Silvers	22,200	3
11	Patino	57,000	9
12	Wang	35,300	2
13	Golden	41,000	6

6. Bonuses are calculated as 2% of salary multiplied by years of service, or (0.02 x Salary x Years). Enter the appropriate bonus formulas by following these steps:
   a. In cell D6, key **=.02*B6*C6** and press Enter. Berenson's bonus is $1120, or 2% of $28,000 salary x 2 years of service.

b. In cell D7, key **=.02***, click cell B7, key *, and click cell C7. Press Enter.

c. Using either step A or B as your entry method, enter bonus formulas for the rest of the employees.

7. Save the workbook as *[your initials]***2-18.xls**.
8. Print the worksheet and close the workbook.

EXERCISE 2-19

Use the SUM function, construct formulas, and use AutoCalculate.

1. Open the file **QCBonus.xls**.
2. In cell A14, key **TOTALS**
3. Key a formula that uses the SUM function to calculate the Salary total by following these steps:
   a. Make B14 the active cell.
   b. Key **=SUM(B6:B13)** and press Tab.
4. Use the mouse to build a SUM formula that calculates the total years of experience by following these steps:
   a. In cell C14, enter **=SUM(**
   b. Click cell C6, hold down Shift, and click cell C13.
   c. Press Tab.
5. Use the AutoSum button to calculate the total of the bonuses by following these steps:
   a. In cell D14, click the AutoSum button Σ.
   b. Press Enter.
6. Clear the contents of cell B14.
7. Use AutoCalculate to calculate the salary total by following these steps:
   a. Select cells B6 through B13.
   b. Jot down the number displayed in the status bar. (The number in the status bar should be preceded by "SUM=." If it is not, right-click the status bar and choose Sum from the AutoCalculate menu.)
   c. Select cell B14 and use the AutoSum button to enter the total. This number should be the same as the number you jotted down.
8. Save the workbook as *[your initials]***2-19.xls**.
9. Print the worksheet and close the workbook.

EXERCISE 2-20

Create formulas, print formulas, and interpret formulas.

1. Open the file **Stock.xls**.
2. In cell A21, key **Totals**
3. In cell B21, create a formula that totals the years of experience of the researchers.
4. In cell C21, create a formula that totals the number of shares of stock awarded.
5. Save the workbook as *[your initials]***2-20.xls**.
6. Print the worksheet.
7. Examine the formulas in column C to see how the shares of stock were calculated for each researcher. On the printout, write an explanation of how researchers are awarded shares of stock.
8. Close the workbook.

Lesson Applications

EXERCISE 2-21

Enter data in selected cells and use the SUM function.

1. Open the file **QCPay1.xls**.
2. Select cells B6:C13 and delete their contents.
3. Key the data as shown in Figure 2-24.

FIGURE 2-24

	A	B	C	D
5	Name	Rate	Hours	Pay
6	Berenson	9.25	40	
7	Alvarez	9.46	40	
8	Czerny	10.54	38	
9	Teij	10.64	40	
10	Silvers	9.50	37.5	
11	Patino	10.00	40	
12	Wang	9.88	40	
13	Golden	9.96	40	

4. Create formulas that calculate the Pay for each employee (Rate x Hours).
5. Key **Total** in cell A15.
6. In cell C15, use the SUM function to calculate the total Hours.
7. In cell D15, calculate the total Pay using the AutoSum button. Be sure to adjust the range to add the data in column D.
8. Save the workbook as *[your initials]***2-21.xls**.
9. Print the worksheet and close the workbook.

EXERCISE 2-22

Enter data, construct formulas, use the SUM function, and use AutoCalculate.

1. Open the file **QCPay2.xls**.
2. Key the headings and data as shown in Figure 2-25.

FIGURE 2-25

	E	F
5	Overtime	O.T. Pay
6	2	
7	3	
8	0	
9	1.5	
10	0	
11	4.25	
12	2.5	
13	3	

3. Use AutoCalculate to total the number of hours in column C and enter this number into cell C15. Use the same method to enter the Pay total in cell D15.
4. In cell E15, use the SUM function to calculate the total Overtime hours. (If you use the AutoSum button, remember to adjust the suggested cell range.)
5. Create a formula for each employee to calculate his or her O.T. Pay. Use the formula "Rate times Overtime times 1.5." (Overtime pay is typically calculated as "time and a half"—that is, at a rate of 1.5 hours.)
6. In cell F15, use the SUM function to calculate the total amount of overtime pay.
7. Save your workbook as *[your initials]***2-22.xls**.
8. Print the worksheet and close the workbook.

EXERCISE 2-23

Enter data, use AutoComplete and Pick From List, construct formulas, use the SUM function, and use AutoCalculate.

1. Open the file **R&DStaf.xls**.
2. Key the information shown in Figure 2-26, using AutoComplete and Pick From List where possible.

FIGURE 2-26

	B	C	D	E	F
5	Clearance	Level	Years	Vacation Days	Manager
6					
7	None	D15	2		Tang
8	Mid	B23	2		Richards
9	Top	A43	3		Tang
10	Mid	B23	3		Tang
11	Top	A43	5		Stevens
12	Mid	B23	5		Stevens
13					
14	Top	A43	6		Richards
15	Mid	B23	6		Stevens
16	None	D15	8		Tang
17					
18	None	B23	14		Stevens
19	None	C15	15		Richards
20	Mid	D15	19		Tang

3. Calculate the amount of Vacation Days due each employee using the following information:

For 1 to 5 years: (Years*0.1 + 5)

For 6 to 10 years: (Years*0.1 + 10)

For more than 10 years: (Years*0.15 + 15)

4. Use AutoCalculate to calculate the total Vacation Days and enter this number in the appropriate cell.
5. Use the SUM function to calculate the total Years.
6. Save your workbook as *[your initials]***2-23.xls**.
7. Print worksheet and close the workbook.

EXERCISE 2-24

Enter data, construct formulas, and use AutoSum.

Alpha Pharmaceuticals' marketing director wants to compare the company's sales with national sales for each product. One way to make this comparison is to calculate market share by dividing Alpha's sales by national sales. Prepare a worksheet that shows market share as a percentage of national sales.

1. Open the file **MktShare.xls**.
2. Key **1997 Market Share** in cell A2.
3. Select the cell range B8:C10 and key the data shown in Figure 2-27.

FIGURE 2-27

	A	B	C
8	Aspirin	19.671	4.085
9	Acetaminophen	25.093	7.314
10	Ibuprofen	29.384	7.457

4. In cell D8, calculate Alpha's market share for aspirin by creating a formula to divide cell C8 by cell B8.
5. Create formulas to calculate the market share in cells D9 and D10.
6. Using either AutoCalculate or the SUM function, calculate the total pain reliever sales for national sales and Alpha sales in cells B12 and C12, respectively.
7. Calculate Alpha's total market share for pain relievers in cell D12.
8. Save the workbook as *[your initials]***2-24.xls**.
9. Print the worksheet and close the workbook.

EXERCISE 2-25

Enter data, construct formulas, and use AutoSum.

To prepare for an annual financial planning meeting, the marketing director of Alpha Pharmaceuticals has asked you to create a worksheet that calculates projected national sales for aspirin, acetaminophen, and ibuprofen for 1998 and 1999. These projected sales will be based on 1997 sales information.

1. Create an appropriate heading for the worksheet, with an indicator that the sales figures are expressed in millions.
2. Enter the information in Figure 2-28 as 1997 data. Be sure to widen column A so the characters in "Acetaminophen" fit.
3. Make sure the text "1997" is entered as a label, and not a number, so it is excluded from calculations. (This step also applies to other cells in the worksheet containing years.)

FIGURE 2-28

Product	1997
Aspirin	4.085
Acetaminophen	7.314
Ibuprofen	7.457

4. For 1998 and 1999 projected sales, show a 2% increase over the previous year's sales for aspirin and acetaminophen, and a 3% increase each year for ibuprofen.
5. Calculate total sales of pain relievers for each year.
6. Save the workbook as *[your initials]***2-25.xls**.
7. Print the worksheet and close the workbook.

Enhancing a Simple Worksheet

OBJECTIVES

After completing this lesson, you will be able to:

1. Select multiple columns and rows.
2. Insert cells, columns, and rows.
3. Delete cells, columns, and rows.
4. Use the Undo and Redo commands.
5. Use shortcut menus.
6. Move data.
7. Format numbers.
8. Apply text attributes and cell borders.

Estimated Time: 1 hour

This lesson teaches easy ways to modify a worksheet by inserting and deleting cells, columns, and rows; changing the number of decimal places displayed; and applying basic text and alignment attributes.

Selecting Multiple Columns and Rows

As you learned in Lesson 2, clicking a row or column heading selects that row or column. You can also select several columns and rows at the same time.

EXERCISE 3-1 Select Multiple Columns and Rows with the Mouse

1. Open the file **USSales1.xls**.
2. Click column heading A to select the column.
3. Click and drag over row headings 2, 3, and 4. The column is deselected and the three rows are selected.
4. Click column heading B, hold down Shift, and click column heading E. Columns B through E are selected.
5. Drag over row headings 2 and 3 to select those rows.
6. Hold down Ctrl and click column heading B. Two rows and one column are selected.

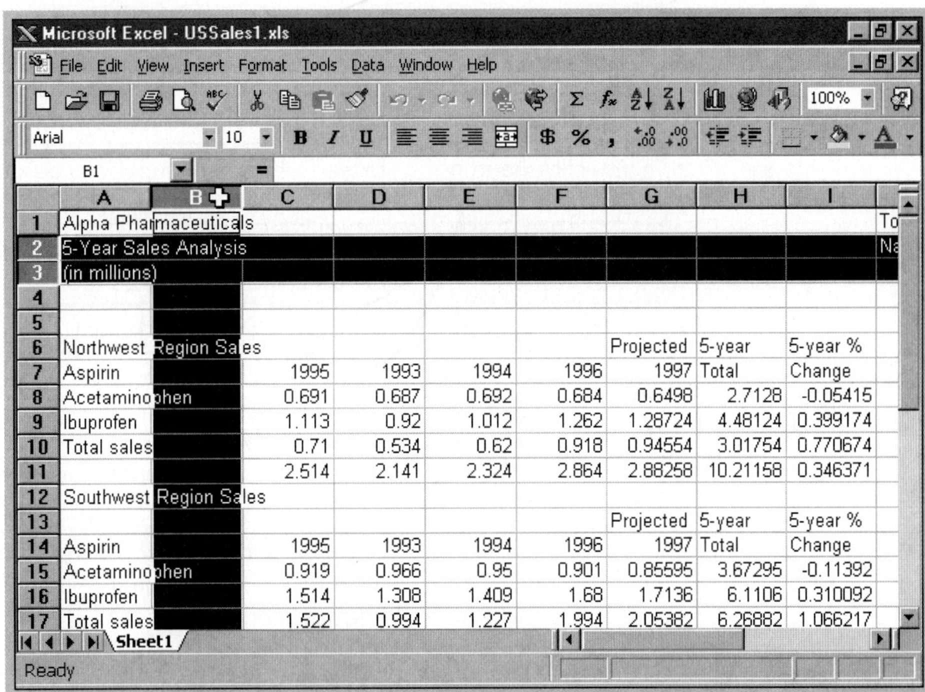

FIGURE 3-1 Selecting columns and rows with the mouse

7. Click any cell in the worksheet to deselect the columns and rows.

EXERCISE 3-2 Select Multiple Columns and Rows with the Keyboard

1. In cell C7, press Shift+Spacebar to select row 7.
2. Select cell D5. Row 7 is deselected.

3. Press Ctrl+Spacebar to select column D.
4. While holding Shift, press → three times. The selection is extended through column G.
5. Select cell B7.
6. Press Shift+→ twice to select cells B7 through D7.
7. Press Ctrl+Spacebar to select columns B through D.
8. Use the keyboard to select cells C7 through E9 and press Shift+Spacebar. Rows 7 through 9 are selected.
9. Press any arrow key to deselect the rows.

TABLE 3-1 Selecting Columns and Rows

ACTION	RESULT
Click heading	Selects a column or row.
Drag across headings	Selects multiple columns or rows.
Shift+click heading	Extends the selection to include adjacent columns or rows.
Ctrl+click heading	Extends the selection to include nonadjacent columns or rows.
Click Select All button	Selects the entire worksheet.
Shift+Spacebar	Selects the current row.
Ctrl+Spacebar	Selects the current column.
Shift+Arrow keys, PgUp or PgDn	Extends the row or column selection (first select a row or column).
Shift+Double-click	When the arrow cursor is displayed, selects the filled column or row in the direction of the vertical edge clicked.

Inserting Cells, Columns, and Rows

You can add cells, columns, and rows to a worksheet to make room for more data or to make the worksheet easier to read. You can do this using the Insert menu or the keyboard shortcut Ctrl+[+] (the plus key on the numeric keypad).

EXERCISE 3-3 Insert a Single Cell

A section of the **USSales1.xls** worksheet shows 10 years of national pain-reliever sales, but contains some errors. When the row labels in column J were keyed, "1989" was skipped. You can insert a cell to correct this problem.

1. Press Alt+PgDn to bring columns J through R into view.
2. Select cell J7. Notice that cell J6 contains "1988" and cell J7 contains "1990."
3. Choose Cells from the Insert menu. The Insert dialog box opens.

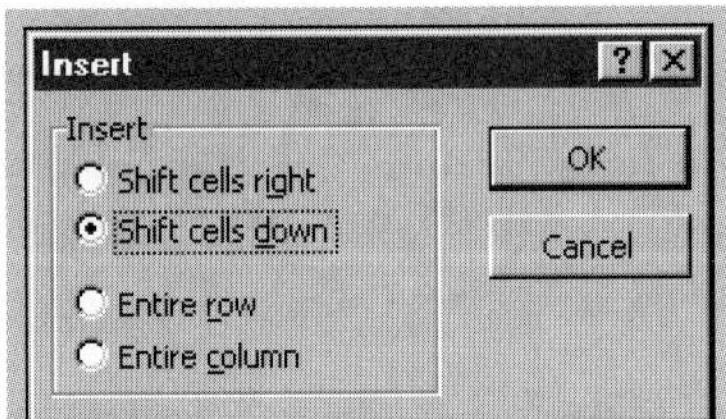

FIGURE 3-2 Insert dialog box

4. Click Cancel and press Ctrl+(+) on the numeric keypad. The Insert dialog box opens again.
5. Choose Shift cells down and click OK. An empty cell appears at cell J7. The labels below shift down one cell.
6. Key **1989** in cell J7 and press Enter.

EXERCISE 3-4 Insert an Entire Column and Row

You can insert an entire row or column in a worksheet at the position of the active cell. Use the Insert menu or the keyboard shortcut Ctrl+(+) on the numeric keypad.

1. Select cell A19.

TIP: Remember, you can use the key combination Alt+PgUp to move one screen left.

2. Choose Rows from the Insert menu. A blank row appears at row 19 and all the information below this row moves down one row.
3. Select row 19 and press Ctrl+(+). Another row is inserted automatically.
4. Press F5 to open the Go To dialog box.
5. Key **J1** and click OK (or press Enter).
6. Click the column J heading to select the entire column.
7. Choose Columns from the Insert menu (or press Ctrl+(+)). A blank column appears at column J and all the information beyond column J moves right one column.

EXERCISE 3-5 Insert Multiple Cells, Columns, and Rows

To insert several cells, columns, or rows in the same operation, select them before choosing a command. For example, if you select two rows, choosing Rows from the Insert menu (or pressing Ctrl+[+]) inserts two blank rows.

When you insert rows or columns, be careful not to separate blocks of data by mistake. Rows and columns span the entire worksheet, not just the visible portion of your screen. Rows extend 256 cells across and columns stretch 65,536 cells down.

1. Select rows 28 and 29 and press Ctrl+[+]. Two blank rows are inserted to separate "Northeast Region Sales" from "Southeast Region Sales."
2. Select rows 12 and 13.
3. Click the right side of the horizontal scroll bar (at the bottom of the screen). Notice that inserting rows here would break up data inappropriately in columns K through O.

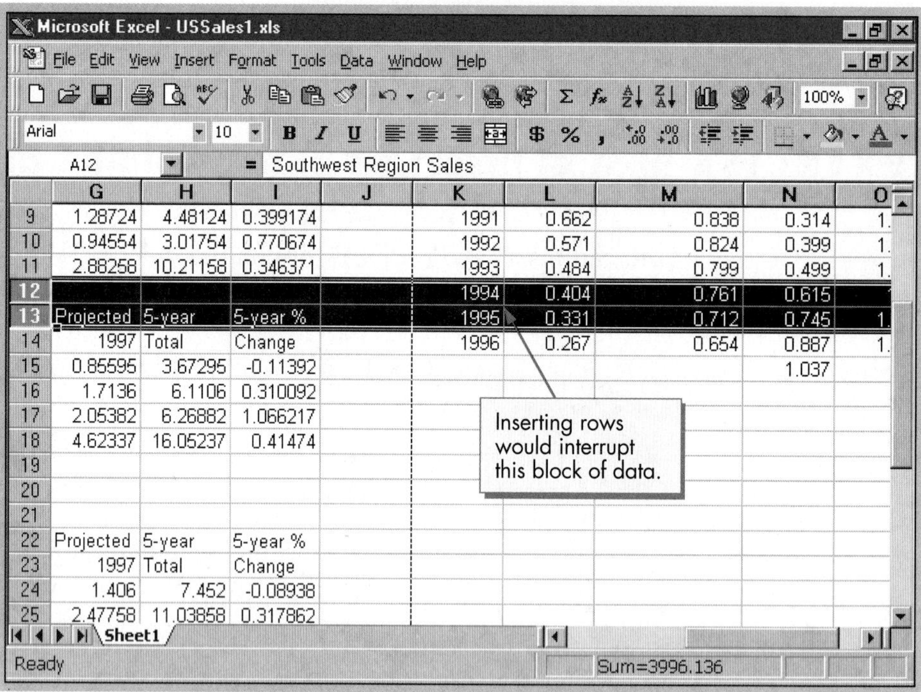

FIGURE 3-3 Selecting to insert multiple rows

4. Deselect the rows and scroll back to view columns A through I.
5. Select cells A12 through I13 and press Ctrl+[+].
6. In the Insert dialog box, choose Shift cells down and click OK. Blank cells appear at cells A12 through I13 and all the data from cells A12 through I13 move down two cells.

7. Press Alt+PgDn to view the 10-year historical data. Notice that no blank cells interrupt the data.

Deleting Cells, Columns, and Rows

You can delete cells, columns, and rows in much the same way that you insert them. Choose Delete from the Edit menu or press Ctrl+- (the minus sign on the numeric keypad).

When you delete cells, those cells are removed from the worksheet and the surrounding cells move to fill the space. If the deleted cells contained data, the data is also removed from the worksheet. In contrast, clearing the contents of cells removes the information contained in those cells, but allows the cells to remain in the worksheet.

NOTE: Never clear contents by keying a blank space in a cell. Although the cell appears blank, it actually contains a label. This label may ultimately affect calculations.

EXERCISE 3-6 Delete Cells, Columns, and Rows

1. Select cell N8. This cell contains the same entry as cell N7. The data in column N extends one row below the data in the other columns.
2. Choose Delete from the Edit menu. The Delete dialog box opens.

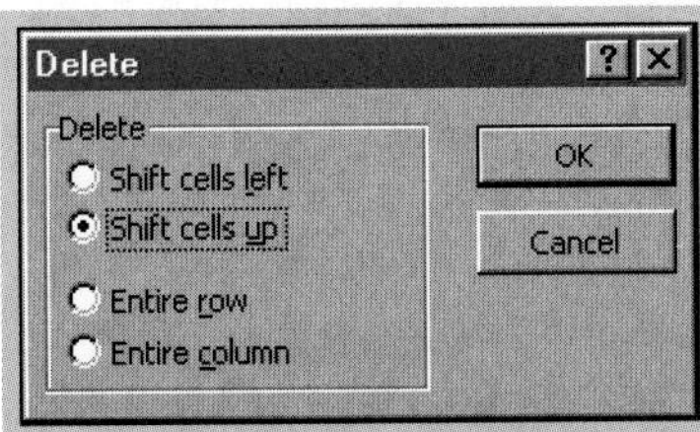

FIGURE 3-4
Delete dialog box

3. Choose Shift cells up and click OK. Cell N8 is deleted and the cells move up to fill the gap.
4. Select column B and choose Delete from the Edit menu. Column B is deleted.
5. Select column B, if necessary, and press Ctrl++ to insert the column.
6. Press Ctrl+- to delete column B again.
7. Select column A.
8. Adjust the width of column A to accommodate the width of the label in cell A8 by choosing Column from the Format menu, choosing Width, and then keying **13** in the text box. Click OK.

NOTE: A well-designed worksheet should not contain blank columns, but should have column widths that are adjusted to fit text.

Using the Undo and Redo Commands

The Undo command reverses the last action you performed on the worksheet. If you deleted a column, for example, Undo brings back the column and its data. If you accidentally overwrite existing data in a cell, Undo restores the original cell contents. To use the Undo command, it is best to choose it immediately after the action you want to undo. The Redo command reverses the action of the Undo command. (You can "undo" Undo.)

You can also use these commands to undo and redo multiple actions at once. You can select Undo and Redo multiple times to step back through you last actions. Undo and Redo reverse actions sequentially. That is, to reverse a specific action, you must reverse any that came before it first.

To use the Undo command, click the Undo button on the Standard toolbar, press Ctrl+Z, or choose Undo from the Edit menu. To use the Redo command, click the Redo button on the Standard toolbar, press Ctrl+Y, or choose Redo from the Edit menu. To undo or redo multiple actions, click the down arrows on the Undo and Redo buttons and select the actions you want to undo or redo from the drop-down list.

NOTE: Undo and Redo are convenient tools, but their usefulness is limited. It is always best to save your worksheet frequently. If you then make an unrecoverable error, you can simply close the worksheet without saving it and then reopen it.

EXERCISE  3-7 Use the Undo and Redo Commands

1. Save the worksheet as *[your initials]***3-7.xls**. Note that both the Undo and Redo buttons are shaded since there are no actions yet to undo or redo.
2. Select column C by clicking its column heading.
3. Choose Delete from the Edit menu. The column is deleted. Notice that the shading on the button is gone.
4. Choose Undo Delete from the Edit menu (or press Ctrl+Z). The column is restored. Notice that the shading on the Redo button has disappeared and the Undo button is shaded. (If Undo did not work, close the worksheet without saving it and open it again.)
5. Choose Redo Delete (or press Ctrl+Y). The undo is reversed and the column is deleted again.
6. Select cell B11 and press Delete. The contents of B11 are cleared.

7. Click the down arrow on the Undo button to see the drop-down list. Notice that the most recent action, which was clearing cell B11, is at the top of the list.

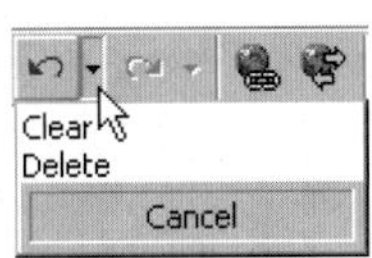

FIGURE 3-5
Undo drop-down list

8. Click Delete on the drop-down list. The contents of cell B11 and column C are restored.

9. Click . This reverses the last undo; and column C is deleted again.

10. Click again. The column is restored.

11. Click any cell to deselect column C.

Using Shortcut Menus

Shortcut menus provide quick access to commands you use often, bypassing the menu bar. To display a shortcut menu, select a cell, a cell range, a row, or a column, and right click the selection or press Shift + F10. The commands you are most likely to use are listed in the shortcut menu. To choose a command, click it with the left mouse button.

EXERCISE 3-8 Use Shortcut Menus

All the row labels in column A, starting in cell A7, are positioned one cell too high. To correct this problem, you can insert a cell at cell A7.

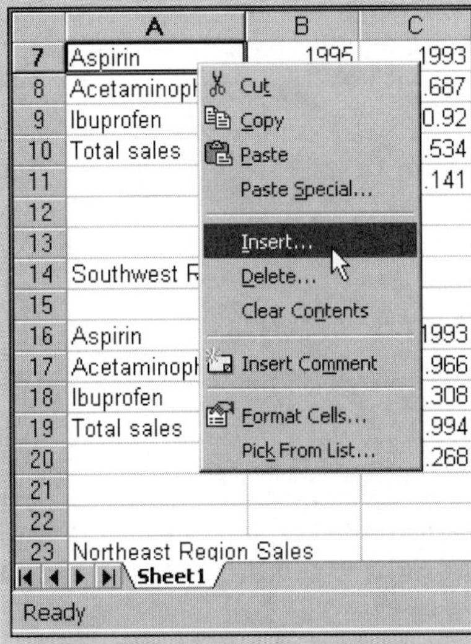

FIGURE 3-6
Shortcut menu for cell ranges

1. Make cell A7 the active cell.

2. While pointing inside cell A7, click the right mouse button. The shortcut menu appears.

3. Use the left mouse button to choose Insert from the shortcut menu.

4. In the Insert dialog box, choose Shift cells down and click OK. The row labels are positioned correctly.

Moving Data to a New Location

You can easily move the contents of cells to another location without rekeying data. One way is to cut and paste the information, which is a two-step operation. First, you *cut* selected cells. You then move to a new location and *paste* the data in the cells at the new location. You can also copy a selection and paste a copy of it in a new location. Lesson 5 discusses copying in detail.

Excel provides several ways to issue the cut and paste commands, including:

- The toolbar buttons Cut and Paste
- Keyboard shortcuts Ctrl+X to cut and Ctrl+V to paste
- The shortcut menu

When you cut or copy data from selected cells, it is stored temporarily on the *Clipboard*, an area in the computer's active memory. The Paste command transfers the contents of the Clipboard to the location you choose.

EXERCISE 3-9 Move Data Using Cut and Paste

1. Right click cell A3.
2. Choose Cut from the shortcut menu. A moving border surrounds cell A3.
3. Click cell A4 and click the Paste button on the Standard toolbar. Cell A3 is cleared, the moving border disappears, and the contents of cell A3 appear in cell A4.
4. Click to undo the Paste command. The moving border marks cell A3 and cell A4 becomes the active cell again.
5. Press Enter. The text is moved. Pressing Enter has the same effect as the Paste command when the moving border marks a range of cut cells.
6. Click to restore the text to cell A3. Press Esc to remove the moving border.

EXERCISE 3-10 Move Data Using Insert Cut Cells

When you paste data to a cell range, any data contained in the range is overwritten by the new data. To insert data at a location that already contains data, use the Insert Cut Cells command. This command causes the existing cells to be shifted down or to the right when data is moved to that location.

1. Save the worksheet as *[your initials]***3-10.xls**.

2. Select cells B7 through B11.
3. Choose Cut from the shortcut menu.
4. Select cell E7.
5. Press Ctrl+V, the keyboard shortcut for Paste. The "1996" data in cells E7 through E11 is overwritten by the "1995" data. Because the formulas in columns F, G, and H referenced the "1996" data, the notation #REF! appears in the cells that contain formulas, indicating a reference error.
6. Click [Undo]. The data is restored and the reference errors are no longer displayed.
7. With the moving border again surrounding cells B7 through B11, and cells E7 through E11 selected, choose Cut Cells from the Insert menu or choose Insert Cut Cells from the shortcut menu. The "1995" data is inserted between the "1994" and "1996" data. The formulas are not disturbed by the move.

FIGURE 3-7
Inserting cut cells

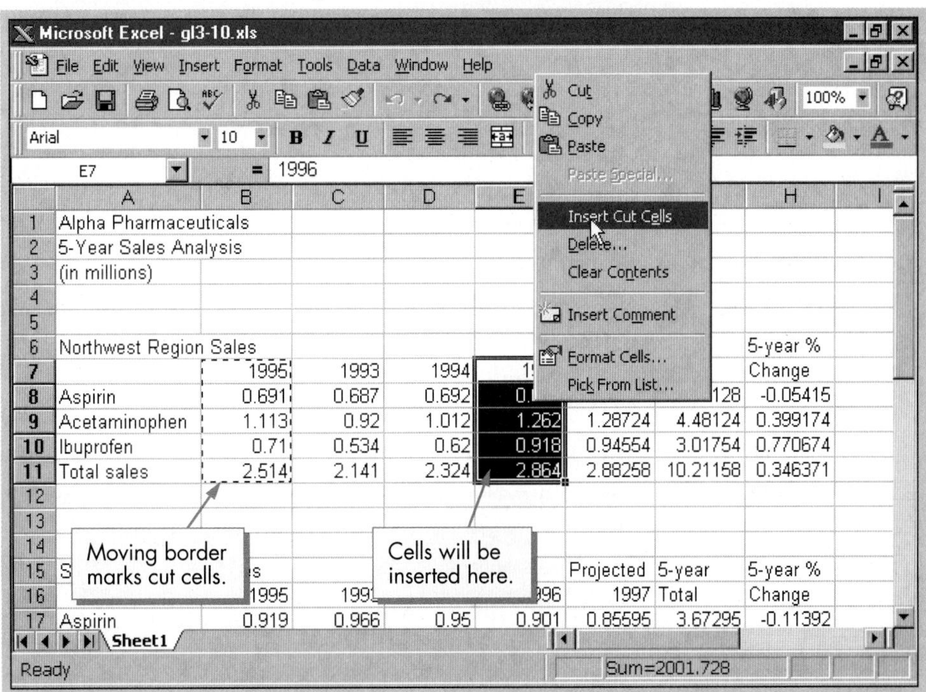

EXERCISE 3-11 Move Data Using Drag and Drop

When you move the white-cross pointer slowly across the border of an active cell or selected cells, it changes to an arrow. This arrow is the drag-and-drop pointer, which you use to move data to a new location. Old data is replaced with moved data when you release the mouse button.

1. Select cells A1 through A3.
2. Slowly move the white-cross pointer across the selection's border until the white cross changes into an arrow.

NOTE: If the arrow pointer does not appear, choose Options from the Tools menu, click the Edit tab, and click the Allow cell drag and drop check box to select the option.

3. Press and hold the left mouse button.
4. Move the arrow to cell D1. A light gray border surrounds cells D1 through D3.

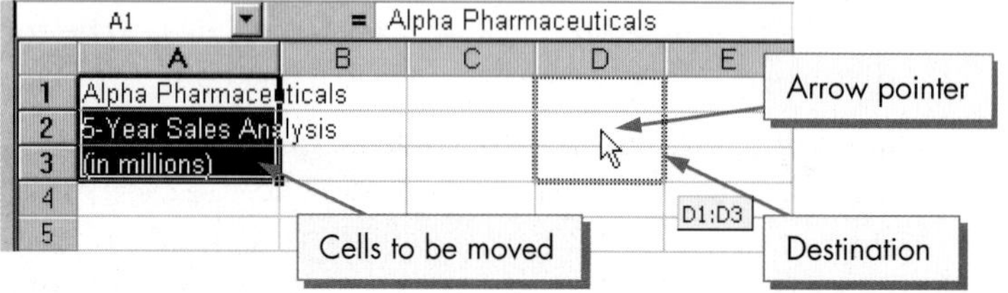

FIGURE 3-8 Using the drag-and-drop method to move data

5. Release the mouse button. The data is moved and cells A1 through A3 are cleared.
6. Select cells B16 through B20.
7. Move the mouse pointer to the border of the selection until you see the arrow pointer.

FIGURE 3-9 Using the drag-and-drop method to insert cut cells

Sales				Proje
1995	1993	1994	1996	
0.919	0.966	0.95	0.901	0.8
1.514	1.308	1.409	1.68	1.
1.522	0.994	1.227	1.994	2.0
3.955	3.268	3.586	4.575	4.6

I-beam marks destination

8. Hold down Shift and drag the I-beam to the vertical gridline between columns D and E, with the top of the I-beam between rows 15 and 16. Notice that you are dragging an I-beam, not a rectangle.
9. Release the mouse button and then release Shift. You inserted the cut cells. The "1995" data is inserted between the "1994" and "1996" data.

EXERCISE 3-12 Check Cell References and Formulas after Moving Data

When you move formulas, the cell references in the formulas remain the same, as do the calculations performed by those formulas. When you move cells that are referenced by formulas, Excel updates the formulas automatically so they

reference the new location of the cells. For example, if a SUM function references the range C5:C10, and you move the contents of cell C10 to cell C12, the SUM function changes automatically to reference the range C5:C12. Always check formulas after moving data to ensure they are updated correctly.

1. Select cell G8. The correct formula, =SUM(B8:F8), appears on the Formula Bar.
2. Select cell H8. The correct formula, =(F8-B8)/B8, appears on the Formula Bar.
3. Check formulas throughout the worksheet.

Formatting Numbers: The Basics

You can format numbers to have a similar appearance without changing their mathematical values. For instance, the values resulting from division often have many decimal places, which may not be aligned. If you format cells to show only two decimal places, the results are neat and easy to read. Excel still stores all the undisplayed digits, however, and uses them in future computations. You can redisplay complete values at any time.

The Excel Formatting toolbar offers a convenient way to format numbers. More information on number formats, such as dates, fractions, and custom formats, is presented in Lesson 8: "Formatting Text and Numbers."

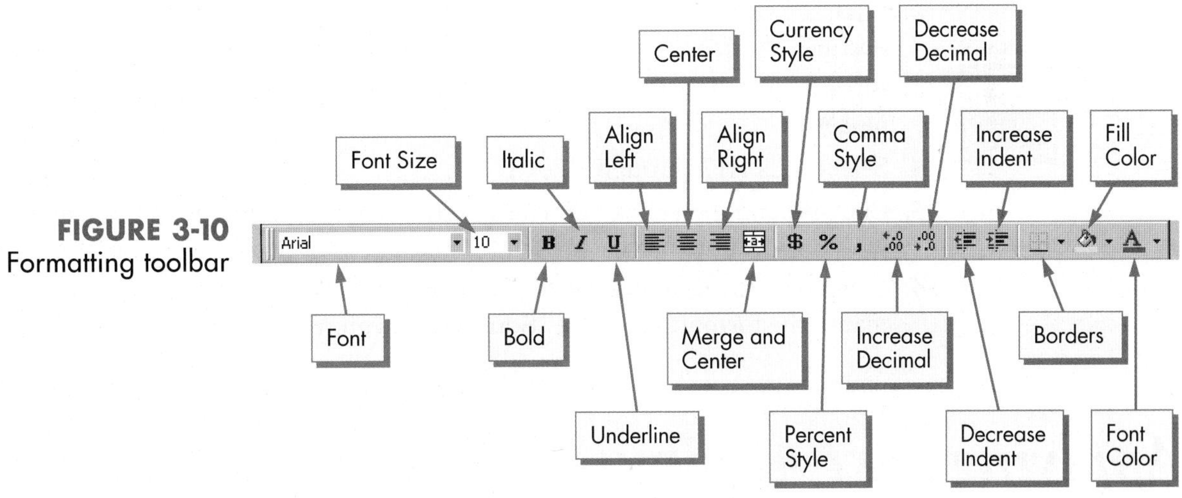

FIGURE 3-10
Formatting toolbar

EXERCISE 3-13 Format Numbers in Comma Style and Percent Style

1. Select cell G8.
2. Click the Comma Style button on the toolbar. Cell G8 is formatted with two decimal places. The Comma Style button inserts commas to separate thousands, if needed, and formats values to have two decimal places.
3. Select cells B8 through G11.
4. Click again. All the selected cells are formatted with two decimal places and the decimals are aligned.

5. Select cells H8 through H11.
6. Click the Percent Style button. The selected cells are formatted as percentages with no decimals.

EXERCISE 3-14 Change the Number of Decimals Displayed

You can use the Increase Decimal and Decrease Decimal buttons on the Formatting toolbar to control the number of decimal places displayed in cells.

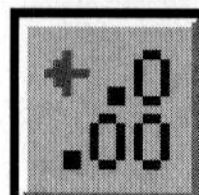

1. Select cells B17 through G20.
2. Click the Decrease Decimal button. The selected cells display two decimal places.
3. Click the Increase Decimal button. The cells display three decimal places.
4. Select cells H17 through H20.
5. Click and then click. The selected cells are displayed as percentages with one decimal place.
6. Using the Formatting toolbar, format all the sales region numbers to match the formatting of the "Southwest Region" numbers.

Applying Text Attributes Using the Toolbar

You can use the buttons on the Formatting toolbar to format text as well as numbers. You can control alignment in a cell, apply bold and italics, draw lines, and change the size of text.

NOTE: Text attributes and borders are discussed in more detail in Unit 3: "Changing the Appearance of a Worksheet."

EXERCISE 3-15 Apply Text Attributes Using the Toolbar

1. Select cells D1 through D3.
2. Click the Center button on the Formatting toolbar. The text in cells D1 through D3 is centered in the cells, but spills over to cells in columns C and E.

3. Select cells D1 and D2.
4. Click the Bold button **B**. The selected text becomes bold.
5. Select cells F6 through H7.

6. Click the Align Right button. The text is aligned with the numbers below it.

TIP: Column titles should always be aligned with their related data.

7. Select cells A6 through H7 and cells A11 through H11.
8. Click **B** to make the selection bold.

FIGURE 3-11 Formatting the worksheet

Microsoft Excel - gl3-10.xls

	A	B	C	D	E	F	G	H
1				**Alpha Pharmaceuticals**				
2				**5-Year Sales Analysis**				
3				(in millions)				
4								
5								
6	**Northwest Region Sales**					**Projected**	**5-year**	**5-year %**
7		**1993**	**1994**	**1995**	**1996**	**1997**	**Total**	**Change**
8	Aspirin	0.687	0.692	0.691	0.684	0.650	3.404	-5.4%
9	Acetaminophen	0.920	1.012	1.113	1.262	1.287	5.594	39.9%
10	Ibuprofen	0.534	0.620	0.710	0.918	0.946	3.728	77.1%
11	**Total sales**	**2.141**	**2.324**	**2.514**	**2.864**	**2.883**	**12.726**	**34.6%**
12								
13								
14								
15	Southwest Region Sales					Projected	5-year	5-year %
16		1993	1994	1995	1996	1997	Total	Change
17	Aspirin	0.966	0.950	0.919	0.901	0.856	4.592	-11.4%

Sheet1

Ready

EXERCISE 3-16 Use Format Painter to Copy Attributes

Once you apply a variety of attributes to a cell range—such as bold and italic, alignment, and number styles—you can copy the attributes from one cell range to another using the Format Painter button on the Formatting toolbar.

1. Select cells A6 through H11.
2. Click the Format Painter button. The selection is surrounded by a moving border. You can now copy the formatting of this range to other sales region data in the worksheet.
3. Use the vertical scroll bar to display cells A15 through H20.

NOTE: When you use the Format Painter, use the scroll bar to navigate around the screen instead of the arrow keys to prevent the cells between the source and destination cells from being painted.

4. Using the Format Painter pointer, select cells A15 through H20, the "Southwest Region Sales" data. The formatting is applied to the data.

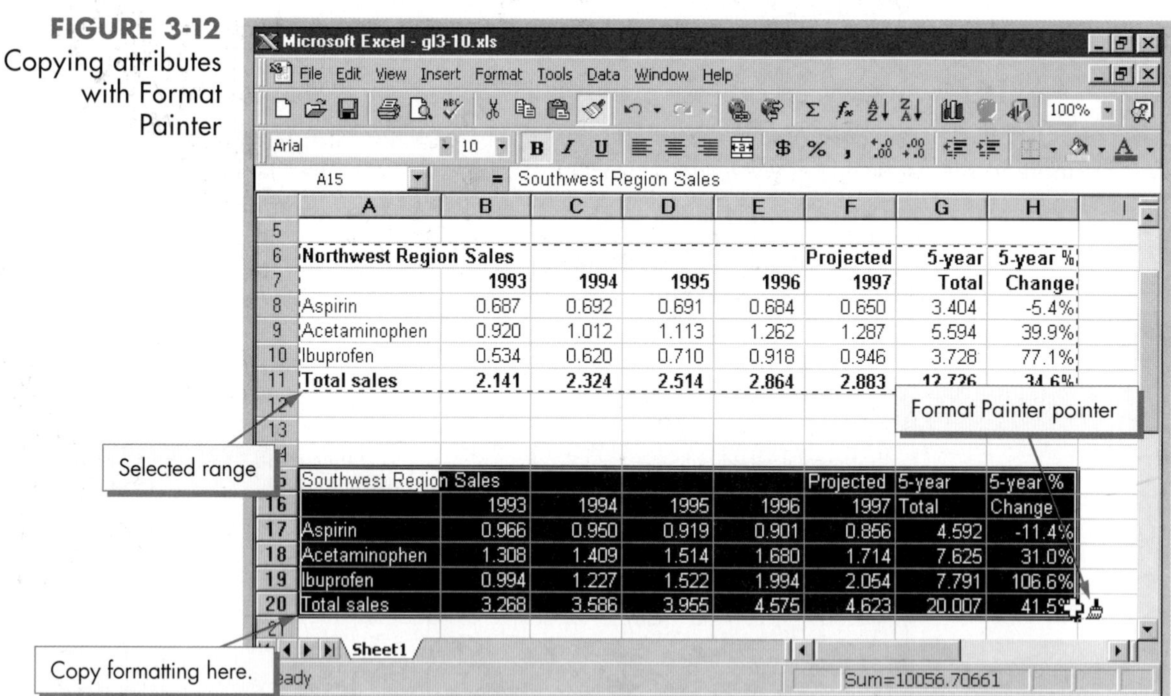

FIGURE 3-12 Copying attributes with Format Painter

5. With the cell range A15 through H20 still selected, double-click. Double-clicking the button when you want to copy formatting multiple times.

6. Use the Format Painter pointer to select cells A24 through H29 and select cells A33 through H38. All the regions now have the same formatting.
7. Press Esc to restore the normal pointer.

EXERCISE 3-17 Apply Borders to the Bottoms of Cells

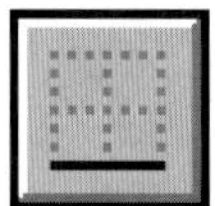

You can create a line to separate data by formatting cells with a bottom border. The easiest way to apply a border is by using the Borders button on the Formatting toolbar.

1. Select cells A7 through H7.

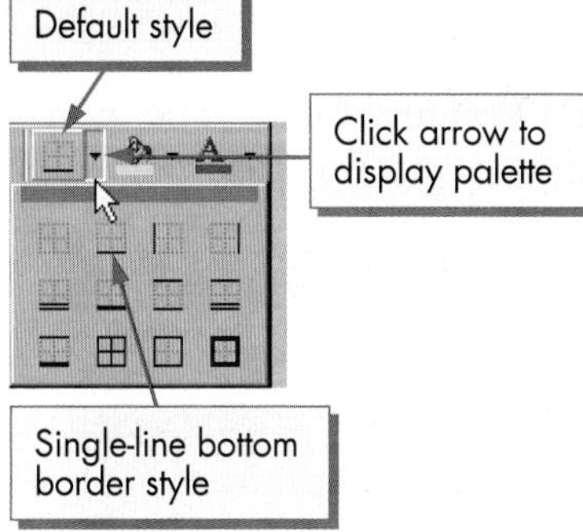

FIGURE 3-13 Borders palette

2. Click the down arrow on the right side of the Borders button. The Borders palette appears.
3. Choose the single-line bottom border style (first row, second column) on the palette. The bottom borders of cells A7 through H7 are formatted as a single solid line. The Borders button default is now single-line bottom border.
4. Apply the same border style to separate the headings from data in the other three regions. Remember, uses the most recently applied border style as a default.
5. Save the file as *[your initials]***3-17.xls**.
6. Print the worksheet and close the workbook.

COMMAND SUMMARY

FEATURE	BUTTON	MENU	KEYBOARD
Insert Cells		Insert, Cells, Rows, or Columns	Ctrl + +
Delete Cells		Edit, Delete	Ctrl + -
Cut		Edit, Cut	Ctrl + X
Paste		Edit, Paste	Ctrl + V
Undo		Edit, Undo	Ctrl + Z
Redo		Edit, Redo	Ctrl + Y

USING HELP

Excel's online Help is extremely comprehensive. The Office Assistant can direct you to Help topics related to the work you are doing, but you can also access Help directly by browsing through the Help Contents window or using the Help Index

Explore the range of topics available in Help Contents

1. Choose Contents and Index from the Help menu.
2. Click the Contents tab, if necessary.
3. Scroll the list of topics, each of which is represented by a book icon.
4. Double-click the topic "Formatting Worksheets." A new group of subtopics is displayed.
5. Double-click "Formatting Text and Cells." The outline expands even further, displaying specific formatting tasks.

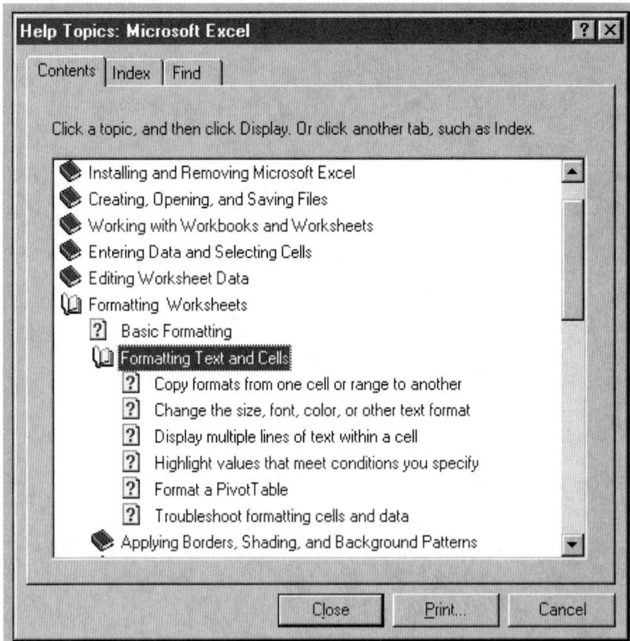

FIGURE 3-14
Formatting Help topics

6. Double click the topic "Copy formats from one cell or range to another." Excel displays a Help window with a how-to description.
7. Review the description and click ☒ to close the window.

Concepts Review

TRUE/FALSE QUESTIONS

Each of the following statements is either true or false. Indicate your choice by circling either T or F.

T F *1.* After selecting a column with the mouse, you can extend that selection only by using the mouse.

T F *2.* You can insert an entire row using the Insert dialog box.

T F *3.* When you delete a cell using the Delete dialog box, both the cell and its contents are removed from the worksheet.

T F *4.* Clicking three times reverses your last three actions.

T F *5.* Double-clicking a cell displays a shortcut menu.

T F *6.* The Cut, Paste, and Copy buttons are located on the Standard toolbar.

T F *7.* The Comma Style button formats numbers to display two decimal places.

T F *8.* You can use to copy both alignment and number formatting from one cell range to another.

SHORT ANSWER QUESTIONS

Write the correct answer in the space provided.

1. To extend a selection using the arrow keys, which key must you hold down?

____

2. To insert multiple rows, you select the number of rows to insert and then press which key combination?

____

3. Which menu command can restore a column you just deleted by mistake?

____

4. When you cut a selection, how is it marked onscreen?

____

5. When you drag to insert cut cells, what do you drag to the new location?

____

6. How many decimal places does the Percent Style button format numbers to display?

____

7. On which toolbar is the bold button located?

____

8. Which keyboard combination selects the current row?

____

CRITICAL THINKING

Answer these questions on a separate piece of paper. There are no right or wrong answers. Support your answers with examples from your own experience, if possible.

1. You want to add a row of sales data for another product to an existing worksheet. Should you insert a row, or just selected cells? Why?
2. If Excel updates formulas automatically after you move cells, why should you check formulas?

Skills Review

EXERCISE 3-18

Select multiple columns and rows; insert and delete cells, columns, and rows; and use the Undo command.

1. Open the file **NWReps1.xls**.
2. Insert a cell to align the labels in column A with the data below by following these steps:
   a. Select cell A8.
   b. Choose Cells from the Insert menu.
   c. Choose Shift cells down in the Insert dialog box and click OK.
3. Insert a column by following these steps:
   a. Select any cell in column B.
   b. Choose Columns from the Insert menu.

4. Delete rows to close up the space between the worksheet heading and the data by following these steps:
   a. Drag over row headings 5 through 8 to select those rows.
   b. Press Ctrl+- (the minus key on the numeric keypad).
5. Choose Undo from the Edit menu to restore the four rows.
6. Delete three rows by following these steps:
   a. Click row heading 5 to select that row.
   b. Press and hold down Shift and click row heading 7.
   c. Press Ctrl+-.
7. Adjust column A to accommodate the longest label in the column.
8. Select and delete column B.
9. Save the workbook as *[your initials]***3-18.xls**.
10. Print the worksheet and close the workbook.

EXERCISE 3-19

Insert cells, use the shortcut menu, and move data.

1. Open the file **NWReps2.xls**. Some data is missing and the quarterly information was keyed in the wrong order. You will move and insert cells to fix these problems and then repair necessary formulas.
2. Insert cells to make room for new data by following these steps:
   a. Select cells A14:H14.
   b. Right click the selection to display the shortcut menu.
   c. Choose Insert.
   d. In the Insert dialog box, choose Shift cells down and click OK.
3. Key the data shown in Figure 3-15.

FIGURE 3-15

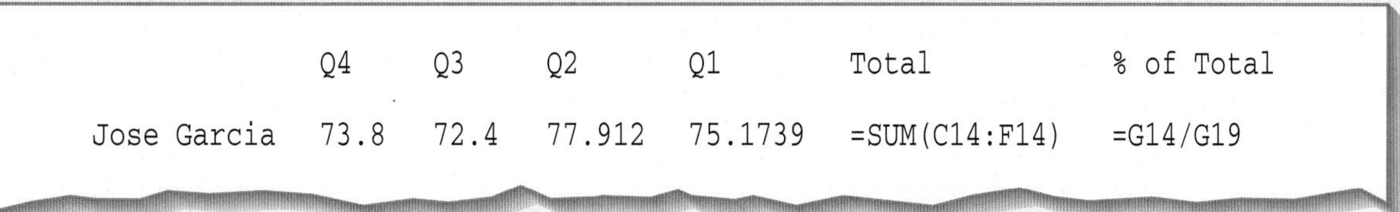

	Q4	Q3	Q2	Q1	Total	% of Total
Jose Garcia	73.8	72.4	77.912	75.1739	=SUM(C14:F14)	=G14/G19

4. Move the "Qtr 1" cells to column B by following these steps:
   a. Select cells F6:F19 and right click the range.
   b. Choose Cut from the shortcut menu.
   c. Right click cell B6 and choose Paste from the shortcut menu.

5. Move the "Qtr 4" cells to column F by following these steps:
   - *a.* Select cells C6:C19.
   - *b.* Move the mouse pointer to the border of the range until it becomes an arrow.
   - *c.* Drag the selection to the range F6:F19 and release the mouse button.
6. Move the "Qtr 1" cells from column B to the blank column C.
7. Reverse the positions of the "Qtr 2" and "Qtr 3" information by following these steps:
   - *a.* Select "Qtr 2" cells E6:E19.
   - *b.* Press Ctrl+X to cut these cells.
   - *c.* Select cell D6, which contains "Qtr 3."
   - *d.* Choose Cut Cells from the Insert menu (or choose Insert Cut Cells from the shortcut menu).
8. Delete the blank column B.
9. Review the formulas in the "Total" column. Correct them, if necessary. (They should sum the sales in all four quarters for each salesperson.)
10. Review the formulas in the "% of Total" column. (They should divide the total sales for each salesperson by the total sales for all salespersons.)
11. Save the workbook as *[your initials]***3-19.xls**.
12. Print the worksheet and close the workbook.

EXERCISE 3-20

Move cells, format numbers, apply text attributes, and apply borders.

1. Open the file **NWReps3.xls**.
2. Format the dollar amounts in comma style and display only one decimal place by following these steps:
   - *a.* Select cells C8:G17.
   - *b.* Click [,] on the Formatting toolbar.
   - *c.* Click [.00→.0] on the Formatting toolbar.
3. Format the first and last rows of dollar amounts in currency style and displaying only one decimal place by following these steps:
   - *a.* Select cells C8:G8 and C19:G19 (use Ctrl to select nonadjacent ranges).
   - *b.* Click [$] on the Formatting toolbar.
   - *c.* Click [.00→.0] on the Formatting toolbar.
4. Format amounts in the "% of Total" column in percent style and displaying one decimal place by following these steps:

a. Select cells H8:H19.

b. Click [%] and then click [.00].

5. Format and align the column labels by following these steps:

a. Select cells A6:H6 and click [B] to make the text bold.

b. With the cells still selected, click the down arrow on the Borders button [Borders] and choose the single-line bottom border.

c. Select cells C6:G6 and click [Align Right] to right-align the text.

6. Format cells A1:A4 and A19:H19 as bold.
7. Delete the blank row 7.
8. In row C18:H18, add a single-line top and a double-line bottom border (which is the last icon on the second row of the border palette) and delete the blank row 17.
9. Delete column B and adjust the column width of column A to fit the longest label in the column.
10. Save the workbook as *[your initials]***3-20.xls**.
11. Print the worksheet and close the workbook.

EXERCISE 3-21

Move cells and rows, format numbers, apply text attributes and borders, copy formats, and use shortcut menus.

1. Open the file **USSales2.xls**.
2. Under "Northwest Region Sales," move row 8 ("Acetaminophen") below row 9 ("Aspirin") to match the sequence in the other three regions. Follow these steps:

a. Right-click row heading 8 and click Cut in the shortcut menu.

b. Right-click row heading 10 and click Insert Cut Cells in the shortcut menu.

3. Move "Northeast Region Sales" before "Southwest Region Sales" by following these steps:

a. Select rows 20 through 26 by dragging with the mouse.

b. Press Ctrl+X to cut the selected rows.

c. Right-click row heading 13 and click Insert Cut Cells in the shortcut menu.

4. Format the title in cells A1:A3 as bold.
5. Format text in the "Northwest Region" by following these steps:

a. Select the row and column labels and the totals (A6:H7, A8:A11, and B11:H11), and make them bold.

b. Right-align cells G6:H7.

c. Apply a double-line bottom border to cells A7:H7.

d. Apply a single-line top and double-line bottom border to cells B11:H11.

6. Format numbers in the "Northwest Region" by following these steps:

a. Select the dollar amounts for "Aspirin" (B8:G8) and "Total sales" (B11:G11). Apply the currency style and add one decimal place to these numbers.

b. To the dollar amounts in cells B9:G10, apply the comma style and add one decimal place. All numbers should have three decimal places.

c. Apply the percent style to cells H8:H11 with one decimal place.

7. Copy the formats for the "Northwest Region" to the other three regions by following these steps:

a. Select cells A6:H11 and double-click the Format Painter button.

b. Using the Format Painter pointer, select the "Northeast Region Sales" range (A13:H18) to copy the formatting.

c. Select the "Southwest Region" range, and then select the "Southeast Region" range.

d. Press Esc to end the process and restore the normal pointer.

8. Save the workbook as *[your initials]***3-21.xls**.

9. Print the worksheet and close the workbook.

Lesson Applications

EXERCISE 3-22

Select rows and columns, move cells and columns, insert and delete rows, move data, format numbers, and apply text attributes and cell borders.

1. Open the file **Share1.xls**.
2. Move the information in column E to column B.
3. Check the formulas now in column B to ensure they divide "Alpha Sales" by "National Sales."
4. Widen column A to accommodate the labels.
5. Insert two rows at row 4.
6. Format the title cells A1 and A2 as bold.
7. Delete the blank row 12.
8. Format the column labels as centered and bold, and apply a single-line bottom border to cells B7:D7.
9. Apply a single-line top and a double-line bottom border to cells B12:D12.
10. Format the row labels and total numbers as bold.
11. Format the "Market Share" numbers in percent style and displaying two decimal places.
12. Format the "National Sales" and "Alpha Sales" numbers in comma style and displaying two decimal places.
13. Delete the blank row 8.
14. Save the workbook as *[your initials]***3-22.xls**.
15. Print the worksheet and close the workbook.

EXERCISE 3-23

Select cells, insert rows, use shortcut menus, move data, format numbers and text, and apply cell borders.

Alpha Pharmaceuticals' auditor reviewed the worksheet that calculates gross pay for the company's Quality Control Division. He noticed that overtime hours were not entered and that employee Silvers is missing from the list. These errors need to be corrected and the worksheet needs to be formatted to make it easier to read.

1. Open the file **QCPay3.xls**.
2. Insert three blank rows, starting at row 3.

3. Move all the data in the "Golden" row between the data for "Czerny" and "Patino."
4. Under "Patino," insert a new row with the data and formulas for employee Silvers as shown in Figure 3-16. (Leave "Overtime" blank.)

FIGURE 3-16

Name	Rate	Hours	Overtime	Regular Pay	Overtime Pay	Total Pay
Silvers	9.50	37.5		=B13*C13	=D13*B13*1.50	=E13+F13

5. Format cell A1 as bold and cell A2 as bold and italic.
6. Right-align the text in rows 6 and 7 (except for "Name" in cell A7, which should be left-aligned).
7. Format rows 6, 7, and 16 as bold.
8. Apply a single-line bottom border to cells A7 through G7 and to cells A15 through G15.
9. Apply the comma style to rows 8 through 16 and display two decimal places.
10. Key the overtime hours for all employees as follows:

Berenson	**2**
Alvarez	**3**
Czerny	**0**
Golden	**3**
Patino	**4.25**
Silvers	**0**
Teij	**1.5**
Wang	**2.5**

11. Use AutoSum to total regular "Hours" and "Overtime" hours. Format the totals in bold, comma style, and displaying two decimal places.
12. Save the workbook as *[your initials]***3-23.xls**.
13. Print the worksheet and close the workbook.

EXERCISE 3-24

Select and insert rows and columns, move data, and format text and numbers.

Alpha Pharmaceuticals' president needs to study U.S. population trends to make sales forecasts. He is especially interested in the over-40 age group, as this group uses more pain relievers than younger people. His population worksheet should be formatted and additional data must be inserted.

1. Open the file **PopData1.xls**.
2. Insert three blank rows at row 3.
3. Move the "1990" data so it is positioned above the "1991" data.
4. Insert three blank rows below the "1986" data to make room for the "1987," "1988," and "1989" data.
5. Key the missing and additional population figures, as shown in Figure 3-17.

FIGURE 3-17

	Total	Over 40
1987	243.07	91.25
1988	245.35	92.61
1989	247.64	93.97
1995	263.87	105.30
1996	266.75	107.42
1997	269.65	109.55

6. Create formulas in cells D10:D12 and D18:D20 to calculate the percentage of the population over age 40. (Hint: Use one of the existing formulas as a model.)
7. Edit cell A1 to read **U.S. Population**
8. Format cells A1:A2 as bold.
9. Format the column headings in row 6 as right-aligned and bold.
10. Format the numbers in columns B and C to display one decimal place.
11. Format the numbers in column D to be displayed as percentages with one decimal place.
12. Save the workbook as *[your initials]***3-24.xls**.
13. Print the worksheet and close the workbook.

EXERCISE 3-25

Historical information on pain-reliever sales for the Northwest Region appears in three separate sections of a worksheet. The Marketing Director asked you to arrange the data into a single table that shows totals by year and by product.

1. Open the file **NWHist1.xls**.
2. Cut the data for "Aspirin" (B3:B14) and paste it beginning in cell D3.
3. Cut the data for "Ibuprofen" (B29:B40) and paste it beginning in cell B3.
4. Cut the data for "Acetaminophen" (B16:B27) and paste it beginning in cell C3.
5. Clear the cells below row 15 in column A.
6. Key **Total** in E3 and create formulas in column E to total each year's sales. (*Hint:* Use AutoSum, but be sure not to add the year.)
7. In cell A15, key **Total**. When AutoComplete suggests "Total Category Sales," press Delete to restore "Total" and press Enter.
8. Create formulas in row 15 that total individual and total product sales.
9. Clear cells A1:A2, which contain the title and key the title as shown in Figure 3-18. Insert enough rows to accommodate the title and to leave two blank lines below it.

FIGURE 3-18

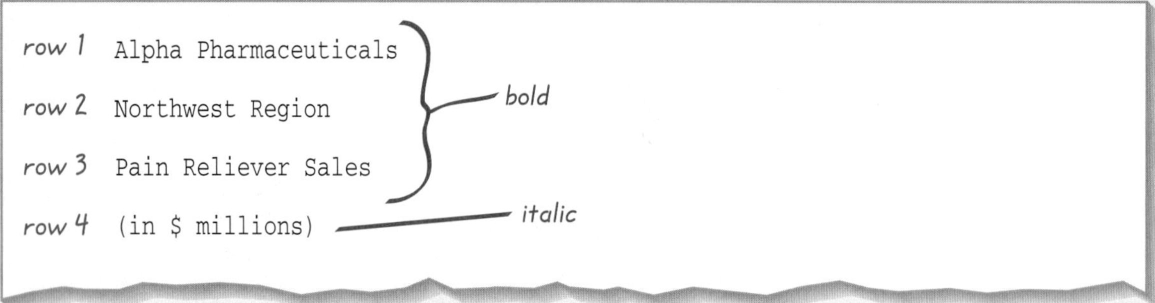

10. Insert the following data below "1996":

    1997 0.209 0.133 0.054
11. Create a formula in column E to total the "1997" sales data.
12. Edit formulas in row 20 to include the data in row 19 in their calculations.
13. Delete the row containing the1986 data.
14. Right-align the column labels and make row and column headings bold. Right-align A19.
15. Apply a single-line heavy bottom border to the column labels (B7:E7).
16. Apply a double-line bottom border to the sales data for "1997" (B18:E18).
17. Format the dollar figures in comma style and displaying two decimal places.
18. Make all totals bold.
19. Save the workbook as *[your initials]***3-25.xls**.
20. Print the worksheet and close the workbook.

Unit 1 Applications

APPLICATION 1-1

Enter and edit data, use AutoSum, create formulas, move data, and format text and numbers.

You have been asked to prepare a statement of assets for Alpha Pharmaceuticals, listing the things of value that the company owned at the end of 1996. The statement will become part of Alpha's balance sheet and be included in Alpha's annual report.

1. Open the file **Assets1.xls**.
2. Change the width of column A to accommodate the label in A6 and the width of column B to accommodate the label in B13.
3. In the cell range C7:C10, key the following data:

   2600
   5960
   4710
   600
4. In cell C11, use AutoSum to create a formula for "Total current assets."
5. In cell C13, key **4980**. In cell C14, key **1520**
6. Cut the text in cell C15 and paste it into cell B15.
7. In cell C15, create a formula that subtracts "Depreciation" from "Property, plant, and equipment."
8. In cell C16, key **1390** for "Other Assets."
9. Italicize the amounts for "Total current assets," "Net fixed assets," and "Other Assets." Create a formula in cell C17 that totals these three amounts. Make that total bold.
10. Right-align the labels "Total current assets" and "Net fixed assets." Make both labels italic.
11. Format cells A1 and A2 as bold.
12. Format the values in column C in comma style with no decimals.
13. Apply a single-line bottom border to cells C10, C14, and C16.
14. Apply a double-line bottom border to cell C17.
15. Edit the label "(Depreciation)" so it reads **(Less depreciation)**
16. Edit cells so only the first letter of the first word of each label is capitalized. (Do not edit the title, however.)
17. Save the workbook as *[your initials]***u1-1.xls**.
18. Print the worksheet and close the workbook.

APPLICATION 1-2

Enter data, construct formulas, use the Sum function, and format text and numbers.

A statement of liabilities and shareholders' equity shows who has claims on the assets of a company. For instance, you can see the amounts owed to outsiders (long-term debt, current debt, accounts payable) and the amounts claimed by the owners (shareholders' equity). You have been asked to prepare such a statement for Alpha Pharmaceuticals. It will later become part of the company's balance sheet.

1. Open **Liablts1.xls**.
2. Change the width of column B so the label in A15 does not extend beyond the right border of column B.
3. Move the label in cell C13 to cell B13.
4. Enter the data in column C as shown in Figure U1-1, including Sum formulas in cells C8 and C13.

FIGURE U1-1

	A	B	C
5	Long-term liabilities		
6		Long-term debt	690
7		Other long-term liabilities	510
8		Total long-term liabilities	(SUM)
9	Current liabilities		
10		Debt due for repayment	1090
11		Accounts payable	1350
12		Other current liabilities	1760
13		Total current liabilities	(SUM)
14	Shareholders' equity		13320
15	Total liabilities and shareholders' equity		

5. Format cells C8, C13, and C14 as italic, add a single-line bottom border to cells C7, C12, and C14, and add a double-line bottom border to cell C15.

6. Move the current liabilities (rows 9 through 13) before the long-term liabilities (rows 5 through 8). (Hint: Cut the cells and use Cut Cells from the Insert menu to insert them in the new location.)
7. Check to make sure the formulas are still correct.
8. Create a formula in cell C15 that adds "Total current liabilities," "Total long-term liabilities," and "Shareholders' equity." Format the cell as bold.
9. Insert a new row at row 1. Change the first two lines of the title to read as follows:

   Alpha Pharmaceuticals
   Liabilities and Shareholders' Equity
10. Format the first three lines of the title as bold.
11. Format all the values in comma style with no decimals.
12. Save your workbook as *[your initials]***u1-2.xls**.
13. Print the worksheet and close the workbook.

APPLICATION 1-3

Edit data, move data, insert and delete rows, construct formulas, and use AutoCalculate.

A balance sheet shows a company's total assets equal the sum of its liabilities and shareholders' equity. You have been asked to construct a balance sheet for Alpha Pharmaceuticals using its asset statement and its statement of liabilities and shareholders' equity. To see the relative size of each item on the balance sheet, you should show the asset ratio for each item. The asset ratio is simply the item divided by the total assets.

1. Open the file **Balance1.xls**.
2. Sheet1 contains Alpha's asset statement. Click the Sheet2 tab to see the statement of liabilities and shareholders' equity.
3. On Sheet2, delete rows 1 through 5, including the title and the blank row.
4. Cut the rest of the material (cells A1:C10).
5. Click the Sheet1 tab and paste the material below the asset statement, beginning in cell A19.
6. Edit cell A1 to read **Balance Sheet for Alpha Pharmaceuticals**
7. Insert a row at row 19, format blank cell A19 as bold, and key **Liabilities and Owners' Equity**
8. Format cell A5 (which contains the label "Assets") as bold.
9. Insert a new row at row 5.
10. Key $ (dollar sign) in cell C5 and key % **Assets** in cell D5. Format both cells as bold and centered.

11. In cell D8, enter the formula **=C8/C18**. (Cell C18 contains the value for total assets. The formula gives the percentage of total assets represented by the value in cell C8—that is, the asset ratio.)
12. In column D, create asset ratio formulas for all the remaining assets in the balance sheet. Be sure to divide by total assets (C18).
13. Format column D in percent style to display one decimal place.
14. Format column C in comma style to display no decimals.
15. Use AutoCalculate to verify the subtotals.
16. Save your workbook as *[your initials]***u1-3.xls**.
17. Print the worksheet and close the workbook.

APPLICATION 1-4

Enter data in a selected range, construct formulas, use AutoSum, format text and numbers, and insert columns and rows.

In addition to a balance sheet, Alpha Pharmaceuticals' annual report will include an income statement. An income statement shows the revenues, expenses, and net income for a company over a period of time. You have been asked to prepare this statement and to format it attractively.

1. Open a new workbook.
2. In the cell range A1:B10, key the data shown in Figure U1-2.
3. Change the width of column A to accommodate the label in A7.
4. Move the entire block of labels and numbers so "Revenue" appears in cell A7.
5. Starting in cell A1, key the following title:

   Income Statement
   Alpha Pharmaceuticals
   1996
   (Dollars in thousands)
6. Left-align the label in A3 if it was entered as a value.
7. Format the first three lines of the title as bold.
8. In cell B13, create a formula that subtracts cells B8:B12 (which are expenses and cost of goods sold) from "Revenue" (cell B7).
9. In cell B16, create a formula that subtracts both interest and taxes (cells B14:B15) from "Earnings before interest and taxes" (cell B13).
10. Key $ in cell B6 and % in cell C6. Format both cells as bold and centered.
11. In column C, create formulas that divide each item in column B by "Revenue" (B7). (Hint: The first three formulas are **=B7/B7**, **=B8/B7**, and **=B9/B7**.)

FIGURE U1-2

	A	B
1	Revenue	34050
2	Cost of goods sold	20410
3	Sales expenses	2400
4	Administrative expense	5210
5	Depreciation	480
6	Other expenses	200
7	Earnings before interest and taxes	
8	Interest expense	310
9	Income taxes	1930
10	Net income	

12. Format column C in percent style to display one decimal place.
13. Format column B in comma style to display no decimals.
14. Apply single-line bottom borders to cells B12:C12 and B15:C15. Apply double-line bottom borders to cells B16:C16.
15. Proofread the worksheet.
16. Save the workbook as *[your initials]***u1-4.xls**.
17. Print the worksheet and close the workbook.

APPLICATION 1-5

Enter data; construct formulas; use AutoSum; format text and numbers; and insert and delete cells, columns, and rows, as needed.

Prepare an income statement for yourself, your household, or another individual.

1. In a new worksheet, enter the income categories and data. Figure U1-3 (on the next page) lists suggested categories to include. (You **must** include categories shown in bold.)

FIGURE U1-3

Income (include at least two subcategories)

Job1

Job2

Investments

Interest

Total income

Expenses (include at least three subcategories)

Food

Housing

Utilities

Transportation

Clothing

Insurance

Medical

Loan payments

Entertainment

Total expenses

Earnings before taxes

Taxes

Net income

2. Complete the worksheet by including the following information and formatting:
   - A title identifying the name of the statement and the period of time it covers.
   - Column labels for dollar amounts and for percentage of income.
   - Bottom borders on cells before subtotals and totals.
   - Numbers and text formatted appropriately.
   - Attractive and clear layout.
3. Save your workbook as *[your initials]***u1-5.xls**.
4. Print the worksheet and close the workbook.

UNIT 2

Developing a Worksheet

Beautiful Belle Company

Sun Soft Heats Up Skin Care Market

The Beautiful Belle Company, also known as BBC, manufactures a moderately priced line of cosmetics. BBC is currently promoting a product named "Sun Soft." It's a 100%-natural hypo-allergenic lotion that has refined almond and sesame oils as its main ingredients. Although it's not proven, and can't be used in advertising, researchers have recently claimed that these oils are beneficial in protecting against skin cancer.

BBC is test-marketing Sun Soft in its Southwest region. Renata Santo, BBC's Southwest regional-sales manager, has decided to concentrate her efforts in the Phoenix area. However, Phoenix is a challenging market for Soft Sun, because a competing product, Corn Silk Cream, has a significant market share of skin care products there.

For the test marketing, Renata will need the following:

- ✔ A worksheet to keep track of weekly sales of Sun Soft and the competing product, Corn Silk Cream, over a two-month period. **(Lesson 4)**
- ✔ Once the test is complete, a worksheet that tracks Sun Soft sales in relation to Corn Silk Cream sales for three months. **(Lesson 5)**
- ✔ A worksheet that shows sales of selected creams for four quarters, with sales broken down by months and by product. **(Lesson 6)**
- ✔ A worksheet that compares Sun Soft sales by quarter for the last three years. **(Lesson 7)**

Designing and Printing a Worksheet

OBJECTIVES

After completing this lesson, you will be able to:

1. **Plan a worksheet on paper.**
2. **Put a worksheet plan on screen.**
3. **Keep row and column labels in view.**
4. **Select display options.**
5. **Create user documentation.**
6. **Protect files.**
7. **Print workbooks and print areas.**
8. **Print formulas.**

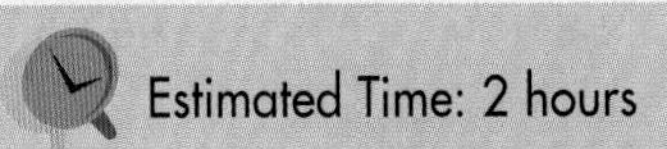

Creating a worksheet requires careful planning. A well-designed worksheet is easy to read, the data is arranged in a logical order, and the results are readily apparent. Decide what you want to accomplish with the worksheet before you create it. Designing the worksheet with a specific purpose in mind will help you decide what you want Excel to do with the data you enter. You can then choose from a variety of print settings so the final, printed worksheet has the appearance you intended.

Planning a Worksheet on Paper

To design a worksheet that meets your goals, start your planning using pencil and paper. Even experienced users often sketch a worksheet before they key any data. Your plan should include:

- titles that indicate who the spreadsheet is for and what it is about
- an entry area, if necessary, to accommodate single input items such as a date, division, or department (optional area)
- the worksheet body, the input and output area that contains multiple entries, labels, and formulas

The procedures in this lesson generate a worksheet to help the sales manager of a small manufacturing company analyze the results of a two-month test-marketing program. The purpose of the worksheet is to compare test-market sales with those of a competing product.

EXERCISE 4-1 Sketch the Planned Worksheet

1. Write the worksheet heading **Sun Soft vs. Corn Silk Sales** at the top left corner of a blank piece of paper. The heading of the worksheet must clearly state the purpose of the worksheet and provide a concise overview of its contents. In this case, the heading names the products and promises a competitive analysis based on sales.
2. Write the subtitles **April through May, 1997** and **(Broken down by gender)** on two separate rows under the heading.

NOTE: In some cases, your worksheet might require an entry area, where you can incorporate single items such as the date, division, or department into a worksheet. This worksheet does not require an entry area; it is optional.

3. Consider the structure of your worksheet. Its purpose is to store weekly sales information over a two-month period and make calculations that provide useful competitive information. Although there are no hard-and-fast rules for worksheet design, it is generally a good idea to put items that are being compared in columns and repetitive items in rows.

NOTE: An analysis comparing two categories usually looks better when the categories are placed side by side. This design makes it easy for a user to glance back and forth to evaluate the information quickly.

4. Plan the structure of your worksheet body by determining the placement of data in columns and rows. The first column of the body holds the date labels. The next two columns hold Sun Soft data broken down by gender. The last two columns hold Corn Silk data broken down by gender.
5. Define the labels that identify the rows of the worksheet. For your worksheet, the labels are the weekly dates for the two-month analysis.
6. Skip several rows to allow for additional column labels. Write the following labels in a column along the left side of the page.

   April 5

   April 12

   April 19

   April 26

   Subtotal

   May 3

   May 10

   May 17

   May 24

   May 31

   Subtotal

   Grand total
7. Define the column headings. You are comparing products based on gender.
8. Move approximately two rows above the row labels. Write **Sun Soft Lotion.** On the same row but further to the right, write **Corn Silk Cream**.
9. In the row beneath the column heading **Sun Soft Lotion,** write the labels **Men**, **Women**, and **Total**. In the same row beneath the heading **Corn Silk Cream,** repeat the same three labels. (See Figure 4-1 on the next page.) The basic design of your worksheet is now complete.
10. Decide which formulas to use and where to put them on the worksheet. Our worksheet calculates monthly subtotals and a grand total of sales for both months. It also calculates total sales to men and women for both the test product and the competing product. Use F for formula locations. You'll use the SUM function to calculate these values.

FIGURE 4-1
Preliminary worksheet design

Sun Soft vs. Corn Silk Sales
April through May, 1997
(Broken down by gender)

	Sun Soft Lotion			Corn Silk Cream		
	Men	Women	Total	Men	Women	Total
April 5						
April 12						
April 19						
April 26						
Subtotal						
May 3						
May 10						
May 17						
May 24						
May 31						
Subtotal						
Grand total						

FIGURE 4-2
Final worksheet design

Sun Soft vs. Corn Silk Sales
April through May, 1997
(Broken down by gender)

	Sun Soft Lotion			Corn Silk Cream		
	Men	Women	Total	Men	Women	Total
April 5			F			F
April 12			F			F
April 19			F			F
April 26			F			F
Subtotal	F	F	F	F	F	F
May 3			F			F
May 10			F			F
May 17			F			F
May 24			F			F
May 31			F			F
Subtotal	F	F	F	F	F	F
Grand total	F	F	F	F	F	F

Putting the Worksheet Plan on Screen

Once you sketch the overall plan and know what data and formulas you will include, you are ready to build the worksheet in Excel.

After your worksheet is set up onscreen, you can validate the data, choose cells by content, and name the worksheet tabs.

EXERCISE 4-2 Enter Row and Column Labels

1. Open the workbook **TestMkt.xls**.

NOTE: Usually you create a new workbook when you implement a sketch in Excel; however, throughout this lesson you build on an existing workbook that has the default font size and column width correctly adjusted.

2. In cell A1, edit the title to read **Sun Soft vs. Corn Silk Sales**
3. In cell A2, edit the subtitle to read **April through May, 1997**
4. In cell A3, edit the second subtitle to read **(Broken down by gender)**. This subtitle should remain bold italic.

NOTE: A worksheet title should not be longer than three lines and there should be some visible difference from one line of the title to the next. Formatting text is discussed in a later lesson.

5. In cell B5, key **Sun Soft Lotion**
6. In cell E5, key **Corn Silk Cream**
7. In cells B6, C6, and D6, key the following labels center-aligned:

   Men Women Total
8. In cells E6, F6, and G6, key the same labels a second time. Center-align these labels.
9. In cell A7, key **April 5**. Notice that the date appears in the cell as "5-Apr" and is displayed on the formula bar as "4/5/1997" (or the current year).

TIP: You can change the date format of selected cells. Choose Cells from the Format menu and click the Number tab. Choose Date in the Category list, select the Type of format, and click OK.

10. In cells A8 through A10, key the following dates:

April 12

April 19

April 26

11. In cells A13 through A17, key the following dates:

May 3

May 10

May 17

May 24

May 31

12. To complete the worksheet design, key **Subtotal** in cells A11 and A18, and **Grand total** in cell A20. You use these rows to summarize the data.

FIGURE 4-3
Worksheet plan with labels entered

	A	B	C	D	E	F	G	H	I	J	K
1	Sun Soft vs. Corn Silk Sales										
2	April through May, 1997										
3	*(Broken down by gender)*										
4											
5		Sun Soft Lotion			Corn Silk Cream						
6		Men	Women	Total	Men	Women	Total				
7	5-Apr										
8	12-Apr										
9	19-Apr										
10	26-Apr										
11	Subtotal										
12											
13	3-May										
14	10-May										
15	17-May										
16	24-May										
17	31-May										
18	Subtotal										
19											
20	Grand total										
21											

Sheet1 / Sheet2 / Sheet3

EXERCISE 4-3 Enter Test Data

The body of the worksheet consists of data. You can enter test data into the worksheet to test formula calculations. *Test data* should consist of numbers that are easy to calculate in your head so you can tell at a glance whether your formulas are correct.

1. Key the following test data for Sun Soft in columns B and C in the appropriate rows as shown below. Start with **1000** in cell B7.

April 5 **1000** **2000**
April 12 **1000** **2000**
April 19 **1000** **2000**
April 26 **1000** **2000**
May 3 **1000** **2000**
May 10 **1000** **2000**
May 17 **1000** **2000**
May 24 **1000** **2000**
May 31 **1000** **2000**

2. Key the following test data for Corn Silk in columns E and F beside the appropriate row labels as shown below. Start with **1000** in cell E7.

April 5 **1000** **2000**
April 12 **1000** **2000**
April 19 **1000** **2000**
April 26 **1000** **2000**
May 3 **1000** **2000**
May 10 **1000** **2000**
May 17 **1000** **2000**
May 24 **1000** **2000**
May 31 **1000** **2000**

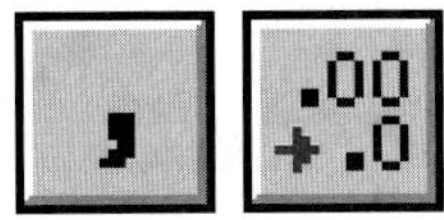

3. Select all the numbers and format them for commas and no decimal places. (Press Ctrl when you click the mouse to select nonadjacent cells.) Click , on the Formatting toolbar, then click .00→.0 until you can see the numbers and no decimal places remain.

FIGURE 4-4
Worksheet plan with data entered

	A	B	C	D	E	F	G	H	I	J	K
1	**Sun Soft vs. Corn Silk Sales**										
2	**April through May, 1997**										
3	***(Broken down by gender)***										
4											
5		Sun Soft Lotion			Corn Silk Cream						
6		Men	Women	Total	Men	Women	Total				
7	5-Apr	1,000	2,000		1,000	2,000					
8	12-Apr	1,000	2,000		1,000	2,000					
9	19-Apr	1,000	2,000		1,000	2,000					
10	26-Apr	1,000	2,000		1,000	2,000					
11	Subtotal										
12											
13	3-May	1,000	2,000		1,000	2,000					
14	10-May	1,000	2,000		1,000	2,000					
15	17-May	1,000	2,000		1,000	2,000					
16	24-May	1,000	2,000		1,000	2,000					
17	31-May	1,000	2,000		1,000	2,000					
18	Subtotal										
19											
20	Grand total										
21											

Sheet1 / Sheet2 / Sheet3

EXERCISE 4-4 Enter Formulas

Once the worksheet data is entered, you can enter formulas to automate the calculations. Since you are adding rows and columns, this is a good time to use the SUM function or Σ.

1. Select cells D7 through D10 and click Σ on the Standard toolbar. The SUM function is entered in each cell and the total values are displayed. Add the totals in your head to check the values as you go through the remaining steps.
2. Select cells B11 through D11 and click Σ. This totals the three separate ranges in the same step.
3. Select cells B13 through D18 (the data cells and the cells for their totals).
4. Click Σ. Excel automatically sums the rows and columns of selected data.
5. Select cells E7 through G11, hold down Ctrl, and select cells E13 through G18.
6. Release Ctrl and click Σ to enter the totals for the two cell ranges at the same time. All the totals and subtotals for Corn Silk are now entered.
7. Move to cell B20 and click Σ. Excel suggests cell B18, the second subtotal to be included in the formula.
8. Hold down Ctrl and click cell B11, the first subtotal to include it in the formula.
9. Release Ctrl and press Enter. Excel totals the two subtotals. The formula =SUM(B18,B11) appears in the Formula Bar for cell B20.

FIGURE 4-5
Worksheet with formulas

	A	B	C	D	E	F	G	H	I	J	K
1	**Sun Soft vs. Corn Silk Sales**										
2	**April through May, 1997**										
3	***(Broken down by gender)***										
4											
5		Sun Soft Lotion			Corn Silk Cream						
6		Men	Women	Total	Men	Women	Total				
7	5-Apr	1,000	2,000	3,000	1,000	2,000	3,000				
8	12-Apr	1,000	2,000	3,000	1,000	2,000	3,000				
9	19-Apr	1,000	2,000	3,000	1,000	2,000	3,000				
10	26-Apr	1,000	2,000	3,000	1,000	2,000	3,000				
11	Subtotal	4,000	8,000	12,000	4,000	8,000	12,000				
12											
13	3-May	1,000	2,000	3,000	1,000	2,000	3,000				
14	10-May	1,000	2,000	3,000	1,000	2,000	3,000				
15	17-May	1,000	2,000	3,000	1,000	2,000	3,000				
16	24-May	1,000	2,000	3,000	1,000	2,000	3,000				
17	31-May	1,000	2,000	3,000	1,000	2,000	3,000				
18	Subtotal	5,000	10,000	15,000	5,000	10,000	15,000				
19											
20	Grand total	9,000	18,000	27,000	9,000	18,000	27,000				
21											

Sheet1 / Sheet2 / Sheet3 /

10. Select cells C7 through C20 and click [Σ]. The formula in cell C20 adds the two subtotals in column C.
11. Do the same for column D.
12. Select cells E7 through G20 and click [Σ]. Examine the formula in cell G20, which adds the grand totals of columns E and F instead of summing the subtotals of column G (which would produce the same result).

EXERCISE 4-5 Validate Data

You can control the type of data entered in cells, such as whole numbers, date, time, and text length. If you or someone else tries to enter data into a cell that is validated, you can have Excel display a prompt specifying the type of data to enter. Excel returns an error message if incorrect data is keyed.

1. Select all the cells containing **1,000**. (Press Ctrl and click the mouse to select nonadjacent cells.)
2. Choose Validation from the Data menu to open the Data Validation dialog box.

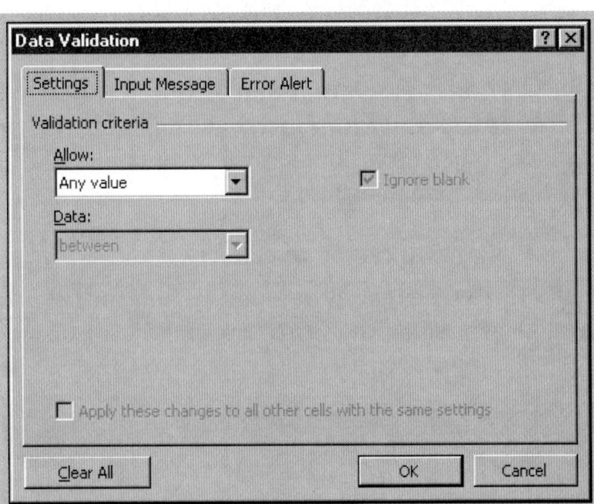

FIGURE 4-6 Data Validation dialog box

3. Click the Settings tab, if necessary, and choose Whole number from the Allow drop-down list.
4. Choose equal to from the Data drop-down list and key **1000** in the Value drop-down list.
5. Click the Input Message tab.
6. Under Title, key **Hey Users**

7. In the Input Message text box, key **Enter 1000 for the test data** and click OK. Notice the message box that appears over the last set of cells with the input message you created.
8. Select any cell containing **1,000**. Notice that the same message box appears.

NOTE: You are taught to validate test data here, but be aware you would not normally validate test data in a worksheet.

9. Change the number to **2,000**. When you try to enter the number in the cell, a message dialog box appears indicating the value you entered is not valid. Click Cancel.

NOTE: To turn off data validation, click the Clear All button at the bottom of the Data Validation dialog box. This also clears any message you created.

EXERCISE 4-6 Select Cells by Content

Once your worksheet is set up, you may find it useful to select cells by content. You can use this method to select a cell or group of cells that have common characteristics (such as validated data or formulas), whether they are adjacent on the worksheet or not.

1. Press Ctrl+Home to return to cell A1.
2. Choose Go To from the Edit menu. When the Go To dialog box opens, click Special to open the Go To Special dialog box.

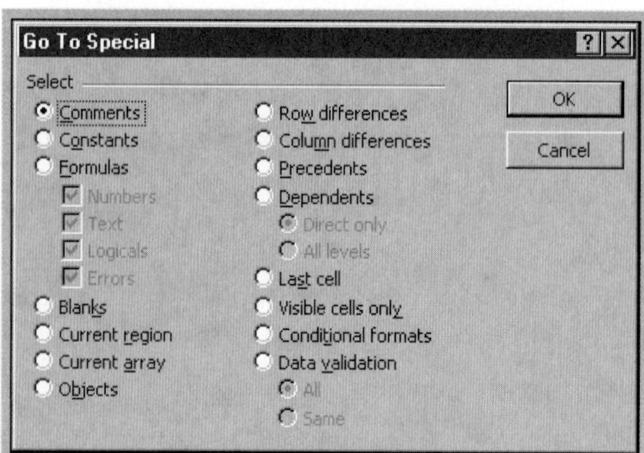

FIGURE 4-7 Go To Special dialog box

TIP: You can also press Ctrl+G to open the Go To dialog box and then click Special to open the Go To Special dialog box.

3. Click Data validation and click OK. All the cells with validated data are selected. Press Ctrl+Home.

4. Try this for the cells with formulas by choosing Formulas in the Go To Special dialog box. (Make sure you choose Numbers under the Formulas option and deselect the others.)

EXERCISE 4-7 Name Worksheet Tabs

As you learned in Lesson 1, each new Excel workbook opens with three sheets that are named Sheet1 through Sheet3 by default. When you work with more than one worksheet, it's a good idea to name worksheet tabs so their purpose is obvious.

1. Double-click the Sheet1 tab. Sheet1 is already named and the tab name is highlighted.
2. Key **Sales Comparison** over the Sheet1 tab name.
3. Double-click the Sheet2 tab. Sheet2 is active and the tab name is highlighted.
4. Key **User Information** over Sheet2. (You use this sheet later in the lesson.)
5. Click the Sales Comparison tab to make this worksheet active again.

NOTE: Sheet names should describe exactly what the sheet includes using only a word or two. Sheet names can be up to 31 characters long, including spaces.

Keeping Row and Column Labels in View

Frequently, the rows and columns of a worksheet extend beyond the display screen. You can split the worksheet into multiple *panes* so you can see row and column labels as you key data or formulas. Using multiple panes you can also scroll through data to locate and select cells to be included in calculations. You do this using *split bars*. For example, when you create a grand total, you might need to scroll to the top of a large worksheet to include one or more subtotals.

EXERCISE 4-8 Split a Worksheet into Panes

1. Move to cell A7 on the Sales Comparison worksheet, just under the column labels.

2. Choose Split from the Window menu. The screen is split into two horizontal panes by a split bar. Each pane has its own vertical scroll bar, permitting it to be scrolled on its own.

TIP: You can also split a worksheet vertically by selecting an entire row first.

3. Click the down vertical scroll arrow for the bottom pane to move row 13 directly under the column labels. Splitting the screen under the column labels makes it easier to enter formulas for the May subtotal and the grand total.
4. Experiment with the scroll buttons in both panes.

FIGURE 4-8
Screen split horizontally

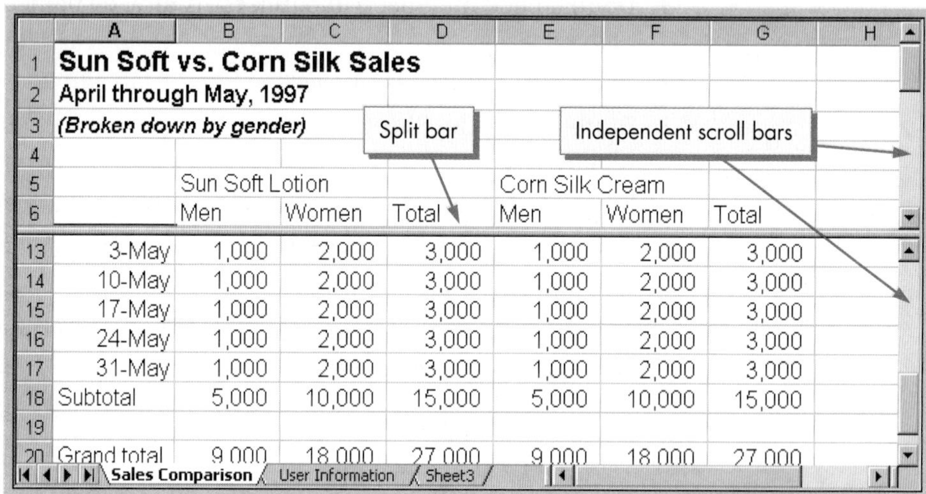

	A	B	C	D	E	F	G	H
1	Sun Soft vs. Corn Silk Sales							
2	April through May, 1997							
3	(Broken down by gender)							
4								
5		Sun Soft Lotion			Corn Silk Cream			
6		Men	Women	Total	Men	Women	Total	
13	3-May	1,000	2,000	3,000	1,000	2,000	3,000	
14	10-May	1,000	2,000	3,000	1,000	2,000	3,000	
15	17-May	1,000	2,000	3,000	1,000	2,000	3,000	
16	24-May	1,000	2,000	3,000	1,000	2,000	3,000	
17	31-May	1,000	2,000	3,000	1,000	2,000	3,000	
18	Subtotal	5,000	10,000	15,000	5,000	10,000	15,000	
19								
20	Grand total	9,000	18,000	27,000	9,000	18,000	27,000	

5. Choose Remove Split from the Window menu. The original view of the worksheet is restored.

NOTE: The Split option on the Window menu changes to Remove Split when a worksheet is split into panes.

6. Move to cell B7.
7. Choose Split from the Window menu. The window splits above and to the left of the active cell. In four panes, you can see both row and column labels at the same time. Scroll to move row 13 just below column labels.

TIP: To create a vertical split only, select a column other than column A (or select a cell in row 1 other than cell A1) before choosing Split from the Window menu.

FIGURE 4-9
Screen split horizontally and vertically

	A	B	C	D	E	F	G	H
1	**Sun Soft**	**vs. Corn Silk Sales**						
2	**April throug**	**gh May, 1997**						
3	***(Broken dov***	***vn by gender)***						
4								
5		Sun Soft Lotion			Corn Silk Cream			
6		Men	Women	Total	Men	Women	Total	
13	3-May	1,000	2,000	3,000	1,000	2,000	3,000	
14	10-May	1,000	2,000	3,000	1,000	2,000	3,000	
15	17-May	1,000	2,000	3,000	1,000	2,000	3,000	
16	24-May	1,000	2,000	3,000	1,000	2,000	3,000	
17	31-May	1,000	2,000	3,000	1,000	2,000	3,000	
18	Subtotal	5,000	10,000	15,000	5,000	10,000	15,000	
19								
20	Grand total	9,000	18,000	27,000	9,000	18,000	27,000	

EXERCISE 4-9 Freeze Panes

You use the Freeze Panes command on the Window menu to freeze row labels, column labels, or both. A single set of scroll arrows and buttons moves data only, but leaves labels in place.

1. Choose Remove Split from the Window menu.
2. Move to cell B7, if necessary.
3. Choose Freeze Panes from the Window menu. Single lines divide the worksheet, marking frozen areas.
4. Experiment with the scroll buttons and the arrow keys.
5. Choose Unfreeze Panes from the Window menu to restore the original view of the worksheet.

EXERCISE 4-10 Use Split Boxes and Split Bars

Another way to split a screen into multiple panes is to use the horizontal and vertical *split boxes*. The horizontal split box appears in the upper right corner of the document window; it is the gray, rectangular box located above the vertical scroll arrow. The vertical split box is found at the far right of the horizontal scroll bar at the bottom of the document window.

Clicking a split box produces a split bar, which you can drag to the desired position on the worksheet to split the screen. Double-click a split box to position the split bar automatically.

1. Move to cell B7, if necessary.
2. Move the mouse pointer to the horizontal split box at the top of the vertical scroll bar. The mouse pointer changes to a split pointer ⇕.

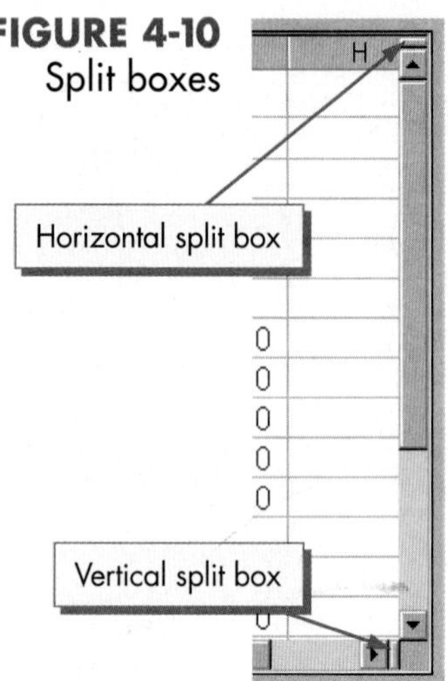

FIGURE 4-10
Split boxes

3. Double-click the split box. A split bar appears above the active cell.
4. Move the mouse pointer to the vertical split box at the right of the horizontal scroll bar.
5. Double-click the split box and the split bar appears between column A and B.
6. Move the mouse pointer to the intersection of the two split bars. The pointer becomes a four-headed arrow ✥.
7. Double-click the intersection of the two split bars to remove the split.

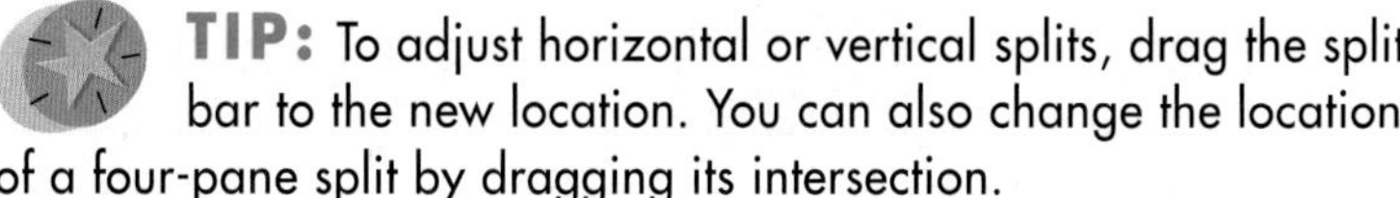

TIP: To adjust horizontal or vertical splits, drag the split bar to the new location. You can also change the location of a four-pane split by dragging its intersection.

Selecting Display Options

You can change how a worksheet is displayed on the screen so it is easier to work with. *Zoom* options change the magnification of the display. You can enlarge it to see more detail or reduce it to show more of the worksheet at one time.

You can also choose to display gridlines and row and column headings.

EXERCISE 4-11 Zoom to Magnify and Reduce the Display

Zoom acts like a magnifying glass. The size of the characters displayed on the screen is expressed in terms of percentages. Higher percentages display larger characters, but less of the worksheet. Lower percentages display smaller characters and show more of the worksheet on the screen. Zoom does not affect the size of the printed worksheet.

Excel provides two ways to use zoom:

- Use the Zoom Control button on the Standard toolbar.
- Choose Zoom from the View menu.

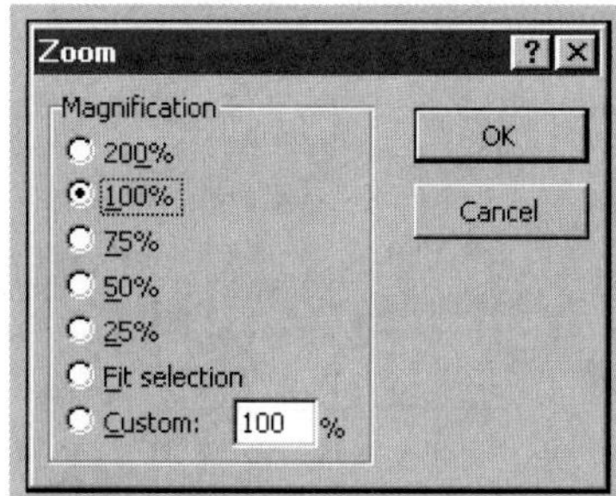

FIGURE 4-11
Zoom dialog box

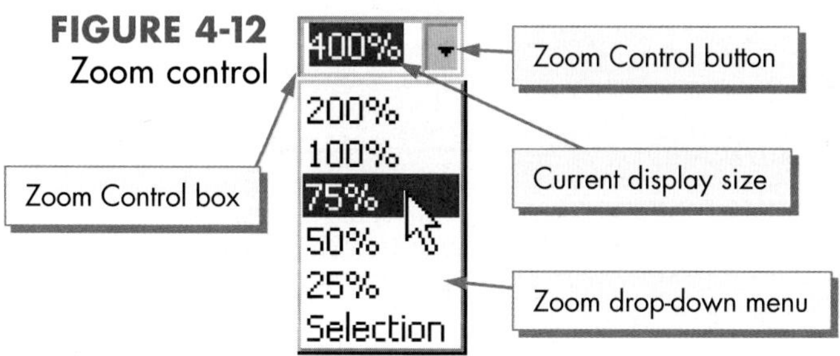

FIGURE 4-12
Zoom control

1. Choose Zoom from the View menu and the Zoom dialog box opens.
2. In the Zoom dialog box, click 75% and click OK. The displayed text becomes smaller and you can see more of the worksheet. The Zoom Control box 75% now displays "75%."
3. Move to cell D7.
4. Choose Zoom from the View menu.
5. Click Custom, key **400**, and click OK. 400% is the largest display type you can specify.
6. Click the Zoom Control button (the arrow at the right of the Zoom Control box) on the Standard toolbar and click 75% on the drop-down menu.

EXERCISE 4-12 Remove Gridlines and Headers from the Screen

You can use other Excel options to vary the on-screen appearance of the worksheet. For example, you can choose to display cell gridlines or row and column headings.

1. Press Ctrl+Home and choose Options from the Tools menu. The Options dialog box appears.
2. Click the View tab, if necessary. See Figure 4-13 on the next page.
3. Under the Window options, click the Gridlines check box and the Row & column headers check box to clear them. Click OK. You removed gridlines and row and column headings from the worksheet display.
4. Move about the worksheet using the Arrow keys. Note that even though the gridlines are not visible, each cell is outlined when active. In addition, although the row and column headers are not visible, the address of the active cell appears in the reference area of the Formula Bar.
5. Move to cell D20, which contains a formula. Note that the contents of the cell appear in the entry area of the Formula Bar.

FIGURE 4-13
Options dialog box

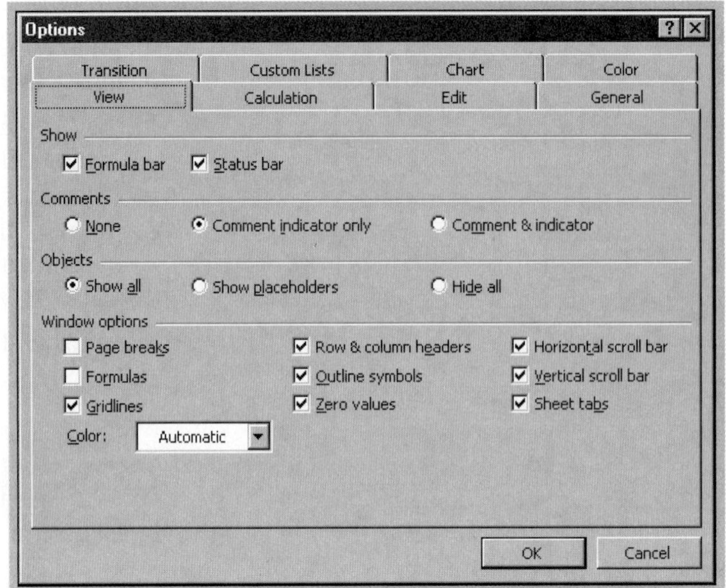

6. Reset the options in the Options dialog box so both gridlines and row and column headings are displayed on the worksheet.

Creating User Documentation

Once you create a worksheet, you may want others to be able to use it. You can provide users with basic information about this worksheet or an entire workbook on a separate worksheet in the workbook. You might label this worksheet User Information or something similar. This sheet should include file information, the purpose of the spreadsheet, and instructions to the user. It should be easy to read.

EXERCISE 4-13 Create User Documentation

1. Click the **User Information** tab to move to the second worksheet, and change the view to 75% using 75%. The varying column widths in the worksheet are already adjusted to create an easy-to-read final worksheet.

2. In cell A1, key **User Information** in bold.

3. Key the following labels as bold and right-aligned in column B, beginning in cell B3. Leave a row space between **Date created:** and **Date revised:** and a row space between **Revised by:** and **Contact for Help:**

Created by:

Date created:

Date revised:

Revised by:

Contact for Help:

4. Key the following labels in bold in cells A11 and A14.

   Purpose

   User Instructions:

5. In column C, starting in cell C3, key the information requested. For example, key your name beside "Created by:" and so on down column C. Make these items left-aligned.
6. In cell B12, key the purpose of this worksheet under the label **Purpose**. Below this, key any user instructions you want to document for another user or for yourself beginning in cell B15. It's a good idea to number these instructions for clarity. Put each numbered item in a separate cell.
7. Turn off gridlines for viewing using the View Options in the Options dialog box.

FIGURE 4-14 Worksheet documentation

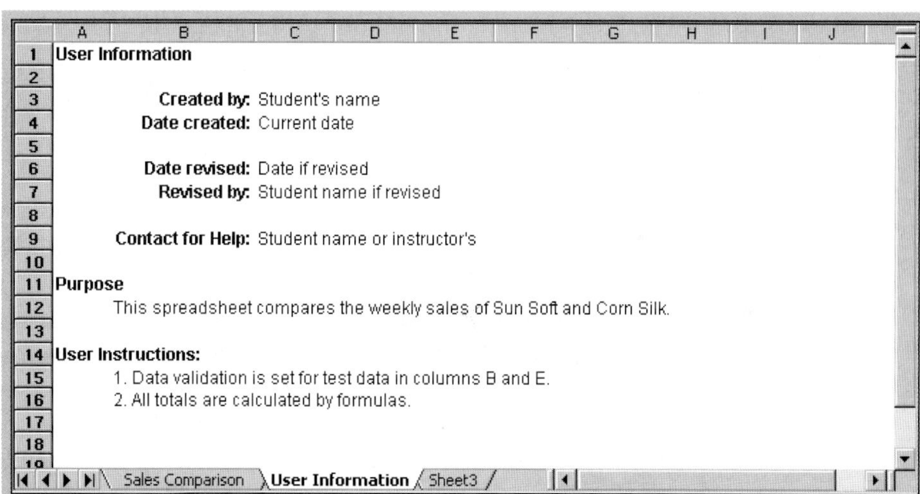

Protecting Files

Workbooks often include formats and formulas that you don't want changed. You can protect a file so users can key only in the areas you leave unlocked.

Protecting a file is a two-step process:

- Unlock areas for data entry
- Protect the file

EXERCISE 4-14 Unlock Data Entry Areas

1. Click the Sales Comparison tab and select the cells that contain test data.
2. Choose Cells from the Format menu and click the Protection tab in the Format Cells dialog box.
3. Clear the Locked check box and click OK. The selected cells are unlocked. When you protect the workbook, they remain available to users.
4. Press Ctrl+Home to return to cell A1.

NOTE: By default, all cells are locked in a workbook. Locked cells become inaccessible only after you protect the worksheet.

EXERCISE 4-15 Protect a Worksheet

The Protection command on the Tools menu offers two options:

- Protect Workbook prevents a user from adding, deleting, renaming, or moving worksheets and from resizing or moving windows.
- Protect Sheet prevents a user from changing data in a worksheet.

1. Point to Protection on the Tools menu and choose Protect Sheet from the cascading menu. The Protect Sheet dialog box appears.
2. In the Password text box, key *[your initials]*. The text box displays asterisks instead of the characters you key to ensure the secrecy of your password. A password can be up to 255 characters long and can include any combination of letters, numerals, and symbols. Passwords are case-sensitive, so you must remember whether you use uppercase or lowercase characters.
3. Click OK and the Confirm Password dialog box appears.
4. Rekey *[your initials]* in this dialog box and click OK.
5. Press Tab repeatedly to move to the cells that are available for data entry.

FIGURE 4-15 Protect Sheet dialog box

Printing Workbooks and Print Areas

In Excel, you can control how your work is printed. You can:

- Preview a worksheet or an entire workbook before printing.
- Change page orientation.
- Position the print area on the page.
- Create headers and footers.
- Print with or without gridlines or row and column headings.
- Print all or part of a worksheet or workbook.

EXERCISE 4-16 Preview the Workbook before Printing

Preview a worksheet before you print it so you can see the page layout, headers and footers, print formatting, and page breaks. Although it is always a good idea to preview a worksheet, it makes particular sense if it contains graphics, drawings, or charts. After all, it takes less time to preview a complex worksheet than to print it.

1. Make the Sales Comparison worksheet active, if necessary.
2. Choose Print Preview from the File menu or click the Print Preview button on the Standard toolbar. At the top of the print preview screen, the Next button is dimmed. The current worksheet fits on one page and the second worksheet is not available.
3. Click the Print button to open the Print dialog box, select Entire workbook under Print what, and click the Preview button. Print Preview labels the current worksheet "Preview: Page 1 of 2," and the Next button becomes available. See Figure 4-16 on the next page.
4. Click Next. The User Information sheet ("Preview: Page 2 of 2") is displayed.
5. Click Zoom at the top of the preview screen (or click the reduced document). The worksheet is displayed in actual size.

TIP: Click the magnifier pointer on the full-page document to Zoom to actual size. Click the arrow pointer on the enlarged document to Zoom to the reduced display.

6. Use the scroll arrows to view other parts of the worksheet in actual size.

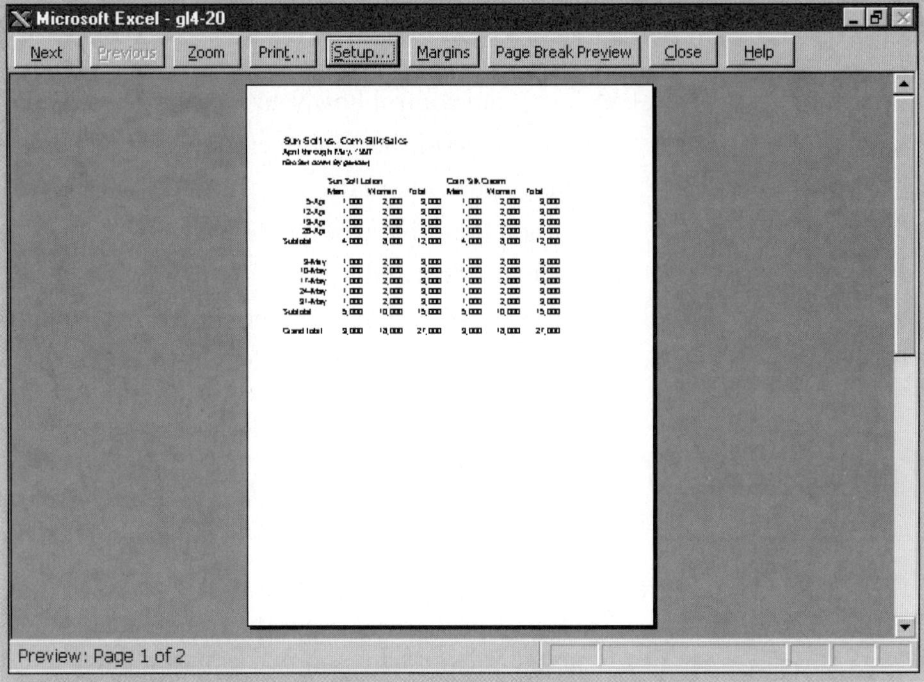

FIGURE 4-16 Print preview display

7. Click Previous to display page 1 again.
8. Click Zoom (or click the document) again to return the worksheet to full-page size.
9. Click Close to close the Preview window.

EXERCISE 4-17 Choose a Page Orientation

One of the most useful print functions offered by Excel is *page orientation*, which you use to print worksheets in either *portrait* or *landscape* orientation. In portrait orientation, the page is vertical, 8½″ × 11″. In landscape orientation, the page is horizontal, 11″ × 8½″. You print worksheets with relatively few columns in portrait orientation. Wide worksheets require landscape orientation.

1. Choose Page Setup from the File menu to open the Page Setup dialog box.

NOTE: The Setup button at the top of the Print Preview screen also opens the Page Setup dialog box.

2. Click the Page tab, if necessary.

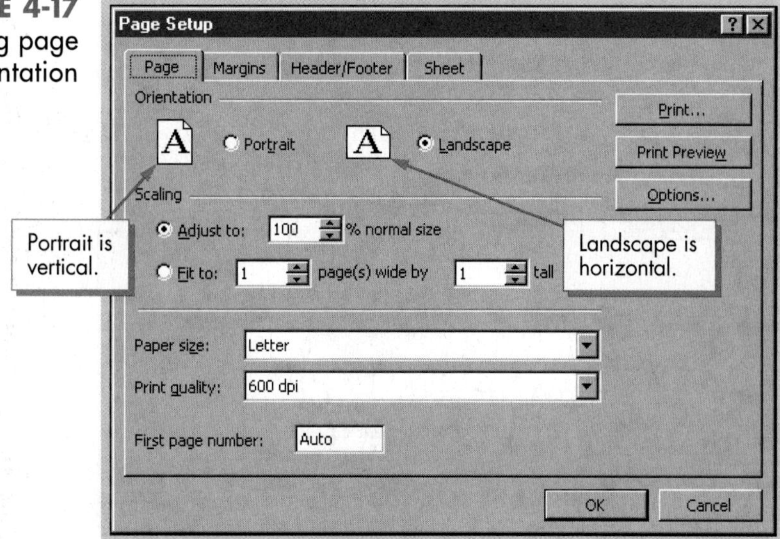

FIGURE 4-17 Choosing page orientation

3. Click Landscape and click OK. The worksheet might look better in landscape orientation, especially if its width exceeds its length.
4. Click .

NOTE: Page Setup options apply only to the current worksheet.

EXERCISE 4-18 Center the Print Area on a Page

You can center worksheets on a page to improve the page layout. This is especially useful when worksheets are relatively small or all the pages are the same size.

1. Click Setup and click the Margins tab.
2. Click the Horizontally and Vertically check boxes. The Preview area in the dialog box displays the centered settings.

NOTE: Normally a worksheet is centered horizontally, but not vertically. We have done it here for teaching purposes only. You may opt to vertically center a worksheet if it contains a chart or other graphics that you learn more about later.

FIGURE 4-18
Center on page options

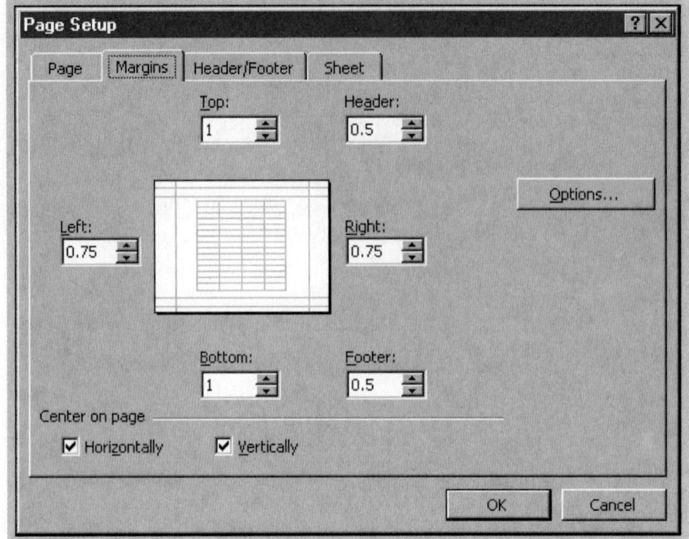

EXERCISE 4-19 Enter a Header and a Footer

Headers and footers provide helpful information about a printed document. You can format these features in Excel using the Page Setup dialog box or the Setup button on the Print Preview screen.

1. Click the Header/Footer tab.
2. Click Custom Header. The insertion point is automatically positioned in the Left Section box so you can change the header.
3. Key your name in the Left Section box. This portion of the header appears in the upper left corner of the printed page.
4. Press Tab. The insertion point moves to the Center Section box.

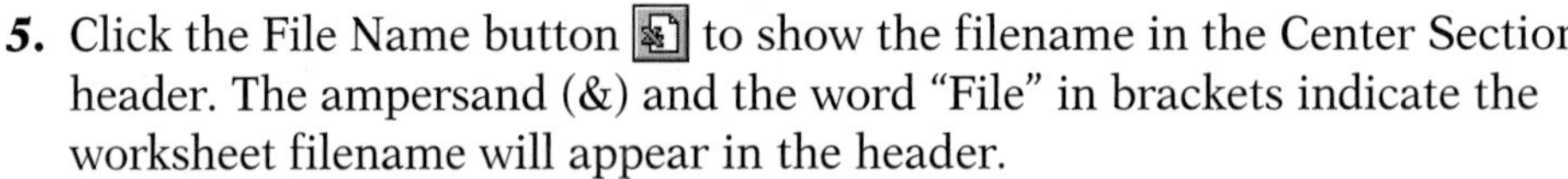

5. Click the File Name button to show the filename in the Center Section header. The ampersand (&) and the word "File" in brackets indicate the worksheet filename will appear in the header.

6. Press Tab and click the Date button to include the current date in the Right Section header. See Figure 4-19 on the next page.
7. Click OK. Your changes appear in the Header text box.
8. Click Custom Footer and press Tab. The insertion point moves to the Center Section box of the Footer dialog box.

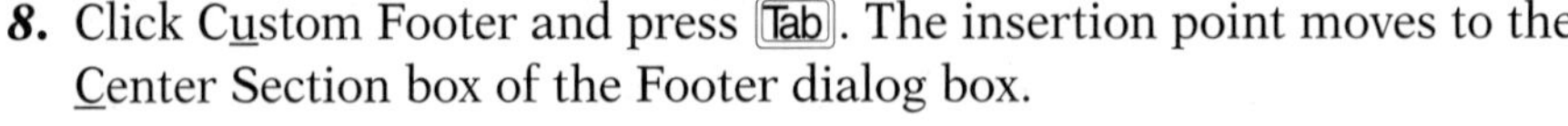

9. Click the Sheet Name button to include the current sheet name in the footer, which is represented by &Tab.

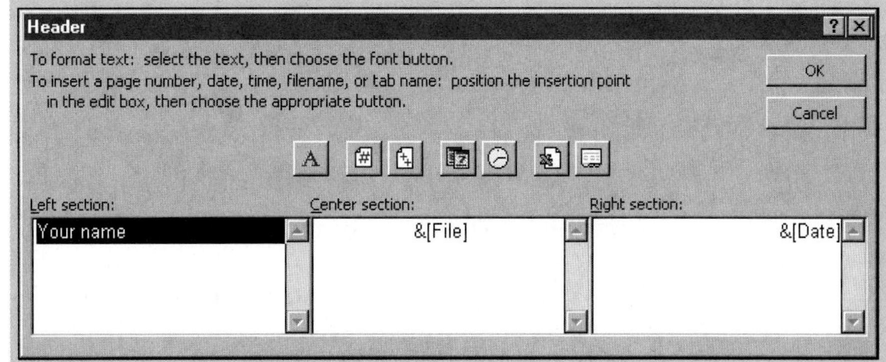

FIGURE 4-19
Creating a custom header

10. Click OK. Your changes appear in the Footer text box.

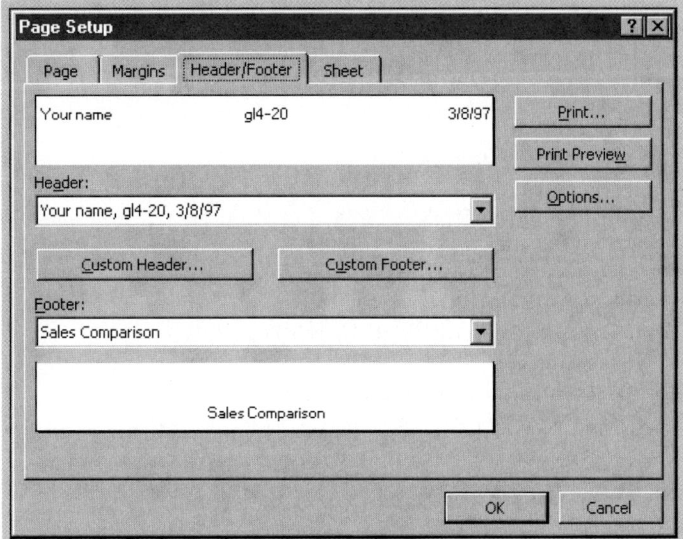

FIGURE 4-20
New header and footer

11. Click OK to close the Page Setup dialog box.
12. Close the Print Preview window.
13. Move to the User Information sheet. Use Page Setup to make the same changes to the header and footer of this sheet.

TIP: The default for headers and footers is none. If you have a header or footer you want to delete from a worksheet, select (none) under Header or Footer to remove it.

EXERCISE 4-20 Print a Workbook

Now that you set up the worksheet, it's time to print. You can print single sheets or multiple sheets of a workbook.

1. Save the workbook as *[your initials]***4-20.xls**.

TIP: Save a workbook immediately before or after printing to preserve the current print settings.

2. Choose Print from the File menu or press Ctrl+P to open the Print dialog box. The dialog box displays Excel's default settings and identifies the designated printer.

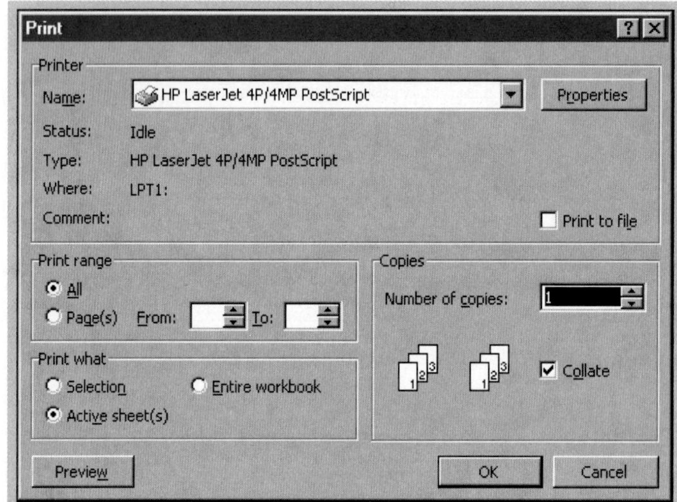

FIGURE 4-21 Print dialog box

TIP: You can click [Print button] on the Standard Toolbar to print the current worksheet automatically or choose Print from the Print Preview screen to open the Print dialog box.

3. Click Entire Workbook and click OK to print both sheets of your workbook. The Printing dialog box appears as your workbook is sent to the printer.
4. Click Cancel to stop the print job.

EXERCISE 4-21 Change the Print Area

Excel automatically prints the entire worksheet unless you specify otherwise. Sometimes you may want to print a specific range of cells—called a *print area*.

If you select multiple print areas, each area begins printing on a separate page. Headers and footers also appear when you print an area.

1. Move to the Sales Comparison sheet, if necessary.
2. Select cells A5 through D11.
3. Choose Print from the File menu.
4. Click Selection.
5. Click OK. Excel prints the selected portion of the worksheet.

TIP: You can also define a print area by selecting a range of cells, choosing Print Area from the File menu, and choosing Set Print Area. Clicking [Print] on the Standard toolbar prints the current print area. To deselect the print area, choose File, Print Area, and then Clear Print Area.

6. Select cells A6 through D11.
7. Hold down Ctrl, select cells A13 through D18, and release Ctrl. Two areas are selected.
8. Choose Print from the File menu.
9. Click Selection and click OK. Excel prints the selected portions of the worksheet on two separate pages.

Printing Formulas

You may want to display formulas onscreen or in your printed worksheet for documentation purposes or to find and correct problems. You can either check the Formulas box on the View tab of the Options dialog box or use the keyboard shortcut Ctrl+`.

EXERCISE 4-22 Set View for Formulas

1. Press Ctrl+Home and choose Options from the Tools menu.
2. Select the View tab, if necessary.

NOTE: View options affect the onscreen appearance of your worksheet. The Formulas option, however, also affects the printed worksheet. You must control most print options—such as row and column headings and gridlines—through the Page Setup dialog box.

3. Click the Formulas check box and click OK. Excel displays all formulas entered in their appropriate worksheet cells. Note that the column widths change to accommodate the wider formulas. As a result, only a portion of the worksheet fits onscreen. Also, the dates change to serial dates and the title is not fully visible.

NOTE: Column widths may not always be automatically widened enough to accommodate extremely wide formulas. In this case you will need to manually widen the columns so you can see the formulas onscreen and on the printed worksheet.

FIGURE 4-22
Formulas displayed in worksheet

	A	B	C	D	E	
1	**Sun Soft vs. Corn**					
2	**April through May, 199**					
3	***(Broken down by gende***					
4						
5		Sun Soft Lotion			Corn Silk Cream	
6		Men	Women	Total	Men	W
7	35525	1000	2000	=SUM(B7:C7)	1000	2
8	35532	1000	2000	=SUM(B8:C8)	1000	2
9	35539	1000	2000	=SUM(B9:C9)	1000	2
10	35546	1000	2000	=SUM(B10:C10)	1000	2
11	Subtotal	=SUM(B7:B10)	=SUM(C7:C10)	=SUM(B11:C11)	=SUM(E7:E10)	=
12						
13	35553	1000	2000	=SUM(B13:C13)	1000	2
14	35560	1000	2000	=SUM(B14:C14)	1000	2
15	35567	1000	2000	=SUM(B15:C15)	1000	2
16	35574	1000	2000	=SUM(B16:C16)	1000	2
17	35581	1000	2000	=SUM(B17:C17)	1000	2
18	Subtotal	=SUM(B13:B17)	=SUM(C13:C17)	=SUM(B18:C18)	=SUM(E13:E17)	=
19						

Sales Comparison / User Information / Sheet3

4. Press Ctrl+`. The worksheet is displayed normally. (The ` key is found to the left of the 1 key.)
5. Press Ctrl+` to display formulas once again.

EXERCISE 4-23 Print with Grids and Headings

To help you verify that each formula is in the right place, you can add gridlines and row and column headings to your worksheet printout using Page Setup.

1. Choose Page Setup from the File menu and click the Sheet tab, if necessary.
2. Click Gridlines and Row and column headings in the Print area of the dialog box.

3. Move to the Page tab and click Landscape, if necessary.
4. Click Fit to and make sure the text boxes to the right show 1 page(s) wide by 1 tall.

NOTE: Fit to shrinks the size of printed characters so the worksheet fits on the number of pages you indicate. In some worksheets this makes the text too small to read.

5. Click the Print Preview button to view the worksheet before printing. Click Zoom to take a closer look.
6. Click the Print button to open the Print dialog box and click OK.
7. Close the workbook. Don't save the changes.

TIP: If you save settings that print formulas, you have to change settings the next time you want to print the normal worksheet.

COMMAND SUMMARY

FEATURE	BUTTON	MENU	KEYBOARD
Go To Special		Edit, Go To, Special	Ctrl+G
Split		Window, Split	
Freeze Panes		Window, Freeze Panes	
Zoom	100%	View, Zoom	
Print Preview		File, Print Preview	
Page Setup		File, Page Setup	
Protect Workbook		Tools, Protection, Protect Workbook	
Protect Worksheet		Tools, Protection, Protect Worksheet	
Print		File, Print	Ctrl+P
Display Formulas		Tools, Options	Ctrl+`
Set View		Tools, Options	

USING HELP 

This lesson showed you how to print worksheets with different display options and with varying print areas. But what happens if you have trouble printing something just the way you need it? Excel includes troubleshooting help you can access through the Office Assistant.

To find out how to troubleshoot some print problems, use the Office Assistant:

1. Click [?].
2. Key **How can I learn more about printing?** in the Office Assistant text box and click Search.
3. Select Troubleshoot printing. Notice that the Microsoft Excel dialog box opens with Troubleshoot printing topics listed.

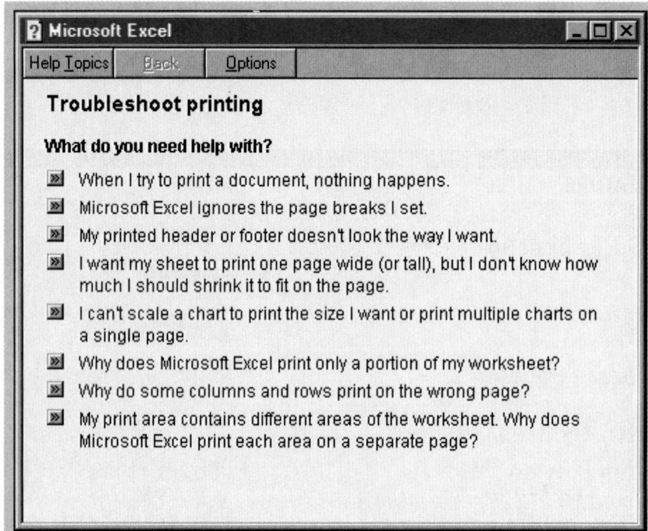

FIGURE 4-23
Microsoft Excel dialog box with Troubleshoot printing topics

4. Click beside a topic of interest to open that topic's Help dialog box.
5. Select Back to return to the previous dialog box and search through other options. Close the dialog box when you finish and close the Office Assistant.

Concepts Review

TRUE/FALSE QUESTIONS

Each of the following statements is either true or false. Indicate your choice by circling T or F.

T F *1*. It's best to begin entering data in Excel before you design a worksheet with pencil and paper.

T F *2*. You should place comparative information in rows.

T F *3*. The Formula Bar displays the current cell's contents and the name box displays the cell address.

T F *4*. It's possible to select cells based on their contents, such as all cells containing formulas.

T F *5*. You use Zoom to speed up the printing process.

T F *6*. You can only validate data that is made up of whole numbers.

T F *7*. You can select page orientation from the Print Preview dialog box.

T F *8*. You can validate data using Validation on the Data menu.

SHORT ANSWER QUESTIONS

Write the correct answer in the space provided.

1. What name is given to simple numbers you can add in your head that are used to verify the accuracy of formulas?

___

2. Which function would you use to keep other users from changing formulas in a worksheet?

___

3. Which command enables you to divide a worksheet into two parts?

___

4. Which command enables you to keep row and column labels in one place while you scroll data?

___

5. What do you call a range of cells to be printed?

____

6. Which part of the screen identifies each worksheet of an Excel workbook?

____

7. Which dialog box enables you to enter a custom header and footer?

____

8. Which page orientation displays the worksheet horizontally?

____

CRITICAL THINKING

Answer these questions on a separate piece of paper. There are no right or wrong answers. Support your answer with examples from your own experience, if possible.

1. Planning and sketching a worksheet with pencil and paper might seem like a waste of time in the "computer age." What might happen if you skip the planning stage? In what types of situations would it be especially important to plan and sketch the worksheet before entering data in Excel?
2. Describe a project or work situation in which you would have liked to have documentation available. What problem were you trying to solve? How would good documentation of the project have helped you?

Skills Review

EXERCISE 4-24

Plan a worksheet in pencil, enter labels, data validation, test data, and formulas onscreen, select cells by content, and name the worksheet tab.

1. Plan and sketch a worksheet showing sales for each month of the first quarter for five sales representatives by following these steps:
   a. Write the worksheet heading **First Quarter Sales** at the top of a blank page.
   b. Write the entry area item **Report date: *[current date]*** two rows below the heading in the first column and use the current date.

c. Write the following labels in a column along the left side of your page two rows below the entry area item:

Sales Rep

Davis

Jackson

Miller

Pierce

Brown

Total

d. Write the labels **January**, **February**, **March**, and **Total** in a row to the right of the label **Sales Rep**

e. Write **F**'s in the cells that contain row and column totals.

2. Enter row and column labels onscreen by following these steps:

a. Open a new Excel workbook.

b. Key the heading **First Quarter Sales** in cell A1 in bold.

c. Key the entry area item in cell A3.

d. Key the row labels from your paper sketch in cells A5 through A11.

e. Key the column labels from your paper sketch center-aligned in cells B5 through E5.

3. Enter data validation in the test data cells.

a. Select cells B6 through D10.

b. Open the Data Validation dialog box and click the Settings tab.

c. Allow for whole numbers between 1000 and 3000.

d. Click the Input message tab and key **Test data between 1000 and 3000** as the input message with no title.

e. Click OK.

4. Enter the test data shown in Figure 4-24 (on the next page) in the worksheet and format it for comma style and no decimals using [,] and [.00→.0].

5. Enter formulas onscreen using the following steps:

a. Select cells E6 through E10 and click [Σ].

b. Select cells B11 through E11 and click [Σ].

6. Select formula cells by content.

a. Press Ctrl+Home.

b. Press Ctrl+G.

c. Click Special.

d. Click Formulas and deselect Text, Logicals, and Errors.

e. Click OK.

FIGURE 4-24

	B	C	D
6	1000	2000	3000
7	1000	2000	3000
8	1000	2000	3000
9	1000	2000	3000
10	1000	2000	3000

7. Name the worksheet tab.

   a. Double-click the Sheet1 tab.

   b. Key Quarter 1.

8. Save the workbook as *[your initials]***4-24.xls**.

9. Print the worksheet and close the workbook.

EXERCISE 4-25

Split a worksheet into panes, freeze panes, use Zoom, and remove gridlines and headers from the screen.

1. Open the file **Expense1.xls**.

2. Split the worksheet into panes by following these steps:

   a. Move to cell B10.

   b. Choose Split from the Window menu.

   c. Click the down vertical scroll arrow for the bottom pane until the Total row for the Phoenix office becomes visible.

3. Freeze the worksheet panes by following these steps:

   a. Choose Freeze Panes from the Window menu.

   b. Click the horizontal scroll bar to compare data for the two offices.

4. Change the size of the worksheet onscreen by choosing Zoom from the View menu and choosing 75%.

5. Remove gridlines from the screen by following these steps:

   a. Choose Options from the Tools menu.

   b. When the Options dialog box appears, click the View tab, if necessary.

c. Clear the Gridlines and Row & column headers check boxes and click OK.

6. Save the workbook as *[your initials]***4-25.xls**.
7. Print the worksheet and close the workbook.

EXERCISE 4-26

Create user documentation, unlock data entry areas, turn off gridlines for viewing, and protect a worksheet.

1. Open the file **Expense2.xls**. Look at the first two sheets.
2. Create documentation for the worksheet by following these steps:
   a. Click the Documentation tab and key **User Information** in cell A1 in bold. (Column widths are already adjusted for easy reading.)
   b. Key the following labels in bold and right-align them in column B. Key the information left-aligned in column C.

FIGURE 4-25

	B	C
3	Created by:	Jaime Santo
4	Date created:	29-Jun
5		
6	Date revised:	Date if revised
7	Revised by:	Student name
8		
9	Contact for Help:	Jaime Santo

3. Key the labels in bold in column A and the information in column B (see Figure 4-26 on the next page). (To create a line break in cell B15, press Alt+Enter after the first line.)
4. Turn off gridlines for viewing.
   a. Choose Options under the Tools menu.
   b. Click the View tab.
   c. Clear the Gridlines check box and click OK.

FIGURE 4-26

	A	B
11	Purpose	
12		This worksheet shows projected increases in Q1 expenses.
13		
14	User Instructions:	
15		1. Note total formulas in row 10 in both sheets. 2. Note percentage formulas in column D in both sheets.

5. Unlock data entry for the Quarter cells in the San Francisco Increase sheet.
   - *a.* Click the San Francisco Increase worksheet tab.
   - *b.* Select cells B4 through C9.
   - *c.* Open the Format Cells dialog box and click the Protection tab.
   - *d.* Clear the Locked box and click OK.
6. Protect the worksheet.
   - *a.* Choose Protection from the Tools menu.
   - *b.* Choose Protect Sheet.
   - *c.* Enter *[your initials]* in the password section of the Protect Sheet dialog box and click OK.
   - *d.* Enter *[your initials]* again in the Confirm Password dialog box and click OK.
   - *e.* Press Ctrl+Home and test the protection by pressing Tab.
7. Save the workbook as *[your initials]***4-26.xls**.
8. Print the entire workbook by following these steps:
   - *a.* Press Ctrl+P.
   - *b.* Select Entire Workbook in the Print dialog box and click OK.
9. Close the workbook.

EXERCISE 4-27

Choose page orientation, center the print area, change headers and footers, and print with and without gridlines, headings, and formulas.

1. Open the file **Revenue.xls**.

2. Choose landscape orientation by following these steps:
   a. Choose Page Setup from the File menu.
   b. Click the Page tab, if necessary.
   c. Click Landscape.
   d. Click Print Preview to view the entire worksheet on one page.
3. Center the print area on the page by following these steps:
   a. While still in Print Preview, click Setup.
   b. Click the Margins tab.
   c. Click the Horizontally and Vertically check boxes.
4. Change the headers and footers by following these steps:
   a. Click the Header/Footer tab in the Page Setup dialog box and click Custom Header.
   b. Key your name in the Left section box and press Tab.
   c. Click [icon] in the Center section of the header and press Tab.
   d. Click [icon] in the Right section of the header and click OK.
   e. Click Custom Footer and press Tab.
   f. Click [icon] and click OK, then click Close.
   g. Save the workbook as *[your initials]*4-27.xls.
5. Print the worksheet without gridlines by following these steps. (*Hint:* The default is that gridlines are turned off for printing. In this worksheet they are on.)
   a. Choose Page Setup from the File menu. Then click the Sheet tab in the Page Setup dialog box.
   b. Clear the Gridlines check box and click Print Preview to view the worksheet in Print Preview.
   c. Click Print to open the Print dialog box and click OK to print the worksheet.
6. Change the print area and print the worksheet with headings and formulas by following these steps:
   a. Select columns A through D, choose Print Area from the File Menu, and choose Set Print Area.
   b. Choose Options from the Tools menu and select the View tab, if necessary.
   c. Check the Formulas box and click OK.
   d. Choose Page Setup from the File menu and click the Sheet tab, if necessary.
   e. Check the Gridlines and Row and column headings boxes.
   f. Click the Page tab and choose Landscape, if necessary, and click OK.

g. Click Print Preview to view the worksheet before printing. Click Zoom to take a closer look.

h. Click Print to open the Print dialog box and click OK to print.

7. Press Ctrl+` to toggle from Formula view to Normal view.
8. Choose Print Area from the File menu and choose Clear Print Area.
9. Clear the Gridlines and Row and column headings settings in the Page Setup dialog box.
10. Close the workbook without saving it.

Lesson Applications

EXERCISE 4-28

Enter a label and data, add formulas, change headers and footers, and print horizontally centered with and without formulas, grids, and row and column headings.

Nate Rosario, the controller for the Beautiful Belle company, needs to prepare a forecast of profits (or net income) for the next five years.

1. Open the file **NetInc1.xls**.
2. Insert a row between the "Administration" and "Marketing" labels.
3. Label the new row **Salaries** and insert the data below.

   550 650 780 870 900
4. Insert Total Expenses formulas that sum the Administration, Salaries, Marketing, and Research expenses for each year.
5. Insert Net Income formulas for each year. Calculate net income by subtracting Total Expenses from Sales.
6. Apply a single-line bottom border to the research data (just above the total expense cells).
7. Format the labels "Sales," "Expenses," and "Net Income" in italic, and format the net income figures in bold.
8. Center the worksheet horizontally on the page and make sure it is set to print without gridlines.
9. Remove the footer and create a new header that includes your name on the left, the filename in the center, and the date on the right.
10. Save the workbook as *[your initials]***4-28.xls** and print the worksheet.
11. Create a formula printout that fits on one page which shows all formulas with gridlines and row and column headings in landscape orientation.
12. Close the workbook without saving it.

EXERCISE 4-29

Enter data and labels, create and enter formulas, select cells by content, set up the worksheet to print in portrait orientation, and print it with gridlines, row and column headings, and formulas.

The executives at Beautiful Belle want to examine third-quarter sales data by comparing the differences in male and female purchasers of Sun Soft and Corn Silk products.

1. Open the file **Totals.xls**.
2. Insert rows between the July and Subtotals rows shown in Figure 4-27. Then enter the data for the months of August and September making the appropriate corrections.

FIGURE 4-27

		Sun Soft	Corn Silk
Men	July	11,685	9,350
	AUGUST	12,550	9,800
	September	8,794	12,810
	Subtotal	11,685	9,350
Women	July	24,030	49,400
	Augst	22,104	38,465
	September	24,366	18,700
	Subtotal	24,030	49,400

3. Check and correct the subtotal formulas, if necessary.
4. Insert two rows above the Grand Total row and key the labels **August** and **September** under Total.
5. Create formulas that calculate the August and September totals.
6. Select cells with formulas using select by content (Go To Special dialog box) and make them all italic.
7. Set up the worksheet to print in portrait orientation with gridlines. (The default orientation is portrait; however, this worksheet's orientation is landscape.)
8. Center the worksheet horizontally.
9. Create a new header that includes your name on the left, the filename in the center, and the date on the right.
10. Save the workbook as *[your initials]***4-29.xls** and print the worksheet.
11. Create a formula printout that shows all formulas with gridlines and row and column headings in landscape orientation.
12. Close the workbook without saving it.

EXERCISE 4-30

Freeze panes, enter data and formulas, use Zoom, use set-up options, preview the worksheet, protect the worksheet, print it with and without formulas.

The Beautiful Belle Company wants to extend the comparative-sales worksheet to include test-marketing data for Sun Soft and Corn Silk through July.

1. Open the file **MktTest.xls**.
2. Edit the title in cell A2 to read **April through July, 1997**.
3. Add new rows to the Sales Comparison worksheet by selecting cells A21 through A32 and choosing Rows from the Insert menu.
4. Freeze panes in cell A8 so column headings remain visible.
5. Enter the data shown in Figure 4-28 beginning in row 21. Make sure the numbers are formatted to match the others.

FIGURE 4-28

	A	B	C	D	E	F	G
		Sun Soft			Corn Silk		
		Men	Women	Total	Men	Women	Total
21	7-Jun	2,300	3,400		1,250	1,050	
22	14-Jun	2,200	5,200		1,370	1,100	
23	21-Jun	1,950	4,300		1,290	1,000	
24	28-Jun	2,700	5,800		1,400	950	
25	Subtotal						
26							
27	5-Jul	2,500	4,500		1,500	1,100	
28	12-Jul	2,735	6,900		1,550	1,300	
29	19-Jul	2,800	5,430		1,650	1,550	
30	26-Jul	3,200	5,700		1,780	1,760	
31	Subtotal						

6. Enter or revise formulas to calculate totals, subtotals, and grand totals. (Grand totals must reflect the two new months' data.)
7. Reduce the size of the worksheet to 50%.
8. View the worksheet in Print Preview.
9. Set the worksheet to print in landscape orientation without gridlines or row and column headings.
10. Close Print Preview. Change the display to 75% using the Zoom Control box on the toolbar.
11. Protect the worksheet leaving only the cells containing weekly sales numbers available for entry. Make any cells containing formulas unavailable.
12. Center the worksheet horizontally and create a header that includes your name on the left, the filename in the center, and the date on the right.
13. Save the workbook as *[your initials]***4-30.xls** and print the worksheet.
14. Create a formula printout that fits on one page which shows all formulas with gridlines and row and column headings in landscape orientation. (Adjust the width of column A to make the formulas fit on one page.)
15. Close the workbook without saving it.

EXERCISE 4-31

Sketch a worksheet plan, enter the plan in a worksheet, validate data, select all formula cells, create documentation, name sheet tabs, use print preview and page set-up options, print the workbook, and print formulas.

The Beautiful Belle Company wants a worksheet that calculates the difference between monthly sales of Sun Soft and Corn Silk products to men and women for their Northeast division. The worksheet should also calculate the difference in total sales by gender to both groups.

1. Sketch a worksheet to calculate these values. Title the worksheet **Sun Soft vs. Corn Silk Sales**, and add an entry area item that includes **Northeast Division 1997** two rows below the title and two rows above the column labels. The report is in two sections, **Men** and **Women**, which should go in the first column. Each section should have the following row labels: **April**, **May**, **June**, and **July**, which should begin beside "Men" and "Women" in the second column. The last row of each section should be a **Subtotal** row and the last row in the worksheet should be a **Total** row. There should be three columns of data labeled **Sun Soft**, **Corn Silk**, and **Difference**.
2. Write formulas in this worksheet plan in the subtotal rows and the total rows. Abbreviate using an F.

3. Key the title and labels in a new Excel worksheet. Use text formatting to distinguish the title, entry area item, and labels from other worksheet data.
4. Input data validation for the cells that contain sales data for men and women. Validate for whole numbers greater than 500. (*Hint:* Insert a message to input men's figures in the men's area and women's figures in the women's area.)
5. Key the following sales data for men formatted in comma style with no decimals:

		Sun Soft	**Corn Silk**	**Difference**
Men	April	**3,300**	**6,600**	
	May	**6,450**	**8,150**	
	June	**9,150**	**5,310**	
	July	**11,235**	**6,480**	

6. Key the following sales data for women formatted in comma style with no decimals:

		Sun Soft	**Corn Silk**	**Difference**
Women	April	**3,300**	**6,600**	
	May	**6,800**	**8,000**	
	June	**18,700**	**4,100**	
	July	**22,530**	**5,710**	

7. Create the formulas to calculate the men's and women's subtotals. (*Hint:* Use AutoSum.)
8. Create the formulas to calculate differences between Sun Soft and Corn Silk subtotals only. Format the figures in comma style, no decimals.
9. Create the formulas to calculate the totals for each section. (*Hint:* Add men's and women's subtotals.) Format the figures in comma style, no decimals, if necessary.
10. Create the formula for the difference between product totals.
11. Select all cells containing formulas and make them italic. (*Hint:* Select the cells by content to be sure you have them all.)
12. Rename the Sheet1 tab **Sales by Gender**.
13. Rename the Sheet2 tab **User Information**.
14. Create user information as follows using the basic layout you learned in the lesson to place the documentation elements. (Don't worry about column width when placing these elements, but follow the basic design you learned in the lesson.)

User Information

Created by:	**Jane Doe**
Date created:	**8/13/97**
Date revised:	***[current date]***
Revised by:	***[your name]***
Contact for Help:	**Jane Doe**
Purpose	**Compare Sun Soft vs. Corn Silk sales data by gender.**
User Instructions:	**1. Note formulas in subtotal, total cells.**
	2. Difference formulas are only present for subtotals and totals.

15. Turn off gridlines for viewing.

16. Center the Sales by Gender sheet horizontally.

17. Create headers that show your name on the left, the filename in the center, and the date at the right on both sheets.

18. Preview the workbook.

19. Print the entire workbook and save it as *[your initials]***4-31.xls**.

20. Display the formulas in the Sales by Gender worksheet. Print the sheet on one page in landscape orientation, showing gridlines and row and column headings.

21. Close the workbook without saving it. Submit four pages: the plan, the two worksheets, and the formula view.

Copying Data and Using Toolbars

OBJECTIVES

After completing this lesson, you will be able to:

1. **Build a worksheet with copy and paste.**
2. **Copy using drag and drop.**
3. **Copy using Fill and AutoFill.**
4. **Use Excel's toolbars.**

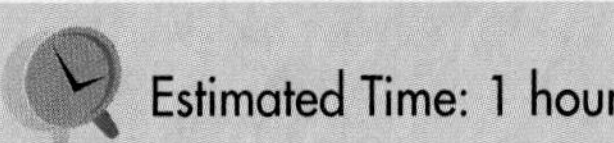

Designing and developing worksheets in Excel often involves repeating many basic elements, including cells, formulas, and formatting. You can copy these elements to build a worksheet quickly and easily. This lesson also demonstrates the versatility of Excel's toolbars and different ways to display them.

Building a Worksheet with Copy and Paste

You can cut, copy, and move cell contents in Excel. A copy is an exact duplicate of the element you select that can be pasted or inserted into other locations of a worksheet or the document area of other Windows applications. The data remains in the original location, but also resides on the Clipboard. Unlike cutting or moving, you don't affect the original element when you copy it. Information is erased from the Clipboard when you initiate a new Cut or Copy command.

You can choose the Copy and Paste commands three ways:

- Use the Edit menu.
- Use the keyboard shortcuts Ctrl+C for Copy and Ctrl+V for Paste.
- Click the Copy and Paste buttons on the Standard toolbar.

EXERCISE 5-1 Copy and Paste Using the Edit Menu

In this exercise you construct a worksheet with both detail and summary comparisons of 1997 second-quarter sales for the test product, Sun Soft Lotion, and its competing product, Corn Silk Cream.

1. Open the file **Compare.xls**.
2. Select cells A6 through B9 as the *source range*. The source range is the area of the worksheet from which you copy or remove data.
3. Choose Copy from the Edit menu. A moving border surrounds the selected cells. The contents of the cells you just copied now appear on the Clipboard.

FIGURE 5-1 Source range selected

	A	B	C	D	E	F	G	H	I
1									
2									
3									
4			Sun Soft	Corn Silk	Difference				
5									
6	Men	April	6000	1000					
7		May	2000	5000					
8		June	1000	4000					
9		Subtotal	9000	10000					
10									
11			8000	7000					
12			4000	5000					
13			3000	11000					
14									
15									
16	Total	Jan							
17		Feb							

Sheet 1

4. Select cell A11. This cell is in the upper left corner of the *target range*. The target range is the new location for the data you copy or move.
5. Choose Paste from the Edit menu. A copy of the data from the source range appears in the target range. A copy of the data also remains on the Clipboard. To show this, Excel displays a moving border around the source range.

TIP: Copy and Paste are available from the shortcut menu. Right click the selected source or target and choose a command.

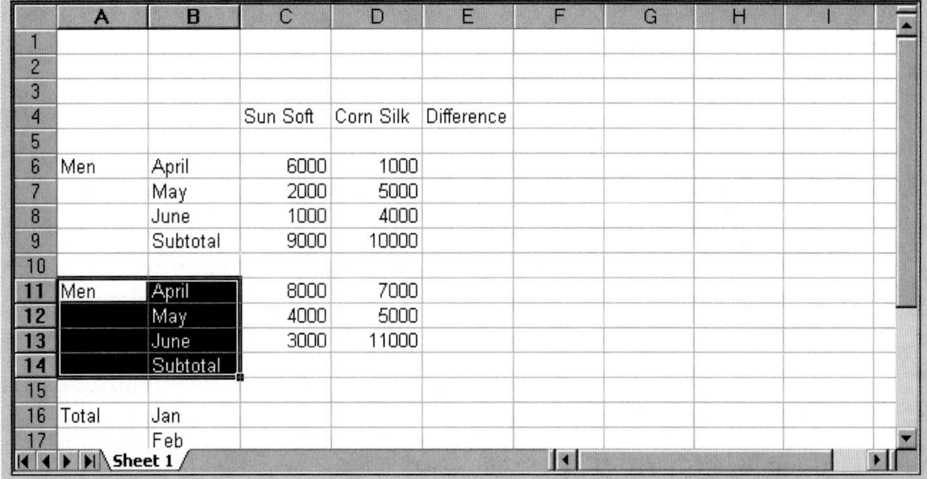

FIGURE 5-2 Source range copied to target range

6. Press Esc to remove the moving border around the source range.
7. Edit cell A11 to read **Women**.

NOTE: When the moving border is no longer displayed, you cannot paste the data from the Clipboard.

EXERCISE 5-2 Overwrite and Insert with Copy and Paste

The Copy and Paste commands overwrite existing cell data. You can also use Copy to insert new cells and data between existing cells.

1. Select cells B11 to B13 and press Ctrl + C.
2. Select cells B16 to B18 and press Ctrl + V. The months "Jan" through "March" are replaced by "April" through "June."
3. Press Esc to exit Copy mode.

TIP: You can simply select cell B16 and press Enter. The contents are pasted in cells B16 to B18 and the moving border is removed from the copied cells automatically. You would not have to press Esc.

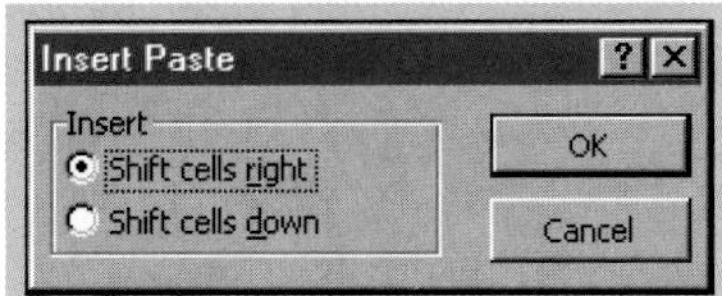

FIGURE 5-3 Insert Paste dialog box

4. Select cell A16 and choose Copy from the Edit menu.
5. Select cell E4 and choose Copied Cells from the Insert menu.

6. Select Shift cells right and click OK in the Insert Paste dialog box. The copy of "Total" appears in cell E4 and the word "Difference" shifts one cell to the right.
7. Press Esc to exit Copy mode and delete the label "Difference."

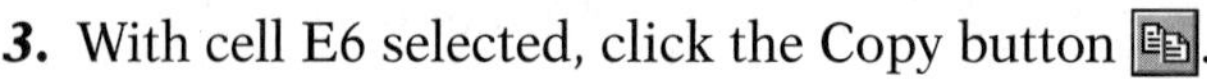

EXERCISE 5-3 Copy and Paste Using the Toolbar

Like the Copy and Paste commands on the Edit menu, you can use the Copy and Paste buttons to copy cell values, formulas, and formatting.

1. Select all cells with numbers and format them for comma style with no decimals.
2. Use Σ to total April sales for Sun Soft and Corn Silk in cell E6.
3. With cell E6 selected, click the Copy button.
4. Select cell E7 and click. Excel copies the formula and the formatting; it also adjusts the cell references so the formula is =SUM(C7:D7). This change in cells is called a *relative cell reference*. With relative referencing, Excel knows if a formula sums a row of numbers, and you copy the formula to a new row, you intend to add the numbers in the new row rather than the numbers in the original row. This type of referencing occurs with any method of copying and pasting formulas..
5. Select cell E8 and click.
6. Select cell E9 and press Enter. Excel pastes the contents and completes the copy action, erasing the Clipboard. All the copied formulas are adjusted with relative cell references and the cell formatting is also copied.

NOTE: You can use the Paste Special command on the Edit menu to paste certain aspects of a cell's contents, including its formatting, values only, validation, or everything except borders to name a few. This is a handy tool if you need to be specific about what you are pasting.

Copying Using Drag and Drop

You can also copy data and formulas using drag-and-drop. This is an easy way to copy information using the mouse. Note that you can make only a single copy using this method.

EXERCISE 5-4 Copy Using Drag and Drop

1. Select cells E6 through E8.
2. Move the mouse pointer across the border of the selection until it becomes an arrow.

TIP: Avoid the lower right corner of the selection.

3. Press and hold down Ctrl. The pointer becomes the drag-and-drop pointer, with a tiny cross appearing to the right of the arrow. When the cross is present, you're copying data, not moving it.
4. Drag the selected cells to cells E11 through E13. Note the gray outline in the shape of the source range and the yellow message box containing the cell addresses as you move the mouse.
5. When the selected cells are positioned at the target range, release the mouse button and the Ctrl key.

TIP: You must hold down the Ctrl key to copy while dragging. Notice the + sign that appears to the right of the arrow pointer.

6. Select cells C9 to E9.
7. Drag and drop this information into cells C14 to E14. Excel copies both the formula and its formatting and adjusts the cell references accordingly.

FIGURE 5-4 Copying using the drag-and-drop method

	A	B	C	D	E	F	G	H	I
4			Sun Soft	Corn Silk	Total				
5									
6	Men	April	6,000	1,000	7,000				
7		May	2,000	5,000	7,000				
8		June	1,000	4,000	5,000				
9		Subtotal	9,000	10,000	19,000				
10									
11	Women	April	8,000	7,000	15,000				
12		May	4,000	5,000	9,000				
13		June	3,000	11,000	14,000				
14		Subtotal							
15					C14:E14				
16	Total	April							
17		May							
18		June							
19									
20									

Sheet 1

8. Verify that the formulas are correct for the new location.

Copying Using Fill and AutoFill

Worksheets frequently contain repetitive formulas. Instead of copying each formula using Copy and Paste, the Fill and AutoFill commands are often a quicker technique.

EXERCISE 5-5 Copy Using the Fill Command

1. Enter the formula **=C6+C11** in cell C16.
2. Select cells C16 through C18. Be sure to select the cell that contains the desired formula and all cells to which that formula is to be copied. These cells must be adjacent to one another to use the Fill command.
3. Choose the Fill command from the Edit menu and choose Down from the cascading menu (or press Ctrl+D). Excel copies the formula to the selected cells and adjusts the cell references.

FIGURE 5-5 Using Fill to copy formulas (with formulas displayed)

	A	B	C	D	E
4			Sun Soft	Corn Silk	Total
5					
6	Men	April	6000	1000	=SUM(C6:D
7		May	2000	5000	=SUM(C7:D
8		June	1000	4000	=SUM(C8:D
9		Subtotal	=SUM(C6:C8)	=SUM(D6:D8)	=SUM(C9:D
10					
11	Women	April	8000	7000	=SUM(C11:
12		May	4000	5000	=SUM(C12:
13		June	3000	11000	=SUM(C13:
14		Subtotal	=SUM(C11:C13)	=SUM(D11:D13)	=SUM(C14:
15					
16	Total	April	=C6+C11		
17		May	=C7+C12		
18		June	=C8+C13		
19					
20					

Sheet 1

4. Click outside the selection.
5. Select cells C16 through E16.
6. Choose Fill from the Edit menu and choose Right from the cascading menu (or press Ctrl+R).
7. Click outside the selection.
8. To view the formulas you copied, press Ctrl+` (or choose Options from the Tools menu, click Formulas, and click OK).

NOTE: It's a good idea to check the formulas in cells that are copied to ensure they have the correct relative references. If possible, enter test data before keying in actual data or turn on formulas for viewing.

EXERCISE 5-6 Copy Using the AutoFill Command

Using AutoFill, you can copy a formula in a single cell to multiple cells in a single step. Drag and drop is a good way to copy when the source area and the target area are not adjacent but both are the same size. AutoFill, on the other hand, should be used for copying to adjacent cells.

1. Press Ctrl + ` to clear the formulas from the screen.

TIP: You can also choose Options from the Tools menu and click to clear the Formulas checkbox.

2. Select cell D16 and position the mouse pointer on the *fill handle*, which is the small box in the lower right corner of the cell. The mouse pointer changes to a black cross.

FIGURE 5-6 Using AutoFill to copy formulas

	A	B	C	D	E	F	G	H	I
4			Sun Soft	Corn Silk	Total				
5									
6	Men	April	6,000	1,000	7,000				
7		May	2,000	5,000	7,000				
8		June	1,000	4,000	5,000				
9		Subtotal	9,000	10,000	19,000				
10									
11	Women	April	8,000	7,000	15,000				
12		May	4,000	5,000	9,000				
13		June	3,000	11,000	14,000				
14		Subtotal	15,000	23,000	38,000				
15									
16	Total	April	14,000	8,000	22,000				
17		May	6,000						
18		June	4,000						
19									
20									

Sheet 1

Fill handle

3. Drag the fill handle until cells D17 and D18 are both selected. The cells are bordered in gray.
4. Release the mouse button. Excel copies the formula from cell D16 to cells D17 and D18.
5. Copy the formula in cell E16 to cells E17 and E18 using the same method.

6. In cells A1 and A2, key the following title:

   Sun Soft/Corn Silk Sales Comparison
   Quarter 2-1997

7. Create a header that includes your name in the left section, the filename in the center section, and the date in the right section.
8. Center the worksheet horizontally on the page.
9. Save the workbook as *[your initials]***5-6.xls** and print the worksheet.
10. Create a formula printout with gridlines and row and column headings in landscape orientation, then turn off formulas for viewing.

Using Toolbars in Excel

To this point, you used Excel's predefined Standard and Formatting toolbars to make your work easier. Excel provides many other predefined toolbars that make chart construction, drawing, accessing the World Wide Web, and other functions faster and more convenient. You can control how toolbars appear on the screen and what functions they perform.

TABLE 5-1 Predefined Toolbars in Excel

TOOLBAR NAME	FUNCTION
PivotTable	Retrieve and analyze data from databases.
Chart	Create and modify charts. It automatically displays when you work on a chart.
Reviewing	Create and edit comments in files that can be sent as e-mail.
Forms	Create custom forms.
Stop Recording	Stop recording a macro.
External Data	Work with data imported from an external database.
Auditing	Trace precedents, dependents, and errors within formulas.
Full Screen	Return to Normal view after displaying the full screen.
Circular Reference	Identify circular references in cells.
Visual Basic	Work with macros.
Web	Access the World Wide Web.

continues

TABLE 5-1 Predefined Toolbars in Excel *continued*

TOOLBAR NAME	FUNCTION
Control Toolbox	Create controls to run macros.
Drawing	Create graphic objects. It contains standard drawing tools such as line, arc, and rectangle.
WordArt	Create display type or word as art.
Picture	Control the look of images imported into Excel.
Shadow Settings	Place shadows behind graphics.
3-D Settings	Create a 3-D effect with graphics.

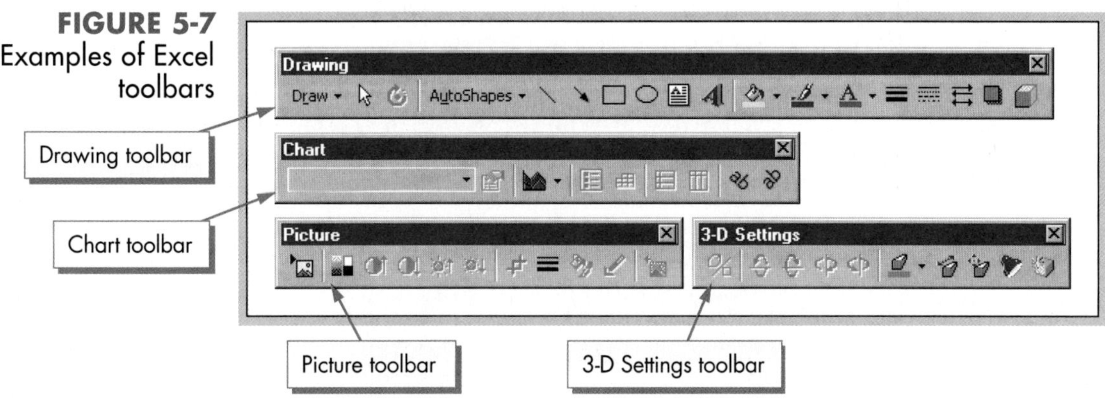

FIGURE 5-7 Examples of Excel toolbars

EXERCISE 5-7 Display Multiple Toolbars

Sometimes it's useful to display several toolbars simultaneously. For example, your worksheet may contain multiple formulas and be designed to be sent to someone outside your company. In that case, the Auditing toolbar helps you trace multiple calculations and the Reviewing toolbar is handy to add comments to the worksheet and attach it to an e-mail message.

1. Choose Toolbars from the View menu. The Toolbars cascading menu opens. (See Figure 5-8 on the next page.)
2. Choose Customize. In the Customize dialog box, click Toolbars, if necessary, to see the complete list of existing toolbars. The Office Assistant may open to see if you want help. If it does, it closes when you close the dialog box. (See Figure 5-9 on the next page.)

FIGURE 5-8
Toolbars cascading menu

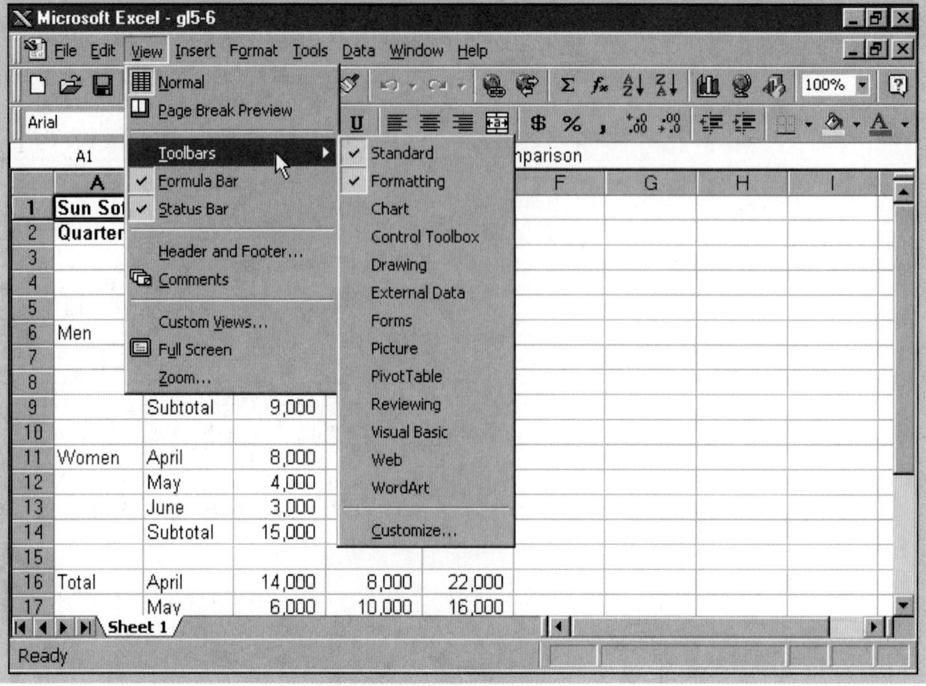

FIGURE 5-9
Customize dialog box

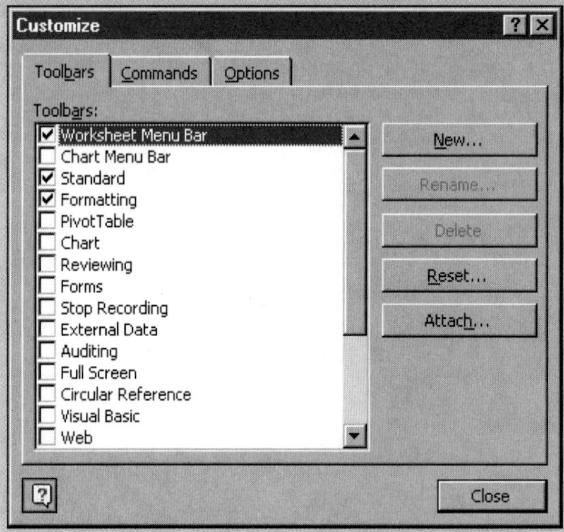

3. Click beside Auditing to display the Auditing toolbar. Click Close in the Customize dialog box.
4. Move the pointer across each button on the Auditing toolbar to identify its name and function.

TIP: Remember, to identify a toolbar button, point to the button and pause for a few seconds. A small box containing the name of the button appears under the button.

5. Change the view of the document to 75%, select cell C14, and click the Trace Precedents button. An arrow appears onscreen, tracing the precedents for cell C14 (the cells to which the formula in cell C14 refers).

6. With the same cell selected, click the Trace Dependents button. An arrow appears onscreen tracing the cells that are dependent upon the value in cell C14.

FIGURE 5-10
Using the Auditing toolbar

	A	B	C	D	E
1	Sun Soft/Corn Silk Sales Comparison				
2	Quarter 2-1997				
3					
4			Sun Soft	Corn Silk	Total
5					
6	Men	April	6,000	1,000	7,000
7		May	2,000	5,000	7,000
8		June	1,000	4,000	5,000
9		Subtotal	9,000		
10					
11	Women	April	8,000	7,000	15,000
12		May	4,000	5,000	9,000
13		June	3,000	11,000	14,000
14		Subtotal	15,000	23,000	38,000
15					
16	Total	April	14,000	8,000	22,000
17		May	6,000	10,000	16,000

Sheet 1

Auditing

Remove All Arrows button

Trace Precedents button

Trace Dependents button

NOTE: Audit arrows are not saved with the file, but you can redisplay them at any time.

7. Click the Remove All Arrows button.

8. Click the right mouse button on any visible toolbar. The Toolbar shortcut menu appears.

9. Click beside Reviewing. The Reviewing toolbar appears. (This toolbar is also listed in the Toolbars cascading menu.)

NOTE: You can customize toolbars in the Customize dialog box. Just click the Commands to add buttons to other toolbars. Let the Office Assistant help you learn how to customize toolbars.

EXERCISE 5-8 Move and Reshape Toolbars

Toolbars can appear either "docked" or "floating." A *docked toolbar* appears in a fixed position outside the work area (like the Standard and Formatting toolbars). A *floating toolbar* appears over the work area. You can dock a floating toolbar by dragging it out of the work area. You can float a docked toolbar by dragging it into the work area. You can also reshape a floating toolbar.

1. Position the pointer on the title bar of the Auditing toolbar (not on a toolbar button), click the left mouse button, and drag the toolbar to a position on the Formula Bar. The Auditing toolbar is docked below the Formatting toolbar.

FIGURE 5-11
Docked and floating toolbars

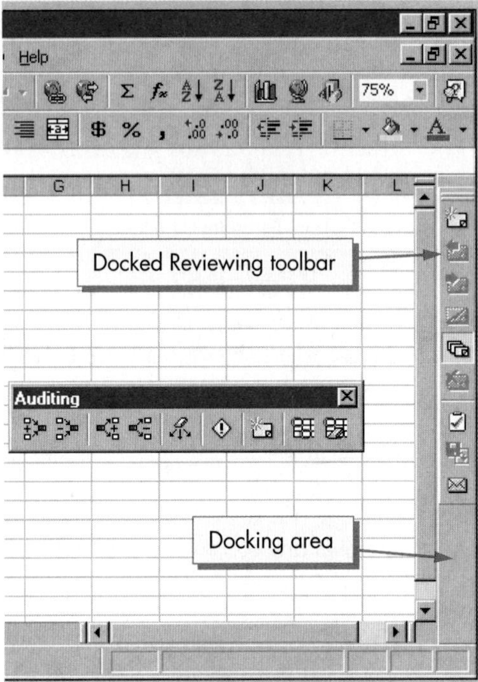

2. Position the pointer between two buttons on the docked Auditing toolbar (not on a button) and hold down the left mouse button. The Auditing toolbar is selected and a light border surrounds it.
3. Drag the toolbar into the work area and release the left mouse button. The Auditing toolbar is floating.
4. Drag the Reviewing toolbar to the far right side of the screen, until it is vertically positioned over the scroll bar. Excel docks the toolbar on this side of the screen and the worksheet window is resized to accommodate it.
5. Double-click the horizontal gray bars in the toolbar to float it. Excel resizes the worksheet window.

NOTE: Double-clicking the title bar of a toolbar converts it from floating to docked. Double-clicking the two gray bars in a docked toolbar converts it to floating. Double-clicking a docking area displays the Customize dialog box. If this occurs, click Cancel and click the background area of the toolbar again.

6. Position the pointer on the left side of the bottom border of the Auditing toolbar so the pointer changes to a double-headed arrow.
7. Drag the bottom border down about 1/2 inch and release the mouse button. The toolbar buttons are grouped in rows.
8. Drag the bottom border down even further, until the toolbar becomes a column of buttons. Reshape it again into a more rectangular arrangement and then back to its original shape.

EXERCISE 5-9 Close Toolbars

There's no restriction on the number of toolbars you can display in Excel, but it may be hard to read the worksheet if too many are open.

1. Click the right mouse button on any visible toolbar. The Toolbar menu appears. Notice the check mark located next to the open Reviewing toolbar. (Remember, the Auditing toolbar is listed in the Customize dialog box.)
2. Click Reviewing to deselect it. Excel closes the Reviewing toolbar. Be sure the Standard and Formatting toolbars remain checked.
3. Click the Close button in the upper right corner of the Auditing toolbar to close it.
4. Close the file without saving it.

COMMAND SUMMARY

FEATURE	BUTTON	MENU	KEYBOARD
Copy		Edit, Copy	Ctrl+C
Fill right		Edit, Fill	Ctrl+R
Fill down		Edit, Fill	Ctrl+D
Trace Precedents			
Trace Dependents			
Remove All Arrows			

USING HELP

This lesson showed you how to use Excel's AutoFill feature to copy data into adjacent cells. AutoFill is a powerful tool you can also use to create a data series such as numbers, dates, or text.

For example, you can start with the month Jan-97 in a cell and build a series that places Feb-97, Mar-97, and so on in adjacent cells. You can also create custom AutoFill series to build complex worksheets quickly.

To find out how AutoFill can create a series of data, use the Office Assistant:

1. Click [?].
2. Enter **AutoFill dates** in the Office Assistant text box and click Search.

3. Select Types of series that Microsoft Excel can fill in for you. Notice that the Microsoft Excel Help window opens.

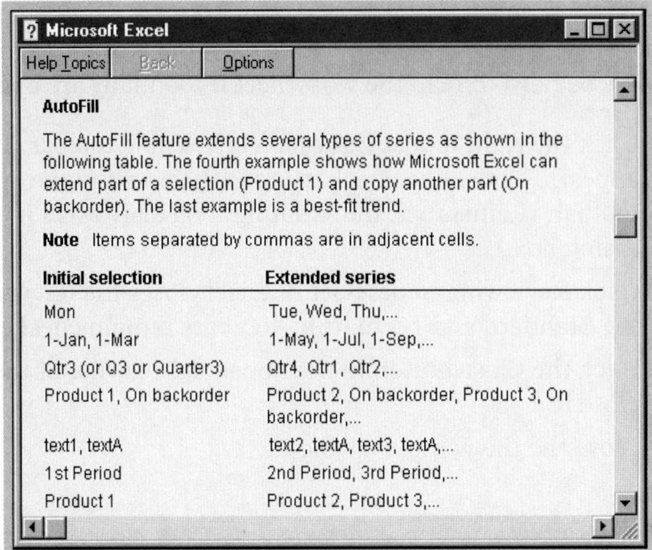

FIGURE 5-12
Microsoft Excel Help window

4. Scroll to the AutoFill section and read the information, paying attention to the Extended Series that you can generate.
5. Close the dialog box when you finish and close the Office Assistant.

Concepts Review

TRUE/FALSE QUESTIONS

Each of the following statements is either true or false. Indicate your choice by circling T or F.

T F *1*. Copying a cell moves its data to a new location in the worksheet.

T F *2*. You can paste cells using keyboard shortcuts, menu commands, or toolbar buttons.

T F *3*. When you copy cells, you must first indicate the source range.

T F *4*. The target range is the new location for data that you copy, cut, or move.

T F *5*. A relative cell reference is automatically adjusted in any formula you copy.

T F *6*. To copy cells using the drag-and-drop method, use the mouse pointer and the Alt key.

T F *7*. You should use AutoFill to copy only to adjacent cells.

T F *8*. A docked toolbar appears in a position outside the work area.

SHORT ANSWER QUESTIONS

Write the correct answer in the space provided.

1. Which keyboard command copies the active cell?

____

2. Which button copies the active cell?

____

3. When you copy data, the information remains in the original location and is also copied to what location not visible in the worksheet?

____

4. What appears around selected cells to highlight them after you choose the Copy command?

____

5. Which key do you use with the mouse to copy data when using the drag-and-drop method?

---

6. Which keyboard shortcut copies and fills cells to the right?

---

7. Which part of the cell do you drag to copy data using AutoFill?

---

8. Name the two predefined toolbars that appear on screen by default when you first open Excel.

CRITICAL THINKING

Answer these questions on a separate piece of paper. There are no right or wrong answers. Support your answer with examples from your own experience, if possible.

1. What are some of the potential dangers posed by relative cell references when you build a worksheet? What are the advantages? How can you effectively manage this feature?

2. Think of some other ways you might be able to use the Copy, Fill, and AutoFill features. Name at least one new way that you might use these powerful tools.

Skills Review

EXERCISE 5-10

Copy and paste using the Edit menu and the toolbar.

1. Open the file **Bonus.xls**.

2. Key the following data in cells B7 through B10:

1500

1800

1800

1500

3. Format cell B7 in currency style with no decimal places. Format cells B8 through B10 in comma style with no decimal places. (*Hint:* Numbers do not fit in cell B7 until you decrease decimals.)
4. Enter the formula **=B7*C7** in cell D7.
5. Copy the formula in cell D7 using the Copy and Paste commands by following these steps:
   a. Select cell D7.
   b. Choose Copy from the Edit menu.
   c. Select cells D8 and D10 and choose Paste from the Edit menu.
   d. Press Esc to remove the moving border from the source range.
6. Format cell D7 in currency style and keep the two decimal places.
7. Select cells B11 and D11 and click Σ.
8. Copy and paste data and formulas using the toolbar by following these steps:
   a. Select cells B7 through D7 as the source range.
   b. Click [Copy].
   c. Select cell B12 as the first cell of the target range.
   d. Click [Paste].
   e. Press Esc to remove the moving border from the source range.
9. Copy data and formulas by following these steps:
   a. Select cells B8 through D8 and choose Copy from the Edit menu.
   b. Select cell B13 and press Ctrl+V.
   c. Select cell B14 and click [Paste].
   d. Select cells B15 through D16 and press Enter.
10. Key the following data in cells B12 through B16, overwriting the data you previously copied:

    2800

    1800

    1700

    2750

    4200
11. Use AutoSum to total the May revenues in cell B17 and the May commissions in cell D17.
12. Key **Total** in cell A18 in bold and use AutoSum to total all revenues in cell B18 and all commissions in cell D18.
13. Format the unlabeled subtotals (cells B11, B17, D11, and D17) as italic.
14. Format the totals (cells B18 and D18) as bold.

15. Add a header with your name in the left section, the filename in the center section, and the date in the right section.
16. Save the workbook as *[your initials]***5-10.xls** and print the worksheet.
17. Create a formula printout with gridlines and row and column headings, and close the workbook without saving it.

EXERCISE 5-11

Copy and paste using the menus, the toolbar, keyboard shortcuts, and drag and drop.

1. Open the file **SalesUp.xls**.
2. In cell C7, enter the formula **=B7*1.015**.
3. Copy this formula into cells C8 through C16 by following these steps:
   - *a.* Select cell C7 and choose Copy from the Edit menu.
   - *b.* Select cells C8 through C16 and choose Paste from the Edit menu.
   - *c.* Press Esc to remove the moving border from the source range.
   - *d.* Format cells C7 through C16 in comma style with no decimal places.
4. Copy formulas using drag and drop by following these steps:
   - *a.* Select cells C7 through C16.
   - *b.* Move the mouse pointer across the border of the selection until it becomes an arrow.
   - *c.* Press and hold down the Ctrl key to change the pointer to the drag-and-drop pointer.
   - *d.* Drag the source range to the target range, cells D7 through D16.
5. In cell E7, enter the formula **=B7*1.22**.
6. Copy this formula into cells E8 through E16 by following these steps:
   - *a.* Select cell E7 and press Ctrl+C.
   - *b.* Select cells E8 through E16 and press Enter.
   - *c.* Format cells E7 through E16 in comma style with no decimal places.
7. Copy formulas using the toolbar by following these steps:
   - *a.* Select cells C7 through D16 as the source range.
   - *b.* Click .
   - *c.* Select cell F7.
   - *d.* Click .
   - *e.* Press Esc.
8. Create a "Total" row by following these steps:
   - *a.* Key **Total** in cell A17. Format the text as bold.

b. Select cells B17, C17, D17, E17, F17, and G17 and click Σ.

c. Format the totals as bold and currency style with no decimal places.

9. Add a header with your name in the left section, the filename in the center section, and the date in the right section.
10. Save the workbook as *[your initials]* **5-11.xls** and print the worksheet.
11. Create a formula printout in landscape orientation that fits on one page with gridlines and row and column headings and close the workbook without saving it. (Use the Fit to option in the Page Setup dialog box so the formula printout remains on one page.)

EXERCISE 5-12

Copy formulas using the Fill command and AutoFill.

1. Open the file **NetInc2.xls**.
2. Enter the following formulas in cells B9 through B11:

   =B6*0.2

   =B6*0.35

   =B6*0.3
3. Format cells B9 through B11 in comma style with no decimal places.
4. Select cell B12, click Σ, and press Enter.
5. Select cells B9 through F12.
6. Choose the Fill command from the Edit menu and choose Right from the cascading menu.
7. Enter the formula **=B6-B12** in cell B14 to calculate the net income for the year 1997 ("Sales" - "Total Expenses"). The cell is already formatted.
8. Use AutoFill to copy the formula in cell B14 to cells C14 through F14 by following these steps:

   a. With cell B14 selected, position the mouse pointer on the fill handle.

   b. Drag the fill handle to select cells C14 through F14.

   c. Release the mouse button.
9. Add bold formatting to the Total Expenses and Net Income figures.
10. Add a header with your name in the left section, the filename in the center section, and the date in the right section.
11. Save the workbook as *[your initials]* **5-12.xls** and print the worksheet.
12. Create a formula printout in landscape orientation that fits on one page with gridlines and row and column headings and close the workbook without saving it.

EXERCISE 5-13

Open multiple toolbars, move and reshape toolbars, and use the Audit toolbar.

1. Open the file **Q4.xls**.
2. Open multiple toolbars using the following steps:
   a. Choose Toolbars from the View menu to open the Toolbars cascading menu.
   b. Select the Chart toolbar. Repeat the steps to select the Drawing toolbar.
   c. If necessary, drag one toolbar down or up to reveal the hidden toolbar.
   d. Right click the title bar of the Chart toolbar. Select the Forms toolbar from the shortcut menu.
   e. Right click a line between two buttons of the Forms toolbar and select Customize from the shortcut menu.
   f. Select Auditing and click Close.
3. Move and reshape toolbars by following these steps:
   a. Double-click the title bar of the Chart toolbar to dock it.
   b. Drag the Auditing toolbar onto the Formula Bar to dock it.
   c. Drag the Forms toolbar to the left side of the screen over the row heading to dock it.
   d. Drag the bottom border of the Drawing border down until it becomes square. The toolbar should contain five rows of buttons. Drag it back to its original shape. (This toolbar may already be a square. If so, practice resizing it and return it to a long rectangular shape.)
   e. Float all the toolbars except the Auditing toolbar by double-clicking the double gray bars in the toolbar.
4. Close the Chart toolbar by right clicking the Chart title bar and deselecting Chart on the Toolbar shortcut menu. Do the same for the Forms toolbar.
5. Close the Drawing toolbar by clicking the close button in the upper right corner of the title bar.
6. Use the Auditing toolbar to trace formula paths by following these steps:
   a. Select cell D14 and click the Trace Precedents button.
   b. Select cell D6 and click the Trace Dependents button.
7. Float the Auditing toolbar by double-clicking the double gray bars and close it by clicking the close button.
8. Add a header with your name in the left section, the filename in the center section, and the date in the right section

9. Center the worksheet horizontally.
10. Save the workbook as *[your initials]***5-13.xls**.
11. Print the worksheet, including the tracing arrows, and then close the workbook.

Lesson Applications

EXERCISE 5-14

Use the Copy and Paste commands, copy using drag and drop, and copy using Fill and AutoFill.

The Beautiful Belle Company needs to break down its revenues by product line and by region. The worksheet must also show product totals and subtotals, regional totals, and the grand total.

1. Open the file **Product.xls.**
2. Create a formula that totals the revenues for the Monterey product line.
3. Copy the formula to cell D16 using and .
4. Copy the formula from cell D16 to cells D17 through D20 using the Fill, Down command.
5. Select cells D17 through D20. Copy this range to cells D9 through D12 using the drag-and-drop method.
6. Create a formula that finds the subtotal for Creams sold in the Northwest territory.
7. Copy this formula to cells C13 and D13 using AutoFill.
8. Copy cells A13 through D13. Paste them in cells A21 through D21 using Ctrl+C and Ctrl+V.
9. Enter a formula to add the subtotals for Creams and Fragrances in cell B23.
10. Copy this formula to cells C23 and D23 using AutoFill.
11. Add a header with your name in the left section, the filename in the center section, and the date in the right section.
12. Change the view to 100% and format the numbers in the subtotal and total rows as bold.
13. Save the workbook as *[your initials]***5-14.xls** and print the worksheet.
14. Create a formula printout in landscape orientation with gridlines and row and column headings and close the workbook without saving it.

EXERCISE 5-15

Copy using the Fill command, toolbar buttons, drag and drop, and AutoFill.

1. Open the file **Frgrnce.xls.**

2. Copy the labels as shown in Figure 5-13 to cells A15 through A21. (Copy the labels only. Don't copy the values.)

FIGURE 5-13

	A
6	Fragrances
7	Pacifica
8	Taos
9	High Sierra
10	Carmel
11	Santa Barbara
12	Total

3. Create a formula that finds the 1997 total revenues for the Pacifica product line (cell D7).

4. Copy this formula to cells D8 through D11 using the Fill, Down command.

5. Enter the formula **=B7*1.1** in cell B16 (Pacifica 1998 sales in the Northwest).

6. Copy and paste this formula to cell C16 using the toolbar buttons.

7. Select cells B16 through C20 and copy the formulas using the Fill, Down command.

8. Copy the formulas from cells D7 through D11 to cells D16 through D20 using drag and drop.

9. Format all the numbers in row 16 in currency style with no decimals. Format numbers in cells B17 through C20 in comma style with no decimals.

10. Create a formula in cell B21 that finds the projected total revenues for the Northwest territory in 1998.

11. Copy this formula to cells C21 and D21 using AutoFill.

12. Copy cells B21 through D21 and create total formulas for 1997 using the drag-and-drop method.

13. Format the numbers in the total rows in bold.

14. Add a header with your name in the left section, the filename in the center section, and the date in the right section.
15. Save the workbook as *[your initials]***5-15.xls** and print the worksheet.
16. Create a formula printout in landscape orientation that fits on one page with gridlines and row and column headings and close the workbook without saving it.

EXERCISE 5-16

Copy using Fill, AutoFill, and drag and drop.

Build a worksheet to compare sales by quarter for Sun Soft for the years 1996 through 1998. Create formulas that calculate total sales for each year. Include a percentage change for 1996 to 1997 and 1997 to 1998.

1. Open the file **Change%.xls**.
2. Enter the labels and data as shown in Figure 5-14 with the corrections. Format the numbers as comma style with no decimals as shown in the figure.

FIGURE 5-14

	A	B	C	D
4		1996	1997	1998
5	Qtr 3 (1)	64,955	96,500	80,530 (tr)
6	~~Quarter 3~~ Qtr 2	70,130	90,130	100,540
7	Qtr 3	110,140	150,350	180,020
8	Qtr 3 (4)	95,600	120,040	135,060

3. Create a formula that totals the four quarters for 1996 in cell B10. (Do not include the column label if you use AutoSum.)
4. Copy the formula to total 1997 and 1998 sales using AutoFill and format the three totals in comma style with no decimals, if necessary.
5. In cell E5, enter a formula that calculates the 1996 to 1997 change in sales as a percentage of 1996 sales. (*Hint:* Subtract 1996 sales from 1997 sales and divide the difference by 1996 sales.)

6. Format the formula in percent style with one decimal place using the Formatting toolbar.
7. Copy the formula to Qtr2 through Qtr4 for 1997 using the Fill, Down command.
8. Copy the formula to Qtr1 through Qtr4 for 1998 using the Fill, Right command.
9. Create totals for the 1997 and 1998 percentage changes by copying the Qtr4 formulas to row 10 using drag and drop.
10. Format the row labels as bold and key the row label **Total** in row 10 in bold.
11. Change the page orientation to portrait. (This worksheet's default orientation was previously changed to landscape.) Center the page horizontally.
12. Add a header with your name in the left section, the filename in the center section, and the date in the right section.
13. Save the workbook as *[your initials]***5-16.xls** and print the worksheet.
14. Create a formula printout in landscape orientation that fits on one page with gridlines and row and column headings and close the workbook without saving it.

EXERCISE 5-17

Copy and paste formulas, use Fill or AutoFill, copy using drag and drop, and use toolbars.

Construct a worksheet comparing second-quarter sales for Sun Soft and Corn Silk for 1996, 1997, and 1998.

1. Plan the worksheet on a sheet of paper. Create a two-line title that explains the worksheet, and in the body of the worksheet include labels for Sun Soft and Corn Silk sales comparisons for 1996, 1997, and 1998. Also include labels for a calculated percentage of Sun Soft as a Percent of Corn Silk for 1996, 1997, and 1998. (These should be the column labels, nine columns altogether.)
2. Include labels for the second quarter months plus a total line. (These should be the row labels, four rows altogether.)
3. Use F for formula locations.
4. Transfer the design to the computer by keying titles and labels. Format them attractively.
5. Input test data in the Sun Soft months for 1996, 1997, and 1998. Format the data for commas with no decimals.

6. Copy and paste the test data to the Corn Silk months for 1996, 1997, and 1998.
7. Calculate the three-month total for Sun Soft in 1996. Copy that formula to the appropriate cells for Sun Soft and Corn Silk.
8. Calculate Sun Soft's sales as a percentage of Corn Silk sales for April 1996. (*Hint:* Divide Sun Soft sales by Corn Silk sales.)
9. Format that formula in percent style with no decimal places.
10. Use Fill or AutoFill to copy the percentage change to the rest of the months for 1996 through 1998.
11. Use drag and drop to copy the formula to the Percent Total .
12. Check your formulas for accuracy and enter the data in Figure 5-15 into the monthly quarter cells for 1996, 1997, and 1998.

FIGURE 5-15

	Sun Soft			Corn Silk		
	1996	1997	1998	1996	1997	1998
April	19,650	24,800	36,540	33,550	28,150	26,540
May	22,630	31,300	24,000	23,260	18,440	16,500
June	27,850	34,030	31,250	29,360	25,040	21,350

13. Reduce the view to 75% and set up the worksheet to print in landscape orientation centered horizontally on one page.
14. Name the worksheet tab **Comparison**.
15. Name the Sheet2 tab **User Information** and create documentation that includes the following: File Information (Created by, Date created, Date revised, Revised by, Contact for help); Purpose of spreadsheet (paragraph form); and Instructions to User (special instructions needed by user to enter data correctly). Style the documentation for easy reading.
16. Add the standard header to both sheets including your name, filename, and date.
17. Save the workbook as *[your initials]***5-17.xls**.
18. Use the Auditing toolbar to trace the precedents for the April 1998 percentage change formula.
19. Print the workbook, including the precedent arrows. Remove the precedent arrows, and then close the Auditing toolbar.

20. Create a formula printout of the Comparison sheet in landscape orientation with grids and row and column headings. Add a footer for multiple pages, if necessary, consisting of "Page 1 of ?". (Choose it from the built-in, drop-down footer list in the Page Setup dialog box.)

21. Close the workbook without saving it. Submit your plan, worksheet, user documentation, and formula printout.

NOTE: The worksheet plan and final version of this spreadsheet both contain empty columns. This makes the worksheet easier to read, but does not necessarily reflect effective worksheet design. Your design may differ from this.

Range Names

OBJECTIVES

After completing this lesson, you will be able to:

1. **Name ranges and constants.**
2. **Use names in formulas.**
3. **Change and delete range names.**
4. **Navigate in the worksheet using range names.**
5. **Paste names into worksheets.**

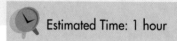

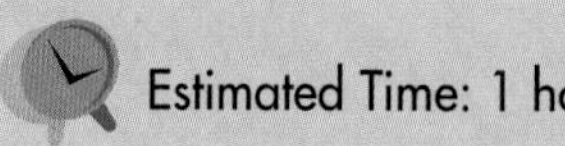
Estimated Time: 1 hour

Instead of trying to remember a particular cell address, such as E17, or a cell range, such as I7:J43, you can use a name to designate a location. For example, you could name a cell that contains a formula "total," and use the name "total" to refer to the cell when you create other formulas. In addition to naming cells, you can also assign names to constants. For example, you could assign the name "rate" to the constant 0.07. Naming cells also makes it easier to find a particular location in the worksheet.

Naming Ranges and Constants

A *range name*—the name you give to a cell or range of cells—must begin with a letter. Although range names can be from 1 to 255 characters long, it is best to keep them short, but still recognizable. Range names must *not*:

- Have the form of a cell reference, such as q1 or A13.
- Be "R" or "C" as a single-letter name.
- Contain spaces.
- Contain hyphens (-) or special characters ($, %, &, #).

To separate parts of a name such as "saleseast," you can use capital letters, a period, or an underline (for example, "SalesEast," "sales.east," or "sales_east").

TABLE 6-1 Examples of Valid and Invalid Names

VALID NAMES	INVALID NAMES
Total.Sales	Total Sales
east_sales	east-sales
EntertainPct	Entertain%
qt1	q1
First	1st
X	R

EXERCISE 6-1 Name an Individual Cell

You can name ranges using the Define Name dialog box or by keying the name in the name box at the left of the Formula Bar.

1. Open the file **97Sales.xls**.
2. Move to cell E9.

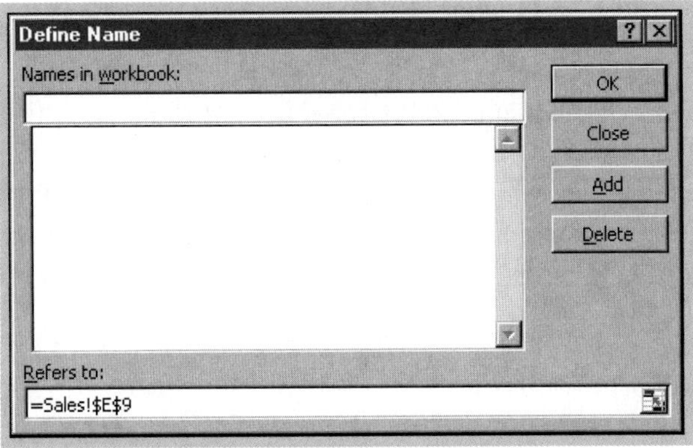

FIGURE 6-1 Define Name dialog box

3. Choose Name from the Insert menu.
4. Choose Define from the cascading menu. The Define Name dialog box appears.

5. Key **qt1** in the Names in workbook text box and click OK. The name appears in the name box at the left of the Formula Bar.
6. Move to cell E18 and click in the name box at the left of the Formula Bar. The cell address is selected.
7. Key **qt2** and press Enter. The name appears in the name box.
8. Name cell E27 **qt3** using the Define Name dialog box.
9. Name cell E36 **qt4** by keying the text directly into the name box at the left of the Formula Bar.

EXERCISE 6-2 Name a Group of Cells

You can name any group of cells. Excel suggests a name for the range based on the title of the selected column or row. If you don't want the suggested name, you can assign a different name to the range.

1. Select all the totals for "New Century," which appear in cells E5, E14, E23, and E32.

NOTE: To select nonadjacent cells, press Ctrl while selecting the cells.

2. Choose Name from the Insert menu.
3. Choose Define. The Define Name dialog box opens. Notice that Excel suggests the name Total.
4. Key **New_Century** in the Names in workbook text box and click OK.
5. Select cells E6, E15, E24, and E33.
6. Click in the name box at the left of the Formula Bar.
7. Key **Golden** and press Enter.
8. Name cells E7, E16, E25, and E34 **Monterey**, and name cells E8, E17, E26, and E35 **Herbal**.

TIP: You can use the Label Ranges dialog box (Insert menu, Name submenu, Label command) to specify ranges that contain column and row labels on your worksheet. When you label a range using the Label Ranges dialog box, and the range contains a year or a date as a label, Excel defines the date as a label by placing single quotation marks around the label when you type the label in a formula.

EXERCISE 6-3 Name a Constant

In addition to assigning names to cells or ranges of cells, you can assign names to *constants*. Constants are unchanging values used in formulas. Named constants don't appear in the worksheet. For example, if you assign the name "rate" to the constant .075, you could then use the name "rate" in formulas instead of the value. When you change the constant value assigned to "rate," any formula that contains "rate" automatically changes to include the new value.

1. Press Ctrl+F3 to open the Define Name dialog box.
2. Key **pro** in the Names in workbook text box.
3. Edit the text to read **=.12** in the Refers to text box.
4. Click OK. The value 0.12 is assigned the name "pro." This name is used to increase the sales figures by 12%.

NOTE: You cannot name a constant in the Formula Bar name box.

Using Names in Formulas

Once you create names for cell references or constants, you can use these names in formula calculations. Key the formula in the normal way, but key the name instead of the cell reference. To use constants, key the name for the constant wherever you would key the constant in the formula.

EXERCISE 6-4 Create Formulas Including Names

1. In cell B41, key **=sum(new_century)** and press Enter. Once you enter the formula in the cell, Excel converts the name to include uppercase letters as you created it.

TIP: You can use F3 to place a name in a formula. For instance, key **=sum(**, press F3, select the name from the list, click OK, and finish the formula.

2. In cell B42, key **=sum(golden)**
3. In cell B43, key **=sum(monterey)**

4. In cell B44, key **=sum(herbal)**
5. In cell C41, calculate a 12% projected sales increase for 1998 by keying **=B41*(1+pro)**. (B41 is the 1997 total and "1+pro" equals 1.12, since you earlier defined "pro" to be 0.12.)
6. Copy this formula to cells C42, C43, C44, and C45. Format cell C45 as bold; it equals zero for now.
7. In cell B45, use the cell names you created by keying **=qt1+qt2+qt3+qt4**

FIGURE 6-2
Total projected 1998 sales, so far.

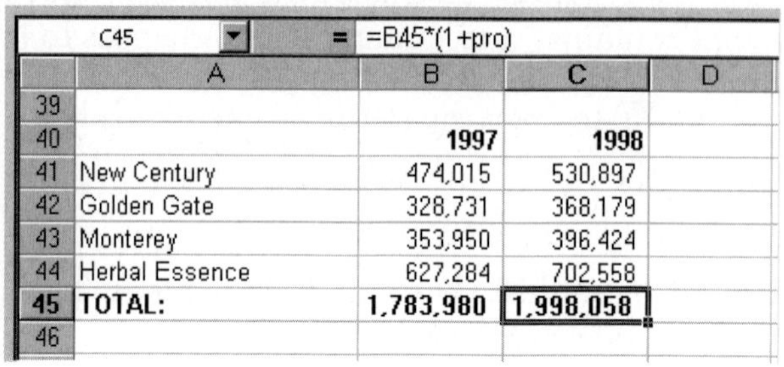

C45 = =B45*(1+pro)

	A	B	C	D
39				
40		**1997**	**1998**	
41	New Century	474,015	530,897	
42	Golden Gate	328,731	368,179	
43	Monterey	353,950	396,424	
44	Herbal Essence	627,284	702,558	
45	**TOTAL:**	**1,783,980**	**1,998,058**	
46				

8. In cells D32 through D35, enter the data as shown below. When you finish, the total for 1998 in cell C45 should be 2,199,716.

	Dec
New Century	**79,658**
Golden Gate	**22,457**
Monterey	**32,568**
Herbal Essence	**45,369**

Changing and Deleting Range Names

You can change a name or delete one that you no longer need. When you change a name, Excel does not replace the old name with the new name in relevant formulas. The old formulas remain valid, however, unless you delete the old name.

EXERCISE 6-5 Change and Delete Range Names

1. Press Ctrl+F3 to open the Define Name dialog box.
2. Choose **New_Century** from the Names in workbook list box.
3. Delete **New_** from the name. "Century" remains in the Names in workbook text box.

4. Click OK.
5. Move to cell B41. The name New_Century is not changed.
6. Choose Name from the Insert menu and then choose Define.
7. Choose "New_Century" from the Names in workbook list box.
8. Click Delete and click OK. The formulas that refer to New_Century display the #NAME? error message.

NOTE: You can use the Undo command to reverse the deletion of a name.

9. In cell B41, double-click New_Century in the Formula Bar to select it and key **century** to change the formula to reflect the new range name. The editing could also be done in the cell.
10. Click the check box in the Formula Bar. The #NAME? error message is no longer displayed in cell B41 or cell C41 and the formulas calculate correctly.

TIP: You can use find and replace to change range names in formulas.

Navigating Using Range Names

Named ranges not only make calculations easier, but also enable you to move around a worksheet more quickly. For example, you can assign a name to a cell and then locate the cell by choosing Go To from the Edit menu (or pressing F5). Excel opens the Go To dialog box, which lists all named cells in the worksheet. It also lists the last four cell addresses the Go To command located. You can also use the Name box drop-down list to move to named ranges.

EXERCISE 6-6 Move to Named Ranges

1. Select cells B4 through E9.
2. Choose Name from the Insert menu and choose Define.
3. Key **one** in the Names in workbook text box and click OK.
4. Select cells B13 through E18.
5. Click in the Name box, key **two**, and press Enter.
6. Name cells B22 through E27 **three**, cells B31 through E36 **four**, and cells B40 through C45 **grandtot**.

7. Choose Go To from the Edit menu or press F5 or press Ctrl+G. The Go To dialog box appears.

FIGURE 6-3
Go To dialog box

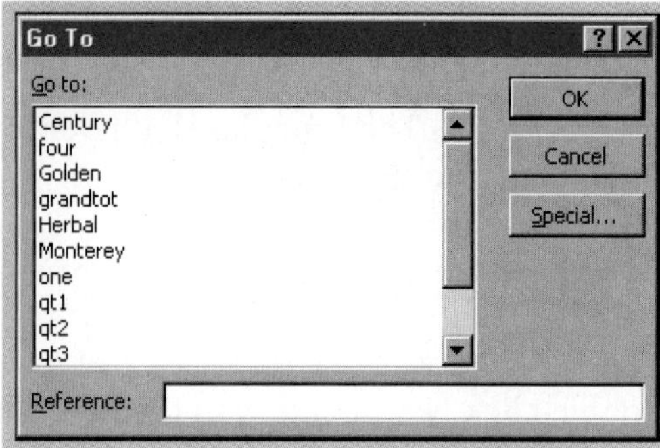

8. Double-click the named range "one." Excel moves to the selected range or cell.

FIGURE 6-4
Name box drop-down list

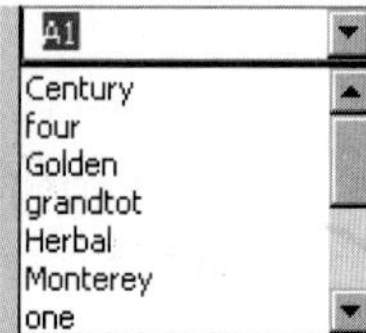

9. Press Ctrl+Home to move to cell A1. Click the Name box arrow. The drop-down list appears.
10. Click the named range "one."
11. Practice moving to named ranges using both the Go To command and the Name box drop-down list.

Pasting Names into Worksheets

You can use the Define Name dialog box to display a list of named ranges and constants to see how a worksheet is set up. Using the Paste Name dialog box, you can paste a list of range names and references into a worksheet as documentation. You can also use this dialog box to paste range names and constants into formulas.

EXERCISE 6-7 Paste Range Names into Worksheets

Before pasting a list of range names, move to a clear area of your worksheet, such as a sheet you created to provide worksheet documentation.

1. Move to cell A18 in the sheet named User Information.
2. Key the label **Range names** in bold and press Enter.
3. Move to cell B19 and key **The following range names have been created in the Sales worksheet.**

4. Move to cell B21 and key **Name** in bold. In cell C21, key **Location** in bold.
5. Move to cell B22, choose Name from the Insert menu, and choose Paste. The Paste Name dialog box appears.

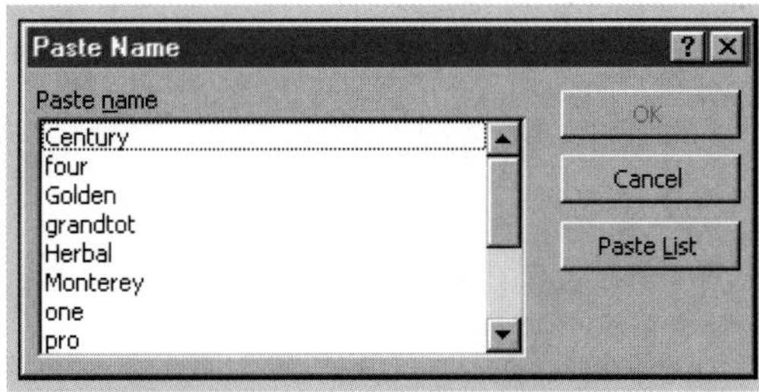

FIGURE 6-5
Paste Name dialog box

6. Click the Paste List button. The list of named ranges is pasted into the Documentation worksheet. You can key descriptions of the named ranges into the worksheet as necessary.
7. Change the view to 75% so you can see all the range names.

FIGURE 6-6
Names pasted into a worksheet

	A	B	C	D	E	F	G	H
18	**Range Names**							
19		The following range names have been created in the Sales worksheet:						
20								
21		**Name**	**Location**					
22		Century	=Sales!$E$5,Sales!$E$14,Sales!$E$23,Sales!$E$32					
23		four	=Sales!$B$31:$E$36					
24		Golden	=Sales!$E$33,Sales!$E$24,Sales!$E$15,Sales!$E$6					
25		grandtot	=Sales!$B$40:$C$45					
26		Herbal	=Sales!$E$35,Sales!$E$26,Sales!$E$17,Sales!$E$8					
27		Monterey	=Sales!$E$7,Sales!$E$16,Sales!$E$25,Sales!$E$34					
28		one	=Sales!$B$4:$E$9					
29		pro	=0.12					
30		qt1	=Sales!$E$9					
31		qt2	=Sales!$E$18					
32		qt3	=Sales!$E$27					
33		qt4	=Sales!$E$36					
34		three	=Sales!$B$22:$E$27					
35		two	=Sales!$B$13:$E$18					
36								

8. In the documentation worksheet, key today's date for "date revised" and key your name for "Revised by." Turn off gridlines for viewing.
9. In cell B44 of the Sales worksheet, key **=sum(**
10. Press F3 to open the Paste Name dialog box.
11. Double-click the name "Herbal" in the Paste Name list box and press Enter. The formula is complete.
12. Add the standard header containing your name, filename, and date to both worksheets.
13. Save the workbook as *[your initials]***6-7.xls**.
14. Print the entire workbook, then create the standard formula printout with grids and row and column headings. (Add a Page of ? footer to the formula printout if it exceeds one page.)
15. Close the workbook without saving it.

COMMAND SUMMARY

FEATURE	BUTTON	MENU	KEYBOARD
Define Name		Insert, Name, Define	Ctrl+F3
Go To		Edit, Go To	F5 or Ctrl+G
Paste Name		Insert, Name, Paste	F3

USING HELP

In this lesson you were given a tip on using the Label Ranges dialog box. To find out more about how and when to use the feature, ask the Office Assistant.

To find out how and when to use the Label Ranges dialog box

1. Click [?].
2. Key **label ranges** in the text box and click Search.
3. Select "About labeling ranges using the Label Ranges dialog box."
4. The Office Assistant displays information that shows you how to use the Label Ranges dialog box.

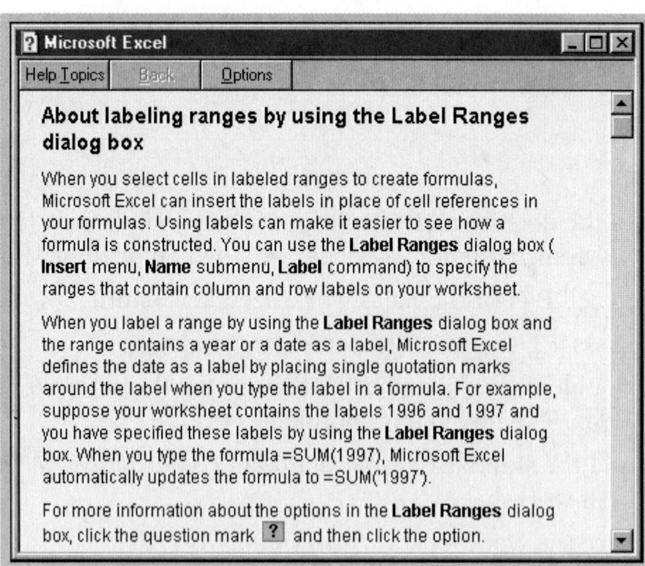

Microsoft Excel
Help Topics
Back
Options
About labeling ranges by using the Label Ranges dialog box
When you select cells in labeled ranges to create formulas, Microsoft Excel can insert the labels in place of cell references in your formulas. Using labels can make it easier to see how a formula is constructed. You can use the Label Ranges dialog box (Insert menu, Name submenu, Label command) to specify the ranges that contain column and row labels on your worksheet.
When you label a range by using the Label Ranges dialog box and the range contains a year or a date as a label, Microsoft Excel defines the date as a label by placing single quotation marks around the label when you type the label in a formula. For example, suppose your worksheet contains the labels 1996 and 1997 and you have specified these labels by using the Label Ranges dialog box. When you type the formula =SUM(1997), Microsoft Excel automatically updates the formula to =SUM('1997').
For more information about the options in the Label Ranges dialog box, click the question mark ? and then click the option.

FIGURE 6-7 Microsoft Excel dialog box with Label Range information

5. Read the information and close the dialog box and the Office Assistant.

Concepts Review

TRUE/FALSE QUESTIONS

Each of the following statements is either true or false. Indicate your choice by circling T or F.

T F *1.* A range name can include spaces and hyphens.

T F *2.* A cell or range name can include as many as 255 characters.

T F *3.* Named cells can contain only formulas.

T F *4.* Range names can include special characters like $, &, and #.

T F *5.* Names applied to constants can later be used in formulas.

T F *6.* You can use range names to replace cell references in formulas.

T F *7.* When you change a name, Excel automatically replaces the old name with the new name in the appropriate formulas.

T F *8.* The Go To dialog box lists all named cells in the worksheet.

SHORT ANSWER QUESTIONS

Write the correct answer in the space provided.

1. Which command enables you to move to the location of a named cell in the worksheet?

____

2. What do you call an unchanging value in a formula?

____

3. Which keyboard combination do you use for the Define Name command?

____

4. Which keyboard combination do you use for the Paste Name command?

____

5. Which menu commands do you use to name a range?

____

6. Which dialog box is opened by pressing F5?

____

7. Which menu commands do you use to paste a range name?

____

8. With what must the name you give to a cell or range begin?

____

CRITICAL THINKING

Answer these questions on a separate piece of paper. There are no right or wrong answers. Support your answer with examples from your own experience, if possible.

1. What are some of the possible disadvantages related to using range names and cell names in formulas? How can you avoid these potential drawbacks?

2. Describe potential uses for range names in Excel other than those described in this lesson. Explain how you would apply each use in a worksheet.

Skills Review

EXERCISE 6-8

Create names for cell ranges and constants, and use names in formulas.

1. Open the file **Lotions.xls**.

2. Create names for cell ranges by following these steps:

a. Select cells B7 through D7.

b. Choose Name from the Insert menu and choose Define.

c. Excel suggests the name "Cypress" in the Names in workbook text box. Click OK.

d. Select cells B8 through D8.

e. Choose Insert, Name and then choose Define.

f. Excel suggests the name "Jojoba" in the Names in workbook text box. Click OK.

g. Select cells B9 through D9.

h. Press Ctrl+F3.

i. Excel suggests the name "Sesame" in the Names in workbook text box. Click OK.

j. Select cells B10 through D10.

k. Choose Insert, Name and then choose Define.

l. Edit the suggested name "Joshua_Tree" in the Names in workbook text to **Joshua** and click OK.

3. Create names for constants by following these steps:

a. Choose Insert, Name and then choose Define.

b. Key **slow** in the Names in workbook text box.

c. Edit the text to read **=1.05** in the Refers to text box. Click the Add button.

d. Edit the text in the Names in workbook text box to read **moderate**

e. Edit the text to read **=1.1** in the Refers to text box. Click Add.

f. Edit the text in the Names in workbook text box to read **fast**

g. Edit the text to read **=1.15** in the Refers to text box. Click OK.

4. Use names in formulas by following these steps:

a. Key **=sum(cypress)** in cell E7.

b. Key **=sum(jojoba)** in cell E8.

c. Key **=sum(sesame)** in cell E9.

d. Key **=sum(joshua)** in cell E10.

5. Build formulas with range names and constant names by following these steps:

a. Key **=cypress*slow** in cell B17.

b. Use AutoFill to copy this formula to cells C17 and D17.

c. Key **=jojoba*moderate** in cell B18.

d. Use AutoFill to copy this formula to cells C18 and D18.

e. Key **=sesame*fast** in cell B19.

f. Use AutoFill to copy this formula to cells C19 and D19.

g. Key **=joshua*slow** in cell B20.

h. Key **=joshua*moderate** in cell C20.

i. Key **=joshua*fast** in cell D20.

j. Use AutoSum and AutoFill to enter formulas for the totals of each type of lotion in cells E17 through E20. Format column E in currency style, no decimals, if necessary.

6. Add the standard header including your name, filename, and date.

7. Save the workbook as *[your initials]***6-8.xls** and print the worksheet.

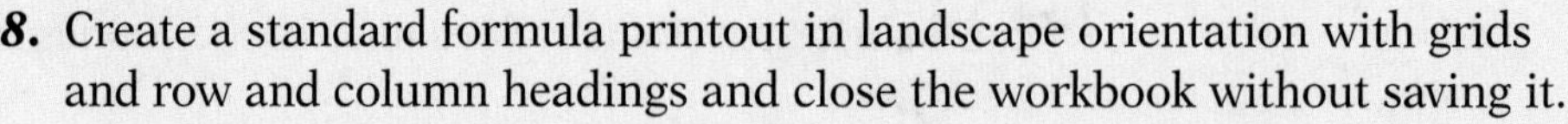

8. Create a standard formula printout in landscape orientation with grids and row and column headings and close the workbook without saving it.

EXERCISE 6-9

Use names in formulas, change range names, and delete range names.

1. Open the file **Powders.xls**.
2. Use names in formulas by following these steps:
   - *a.* Key **=sum(sahara)** in cell E6.
   - *b.* Key **=sum(marin)** in cell E7.
   - *c.* Key **=sum(mohave)** in cell E8.
   - *d.* Key **=sum(april_fresh)** in cell E9.
   - *e.* Key **=sum(spring_day)** in cell E10.
   - *f.* Key **=april_fresh+spring_day** in cell B12.
3. Use AutoFill to copy the formula from cell B12 to cells C12 and D12.
4. Use AutoSum to enter a formula that totals the new products in cell E12.
5. Change range names by following these steps:
   - *a.* Choose Insert, Name and then choose Define.
   - *b.* Choose "April_Fresh" from the Names in workbook list box.
   - *c.* Delete "_Fresh" from the name. Click Add.
   - *d.* Choose "Spring_Day" from the Names in workbook list box, change the name to **Spring**, and click OK.
6. Delete range names by following these steps:
   - *a.* Press Ctrl+F3.
   - *b.* Choose "April_Fresh" from the Names in workbook list box and click Delete.
   - *c.* Choose "Spring_Day" from the Names in workbook list box, click Delete, and click OK.
7. Use the new range names in formulas by following these steps:
   - *a.* Move to cell E9.
   - *b.* Double-click "April_Fresh" in the formula to select it and key **april**.
   - *c.* Press Enter.
   - *d.* In cell E10, change the name "Spring_Day" in the formula to **spring**.
   - *e.* Change the formula in cell B12 to **=april+spring**.
   - *f.* Copy the new formula in cell B12 to cells C12 and D12.

8. In cell A13, key **Grand Total**. In cells B13 through E13, calculate the totals for each month and for the three-month period. Do not include the "New Product Totals" in the "Grand Totals."
9. Add the standard header including your name, filename, and date, and center the worksheet horizontally on the page.
10. Save the workbook as *[your initials]***6-9.xls** and print the worksheet.
11. Create a standard formula printout that fits on one page with grids and row and column headings and close the workbook without saving it.

EXERCISE 6-10

Name a range of cells and navigate in the worksheet using range names.

1. Open the file **Credit.xls**.
2. Starting in row 24, add the following data for each customer into the worksheet:

Hall, Martha	**240**	**9%**
Spencer, Jon	**150**	**10%**
May, Violet	**23**	**7%**
Bernard, Frank	**542.21**	**13%**
Brown, JoAnne	**500**	**11%**

3. Name a range of cells by following these steps:
   - ***a.*** Select cells A24 through C24.
   - ***b.*** Choose Insert, Name and then choose Define.
   - ***c.*** Excel suggests the name "Hall_Martha" in the Names in workbook text box. Click OK.
4. Use the Go To command to navigate with names in the worksheet by following these steps:
   - ***a.*** Choose Go To from the Edit menu.
   - ***b.*** Double-click the range "Ferrara_Joseph."
   - ***c.*** Press F5.
   - ***d.*** Double-click the range "fifteen." All new customers with credit at the 15% interest rate are selected.
5. Add the standard header including your name, filename, and date, and center the worksheet horizontally on the page.
6. Save the workbook as *[your initials]***6-10.xls**.
7. Print the worksheet and close the workbook.

EXERCISE 6-11

Name constants, paste names into a formula, and paste names into a worksheet.

1. Open the file **Freight1.xls**.
2. Name constants using the following steps:
   a. Choose Insert, Name then choose Define.
   b. Key **mileage** in the Names in workbook text box.
   c. Edit the text to read **=4** in the Refers to text box.
   d. Click Add.
   e. Key **weight** in the Names in workbook text box.
   f. Edit the text to read **=.0015** in the Refers to text box.
   g. Click OK.
3. Change a formula by inserting the newly named constants using these steps:
   a. Select and delete cell D7.
   b. Key **=(b7/mileage)*(c7*weight)** and press Enter.
4. Using AutoFill, copy the new formula in cell D7 to cells D8 through D16.
5. Paste names into a worksheet by following these steps:
   a. Move to cell A18 in the sheet labeled **User Information**.
   b. Key the label **Constant names** in bold and press Enter.
   c. In cell B19, key **These are the constant names used in the spreadsheet.**
   d. In cell B21, key **Name** in bold and in cell C21 key **Refers to** in bold.
   e. In cell B22, choose Name from the Insert menu and choose Paste. The Paste Name dialog box appears.
   f. Click the Paste List button.
   g. Change the "Date revised" to today's date and key your name for "Revised by."
   h. Turn off gridlines for viewing.
6. Add the standard header including your name, filename, and date to both worksheets, and center the first worksheet horizontally on the page.
7. Save the workbook as *[your initials]*6-11.xls and print the entire thing.
8. Create a standard formula printout in landscape orientation with grids and row and column headings, and close the workbook without saving it.

Lesson Applications

EXERCISE 6-12

Name constants, use names in formulas, define range names, change range names, and paste range names into the worksheet.

Complete and revise Beautiful Belle's fuel estimation worksheet, so managers can better control the costs associated with product shipments.

1. Open the file **Freight2.xls**.
2. Enter the data into the worksheet as shown in Figure 6-8 with the following corrections.

FIGURE 6-8

Seattle	827	Van	524
Denver	1270	Light truck	1642
Portland	652	Semi	2159
Albuquerque	11‸7 (2)	Van	312
Los Angeles	403	semi	~~44~~2493
Phoenix	800	‸Semi	2200
Dallas	1806	semi	3200
Salt‸Lake City (#)	759	Semi	3200
Mexico City	2419	Semi	2047
Topeka	1811	Van	750

3. Name the following constants:

   Van = 16

   Truck = 10

   Semi = 6
4. Substitute the appropriate names (**Van, Truck,** or **Semi**) for the name "mileage" in the Fuel Estimate formulas in column E.
5. Enter the following labels in cells A18 through A21. Make "Territories" bold.

Territories
Northwest
Southwest
Midwest

6. Key **Total Fuel** in cell B18.
7. Define the range name "Northwest" to include the values in the Fuel Estimate column for the following cities: Seattle, Portland, and Salt Lake City.
8. Define the range name "Southwest" to include Fuel Estimates for the following cities: Albuquerque, Los Angeles, Phoenix, and Mexico City.
9. Define the range name "Midwest" to include Fuel Estimates for the following cities: Denver, Dallas, and Topeka.
10. Create a formula using range names to calculate the total estimated fuel for each territory: "Northwest," "Southwest," and "Midwest."
11. Format cells containing these formulas as comma style with two decimal places and any cells containing values other than formulas as comma style, no decimals.
12. Paste the range names somewhere at the bottom of the worksheet so your teacher can check your work, if necessary.
13. Add the standard header including your name, filename, and date, and center the worksheet horizontally on the page.
14. Save the workbook as *[your initials]***6-12.xls** and print the worksheet.
15. Create a standard formula printout with grids, row and column headings, and a Page 1 of ? footer for multiple pages, if necessary.
16. Close the workbook without saving it.

NOTE: The formula printout may cut off range name locations. You learn how to adjust row and column width in Lesson 8, so you can disregard this for now.

EXERCISE 6-13

Define range names, build formulas using range names, change and delete range names, navigate in a worksheet using range names, and paste range names into the worksheet.

Develop a worksheet that audits selected Beautiful Belle product sales by store.

1. Open the file **Stores.xls**.

2. Define range names for each city in the worksheet by highlighting the corresponding cells in the Amount column.
3. In cells A27 through A33, enter the labels shown below. Format the labels in bold.

   Store Totals
   Dallas
   New York
   Chicago
   San Francisco
   Boston
   Indianapolis

4. Use these range names to build formulas that calculate the total sales for each store. Enter the formulas in column B beside the appropriate label and format the results in comma style.
5. Change the range name "Dallas" to **Denver**.
6. Delete the range name "Dallas."
7. Change the name "Dallas" to **Denver** in the formula that calculates the store total.
8. Change the labels in the Store column and Store Totals column from "Dallas" to **Denver**.
9. Use the Go To command to highlight the Denver sales amounts.
10. Paste the range names somewhere at the bottom of the worksheet so your teacher can check your work, if necessary.
11. Add the standard header including your name, filename, and date, and center the worksheet horizontally on the page.
12. Save the workbook as *[your initials]***6-13.xls** and print the worksheet.
13. Create a standard formula printout that fits on one page in landscape orientation with grids and row and column headings and close the workbook without saving it.

NOTE: The formula printout may cut off range name locations. You learn how to adjust row and column width in Lesson 8, so you can disregard this for now.

EXERCISE 6-14

Create range names, build formulas using range names, paste names into the worksheet, and use the Go To command to navigate in the worksheet.

Construct a worksheet for the Beautiful Belle Company that calculates the total sales and commissions paid over four quarters.

1. Open the file **Cmsions.xls**.
2. In cell C16, use the AutoSum button to add the column.
3. Use Autofill to copy the SUM formula to cells D16 through J16.
4. Create the name **rt** for the constant **.07** (7%).
5. Create formulas using the constant name "rt" in cells D4, F4, H4, and J4 that calculate the commission due for each quarter. Copy the formula using AutoFill to complete the columns.
6. Create the names **sq1**, **sq2**, **sq3**, and **sq4** for the total sales for each quarter.
7. Create a formula in cell B17 that uses names to calculate the total sales for the year.
8. Create the names **com1**, **com2**, **com3**, and **com4** for the total commissions for each quarter.
9. Use the commission range names to create a formula in cell B18 that calculates the total commissions for the year.
10. In cell B21, paste all the names you created on the worksheet.
11. Key the following information in cells A21, A25, and A26:

    commission q1

    commsn rate

    sales q1
12. Use the Go To command to locate the cell named "sq4."
13. If necessary, set up the worksheet to print without gridlines in landscape orientation on a single page.
14. Add the standard header including your name, filename, and date.
15. Save the workbook as *[your initials]***6-14.xls**.
16. Print the worksheet, then create a standard formula printout with grids and row and column headings. Use the Page 1 of ? footer for multiple pages. Do not fit the formula printout on one page.
17. Close the workbook without saving it.

EXERCISE 6-15

Name cells, create formulas using named cells, and paste range names into the user documentation.

In an effort to understand its expenses by region, the Beautiful Belle Company needs to calculate quarterly, biannual, and yearly total expenses based on its 1997 expense information.

1. Create a worksheet sketch that includes a title, row and column labels, and an area for data and formulas. The worksheet should include January through December expense information (columns) for the Southeast, Northeast, and Northwest regions (rows). (*Hint:* Use abbreviations and start a new section for the second half of the year.) There should also be areas for monthly totals, quarterly totals, and half-year totals for each section. Use F for formula locations.
2. Transfer the sketch into Excel by keying and formatting the labels appropriately. Key the data from Figure 6-9 in the worksheet formatted in comma style, no decimals.

FIGURE 6-9

	Jan	Feb	Mar	Apr	May	Jun
S.E.	32,098	189,074	156,976	82,514	188,365	174,958
N.E.	11,098	294,651	192,634	99,254	201,648	89,254
N.W.	132,098	486,277	326,584	135,698	543,958	142,360
	Jul	Aug	Sept	Oct	Nov	Dec
S.E.	124,725	93,581	54,321	42,587	748,512	154,879
N.E.	124,521	84,516	68,954	859,641	365,894	254,369
N.W.	123,695	99,365	67,987	102,587	411,758	254,879

3. Include calculations for monthly total expenses.
4. Name each cell containing a monthly total.
5. Below the monthly data, use your cell names to calculate quarterly expenses based on the monthly totals for all regions.
6. Below the quarterly totals, use cell names to calculate half-year expenses.
7. Format the remaining cells in comma style with no decimal places.
8. Format the cells above monthly totals with bottom borders.
9. Rename Sheet1 **Regions** and rename Sheet 2 **User Information**
10. In the User Information worksheet, create documentation that includes the following: File Information (Created by, Date created, Date revised, Revised by, Contact for help); Purpose of spreadsheet (paragraph form); Instructions to User (special instructions needed by the user to enter

data correctly), and Range Names (names used in the worksheet and their location). Style the documentation for easy reading.

11. Add the standard header including your name, filename, and date to both worksheets, and center the Regions worksheet horizontally on the page.
12. Save the workbook as *[your initials]***6-15.xls**.
13. Print the entire workbook, then create a standard formula printout with grids and row and column headings. Use the Page 1 of ? footer for multiple pages. Do not fit the formula printout on one page.
14. Close the workbook without saving it.

Spelling, Find/ Replace, and File Management

OBJECTIVES

After completing this lesson, you will be able to:

1. Check spelling.
2. Use AutoCorrect.
3. Find and replace data.
4. Find files.
5. Rename, copy, and delete files in Excel.

Creating and building a workbook is only the beginning of effective data management and analysis. You must make your workbooks accurate and easy to use, and Excel can help. Excel provides automated dictionaries to check your spelling. It also provides a Find and Replace function you can use to make global changes and revisions.

Excel's Open dialog box lets you find files easily and offers many other file-management functions.

Checking Spelling

Excel's spell-checker scans the active worksheet and highlights words not found in any of its dictionaries. It also finds repeated words. A Spelling dialog box provides a choice of options for handling the highlighted word, as shown in Table 7-1.

TABLE 7-1 Spell-Checking Options

BUTTON	ACTION
Ignore	Do not take any action; do not change the spelling. If it is a repeated word, do not delete or change it.
Ignore All	Do not take any action for all occurrences of this word in the worksheet.
Change	Change the current spelling of this word to the spelling highlighted in the Change To box.
Delete	Delete a repeated word.
Change All	Change all occurrences of this word to the spelling highlighted in the Change To box.
Add	Add this word to the dictionary. Once added, Excel no longer highlights this word as "Not in Dictionary."
Suggest	Display a list of proposed suggestions.
Undo Last	Reverse the last action.
Cancel/Close	End spell-checking.
AutoCorrect	Add to the list of corrections that AutoCorrect makes as you key text in a worksheet.

You can customize the spell-checker so it works smarter for you. Adding words to a dictionary is especially useful for worksheets that contain data from specific fields, such as law, real estate, or science. You can also turn off the Suggestions list box choice and ignore words that contain numbers or all uppercase letters.

EXERCISE 7-1 Spell-Check the Entire Worksheet

Excel begins spell-checking at the active cell. If you begin spell-checking in the middle of the worksheet, a dialog box appears when the spell-checker reaches the end. You can continue spell-checking at the beginning of the worksheet.

1. Open the file **Change%2.xls**.

2. Select cell A1 to begin spell-checking from the beginning of the worksheet.
3. Choose Spelling from the Tools menu or press F7. Excel locates the first word not found in its dictionary, "introducsion." The correct spelling appears in both the Change to text box and the Suggestions drop-down list box.

FIGURE 7-1
Spelling dialog box

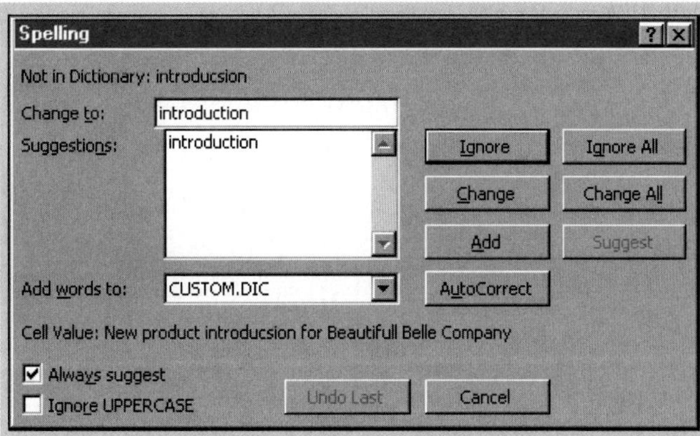

4. Click Change. Excel changes the word to "introduction" and locates the next word not found in its dictionary.

TIP: You may want to view a word in the worksheet before you change its spelling. To move the Spelling dialog box out of the way, drag its title bar.

5. Continue spell-checking until you reach the end of the worksheet. Click Ignore if no change is required. If the correct spelling appears in the Suggestions drop-down list box but not in the Change to text box, select the correct word from the list and click Change.

NOTE: If the correct word does not appear in the drop-down list, key it directly into the Change to text box and click Change.

6. When the spell-check is completed, click OK in the dialog box.

EXERCISE 7-2 Spell-Check a Range in the Worksheet

To spell-check a range in a worksheet, highlight the range to be checked and choose Spelling from the Tools menu. Excel checks only the highlighted range.

1. Move to the User Information sheet and select cells A1 through D7.

2. Click the Spelling button on the Standard toolbar. The Spelling dialog box appears. Excel locates "Creted," the first word in the selected range not found in its dictionary.
3. Click Change to change the misspelled word to "Created." Excel locates "Dat," the next word not found in its dictionary.
4. Click Date in the Suggestions drop-down list box, if necessary, and click Change.
5. Click Change to correct "Revisd" to "Revised."
6. Key **by** in the Change to text box and click Change. A dialog box appears when the spell-check of the range is complete.
7. Click OK.

Using AutoCorrect

The AutoCorrect feature automatically corrects your spelling as you key text. You can customize AutoCorrect by adding words you commonly misspell to Excel's list. You can also turn off AutoCorrect, if desired.

EXERCISE 7-3 Use AutoCorrect to Correct Typos

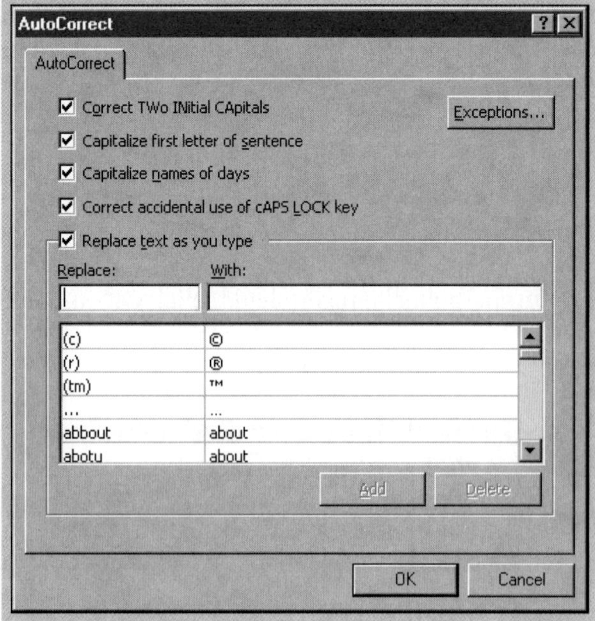

FIGURE 7-2 AutoCorrect dialog box

1. Choose AutoCorrect from the Tools menu. The AutoCorrect dialog box appears.
2. Clear the Replace text as you type check box and click OK. The AutoCorrect feature is deselected and Excel does not correct spelling automatically.
3. Key **Purpse** in bold in cell A9 and press Enter. Remember to type the word exactly as shown. With Auto-Correct deselected, the spelling error remains in the cell.

4. Choose AutoCorrect from the Tools menu.
5. Click the Replace text as you type check box to select it and click OK. AutoCorrect becomes active again, but does not correct existing text.
6. Key the following text in cell B10 exactly as shown to see AutoCorrect at work:

   Analyze teh sale groth of new product line

   AutoCorrect changes the word "teh" to "the" as you type. Note, however, that the misspelled word "groth" was not corrected. In addition, errors in sentence syntax, such as the word "sale" in this entry, are not corrected by AutoCorrect or the spell-checker.

EXERCISE 7-4 Train AutoCorrect for Your Common Typos

You can train AutoCorrect to automatically correct a word you misspell often. Simply add the misspelling and its correction to AutoCorrect's list of words.

1. Select cells A9 through B10 in the User Information worksheet.
2. Click [spelling button]. Excel suggests "Purpose" to correct the first word in the range that does not match its dictionary.
3. Double-click Purpose in the Suggestions drop-down list box (another way to select a word). Excel finds "groth," the next word in the range not found in its dictionary and suggests "growth."
4. Click AutoCorrect. Excel changes the spelling of the word and adds this correction to AutoCorrect's list of words to correct as you type. A dialog box appears when the spell-check of the range is complete.
5. Click OK.
6. Move to cell B10 again and change the word "sale" to **sales.**
7. Choose AutoCorrect from the Tools menu.
8. Key the following words in the Replace and With text boxes and click Add (see Figure 7-3 on the next page). Be sure to type the words exactly as shown.

   produtc **product**

9. Scroll up the Replace and With text boxes to confirm that the word "groth" was added to the AutoCorrect list.
10. Choose "groth" and click Delete to remove it from the list.
11. Click OK, return to cell A1, and turn off gridlines for viewing.

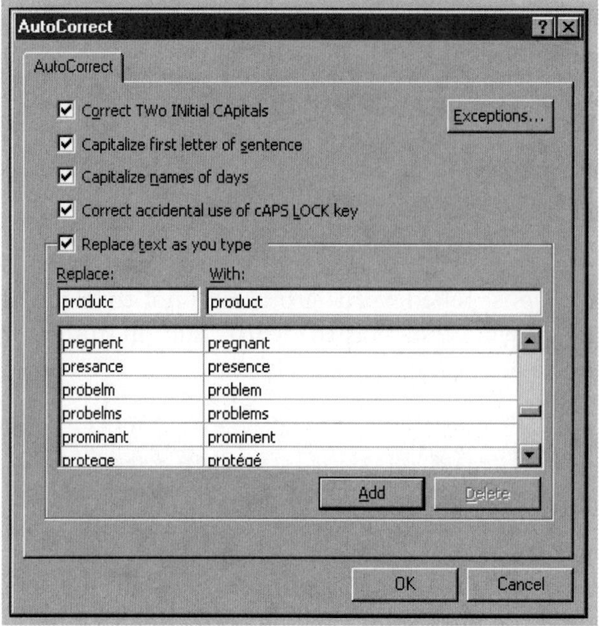

FIGURE 7-3 Adding a new AutoCorrect listing

TIP: You can also use AutoCorrect to create abbreviations that speed data entry. For example, assume that you type the phrase "Pending Release" frequently in your worksheets. Just add the abbreviation "pr" to the Replace text box and the full phrase "Pending Release" to the With text box in the AutoCorrect dialog box.

Finding and Replacing Data

Find and Replace are handy tools for updating worksheets. Find locates occurrences of a *character string*—a sequence of characters in a formula or text. You can use Find to return to a particular location in a worksheet, to verify that text is consistent, or to check that a formula appears in all intended locations.

Replace locates occurrences of a character string and replaces them, either one at a time or globally. As a result, it can change a formula that occurs in multiple cells. You can also use Replace to change repeated labels, such as a category or product names.

EXERCISE 7-5 Find Data in a Worksheet

You can use the Find command in relatively long worksheets that contain too many formulas and values to check individually. Find is especially useful in locating all instances of a formula or error in a worksheet. Excel uses the asterisk (*) as a *wildcard* symbol, which instructs Excel to allow any combination of letters or numbers to replace it. If, for example, Excel was searching for 7-*, it would locate 7-1, 7-2, 7-A, 7-SOFT, and so on.

All error values begin with # (the number sign), so you can key **#** in the Find what text box to locate error values in a worksheet. You can also look for specific error values, such as #DIV/0!, the error value produced by division by zero.

1. In the Sun Soft worksheet, choose Find from the Edit menu (or press Ctrl+F). The Find dialog box appears.

FIGURE 7-4
Find dialog box

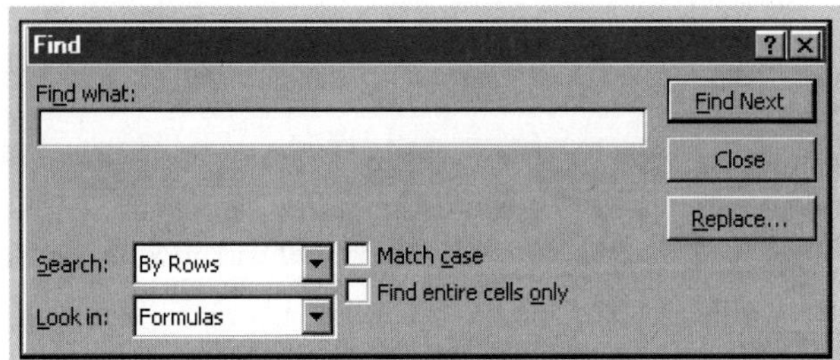

2. Key **=SUM(C7:C10)** in the Find what text box.
3. Choose Formulas from the Look in drop-down list box, if necessary. Make sure the Match case box is not checked so Excel does not try to match the case (upper or lower) of the word you keyed.
4. Click Find Next. Excel finds the formula in cell C12 and displays the cell reference in the name box and the formula in the Formula Bar.

TIP: Drag the Find dialog box out of the way so you can see the selected cell in the worksheet.

5. Edit the text in the Find what text box to read "**=SUM(*7:*10)**" and click Find Next. Excel selects cell D12.
6. Click Find Next to find the next occurrence of the formula. Excel selects cell B12.

NOTE: You cannot edit the worksheet when the Find dialog box is open. If you close the Find dialog box, however, you can repeat the last search by pressing F4.

7. Click Find Next. Excel selects cell C12 again.
8. Choose Values from the Look in drop-down list box.

9. Key **#** in the Find what text box (replacing the formula) and click Find Next. Excel returns cell E7, which contains a formula that attempts to perform division by zero. (The formula "C7/B7" is a division by zero, because cell B7 is empty.)
10. Close the Find dialog box.
11. In cell B7, key **57,809** to correct the error.

EXERCISE 7-6 Replace Data in a Worksheet

You can replace character strings globally or one at a time.

1. Select cell A6 and choose Replace from the Edit menu (or press Ctrl+H). The Replace dialog box appears. The Find what text box contains # (the number sign), which is the last entry in the Find dialog box.

FIGURE 7-5
Replace dialog box

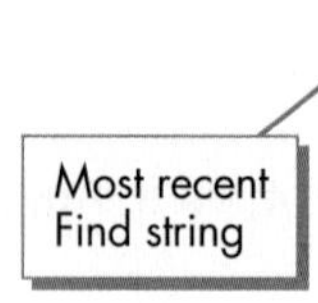

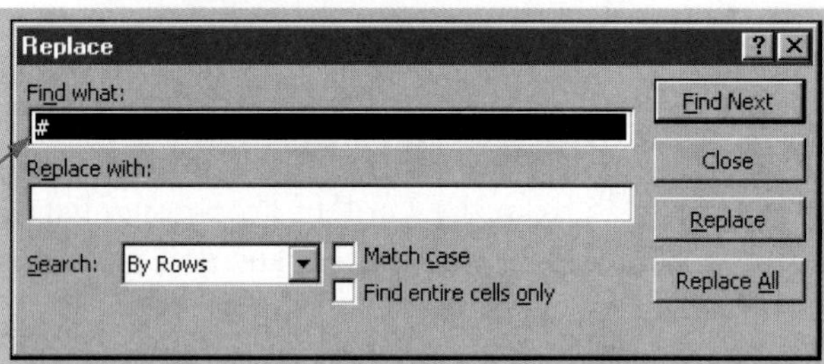

2. Key **1995** in the Find what text box (replacing #), press Tab, and key **Year 1** in the Replace with text box.
3. Click Find Next.

TIP: Drag the Replace dialog box out of the way so you can see the selected cell in the worksheet.

4. Click Replace. The worksheet displays "Year 1" in cell B6.
5. Close the Replace dialog box and right-align the label. (See Figure 7-6 on the next page.)
6. Select cell B6, if necessary.
7. Choose Find from the Edit menu, edit the date in the Find what text box to read **1996**, and click Find Next. Cell C6 is selected.
8. Click Replace to expand to Find dialog box to the Replace dialog box.
9. Make the Replace with text box read **Year 2** and choose Replace All. Both occurrences of "1996" are replaced with "Year 2."

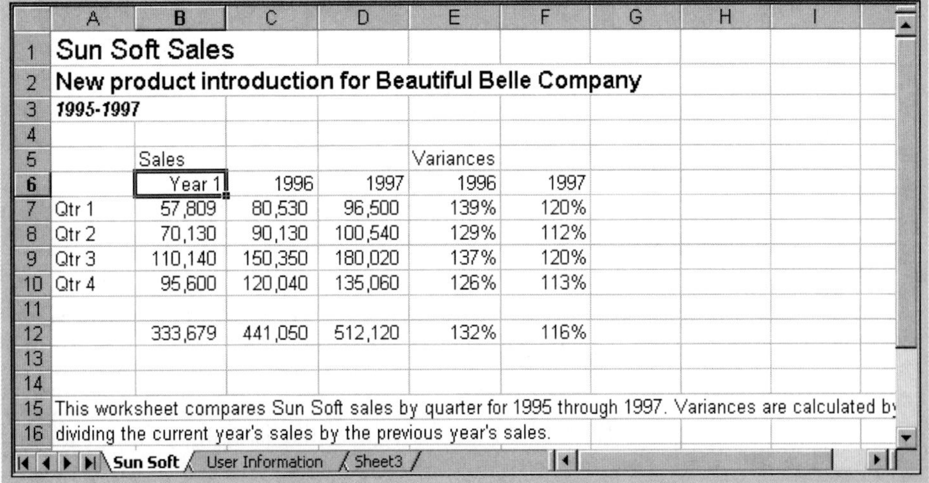

	A	B	C	D	E	F	G	H	I
1	Sun Soft Sales								
2	New product introduction for Beautiful Belle Company								
3	*1995-1997*								
4									
5		Sales			Variances				
6		Year 1	1996	1997	1996	1997			
7	Qtr 1	57,809	80,530	96,500	139%	120%			
8	Qtr 2	70,130	90,130	100,540	129%	112%			
9	Qtr 3	110,140	150,350	180,020	137%	120%			
10	Qtr 4	95,600	120,040	135,060	126%	113%			
11									
12		333,679	441,050	512,120	132%	116%			
13									
14									
15	This worksheet compares Sun Soft sales by quarter for 1995 through 1997. Variances are calculated by								
16	dividing the current year's sales by the previous year's sales.								

Sun Soft / User Information / Sheet3

FIGURE 7-6
Worksheet with new value

10. Choose Replace from the Edit menu. Edit the Find what box to read **1997** and edit the Replace with box to read **Year 3**.
11. Click Find Next. Excel moves to cell D6.
12. Click Replace and Excel moves to cell F6.
13. Replace "1997" in cell F6 with **Year 3**.
14. Close the Replace dialog box and right-align the rest of the column labels.
15. Change the title to reflect **Year 1-Year 3** and the text in cell A15 to reflect the same.
16. Add the standard header with your name, filename, and date to both worksheets.
17. Save the workbook as *[your initials]***7-6.xls.**
18. Print the entire workbook and then close it.

Finding Files

You can use Excel's Open dialog box to find a file, even if you do not remember its exact name. You can also display different types of details about files to determine which file to open.

TABLE 7-2 Open Dialog Box Buttons

BUTTON	BUTTON NAME/ACTION
	Up One Level moves up the file tree shown in the Look in drop-down list.
	Search the Web accesses the World Wide Web.
	Look in Favorites displays a list of folders and files specified as your "favorites."
	Add to Favorites adds the selected item to your Favorites list.
	List displays only folder names and filenames (no details).
	Details displays the filenames and descriptive details like size, type, and date last modified.
	Properties displays filenames and properties of the selected file.
	Preview displays filenames and a window of the contents of the selected file.
	Commands and Settings offers a menu of options.

If you choose Search Subfolders from the Commands and Settings menu, Excel looks in the current folder and any subfolders. You can also have Excel search for files that contain specific words or phrases. To take this approach, you key the text in the Text or property text box before you start your search.

EXERCISE 7-7 Find a Workbook

Excel can search for specific filenames or for filenames containing a certain pattern. For example, you can search for all filenames with a specific prefix or extension.

1. Click [Open] or choose Open from the File menu or press Ctrl+O. The Open dialog box appears. (See Figure 7-7 on the next page.)
2. Specify your Student Template Disk in the Look in drop-down list.
3. In the File name text box, key **Frgrnce**.
4. Choose Microsoft Excel Files (*.xl*; *.xls; *.xla;) from the Files of type drop-down list, if necessary.
5. Click Find Now. The filename, "Frgrnce," is displayed in the list box, and the search results, "1 file(s) found," are displayed in the status bar at the bottom of the dialog box.

FIGURE 7-7
Open dialog box

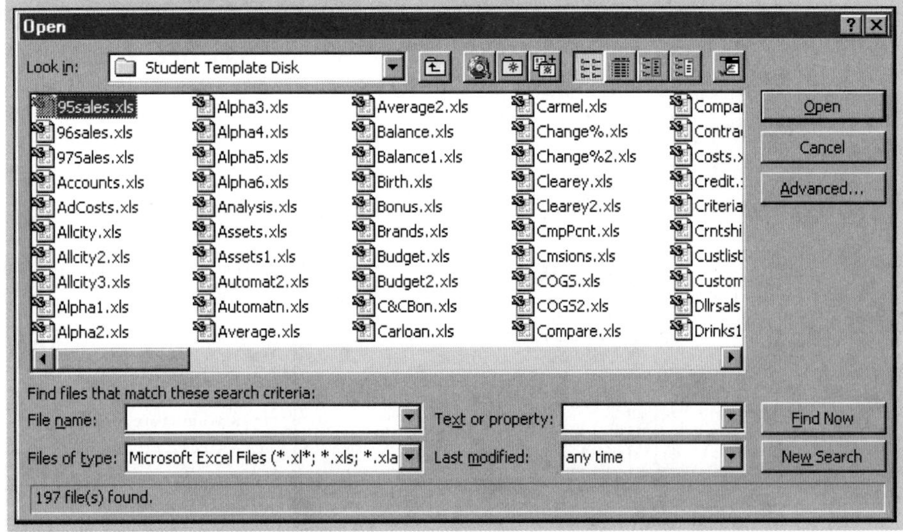

6. Key **F*** in the File name text box and click Find Now. All Excel files that begin with "F" are displayed.

TIP: The asterisk * is the wildcard character, so F* means any filename beginning with "F". You could key *[your initials]***6*** to search for all your answer files in Lesson 6, for example.

7. Select one of the files displayed and click Open. The workbook opens.
8. Close the workbook.

TIP: When you double-click the Find Fast icon in the Windows Control Panel you open the Find Fast utility. Find Fast creates indexes to speed up file searches by content, properties, or both. For information about using Find Fast, refer to Help in the Find Fast dialog box.

Renaming, Copying, and Deleting Files

You can open, copy, print, rename, or delete files directly from the Open dialog box. However, when a file is already open, you cannot rename it.

EXERCISE 7-8 Rename, Copy, and Delete a File Using the Open Dialog Box

1. Choose Open from the File menu.

2. Choose the correct drive and folder (if necessary) from the Look in drop-down list box or key the location directly in the text box.
3. Click the icon for the file *[your initials]***7-6.xls**, which you saved earlier in this lesson. The file is selected.

4. Click the Preview button. The upper left corner of the selected file appears in the Preview box.

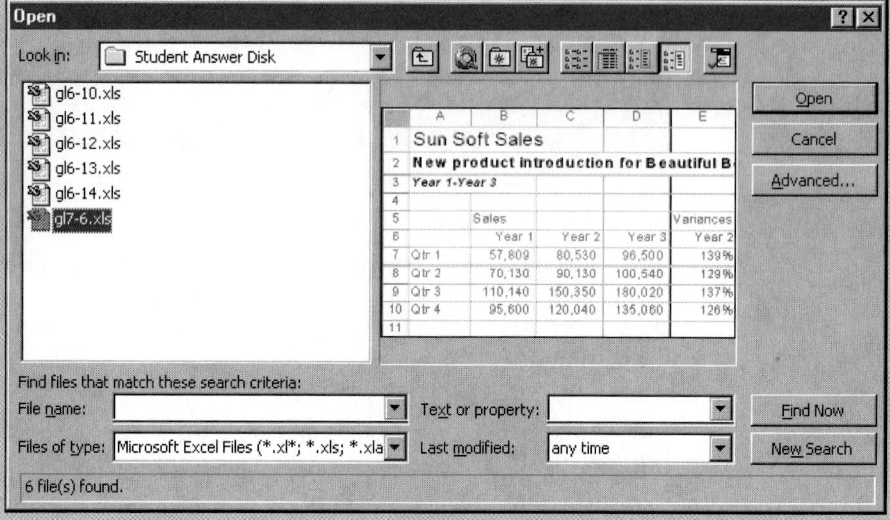

FIGURE 7-8
File preview in the Open dialog box

5. With the file *[your initials]***7-6.xls** still selected, press Ctrl+C. The file is copied to the Clipboard, although nothing appears on the screen.
6. Press Ctrl+V to paste a copy of the file into the current folder.

7. Click the file **Copy of** *[your initials]***7-6.xls** to select it, if necessary, and click the Commands and Settings button.
8. Click Print. Excel opens the file, prints the active worksheet in the workbook, and then closes the file and the Open dialog box.

TIP: You can also right click a filename and choose Print from the shortcut menu.

9. Click to open the Open dialog box again.
10. Right click the file **Copy of** *[your initials]***7-6.xls** to open the shortcut menu.
11. Choose Rename, key *[your initials]***7-8.xls**, and press Enter. Excel changes the filename.

NOTE: Be sure to key the file extension (.xls) when you rename a file. Otherwise, that file cannot be recognized as a file of its type.

12. Right click the file *[your initials]***7-8.xls** to open the shortcut menu.
13. Choose Delete. A dialog box appears asking if you're sure you want to delete the file.
14. Click Yes. The file is deleted.

TIP: You may want to access other information about your files. Explore the other buttons available in the Open dialog box to access information such as file size, type, and date modified, file author, or when a file was created.

COMMAND SUMMARY

FEATURE	BUTTON	MENU	KEYBOARD
Spell-check	[ABC✓]	Tools, Spelling	F7
Find		Edit, Find	Ctrl+F
Replace		Edit, Replace	Ctrl+H
Repeat (last) Find			F4
AutoCorrect		Tools, AutoCorrect	
Find and Manage files	[Open]	File, Open	Ctrl+O

USING HELP

What if you need a file that you printed last week and all you can remember is that it included the word "variance?" Excel includes advanced search tools that can help. You can even save a search if you think you'll use it more than once.

To find out how to perform advanced searches for files from the Open dialog box, try using the Office Assistant:

1. Click [?].
2. Enter **find files** in the text box and click Search.
3. Select "Find files."

   The Office Assistant displays information that shows you how to find files, including advanced features and Find Fast (which was introduced earlier in the lesson).

FIGURE 7-9
Microsoft Excel dialog box with Find files information

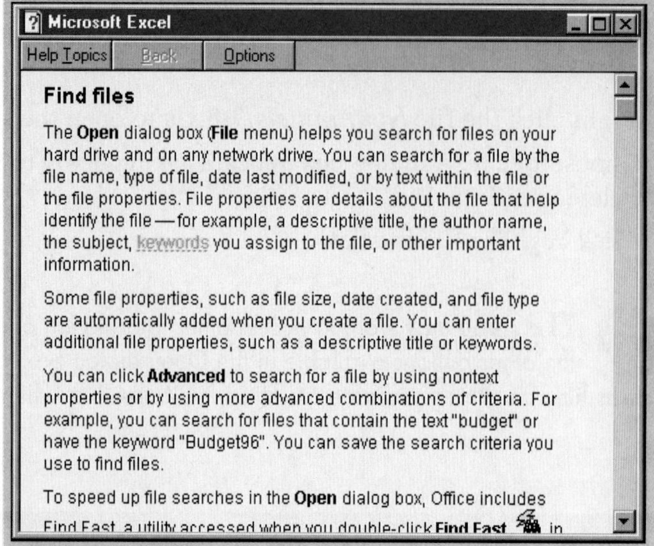

Microsoft Excel
Help Topics
Back
Options
Find files
The Open dialog box (File menu) helps you search for files on your hard drive and on any network drive. You can search for a file by the file name, type of file, date last modified, or by text within the file or the file properties. File properties are details about the file that help identify the file — for example, a descriptive title, the author name, the subject, keywords you assign to the file, or other important information.
Some file properties, such as file size, date created, and file type are automatically added when you create a file. You can enter additional file properties, such as a descriptive title or keywords.
You can click Advanced to search for a file by using nontext properties or by using more advanced combinations of criteria. For example, you can search for files that contain the text "budget" or have the keyword "Budget96". You can save the search criteria you use to find files.
To speed up file searches in the Open dialog box, Office includes

4. Read the information and close the dialog box and the Office Assistant.

Concepts Review

TRUE/FALSE QUESTIONS

Each of the following statements is either true or false. Indicate your choice by circling T or F.

T F *1.* Excel's spell-checker automatically deletes repeated words.

T F *2.* You access the Find and Open commands from the same menu.

T F *3.* You can add words to customize Excel's spell-checking dictionaries.

T F *4.* A character string is a sequence of characters in a formula or worksheet text.

T F *5.* All error values in Excel begin with the number sign (#).

T F *6.* You can use a wildcard to indicate text that will be automatically replaced throughout the worksheet.

T F *7.* AutoCorrect identifies common typos and automatically changes them to the correct spelling.

T F *8.* Using the Open dialog box, you can copy worksheets, but you can't print them.

SHORT ANSWER QUESTIONS

Write the correct answer in the space provided.

1. Which key starts Excel's spell-checker?

____

2. Which menu commands do you use to open the Replace dialog box?

____

3. Which keystroke combination do you use to open the Find dialog box?

____

4. Which Excel dialog box offers file-management tools?

____

5. Which keystroke combination do you use to access the Open dialog box?

____

6. How can you instruct Excel to allow any combination of letters or numbers to replace a symbol in a search?

____

7. How do you look at a worksheet without opening it?

____

8. How do you print from the Open dialog box?

____

CRITICAL THINKING

Answer these questions on a separate piece of paper. There are no right or wrong answers. Support your answer with examples from your own experience, if possible.

1. Describe a work situation in which Excel's Replace feature would be useful. Can Replace All be too much of a good thing?
2. Why do you think there are several ways to perform operations in Excel and other Windows applications?
3. What are the implications of features such as AutoCorrect that seem to do the thinking for you?

Skills Review

EXERCISE 7-9

Spell-check a worksheet, spell-check a range, and correct typos with AutoCorrect.

1. Open the file **MktExp.xls.**
2. Spell-check the worksheet by following these steps:
   a. Move to cell A1, if necessary, and click [ABC✓].
   b. Select or key appropriate spellings in the Change To text box and click Change. Remember, Excel's suggested replacement may not be the correct word for your worksheet.
   c. Click OK when the spell-check is finished.
3. Key the text as shown in Figure 7-10, starting at cell A16.

FIGURE 7-10

	A	B	C	D	E
16	Pacifica	9200	9800	10000	12000
17	Taos	5000	5000	7500	8500
18	High Sierra	3000	4000	6000	7500
19	Carmel	9550	9550	12500	12500
20	Santa Barbara	2300	2500	6000	9000

4. Key **Total** in cell F15 and center-align it.
5. Spell-check the range you just entered using these steps:
   - ***a.*** Select cells A16 through E21.
   - ***b.*** Choose Spelling from the Tools menu (or press F7).
   - ***c.*** Change any misspelled words. If you're a good typist, the range may not include any misspelled words. Remember, Excel's suggested replacement may not be the correct word for your worksheet.
   - ***d.*** Click OK when the spell-check is finished.
6. Enter formulas to find the product and quarterly totals by following these steps:
   - ***a.*** Select cell F7. Click Σ twice.
   - ***b.*** Copy this formula to cells F8 through F12 using AutoFill.
   - ***c.*** Select cell B12. Click Σ twice.
   - ***d.*** Copy this formula to cells C12 through F12 using AutoFill.
   - ***e.*** Copy the range F7 through F11 to cells F16 through F20 by dragging the range.
   - ***f.*** Use Σ to calculate totals in cells B21 through F21.
7. Key **Subtotal** in cell A21.
8. Use AutoCorrect to correct typos by keying the following text, exactly as shown, in cell A24:

   Acn we acheive any ohter cost savings in teh third quater?
9. Format the individual product expenses in comma style with no decimal places.
10. Format the totals in currency style with no decimal places.
11. Add the standard header with your name, filename, and date, and center the worksheet horizontally on the page.

12. Save the workbook as *[your initials]***7-9.xls** and print the worksheet.
13. Create a formula printout that fits on one page in landscape orientation with grids and row and column headings.
14. Close the workbook without saving it.

EXERCISE 7-10

Train AutoCorrect to correct common typos, and find and replace values in a formula.

1. Open the workbook **AdCosts.xls**.
2. Train AutoCorrect for common typos by following these steps:
   - *a.* Choose AutoCorrect from the Tools menu.
   - *b.* Key the following words in the Replace and With text boxes and click Add. Be sure to type the words exactly as shown.

     diretc **direct**

     mial **mail**
   - *c.* Click OK.
3. Key the following misspelling in cell A10 and watch AutoCorrect at work:

   Diretc Mial
4. Key the following amounts in the cells indicated:

   B10: **1000** D10: **1500** E10: **2000**
5. Copy the formula from cell F9 to cell F10 using AutoFill.
6. Find and replace data in the worksheet using these steps:
   - *a.* Select cell A1 and choose Find from the Edit menu.
   - *b.* Key **=SUM(*7:*9)** in the Find what text box.
   - *c.* Choose Formulas from the Look in drop-down list box, if necessary. Make sure the Match case box is not checked.
   - *d.* Click Find Next. Excel finds the formula in cell B11.
   - *e.* Click Replace.
   - *f.* Edit the text, if necessary, in the Replace with text box to read **=SUM(B7:B10)** and then click Replace.
   - *g.* Click Close.
7. Copy the formula from cell B11 to cells C11 through F11 using AutoFill.
8. Format the individual expenses in comma style with no decimal places.
9. Format the totals in row 11 in currency style with no decimal places and the totals in column E in comma style, no decimals.

10. Delete the AutoCorrect entries you made in this exercise by following these steps:
    a. Choose AutoCorrect from the Tools menu.
    b. Select "diretc" in the scroll box and click Delete.
    c. Select "mial" in the scroll box and click Delete.
11. Add the standard header with your name, filename, and date, and center the worksheet horizontally on the page.
12. Save the workbook as *[your initials]***7-10.xls** and print the worksheet.
13. Create a formula printout that fits on one page in landscape orientation with grids and row and column headings .
14. Close the workbook without saving it.

EXERCISE 7-11

Find and open a file, and find and replace data.

1. Find a file containing the word "inventory" and open it by following these steps:
    a. Choose Open from the File menu.
    b. Choose the drive containing your student files (if necessary) from the Look in drop-down list box or key the location directly in the text box.
    c. Click the Details button, if necessary.
    d. Click the Commands and Settings button and check Search Subfolders in the menu, if necessary.
    e. In the Text or property box, key **inventory**.
    f. Click Find Now. This may take a while. Notice the progress of the search in the Open dialog box's status bar.
    g. Select **InvntyQ1.xls** in the Name list and click Open.
2. Find and replace data in the worksheet using these steps:
    a. In cell A1, choose Replace from the Edit menu.
    b. Key **subtotal** in the Find what text box.
    c. Key **Monthly subtotal** in the Replace with text box.
    d. Select By columns from the Search drop-down list box.
    e. Click Find Next. Excel selects cell A13.
    f. Click Replace. Excel selects cell A22.
    g. Move the Replace dialog box out of the way to see the selected cell, if necessary.
    h. Click Replace again. Excel selects cell E6.

3. Change the text to be replaced by following these steps:
   a. Key **Product subtotal** in the Replace with text box.
   b. With cell E6 selected, click Replace. Excel selects cell E16.
   c. Click Replace again.
   d. Click Close.
4. Add the standard header with your name, filename, and date.
5. Save the workbook as *[your initials]***7-11.xls** and print the worksheet.
6. Close the workbook without saving it.

EXERCISE 7-12

Copy, rename, delete, and print a file using the Open dialog box.

1. Copy a file using the Open dialog box by following these steps:
   a. Open the Open dialog box.
   b. In the Look in box, choose the drive that contains your student files.
   c. Click the icon for the file **COGS.xls** to select it and press Ctrl+C.
   d. Press Ctrl+V to paste a copy of the file into the same drive or folder.
2. Rename a file using the Open dialog box by following these steps:
   a. Right click the file **Copy of COGS.xls** to open the shortcut menu.
   b. Choose Rename, key *[your initials]***7-12.xls**, and press Enter.
3. If necessary, cut this file (Ctrl+X) and paste it (Ctrl+V) into your answer folder.
4. Copy this file, *[your initials]***7-12.xls**, into its current folder (see steps 1c and 1d).
5. Print the copy of your file using the Open dialog box by following these steps:
   a. Click the file **Copy of** *[your initials]***7-12.xls** to select it.
   b. Click [icon].
   c. Click Print in the Commands and Settings menu.
6. Delete the copy of your file by following these steps:
   a. Open the Open dialog box and right click the file **Copy of** *[your initials]***7-12.xls** to open the shortcut menu.
   b. Choose Delete. A dialog box appears asking if you're sure you want to delete the file.
   c. Click Yes and close the Open dialog box.

Lesson Applications

EXERCISE 7-13

Find and open a file, find and replace data, and spell-check a worksheet.

Correct and complete Beautiful Belle's cost of goods sold worksheet for the second quarter.

1. Find and open **COGS2.xls**.
2. Key the data for fragrances as shown in Figure 7-11.

FIGURE 7-11

	A	B	C	D
15	Pacifica	6652	1665	9816
16	Taos	6654	4455	224
17	High Sierra	6698	4334	7358
18	Carmel	211	3669	10322
19	Santa Barbara	3983	1112	4983

3. Use AutoSum and AutoFill to enter formulas that calculate monthly and product subtotals for the new data.
4. Replace the month labels "Jan," "Feb," and "Mar" with **Apr**, **May**, and **Jun**, respectively.
5. Spell-check the entire worksheet, correcting any misspellings.
6. Format all numbers in comma style with no decimal places, if necessary.
7. Add the standard header with your name, filename, and date, and center the worksheet horizontally on the page.
8. Save the workbook as *[your initials]***7-13.xls** and print the worksheet.
9. Create a formula printout that fits on one page in landscape orientation with grids and row and column headings .
10. Close the workbook without saving it.

EXERCISE 7-14

Find and open a file, train AutoCorrect to convert abbreviations into words, and use the Open dialog box to rename and print a file.

Create a worksheet showing the sales history for the Carmel product line.

1. Find and open the file **Carmel.xls**.
2. Train AutoCorrect to convert the following abbreviations into complete words:

Abbreviation	Complete word
Qtr.	**Quarter**
Tot	**Total**

3. Key the data as shown in Figure 7-12 with the corrections. Center-align the column labels.

FIGURE 7-12

	A	B	C	D	E	F
5		Qtr. 1	Qtr. 2	Qtr. 3	Qtr. 4	Tot
6	1997	26544	25799	30124	35,666	
7	1998	30118	69765	~~45621~~ 46,552	50,217	
8	1999	54339	26001	35612	58,378	

4. Enter formulas to find the annual and quarterly totals.
5. Format the worksheet in comma style with no decimal places.
6. Spell-check the worksheet.
7. Delete the AutoCorrect entries you made in this exercise (Qtr and Tot).
8. Add the standard header with your name, filename, and date, and center the worksheet horizontally on the page.
9. Save the workbook as *[your initials]***7-sales.xls** and close it.
10. Use the Open dialog box to rename the file *[your initials]***7-sales.xls** as *[your initials]***7-14.xls**.
11. Print the active worksheet from the Open dialog box.

EXERCISE 7-15

Find and open a file, find and replace data, spell-check a worksheet, and print a workbook from the Open dialog box.

The Beautiful Belle Company's product sales analysis should be for the year 1997, not 1996. In addition, the company president wants to change the terms "Men" and "Women" in the worksheet to "Males" and "Females."

1. Find and open the file **Compare2.xls**.
2. Replace the column label **Men** with **Males**.
3. Replace the column label **Women** with **Females**.
4. Replace all occurrences of **1996** with **1997**.
5. Spell-check the worksheet.
6. Check the dates in cell A22 to verify the change in year.
7. Add the standard header with your name, filename, and date.
8. Save the workbook as *[your initials]***7-15.xls** and close it.
9. Print the active sheet from the Open dialog box.

EXERCISE 7-16

Find and open a file, replace labels, spell-check a worksheet, and use the Open dialog box to rename and print a worksheet.

A six-month sales analysis of Sun Soft sales that covers the wrong six months has been created. The worksheet also contains several spelling errors. Make the necessary corrections and use the Open dialog box to copy, rename, and print the worksheet.

1. Sketch on paper a worksheet for a six-month sales comparison for Sun Soft sales based on men and women. Create a title, column labels for comparison, and initial row labels with the wrong months (Jun, Jul, Aug, Sept, Oct, Nov). Include a place for totals for the months and for gender.
2. Transfer your sketch to Excel and format the title and labels accordingly.
3. Insert the data in Figure 7-13 (on the next page) and format the numbers in comma style, no decimals. Correct the row labels as shown.
4. Create formulas that calculate month totals and gender totals.
5. Key **Results indcate that theer is moer brand loyelty among wemen than men** two rows below the last row of data. (You will correct the misspellings in the next step.)

FIGURE 7-13

	Women	Men
~~Jun~~ Jul.	2500	4200
~~Jul~~ Aug.	5000	4000
~~Aug~~ Sep.	6500	2000
~~Aug~~ Oct.	5500	2000
~~Sept~~ Nov.	6000	2800
~~Nov~~ Dec.	5600	4000

6. Spell-check the worksheet. Make the necessary corrections.
7. Create the standard header with your name, filename, and date, and center the worksheet horizontally.
8. Rename Sheet1 **Compare** and rename Sheet 2 **User Information**.
9. In the User Information worksheet, create documentation which includes the following: File Information (Created by, Date created, Date revised, Revised by, Contact for help); Purpose of worksheet (paragraph form); and Instructions to User (special instructions needed by user to enter data correctly). Style the documentation for easy reading and spell-check your work.
10. Print the documentation worksheet and make the Compare worksheet active.
11. Save the workbook as *[your initials]***7-compare** and close it.
12. Use the Open dialog box to rename the file *[your initials]***7-16.xls**.
13. Print the active worksheet in *[your initials]***7-16.xls** from the Open dialog box.
14. Open the file again and create a formula printout with grids and row and column headings.
15. Close the workbook without saving it.

NOTE: When you turn on formulas for printing the data you keyed, the results of the comparison get cut off as well as the title, which has been standard up to this point. In Lesson 8, you learn column width adjustment so you can remedy this.

Unit 2 Applications

APPLICATION 2-1

Sketch a worksheet, enter labels in a new Excel worksheet, validate data, create and enter formulas, center the worksheet, print the worksheet, display formulas, create a custom header, and print in landscape orientation showing column and row labels and gridlines.

The Beautiful Belle Company wants to construct a worksheet that calculates the difference between first quarter monthly sales for men and women for two of its products: Pacifica and Taos. The worksheet should also calculate the difference in total sales.

1. Sketch the worksheet giving it a title (**Pacifica vs. Taos Sales**), column labels (**Pacifica**, **Taos**, and **Difference**), and row labels (see Figure U2-1 on the next page). Use F for formulas, but note that differences should only be figured in subtotal rows and the total row in the Total section.
2. Open a new worksheet.
3. Key the title and labels into the worksheet. Format the labels using bold or italic, and center-alignment where necessary.
4. Key the data as shown in Figure U2-1 in the appropriate rows and columns.
5. Validate the data of all the subtotal cells in the men and women sections so that they contain whole numbers greater than –25,000. Include an input message.
6. Create a formula that calculates the men's subtotal for "Pacifica."
7. Create formulas that calculate totals for January, February, and March. Key the actual formulas.
8. Using the AutoSum button on the toolbar, create a formula that calculates the women's subtotal for "Pacifica" and formulas that calculate subtotals for men's and women's "Taos" sales.
9. Calculate the difference between "Pacifica" and "Taos" sales in the "Subtotal" rows. ("Pacifica" minus "Taos.")
10. Calculate a grand total for "Pacifica," "Taos," and the difference between them in the Total section.
11. Format all values in comma style, no decimals.
12. Preview the worksheet.
13. Center the page horizontally.

FIGURE U2-1

		Pacifica	Taos	Difference
Men	January	7,985	16,544	
	February	2,697	9,800	
	March	10,655	9,402	
	Subtotal			
Women	January	9,557	20,550	
	February	10,665	14,675	
	March	9,418	16,550	
	Subtotal			
Total	January			
	February			
	March			
	Total			

14. Add a standard header including your name, filename, and date.
15. Save the workbook as *[your initials]***u2-1.xls**.
16. Print the worksheet.
17. Create a formula printout that fits on one page with grids and row and column headings in landscape orientation.
18. Close the workbook without saving it. Submit the worksheet sketch, the normal worksheet, and the formula printout.

APPLICATION 2-2

Copy using drag and drop, the toolbar, the Fill command, AutoFill, and keyboard shortcuts; freeze column titles; insert data; create a custom header; open and dock the Auditing toolbar; and trace precedents for a cell.

Complete a worksheet that compares Pacifica and Taos product sales in the second quarter for two consecutive years.

1. Open the file **PacTaos.xls**.
2. Copy cells B8 through B20 to cells G8 through G20 using the drag-and-drop method.
3. Key the 1998 product data as shown in Figure U2-2.

FIGURE U2-2

		H	I
		Pacifica	Taos
8	April	11,600	10,650
9	May	13,500	8,401
10	June	14,877	11,650
13	April	15,400	19,680
14	May	19,102	12,120
15	June	21,241	15,611

4. Freeze column titles.
5. Copy the formula in cell E8 to cell J8 using the Copy and Paste buttons on the Standard toolbar.
6. Using the Fill command, copy the formula to cells J9 through J11.
7. Use the drag-and-drop method to copy the formulas in cells J8 through J11 to cells J13 through J16.
8. Create a formula that subtotals men's 1998 "Pacifica" sales.
9. Copy the formula in cell H11 to cell I11 using AutoFill.
10. Copy both of these formulas to subtotal women's sales using the Copy and Paste commands.
11. Using drag and drop, copy the formulas for calculating the monthly totals for April 1997 to April 1998.
12. Select cells H18 through H20 and calculate the totals for the remaining months using Fill, Down.
13. Select cells H18:I20 and Fill, Right.
14. Create a grand total for 1998 "Pacifica" sales for the second quarter and copy it to cell I22 using AutoFill.

15. Copy the difference formula from cell J16 to J18 and then to J19, J20, and J22 in the "Second-Quarter Total" row using the Copy and Paste buttons.
16. Add a standard header including your name, filename, and date.
17. Save the workbook as *[your initials]***u2-2.xls**.
18. Activate the Auditing toolbar and dock it. Trace the precedents for cell E22.
19. Close the Auditing toolbar using the Toolbar shortcut menu.
20. Print the worksheet, including the tracing arrow.
21. Create a formula printout with gridlines, row and column headings, and Page 1 of ? footer. (The tracing arrow is still present.)
22. Close the workbook without saving it.

APPLICATION 2-3

Use AutoSum and AutoFill, create range names, build formulas using names, paste names into the worksheet, rename worksheet tabs, create documentation, spell-check, navigate the worksheet using names, create custom headers, and print formulas.

Create a worksheet that calculates commissions for Beautiful Belle's Southwest region and summarizes yearly sales, commissions, and net sales—that is, gross sales minus commissions.

1. Open the file **SW.xls**.
2. In cell C15, use the AutoSum button to add the column.
3. Use AutoFill to copy the SUM formula to cells D15 through J15.
4. Create the name **rt** for the constant **.07** to calculate quarterly commissions due.
5. Create formulas using the constant name in cells D5, F5, H5, and J5 to calculate the commission due for each quarter. To complete the columns, copy the formula using AutoFill.
6. Create the names **sq1**, **sq2**, **sq3**, and **sq4** for the total sales for each quarter.
7. Create a formula in cell B17 that calculates the total sales for the year. Use names in the formula.
8. Create the names **com1**, **com2**, **com3**, and **com4** for the total commissions for each quarter.
9. Use the commission range names to create a formula in cell B18 that calculates the total commissions for the year.

10. Create a formula in cell B19 that calculates the annual net sales—that is, gross sales minus commissions—for the Southwest territory.
11. Rename the Sheet1 tab **Commission**.
12. Rename the Sheet2 tab **User Information**.
13. Key the data from Figure U2-3 into the User Information sheet, including the corrections. Place the data in the worksheet so it is easy to read. Include formatting that might make it easy to read.

FIGURE U2-3

```
User Information

Creted by:            Jenny Bissell

Date created:         5/11/97

Date rvised:          5/12/97

Revised by:           5/12/97 Ray Maskis

Purpose:              Calculate comission for SW territory based on sales
                      by quarter.

User insturctions:    Note range and constant names below.
```

14. After the last line of text from Figure U2-3, skip a row and paste all the names you created into the worksheet.
15. Spell-check the User Information worksheet.
16. In the Commission worksheet, use the Go To command to locate the cell named "sq4."
17. Spell-check the worksheet.
18. Add the standard header including your name, filename, and date to both worksheets.
19. Save the workbook as *[your initials]***u2-3.xls**.
20. Print the entire workbook.
21. Create a formula printout of the Commissions worksheet with gridlines, row and column headings, and a Page 1 of ? footer. Do not fit this on one page.
22. Close the workbook without saving it.

APPLICATION 2-4

Find and open a file, replace labels, spell-check the worksheet, train AutoCorrect to recognize typos, use AutoSum and AutoFill to enter formulas, create a custom header, change print settings, and use the Open dialog box to copy a file and print a worksheet.

Find and adapt a workbook to total fourth quarter cream and fragrance sales for Beautiful Belle.

1. Open the file **Prdcts.xls**.
2. Spell-check the worksheet.
3. Train AutoCorrect to recognize the misspelled word **Otcober**
4. Edit "July" with **Otcober**
5. Delete the AutoCorrect entry.
6. Use the Replace command to replace all occurrences of "August" and "September" with **November** and **December**, respectively.
7. Use AutoSum and AutoFill to enter formulas for the "Totals" rows and columns.
8. Replace "Third" with **Fourth**.
9. Add the standard header including your name, filename, and date.
10. Save the workbook as *[your initials]***u2-4.xls**.
11. Create a formula printout with grids and row and column headings in landscape orientation.
12. Close the workbook without saving it.
13. Use the Open dialog box to create a copy of *[your initials]***u2-4.xls** and print the active worksheet from the Open dialog box.
14. Delete the copy of your file.

APPLICATION 2-5

Design a worksheet and transfer it to Excel, check spelling, and copy and paste data and formulas. Create range names and create formulas using range names. Use AutoSum and AutoFill, find and replace data, create documentation, paste range names into a worksheet, create custom headers, change print settings, and use the Open dialog box to copy and print a worksheet.

Imagine you are a product manager for the Beautiful Belle Company charged with projecting revenue for three new lines of shampoo being launched in the third quarter of the current year. You need to create an initial worksheet design for the third quarter and enter data. After you transfer the design to Excel, your boss needs to add information to the worksheet for fourth quarter projections; this information is not included in your initial design.

1. Sketch a worksheet that contains an appropriate title, a single-entry area (Quarter:), column labels for three types of shampoo, and row labels for the third quarter (abbreviate these). You also need a column and a row for product and month totals. Use F for formulas.
2. Transfer the title and labels to Excel, formatting them as necessary. Key **Third** beside "Quarter:" in the single-entry area and enter the data in Figure U2-4.

FIGURE U2-4

	Jaz	Britely	Frezia	Total
Jul	5800	6800	6000	
Aug	3200	7200	4500	
Sept	2800	8400	3800	
Total				

3. Spell-check the worksheet and make any necessary corrections.
4. Use AutoSum and AutoFill to create formulas that calculate the monthly totals.
5. Use AutoSum and AutoFill to create formulas that calculate the product line totals for the third quarter.
6. Create a formula that calculates the total projected sales for the three new products in the third quarter.
7. Copy the range that contains labels and data including the single-entry item and paste it into the worksheet beneath the third-quarter data.
8. In the pasted text, replace "Third Quarter" with **Fourth Quarter** and replace "Jul," "Aug," and "Sept," with **Oct**, **Nov**, and **Dec**, respectively.
9. Create the name **rt** for the constant **1.1** that you will use to calculate projected sales growth for the fourth quarter.
10. Create an appropriate range name for the first product value for "Jul."
11. Create an appropriate range name for the first product value for "Aug."

12. Create an appropriate range name for the first product value for "Sept."
13. Create formulas that use the range names for the first product and the name **rt** to calculate projected sales growth for the fourth quarter.
14. Create similar formulas for the other two products and format all numbers in comma style, no decimals.
15. Rename the worksheet tab **Projections** and name the Sheet2 tab **User Information**.
16. Create user documentation on the User Information sheet and include a pasted list of named ranges.
17. Add the standard header with your name, filename, and date to both worksheets and horizontally align the Projections worksheet on the page.
18. Save the workbook *[your initials]***u2-5.xls** and print the User Information worksheet only.
19. Display formulas in the Projections sheet. Trace the precedents to the first shampoo sales projection for October.
20. Create a formula printout with grids and row and column headings in landscape orientation, turn off the formula display, and close the Auditing toolbar.
21. Use Page Setup to change the print settings to print in portrait orientation, without gridlines and without row and column headings.
22. Save and close the workbook.
23. Use the Open dialog box to create a copy of the file.
24. Print the file **Copy of** *[your initials]***u2-5.xls** from the Open dialog box.
25. Delete the file **Copy of** *[your initials]***u2-5.xls**.
26. Submit the worksheet sketch, the normal worksheet, and the formula printout.

UNIT

3

Changing the Appearance of a Worksheet

Short-Camper Gear Stands Tall in Sales

Clearey & Clayton produces camping gear for backpacking, boating, skiing, and other wilderness activities. The business got its start when Bettina Clearey, a former fashion designer, sewed her own backpack to accommodate her petite 5-foot frame. She soon found there was a huge demand for scaled-down camping equipment. John Clayton, an advertising executive, became her partner and Clearey & Clayton was formed.

Clearey & Clayton's products were so well designed that it wasn't long before the company become one of the largest suppliers of camping gear in the country. Their best-selling products are their backpacks, sunglasses, camping chairs, kayaks, duffel bags, and mountaineering tents.

To increase their market share, Clearey & Clayton need to create the following worksheets to use as promotional material.

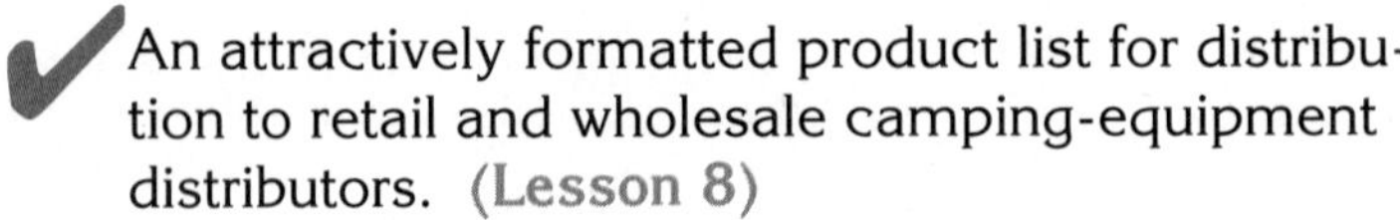

- ✔ An attractively formatted product list for distribution to retail and wholesale camping-equipment distributors. (Lesson 8)
- ✔ An attractively formatted order blank to be included in a mail-order catalog. (Lesson 9)

Formatting Text and Numbers

OBJECTIVES

After completing this lesson, you will be able to:

1. **Format numbers.**
2. **Suppress the display of zero values.**
3. **Work with stored numbers.**
4. **Align text.**
5. **Change column width and row height.**
6. **Hide columns and rows.**

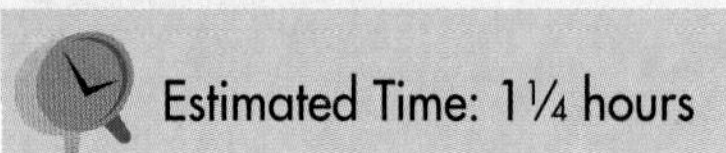

You can change the appearance of a worksheet by formatting numbers and text in different ways. Number formats include commas, dollar signs, and decimal places. Text formats include alignment in a cell, alignment over a group of cells, and text wrap within a cell. You can also change column width and row height.

Formatting Numbers

The default *format*—that is, the attributes of text or numbers, such as font style, underlining, bold, number of decimal places, or alignment—is called the Normal style. For numbers, the General format code is used. With this format, numbers are right-aligned; decimals, commas, and dollar signs are not displayed unless keyed; and the font is 10-point Arial.

NOTE: The default format for text in the Normal style is left-aligned, 10-point Arial.

In Lesson 3, you used the Formatting toolbar to perform basic number formatting. In this lesson, you choose from additional standard formats and create custom formats using the Number options in the Format Cells dialog box. You can apply number formats to entire columns, rows, worksheets, or individual cells.

EXERCISE 8-1 Choose a Number Format

1. Open the file **TWOut.xls**.
2. Select cells D8 through E10 and cells D13 through E14. (*Hint:* Press Ctrl to select the second set of cells.)
3. Choose Cells from the Format menu.
4. In the Format Cells dialog box, click the Number tab, if necessary. The Number options appear.

FIGURE 8-1 Number options in the Format Cells dialog box

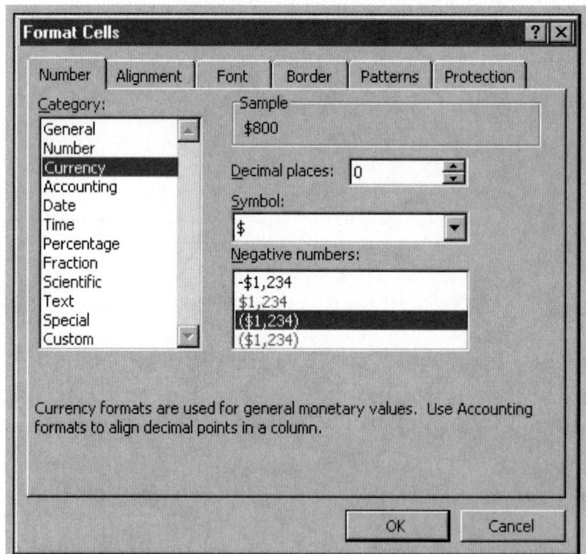

5. Choose Currency from the Category list box.

NOTE: The Currency format is used for general monetary values. The Accounting format aligns currency symbols and decimal points in a column.

6. Choose the third format code ($1,234.00) in the Negative Numbers list.

TIP: The options in the Negative Numbers list indicate how Excel handles negative numbers. For example, if you are "in the red" and want to show a loss in 1997, Quarter 4, the second or last options in red are good choices. (If you don't have a color printer and plan to print the worksheet, avoid all the red options.)

7. Notice that the default Symbol is the $. With this option, a dollar sign appears beside each number in the selected cells.
8. Key 0 beside Decimal Places to have numbers appear without decimal places.
9. Click OK. The numbers in cells E13 and E14 now contain commas that separate thousands from hundreds and all selected cells have dollar signs next to the values.

EXERCISE 8-2 Create a Custom Format

You can create custom format codes to meet special needs. For example, you can insert dashes within Social Security numbers or parentheses and dashes to indicate area codes and phone numbers. You can include text in a code by surrounding it with quotation marks. You can even hide numbers so they are used in calculations but do not appear in the worksheet cells.

TABLE 8-1 Examples of Custom Format Codes

FORMAT CODE	NUMBER	DISPLAY
000-00-0000	123456789	123-45-6789
(000) 000-0000	2035551234	(203) 555-1234
"Purchase No." 0000	1234	Purchase No. 1234
#.##	0.7	.7
#.##	5211.129	5211.13
#.0#	15	15.0
#.0#	1234.568	1234.57
0.0%	.7889	78.9
00000	06477 (ZIP CODE)	06477
#,##0;#,##0-	-1234	1,234-
#.#0	18.1	18.10
;;	1234	No value displayed

NOTE: A pound sign in a format code represents an integer or whole number, a zero represents leading or trailing zeros that fall immediately before or after the decimal position, and format codes for positive and negative numbers are separated by a semicolon. The ;; format suppresses number display in the cell, but the formula still appears in the Formula Bar.

In this exercise, you insert dashes and create item numbers.

1. Select cells B8 through B10 and cells B13 through B14.
2. With the white cross over one of the highlighted cells, click the right mouse button and choose Format Cells from the shortcut menu. The Format Cells dialog box appears.

FIGURE 8-2
Shortcut menu with Format Cells highlighted

TIP: You can also press Ctrl+1 to open the Format Cells dialog box.

3. Click the Number tab, if necessary, and choose Custom from the Category list box.
4. Choose the format code 0.00 from the Type list. The Type text box appears.
5. Position the insertion point in the Type text box and delete the period from the code. After the three zeros, key **0-000**. The new code should read 0000-000.
6. Click OK. Dashes appear in cells B8 through B10 along with the numbers.
7. Key the following data in cells B13 and B14:

   5217988

   5218088

   Notice that the new format now applies to these numbers.

NOTE: The Custom Category list is a good source for format codes. The original format code you edited, 0.00, is still available for use in this workbook, and the new code you created is added to the end of the list. If you need the new code for another workbook, you must re-create it in that workbook.

Suppressing the Display of Zero Values

When a large worksheet contains many zero entries, it can be hard to read. You can suppress the zero values in the worksheet to make it more readable.

EXERCISE 8-3 Suppress the Display of Zero Values

1. Scroll down to rows 17 through 19. Notice the zero values in columns D and E.
2. To hide these zeros, choose Options from the Tools menu.
3. In the Options dialog box, click the View tab, if necessary. The View options appear.
4. Click the Zero values check box to clear it.

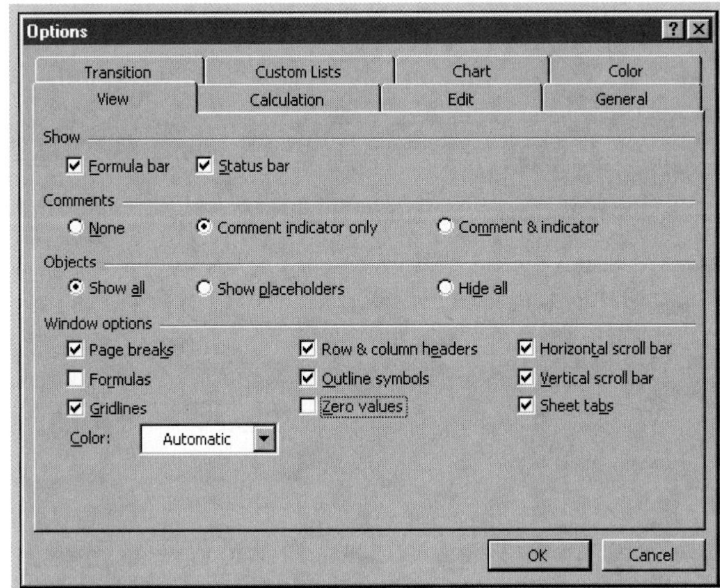

FIGURE 8-3 View options in the Options dialog box

5. Click OK. The zeros in cells D17 through E19 disappear.

NOTE: The Zero values setting works for only the active worksheet—not the entire workbook. You can restore the zeroes by clicking the Zero values check box a second time.

Working with Stored Numbers

When you key a number, Excel rounds it according to the cell's format. For instance, if you key **30** and the cell is formatted for two decimal places, Excel displays 30.00. Similarly, if the cell is formatted for no decimal places and you key **9.9**, Excel displays 10. Excel stores the number that you key (9.9) internally and uses that number in calculations. This characteristic is called *full precision*.

Sometimes, if you change numbers in a worksheet column after the column is totaled, and Excel rounds the new numbers up or down, the total may appear to be incorrectly calculated. To avoid this, you can store numbers as the rounded values that appear onscreen (10). This option is called *Precision as Displayed.*

EXERCISE 8-4 Calculate Using the Precision as Displayed Option

1. Key the following data to replace the numbers in cells D13 and D14:
   1000.45 **2000.35**
   Notice that the total for column D is now incorrect. The numbers stored internally in full precision are used in the arithmetic rather than the displayed numbers.
2. Choose Options from the Tools menu.
3. In the Options dialog box, click the Calculation tab.

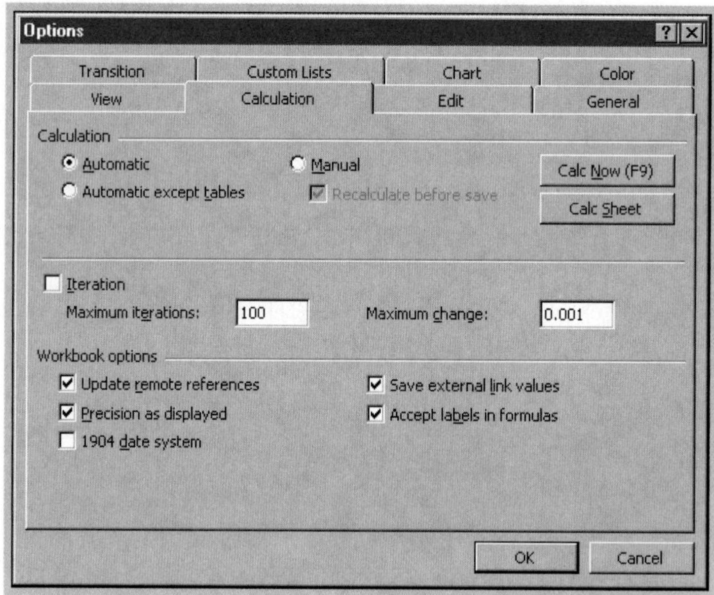

FIGURE 8-4 Calculation options in the Options dialog box

4. Click the Precision as displayed check box to turn on this option and click OK.
5. Click OK at the prompt that says data will permanently lose accuracy. The sum in Column D is now correct.

NOTE: Once you calculate with the Precision as Displayed option, you cannot restore values to full precision. In addition, this choice affects the entire workbook, not just the worksheet in which you change the setting.

Aligning Text

You can change the Normal style for text alignment (left-aligned) several ways. You can realign text within a cell or across cells. You can also rotate text or wrap it onto several lines in a cell.

EXERCISE 8-5 Align Text in a Cell

You use the Alignment command to align text to the left, right, or center of a cell. You can also align text vertically with the top, bottom, or center of the cell. In addition, wrapped text can be justified to fill the entire width of a cell, with even margins appearing on each side of the cell contents.

1. Select cells A4 through E4 and cells A7 and A12.
2. To center the text horizontally in these cells, click the Center button on the Formatting toolbar.
3. Select cells A8 through A10 and cells A13 through A14.
4. Click the Align Right button on the Formatting toolbar. All the text is now right-aligned.
5. To center text vertically in cells A4 through E4, select these cells.
6. Press Ctrl+1 to open the Format Cells dialog box.
7. Click the Alignment tab, if necessary. The Alignment options appear. (See Figure 8-5 on the next page.)
8. Choose Center from the Vertical drop-down list. Center under Horizontal is already selected because you applied this formatting in step 2.
9. Click OK. Although you cannot see it on the screen, the text is centered vertically in the cells. (You see the effects of this alignment in Exercise 8-9.)

NOTE: Both text and numbers can also be left-aligned. In addition, you can align titles over lists of data to make reading easier. If a list is left-, right-, or center-aligned, the title should have the same alignment as the list. If a list is extremely wide and left- or right-aligned, the title can be centered.

FIGURE 8-5
Alignment options in the Format Cells dialog box

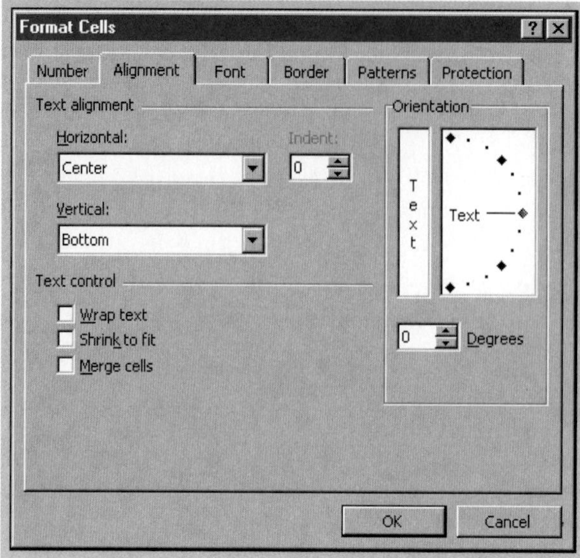

EXERCISE 8-6 Center Text Over a Range of Columns

If you want to center the title of a worksheet over all its columns or center other text over a range of columns, you can use one of two methods. You use the Merge and Center button  on the Formatting toolbar to merge a selected range of cells and center a title within the merged cell. You can also center a title across a range of cells without merging the cells using the Alignment tab in the Format Cells dialog box.

NOTE: The title should appear or be entered in the column furthest to the left of the range of columns over which you want to center it.

1. Position the mouse pointer in cell A1 and key **Clearey & Clayton** and make it bold.
2. Select cells A1 through E1.
3. Press Ctrl+1 to open the Format Cells dialog box.
4. Click the Alignment tab, if necessary.
5. Choose Center Across Selection from the Horizontal drop-down list.
6. Click OK. The text in A1 is centered across cells A1 through E1. If the screen gridlines are turned on, they do not display between the columns that contain the centered title. If you click the pointer across the row, you notice there are still separate cells within the range. In the next steps, you merge selected cells into a single cell.

7. In cell A2, key **Product List** and make it bold.
8. Select cells A2 through E2. These selected cells include the range of cells in which you center the subtitle.
9. Click [Merge and Center]. The text becomes a subtitle for the worksheet. Again, notice that if the screen gridlines are turned on, they do not display between the columns that contain the centered title. Also notice that the cell pointer shows that the range is now a single cell.
10. To remove the formatting, click [Undo]. Notice that that the individual cells in the range are redisplayed.
11. Press Ctrl+1 to open the Format Cells dialog box.
12. Choose Center Across Selection from the Horizontal drop-down list.
13. Click OK. The subtitle is now centered across A2 through E2. The cells in the range are not merged.

TIP: You can also open the Alignment dialog box by choosing Format Cells from the shortcut menu after you select the text to be aligned. You can then select Center Across Selection from the Horizontal drop-down list to apply the same formatting. You can click the Merge cells check box to also merge the selected cells. (Remember to position the white cross in a highlighted cell when you click the right mouse button.)

EXERCISE 8-7 Wrap Text on Several Lines Within a Cell

When you key a line of text that is too wide for a column (for example, column A), the text extends into the next column (B), if it's blank. If the next column is not blank, the text to the right in column A is hidden from view. If you don't want to widen the column, you can wrap the text on several lines within the cell.

1. Key the text shown in Figure 8-6 in cell C8. Do not press Enter at the end of each line.

FIGURE 8-6

```
This tent is designed for spring, summer, and fall. It has a separate rain
fly and fiberglass poles. Packed size is 18" x 5.5". Weight: 4.5 lbs.
```

2. Press Enter. The text is hidden by the next column.

3. To make the text wrap in the cell, select cell C8 and open the Format Cells dialog box.
4. Click the Alignment tab, if necessary.
5. Click the Wrap Text check box to select it and click OK. The text wraps in the cell and the height of the other cells in the row is adjusted.

NOTE: When you wrap text on several lines within a cell, row height adjusts to accommodate the font size. If you change the font size or column width after wrapping the text, the row height does not change.

EXERCISE 8-8 Rotate Text Within a Cell

At some point, you may find it useful to rotate text within a cell. This option highlights the information in that cell and can narrow the column containing the text.

1. Select cell A7.
2. Open the Format Cells dialog box. Click the Alignment tab, if necessary.
3. Under Orientation, drag the indicator in the right window to a 45-degree position and click OK. "Tents" rotates upward.
4. Press Ctrl+Z to undo the formatting.

EXERCISE 8-9 Create Line Breaks Within a Cell

Text wraps to the next line when it reaches the end of the column. If you want it to go to the next line before this point, you must create a *line break*, or a forced movement of the cursor to the next line down within the cell. Line breaks are also useful to make wide columns narrow.

1. Select cells D4 and E4.
2. Open the Format Cells dialog box using the shortcut menu.
3. Click the Alignment tab, if necessary.
4. Click the Wrap text check box and click OK.
5. To create a line break in cell D4, key **Wholesale**, and press Alt+Enter.
6. Key **Price** and press Enter. A line break appears after "Wholesale."
7. Repeat these steps for cell E4. In this cell, key **Suggested**, press Alt+Enter to create a line break, key **Retail Price**, and press Enter. Notice how the

text in the other cells in row 4 is vertically centered, which you did in Exercise 8-5.

Changing Column Width and Row Height

You can increase column width to display text that won't fit in the current column or to make a worksheet more readable. You can also decrease column width to make room for other columns. Additionally, you can adjust row height to create proper spacing between rows or to adjust to a new font size when working with wrapped text.

Excel provides three ways to change column width and row height:

- Using the mouse
- Using the Column Width and Row Height dialog boxes
- Using the AutoFit option to maximize the columns visible on the screen and those that print on each page

EXERCISE 8-10 Change Column Width and Row Height with the Mouse

1. Scroll the worksheet to display columns C and D, if necessary.
2. To increase column width, move the pointer to the divider line between column C and column D in the lettered gray area that frames the worksheet.
3. When the pointer becomes a two-headed arrow ✛, drag until the column width increases about 0.5 inch or to approximately 17.00. (The column size displays in a ScreenTip immediately above the pointer.)

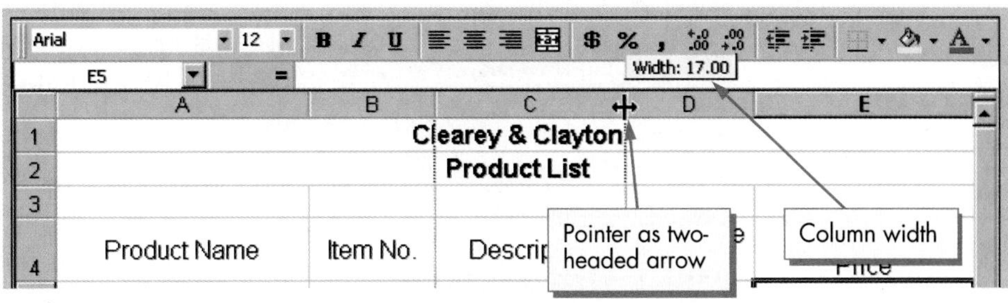

FIGURE 8-7 Changing column width

NOTE: The column-size number refers to the average number of characters of the default text font that fit in a cell. Your numbers may vary if your default text font is different from the standard.

4. Change the document view to 75%. Position the pointer along the divider line between row 8 and row 9 in the numbered gray area.
5. When the pointer becomes a two-headed arrow, drag up until the row height decreases to about 147.00.
6. Change the document view back to 100%.
7. Position the pointer along the divider line between row 4 and row 5 and with the two-headed arrow, drag down until the row height increases about 0.5 inch to 45.00.
8. To change more than one column at once, select columns C, D, and E.
9. Position the pointer at the top right border of any selected column until the pointer becomes a two-headed arrow. Drag to decrease the column width about 0.5 inch. The width of all selected columns decreases by the same amount.

NOTE: When a column is not sufficiently wide to accommodate the number of characters in a cell, values (numbers) are displayed with the # symbol. This does not affect the actual content of the cell. To remove the # characters, simply widen the column.

10. With the columns still selected, increase the width by the same amount. The columns are now all the same width.

EXERCISE 8-11 Use the Column Width and Row Height Dialog Boxes

1. Select column B.

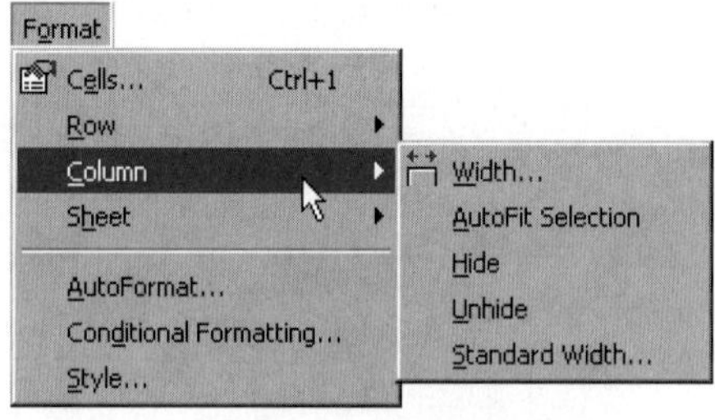

FIGURE 8-8 Column cascading menu

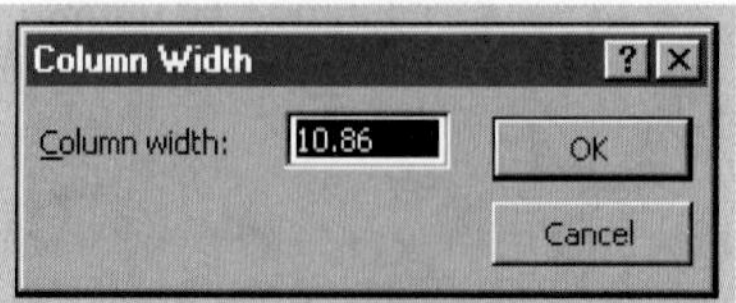

FIGURE 8-9 Column Width dialog box

2. Choose Column from the Format menu. The Column cascading menu appears.
3. Choose Width. The Column Width dialog box appears.
4. Key **15** in the Column width text box and click OK or press Enter. The column width increases.
5. Select rows 7 and 12.

TIP: To select nonadjacent rows or columns, press Ctrl when you select subsequent rows or columns.

6. Choose Row from the Format menu. The Row cascading menu appears.
7. Choose Height. The Row Height dialog box appears.
8. Key **30** in the Row height text box and click OK. The row height increases.

EXERCISE 8-12 Use AutoFit and Shrink to Fit

The AutoFit option is a fast way to adjust the column width so the longest item fits exactly in the column. This feature helps maximize the number of columns you can see on your screen and print on a page. You can also adjust row height using the AutoFit option. If you prefer not to change the size of a row or a column, you can use the Shrink to Fit alignment option.

1. Position the pointer on the right border of column B in the Column Heading until it turns into a two-headed arrow and double-click. The column width adjusts to fit the items in the cells.
2. To change the height of row 4 to fit the items in the cells, position the pointer on the bottom border of row 4 in the Row Heading until the pointer turns into a two-headed arrow and double-click. The row height adjusts to fit the items in the cells.
3. To change columns C and D at the same time, select both columns.
4. Choose Column from the Format menu. The Column cascading menu opens.
5. Choose AutoFit Selection. The column widths of both columns are adjusted.

NOTE: You can also double-click with the two-headed arrow positioned on the right border of column C or D to change the column widths to fit the items in the cells.

6. Delete row 6.
7. Select cell C18 and key **Model Discontinued**. The text is too large to fit in the cell. Instead of changing the column width or row height, you can use the Shrink to Fit feature.
8. With cell C18 selected, choose Cells from the Format menu and click the Alignment tab, if necessary.
9. Select the Shrink to fit check box and click OK. The contents of C18 shrink to fit the size of the cell.

EXERCISE 8-13 Reset Column Width and Row Height

You may sometimes need to return column widths or row heights to their original settings.

1. To return column B to its standard size, select column B.
2. Choose Column from the Format menu. The Column cascading menu appears.
3. Choose Standard Width. The Standard Width dialog box appears and a number appears next to Standard Column Width. This value is the default standard width for all columns that are not set individually. (The standard width varies for different computers.)
4. Click OK.
5. Choose Column from the Format menu and choose Width. The Column Width dialog box appears.
6. Enter the default width in the text box and click OK. The column is sized down to the standard width.
7. Press Ctrl+Z to undo the column size change.
8. Select rows 6 and 11.
9. Choose Row from the Format menu. The Row cascading menu appears.
10. Choose Height and key **15**, the standard row height, in the Row Height dialog box. (The standard row height may vary depending on your computer. Use 15 for this exercise.)
11. Click OK. The row height is resized.
12. Press Ctrl+Z to undo the row height size change.

Hiding Columns and Rows

You can hide rows or columns temporarily so they do not print or appear on the screen. You may want to hide the salaries column when you print a payroll worksheet, for example, or you may want nonconsecutive rows to appear consecutively when you view them on your screen.

EXERCISE 8-14 Hide Columns and Rows

1. Select column D and choose Column from the Format menu.

2. Click Hide. Column D becomes invisible.
3. Select columns C through E, which appear on either side of the hidden column. Use the Shift key so column D is included in the range. (You can also select both columns by clicking and dragging.)
4. Choose Column from the Format menu and click Unhide. Column D reappears.
5. Select row 4 and choose Row from the Format menu
6. Click Hide. The row is hidden from view.
7. Select rows 3 through 5, which are on either side of the hidden row.
8. Choose Row from the Format menu and click Unhide. The row becomes visible again.
9. Make sure gridlines are turned on for printing and add the standard header to the worksheet with your name, the filename, and the date.
10. Save the workbook as *[your initials]***8-14.xls**.
11. Print the worksheet and close the workbook.

COMMAND SUMMARY

FEATURE	BUTTON	MENU	KEYBOARD
Format cells		Format, Cells	Ctrl+1
Right-align		Format, Cells	
Center		Format, Cells	
Left-align			
Center across columns		Format, Cells, Center across selection	
Hide rows		Format, Row, Hide	Ctrl+9
Unhide rows		Format, Row, Unhide	Ctrl+Shift+(
Hide columns		Format, Columns, Hide	Ctrl+0
Unhide columns		Format, Columns, Unhide	Ctrl+Shift+)

USING HELP

You learned how to create custom number formats. Excel can give you more information about their makeup.

Use Excel's Office Assistant to learn more about custom number formats:

1. Press F1 to open the Office Assistant.
2. In the text box, key **Tell me about custom number formats**
3. Click Search and a list of topics appears.
4. Click "Custom number, date, and time format codes." Notice that the Microsoft Excel Help dialog box opens with information about custom number formats.

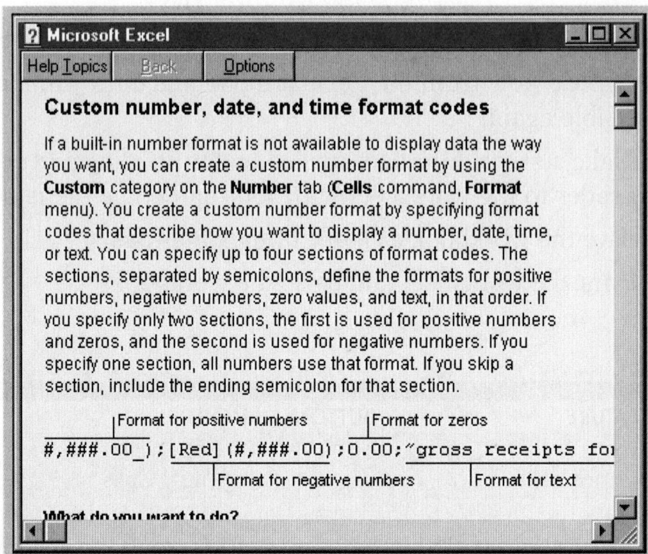

FIGURE 8-10 Microsoft Excel Help dialog box with information on custom numbers

5. Close Help when you finish learning about these formats and close the Office Assistant.

Concepts Review

TRUE/FALSE QUESTIONS

Each of the following statements is either true or false. Indicate your choice by circling T or F.

T F *1.* The default format for numbers is left-aligned, 12-point Palatino.

T F *2.* You cannot insert dashes in custom number formats.

T F *3.* A pound sign in a number format code represents an integer or a whole number.

T F *4.* When you use the Suppress the Display of Zeros option, you can see zeros on an onscreen worksheet but cannot print them.

T F *5.* To center the title of a worksheet over all its columns, you use [button].

T F *6.* A forced movement of the cursor to the next line down within the cell is called a line break.

T F *7.* You can use the mouse to increase column width to display text that doesn't fit in the current column.

T F *8.* You can hide rows or columns temporarily so they do not appear on the screen or print.

SHORT ANSWER QUESTIONS

Write the correct answer in the space provided.

1. What are the keystrokes to open the Format Cells dialog box?

___

2. What do you call Excel's ability to internally store the number you key in a cell and then use this number in calculations?

___

3. Under what menu do you access the Columns cascading menu?

___

4. If you want to align text to the right in a cell, which button do you use?

___

5. What are the keystrokes to create a line break in a cell?

____

6. Which check box do you click to suppress the display of zero values?

____

7. On which toolbar is [icon] located?

____

8. To rotate text in a cell, which dialog box do you open?

____

CRITICAL THINKING

Answer these questions on a separate piece of paper. There are no right or wrong answers. Support your answer with examples from your own experience, if possible.

1. If you had to present a projected quarterly report of revenues in 1998, what components would you include? How would you align various components in the report? Why?
2. You can change the column width and row height in Excel three different ways—using the mouse, with dialog boxes, or using the AutoFit option. Which approach do you prefer? Describe instances of using each option in the same worksheet.

Skills Review

EXERCISE 8-15

Format numbers.

1. Open the file **Employee.xls**.
2. Apply the first currency number format to column D by performing the following steps:
   - *a.* Select the values in column D.
   - *b.* Press Ctrl+1.
   - *c.* Click the Number tab, if necessary.
   - *d.* Select Currency from the Category list.

e. Select None for Symbol.

f. Click OK.

3. Precede the numbers in column B with the abbreviation "No." by completing the following steps:

a. Select the values in column B.

b. Press Ctrl+1.

c. Select Custom from the Category list.

d. Click the 0.00 format.

e. Delete the period in the format code of the Type text box.

f. Add three zeros to the format code. Key **No.** and a space enclosed in quotation marks in front of the six zeros.

g. Click OK.

4. Format the numbers in column C to appear as Social Security numbers.

a. Select the values in column C.

b. Open the Format Cells dialog box.

c. Select Special from the Category list.

d. Select Social Security Number.

e. Click OK.

5. Delete row 2.

6. Add the standard header to the worksheet with your name, the filename, and the date.

7. Horizontally center the worksheet.

8. Save the workbook as *[your initials]***8-15.xls**.

9. Print the worksheet and close the workbook.

EXERCISE 8-16

Suppress the display of zero values and work with stored numbers.

1. Open the file **Sales.xls**.

2. Suppress zeros in the worksheet by completing the following steps:

a. Choose Options from the Tools menu.

b. Click the View tab.

c. Click Zero values to deselect it.

d. Click OK.

3. Change the total in column C to reflect the correct total for the column. (It is now being calculated using full precision.) Use the Precision as Displayed option by completing the following steps:

a. Choose Options from the Tools menu.

b. Click the Calculation tab.

c. Click Precision as displayed to select it.

d. Click OK.

e. Click OK when the prompt appears that describes how the data will permanently lose its accuracy.

4. Add the standard header to the worksheet with your name, the filename, and the date.
5. Save the workbook as *[your initials]***8-16.xls**.
6. Print the worksheet and close the workbook.

EXERCISE 8-17

Align text and change column width and row height.

1. Open the file **States.xls**.
2. Center "Clearey & Clayton Sales Comparison" over columns A through F by doing the following:

   a. Select cells A1 through F1.

   b. Click [Merge and Center button].

3. Key **Please note that this is for the sale of tents only** in cell A12 and make the text wrap in the cell by completing the following steps:

   a. Key the text in cell A12 and press Enter.

   b. Select cell A12.

   c. Press Ctrl+1 to open the Format Cells dialog box.

   d. Click the Alignment tab.

   e. Click Wrap text.

   f. Click OK.

4. Change the width of column F using the AutoFit option by double-clicking with the two-headed arrow on the divider line between columns F and G in the lettered gray area that frames the worksheet.
5. Change the width of column A using the mouse by completing the following steps:

   a. With the two-headed arrow, drag the right border of column A just past the "o" in "Mexico."

   b. Release the mouse button.

6. Change the height of row 12 by dragging the bottom border of the row up with the two-headed arrow to approximately 60.75.

7. Add the standard header to the worksheet with your name, the filename, and the date.
8. Horizontally center the worksheet.
9. Save the workbook as *[your initials]***8-17.xls**.
10. Print the worksheet and close the workbook.

EXERCISE 8-18

Hide and unhide columns and rows.

1. Open the file **Clearey.xls**.
2. Hide column C by performing the following steps:
   a. Select column C.
   b. Choose Column from the Format menu to open the Column cascading menu.
   c. Choose Hide.
3. Hide row 5 by completing the following steps:
   a. Select row 5.
   b. Choose Row from the Format menu to open the Row cascading menu.
   c. Choose Hide.
4. Hide row 4.
5. Insert five rows after the entry "Hankle, Michele" and key the information shown in Figure 8-11 in columns A and B.

FIGURE 8-11

Jenkins, Ross	125,950
Latham, Mary	256,857
Norton, Marie	301,205
Peters, Joanne	187,500
Ravin, Mike	99,500

6. Hide rows 11 and 12.
7. Unhide rows 4 and 5 by completing the following steps:
   a. Select rows 3 through 6 using Shift.
   b. Choose Row from the Format menu.

   c. Choose Unhide from the Row cascading menu.

8. Add the standard header to the worksheet with your name, the filename, and the date.

9. Horizontally center the worksheet on the page.

10. Save the workbook as *[your initials]***8-18.xls**.

11. Print the worksheet and close the workbook.

Lesson Applications

EXERCISE 8-19

Hide a column, format numbers, and change column width and row height.

Clearey & Clayton likes to keep the phone numbers and Social Security numbers of its employees in a separate list. Format the following worksheet for readability and apply phone number and Social Security formatting.

1. Open the file **Employee.xls**.
2. Hide column B.
3. Clear column D and key the text shown in Figure 8-12, including the corrections, beginning in cell D3.

FIGURE 8-12

Phone (bf)

9085515532 (tr)

9085553474

~~9085551234~~

9085559002 (tr)

9085556453

9085550984

9085589 34 (54)

9085559342

~~9085550902~~

9085550221

~~9085555553~~

809555124 (98, 5)

908555 6486

4. Format the numbers in column C as Social Security numbers and the numbers in column D as phone numbers with the area code enclosed in parentheses.
5. Use the AutoFit option to change the width of columns C and D as necessary.
6. Increase the height of rows 4 through 13 to 18 points.
7. Center the headings in cells C3 and D3.
8. Add the standard header to the worksheet with your name, the filename, and the date.
9. Horizontally center the worksheet.
10. Save the workbook as *[your initials]***8-19.xls**.
11. Print the worksheet and close the workbook.

EXERCISE 8-20

Suppress the display of zero values, format numbers, hide rows, work with stored numbers, and align text.

Bettina Clearey would like a printout of sales amounts for tents and kayaks for the first four months of the year. Format the worksheet to remove the extra months and have the numbers represent sales amounts with rounded-off column totals.

1. Open the file **Kayaks.xls**.
2. Suppress the zeros found in column E and hide rows 8 through 17.
3. Format cells B4 through E7 to have no dollar signs.
4. Format the Totals row as accounting, with a leading dollar sign but no decimal places.
5. Change the amount in cell B5 to **30,056.95**, the amount in cell B6 to **34,677.55**, and the amount in cell B7 to **$458.65**.
6. Correct the total for column B. (Use the Precision as Displayed option.)
7. Right-align the column headings in B3 through E3.
8. Key the title **Tents and Kayaks** in cell A1, make it bold, and center it over the worksheet columns.
9. Add the standard header to the worksheet with your name, the filename, and the date.
10. Horizontally center the worksheet.
11. Save the workbook as *[your initials]***8-20.xls**.
12. Print the worksheet and close the workbook.

EXERCISE 8-21

Align text, format numbers, change column width and row height, suppress the display of zero values, and hide rows.

Clearey & Clayton also sells chairs for camping. Format the worksheet to show the sales figures and totals for January through April for their five best-selling chairs. Resize rows and columns and add a worksheet title and column headings for readability.

1. Open the file **Monthly.xls**.
2. Key the titles **Clearey & Clayton** in cell A1 and **Monthly Sales of Camp Chairs** in cell A2. Center these titles over the entire worksheet without merging the cells and make them bold.

TIP: Put each line of the title in its own row in the first cell of the row, and align the entire title at the same time.

3. Enter the following data as column headings over columns B through E: **Ultimate** **Rester Chair** **Travel Chair** **Crazy Chair**
4. Format the headings in columns B through F for word wrap and center-align them vertically and horizontally.
5. Center-align column A vertically.
6. Format the sales figures as currency without dollar signs or decimals.
7. Use the AutoFit feature to adjust the width of the Totals column.
8. Adjust the height of row 5 to put additional space between the column headings and the data that follows them.
9. Suppress the display of zeros for months that have no data.
10. Hide the rows for months that have no data and the blank row above the totals.
11. Add the standard header to the worksheet with your name, the filename, and the date.
12. Save the workbook as *[your initials]***8-21.xls**.
13. Print the worksheet and close the workbook.

EXERCISE 8-22

Change column width and row height, hide columns and rows, format numbers, suppress the display of zero values, and align text.

At the beginning of each quarter, Bettina Clearey likes to see comparisons of the present year's last quarter versus the same quarter for the previous year for each member of the sales force. She also wants to see bonus amounts included in the sales figures.

1. Create a spreadsheet sketch that includes a worksheet title, row and column labels, and an area for data and formulas. The worksheet should include each member of the sales force (rows). The information for each sales person (columns) should include 1st Quarter 1996 sales, 1st Quarter 1997 sales, the Change between the two quarters, their 1996 Bonus, and a cell for Notes. (*Hint:* Use abbreviations for the quarterly headings.) Use a formula to compute the difference between the most recent quarter and the previous quarter.
2. Transfer the sketch into Excel by keying the labels and formatting them. Then key the data from Figure 8-13 in the worksheet with the values formatted in comma style, no decimals.

FIGURE 8-13

	Title	Q1-1996	Q1-1997	Bonus
Adams, John	Marketing Rep	78,655	80,066	0
Christian, Susan	Sales Mgr	46,098	45,001	500
Clayton, John	Marketing Rep	22,099	23,046	0
Clearey, Bettina	Sales Mgr	77,988	77,649	0
Delaney, George	Sales Mgr	79,988	78,098	900
Gilbertson, Sam	Sales Mgr	91,434	91,938	900
Hankie, Michele	Marketing Rep	56,987	55,875	0
Walker, Jim	Marketing Rep	45,324	44,654	0
Williamson, Lee	Sales Mgr	76,909	77,988	900

3. Use AutoFit to adjust all the columns in a single step.
4. Hide the "Title" column.
5. Set the height of the rows containing the names of the salespeople to approximately 20 points.
6. Adjust the row height of the column headings to approximately 30 points and center their contents vertically.

7. Using the mouse, widen each column individually to make it easier to read.
8. Format all values as comma style with no decimal places displayed and with negative numbers displayed in red within parentheses.
9. Format the values in the "Bonus" column as currency with dollar signs and no decimal places, using the shortcut menu.
10. Suppress the zeros in the worksheet. Set the cells in the "Notes" column for Wrap Text.
11. In the "Notes" cell for John Adams, key **Best improvement over last year**. Adjust row height and column width so the note wraps to three lines.
12. Right align the column headings for all columns containing numeric data. Center the title and subtitle over the worksheet.
13. Rename Sheet1 **Sales** and rename Sheet2 **User Information**
14. In the User Information worksheet, create documentation that includes the following: File Information (Created by, Date created, Date revised, Revised by, Contact for help); Purpose of spreadsheet (paragraph form); Instructions to User (special instructions needed by user to enter data correctly). Style the documentation for easy reading.
15. Add the standard header including your name, the filename, and the date to both worksheets, center the worksheets horizontally on the page, and turn on the gridlines for the Sales worksheet.
16. Save the workbook as *[your initials]***8-22.xls**.
17. Print the workbook and create a standard formula printout using landscape orientation with gridlines and row and column headings.
18. Close the workbook without saving.

Changing Fonts, Patterns, Colors, and Formats

OBJECTIVES

After completing this lesson, you will be able to:

1. Work with fonts.
2. Add borders.
3. Use patterns and colors.
4. Color borders.
5. Copy cell formatting.
6. Work with styles.

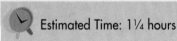

Estimated Time: 1¼ hours

You can enhance the appearance of a worksheet by changing fonts and point size, adding borders and shading, and coloring cell borders. After you make such changes to one cell, you can copy the format to other cells. You can also create a style and apply it to one or several cells.

Working with Fonts

A *font* is a type design applied to an entire set of characters, including all letters of the alphabet, numerals, punctuation marks, and other keyboard symbols. Fonts can be plain like Arial (Excel's default font) or ornate like Times New Roman.

FIGURE 9-1 Examples of fonts

ABCDEFGHIJKLMNOPQRSTUVWXYZ
abcdefghijklmnopqrstuvwxyz
1234567890!@#$%

Times New Roman

ABCDEFGHIJKLMNOPQRSTUVWXYZ
abcdefghijklmnopqrstuvwxyz
1234567890!@#$%

Courier New

ABCDEFGHIJKLMNOPQRSTUVWXYZ
abcdefghijklmnopqrstuvwxyz
1234567890!@#$%

Arial

TIP: There are two types of fonts available: TrueType fonts and PostScript fonts. For PostScript fonts to print correctly, you must have a PostScript printer. If you don't have one or are unsure of your printer set-up, select TrueType fonts so your workbook prints as it appears on your screen. (TrueType fonts have TT beside them in the Font drop-down list that you use in the first exercise.)

Fonts are also available in a variety of sizes, which are measured in points to give the *point size* of the font. There are 72 points to an inch. Like other character formatting, you can use different fonts and font sizes in the same document.

FIGURE 9-2 Examples of different point sizes

Excel provides two ways to choose fonts and font size:

- Formatting toolbar
- Font dialog box

EXERCISE 9-1 Choose Fonts and Font Size Using the Formatting Toolbar

The easiest way to choose fonts and font sizes is with the Formatting toolbar. You can also apply bold, italic, and underlining to worksheet data from the Formatting toolbar.

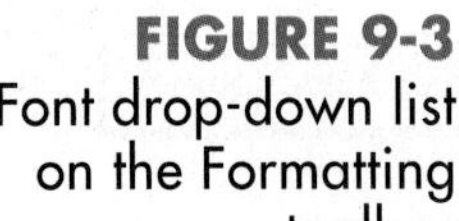

FIGURE 9-3
Font drop-down list on the Formatting toolbar

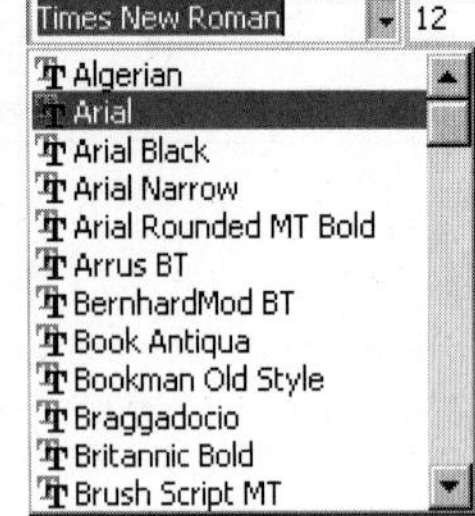

1. Open the file **Order.xls**.
2. Select cells A1 through A2.
3. Click the down arrow in the Font box on the Formatting toolbar to open the drop-down list. Scroll up and choose the font Arial.
4. To apply bold formatting to the worksheet title, click the Bold button **B** on the Formatting toolbar while cells A1 and A2 are still selected. The title becomes boldface Arial.

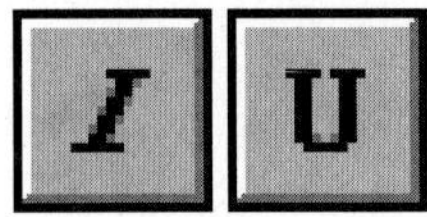

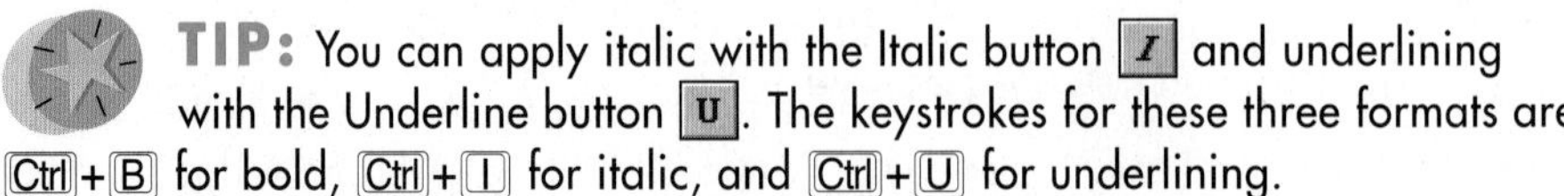

TIP: You can apply italic with the Italic button *I* and underlining with the Underline button U. The keystrokes for these three formats are Ctrl+B for bold, Ctrl+I for italic, and Ctrl+U for underlining.

5. To change the font size, with cells A1 and A2 still selected, click the down arrow to open the Font Size drop-down list and choose 14 point. The first two rows stand out as worksheet titles.

FIGURE 9-4
Changing font size from the Font Size drop-down list

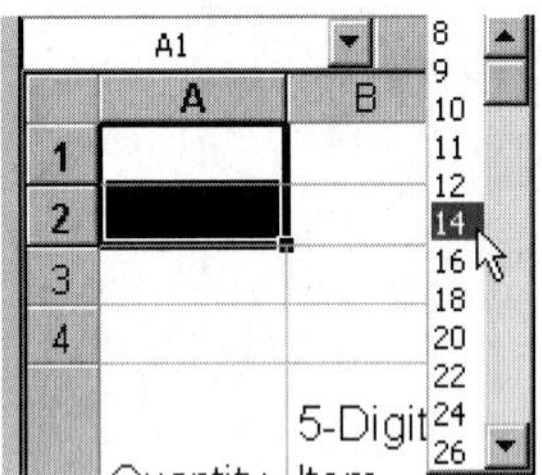

TIP: It's a good idea to use plain fonts such as Arial and Helvetica (if it is available). Good worksheet design uses the same font throughout, changing the font size or adding italic when needed. If you want to use a more ornate font, choose a font such as Times New Roman.

EXERCISE 9-2 Choose a Font and Font Size Using the Format Cells Dialog Box

The Font options in the Format Cells dialog box give you a wider variety of options than are available on the Formatting toolbar. You can preview the options as you choose them. You can even apply formatting to selected text within a cell.

1. Select rows 5 through 17.
2. Open the Format Cells dialog box. (Press Ctrl+1 or choose Cells from the Format menu.)
3. Click the Font tab, if necessary.
4. Use the arrow to scroll down under the Font list box.
5. Choose Times New Roman.

6. Choose Regular under the Font Style list box. (The font appears without formatting such as bold or italic.) The Preview box displays the font size and style you select.

NOTE: You can change the font size by selecting a different point size under Size. For this worksheet, leave the font size at 12 points.

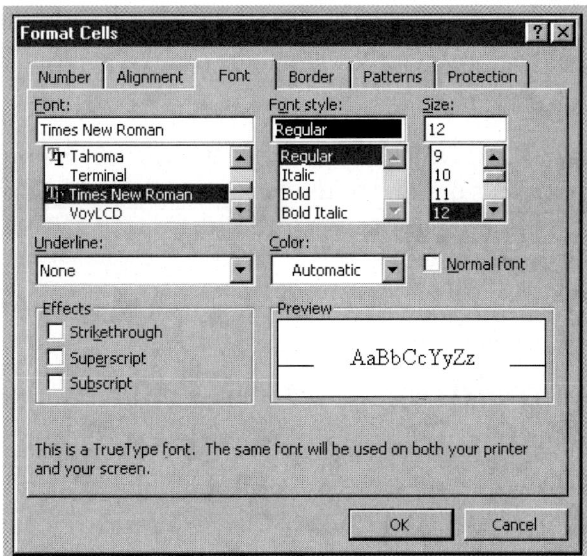

FIGURE 9-5
Changing the font with the Font options in the Format Cells dialog box

7. Click OK. The rows are formatted for 12-point Times New Roman. Next, you change the font of selected characters in a cell.
8. Select cell C5.
9. Select the text "1st Choice" in the Formula Bar by dragging across it with the mouse.
10. Choose Cells from the Format menu. The Format Cells dialog box is displayed.
11. Choose a Font Style of Bold Italic and click OK. The selected text in C5 changes. Select any cell in the worksheet to show the new formatting in the cell. Note that you can also format selected characters in a cell as you enter them by choosing Format, Cells from the menu.
12. Use [Undo] to restore the selected text to its previous format.

TIP: You can use the Font options in the Format Cells dialog box to underline, color, and create character effects. Choose some of these options and apply them to the text in one of the cells. Make sure you press Ctrl+Z to undo the formatting.

Adding Borders

You can add borders to the right, left, top, or bottom of a cell, to each cell in a range of cells, or around any group of cells for an outline effect. Borders can add emphasis and make a worksheet easier to read or understand. Cells share borders, so adding a border to the bottom of cell A1 has the same effect as adding a border to the top of cell A2.

Excel provides two ways to add borders to a selected cell or cells:

- Use the Format Cells dialog box.
- Use [Borders button].

You already learned to apply simple bottom borders using [Borders button] in Lesson 3. Using the Border options in the Format Cells dialog box, you have additional options, such as a wider variety of border line weights and border colors that you apply in Exercise 9-8.

EXERCISE 9-3 Add Borders to Cells

1. Select cells A15 through G15 and choose Cells from the Format menu.
2. Click the Border tab, if necessary. The Border options appear.

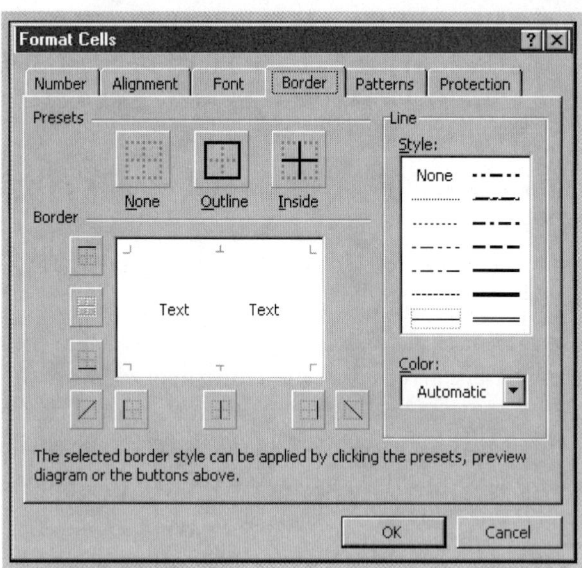

FIGURE 9-6 Border options in the Format Cells dialog box

3. Click the second darkest single-line border style (the fifth Line Style option on the right).

4. Click the top Border box and click OK.
5. Click anywhere in the worksheet to deselect the selection. Notice the rule that appears above row 15.
6. To add borders using [button], select cells A15 through B15.
7. Click the arrow to the right of [button] on the Formatting toolbar.
8. Click the border in the middle row, second from the left (the darker bottom border).
9. Select cell E15.
10. Click [button] and select None for borders (the top left choice). Select any other cell and notice that the top border disappears in cell E15. (You can also create this effect by selecting the bottom right box under Style in the Border options of the Format Cells dialog box.)

NOTE: Each border option adds borders to cells. When you select None from the border options, the border tool removes all borders from selected cells. The last border used is displayed in the button. You can select that border by clicking the button rather than the arrow.

EXERCISE 9-4 Add Gridline Borders to Cells

Gridlines are lines displayed on every border of a range of cells. The default is for gridlines to be displayed on the entire worksheet. You turn this option off and display borders for a range of selected cells. By removing gridlines around every cell and using them on only cells that need them, the worksheet looks cleaner and is easier to read.

1. Choose Options from the Tools menu.
2. Click the View tab, if necessary. The View options in the Options dialog box appears.
3. Click Gridlines to turn off gridlines.
4. Click OK. No gridlines appear in the worksheet.
5. Select cells A5 through G13.
6. Press Ctrl+1 to open the Format Cells dialog box.
7. Click the Border tab, if necessary.
8. To apply gridline borders to the cells, click Outline and Inside. Gridline borders appear around the selected cells. Then click OK, and select any cell to see the gridline borders. (See Figure 9-7 on the next page.)
9. Select cells F14 through G17.
10. Click the arrow to the right of [button].

FIGURE 9-7
Cells with gridlines

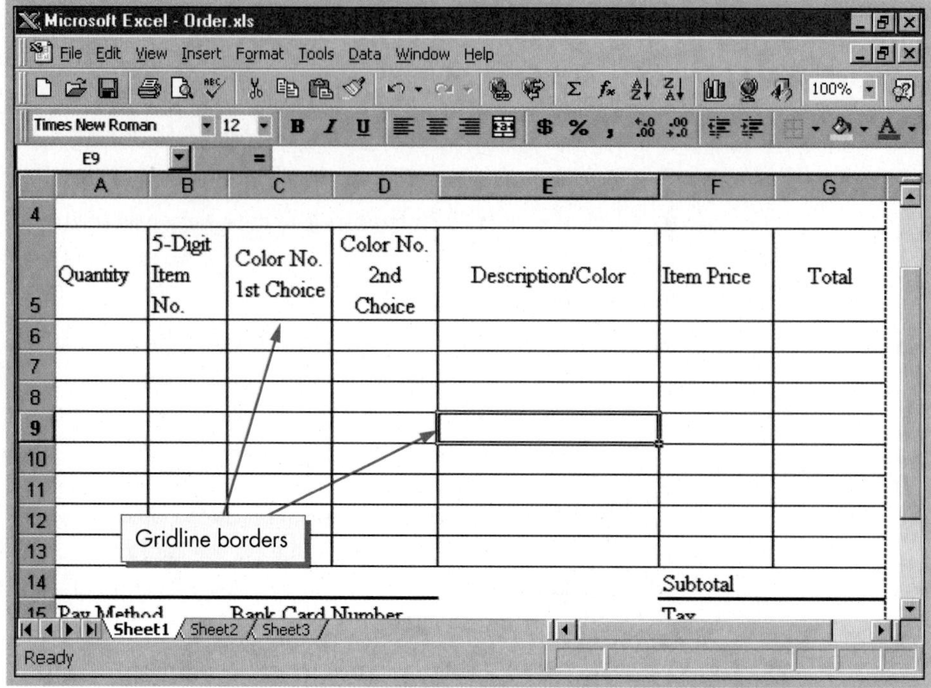

11. Click the gridline border (last row, second from the left). Gridline borders are added to the cells.

TIP: You can drag the  drop-down palette to any location on the worksheet for easy access when styling with borders.

EXERCISE 9-5 Outline Cells

You can outline any group of selected cells, placing a border on the outer edges of these cells.

1. Select cells A15 through B17.
2. Open the Format Cells dialog box.
3. Click the Border tab, if necessary.
4. Click Outline under Presets and click OK. The cells are outlined.

Using Patterns and Colors

You can shade cells with a variety of gray or colored patterns. You can also give cells a solid color. Patterns and colors can improve the appearance of a worksheet and make the data easier to read. It can also give the worksheet a more interesting appearance.

EXERCISE 9-6 Add a Shading Pattern

1. Select cells A5 through G5.
2. Press Ctrl+1 to open the Format Cells dialog box.
3. Click the Patterns tab, if necessary. The Patterns options appear.
4. Click the arrow in the Pattern box. A palette of patterns and colors appears.

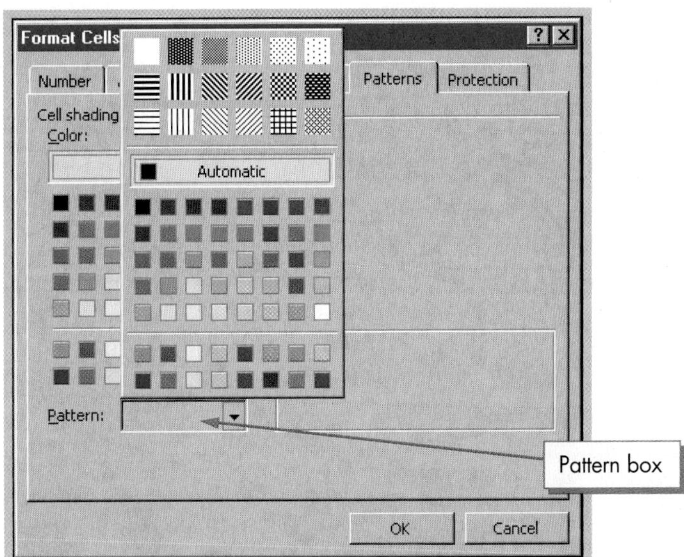

FIGURE 9-8 Pattern options in the Format Cells dialog box

5. Choose the 12.5% gray dotted pattern in the top row, second cell from the right and click OK. The cells contain a dotted pattern.
6. Open the Pattern options again. Click the arrow in the Pattern box to apply a color to the dotted pattern. (Cells A5 through G5 should still be selected.)
7. Choose Light Green (fifth row of colors, fourth cell from the left) and click OK. The pattern is made up of green dots.
8. Click **B**. Text usually looks better in bold against a shaded background.

EXERCISE 9-7 Add Background Colors

You can choose background colors for plain cells or cells with patterns. If you choose colors for cells with patterns, the color appears behind the pattern.

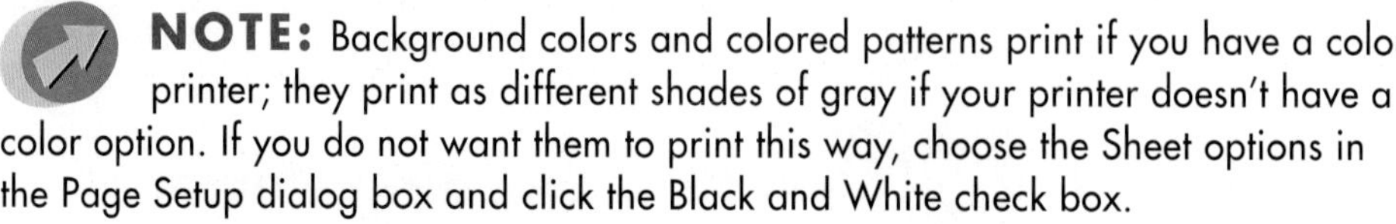

NOTE: Background colors and colored patterns print if you have a color printer; they print as different shades of gray if your printer doesn't have a color option. If you do not want them to print this way, choose the Sheet options in the Page Setup dialog box and click the Black and White check box.

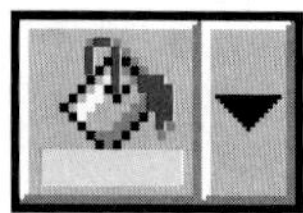

1. Select cells A1 through G2.
2. Click the arrow next to the Fill Color button on the Formatting toolbar.
3. Choose Turquoise (fourth row, fifth cell from the left). Select any other cell to see that the cells have a solid turquoise background.
4. Select cells F17 through G17.
5. Open the Format Cells dialog box.
6. Click the Patterns tab, if necessary.
7. Choose Yellow (fourth row, third cell from the left) from the Color box and click OK. Select any other cell to see that these cells are yellow.

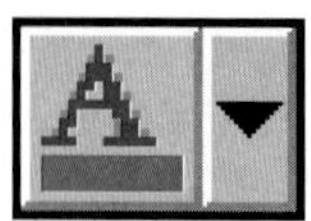

TIP: When you use dark colors or heavy shading patterns in cells, it can be hard to read the text. Either increase the font size, make text bold, or change the font to a light color or white with the Font Color button on the Formatting toolbar. Click the arrow next to the button to see the available font colors. Note, however, that some printers have trouble printing white text on black backgrounds.

Coloring Borders

Borders can also be colored. Colored gridlines draw attention to important areas of a worksheet.

EXERCISE 9-8 Color Cell Borders

1. Select cells C15 through D15.
2. Open the Format Cells dialog box.

3. Click the Border tab, if necessary.
4. Click the arrow under the Color box. The color palette opens.
5. Choose red from the color palette.
6. Click Outline to apply an outline around the cells.
7. Click the thickest border style and click OK. Select any other cell to see that the cells have a thick red outline.
8. Repeat this process for cells C16 through D16 and cells C17 through D17.

Copying Cell Formatting

You can copy the formatting of a cell, like its shading or color. Excel provides two ways to copy these characteristics:

- Use the Format Painter button on the Standard toolbar.
- Use the Copy and Paste Special options from the Edit menu.

EXERCISE 9-9 Use Copy and Paste Special

1. Select cells C15 through D17.
2. Choose Copy from the Edit menu or press Ctrl+C.
3. Select cells A15 through B17.
4. Choose Paste Special from the Edit menu. The Paste Special dialog box opens.
5. Click the Formats option button and click OK. Press Esc to turn off Paste Special. Select any other cell and notice that the cells A15 through B17 have a thick red outline.

TIP: You can also use Paste Special to copy formulas, values, notes, everything in the cell, or everything except the borders, as well as the formatting of a selected cell or cells.

EXERCISE 9-10 Use the Repeat Command

Once a cell is formatted, you can use the Repeat command on the Edit menu to apply the same format to another cell or range of cells. You can also use this command to repeat other procedures.

1. Select cells F14 through G14.

2. Apply the same yellow background color to these cells as the color in cell F17. (Use [Fill Color button] on the Formatting toolbar and select the yellow in the fourth row.)
3. Select cells F15 through G16.
4. Choose Edit, Repeat Format Cells from the menu to repeat the formatting. Select any other cell and notice that cells F15 through G16 have a yellow background.

TIP: The AutoFormat feature applies formatting automatically. When you click AutoFormat under Format, Excel applies a built-in set of formats to a selected range of cells. You can choose from 16 preset formats as well as options that can be turned off and on. It's a quick, easy, and fun feature to apply.

Working with Styles

A *style* is a set of formatting instructions that you can apply to the cells of a worksheet. Styles make it easier to apply formatting and ensure consistency of formatting throughout the worksheet.

In every workbook, Excel maintains a list of style names and their formatting specifications. Every workbook contains six predefined styles for numbers and text: Comma, Comma [0], Currency, Currency [0], Normal, and Percent. The first four styles are used for accounting formatting. You can apply these styles as they are, modify them, or create your own styles.

EXERCISE 9-11 Work with Styles

The default style for a workbook is called *Normal style*. Unless you change your system's default, Normal contains these formatting specifications: general Number format, 10-point Arial, general bottom-alignment, no borders, no shading, and no protection.

1. Key the items shown in Figure 9-9 in rows 6 through 8.

FIGURE 9-9

2	34521	Blue	Red	Sierra backpack	25
1	24375	Green	Brown	Round top	250
2	12432	Black	Blue	Kiowe	400

2. Select cells A6 through E6.
3. Choose Style from the Format menu. The Style dialog box opens.

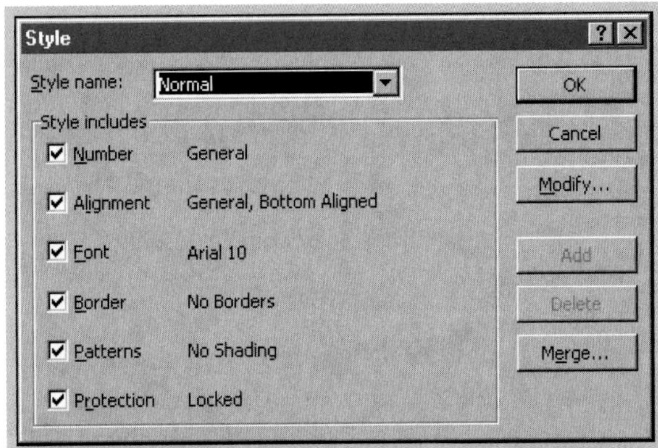

FIGURE 9-10
Style dialog box

4. Key **INVOICE** in all caps in the Style Name text box. The settings change to reflect the formatting of selected cells.
5. Click Modify to open the Format Cells dialog box.
6. Click the Font tab and change the Font to regular, 12-point Arial. Do not click OK yet.
7. Click the Alignment tab and choose Left Horizontal alignment.
8. Click OK. The settings beside the check boxes change.
9. Click Add to add the style to the style list and click OK. Notice that the cells are now left-aligned, 12-point Arial.

TIP: To create a style based on an example cell, select the cell that has the formatting you want in the style, open the Style dialog box, and key a new style name. You don't have to add it to the list. Just close the dialog box by clicking OK and the style becomes available for use in the workbook.

10. To apply the INVOICE style, select cells A7 through E8.
11. Open the Style dialog box.
12. Choose INVOICE from the Style Name drop-down list.
13. Click OK. The style is applied to these cells.
14. You can also delete unnecessary styles from the style list. Open the Style dialog box and choose Comma from the list of styles.
15. Click Delete and the style is removed from the list. Repeat this process for Comma [0], Currency, Currency [0], and Percent. Only the Normal and INVOICE styles remain in the list.
16. Add the standard header to the worksheet with your name, the filename, and the date.

17. Save the workbook as *[your initials]***9-11.xls**.
18. Print the worksheet and close the workbook.

COMMAND SUMMARY

FEATURE	BUTTON	MENU	KEYBOARD
Bold	B	Format, Cells	Ctrl+B
Italic	I	Format, Cells	Ctrl+I
Underline	U	Format, Cells	Ctrl+U
Add borders		Format, Cells	
Add outline border		Format, Cells	Ctrl+Shift+&
Remove all borders		Format, Cells	Ctrl+Shift+_
Add background color		Format, Cells,	
Copy cell formatting		Edit, Copy, Paste Special	
Repeat formatting		Edit, Repeat	Ctrl+Y

Concepts Review

TRUE/FALSE QUESTIONS

Each of the following statements is either true or false. Indicate your choice by circling T or F.

T F *1*. A font is a type design applied to an entire set of characters, excluding punctuation marks.

T F *2*. The easiest way to choose fonts is with the Formatting toolbar.

T F *3*. You can add borders to only the right and left sides of a cell.

T F *4*. You can copy cell formatting using Copy and Paste Special options.

T F *5*. You cannot outline any group of selected cells.

T F *6*. You cannot choose colors for cells with patterns.

T F *7*. You can add color to Borders.

T F *8*. A style is a set of formatting instructions that you can apply to text.

SHORT ANSWER QUESTIONS

Write the correct answer in the space provided.

1. What do you call a list of style names and their formatting specifications?

____

2. Which command do you use to repeat a command?

____

3. Where are Font options located?

____

4. What do you call lines on every border of a range of cells?

____

5. Where is [button] located?

____

6. What is the default font in Excel?

____

7. How many points are there in one inch?

____

8. Which button do you use to apply bold formatting to items in cells?

____

CRITICAL THINKING

Answer these questions on a separate piece of paper. There are no right or wrong answers. Support your answer with examples from your own experience, if possible.

1. You have just been given a spreadsheet that lists sales of all products made by the water ski company for which you work. You need to make certain areas of the worksheet stand out. The list needs to be printed and you do not have a color printer. How might you enhance these areas of the worksheet?
2. Excel provides many ways to use color in worksheets. Do you find that using color is helpful in drawing attention to a specific area? What colors look best to you? When do they become overwhelming?

Skills Review

EXERCISE 9-12

Work with fonts.

1. Open the file **Market.xls**.
2. Change the title in cells A1 through A3 to 16-point, bold Arial using the Formatting toolbar:
   a. Select cells A1 through A3.
   b. Click the arrow beside the Font box on the Formatting toolbar.
   c. Choose Arial from the drop-down list.
   d. Click the arrow beside the Font Size box.
   e. Choose 16.
   f. Click **B**.

3. Change the column titles to 14-point, italic Times New Roman using the Format Cells dialog box:
   a. Select cells A5 through C5.
   b. Open the Format Cells dialog box. (Press Ctrl+1.)
   c. Click the Font tab, if necessary.
   d. Choose Times New Roman under Font, Italic under Font Style, and 14 under Size.
   e. Click OK.
4. Change the font in rows 6 through 14 to Times New Roman.
5. Add the standard header to the worksheet with your name, the filename, and the date.
6. Save the workbook as *[your initials]***9-12.xls**.
7. Print the worksheet and close the workbook.

EXERCISE 9-13

Add borders and use patterns.

1. Open the file **Market2.xls**.
2. Turn off the display of gridlines. (Open the Options dialog box under the Tools menu, click the View tab, and deselect Gridlines.)
3. Add gridline borders to cells A5 through C14 using [Borders button]:
   a. Select cells A5 through C14.
   b. Click the arrow to the right of [Borders button].
   c. Choose gridline borders (third row, second from left).
4. Outline the worksheet title with a double-line border using the Format Cells dialog box:
   a. Select cells A1 through C3.
   b. Open the Format Cells dialog box. (Press Ctrl+1.)
   c. Click the Border tab, if necessary.
   d. Choose the double-line border.
   e. Choose Outline.
   f. Click OK.
5. Add a dotted yellow pattern to the title box:
   a. Select cells A1 through C3, if necessary.
   b. Open the Format Cells dialog box.
   c. Click the Patterns tab.
   d. Click the arrow in the Pattern box to open the Pattern palette.

e. Choose the 25% gray pattern (the fourth dotted pattern from the left in the top row).

f. Click the arrow in the Pattern box to open the Pattern palette again.

g. Choose yellow in the fourth row of colors.

h. Click OK.

6. Make the titles in A1 through A3 bold.
7. Add the standard header to the worksheet with your name, the filename, and the date.
8. Horizontally center the worksheet.
9. Save the workbook as *[your initials]***9-13.xls**
10. Print the worksheet and close the workbook.

EXERCISE 9-14

Color borders and copy cell formatting.

1. Open the file **Clearey2.xls**.
2. Color the border around the worksheet title blue:

a. Select cells A1 through C1.

b. Open the Format Cells dialog box.

c. Click the Border tab, if necessary.

d. Select the third thickest single-line border.

e. Click the arrow beside the Color box.

f. Choose the royal blue in the top row.

g. Choose Outline and click OK.

3. Copy the outline border color from the title to the column headings using Copy and Paste Special:

a. Select cells A1 through C1.

b. Click [Copy button].

c. Select cells A3 through C3.

d. Choose Paste Special from the Edit menu.

e. Select Formats and click OK.

4. Color the outline border around the rest of the worksheet, cells A4 through C13, using the same border format as in the previous steps.
5. Format the worksheet, except for the title, as left-aligned.
6. Add the standard header to the worksheet with your name, the filename, and the date.

7. Save the workbook as *[your initials]***9-14.xls**.
8. Print the worksheet and close the workbook.

EXERCISE 9-15

Work with styles.

1. Open the file **Months.xls**.
2. Key the text shown in Figure 9-11 in rows 13 through 15.

FIGURE 9-11

Oct	745	456	677
Nov	345	7465	3532
Dec	2456	5678	867

3. Create a style named "months" that is 12-point Times New Roman, center-aligned vertically, with a currency number format containing no "$" and no decimals:
   a. Open the Style dialog box under the Format menu.
   b. Key **months** for Style Name.
   c. Click Modify and click the Number tab.
   d. Choose Currency. Deselect $ and key **0** for Decimals.
   e. Click the Alignment tab.
   f. Select General under Horizontal, if necessary, and Center under Vertical.
   g. Click the Font tab.
   h. Choose Times New Roman, Regular, 12 point and click OK.
   i. Click Add and click OK.
4. Apply the style to rows 4 through 15:
   a. Select rows 4 through 15.
   b. Open the Style dialog box.
   c. Choose months from under Style Name.
   d. Click OK.
5. Delete rows 1 and 2.

6. Vertically center the headings and right-align the headings for columns B, C, and D.
7. Use AutoFit to adjust the widths of the columns.
8. Insert three blank rows at the top of the worksheet. In cell A1 key the title **Clearey & Clayton** and in cell A2 key **Top-selling Products**. Center the titles across the worksheet and format them in 14-point bold.
9. Add the standard header to the worksheet with your name, the filename, and the date.
10. Save the workbook as *[your initials]***9-15.xls**.
11. Print the worksheet and close the workbook.

Lesson Applications

EXERCISE 9-16

Work with fonts, add borders, and color borders.

A worksheet that gives a sales comparison for the years 1995, 1996, and 1997 in seven of Clearey & Clayton's biggest states is needed for a sales meeting next week. Format the worksheet so the printout of this comparison is attractive and easy to follow.

1. Open the file **States.xls**.
2. Use the Formatting toolbar to make the title 16-point, bold italic Arial.
3. Center the title over the columns and place a blue outline around it.
4. Increase column F using AutoFit, so the text fits in the column.
5. Apply a gridline border around cells A3 through F10 using ▦.
6. Delete column B and increase the size of column A using Best Fit.
7. Horizontally center the worksheet on the page and add the standard header to the worksheet with your name, the filename, and the date.
8. Save the workbook as *[your initials]***9-16.xls**.
9. Print the worksheet and close the workbook.

EXERCISE 9-17

Work with fonts, add borders, and use patterns and colors.

Nine of the top performers at Clearey & Clayton are monitored based on sales. Format this comparison of 1996 and 1997 sales in an easy-to-read worksheet for the Board of Directors meeting next month.

1. Open the file **Perform.xls**.
2. Change the title in the first row to 14-point, bold Arial.
3. Make the rest of the worksheet title 12-point, bold Arial.
4. Change the text in cells A5 through F14 to 12-point Times New Roman.
5. Place borders on the left, right, top, and bottom sides of cells A5 through F5.
6. Apply a gray pattern to these cells. (Make sure the pattern is light enough so you can see the text. Do not add a color background.)

7. Do the same for the worksheet title, but use green as the color. (Apply this pattern to cells A1 through F3.)
8. Give the column headings a yellow background using [Fill Color button]. (The colored pattern should remain in place.)
9. Increase the height of row 5 and center the text vertically.
10. Increase the width of column B so the worksheet title appears more evenly centered in the patterned area. Make sure the "Difference" column fits on page 1.
11. Add the standard header to the worksheet with your name, the filename, and the date.
12. Save the workbook as *[your initials]***9-17.xls**
13. Print the worksheet and close the workbook.

EXERCISE 9-18

Work with fonts, add borders, copy cell formatting, and use patterns and colors.

The New York and San Diego store locations of Clearey & Clayton are the company's largest. For this reason, the head office maintains a worksheet for each quarter's budget for these two stores. In the past, the format of the spreadsheet was dreary and hard to review. Change this worksheet and make the information easy to pick out.

1. Open the file **Budget.xls**.
2. Turn off the display of gridlines on the screen.
3. Change the font for the entire worksheet to 12-point Times New Roman.
4. Change the font in cells A1 and A2 to 14-point Times New Roman bold.
5. Add top and bottom borders to rows C4 through G4 and cells C6 through G6.
6. Copy the formatting of these rows using [Format Painter button] or Copy and Paste Special to the rows for "Equipment" and "Advertising" under the "New York, NY" section only.
7. Add a light shading pattern to cells C6 through G6, C8 through G8, and C10 through G10.
8. Enclose cells C4 through G18 in an outline.
9. Copy the format of cells C5 through G10 to cells C12 through G17.
10. Change cells C4 through G4 to bold with a turquoise background and right-align the headings over the columns.
11. Increase the width of the "Totals" column so it appears somewhat larger than columns D, E, and F.

12. Make the worksheet titles left-aligned.
13. Delete row 11 and increase the height of the new row 11 to slightly more than twice its current height.
14. Add the standard header to the worksheet with your name, the filename, and the date.
15. Save the workbook as *[your initials]***9-18.xls**.
16. Print the worksheet and close the workbook.

EXERCISE 9-19

Work with fonts, use patterns and colors, add borders, and work with styles.

One very important item to track is employee birthdays, especially since the company owners at Clearey & Clayton love to surprise employees with their favorite cake on or around the big day. Format the following worksheet so the birthdays are easier to read.

1. Create a worksheet sketch that includes a title, column labels, and an area for data. The worksheet should include each employee's name (rows) and a column for his or her birth date.
2. Transfer the sketch into Excel by keying the labels and formatting them. Then key the data from Figure 9-12 in the worksheet.

FIGURE 9-12

Adams, John	2/13/58
Bilton, Angela	12/23/52
Christian, Susan	4/28/58
Delaney, George	6/19/65
Gilbertson, Sammie	11/30/70
Hankle, Michele	8/12/63
Rishi, Joanie	3/10/59
Robertson, Bill	9/15/64
Walker, Idgi	7/19/70
Williamson, Lobella	6/23/71

3. Use AutoFit to adjust the width of the columns to an appropriate size.
4. Turn off the default display of gridlines. Change the font of the worksheet title, make it bold, and center the title across the worksheet.
5. Give the titles a simple patterned background and a light background color. (Do not create a colored pattern.)
6. Insert a blank row after the title. Make sure you clear the pattern and colors from the inserted row.
7. Place a left, right, and top border around the cells containing the column headings.
8. Create a style called "employee." Choose whatever font you like, but keep it 12-point, Regular. Make the text left-aligned with borders on the left, right, top, and bottom.
9. Left-align the column headings, if necessary, and make them bold.
10. Apply the "employee" style to the cells containing the employee names and their birth dates.
11. If necessary, change the font of the worksheet title to the same font as the "employee" style. Change the font size of the title to 14-point.
12. Add an outline border around the entire worksheet, including the titles. Adjust the column widths, if necessary, to make the data easier to read.
13. Rename Sheet1 **Birthdays** and rename Sheet2 **User Information**
14. In the User Information worksheet, create documentation that includes the following: File Information (Created by, Date created, Date revised, Revised by, Contact for help); Purpose of spreadsheet (paragraph form); Instructions to User (special instructions needed by user to enter data correctly). Style the documentation for easy reading.
15. Center the worksheet horizontally and add the standard header to the worksheet with your name, the filename, and the date.
16. Save the workbook as *[your initials]***9-19.xls**.
17. Print the worksheet and close the workbook.

Unit 3 Applications

APPLICATION 3-1

Format numbers, suppress the display of zero values, align text, change column width, and add a border.

John Clayton needs to construct a worksheet for the bank showing employee bonuses. He asked you to make the worksheet attractive.

1. Open the file **C&CBon.xls**.
2. Choose a currency format for columns B through E that does not have dollar signs, but does have decimal places.
3. Suppress zeros in the worksheet.
4. Left-align the text in cells A4 through A13 and center the worksheet title over the columns. Make the title bold.
5. Make the column headings bold and right-align the headings in columns B through E.
6. Use AutoFit to adjust all columns that need widening.
7. Delete row 2 and add a gridline border around the cells that contain data in the worksheet, including the title.
8. Turn off the default gridlines for viewing.
9. Add the standard header to the worksheet with your name, the filename, and the date.
10. Save the workbook as *[your initials]***u3-1.xls**.
11. Print the worksheet and close the workbook.

APPLICATION 3-2

Hide a column, color borders, use patterns and colors, change row height, and work with fonts.

John Clayton must include the first-quarter budget in a report he is presenting to the Board of Directors. He wants you to make the worksheet attractive.

1. Open the file **Budget2.xls**.
2. Hide column G.
3. Add a background color to the title of the worksheet. Make sure the title text is readable.

4. Add thick red top and bottom borders to the column heading row (cells A4 through H4).
5. Make the cell background a shaded blue pattern in the same row.
6. Make the background color in cells A5 through H18 the lightest green you can find.
7. Change the font size for the entire worksheet to 12 point.
8. Increase the height of row 4 and row 12 by about 50% of their current height.
9. Turn off default gridlines for viewing.
10. Right-align the column headings and make them bold.
11. Add the standard header to the worksheet with your name, the filename, and the date.
12. Save the workbook as *[your initials]***u3-2.xls**.
13. Print the worksheet and close the workbook.

APPLICATION 3-3

Work with fonts, add borders, color borders, format numbers, change column width and row height, and change alignment.

Bettina Clearey is meeting with an insurance salesperson. She wants to provide the agent with an attractive list of employee insurance plans.

1. Open the file **Insure.xls**.
2. Create a worksheet title and center it over the columns. Make it 16-point, bold Arial.
3. Add a thick blue outline around the title.
4. Format the policy numbers to have dashes after the first two numbers and after the next three numbers.
5. Increase the row height by slightly less than twice the current height for the rows containing the employee names and insurance information.
6. Make the column titles wrap to the next line and adjust the row height if you cannot read them now.
7. Left-align the employee names.
8. Increase the width of column D so the column heading fits and left-align the text in the column.
9. Vertically center the column headings.
10. Make sure a blank row appears between the title and the body of the worksheet.

11. Turn off gridlines for viewing.
12. Add the standard header to the worksheet with your name, the filename, and the date.
13. Save the workbook as *[your initials]***u3-3.xls**.
14. Print the worksheet and close the workbook.

APPLICATION 3-4

Work with fonts, copy cell formatting, work with styles, hide rows, and work with stored numbers.

John Clayton wants to show the sales force the monthly camp chair sales in an attractive worksheet format.

1. Open the file **Monthly2.xls**.
2. Create a worksheet title in 14-point, bold Arial and center it over the columns.
3. Enter the following data as headings over columns B through E:

   Ultimate   **Rester Chair**   **Travel Chair**   **Crazy Chair**
4. Copy the formatting in cell A5 to the rest of the month cells in column A.
5. Create a style named "new" based on cell B5. Change the number format to currency with no dollar signs and no decimal places. Change the alignment to right-aligned and create a green border similar to the one in cell A5.
6. Apply the "new" style to cells B5 through F16.
7. Hide rows 9 through 16.
8. Turn on the Precision as Displayed option to correct the total in column B.
9. Delete row 17. Copy the formatting in row 4 to the totals row.
10. Turn off the default display of gridlines.
11. Adjust the widths of columns B through E so all the headings display appropriately and right-align the column headings.
12. Add the standard header to the worksheet with your name, the filename, and the date.
13. Save the workbook as *[your initials]***u3-4.xls**.
14. Print the worksheet and close the workbook.

APPLICATION 3-5

Create a worksheet title; create column heads; choose fonts, font size, and font style; and use color backgrounds, borders, and shading.

Bettina Clearey needs to see the projections for 1998 for Clearey and Clayton's nine top-selling tents. Create a spreadsheet sketch that includes a worksheet title, column labels, and an area for data. The worksheet should list each tent (rows) and sales amounts (columns) for the years 1996, 1997, and 1998.

Transfer the sketch into Excel by keying in the labels and formatting them. Key the data in Figure U3-1 with corrections, in order from 1 to 9, as the body of the worksheet (do not key the numbers before the tent name). The number columns are for years 1996, 1997, and 1998.

Be creative in your use of fonts, colors, borders, and cell backgrounds. Make the worksheet as colorful and attractive as possible. Be sure to use colors that do not hide text. Make sure the worksheet is horizontally centered and add the standard header to the worksheet with your name, the filename, and the date.

Rename Sheet1 appropriately and rename Sheet2 User Information. In the User Information worksheet, create documentation that includes the following: File Information (Created by, Date created, Date revised, Revised by, Contact for help); Purpose of spreadsheet (paragraph form); Instructions to User (special instructions needed by user to enter data correctly). Style the documentation for easy reading. Save the workbook as *[your initials]***u3-5.xls**, and print and close the workbook.

FIGURE U3-1

1. Boston **blue** (not bold)	25380	37870	02500
3. Ylelow rover	16920	14320	15000
9. lockerZip Gray	58760	48760	550000
4. Purple ptite	7870	15130	a9500
7. *brown* baskin (ROM)	8320	9380	10000
6. S mall round	9960	178870	12000
2. Green moun(tain)	108920	78560	85000
8. Hikers nighlt	55850	77420	65000
5. Snow bound	78520	65900	60000

UNIT

4

Formula and Template Construction

Custom Boat Covers Keep Business Afloat

For over 40 years, the Dunkirk Canvas Company manufactured sails for boats. Facing increased competition, the company recently began making boat covers. They make covers to fit almost any boat manufactured in the U.S. Each boat cover is custom made, using a special computerized cloth-cutting machine that stores patterns and data about the amount of cloth used in a particular customer's boat cover.

Dunkirk was founded by Frank Bouchard and Mickey Finnegan. The company spent a considerable amount of money buying the cutting machine and is just beginning to see a profit on its boat cover operation. Sales volume has increased so much, however, that the company needs to use independent contractors to make some of its sails. This has caused the company to focus on automating some of its everyday business tasks.

In order to start automating the business records, the Dunkirk Canvas Company needs to produce:

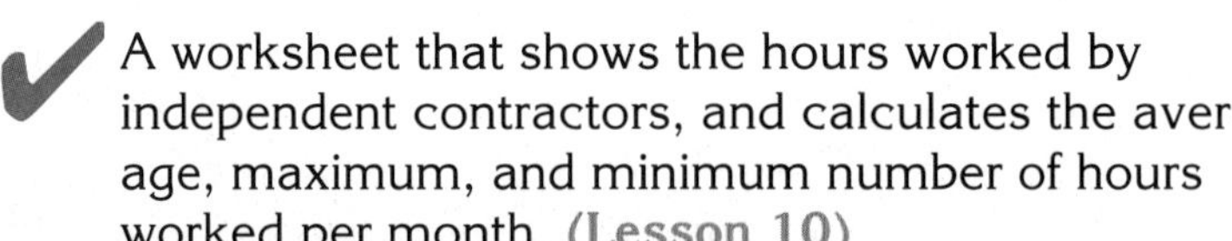

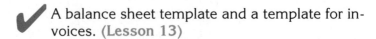

- ✔ A worksheet that shows the hours worked by independent contractors, and calculates the average, maximum, and minimum number of hours worked per month. **(Lesson 10)**
- ✔ Worksheets calculating commissions and markup for canvas goods, bonuses for sales reps, and the costs and prices of some of Dunkirk's products. **(Lesson 11)**
- ✔ Worksheets maintaining employee information and analyzing the present value of a business loan. **(Lesson 12)**
- ✔ A balance sheet template and a template for invoices. **(Lesson 13)**

Using Functions

OBJECTIVES

After completing this lesson, you will be able to:

1. **Enter functions.**
2. **Use the AVERAGE function.**
3. **Use the MIN and MAX functions.**
4. **Use the COUNT function.**
5. **Use the COUNTA function.**
6. **Use the INT and ROUND functions.**
7. **Use nested functions.**

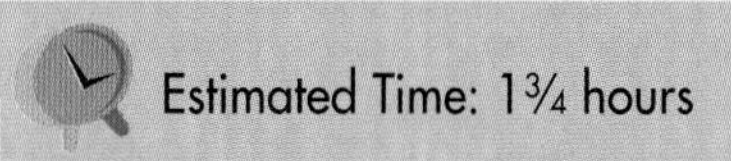

Functions are built-in formulas. Excel provides many functions besides the SUM function introduced in Lesson 2. The SUM function is a mathematical function. This lesson covers the statistical functions AVERAGE, MIN, MAX, COUNT, and COUNTA, as well as two additional mathematical functions, INT and ROUND.

Entering Functions

There are two ways to enter functions in your worksheets. You can key the formulas or use Paste Function. Using Paste Function is easier, but keying formulas helps you learn formula construction.

The values that a function operates on are called *arguments,* which are placed inside parentheses after the function name. A function's arguments can consist of:

- Constants (a number keyed directly in a formula)
- Cell references (such as A10 or A1:A10)
- Additional functions
- Defined names

To use a cell range as an argument, you separate the beginning and ending cell references with a colon. If the function takes more than one argument, the arguments are separated by commas. The value that the function returns is called the *result*.

NOTE: Functions used as arguments are discussed later in this lesson.

Using the AVERAGE Function

Use the AVERAGE function to calculate a mean. The arguments for this function can be cell references, defined names, or constants. For example, in the Dunkirk1 workbook, you track the hours contractors work for the Dunkirk Canvas Company. You could use the AVERAGE function to calculate the average hours worked per month by all contractors.

Use the format =AVERAGE(arguments). The arguments can be one or more cell ranges or constants for which you want to find the average. The AVERAGE function ignores:

- Text
- Blank cells (but not zeros)
- Error values
- Logical values (*logical values* are the values TRUE and FALSE, which are the result of formulas that use comparison operators such as = or >)

TABLE 10-1 Examples of the AVERAGE Function

FUNCTION	CELL DATA	RESULT
=AVERAGE(A1:A3)	A1=10, A2=20, A3=30	20
=AVERAGE(50,60)	(none)	55
=AVERAGE(A1,100)	A1=50	75
=AVERAGE(A1, B2, C1:C2)	A1=2, B2=2, C1=4, C2=4	3

EXERCISE 10-1 Use the AVERAGE Function

1. Open the file **Dunkirk1.xls**.
2. Select cell A15 and key **Average Hours:**
3. Select cell C15 and enter **=AVERAGE(C4:C13)**. Excel displays the error value #DIV/0!. Error values always start with the # symbol and indicate the formula contains some sort of problem. This error indicates there is no data in the specified range to calculate or that division by zero was attempted.

TIP: You can key formulas in lowercase letters for convenience. Excel converts the text to uppercase in the Formula Bar automatically.

4. Key the following data in column C, starting with cell C4:

   10
   N/A
   20
   10
   10
   20
   20
   0
   0
   0

   The result, 10.00, is displayed in cell C15. The cells with zeros are counted in the Average, while the cell containing "N/A" does not affect the average.
5. Compare your result to the result found with AutoCalculate by highlighting the range C4:C13. If the AutoCalculate area at the bottom of the screen does not show Average, click the AutoCalculate area with the right mouse button and select Average. The AutoCalculate value and the number in C15 should both be 10.00.
6. Copy the formula in cell C15 to cells D15 through F15.

Using the MIN and MAX Functions

Use the MIN and MAX functions to find the minimum and maximum values in a range of values. For example, in the Dunkirk1 worksheet, you can use the MIN and MAX functions to return the lowest and highest number of hours worked.

The MIN and MAX functions ignore:

- Text
- Blank cells (but not zeros)
- Error values
- Logical values (such as TRUE and FALSE)

Use the format =MIN(arguments) or =MAX(arguments). The arguments represent the values for which you want to find a minimum or maximum.

TABLE 10-2 Examples of the MIN and MAX Functions

FUNCTION	CELL DATA	RESULT
=MAX(A1:A3)	A1=10, A2=20, A3=30	30
=MAX(A1,B2,C3)	A1=3, B2=6, C3=10	10
=MIN(A1:A3)	A1=2, A2=20, A3=30	2
=MIN(-50,60)	(none)	-50
=MIN(A1,0)	A1=50	0
=MIN(A1,B5,C12)	A1=2, B5=20, C12=50	2

EXERCISE 10-2 Use the MIN Function

1. Select cell A16 and key **Least Hours Worked:**
2. Select C16 and key **=MIN(C4:C13)**
3. Copy the formula in cell C16 to cells D16 through F16.
4. Key the following data in column D, starting with cell D4 and leaving the second-to-last cell blank, as indicated:

   22
   19
   20
   N/A
   21
   20
   15
   30
   (blank)
   10

The results, 0.00 and 10.00, are displayed in cells C16 and D16, respectively. The MIN function ignores the blank cell, D12, and the cells with text, C5 and D7.

5. Select cell D12 and key **0**. That zero is now counted as the minimum value in the column and the result becomes 0.00.

EXERCISE 10-3 Use the MAX Function with Paste Function

In the previous exercises, you keyed the specified formulas. Now you use Paste Function to write the function for you.

1. Select cell A17 and key **Most Hours Worked:**
2. Select cell C17.

3. Click the Paste Function button or press the keys Shift + F3. The Paste Function dialog box appears.

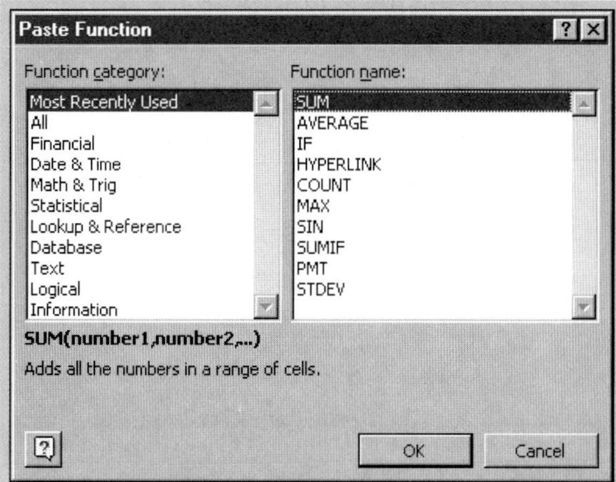

FIGURE 10-1 Paste Function dialog box

4. Choose Statistical from the Function category list box.
5. Choose MAX from the Function name list box.
6. Click OK. The MAX function is displayed in the Formula Bar and the Formula Palette pop-up window is displayed under the Formula Bar. Notice that the Formula Palette provides a text box for each MAX function argument. It describes the function and the text box for each of the function's arguments. You can key the cell reference, defined name, or a constant, click the cell location, or drag across multiple cells. (See Figure 10-2 on the next page.)
7. Key **C4:C13** in the Number1 argument box. As you key the arguments, the cell range is entered in the Formula Bar, the values of the cells are displayed in the text box to the right of the argument box, and the result of the function is displayed in the lower left corner of the Function Palette.

FIGURE 10-2
Function Palette for the MAX function

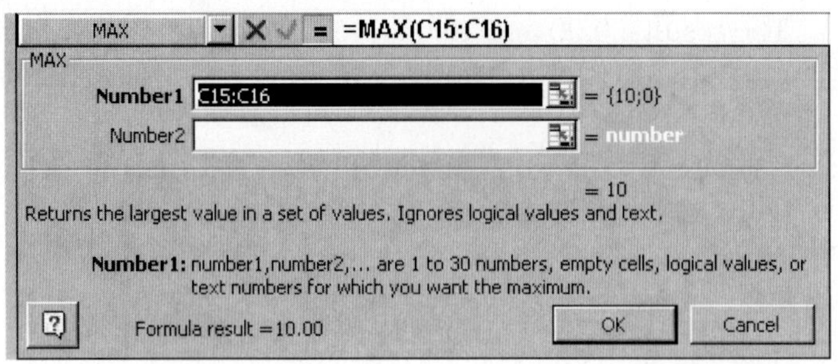

TIP: Instead of keying the cell range, you can move the pointer out of the dialog box and select the cell range in the worksheet by clicking and/or dragging.

8. Click OK.
9. Copy the formula in cell C17 to cells D17 through F17.
10. Key the following data in column E, starting with cell E4 and leaving the second-to-last cell blank, as indicated:

    N/A
    18
    20
    N/A
    21
    23
    19
    10
    (blank)
    10

    The results are displayed in cells C17, D17, and E17. The MAX function ignores the blank cell and the cells that contain text.

Using the COUNT Function

Use the COUNT function to count how many cells contain numbers within a specified range of cells. For example, you can use the COUNT function in the Dunkirk1 worksheet to count how many cells in C4 through C13 contain numbers.

The COUNT function ignores:

- Text
- Blank cells (but not zeros)

- Error values
- Logical values (such as TRUE and FALSE)

Use the format =COUNT(arguments), where the arguments refer to the values you want to count.

TABLE 10-3 **Examples of the COUNT Function**

FUNCTION	CELL DATA	RESULT
=COUNT(A1:A3)	A1 is blank, A2=40, A3=30	2
=COUNT(A1:A3)	A1=31, A2 is blank, A3=N/A	1
=COUNT(A1:A3)	A1=0, A2 is blank, A3=N/A	1
=COUNT(13,21,111)	(none)	3
=COUNT(A1, B2, C1:C2)	A1=2, B2=is blank, C1=4, C2=4	3

EXERCISE 10-4 Use the COUNT Function with Paste Function

1. Select cell A18 and key **Available Contractors:**
2. Select cell C18.
3. Click [fx] or choose Function from the Insert menu. The Paste Function dialog box appears.
4. Choose Statistical from the Function category list box.
5. Choose COUNT from the Function name list box.
6. Click OK. The Formula Palette pop-up window appears.
7. Key **C4:C13** in the Number1 argument box. The cell range is displayed in the Formula Bar and the values of the cells and the result of the function are displayed in the Formula Palette window.
8. Click OK.
9. Copy the formula in cell C18 to cells D18 through F18.
10. Key the following data in column F, starting with cell F4 and leaving the second-to-last cell blank, as indicated:

    20
    15
    15
    20
    N/A

22
N/A
10
(blank)
N/A

The result, 6, is displayed in cell F18. The COUNT function does not count the blank cell or the cells that contain text.

11. Highlight the range F4:F13 and use AutoCalculate, selecting Count Nums. The result should agree with the value in F18.

NOTE: Count Nums in AutoCalculate is the same as the COUNT function.

Using the COUNTA Function

Use the COUNTA function to count how many items are found in a range of cells. Unlike the COUNT function, COUNTA counts cells that contain text as well as cells that contain numbers.

The COUNTA function ignores:

- Blank cells (but not zeros)
- Error values
- Logical values (such as TRUE and FALSE)

Use the format =COUNTA(arguments), where the arguments refer to the values you want to count.

TABLE 10-4 Examples of the COUNTA Function

FUNCTION	CELL DATA	RESULT
=COUNTA(A1:A3)	A1 is blank, A2=40, A3=30	2
=COUNTA(A1:A3)	A1=31, A2=40, A3=N/A	3
=COUNTA(A1:A3)	A1=0, A2 is blank, A3=N/A	2
=COUNTA(A1, B2, C1:C2)	A1=2, B2=is blank, C1=N/A, C2=4	3

EXERCISE 10-5 Use the COUNTA Function

1. Select cell A19 and key **Total Contractors:**

2. Widen column A to accommodate row headings in rows 15 through 19. Do not use Best Fit.
3. Select cell B19 and enter **=COUNTA(B4:B13)**. The COUNTA function counts all the cells that contain text. The result is 10.
4. Copy the formula in cell B19 to cells C19 through F19. The COUNTA function counts text and numbers, but not blank cells.
5. Center the worksheet and add the standard header to the worksheet with your name, the filename, and the date.
6. Save the workbook as *[your initials]***10-5.xls**.
7. Print the worksheet and close the workbook.

FIGURE 10-3
Worksheet with functions entered

F19 = =COUNTA(F4:F13)

	A	B	C	D	E	F	G	H
6	Callahan	Linda	20.00	20.00	20.00	15.00		
7	Kramer	Paul	10.00	N/A	N/A	20.00		
8	Ledder	Sam	10.00	21.00	21.00	N/A		
9	Michals	Mark	20.00	20.00	23.00	22.00		
10	Michals	Bruce	20.00	15.00	19.00	N/A		
11	Openheimer	James	0.00	30.00	10.00	10.00		
12	Smith	Tina	0.00	0.00				
13	Wallace	Michael	0.00	10.00	10.00	N/A		
14								
15	Average Hours:		10.00	17.44	17.29	17.00		
16	Least Hours Worked:		0.00	0.00	10.00	10.00		
17	Most Hours Worked:		20.00	30.00	23.00	22.00		
18	Available Contractors:		9	9	7	6		
19	Total Contractors:	10	10	10	9	9		

Dunkirk1

Ready | Count Nums=1 | CAPS

Using the INT and ROUND Functions

Sometimes the numbers that Excel uses in its calculations do not match the numbers displayed. This discrepancy occurs because Excel stores the full number of decimals keyed or calculated for a cell, even if the cell is formatted for rounded values. For example, if you key 3.569 in a cell formatted for two decimal places, the cell displays 3.57. In calculations, however, Excel uses the full precision, 3.569. You can use the INT (integer) and ROUND functions to control the amount of precision that Excel uses in calculations.

Use the INT function to round a number down to the nearest integer. For example, the INT function rounds 2.99 to 2. Use the format =INT(number), where (number) is the value you want to round down to the nearest integer.

TABLE 10-5 Examples of the INT Function

FUNCTION	CELL DATA	RESULT
=INT(9.7)	(none)	9
=INT(B20)	B20 = -9.7	-10
=INT(A1)	A1 = 100.55	100

Use the ROUND function to round a number to a specified number of decimal places.

Use the format =ROUND(number, num_digits), where number is the number you want to round and num_digits is the number of decimal places to which you want to round the number.

- If num_digits is greater than 0, the number rounds to the specified number of decimal places.
- If num_digits is 0, the number rounds to the nearest integer.
- If num_digits is less than 0, the number rounds to the specified number of places to the left of the decimal point.

TABLE 10-6 Examples of the ROUND Function

FUNCTION	CELL DATA	RESULT
=ROUND(1.55,1)	(none)	1.6
=ROUND(A1,0)	A1=1.55	2
=ROUND(100.55,-1)	(none)	100
=ROUND(-1.555,B10)	B10 = -2	0

EXERCISE 10-6 Use the INT Function

1. Open the file **Dunkirk2.xls**.
2. Select cell E4 and enter **=INT(B4)**. The result is 0.
3. Go to the Formula Bar and edit the formula by adding ***D4** after the ending parenthesis. The result is still 0.
4. Key the following data in column B, beginning in cell B4:

   5.22
   5.52

6.23
6.42
6.86

5. Copy the formula in cell E4 to cells E5 through E8. The INT function in the formula rounds down the column B values to the nearest integer, providing a whole number in column E. The result in E4 is 135.

EXERCISE 10-7 Use the ROUND Function

1. Select cell F4 and enter **=ROUND(C4*D4,0)**. The result is (zero).

TIP: A quick way to ensure that you include all required arguments and parentheses when you enter a function manually is to press Ctrl+Shift+A after you type the equal sign and function name. These keystrokes automatically insert the argument names and parentheses.

2. Key the following data in column C, beginning with cell C4:

5.09
5.45
6.14
6.23
6.51

Excel rounds the total to the nearest integer.

3. Copy the formula in cell F4 to cells F5 through F8. Format cells F4:F8 in Accounting style with the $ symbol and no decimal places. Format D4:E8 in comma style with no decimal places.

FIGURE 10-4
Results of the ROUND function

F8 = =ROUND(C8*D8,)

	A	B	C	D	E	F
1	Dunkirk Canvas Co. - Material Order List					
2						
3	Material	Weight in Lbs. Per Yard	Cost Per Yard	Quantity	Total Lbs.	Total Cost
4	Canvas 101	5.22	5.09	27	135	$ 137
5	Canvas 102	5.52	5.45	120	600	$ 654
6	Canvas 103	6.23	6.14	320	1920	$ 1,965
7	Canvas 104	6.42	6.23	220	1320	$ 1,371
8	Canvas 105	6.86	6.51	550	3300	$ 3,581
9						
10						

4. Center the worksheet and add the standard header to the worksheet with your name, the filename, and the date.
5. Save the workbook as *[your initials]***10-7.xls**.
6. Print the worksheet and close the workbook.

Using Nested Functions

A function used as an argument inside another function is called a *nested function*. Paste Function and the Formula Palette are especially useful for inserting nested functions. In the following exercise, you use nested functions to sum separate groups of items and then take an average of the two sums.

EXERCISE 10-8 Use Nested Functions

1. Open the file **Dunkirk3.xls**.
2. Select cell C8 and click [fx].
3. Choose Most Recently Used from the Function category list box.
4. Choose AVERAGE from the Function name list box. (If AVERAGE does not appear in this list, select the Statistical category to locate it.)
5. Click OK. The Formula Palette is displayed.
6. To insert a function as an argument, click the down arrow next to the Function box on the Formula Bar. A drop-down list is displayed. (The functions displayed in the drop-down list may differ from those shown.)

FIGURE 10-5 Function box drop-down list

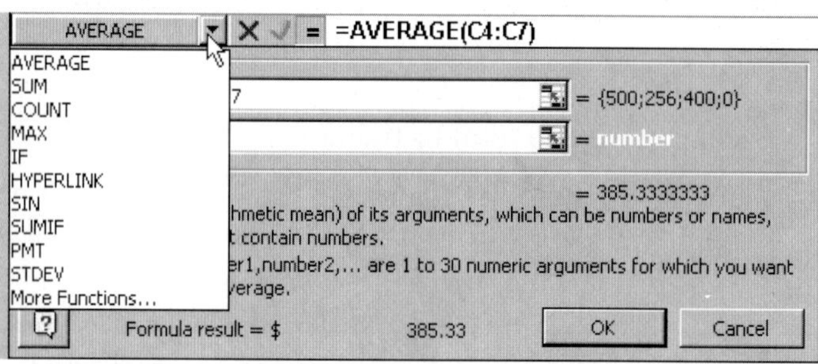

7. Choose SUM. The Formula Bar now shows the argument of the AVERAGE function as a nested SUM function.
8. Key B4:B6 in the Number1 argument box.
9. Click the word AVERAGE in the formula in the Formula Bar so you can continue entering arguments for the AVERAGE function. Notice that as you click on a function name in the Formula Bar, the function's arguments are displayed in the argument boxes in the Formula Palette.

NOTE: When a formula contains nested functions, the argument boxes displayed on the Formula Palette change to show which function is currently selected in the Formula Bar.

10. Click the Number2 argument box to insert another argument for the AVERAGE function.

11. Click the Function box, which now displays SUM. The Formula bar now shows a second argument for the AVERAGE function, which is another nested SUM function. Notice that you did not need to use the drop-down list to select the SUM function because the Function box automatically inserts the most recently used function.

12. Key **C4:C6** in the Number2 argument box and click OK.

FIGURE 10-6
Worksheet with nested functions

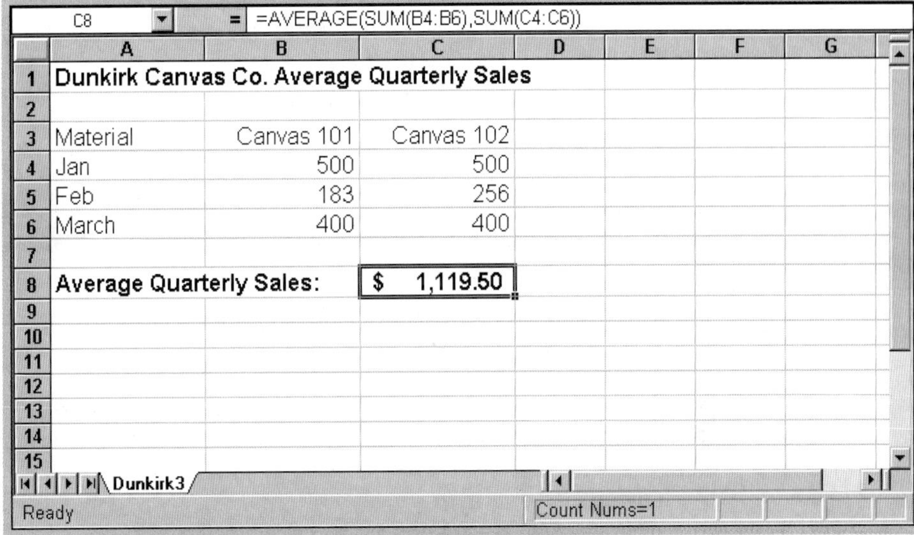

13. Add the standard header to the worksheet with your name, the filename, and the date.

14. Save the workbook as *[your initials]***10-8.xls**.

15. Print the worksheet and close the workbook.

TIP: You can use Paste Function to create and edit formulas that contain functions. To edit an existing formula containing a function, select the desired cell and click [fx]. Excel opens the Formula Palette. As you click each function name in the Formula Bar, the function's arguments appear in the argument boxes. Click OK to enter additional changes and to close the Formula Palette.

COMMAND SUMMARY

FEATURE	BUTTON	MENU	KEYBOARD
Paste Function	[fx]	Insert, Function	Shift+F3
Insert Arguments			Ctrl+Shift+A

USING HELP

This lesson introduced you to seven of Excel's built-in functions and Paste Function, which assists you in entering them. You can use Excel's on-line Help to learn more about specific functions and how to use them.

To view detailed information about an individual function, use on-line Help from the Paste Function dialog box:

1. Click [New] to open a new workbook.
2. Click [fx]. The Paste Function dialog box appears.
3. Choose Statistical from the Function category list box.
4. Choose COUNT from the Function name list box.
5. Click the Office Assistant button in the lower left corner of the dialog box.
6. In the Office Assistant balloon, click Help with this feature and then click Help on selected function.
7. Scroll through the Help information provided, which includes an explanation of the function, its syntax, and examples of its use.

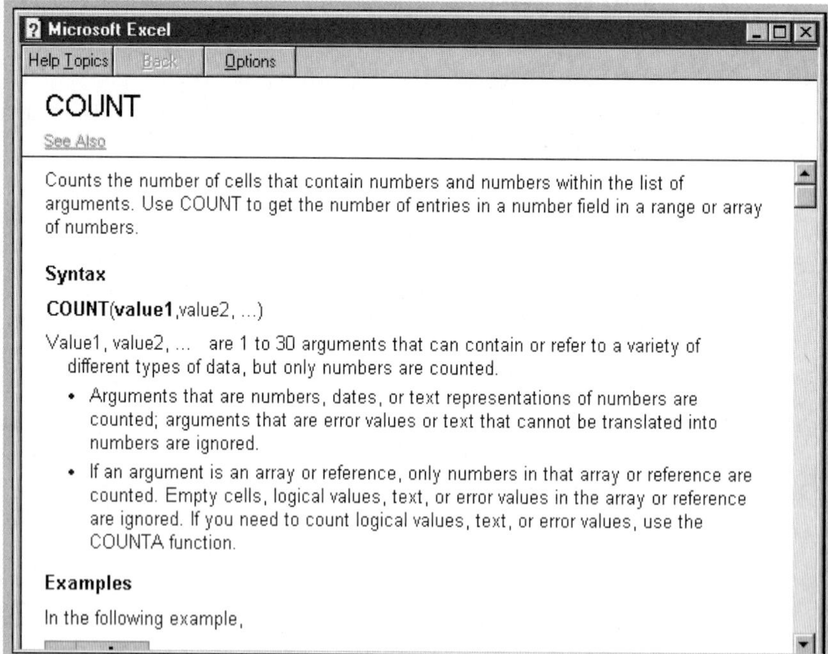

FIGURE 10-7
COUNT function Help screen

8. Close the Help window and close the Office Assistant.
9. Click the Cancel button to close the Paste Function dialog box.

Concepts Review

TRUE/FALSE QUESTIONS

Each of the following statements is either true or false. Indicate your choice by circling T or F.

T F *1.* You can enter functions in a worksheet in only one way—through Paste Function.

T F *2.* The arguments for an Excel function are enclosed in parentheses following the function name.

T F *3.* The arguments for an Excel function can consist of only constants or cell references.

T F *4.* When using Paste Function, all argument boxes shown in the Formula Palette must be completed.

T F *5.* The value returned by a function is called the result.

T F *6.* The MAX function can be found in the Math & Trig function category in the Paste Function dialog box.

T F *7.* The COUNTA function counts cells containing text and cells containing numbers.

T F *8.* The AVERAGE function ignores blank cells and zeros.

SHORT ANSWER QUESTIONS

Write the correct answer in the space provided.

1. Which menu command do you use to access Paste Function?

___

2. What is the value operated on by a function called?

___

3. If a function takes more than one argument, which keyboard character do you use to separate the arguments?

___

4. What name is given to a function which is itself the argument of another function?

___

5. Which category of functions in the Paste Function dialog box contains the AVERAGE, MIN, and MAX functions?

____

6. Which function do you use to calculate a mean?

____

7. Which function do you use to round a number down to the nearest integer?

____

8. Which function do you use to round a number to a specific number of decimal places?

____

CRITICAL THINKING

Answer these questions on a separate piece of paper. There are no right or wrong answers. Support your answers with examples from your own experience, if possible.

1. What advantages and disadvantages do you see in using Excel's Paste Function when developing formulas in your worksheets?
2. Discuss the use of nested functions. When can they be especially useful?

Skills Review

EXERCISE 10-9

Enter formulas using the AVERAGE, MIN, and MAX functions.

1. Open the file **Dunkirk4.xls**.
2. Enter a formula that calculates the average cost per yard by following these steps:
   a. Select cell B16.
   b. Key **=AVERAGE(B4:B14)**
3. Enter a formula that calculates the minimum stock by following these steps:
   a. Select cell F17 and click [fx].
   b. Choose Statistical from the Function category list box.
   c. Choose MIN from the Function name list box.

d. Click OK to display the Formula Palette.

e. Key **F4:F14** in the Number1 argument box.

f. Click OK.

4. Enter a formula that calculates the maximum stock by following these steps:

   a. Select cell F18 and click [fx].

   b. Choose Statistical from the Function category list box.

   c. Choose MAX from the Function name list box.

   d. Click OK.

   e. Key **F4:F14** in the Number1 argument box.

   f. Click OK.

5. Add the standard header to the worksheet with your name, the filename, and the date.
6. Save the workbook as *[your initials]***10-9.xls**.
7. Print the worksheet.
8. Create a formula printout in landscape orientation with grids and row and column headings.
9. Close the workbook without saving.

EXERCISE 10-10

Enter formulas using the COUNT and COUNTA functions.

1. Open the file **Dunkirk5.xls**. Key the data shown in Figure 10-8 beginning in cell C4 (leave cells blank where indicated.)

FIGURE 10-8

	C	D
4	yes	1
5		n/a
6	yes	3
7	yes	2
8		n/a

2. Enter a formula that counts the number of employees whose insurance covers dependents by following these steps:

a. Select cell D10 and click [fx].
b. Choose Statistical from the Function category list box.
c. Choose COUNT from the Function name list box.
d. Click OK.
e. Key **D4:D8** in the Value1 argument box.
f. Click OK.

3. Enter a formula that counts the employees with hospitalization coverage by following these steps:
   a. Select cell C11.
   b. Key the COUNTA function, specifying the range for the argument as C4:C8.
4. Add the standard header to the worksheet with your name, the filename, and the date.
5. Save the workbook as *[your initials]***10-10.xls**.
6. Print the worksheet.
7. Create a formula printout with grids and row and column headings.
8. Close the workbook without saving.

EXERCISE 10-11

Create a formula using the INT and ROUND functions.

1. Open the file **Dunkirk6.xls**.
2. Enter a formula that rounds a 10% increase by following these steps:
   a. Select cell E4 and click [fx].
   b. Choose Math & Trig from the Function category list box.
   c. Choose ROUND from the Function name list box.
   d. Click OK.
   e. Key **B4*1.1** in the Number argument box.
   f. Key **2** in the Num_digits argument box.
   g. Click OK.
3. Copy this formula from cell E4 to cells E5 through E8.
4. Enter a formula that totals the New Total Cost, rounding the total down to the nearest integer by following these steps:
   a. Select cell F4.
   b. Key **=INT(C4*E4)**

5. Copy this formula from cell F4 to cells F5 through F8.
6. Add the standard header to the worksheet with your name, the filename, and the date.
7. Save the workbook as *[your initials]***10-11.xls**.
8. Print the worksheet.
9. Create a formula printout in landscape orientation with grids and row and column headings. Use a Page 1 of ? footer.
10. Close the workbook without saving.

EXERCISE 10-12

Create a formula using nested functions.

1. Open the file **Dunkirk7.xls**.
2. Select cell B8 and key **5126**
3. Select cell C8 and key **6295**
4. Enter a formula using a nested function that finds average annual sales by following these steps:
   - *a.* Select cell B10 and click [fx].
   - *b.* Choose Statistical from the Function category list box.
   - *c.* Choose AVERAGE from the Function name list box.
   - *d.* Click OK.
   - *e.* Click the arrow next to the Function box and choose SUM from the drop-down list.
   - *f.* Key **B5:B8** in the Number1 argument box.
   - *g.* Click the word AVERGE in the Formula Bar.
   - *h.* Click the Number2 argument box.
   - *i.* Click the Function box to select a SUM function as a second argument for the AVERAGE function.
   - *j.* Key **C5:C8** in the Number1 argument box.
   - *k.* Click OK.
5. Add the standard header to the worksheet with your name, the filename, and the date.
6. Save the workbook as *[your initials]***10-12.xls**.
7. Print the worksheet.
8. Create a formula printout with grids and row and column headings. Make sure column B is wide enough to display the formulas.
9. Close the workbook without saving.

Lesson Applications

EXERCISE 10-13

Create a worksheet that includes formulas using the AVERAGE, MIN, MAX, COUNT, and COUNTA functions.

Create a worksheet that calculates weekly commissions for salespeople. It should also include average sales earned, the minimum and maximum sales earned, the number of salespeople selling that week, and the total number of salespeople on the regular sales force.

1. Open the file **Dunkirk8.xls**.
2. Key the data shown in Figure 10-9, beginning in cell B4.

FIGURE 10-9

Callahan	23,098.00	.045
Davis	32,427.00	.055
Jefferson	vacation	.040
Lerner	12,835.44	.056
Matthews	10,098.53	.060
Nicholson	42,098.65	.030
Peters	56,987.54	.050
Stuart	vacation	.065
Vaughn	5,098.87	.133

3. To calculate the commissions, rounding the number to two decimal places, select cell D4 and key **=ROUND(B4*C4,2)**
4. Copy the formula in cell D4 to cells D5 through D12.
5. Key **0** in cells D6 and D11.
6. Select cell A14, and key **AVERAGE:**
7. To calculate the weekly average, select cell B14 and key **=AVERAGE(B4:B12)**

8. Select cell A15 and key **MAX:**
9. To calculate the maximum sales earned by a salesperson, select cell B15 and key **=MAX(B4:B12)**
10. Select cell A16 and key **MIN:**
11. To calculate the minimum sales earned by a salesperson, select cell B16 and key **=MIN(B4:B12)**
12. Select cell A18 and key **Active Salespersons:**
13. To calculate the number of salespersons working that week, select cell B18 and key **=COUNT(B4:B12)**
14. Select cell A19 and key **Total Salespersons:**
15. To calculate the number of salespeople on the regular sales force, select cell B19 and key **=COUNTA(B4:B12)**
16. Format cells B18 and B19 with no decimal places.
17. Select cell A20 and key **% Active:**
18. To calculate the percentage of salespeople working this week, select cell B20 and key **=B18/B19**
19. Format cell B20 for percent with no decimal places.
20. Format the range D4:D12 in comma style with two decimal places.
21. Add the standard header to the worksheet with your name, the filename, and the date.
22. Save the workbook as *[your initials]***10-13.xls**.
23. Print the worksheet.
24. Create a formula printout with grids and row and column headings.
25. Close the workbook without saving.

EXERCISE 10-14

Construct a worksheet that includes formulas using nested AVERAGE, MIN, MAX, INT, or ROUND functions.

Construct a worksheet that analyzes monthly sales by product. For each product, calculate the most units sold and the least units sold by any region. In addition, calculate the average revenue and the total revenue for all regions, rounded to the nearest dollar.

1. Open the file **Dunkirk9.xls**. Key the data shown below, beginning in cell C5:

   Units Sold
   320

254
634
300
720
310
540
230

2. Center the region text in the range B4:B12.
3. In cell A16, key **Most Units**
4. In cell B16, calculate the most units sold for Cover C-9087.
5. In cell C16, calculate the most units sold for Cover C-9088.
6. In cell A17, key **Least Units**
7. In cell B17, calculate the least units sold for Cover C-9087.
8. In cell C17, calculate the least units sold for Cover C-9088.
9. In cell A18, key **Average Units**
10. In cell B18, calculate the average number sold for Cover C-9087.
11. In cell C18, calculate the average number sold for Cover C-9088.
12. In cell A19, key **Total Revenue**
13. In cell B19, calculate the total revenue rounded to the nearest dollar for Cover C-9087. Use 11.5 as the price of each unit.
14. In cell C19, calculate the total revenue rounded to the nearest dollar for Cover C-9088. Use 13.11 as the price of each unit.
15. Format cells B19 and C19 for currency with no decimal places. (Do not use the toolbar for the currency format.)
16. Add the standard header to the worksheet with your name, the filename, and the date.
17. Save the workbook as *[your initials]***10-14.xls**.
18. Print the worksheet.
19. Create a formula printout in landscape orientation with grids and row and column headings.
20. Close the workbook without saving.

EXERCISE 10-15

Create a worksheet that includes formulas using the MIN, MAX, and COUNT functions.

Create a worksheet that shows employees, their salaries, and their job performance ratings.

1. Open the file **Dunk10.xls**. Key the data shown in Figure 10-10.

FIGURE 10-10

Name	Full-time	Part-time Hourly	Performance Rating
Anderson	50,000		3
Boyd		18.00	4
Carlson	35,000		3
Dugan	28,000		4
Evans	45,000		4
Jenkins		10.00	2

2. In cell A11, key **Count:**
3. In cell B11, enter a function that counts the number of full-time employees.
4. In cell C11, enter a function that counts the number of part-time employees.
5. In cell A12, key **Max:**
6. In cell A13, key **Min:**
7. In cells B12 and C12, enter functions that show the highest salary for full-time employees and the highest hourly rate for part-time employees, respectively.
8. In cells B13 and C13, enter functions that show the lowest salary for full-time employees and the lowest hourly rate for part-time employees, respectively.
9. Format column B in accounting style, with dollar signs and no decimal places.
10. Format column C in accounting style, with dollar signs and two decimal places.
11. Format cells B11 and C11 in number style with no decimal places.
12. Add the standard header to the worksheet with your name, the filename, and the date.
13. Save the workbook as *[your initials]***10-15.xls**.
14. Print the worksheet
15. Create a formula printout in landscape orientation with grids and row and column headings.
16. Close the workbook without saving.

EXERCISE 10-16

Construct a worksheet using the AVERAGE, INT, COUNTA, and ROUND functions.

The Dunkirk Canvas Company needs a worksheet that shows transportation charges for the month of May for each of its carriers.

1. Create a spreadsheet sketch that includes a worksheet title, column labels, and an area for data. The worksheet should include each carrier (rows), and columns showing the mileage for each carrier, the charge per mile, and formulas computing the total mileage charges for each carrier. Below the area for data, there should be formulas showing the total number of carriers, the average mileage and total mileage for all carriers, and the total transportation charges for the month.
2. Using a 12-point font for all data, transfer the sketch into Excel by keying and formatting the labels. Then key the following data:

Carrier	Miles	Charge Per Mile
Allied Trans.	5736.5	0.75
United Freight	4397.6	0.47
Eastern Trans.	5107.1	0.95
Coastal Trans.	7130.4	0.49

3. Create a formula to show the total charges for each carrier.
4. Show the total transportation charges for all carriers rounded to the nearest dollar. Use Paste Function to create formulas with nested functions.
5. Use the COUNTA function to show the total number of carriers.
6. Use the INT function to round the total mileage and the average mileage.
7. Format all cells that show the number of miles in Number Style with a comma separator and one decimal place, except for the total and average mileage cells, which should have no decimal places.
8. Format all dollar amounts in the currency style with no decimal places, except for the "Charge Per Mile" cells, which should have two decimal places. Use the Format Cells dialog box—not the toolbar—to apply the formatting.
9. Rename Sheet1 Charges and rename Sheet2 User Information.
10. In the User Information worksheet, create documentation which includes the following: File Information (Created by, Date created, Date revised, Revised by, Contact for help); Purpose of spreadsheet (paragraph form); Instructions to User (special instructions needed by user to enter data correctly). Style the documentation for easy reading.

11. Center the worksheets horizontally and add the standard header to the worksheets with your name, the filename, and the date.
12. Save the workbook as *[your initials]***10-16.xls**.
13. Print the workbook.
14. Create a formula printout of the Charges worksheet in landscape orientation on one page with grids and row and column headings and close the workbook without saving.

Advanced Formulas

OBJECTIVES

After completing this lesson, you will be able to:

1. Use absolute and mixed cell references.
2. Create an IF function.
3. Create an IF function with multiple conditions.
4. Insert text with the IF function.
5. Use the VLOOKUP and HLOOKUP functions.
6. Use comments to annotate a formula.
7. Correct circular references.

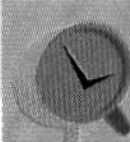

Estimated Time: 1¾ hours

Understanding differences in the types of cell references is the key to making the most of Excel's formula capabilities. As this lesson demonstrates, using the right type of cell reference is important when you copy formulas between cells. This lesson also explains how to use the IF function to create more powerful formulas, how to create lookup tables to automate data-entry tasks, and how to document complicated formulas by attaching comments to cells. Finally, circular cell references—a common error in creating formulas—are explained.

Using Absolute and Mixed Cell References

So far, you have worked primarily with *relative cell references* in formulas. In relative cell references, the cell's address is relative to the address of the cell containing the formula. Excel automatically adjusts relative cell addresses when you copy a formula from one cell to another.

Sometimes, you will not want Excel to adjust the cell references when you copy a formula. In those instances, use *absolute cell references* or *mixed cell references*. In absolute cell references, the addresses of cells remain unchanged when a formula is copied from one cell to another. With mixed cell references, either the row or the column portion of the address is absolute, and the other portion of the address is relative.

NOTE: Cell references of named cells are absolute.

EXERCISE  11-1 Use an Absolute Cell Reference in a Formula

You create absolute cell references by placing dollar signs in front of the column letter and row number (for example, $A$3, $A$4).

TIP: With the insertion point within a cell reference in the Formula Bar, pressing F4 provides a shortcut method for cycling among relative, absolute, and mixed cell references.

1. Open the file **Rates.xls**.
2. Select cell C6.
3. Key **=B6+(B6*G4)**. This formula calculates a 50% markup price for the first yardage item—the markup amount is in cell G4. The result is 37.5.

NOTE: The parentheses in the above formula are not needed since order of precedence dictates the multiplication is performed before the addition. However, the parentheses are included here for clarity.

4. Use AutoFill to copy the formula to cells C7 and C8. The formulas in cells C7 and C8 are incorrect because of the relative reference to cell G4.
5. Double-click cell C6, move the insertion point after the "G" in the formula, and press F4. Dollar signs appear before the "G" and the "4," indicating that both column G and row 4 are absolute references.

Cost	Price	10%
25.00	=B6+(B6*$G$4)	

FIGURE 11-1
Changing a cell address to absolute

NOTE: Pressing F4 doesn't work if the insertion point is positioned in front of the equal sign in the formula. Always move the insertion point within the cell reference that requires the $ signs.

6. Enter the formula and use AutoFill to copy it to cells C7 and C8. The results are 75 and 112.5, respectively. The formulas are now correct, because the absolute cell reference $G$4 does not adjust in its copied locations.

EXERCISE 11-2 View a Named Cell as an Absolute Reference in a Formula

When you use named cells in formulas, Excel makes the reference to the named cell absolute.

1. Select cell G5.
2. Give this cell a name by choosing Insert, Name, Define. The Define Name dialog box is displayed.
3. Key **sixty**. At the bottom of the box, the cell reference is absolute: $G$5.
4. Click OK.
5. Select cell C6 and change the formula to =**B6+(B6*sixty)**
6. Copy the formula to cells C7 and C8. The name "sixty," which always refers to cell $G$5, is copied to each cell, as references to named cells are absolute.

TIP: It is good practice to use named cells for constant values in formulas whenever possible. Names make formulas easier to understand and changing the value of the constant doesn't necessitate changing the formula.

EXERCISE 11-3 Use a Mixed Cell Reference

To create a mixed cell reference, place a dollar sign ($) in front of the part of the cell reference (the row number or column letter) that you want to be absolute.

1. Select cell D6 and key **=C6*D4**. This formula is intended to multiply the price in column C by the commission rate in D4. The result should be 4.00.
2. Copy this formula to cells D6 through F8.
3. Select cell F8. The cell references in the formula are incorrect. The formula should refer to column C, the "Price" column, but now it refers to column E. Similarly, the formula should refer to row 4, which contains the commission rates. Instead, it refers to row 6.

4. Double-click cell D6.
5. Position the insertion point in the cell reference C6 (after the equal sign).
6. Press F4 three times to make the reference to column C absolute. The cell reference changes to $C6.
7. Position the insertion point in the cell reference D4.
8. Press F4 twice to change the cell reference to D$4, making row 4 absolute.
9. Press Enter and copy the formula to cells D6 through F8.

FIGURE 11-2
Copying a formula with mixed cell references

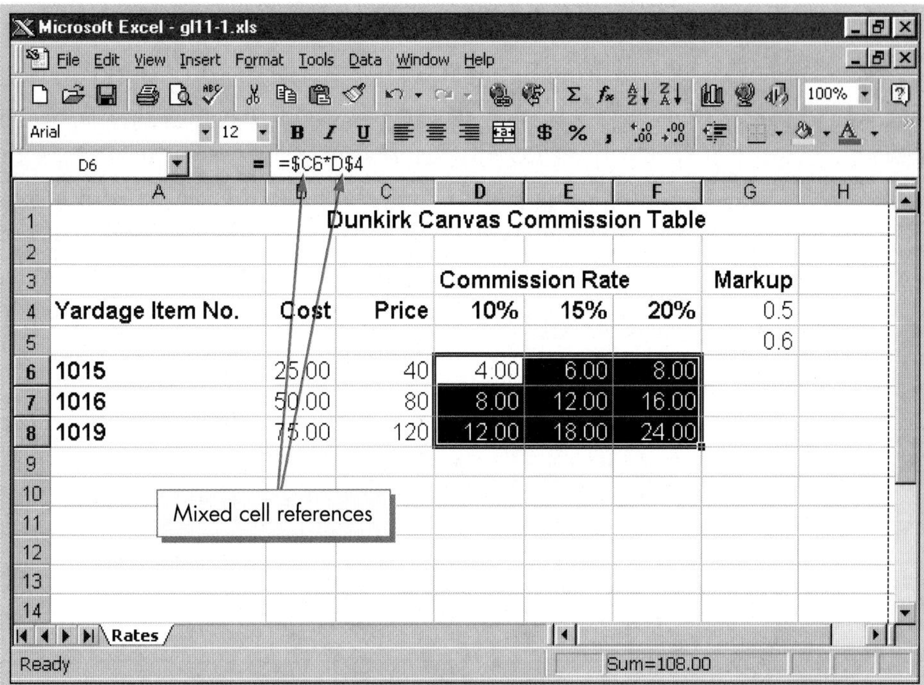

10. Compare the formula in D6 (=$C6*D$4) with the formula in cell F8 (=$C8*F$4).

TIP: You can quickly scan your formulas in the worksheet using Ctrl+` (left single quote) to toggle between displaying the values in your worksheet and displaying the formulas. This is the same as choosing Tools, Options and choosing Formulas from the View tab.

11. Add the standard header to the worksheet with your name, the filename, and the date.
12. Save the workbook as *[your initials]*11-3.xls.
13. Print the worksheet and close the workbook.

Creating an IF Function

You use the IF function to create conditional expressions—that is, formulas of the form "If X, then Y." For example, "If the bill is past 30 days late, then you will pay a late fee of 2%."

The IF function in Excel takes the form, "If X, then Y, otherwise Z." The IF function evaluates whether X is true or false. It returns the value Y if the conditional expression is true and the value Z if it is false. An example is "If cell C5 is greater than 50, then charge a late fee; otherwise, state 'Thank you for your payment.'"

The IF function takes three arguments in this format:

=IF(logical_test, value_if_true, value_if_false)

- Logical_test is the expression that evaluates to true or false. For example, the expression C5>50 is either true or false.
- Value_if_true is the value that is returned if logical_test is true. Value_if_true can be a constant, a formula, text, or a cell reference.
- Value_if_false is the value that is returned if logical_test is false. Value_if_false can be a constant, a formula, text, or a cell reference.

Table 11-1 shows the operators you can use to construct the logical_test portion of the function.

TABLE 11-1 Operators to Use in Functions

OPERATOR	MEANING
=	Equal to
<>	Not equal to
>	Greater than
<	Less than
>=	Greater than or equal to
<=	Less than or equal to

EXERCISE 11-4 Use the IF Function in a Formula

1. Open the file **DunBon.xls**.
2. Select cell D4 and key **=IF(B4>20000,500,0)**. The formula returns a bonus of 500 if the value in B4 is greater than $20,000; otherwise, it

returns a zero. Since Jack Bell's sales are greater than $20,000, he receives a $500 bonus.

FIGURE 11-3 IF function determining who receives bonuses

D4 = =IF(B4>20000,500,0)

	A	B	C	D	E	F	G
1			Dunkirk Canvas Bonus Table				
2							
3	Name	Sales	Rate	Bonus 1	Bonus 2	Bonus 3	Bonus 4
4	Bell, Jack	21,000	10%	500			
5	Brandeis, Sue	0	15%				
6	Caulder, Liz	18,000	10%				
7	Edwards, Tom	20,000	20%				
8	Summers, Lynn	21,305	20%				

3. Copy the formula in cell D4 to cells D5 through D8.

NOTE: No comma or dollar punctuation is allowed for numbers inside the IF function

Using IF Functions with Multiple Conditions

You can use logical functions such as AND, OR, and NOT for the logical_test part of the conditional expression. When you use functions for the logical_test argument, the functions are enclosed in parentheses. Excel then evaluates the conditional formula, starting with the innermost parentheses that enclose the nested arguments.

The AND expression can be summed up as "All conditions must be met." It returns true if all of its conditions test true, and false if one or more of its conditions tests false. Use the format AND(logical_1,logical_2,...), where you can test as many as 30 conditions, beginning with logical_1.

TABLE 11-2 Examples of the AND Function

EXPRESSION	EXCEL RETURNS
AND(1+2=3, 3+3=6)	TRUE
AND(2+2=4, 1+1=3)	FALSE
AND(C2>1, C2<100)	TRUE if cell C2 contains a number greater than 1 and less than 100; otherwise FALSE

The OR expression can be summed up as "At least one condition must be met." Use the format OR(logical_1,logical_2,...), where as many as 30 conditions, beginning with logical_1, can be true or false.

TABLE 11-3 Examples of the OR Function

EXPRESSION	EXCEL RETURNS
OR(1+1=3, 3+3=6)	TRUE
OR(2+0=4, 1+1=1)	FALSE
OR(A1:A3)	TRUE only if the cells in A1:A3 contain at least one formula or expression that evaluates true; otherwise FALSE

When using the AND and OR functions, keep the following points in mind:

- AND and OR ignore empty cells and cells with text.
- If the references in AND or OR contain no logical values, Excel returns the #VALUE! error message.

The NOT expression can be summed up as "Reverse the result of testing a logical condition." Use the format NOT(logical), where logical is an expression or value that can be true or false.

TABLE 11-4 Examples of the NOT Expression

EXPRESSION	EXCEL RETURNS
NOT(A3=0)	TRUE if cell A3 contains any number other than 0; FALSE if cell A3 contains 0
NOT(2+2=4)	FALSE

EXERCISE 11-5 Use AND in a Formula

1. Select cell E4.
2. Click [fx] or choose Function from the Insert menu. The Paste Function dialog box appears.
3. Choose Logical from the Function category list box.

4. Choose IF from the Function name list box.
5. Click OK. The Formula Palette appears.
6. Click the down arrow next to the Function box. Choose More Functions from the drop-down list. The Paste Function dialog box is displayed once again.
7. Choose Logical from the Function category list box.
8. Choose AND from the Function name list box.
9. Click OK. The Formula Palette is redisplayed. Notice that the AND function is in bold in the Formula Bar, which indicates you will enter the arguments for the AND function in the argument boxes on the Formula Palette.

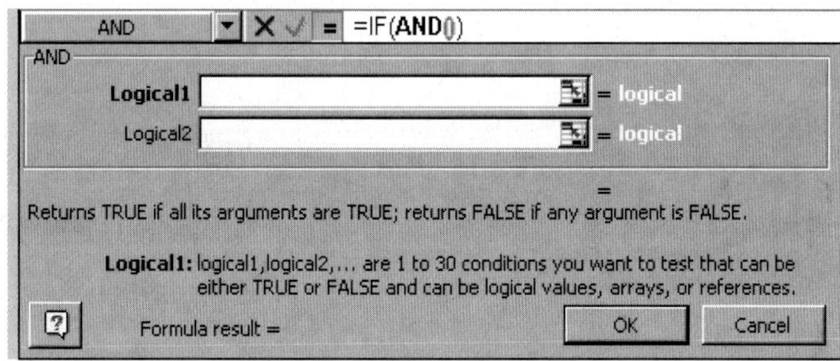

FIGURE 11-4
Formula Palette for the AND function

10. Key **B4>20000** in the Logical1 argument box.
11. Key **C4=.2** in the Logical2 argument box. Notice in the Formula Bar that the AND function was inserted as the "X" part of the "If X, then Y, otherwise Z" conditional expression.
12. Click the IF function name in the formula displayed in the Formula Bar. The Formula Palette now displays the argument boxes for the remaining arguments in the IF function. Notice that the AND function serves as the Logical_test argument.

AND =IF(AND(b4>20000,c4=.2))
IF
Logical_test AND(b4>20000,c4=.2) = FALSE
Value_if_true = any
Value_if_false = any
=
Returns one value if a condition you specify evaluates to TRUE and another value if it evaluates to FALSE.
Logical_test is any value or expression that can be evaluated to TRUE or FALSE.
Formula result =
OK Cancel

FIGURE 11-5
Formula Palette for the rest of the IF function

13. Key **500** in the Value_if_true argument box. It becomes the "Y" part of the conditional expression.
14. Key **0** in the Value_if_false argument box. It becomes the "Z" part of the conditional expression.

NOTE: If you forget to key 0 in the Value_if_false argument box, Excel displays the value FALSE in the worksheet instead of the value 0. To complete the formula, you can edit it manually in the Formula Bar. Key **0** preceded by a comma where the Value_if_false argument belongs.

15. Click OK. Because cell B4 is greater than 20,000, but cell C4 is not 20%, the formula calculates 0 (no bonus).
16. Copy the formula to cells E5 through E8.

EXERCISE 11-6 Use OR in a Formula

1. Select cell F4 and click .
2. In the Paste Function dialog box, choose Logical from the Function category list box and IF from the Function name list box.
3. Click OK. The Formula Palette is displayed.
4. Click the down arrow next to the Function box and choose More Functions from the drop-down list. The Paste Function dialog box is displayed again.
5. Choose Logical from the Function category list box and OR from the Function name list box.
6. Click OK. The Formula Palette is redisplayed.
7. Key **B4>20000** in the Logical1 argument box.
8. Key **C4=.2** in the Logical2 argument box.
9. Click the IF function name in the formula displayed in the Formula Bar. The remaining arguments for the IF function are displayed in the Formula Palette.
10. Key 500 in the Value_if_true argument box.
11. Key 0 in the Value_if_false argument box and click OK. Because one condition was met, the formula calculates a $500 bonus.
12. Copy the formula to cells F5 through F8. Notice the difference in bonus amounts using OR versus AND.

EXERCISE 11-7 Use NOT in a Formula

1. Select cell G4.
2. Key **=IF(NOT(B4=0),500,0)**

3. Copy the formula to cells G5 through G8. Using NOT in the IF formula, all salespeople receive $500 commissions under Bonus Plan 4 unless they have zero sales.

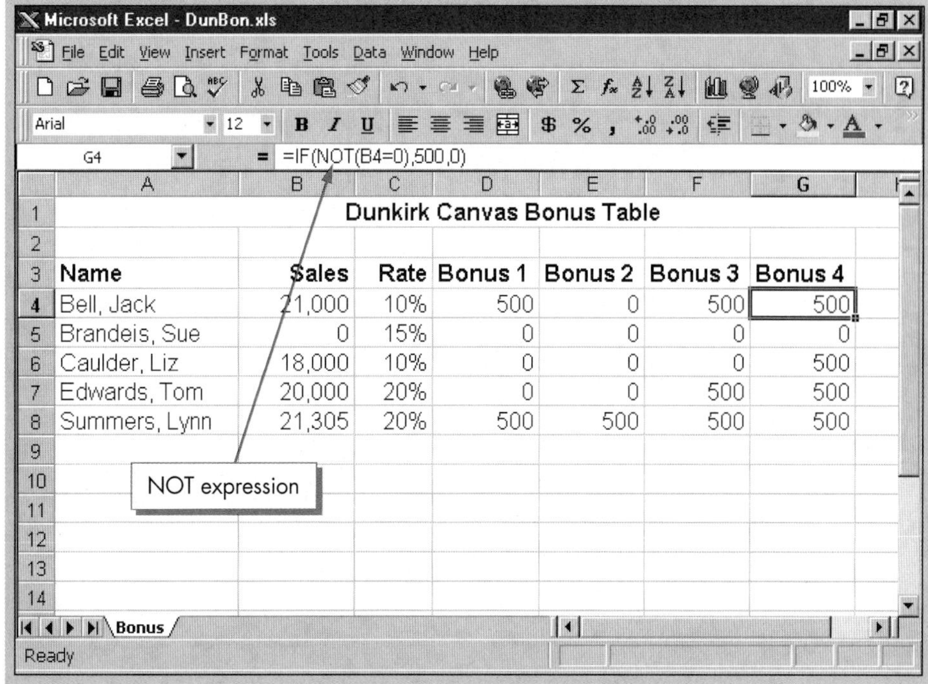

FIGURE 11-6
Using the NOT expression in an IF formula

4. Add the standard header to the worksheet with your name, the filename, and the date.
5. Save the workbook as *[your initials]***11-7.xls**.
6. Print the worksheet and close the workbook.

Using IF Functions to Insert Text

You can create a formula using the IF function that displays text based on whether a condition is true or false. For example, you could display the text "Delinquent Account" if the value in the "Days Overdue" column of a worksheet is greater than 30. To add text in an IF function, you enclose the text in quotes. For example, you could use the following IF statement to display "Current Account" if an account is less than or equal to 30 days late, and "Past Due" if the account is more than 30 days late: IF(G3<=30,"Current Account","Past Due")

You also can replace Excel's error messages with easier-to-understand messages. For example, if a cell contains a formula for division, and the number is divided by zero, the #DIV/0! error message appears. To replace this error message, you can create a formula, such as IF(B2=0,"You cannot divide by zero.",B1/B2). If a user keys 0, the text you defined appears; otherwise, Excel performs the division.

EXERCISE 11-8 Insert Text with an IF Function

1. Open the file **Costs2.xls**.

FIGURE 11-7
Using text in an IF formula

= =IF(D4>40,"Yes","No")

C	D	E	F	G
	Dunkirk Canvas			
Cost/Yard	Hours	OT	Yardage Cost	Labor Cost
7.00	42	Yes	0.00	0.00
9.50	39	No	0.00	0.00
7.00	40	No	0.00	0.00
6.00	44	Yes	0.00	0.00
5.25	50	Yes	0.00	0.00
3.99	20	No	0.00	0.00
6.22	41	Yes	0.00	0.00

2. In cell E4, enter the formula **=IF(D4>40,"Yes","No")**. Because the value in cell D4 is greater than 40, Excel displays "Yes."

3. Copy the formula to cells E5 through E10.

TIP: You can insert a blank as either the true or false statement by using double quotation marks ("") with no space in between.

Using VLOOKUP and HLOOKUP

You can create a table in one area of a worksheet that is used to retrieve values for another area of the worksheet. This operation involves using the VLOOKUP and HLOOKUP functions. For example, you could create a table that lists item numbers and prices in one area of an invoice worksheet. When you key the item number in the item column of the worksheet, Excel looks up the price for the item in the table and automatically places it in the price column. Besides saving work, these functions help prevent data-entry errors.

Use this format:

=VLOOKUP(lookup_value,table_array,col_index_num,range_lookup)

- Lookup_value is the value for which VLOOKUP searches. It can be a value, text string, or cell reference.
- Table_array is the range of cells through which Excel searches for lookup_value. It is a good idea to use a range name for the table. VLOOKUP searches down the far left column in the table for a match to the lookup_value; HLOOKUP searches the top row in the table.

Table_array can contain numbers, text, or logical values. The values in the first column must appear in ascending order (1,2,3...A-Z...FALSE, TRUE) unless an exact match is desired.

- Col_index_num is the column number in the table_array from which the matching value should be returned. A col_index_num of 1 returns the value in the first column in table_array; a col_index_num of 2 returns the value in the second column in table_array; and so on.
- Range_lookup is an optional argument. It is a logical value (TRUE or FALSE) that specifies whether you want VLOOKUP to find an exact match or an approximate match. When it is TRUE or omitted, VLOOKUP finds the largest value that is less than the lookup_value. If you want VLOOKUP to find an exact match for the lookup_value, the range_lookup should be FALSE.

HLOOKUP works just like VLOOKUP, except it searches the top row of the table for the lookup_value, and it uses a row_index_num to indicate the row number in the table from which the matching value is returned. Use the following format:

=HLOOKUP(lookup_value,table_array,row_index_num,range_lookup)

Note the following characteristics of VLOOKUP and HLOOKUP:

- IF VLOOKUP and HLOOKUP cannot find lookup_value, and range_lookup is TRUE, they use the largest value that is less than the lookup_value.
- If lookup_value is less than the least value in the first column of the table_array, VLOOKUP returns the #N/A error value. The same applies to HLOOKUP and the first row of the table_array.

EXERCISE 11-9 Use the VLOOKUP Function

1. Go to the Table worksheet.
2. Select cells A2:B8 and name the range T_Yardage.

TIP: Give range names to your tables and use these names in your VLOOKUP and HLOOKUP functions instead of cell addresses. It is also a good idea to establish a naming convention for table range names to distinguish them from other range names, as in the "T_" portion of the above range name.

3. Return to the Costs worksheet, select cell B4, and key **=VLOOKUP(A4,T_Yardage,2)**

TIP: When entering a formula that uses a named range, you can use F3 to paste the range name into the formula.

4. Copy the formula in cell B4 to cells B5 through B10. Because lookup_value is relative, Excel adjusts the formula and looks up all the corresponding yardage items in the table.

FIGURE 11-8
VLOOKUP function used in the worksheet

B4 = =VLOOKUP(A4,T_Yardage,2)

	A	B	C	D	E	F	G	H	I	J
1					Dunkirk Canvas					
2										
3	No.	Yards	Cost/Yard	Hours	OT	Yardage Cost	Labor Cost	Total Cost	Price	
4	106	35	7.00	42	Yes	245.00	350.00	595.00	892.50	
5	107	44	9.50	39	No	418.00	440.00	858.00	1,287.00	
6	105	72	7.00	40	No	504.00	720.00	1,224.00	1,836.00	
7	101	50	6.00	44	Yes	300.00	500.00	800.00	1,200.00	
8	101	50	5.25	50	Yes	262.50	500.00	762.50	1,143.75	
9	107	44	3.99	20	No	175.56	440.00	615.56	923.34	
10	101	50	6.22	41	Yes	311.00	500.00	811.00	1,216.50	
11										

Using Comments to Annotate Formulas

You can attach a comment to a cell that contains descriptive text. This approach is helpful for explaining complicated formulas or warning other users not to key data in a cell containing a formula.

To create and view the comments in a worksheet, use the Comment option on the Insert menu. You can also use the New Comment button and the Show All Comments button, which are on the Auditing and Reviewing toolbars. In addition, you can use the keyboard shortcut Shift+F2 to create and edit comments.

Cells with comments have a small, red triangle in their upper-right corner. You can print the comments when you print the worksheet by selecting File, Page Setup, and selecting Comments from the Sheet tab. Comments can be printed as displayed on the worksheet or on a separate page at the end of the worksheet.

EXERCISE 11-10 Use a Comment to Annotate a Formula

1. Select cell B4.
2. Choose Comment from the Insert menu or press Shift+F2. A new Comment box appears.

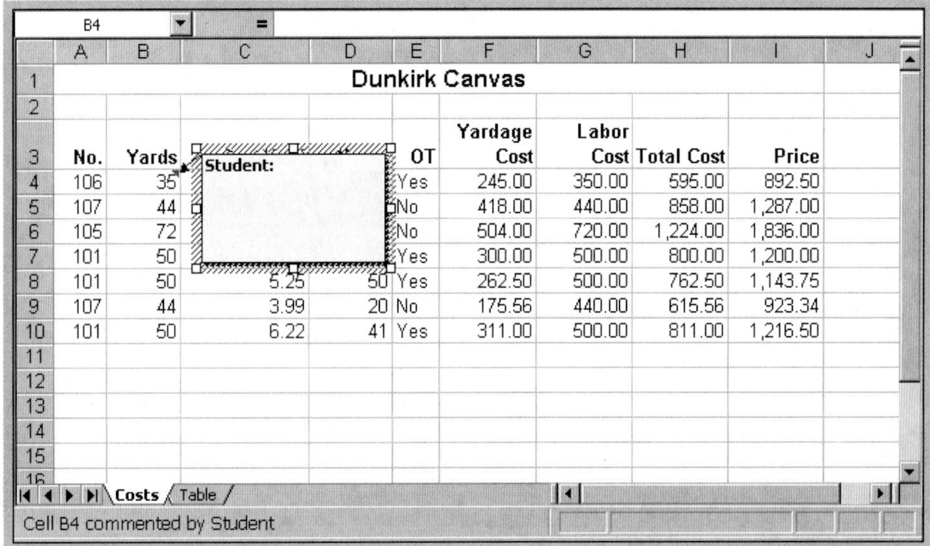

FIGURE 11-9
A new Comment box

NOTE: The name that appears at the top of a new Comment box is the default user name. Although you can change this name in the Comment box when you add your comments, the Status bar continues to show the default user name.

3. Use Backspace to delete the default user name.
4. Key *[your initials]*: and press Enter.
5. Key the following text:

   Do not key data in this column. Change data only in the Yardage Lookup Table on the Table worksheet.
6. Expand the size of the Comment box to display the entire message by using the bottom resize handle on the Comment box.
7. Select any cell in the worksheet. A small, red triangle appears in cell B4 to indicate the presence of a comment.

EXERCISE 11-11 View and Edit the Contents of a Comment

1. Move the pointer over cell B4 without selecting it. The Comment box appears when the pointer is placed over a cell that contains a comment. Notice that the message in the Status bar indicates the presence of a comment.
2. Select cell B4 and choose Edit Comment from the Insert menu or press Shift+F2. The Comment box appears.

3. Select the beginning of the comment and key **IMPORTANT!**
4. Select any cell on the worksheet. The edited comment is applied to cell B4.

Correcting Circular References

A formula cannot contain a reference to its own cell address. For example, the formula =A1+A2+A3 is incorrect if it appears in cell A3. Cell A3 cannot be operated on by a formula and contain the formula simultaneously. Such a reference in a formula, called a *circular reference*, is a fairly common mistake. If you try to enter a formula with a circular reference, Excel produces an error message to let you know that you need to correct the formula.

EXERCISE 11-12 Enter and Correct a Circular Reference and Print Comments on a Sheet

1. Select cell E4.
2. In the Formula Bar, change "D4" to **E4** and enter the formula. Excel displays an error message that describes the presence of a circular reference in the formula.
3. Click Cancel. (Click OK if the Cancel button is not present; Excel displays a slightly different error message if you have already seen the circular reference message and Help screens during your current session.)
4. Change "E4" back to D4 to correct the formula, if necessary.
5. Select File, Page Setup from the menu. Click the Sheet tab if it is not already displayed. Click the down arrow next to Comments and choose At end of sheet. The comments are printed on a separate page after the worksheet.
6. Add the standard header to the worksheet with your name, the filename, and the date. Use a Page 1 of ? footer.
7. Save the workbook as *[your initials]***11-12.xls**.
8. Print the worksheet and close the workbook.

COMMAND SUMMARY

FEATURE	BUTTON	MENU	KEYBOARD
Create a cell comment		Insert, Comment	Shift+F2
Switch between displaying formulas and values		Tools, Options, View	Ctrl+` (left single quote)

Concepts Review

TRUE/FALSE QUESTIONS

Each of the following statements is either true or false. Indicate your choice by circling T or F.

T F 1. Excel automatically adjusts relative cell references in a formula when the formula is copied from one cell to another.

T F 2. $A$3 is an example of a relative cell address.

T F 3. Two types of cell references exist in Excel: relative and absolute.

T F 4. When creating or editing a formula, you press F4 to move through the cell reference types.

T F 5. Cell references of named cells are considered absolute.

T F 6. An IF function takes two arguments.

T F 7. An IF function can use logical functions such as AND, OR, and NOT for the logical_test part of the conditional expression.

T F 8. Excel automatically displays an error message when a circular reference is used in a formula.

SHORT ANSWER QUESTIONS

Write the correct answer in the space provided.

1. Which type of cell reference combines absolute and relative cell addresses?

___

2. Which keyboard character is added to a cell address in a formula when you press F4?

___

3. Which type of cell reference do you use in a formula when you want to copy a formula but do not want the cell reference to change?

___

4. Which function evaluates a condition and provides one answer if the condition is true and another answer if the condition is false?

___

5. Which keyboard character do you use to surround text in an IF function?

____

6. Which functions retrieve a value from a table in another area of the worksheet and place it in the formula cell?

____

7. Which command from the Insert menu do you use to annotate a worksheet cell?

____

8. What type of marker is displayed in a cell that contains a note?

____

CRITICAL THINKING

Answer these questions on a separate piece of paper. There are no right or wrong answers. Support your answers with examples from your own experience, if possible.

1. Think about how the VLOOKUP function was used in this lesson. Could a table be set up in a separate workbook and then be referenced in a VLOOKUP function? How might this option prove useful in a company?
2. When someone sets up a worksheet for another person, are the purpose of the worksheet and how the formulas work always clear? Which Excel command is useful for adding annotations in a worksheet cell? How might this feature be beneficial to you as an employee taking over someone else's work?

Skills Review

EXERCISE 11-13

Use relative, mixed, and absolute cell references.

1. Open the file **DunRev.xls**.
2. Select cell C7.
3. Key **=$B7*C$4+$B7**. This formula contains mixed cell addresses. Each quarterly projection is based on the percentage indicated in row 4 multiplied by the fourth quarter's actual numbers in column B. The fourth-quarter number is then added to the increase.

4. Copy the formula to cells C7 through F8. Because you used mixed cell references, you can key the formula once and copy it to the cell range.
5. Copy the formula from cell B10 to cells C10 through F10.
6. Select cell C15.
7. Key **=B15*F13+B15**. The projections for expenses for each quarter are based on the percentage in cell F13 multiplied by the previous quarter's expenses.
8. Edit the formula in cell C15. Use F4 to make cell reference F13 the absolute cell address, $F$13. The formula should now be: =B15*$F$13+B15.
9. Copy the formula from cell C15 to cells C15 through F16.
10. Copy the formula from cell B18 to cells C18 through F18.
11. In cell F4, key **7%**
12. In cell F13, key **4%**. Changes appear in affected worksheet cells.
13. Add the standard header to the worksheet with your name, the filename, and the date.
14. Save the workbook as *[your initials]***11-13.xls**.
15. Print the worksheet.
16. Create a formula printout in landscape orientation on one page with grids and row and column headings.
17. Close the workbook without saving.

EXERCISE 11-14

Use relative and absolute cell references with an IF function with a single condition.

1. Open the file **Salaries.xls**.
2. In cell F5, key **4%**
3. In cell F6, key **5%**
4. Select cell D5.
5. Key **=IF(C5>3,$F$6,$F$5)**
6. Copy the formula from cell D5 to cells D6 through D8.
7. Format column D in percentage style with no decimal places.
8. Select cell E5.
9. Key **=B5*D5+B5**
10. Copy the formula from cell E5 to cells E6 through E8.
11. Add the standard header to the worksheet with your name, the filename, and the date.
12. Save the workbook as *[your initials]***11-14.xls**.

13. Print the worksheet.
14. Create a formula printout in landscape orientation with grids and row and column headings. Use a Page 1 of ? footer.
15. Close the workbook without saving.

EXERCISE 11-15

Create an IF function with multiple conditions, one of which inserts text.

1. Open the file **Reorder.xls**.
2. Select cell G4 and click [fx].
3. Choose Logical from the Function category list box, choose IF from the Function name list box, and click OK.
4. Click the down arrow next to the Function box and choose OR from the drop-down list.
5. Key **F4<=D4*.10** in the Logical1 argument text box.
6. Key **F4<5** in the Logical2 argument text box and click the IF function name in the formula displayed in the Formula Bar.
7. Key **YES** in the Value_if_true argument text box.
8. Key "" (double quotation marks) in the Value_if_false argument text box. The cell is left blank if the answer is false.
9. Click OK. Copy the formula from cell G4 to cells G5 through G8. The cells in column G that meet either condition contain the answer YES; otherwise, they are left blank.
10. Change the value in cell E4 to 23. Cell G4 is updated with the answer YES.
11. Add the standard header to the worksheet with your name, the filename, and the date.
12. Save the workbook as *[your initials]***11-15.xls**.
13. Print the worksheet.
14. Create a formula printout in landscape orientation with grids and row and column headings. Use a Page 1 of ? footer.
15. Close the workbook without saving.

EXERCISE 11-16

Use relative, absolute, and mixed cell references with the VLOOKUP function; use comments to annotate the formula; and correct a circular reference.

1. Open the file **Vacation.xls**.

2. Key the data by following these steps:
   - *a.* In cell B5, key **8/10/94**
   - *b.* In cell B6, key **2/3/95**
   - *c.* In cell B7, key **5/5/95**
   - *d.* In cell B8, key **6/1/95**
   - *e.* In cell B9, key **10/10/90**
   - *f.* In cell B10, key **4/2/93**
3. Select cell C5 and key **=ROUND((F$1-B5)/365.25,1)**. This formula subtracts the employment date in cell B5 from the current date in cell F1; it then divides by 365.25 to convert the days to years.
4. Copy the formula from cell C5 to cells C6 through C10.
5. Format column C in number style, with one decimal place.
6. Insert a new worksheet, placing it after the Vacation worksheet. Rename the new sheet **Table**.
7. Key the table as shown in Figure 11-10, beginning in cell A1 on the Table sheet.

FIGURE 11-10

	A	B
1	Years of Service	Vacation Days Due
2	1	5
3	2	5
4	3	5
5	4	5
6	5	10
7	6	10
8	7	10
9	8	10
10	9	10
11	10	15

8. Make the titles in row 1 bold and format cell A1 so the text wraps.
9. Name the range A2 through B11 T_Days.
10. On the Vacation sheet, select cell D5 and key **=VLOOKUP(C5,T_Days,2)**
11. Copy the formula from cell D5 to cells D6 through D10.
12. Select cell D4 and choose Comment from the Insert menu.
13. Replace the default user name in the Comment box with *[your initials]*: and press Enter.
14. Key **Maximum vacation is 15 days.** and then select any cell. A red marker appears in cell D4.
15. Select cell B11 and key **Employees with vacation due:**
16. Select cell D11, key **=COUNT(D5:D11)**, and press Enter.
17. Click OK or Cancel to remove the circular reference error message.
18. Edit the formula in cell D11. Change "D11" to **D10**.
19. Add the standard header to both worksheets with your name, the filename, and the date. Use a Page 1 of ? footer.
20. Save the workbook as *[your initials]***11-16.xls**.
21. Print the entire workbook and the comment at the end of the sheet.
22. Create a formula printout in landscape orientation with grids and row and column headings. Do not include the comments with this printout. Use a Page 1 of ? footer.
23. Close the workbook without saving

Lesson Applications

EXERCISE 11-17

Use relative, absolute, and mixed cell references, and use comments to annotate a formula.

Create a worksheet that determines quantity-based discounts received from a supplier. Create formulas with relative and absolute cell addresses that calculate the discount prices.

1. Open a new workbook.

2. Construct the worksheet as shown in Figure 11-11.

FIGURE 11-11

	A	B	C	D	E	F
1	Dunkirk Canvas Company					
2	Material Order List					
3			2%	3%	4%	5%
4	Part No.	Cost Per Yard		Quantity Ordered		
5			50	100	200	Over 200
6	Canvas 101	5.09				
7	Canvas 102	5.45				
8	Canvas 103	6.14				
9	Canvas 104	6.23				
10	Canvas 105	6.51				

3. Format the range B6:F10 in number style, with two decimal places.

4. Right-align the heading for cell F5.

5. Center the titles in A1:A2 across the worksheet and make them bold.

6. Widen columns A and B to accommodate the data and headings.

7. Center the "Quantity Ordered" heading over the four columns below it.

8. Select cell C6 and key **=B6-(B6*C3)**. The formula calculates the new price for a quantity of 50, based on a 2% discount.

9. Edit the formula in cell C6. Change cell reference C3 to the mixed cell reference that adjusts the column, but not the row, when the formula is copied.
10. Change both B6 cell references in the formula to the mixed cell reference that adjusts the row, but not the column, when the formula is copied.
11. Copy the formula from cell C6 to cells C7 through F10.
12. Widen columns to display the values, if necessary.
13. Create a comment in cell A1. Change the default user name to *[your initials]* and key the following text for the comment:

    Call supplier on a monthly basis to review discounts received.
14. Rename the Sheet1 tab Discounts
15. Add the standard header to the worksheet with your name, the filename, and the date. Use a Page 1 of ? footer. Horizontally center the worksheet on the page.
16. Save the workbook as *[your initials]***11-17.xls**.
17. Print the worksheet and the comment at the end of the sheet.
18. Create a formula printout in landscape orientation with grids and row and column headings. Do not include the comments with this printout. Use a Page 1 of ? footer.
19. Close the workbook without saving.

EXERCISE 11-18

Create an IF function with a single condition and correct a circular reference

Construct a worksheet for analyzing overtime. Use formulas that include IF functions that track hours worked and overtime pay.

1. Open a new workbook.
2. Key the worksheet as shown in Figure 11-12.

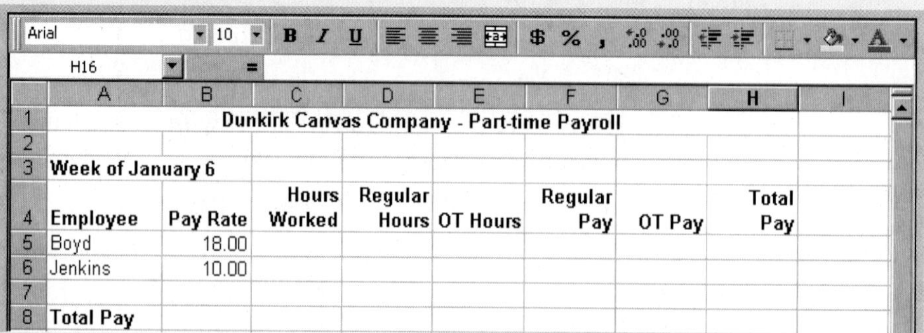

	A	B	C	D	E	F	G	H
1	Dunkirk Canvas Company - Part-time Payroll							
2								
3	Week of January 6							
4	Employee	Pay Rate	Hours Worked	Regular Hours	OT Hours	Regular Pay	OT Pay	Total Pay
5	Boyd	18.00						
6	Jenkins	10.00						
7								
8	Total Pay							

FIGURE 11-12 The worksheet to be keyed.

3. Format the text in cells B4 through F4 to wrap and make the necessary cell format and column format changes as shown in the figure.
4. Select cell D5.
5. Key **=IF(C5>=40,40,C5)**. The result is 0. This formula tests the value in cell C5. If the value is greater than or equal to 40, the number 40 is entered in cell D5 as regular hours worked. If the value is less than 40, the value in cell C5 is entered in cell D5 as regular hours.
6. Copy the formula in cell D5 to cell D6.
7. Select cell E5 and enter a subtraction formula that determines the overtime hours. Copy the formula from cell E5 to cell E6.
8. Select cell F5 and enter a multiplication formula that determines the regular pay. The result is 0 formatted with a hyphen.
9. Copy the formula from cell F5 to cell F6.
10. Select cell G5 and enter a multiplication formula that determines the overtime pay. Overtime hours are paid at 1.5 times the regular pay rate.
11. Copy the formula in cell G5 to cell G6.
12. Select cell H5 and enter a formula that adds regular pay to overtime pay. Copy the formula to cell H6.
13. To test the formulas, select cell C5 and key **43**
14. In cell C6, key **50**
15. Select cell F8 and key **=SUM(F5:F8)**. Click OK or Cancel to remove the circular reference error message.
16. Correct the circular reference error in cell F8. Copy the corrected formula to cells G8:H8.
17. Format the cells H5:H6 and F8:H8 in accounting style with dollar signs and two decimal places. Format F5:G6 in the same style without the dollar sign.
18. Rename the Sheet1 tab to **Part-time payroll**.
19. Add the standard header to the worksheet with your name, the filename, and the date. Horizontally center the worksheet on the page.
20. Save the workbook as *[your initials]***11-18.xls**.
21. Print the worksheet.
22. Create a formula printout in landscape orientation with grids and row and column headings. Use a Page 1 of ? footer.
23. Close the workbook without saving.

EXERCISE 11-19

Create an IF function that inserts text and use the VLOOKUP function.

Construct a worksheet that shows the status of delinquent accounts and calculates a 2% late fee using the IF function. Use a lookup table to insert the company name next to the corresponding company number.

1. Open the file **Accounts.xls**.
2. Use the information shown in Figure 11-13 for the following steps.

FIGURE 11-13

Co. No.	Invoice Date	Amount
1014	6/28/97	24,369.00
1011	5/30/97	13,254.21
1015	8/20/97	34,547.33
1013	4/22/97	6,241.01
1016	9/14/97	27,362.00
1012	7/9/97	14,925.08

Your instructor may give you different "Invoice Dates."

3. Enter the data from Figure 11-13, starting in cells A4, C4, and D4.
4. Select cell E4. This cell contains a formula that calculates the number of days late. Create a better formula that hides the numbers appearing in the "Days Late" column if the invoice date is blank and that calculates days late when an invoice date exists: Key **=IF(C4=0,"",TODAY()-C4)**. The value_if_false argument calculates the days late when an invoice date exists.
5. Copy the formula in cell E4 to cells E5 through E9.
6. Select cell F4.
7. Click [fx] to begin entering a formula that displays "Over 30" for accounts 30 days past due, "Over 60" for accounts 60 days past due, and "Collection" for accounts 90 days past due.
8. Choose Logical from the Function category list box.
9. Choose IF from the Function name list box.
10. Click OK.

11. Key **E4>90** in the Logical_test argument box.
12. Key **"Collection"** in the Value_if_true argument box.
13. Click the Value_if_false argument box, then click the down arrow on the Function box to insert another IF function as a nested argument.
14. Choose IF from the drop-down list.
15. Key **E4>60** in the Logical_test argument box.
16. Key **"Over 60"** in the Value_if_true argument box.
17. Click the Value_if_false argument box, then click the Function box to insert another IF function as a nested argument.
18. Key **E4>30** in the Logical_test argument box.
19. Key **"Over 30"** in the Value_if_true argument box.
20. Key **0** in the Value_if_false argument box.
21. Click OK.
22. Copy the formula in cell F4 to cells F5 through F9.
23. Place a comment in cell F4 explaining how the formula works. Select cell F4 and choose Comment from the Insert menu.
24. Replace the default user name with *[your initials]*: then key the following text in the Comment box:

    Logical tests are for 90, 60, and 30 days past due.
25. Select any cell.
26. Create a name for the constant .02 called **late_fee**.
27. Select cell G4.
28. Create a formula that charges a 2% late fee for accounts more than 60 days past due by keying **=IF(E4>60,D4*late_fee,0)**
29. Copy the formula in cell G4 to cells G5 through G9.
30. Select cells A2:B7 in the Table sheet and name this range **T_Company**. It serves as the table_array in a VLOOKUP function.
31. Select cell B4 in the Accounts sheet.
32. To create a formula that inserts the company name next to the corresponding company number, key **=VLOOKUP(A4,T_Company,2)**
33. Copy the formula in cell B4 to cells B5 through B9.
34. Adjust the column widths so all text shows and the worksheet can print on one page. Format the values in columns D, G and H in number style with two decimal places and commas.
35. Add the standard header to both worksheets with your name, the filename, and the date. Use a Page 1 of ? footer.
36. Save the workbook as *[your initials]***11-19.xls**
37. Print the entire workbook and the comment at the end of the sheet.

38. Create a formula printout with grids and row and column headings. Do not include the comment with this printout. Use a Page 1 of ? footer.
39. Close the workbook without saving.

EXERCISE 11-20

Create an IF function that inserts text and use the VLOOKUP function.

Create a worksheet that lists debits and credits against specific accounts for a monthly journal for the Dunkirk Canvas Company.

1. Create a worksheet sketch that includes a title, column labels, and an area for data. The worksheet should include each account number (rows) and columns showing the account description, its category, debit, and credit. The description and category should be computed with formulas that use a lookup table. The last row of the data area should include a row that will show totals for the debits and credits. Sketch the lookup table on a separate page. The table will have columns for the account number, description, and category.
2. Using a 12-point font for all data, transfer the monthly journal sketch into Excel by keying and formatting the labels. Then key the information shown in Figure 11-14. This is the monthly journal portion of the worksheet.

FIGURE 11-14

Acc#	Description	Category	Debit	Credit
100			100.00	85.00
201			300.00	325.00
101			142.00	

3. Rename the Sheet1 tab Journal, rename Sheet2 Table, and rename Sheet3 User Information.
4. Transfer the sketch of the lookup table to the Table sheet, using a 12-point font and formatting the headings. Then key the information shown in Figure 11-15 (on the next page).
5. Name the table T_Description. Do not include the column headings in the range.

FIGURE 11-15

Acc#	Description	Category
100	Cash	Asset
101	Securities	Asset
102	Notes Receivable	Asset
200	Notes Payable	Liability
201	Taxes Payable	Liability
202	Wages Payable	Liability

6. In the "Description" column on the Journal sheet, create a formula to enter the description automatically when the account number is keyed. Construct the formula so no #N/A messages appear if the "Account Number" column is blank. (*Hint:* Use IF and VLOOKUP with nesting.)
7. In the "Category" column, create another formula to enter the category automatically when the account number is keyed. Construct the formula so no #N/A messages appear if the "Account Number" column is blank.
8. Widen columns B and C to accommodate the results of the formulas.
9. Assume that nine additional rows of data will be entered. Extend the formulas through these rows.
10. Add a row to total the debits and credits.
11. Below the total, enter a formula that displays the message, "Debits do not equal credits," when the total debits do not match the total credits.
12. Enhance the worksheet by adding formatting such as bold and borders. Format the Total values appropriately.
13. In the User Information worksheet, create documentation that includes the following: File Information (Created by, Date created, Date revised, Revised by, Contact for help); Purpose of workbook (paragraph form); Instructions to User (special instructions needed by user to enter data correctly); and Range Names. Style the documentation for easy reading.
14. Add the standard header to all worksheets with your name, the filename, and the date. Horizontally center the worksheets. Use a Page 1 of ? footer.
15. Save the workbook as *[your initials]***11-20.xls**
16. Print the entire workbook.
17. Create a formula printout in landscape orientation with grids and row and column headings. Use a Page 1 of ? footer.
18. Close the workbook without saving.

Working with Dates, Times, and Financial Functions

OBJECTIVES

After completing this lesson, you will be able to:

1. **Use automatic date formats.**
2. **Work with date functions.**
3. **Use date math.**
4. **Work with time functions.**
5. **Work with financial functions.**

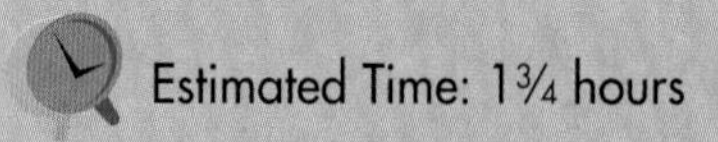

This lesson covers several of Excel's date and time functions and introduces you to calculations involving dates and times. In addition, you see how financial functions assist you in evaluating and analyzing loan and investment terms. You can calculate present and future values of investments, interest rates and amounts, the number of payment periods in an annuity, and payment amounts. Once you become familiar with Excel's financial functions, you can evaluate an investment and even choose the best loan terms.

Working with Dates

In Excel, dates are stored as numbers. Excel uses as a default the 1900 Date System, which uses *serial numbers* from 1 to 2,958,525 to store dates in cells with the date format. Each serial number represents a date: 1 stands for the date January 1, 1900, while the last number, 2,958,525, represents December 31, 9999. Storing dates as numbers enables Excel to perform calculations with dates.

You can key dates in a variety of ways. As with numbers, Excel assigns the closest matching date format to the date you key. The date displayed on the screen may not exactly match the date you keyed, depending on whether your date format matches one of Excel's built-in date formats.

TABLE 12-1 **Excel's Date Formats**

KEYED CHARACTERS	DATE CODE	SCREEN DISPLAY
12-1-97	m/d/yy	12/1/97
12/1/97	m/d/yy	12/1/97
1-Jan-97	d-mmm-yy	1-Jan-97
1-January-1997	d-mmm-yy	1-Jan-97
March-97	mmm-yy	Mar-97
3-97	mmm-yy	Mar-97

EXERCISE 12-1 Use Automatic Date Formats

Excel formats the cells for dates when you enter them.

1. Open a new workbook.
2. In cells A6:E6, key the following data:

   12/1/97 12-1-97 1-Dec-97 1-December-1997 12/97
3. Select cell D6 and choose Cells from the Format menu. Click the Numbers tab, if necessary. In the Format Cells dialog box, Excel chooses the date format code that most closely matches the date you keyed.
4. Click Cancel.

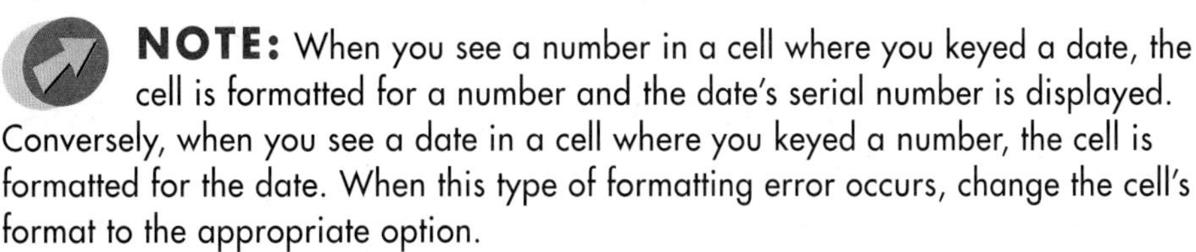

NOTE: When you see a number in a cell where you keyed a date, the cell is formatted for a number and the date's serial number is displayed. Conversely, when you see a date in a cell where you keyed a number, the cell is formatted for the date. When this type of formatting error occurs, change the cell's format to the appropriate option.

Working with Date Functions

Excel's built-in date functions make it possible to use dates in calculations. You can enter functions into your worksheet in the following ways:

- Key the function directly
- Use the Function command on the Insert menu
- Use [fx] to select from several types of date and time functions.

TABLE 12-2 Excel's Date Functions

FUNCTION	DESCRIPTION OF FUNCTION
=DATE()	Returns the serial number of a specified date
=NOW()	Returns the current system date and time
=TODAY()	Returns the current system date
=YEAR()	Returns the year, given a serial number or a date enclosed within quotes
=MONTH()	Returns the month number (e.g., 3 for March), given a serial number or a date
=DAY()	Returns the day number of the month, given a serial number or a date
=WEEKDAY()	Returns the day of the week (e.g., 2 for Monday), given a serial number or a date

EXERCISE 12-2 View the Serial Number of a Date

The DATE function returns the serial number of a particular date in the format "2/2/97." You must enter the arguments of the DATE function in the order of year, month, day.

1. In cell A1, enter **=DATE(97,8,27)**
2. Select cell A1 and choose Cells from the Format menu. Click the Number tab, if necessary, and choose Number in the Category list box. Choose 0 from the Decimal places option box. The Sample box displays the serial number for the date.
3. Click OK. The serial number appears on the screen. The result is 35669.
4. To display the date again, choose Cells from the Format menu.

5. Choose the Date category and the format 3/4/97 and click OK. The date is displayed.

TIP: You can also click the right mouse button and choose Format Cells from the shortcut menu to open the Format Cells dialog box. To generate the d-mmm-yy format, you can use the keyboard shortcut Ctrl+Shift+#.

6. Add the standard header to the worksheet with your name, the filename, and the date.
7. Save the workbook as *[your initials]***12-2.xls** and print the worksheet.
8. Close the workbook.

EXERCISE 12-3 Enter the Current Date

The TODAY function displays the current date stored in your computer. This date is updated each time you recalculate your worksheet. TODAY uses the format TODAY(). Note that the TODAY function (and the NOW function) will produce different results as the day or time changes.

1. Open the file **Employ1.xls**.
2. In cell F1, enter **=TODAY()**

TIP: You can also generate the current day by pressing Ctrl+;. Note that, unlike TODAY(), the current date generated by these keystrokes is not updated when the system clock changes.

Using Date Math

You can use addition, subtraction, multiplication, and division to perform calculations with dates. For example, the formula =TODAY()+30 displays the date 30 days from today. To calculate with a cell formatted for date, simply key the cell reference in the formula. To enter a date directly in a formula, key quotation marks around the date. This format instructs Excel to use the serial number for the date. For example, to calculate the number of days between April 15, 1995 and March 1, 1997, you could use the formula ="3-1-97"-"4-15-95".

When you calculate dates, make sure the dates in the cell are formatted appropriately for a date. Excel uses the stored serial number to calculate no matter how the date is formatted on the screen.

EXERCISE 12-4 Calculate Elapsed Days

1. Select cell E5 and key **=TODAY()-D5**
2. Copy the formula from cell E5 to cells E6 through E10. The results display as dates and times rather then numbers, so the format needs to be changed.

FIGURE 12-1 Calculating differences in dates

E5 = =TODAY()-D5

	A	B	C	D	E
1	Dunkirk Canvas Company				
2	Employee Information				
3					
4	Last	First	Date of Birth	Hire Date	Length of Service
5	Anderson	Carl	03/05/54	02/11/91	2259
6	Boyd	Jennifer	2/6/64	12/20/93	1216

Formula using the TODAY function

3. Format the cells in column E in the General format. The values in cells E5 through E10 show the length of service in days.

TIP: If you want to use the serial number for the current date in a calculation, but you don't want the number to change (as is the case when you use the TODAY() function), a quick way to get the serial value of the current date is to key =TODAY() and press F9 before you enter the function.

EXERCISE 12-5 Convert Days to Years

After the length of service is calculated, you can make the result more meaningful if you convert the days to years.

1. Double-click cell E5 to edit its contents.
2. Enclose the existing formula in parentheses by placing a left parenthesis before the "T" in "Today" and a right parenthesis at the end of the formula.
3. At the end of the formula, key **/365.25**

NOTE: 365.25 is the average number of days in a year, taking into account leap years.

4. Press Enter.
5. Copy the formula from cell E5 to cells E6 through E10.

FIGURE 12-2
Converting number of days into years

E5 = =(TODAY()-D5)/365.25

	A	B	C	D	E
1	Dunkirk Canvas Company				
2	Employee Information				
3					
4	Last	First	Date of Birth	Hire Date	Length of Service
5	Anderson	Carl	03/05/54	02/11/91	6.184804928

EXERCISE 12-6 Use the Integer Part of a Year

You may want to show only the whole number of years elapsed. Use the INT(Number) function to round down to the integer.

1. Select cell E5. The result of the formula is displayed in the General format.
2. Double-click cell E5 to edit the contents of the cell.
3. Position the insertion point after the = symbol and key **INT(**
4. Position the insertion point at the end of the formula and key a closed parenthesis, **)**
5. Press Enter. The number of years elapsed is rounded down to the integer.
6. Copy the formula from cell E5 to cells E6 through E10.

FIGURE 12-3
Rounding down number of years to an integer

7. Center the values in column E and add the standard header to the worksheet with your name, the filename, and the date.
8. Save the workbook as *[your initials]***12-6.xls**.
9. Print the worksheet and close the workbook.

EXERCISE 12-7 Calculate a Future Date

You may need to use the serial number of a specific date in a calculation. You can use the DATE function to calculate the serial number for a given date. The function uses the format DATE(year,month,day).

1. Open a new workbook. You use Excel to calculate the maturity date of a loan based on the issue date of June 6, 1994, and a term of 20 years.
2. Select cell A1 and key **Dunkirk Canvas Company**
3. Select cell A3 and key **Loan**
4. Select cell B3 and key **Maturity Date**
5. Select cell A4 and key **No.100**
6. Make the title and column headings bold and widen column B to accommodate the heading.
7. Select cell B4 and key **=DATE(94,6,6)+20*365.25**
8. Format cell B4 in the date format of March 4, 1997. The calculation determines the loan will mature on June 6, 2014.

EXERCISE 12-8 Calculate the Day of the Week

The WEEKDAY function returns a date's day number of the week. Sunday is 1, Monday is 2, and so on. The function uses the form WEEKDAY(serial_number,return_type), where the serial_number is a date or the cell address of a date.

1. Select cell C3 and key **Weekday**
2. Make the text bold, widen the column to accommodate the heading, and right align the heading.
3. Select cell C4 and enter **=WEEKDAY(B4)**. The result is 6, which represents Friday. In the next steps, you use a lookup table to convert this value to text.

NOTE: The WEEKDAY function's return_type argument is optional. Use it to change the day of the week start number. With a return_type of 2, number 1 represents Monday and number 7 represents Sunday.

4. Build the lookup table by keying the following data in columns A and B, starting in cell A8:

Number	**Day**
1	**Sunday**
2	**Monday**
3	**Tuesday**
4	**Wednesday**
5	**Thursday**
6	**Friday**
7	**Saturday**

5. Name this table T_Days.
6. Edit the formula in cell C4 to read =VLOOKUP(WEEKDAY(B4),T_Days,2) The formula now returns the text "Friday."
7. Right align cells C4:C5 and add the standard header to the worksheet with your name, the filename, and the date.
8. Save the workbook as *[your initials]***12-8.xls**.
9. Print the worksheet and close the workbook.

Working with Time Functions

Excel's time functions operate much like its date functions. Time is stored as a number and is displayed according to the format you select. A time number is stored as a decimal number. For example, the time number for 12:00 noon is 0.5, because it is half of the day (12 hours divided by 24 hours).

You can calculate with time numbers and Excel provides several useful time functions. Note that the time functions, such as TODAY(), are dynamic, changing as the day or time changes when the worksheet is updated or retrieved.

TABLE 12-3 **Excel's TIME Functions**

FUNCTION	DESCRIPTION OF FUNCTION
=NOW()	Returns the current system date and time
=TIME()	Returns the serial number of the specified time
=TIMEVALUE()	Returns the serial number of a time written as text and enclosed in quotation marks
=HOUR()	Returns the hour portion of a given serial number
=MINUTE()	Returns the minute portion of a given serial number
=SECOND()	Returns the second portion of a given serial number

EXERCISE 12-9 Use Automatic Time Formats

The TIME function returns the serial number of a particular time. It uses the format TIME(hour,minute,second).

1. Open the file **Employ2.xls**.
2. Select cell E1 and key **=TIME(7,30,25)**
3. Format cell E1 in number format with two decimal places. Notice how the time number is stored as a fraction of a 24-hour day, which is calculated by taking the number of hours passed in the day and dividing it by 24.

FIGURE 12-4 Time in number format, displaying as a decimal

E1 = =TIME(7,30,25)

	A	B	C	D	E
1	Dunkirk Canvas Company				0.31
2	Part-time Employees - Weekly hours				

Formula using the TIME function

4. Format cell E1 in time format, using the 13:30:55 format. The time displays as 7:30:25.

TIP: You can use the keyboard shortcut Ctrl+Shift+@ to generate the h:mm AM/PM format.

EXERCISE 12-10 Use Time Math

You can calculate with time numbers as well as date numbers. Remember to multiply a time number by 24 to convert it to hours.

1. In the range A6:F6, key the following data, skipping cell E6 and using a space between the time and am/pm:

   1/7/97 7:00 am 11:30 am 12:00 pm 4:00 pm

NOTE: You can key "am" or "pm" in lowercase letters and Excel automatically converts them to uppercase.

2. In cells A7:F7, key the following data, skipping cell E7:

   1/8/97 7:30 am 12:00 pm 12:45 pm 5:00 pm

TIP: You can generate the current time from the computer's clock by pressing Ctrl+Shift+;.

3. Select cell E6 and key **=(D6-C6)*24**. This formula converts the time number difference between Lunch Out and Lunch In to show Lunch Time as a fraction of an hour, rather than as a fraction of a day.
4. Format cell E6 in number format with two decimal places. The date format is replaced by a number format that shows the Lunch Time as a fraction of an hour.
5. Copy the formula from cell E6 to cell E7.
6. Select cell G6 and key **=(F6-B6)*24**
7. Format cell G6 in number format with two decimal places.
8. Double-click cell G6 to edit the formula so it subtracts the lunch time.
9. Position the insertion point at the end of the formula. Key **-E6** and press Enter.
10. Copy the formula from cell G6 to cell G7.
11. Add the standard header to the worksheet with your name, the filename, and the date.
12. Save the workbook as *[your initials]***12-10.xls**.
13. Print the worksheet and close the workbook.

FIGURE 12-5 Completed worksheet with formula converting time number into hours

Microsoft Excel - gl12-10.xls

G6 = =(F6-B6)*24-E6

	A	B	C	D	E	F	G
1	Dunkirk Canvas Company				7:30:25		
2	Part-time Employees - Weekly hours						
3							
4	Jennifer Boyd						
5	Date	Start Time	Lunch Out	Lunch In	Lunch Time (In hours)	Out Time	Hours Worked
6	1/7/97	7:00 AM	11:30 AM	12:00 PM	0.50	4:00 PM	8.50
7	1/8/97	7:30 AM	12:00 PM	12:45 PM	0.75	5:00 PM	8.75

Employ2

Ready

Working with Financial Functions

You can use Excel's financial functions to evaluate and analyze various loan and investment terms. This lesson focuses on the financial functions PMT, PV, RATE, NPER, FV, IPMT, and PPMT. In all financial functions, amounts of payments are represented by negative values if the payments are to be paid out and by positive values if they are to be received.

Many of these functions take the same arguments. Note that some of the argument names are the same as the function names themselves. For clarity, argument names are shown here in lowercase letters within parentheses and function names are in uppercase letters:

- (rate)
  The interest rate per period. To reflect the rate period in which the payments are made, you must enter the annual rate as a fraction that indicates how many payments per year are made. For example, a loan at an 8% annual rate for which the payments are made monthly is shown as 8%/12.
- (nper)
  The number of payment periods in an annuity. For a five-year loan with monthly payments, nper is shown as 5*12.
- (pv)
  The present value of an annuity. It is the total current value of the future payments.
- (fv)
  The future value of an annuity or the balance remaining after the last payment is made. In the case of loans, the future value should be 0 (and, in that instance, it is omitted).
- (type)
  Specifies whether payments are to be made at the beginning of the period (type 1) or at the end of the period (type 0 or omitted from function).

EXERCISE 12-11 Use the PMT Function

The PMT function calculates the amount of each payment for an *annuity*, which is a constant periodic payment paid over a fixed time period. The PMT function uses the format PMT(rate,nper,pv,fv,type).

1. Open the file **Finance.xls**. You'll use different worksheets in this workbook for Exercises 12-11 through 12-17. Display the PMT worksheet.

2. In cell B4, key **10**
3. To calculate the (nper), select cell B5 and key **=B4*12**
4. In cell B6, key **150000** for the present value of the loan.
5. In cell B7, key **13%**
6. In cell B9, enter **=PMT(B7/12,B5,B6)**
7. Adjust the column width, if necessary. The result ($2,239.66) is negative because it represents a value that is owed and negative numbers in this format are displayed in red. When the type argument is omitted, Excel makes the calculation based on a monthly payment made at the end of each month.
8. In cell B10, enter **=PMT(B7/12,B5,B6,0,1)**. The inclusion of the type argument shows the monthly payment of ($2,215.66) when payment is made at the beginning of each month. It is clear from the two formulas that payments are lower when they are made at the beginning of the month.

FIGURE 12-6 Using the PMT function

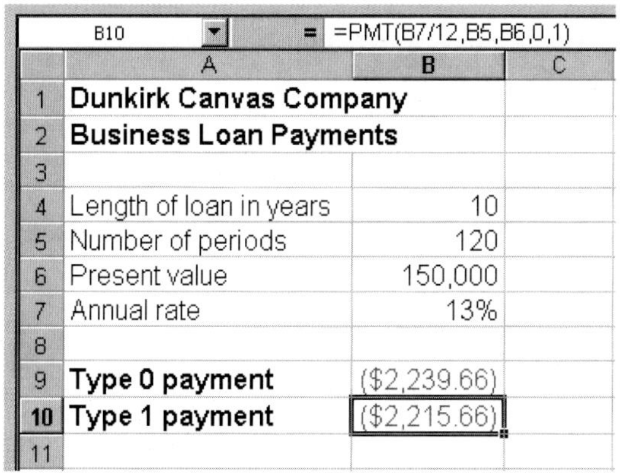

B10 = =PMT(B7/12,B5,B6,0,1)

	A	B	C
1	**Dunkirk Canvas Company**		
2	**Business Loan Payments**		
3			
4	Length of loan in years	10	
5	Number of periods	120	
6	Present value	150,000	
7	Annual rate	13%	
8			
9	**Type 0 payment**	($2,239.66)	
10	**Type 1 payment**	($2,215.66)	
11			

9. Add the standard header to the worksheet with your name, the filename, and the date. Add a Page 1 of ? footer.
10. Save the workbook as *[your initials]***12-11.xls**, but don't close the workbook.

EXERCISE 12-12 Use the PV Function

You use the PV function to determine the value of an annuity at the present time. It uses the format PV(rate,nper,pmt,fv,type). The pmt argument is the payment made each period. It must be entered as a negative value. If both fv and type are 0, you can omit them.

1. Display the PV worksheet by clicking on the PV tab of the workbook you saved in the last Exercise.
2. Select cell B4 and key **9.7%**
3. Select cell B5 and key **10**
4. Select cell B6. The formula in this cell calculates the nper argument.
5. Because the bond pays semi-annually, key **=B5*2**
6. In cell B7, key **-7900**
7. In cell B8, key **100000**
8. Format cells B5:B8 in number style with commas and no decimal places, using the third Negative numbers option. Adjust the column width, if necessary.
9. In cell B9, enter **=PV(B4/2,B6,B7)**. The result returned is $99,715.76.
10. In cell B11, enter **=B9-B8**. The difference between the cost and the actual value of the bond is ($284.24). Because the asking price is higher than the present value of the bond, it is not a good investment.

FIGURE 12-7 Using the PV function

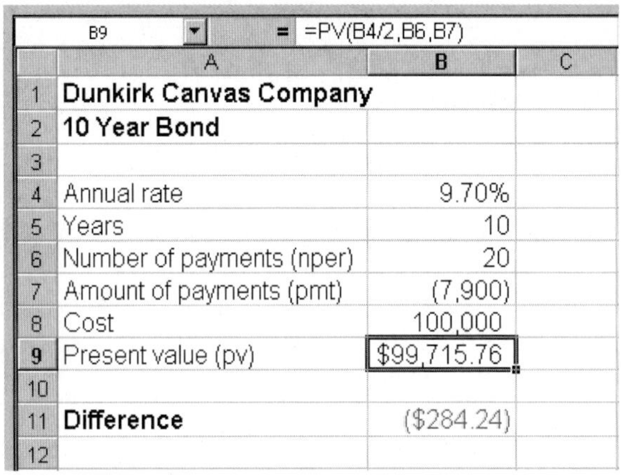

B9 = =PV(B4/2,B6,B7)

	A	B	C
1	**Dunkirk Canvas Company**		
2	**10 Year Bond**		
3			
4	Annual rate	9.70%	
5	Years	10	
6	Number of payments (nper)	20	
7	Amount of payments (pmt)	(7,900)	
8	Cost	100,000	
9	Present value (pv)	$99,715.76	
10			
11	**Difference**	($284.24)	
12			

11. Add the standard header to the worksheet with your name, the filename, and the date. Add a Page 1 of ? footer.

EXERCISE 12-13 Use the RATE Function

You can use Excel's RATE function to calculate the interest rate per period of an annuity. It uses the format RATE(nper,pmt,pv,fv,type,guess). The guess argument is your estimate of the rate. If you omit it, Excel assumes the rate is 10% annually. If the result is not at least 0.0000001 (or 0.00001%), RATE does not find a result, and the #NUM error value is displayed. You can then try entering different values as a guess.

1. Display the RATE worksheet by clicking the RATE tab.
2. Beginning in cell B4, key the following data in column B:

   4
   =B4*12
   -100
   3500
   350

3. Format the range B4:B8 in comma style with no decimal places.
4. In cell B9, enter the formula with the "guess" argument omitted: **=RATE(B5,B6,B7,B8)**
5. Change the format to show the percentage with two decimal places.
6. In cell B11, enter **=B9*12**
7. Format the cell in percent style with two decimal places.

FIGURE 12-8
Using the RATE function

B9 = =RATE(B5,B6,B7,B8)

	A	B	C
1	**Dunkirk Canvas Company**		
2	**Equipment Lease**		
3			
4	Length of lease in years	4	
5	Number of payment periods	48	
6	Amount of payments	(100)	
7	Present value	3,500	
8	Future value of balance	350	
9	Monthly rate of lease	1.11%	
10			
11	**Yearly rate of lease**	13.31%	

8. Add the standard header to the worksheet with your name, the filename, and the date. Add a Page 1 of ? footer.
9. Save the workbook as *[your initials]***12-13.xls**, but do not close it.

EXERCISE 12-14 Use the NPER Function

You use the NPER function to calculate the number of periodic, constant payments for an annuity at an unchanging interest rate. It uses the format NPER(rate,pmt,pv,fv,type). You can omit the pv and fv arguments if they are both zero.

1. Display the NPER worksheet by clicking the NPER tab of the workbook you saved in the previous Exercise.
2. Beginning in cell B4, key the following data in column B:

   3%

   210

   3000
3. In cell B7, enter **=NPER(B4/12,B5,B6,0,1)**. The result is a negative 14 because payments paid out are represented as negative values and payments received are shown as positive values.
4. Format the cell to have no decimal places.

FIGURE 12-9 Using the NPER function

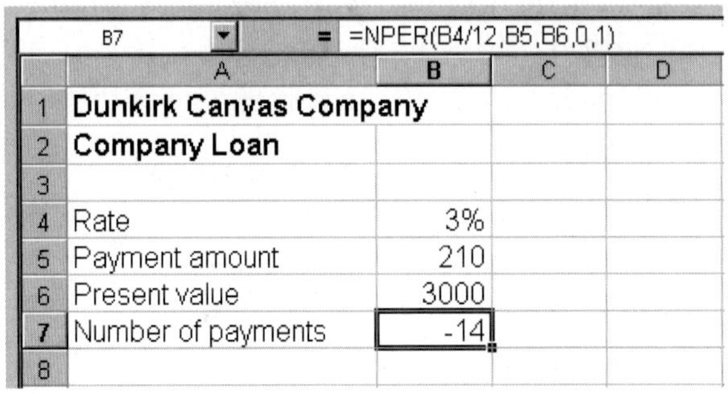

B7 = =NPER(B4/12,B5,B6,0,1)

	A	B	C	D
1	**Dunkirk Canvas Company**			
2	**Company Loan**			
3				
4	Rate	3%		
5	Payment amount	210		
6	Present value	3000		
7	Number of payments	-14		
8				

5. Add the standard header to the worksheet with your name, the filename, and the date. Add a Page 1 of ? footer.

EXERCISE 12-15 Use the FV Function

The FV function calculates the future value of an annuity. It provides the value of an investment or loan after all payments are made over a given period of time at a given interest rate. The FV function uses the format FV(rate,nper,pmt,pv,type).

The pmt argument is the amount of each periodic payment for the annuity and is represented by a negative number because it is paid to the lender.

1. Display the FV worksheet.
2. Beginning in cell B4, key the following data:

   4.5%

   12

   -250

   -500

3. In cell B9, enter **=FV(B4/12,B5,B6,B7,1)**
4. Increase the column width to display the future value of $3,597.11, if necessary.

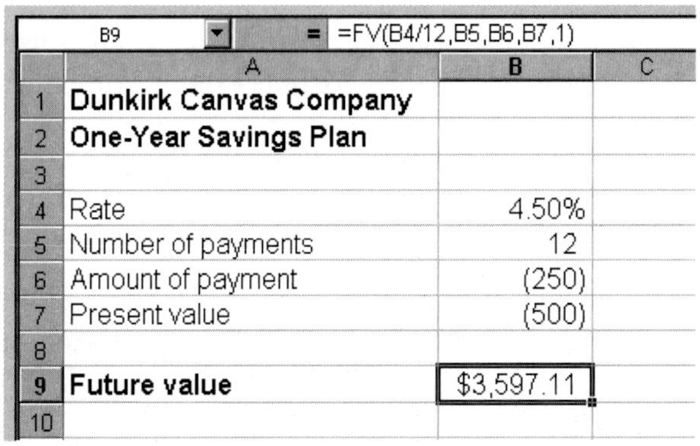

FIGURE 12-10 Using the FV function

B9 = =FV(B4/12,B5,B6,B7,1)

	A	B	C
1	**Dunkirk Canvas Company**		
2	**One-Year Savings Plan**		
3			
4	Rate	4.50%	
5	Number of payments	12	
6	Amount of payment	(250)	
7	Present value	(500)	
8			
9	**Future value**	$3,597.11	
10			

5. Add the standard header to the worksheet with your name, the filename, and the date. Add a Page 1 of ? footer.
6. Save the workbook as *[your initials]***12-15.xls**, but do not close it.

EXERCISE 12-16 Use the IPMT Function

When payments are made to reduce a loan, each payment includes both an interest amount and a portion of the principal. The *principal* is the amount borrowed, or the present value. *Interest* is the amount paid to the lender as the lender's profit; it accrues at a set rate.

The IPMT function calculates the amount of the interest payment for a period of an annuity. It uses the format IPMT(rate,per,nper,pv,fv,type).

The per argument is the period for which you want to calculate the interest amount. It must be a whole number ranging from 1 to the number of payments (nper).

1. Display the PMT worksheet by clicking the PMT tab of the wookbook you saved in the previous Exercise.
2. Beginning in cell A12, key the following data:

   Type 0 Payments

   Interest for the first month

   Principal payment for the first month
3. Increase the width of column A.
4. In cell B13, enter **=IPMT(B7/12,1,B5,B6)**. The result is ($1,625.00), which is the amount of the interest payment for the first month.

EXERCISE 12-17 Use the PPMT Function

The PPMT function calculates the amount of the principal payment for a period of an annuity. It uses the format PPMT(rate,per,nper,pv,fv,type).

1. In cell B14, enter **=PPMT(B7/12,1,B5,B6)**. The result is ($614.66), which is the principal payment for the first month. The result from cell B13 and the result from cell B14 add together to make up the periodic payment.

FIGURE 12-11 Using the IPMT and PPMT functions

B14 = =PPMT(B7/12,1,B5,B6)

	A	B	C
2	**Business Loan Payments**		
3			
4	Length of loan in years	10	
5	Number of periods	120	
6	Present value	150,000	
7	Annual rate	13%	
8			
9	**Type 0 payment**	($2,239.66)	
10	**Type 1 payment**	($2,215.66)	
11			
12	Type 0 Payments		
13	Interest for the first month	($1,625.00)	
14	Principal payment for the first month	($614.66)	
15			

2. Save the workbook as *[your initials]***12-17.xls** and print the entire workbook.
3. Close the workbook.

COMMAND SUMMARY

FEATURE	BUTTON	MENU	KEYBOARD
d-mmm-yy date format		Format, Cells	Ctrl+Shift+#
h:mm AM/PM time format		Format, Cells	Ctrl+Shift+@

Concepts Review

TRUE/FALSE QUESTIONS

Each of the following statements is either true or false. Indicate your choice by circling T or F.

T F *1*. When you key a date in a cell, it is sometimes displayed differently on the screen.

T F *2*. The TODAY function displays the current date and time.

T F *3*. Because Excel stores dates as numbers, date calculations are possible.

T F *4*. In all financial functions, amounts of payments are represented by positive values if the payments are to be paid out.

T F *5*. The function TIMEVALUE() returns the current date and time.

T F *6*. When using the PV(rate,nper,pmt,fv,type) function, you can omit the fv and type arguments if their values are both 0.

T F *7*. When you type a time in a cell, it is stored as a time number and is displayed according to the format you select.

T F *8*. The RATE function, which is used to calculate the interest rate per period of an annuity, always returns a result.

SHORT ANSWER QUESTIONS

Write the correct answer in the space provided.

1. Which function would you use to determine the serial number of a specific date?

____

2. Which function would you use to calculate the amount of each payment for an annuity over a certain period of time at a given interest rate?

____

3. Dates are stored as what type of number so that they can be used in calculations?

____

4. Given a serial number or a date, which function would you use to calculate the day of the week?

____

5. If you want to enter a date directly in a formula, you surround the date with which keyboard symbol?

____

6. How is a time number recorded in a cell?

____

7. When payments are to be made at the beginning of the period, is the type argument in a financial function specified as 1 or 0?

____

8. The PPMT function is used to calculate the amount of which type of payment for a period of an annuity?

____

CRITICAL THINKING

Answer these questions on a separate piece of paper. There are no right or wrong answers. Support your answers with examples from your own experience, if possible.

1. What are some examples of when a business may need to determine elapsed days but needs to calculate only the workdays? Is there a date and time function that performs this calculation?
2. Can you use financial functions to evaluate an adjustable rate mortgage? Why or why not?

Skills Review

EXERCISE 12-18

Use date and time functions and date math.

1. Open the file **Employ3.xls**.
2. Select cell F1 and key the formula for the current date: **=TODAY()**
3. Select cell E5 and key the formula to calculate the years to retirement based on age 65: **=65-INT((TODAY()-C5)/365.25)**

4. Copy the formula from cell E5 to the range E6:E8.
5. Center align the values in column E and add the standard header to the worksheet with your name, the filename, and the date.
6. Save the workbook as *[your initials]***12-18.xls** and print the worksheet.
7. Create a formula printout in landscape orientation with grids and row and column headings.
8. Close the workbook without saving.

EXERCISE 12-19

Use functions that calculate the day of the week and create formulas that place the day of the week in worksheet cells.

1. Open the file **Schedule.xls**.
2. Select cell G5 and key the formula =WEEKDAY(F5).
3. Copy the formula from cell G5 to the range G6:G12.
4. On the Table worksheet, name the lookup table that starts in cell A2 T_Days. Do not include the column headings.
5. On the Schedule worksheet, select cell H5 and enter a formula using a VLOOKUP function to look up the number of the weekday in the T_Days table and return the day of the week to the formula cell.
6. Copy the formula from cell H5 to the range H6:H12.
7. Center align the values in column G.
8. Re-apply a thick bottom border to cells G12:H12, which were changed when the formulas were copied.
9. Add the standard header to the worksheet with your name, the filename, and the date.
10. Save the workbook as *[your initials]***12-19.xls** and print the Schedule worksheet.
11. Create a formula printout of the Schedule worksheet in landscape orientation with grids and row and column headings. Use a Page 1 of ? footer.
12. Close the workbook without saving.

EXERCISE 12-20

Use automatic time formats and time math to compute the total number of hours worked in a day.

1. Open the file **Contract.xls**.
2. Select cell A8 and key **Wallace, M.**

3. In cells D8 and E8, key the following data:

   6:00 am   5:45 pm

4. Select cell L5 and key the formula:
   =SUM((C5-B5),(E5-D5),(G5-F5),(I5-H5),(K5-J5))
5. Copy the formula from cell L5 to the range L6:L8, and restore the bottom border to L8.
6. Add the standard header to the worksheet with your name, the filename, and the date.
7. Save the workbook as *[your initials]***12-20.xls** and print the worksheet.
8. Create a formula printout in landscape orientation with grids and row and column headings. Use a Page 1 of ? footer.
9. Close the workbook without saving.

EXERCISE 12-21

Use financial functions to analyze different payment plans for a loan and calculate the future value of the loan amount.

1. Open the file **Analysis.xls**.
2. In cells B5:B8, key the following data:

   1   =B5*12   10,000   10%

3. Select cell B10 and key **=PMT(B8/12,B6,B7)**
4. Select cell B11 and key **=PMT(B8/12,B6,B7,0,1)**
5. In the range E5:E8, key the following data:

   6%   12   1,000   1,000

6. Select cell E10 and key **=FV(E5/12,E6,E7,E8,1)**
7. Add the standard header to the worksheet with your name, the filename, and the date.
8. Save the workbook as *[your initials]***12-21.xls** and print the worksheet.
9. Create a formula printout with grids and row and column headings. Use a Page 1 of ? footer.
10. Close the workbook without saving.

Lesson Applications

EXERCISE 12-22

Use automatic date formats and use date functions to compute the days late based on the current date.

One of Dunkirk Canvas Company's largest clients is overdue on its accounts. Set up an accounts receivable worksheet for overdue accounts.

1. Open the file **Smith1.xls**.
2. Key the following data in columns B and C, beginning in cell B3:

1,009.65	**6/10/97**
2,376.23	**6/10/97**
34,987.22	**6/12/97**
203,979.00	**6/19/97**
542.18	**7/12/97**
1,409.67	**7/14/97**
311.98	**7/18/97**
2,906.12	**8/14/97**
4,032.86	**8/15/97**
22,091.48	**8/18/97**

3. Create a formula in D3 that adds 30 days to the invoice date.
4. Copy the formula through cell D12 by dragging the fill handle.
5. Create a formula in E3 that subtracts the due date from the current date.
6. Copy the formula to cells E4 through E12.
7. Format the values in column E for number style with no decimal places.
8. In the range F3:F12, use the IF function to enter a formula that displays "Yes" if the invoice is more than thirty days late and "No" if it is not.
9. Add the standard header to the worksheet with your name, the filename, and the date.
10. Save the workbook as *[your initials]***12-22.xls** and print the worksheet.
11. Create a formula printout in landscape orientation with grids and row and column headings. Use a Page 1 of ? footer.
12. Close the workbook without saving.

EXERCISE 12-23

Use automatic date formats and date math to compute the number of days between dates.

In an effort to improve customer service, Dunkirk Canvas Company is researching the number of days it took to ship a product after it was ordered.

1. Open the file **DunShip.xls**.
2. Beginning in cell C5, key the following data:
   9/5/96
   9/5/96
   9/6/96
   9/6/96
   9/6/96
   9/9/96
   9/9/96
   9/10/96
   9/11/96
   9/11/96
   9/11/96
3. Select cell D5 and key a formula that subtracts the date the order was received from the date the order was shipped.
4. Copy the formula from cell D5 to the range D6:D15.
5. Format the values in column D for number style with no decimal places.
6. Select cell A17 and key **Average**
7. Select cell D17 and key a formula using the AVERAGE function to calculate the average turnaround days. Format the cell to display one decimal place.
8. Add the standard header to the worksheet with your name, the filename, and the date.
9. Save the workbook as *[your initials]***12-23.xls** and print the worksheet.
10. Create a formula printout in landscape orientation with grids and row and column headings.
11. Close the workbook without saving.

EXERCISE 12-24

Use automatic date and time format, and date and time math, to compute elapsed times.

Dunkirk Canvas Company needs a worksheet to track customer phone inquiries. It wants to know when the phone call was returned and whether the problem was resolved, using sample phone data collected by the Customer Service Department.

1. Open the file **Customer.xls**.
2. Key the following data in columns C and D, beginning in cell C6:

9-16-97 3:00 pm	**Yes**
9-17-97 9:00 am	**Yes**
9-17-97 12:30 pm	**No**
9-18-97 9:30 am	**Yes**
9-18-97 10:00 am	**No**
9-19-97 8:00 am	**Yes**

3. In cell E6, key a formula to determine the turnaround time. The first part of the formula should subtract the dates and times of the two phone calls (make sure to place parentheses around this part of the formula); the second part should multiply this value by 24.
4. Copy the formula from cell E6 to cells E7:E11.
5. Format the range A5:E11 with an outline border, choosing the third line from the bottom, on the right side of Style list box.
6. Format column E to display one decimal place.
7. Using the same line style, add a border between each column and row in the A5:E11 range.
8. Vertically center the column headings and center align the data in cells D6:E11.
9. Add the standard header to the worksheet with your name, the filename, and the date.
10. Save the workbook as *[your initials]***12-24.xls** and print the worksheet.
11. Create a formula printout in landscape orientation with grids and row and column headings. Use a Page 1 of ? footer.
12. Close the workbook without saving.

EXERCISE 12-25

Use a financial function to calculate mortgage payments at different interest rates.

Dunkirk Canvas Company is in the process of choosing a mortgage loan to finance its expansion. Information was obtained from four banks about their interest rates. A mortgage loan analysis worksheet is needed to calculate the monthly payments based on the following: All loans are 15-year mortgages with payments due at the end of each month, so there will be 180 monthly payments. All loans have a present value of $200,000.

1. Create a spreadsheet sketch that includes a worksheet title, column and row labels, and an area for data. The data area consists of two columns that include labels and data for the following information: the annual rate, the number of periods (nper), and the amount of the loan (pv). In the adjacent columns are column headings for the interest rates of four different banks, labeled Bank 1, Bank 2, etc. Under the data area is a row containing the formulas that compute payments for each of the four banks.
2. Using a 12-point font for all data, transfer the loan analysis sketch into Excel by keying and formatting the labels.
3. Rename Sheet1 **Payments** and rename Sheet2 **User Information**.
4. Key the following information in the data area of the Payments worksheet:

	Bank1	**Bank2**	**Bank3**	**Bank4**
Annual Rate	**11%**	**10.5%**	**9.7%**	**11.3%**
No. of periods (nper)	**180**			
Amount of Loan (pv)	**200000**			
Payment				

5. In the Payment row under each bank, enter formulas using the PMT function to compute the monthly payments. Remember that the annual rate argument must be divided by 12. You can omit the fv and type arguments. Use absolute and mixed cell addresses in the formula for the Bank1 formula and copy it to the remaining three banks. (*Hint:* Use a mixed cell address for the rate and absolute cell addresses for the nper and pv arguments.)
6. Format the worksheet attractively, using the percent style with one decimal place for the rates and currency style with two decimal places for the payment amounts. Use the negative number format that displays values in parentheses.

7. In the User Information worksheet, create documentation that includes the following: File Information (Created by, Date created, Date revised, Revised by, Contact for help); Purpose of spreadsheet (paragraph form); and Instructions to User (special instructions needed by user to enter data correctly).
8. Add the standard header to the worksheets with your name, the filename, and the date. Horizontally center the worksheets.
9. Save the workbook as *[your initials]***12-25.xls** and print the entire workbook.
10. Create a formula printout of the Payments worksheet with grids and row and column headings. Use a Page 1 of ? footer.
11. Close the workbook without saving.

Templates

OBJECTIVES

After completing this lesson, you will be able to:

1. **Create a template.**
2. **Use a template.**
3. **Work with Excel's built-in templates.**

Estimated Time: 1½ hours

Templates are models for worksheets. They include style elements such as fonts, font style, font size, alignment, and borders. They can also include boilerplate text or formulas, such as comments on data included in specific reports. Two basic differences exist between template files and workbook files:

- When you open a template, you open a copy of the template instead of the actual file.
- Template files are assigned an .xlt extension and workbook files are assigned an .xls extension.

You can create your own templates or use the built-in templates provided by Excel. In a Typical installation of Microsoft Excel, the following templates are available from the Spreadsheet Solutions tab when you choose New from the File menu: Invoice and Village Software.

Creating Templates

You create templates by example or by definition, which is similar to how you create styles, as described in Lesson 9. Any worksheet can become a template. To create a template:

- Create a new workbook or complete formatting changes to an existing workbook.
- Choose Save As from the File menu.
- Key the template name in the File name text box and select the folder from the Save in text box.
- From the Save as type list, choose the Template format (.xlt extension).
- Click the Save button.

EXERCISE 13-1 Create a Template by Example

You can create a template from an existing worksheet by making formatting changes and clearing data.

1. Open the file **Balance.xls**.
2. Choose Page Setup from the File menu.
3. Click the Page tab, if necessary, and click Landscape.
4. Click the Margins tab. Key **.65** in both the Left and Right margin text boxes, horizontally center the page, and click OK.
5. Select cells C6 through D6 and change the font size to 12 points.
6. Select cell C6 and edit it to read 1997.
7. Select cell D6 and edit it to read 1998.
8. Clear cells C7 through D11 and cells C14 through D16 and click any cell to deselect the ranges.
9. Add the standard header to the worksheet with your name, the filename, and the date.
10. Choose Save As from the File menu.
11. Key *[your initials]***13-1** in the File name text box. (Do not try to key the .xlt extension to change the file type.)
12. Click the down arrow in the Save as type text box and choose Template from the drop-down list. The filename extension changes to .xlt and the Save in text box displays the Templates folder.

NOTE: Excel stores its built-in template files in a folder called Templates in the MSOffice folder. You can access these templates by choosing File, New. If you save templates to the Templates folder, they are displayed in the New dialog box. You can open a template from any folder, but only the templates saved to the Templates folder appear in the New dialog box.

FIGURE 13-1
Saving a file as a template

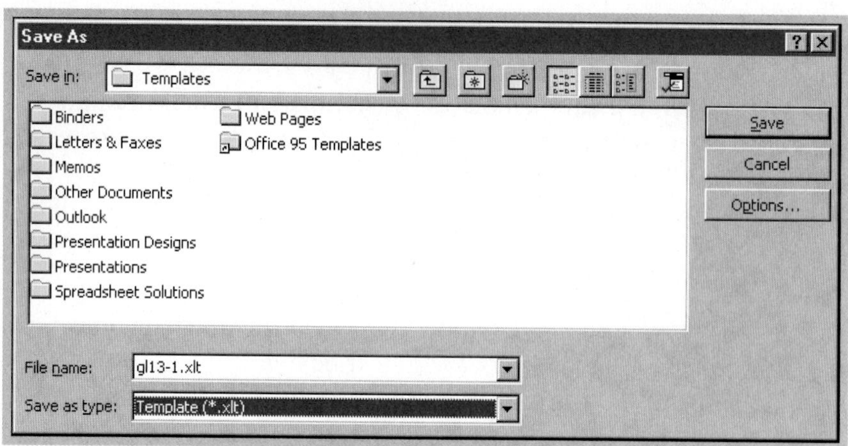

13. Click the down arrow in the Save in text box and click 3½ Floppy (A:). For classroom purposes, student template files are saved to the A: drive.
14. Click Save. The file is saved as a template with an .xlt extension.
15. Print the template and close the workbook.

Using Templates

Templates are similar to regular worksheets in most ways. The difference is that when you open a template, Excel makes a copy of it. Excel appends a number to the template name to make it unique and changes the template extension to the worksheet extension. For example, when you open qtr.xlt, qtr.xlt becomes qtr1.xls.

EXERCISE 13-2 Use a Template

1. Choose Open from the File menu.

NOTE: When the template is saved to the Templates folder on the hard drive, you can access a copy of the template file using the File, New command.

2. Open the template file *[your initials]***13-1.xlt**.
3. Key the following data in columns C and D, starting in cell C7:

186,425	**190,200**
52,949	**60,110**

22,324	**20,211**
695,356	**809,113**
388,385	**355,423**

4. Key the following data in columns C and D, starting in cell C14:

578,325	**555,313**
310,440	**313,445**
456,674	**453,111**

5. Choose Save As from the File menu. Because you are working in the actual template—not a copy of it—you save the file as a workbook file.

NOTE: In a typical situation, when you use the template copy and want to save it, just choose Save from the File menu. The Save As dialog box is automatically displayed with the file type already specified as a Microsoft Excel Workbook.

6. In the File name box, key *[your initials]***13-2**. (Do not try to type .xls to change the file type.)
7. Click the down arrow in the Save as type text box and choose Microsoft Excel Workbook. The file extension changes from .xlt to .xls.
8. Click Save. The file is saved as a workbook file.
9. Print the worksheet and close the workbook.

Working with Built-In Templates

Excel provides several built-in template files that can assist you in running your business, handling finances, and providing consistency in your documentation. These templates may already include text, formatting, formulas, cell notes, and even toolbars. Before you create new templates, look at the ones provided to see if they meet your needs. You can also customize the built-in templates to reflect information about your company. For example, you can add your company logo, name, and address to a template.

EXERCISE 13-3 Open a Copy of the Invoice Template

1. Choose New from the File menu.
2. Click the Spreadsheet Solutions tab.

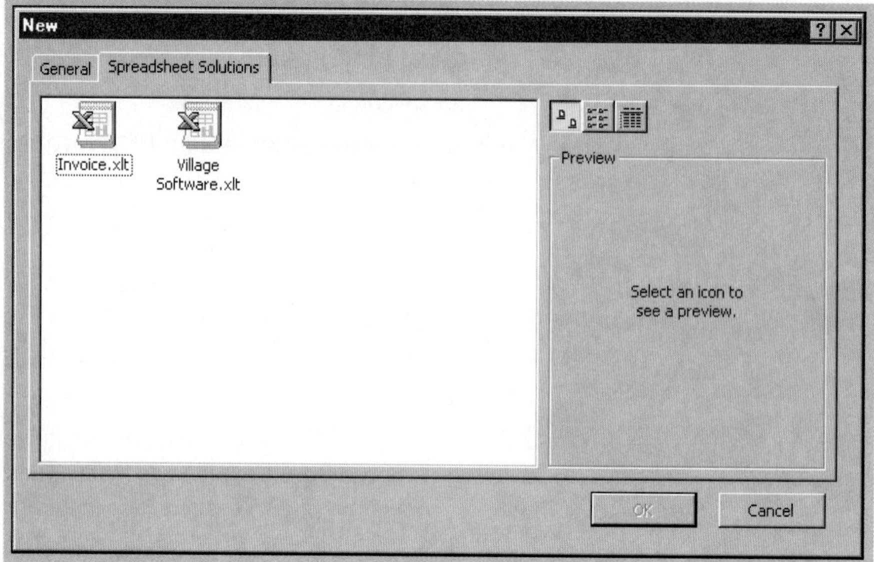

FIGURE 13-2 Available templates in the New dialog box, Spreadsheet Solutions tab

3. Select the template file **Invoice.xlt** and click OK. (Click Enable Macros if a Microsoft Excel dialog box appears before the template is displayed.) A copy of the Invoice template is displayed. The title bar shows the filename as Invoice1, which is a copy of Excel's built-in invoice template. All templates accessed via File, New open a copy of the template, rather than the actual template itself.

EXERCISE 13-4 Customize the Invoice Template

If you plan to use a built-in template repeatedly, you can customize it. In addition to adding your company information, you can change fonts, add default information, and even include your corporate logo. To customize a template and save it for future use, follow these steps:

- Choose New from the File menu, click the Spreadsheet Solutions tab, and click the template you want to use.
- Click the Customize button in the upper right corner of the template and complete the information on the Customize worksheet.
- To permanently save the changes, click the Lock/Save Sheet button on the form. Under Locking Options, click Lock and Save Template.
- Key a name for your customized template in the File name box in the Save Template dialog box and click the Save button. Click OK, then click Close.

1. Click the Customize button in the upper right corner of Invoice1. The Customize Your Invoice worksheet is displayed.

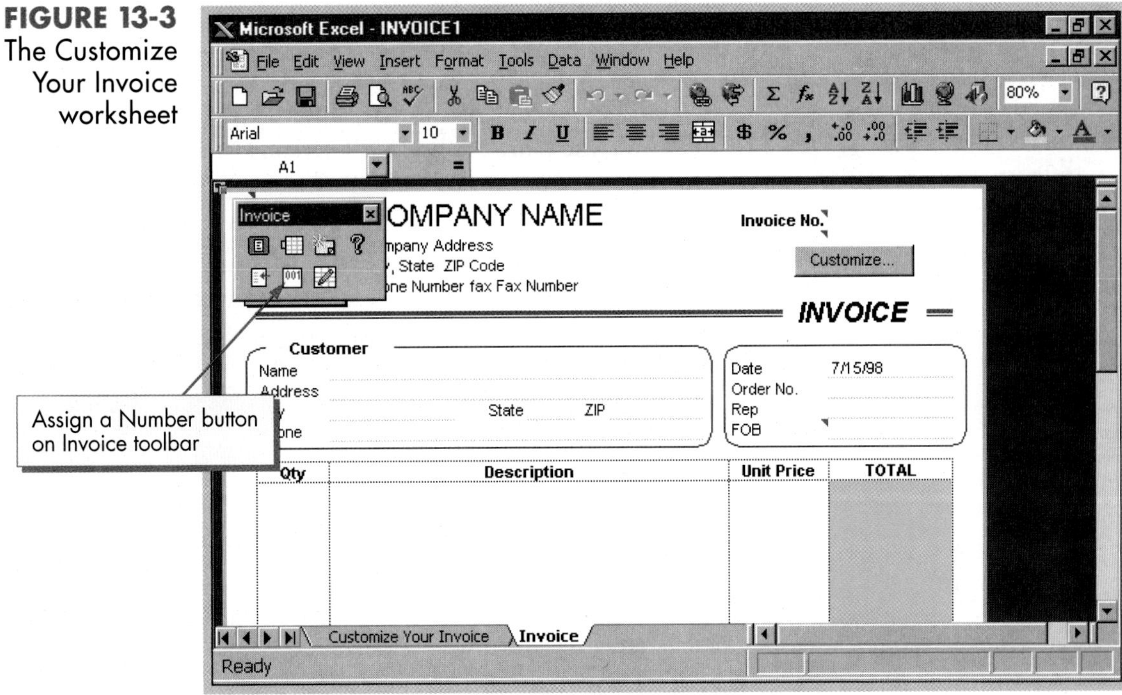

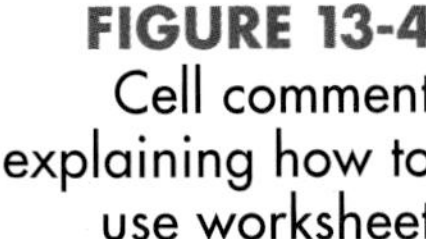

FIGURE 13-3 The Customize Your Invoice worksheet

2. Point to the red triangle at the top center of the worksheet to display the cell comment. It is one of many cell comments that assist you in customizing the template.

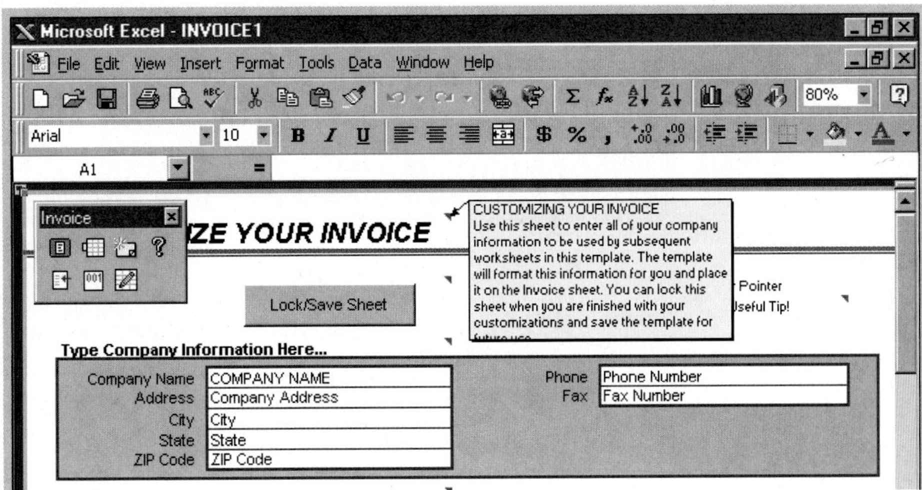

FIGURE 13-4 Cell comment explaining how to use worksheet

3. Scroll through the invoice template to view the areas available for customization.

4. Click the down arrow in the Name Box (next to the Formula Bar), scroll down to the cell named vital1, and select it. This cell is labeled COMPANY NAME and is in the "Type Company Information Here" section of the invoice. All input cells in this section of the invoice are named vital1, vital2, and so on; the Name Box shows you the name of the current cell.

TIP: You can also place the pointer in a named cell by typing the name of the cell in the Name Box and pressing Enter.

5. Key the following information in the cells located in the "Type Company Information Here" section of the invoice, starting with the named cell vital1. Drag the toolbar to another location on the screen if it obstructs your view of the template.

vital1	**Dunkirk Canvas Company**
vital2	**14 River Street**
vital4	**Boston**
vital5	**MA**
vital6	**02205**
vital8	**617-555-4410**
vital9	**617-555-4411**

6. Click the Change Plate Font button at the bottom of the worksheet. The Format Cells dialog box is displayed. Choose Times New Roman from the Font list box. Click OK.

7. Click the Assign a Number button on the Invoice toolbar to assign sequential numbers to each invoice created. A message is displayed.

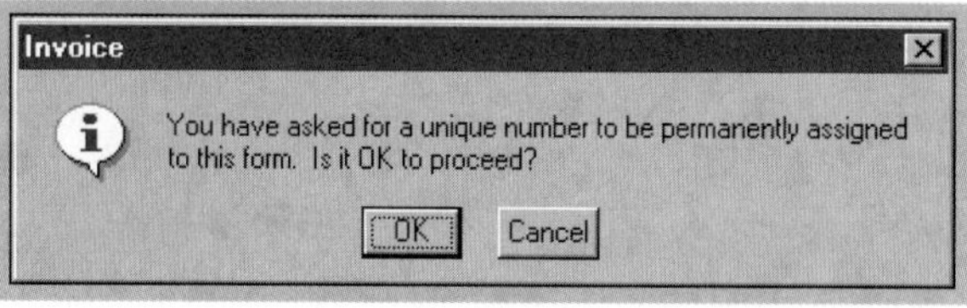

FIGURE 13-5 Message describing how a unique number is assigned to the form

NOTE: If you prefer, you can type your own number in the designated cell on the worksheet.

8. Click OK to continue.

9. Click the Lock/Save Sheet button at the top of the worksheet. Select the Lock and save Template option from the dialog box and click OK. The Save Template dialog box appears.

10. Click the down arrow in the Save in box and click the 3½ Floppy (A:) disk drive.

11. In the File name text box, key *[your initials]***13-4**. The Save as type text box displays Templates. Click the Save button. A message appears with instructions on how to access your customized template.

NOTE: Remember that you are saving templates to the 3½ Floppy (A:) disk drive for classroom purposes only.

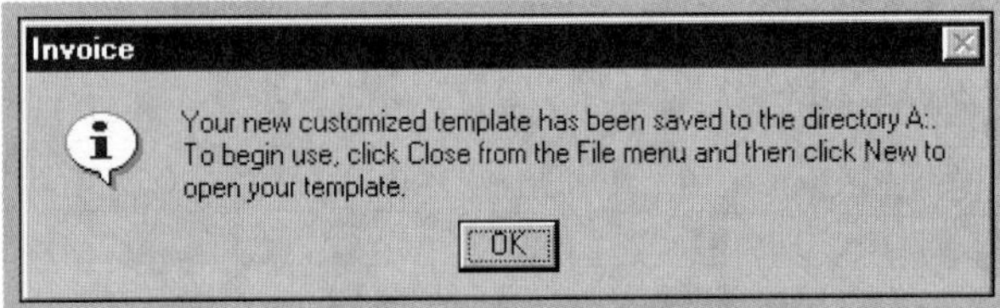

FIGURE 13-6 Message describing how to access a customized template

12. Click OK.

13. Add the standard header to the worksheet with your name, the filename, and the date.

14. Print the template.

EXERCISE 13-5 Enter Data into the Invoice Template

With the template displayed, you can key the necessary information just as you would complete a worksheet, moving from cell to cell using the mouse or pressing the arrow keys, Tab, or Enter.

1. Close the Invoice toolbar.
2. Click the arrow in the Name Box and select the named cell data1, which is the cell adjacent to the "Date" label. The current date is automatically displayed in the cell named data1.
3. Select the cell named data2, which is adjacent to the "Order No." label.
4. Key the following customer information in the cells named data2 through data10:

data2	**1350**
data3	**Davis**
data5	**Atlanta Yacht Club**
data6	**12 Lakeview Road**
data7	**Atlanta**

data8 **GA**

data9 **30358**

data10 **404-555-5555**

The customer information is complete.

5. Select the cell named data11 to key the following order information:

   data11 **25**

   data12 **Cover C-9087**

   data13 **150**

   A formula is included in cell L18. After keying the unit price in cell data13, the "TOTAL" cost is automatically calculated.

6. Scroll to the bottom of the invoice. The "Shipping & Handling" cell is already filled in and the "SubTotal" and "TOTAL" cells contain formulas based on the invoice information. Data entry for the invoice is complete.
7. Click the Fine Print box at the bottom of the form. Delete the text.
8. Click the Farewell Statement box at the bottom of the form. Delete the text.
9. Print the invoice worksheet. If a company logo was not inserted on the invoice form, the logo box does not print.
10. Close the template file without saving the changes. You do not want the newly created Atlanta Yacht Club invoice to become part of the template or to be saved as a workbook.

Concepts Review

TRUE/FALSE QUESTIONS

Each of the following statements is either true or false. Indicate your choice by circling T or F.

T F *1.* Any worksheet can become a template.

T F *2.* Templates can contain style elements, formatting, and frequently-used text, but not formulas.

T F *3.* There are 10 built-in templates provided with the Excel software.

T F *4.* When you open a template file, only a copy of the file is opened to protect the original template.

T F *5.* When you create a template, you can save it in any folder.

T F *6.* You can view a list of available built-in templates by clicking [New] on the Standard toolbar.

T F *7.* You can customize built-in templates with your personal or company information.

T F *8.* Excel's built-in templates are stored in the Templates file folder.

SHORT ANSWER QUESTIONS

Write the correct answer in the space provided.

1. Which Excel command displays a list of built-in templates?

____

2. Which file extension is assigned to Excel template files?

____

3. Which feature does Excel use in its built-in templates to provide you with information and assistance?

____

4. Templates should be saved to which folder if they are to be accessed from the New dialog box?

____

5. When you are creating a template from an existing worksheet, which Excel command would you use to save the file as a template?

____

6. Which button on the Invoice toolbar is used to assign sequential numbering to the invoice number cell?

____

7. When you customize a template, which button do you use to save changes to a template?

____

8. What are the names of the two built-in template files?

____

CRITICAL THINKING

Answer these questions on a separate piece of paper. There are no right or wrong answers. Support your answers with examples from your own experience, if possible.

1. Give some examples of how a company could use Excel's built-in templates. In what ways would it be beneficial if the worksheet cells in the template were linked to a database file?
2. A company creates many worksheets for business and financial analysis. Can you think of examples of worksheets, other than Excel's built-in templates, that can be converted to templates to assist in running a business and to help ensure documentation is consistent?

Skills Review

EXERCISE 13-6

Create a template from an existing workbook file.

1. Open the file **DunBud.xls**.
2. Clear cells B5 and B7 and cells B9 through D11.
3. Add the standard header to the worksheet with your name, the filename, and the date.

4. Choose Save As from the File menu.
5. Key *[your initials]***13-6** in the File name text box.
6. Click the down arrow in the Save as type box and click Template. The Save in text box displays the Templates folder.
7. Click the down arrow to open the Save in box, and click 3½ Floppy (A:). For classroom purposes, student files are saved to the A: drive.
8. Click the Save button. When the file is saved as a template, Excel changes the file extension from .xls to .xlt.
9. Print the template and close the workbook.

EXERCISE 13-7

Use a template to create a workbook file; enter data in the worksheet and save the data without changing the template file.

1. Open the file **DunBudT.xlt**.
2. In columns B, C, and D, key the following data:

B5	**Apr**	C4	**5%**	D4	**5.5%**
B6	**78,375**	C5	**May**	D5	**Jun**
B8	**52,250**	C10	**1,300**	D10	**1,200**
B10	**1,400**	C11	**300**	D11	**350**
B11	**250**	C12	**700**	D12	**700**
B12	**700**				

3. Add the standard header to the worksheet with your name, the filename, and the date.
4. Choose File, Save As to save the worksheet as *[your initials]***13-7.xls**. Remember to change the Save As type to Microsoft Excel Workbook.
5. Print the worksheet and close the workbook.

EXERCISE 13-8

Use a built-in template, customize it, and save it under a different filename.

1. Choose New from the File menu. Click the Spreadsheet Solutions tab.
2. Open the template **Invoice.xlt**. (Click Enable Macros if the Microsoft Excel dialog box appears.)
3. Click the Customize button.
4. Using the Name Box (next to the Formula Bar) to locate cells, key the following data in the named cells shown below:

vital1	**DUNKIRK CANVAS CO.**
vital2	**12 RIVER ST.**
vital4	**BOSTON**
vital5	**MA**
vital6	**02205**
vital8	**(617) 555-4410**
vital9	**(617) 555-4411**

5. Click the Change Plate Font button at the bottom of the form and change the font size to 9 points.
6. Click the Lock/Save Sheet button at the top of the form.
7. Select the Lock and save Template option in the dialog box and click OK.
8. Click the down arrow in the Save in box and click the 3½ Floppy (A:) disk drive.
9. In the File name box, key *[your initials]***13-8**. If the Save as type box does not show Templates, select Templates.
10. Click Save and click OK when the message appears describing how to access your new template.
11. Add the standard header to the template with your name, the filename, and the date.
12. Print the template and close the template file without saving the changes.

EXERCISE 13-9

Create a template from an existing workbook file; enter data in the new template and save the data without changing the template.

1. Open the file **Timecard.xls**.
2. Clear the cells A6:D8, F6:F8, and cell B4.
3. Add the standard header to the template with your name, the filename, and the date. Center the worksheet horizontally on the page.
4. Choose Save As from the File menu and key *[your initials]***13-9t** in the File name text box.
5. Click the down arrow in the Save as type box and click Templates.
6. Click the down arrow in the Save in text box, click 3½ Floppy (A:), and click Save.
7. Print the template and close the workbook.
8. Open the template file *[your initials]***13-9t.xlt**. (Click Enable Macros if the Microsoft Excel dialog box appears.)

9. Key the following data in the cells indicated:

B4	**4/28/97**
A6	**Boyd**
B6	**7:00 am**
C6	**11:30 am**
D6	**12:00 pm**
F6	**4:00 pm**

10. Save the file as a worksheet by choosing Save As from the File menu. In the File name box key *[your initials]***13-9.xls**. Remember to change the Save as type box to Microsoft Excel Workbook.
11. Print the worksheet and close the workbook.

Lesson Applications

EXERCISE 13-10

Create a template from an existing worksheet file.

Dunkirk Canvas Company needs a template created from its current income statement worksheet.

1. Open the file **Income.xls**.
2. Clear the contents of cells B4 through B10, cells B13 through B14, and cell B16. The formulas remain intact.
3. Add the standard header to the template with your name, the filename, and the date.
4. Choose Save As from the File menu.
5. Key *[your initials]***13-10** in the File name text box.
6. Choose Template from the Save file as type drop-down list box and choose the 3½ Floppy (A:) drive from the Save in list.
7. Click Save.
8. Print the template file and close the workbook.

EXERCISE 13-11

Create a template from an existing worksheet and save it as a template file; enter data into the new template and save it as a worksheet file.

Dunkirk Canvas Company needs to create a new financial template from the model for the "Asset & Liability" report.

1. Open the file **Assets.xls**.
2. Copy the contents of the range D6:D11 to the range C6:C11. Copy the contents of the range D14:D16 to the range C14:C16.
3. Delete the contents of the ranges D7:D11 and D14:D16.
4. In cell D6, key **1998**
5. Add the standard header to the template with your name, the filename, and the date.
6. Save the file as a template with the name *[your initials]***13-11.xlt** and print the template.

7. In the range D7:D11, key the following data:

    200,500

    40,220

    10,000

    900,400

    375,500

8. In cells D14:D16, key the following data:

    500,000

    300,500

    475,254

9. Save the file as a workbook with the name *[your initials]***13-11.xls**.
10. Print and close the workbook.

EXERCISE 13-12

Create a customized template from a built-in Excel template.

Dunkirk Canvas Company wants to customize the Purchase Order template.

1. Choose New from the File menu. Click the Spreadsheet Solutions tab.
2. Open the template **Invoice.xlt**. (Click Enable Macros if the Microsoft Excel dialog box appears.)
3. Click the Customize button.
4. Using the Name Box to locate cells, key the following data in the named cells shown below:

vital1	**Dunkirk Canvas Company**
vital2	**14 River Street**
vital4	**Boston**
vital5	**MA**
vital6	**02205**
vital8	**617-555-4410**
vital9	**617-555-4411**

5. Scroll to the "Specify Default Purchase Order Information Here" section.
6. Key VISA in Credit Card #1 text box.
7. Click the Change Font Plate button at the bottom of the form and change the font to 10-point Times New Roman Italic.
8. Click the Lock/Save button on the form

9. Select the Lock and save Template option in the dialog box and click OK.
10. In the File name box, key *[your initials]***13-12**. In the Save as type box, select Templates.
11. Click the down arrow in the Save in list box, choose 3½ Floppy (A:) drive, and click Save.
12. Add the standard header to the template with your name, the filename, and the date. Print and close the file without saving the changes to the template.

EXERCISE 13-13

Customize an existing template and save it as a template file; enter data into the new template and save it as a worksheet.

Dunkirk Canvas Company wants to change its existing Invoice template and use it for new customer accounts. The existing template needs to reflect increased shipping charges and a higher local sales tax.

1. Open the file **Invoice2.xlt**. (Click Enable Macros if the Microsoft Excel dialog box appears.)
2. Close the Invoice toolbar.
3. Delete the 10 in the named cell NO in the upper-right corner of the form.
4. In the "Insert Fine Print Here" text box at the bottom of the form, key **Thank you for your business**
5. Delete the text in the Farewell Statement text box.
6. Click the Customize button at the upper-right corner of the form.
7. Click the Unlock This Sheet button at the upper-left corner of the form and click OK.
8. Using the Name Box to locate the cells, key the following information in the named cells:

   dflt2 **5.25%**

   dflt7 **8.00**
9. Click Lock/Save Sheet and select the Lock but don't save option in the Lock/Save dialog box.
10. Click the Invoice tab and add the standard header to the template with your name, the filename, and the date.
11. Save the template as *[your initials]***13-13t.xlt**.
12. Print the template and close the workbook.

13. Open the template file *[your initials]***13-13t.xlt**. (Click Enable Macros if the Microsoft Excel dialog box appears.)

14. Key the following customer information in the named cells:

data2	**1352**
data3	**Callahan**
data5	**Jensen's Sailboats**
data6	**Marina Drive**
data7	**Boston**
data8	**MA**
data9	**01101**
data10	**617-555-6612**

15. Key the following order information in the named cells:

data11	**20**
data12	**Cover C-9088**
data13	**100**

16. Choose Save As from the File menu and save the template as a worksheet file as *[your initials]***13-13.xls**.

17. Print the worksheet and close the workbook.

Unit 4 Applications

APPLICATION 4-1

Create a worksheet using the functions IF, VLOOKUP, and TODAY; use text comments and date math in the formulas.

The owners of Dunkirk Canvas Company want to make sure their employees receive an annual performance review. They need a worksheet that shows each employee's last review date and whether he or she is due for a review now.

1. Open the file **Reviews.xls**.
2. Select cells A16:C21 and name this range T_Dates.
3. Select cell B5. Write a formula using a VLOOKUP function that looks up the employee name in the table and returns the last review date. Use the T_Dates range name as the table_array argument in the VLOOKUP function.
4. Copy the formula from cell B5 to cells B6 through B10. Format the cells in the date format 3/4/97.
5. Select cell C5. Write a formula using an IF function that determines whether the difference between =TODAY() and the date in cell B5 is greater than or equal to 365. If the answer is true, return the text comment "Yes" to cell C5. If the answer is false, return the text comment "No" to cell C5.
6. Copy the formula from cell C5 to cells C6 through C10.
7. Add the standard header to the worksheet with your name, the filename, and the date.
8. Save the workbook as *[your initials]***u4-1.xls**.
9. Print the worksheet.
10. Create a formula printout in landscape orientation with grids and row and column headings.
11. Close the workbook without saving.

APPLICATION 4-2

Use statistical functions COUNT, COUNTA, MIN, and MAX to analyze worksheet data; use logical functions with multiple conditions, text comments, and nesting.

The Dunkirk Canvas Company sent out an employee survey regarding company benefits. Surveys were returned and are being reviewed. A worksheet is needed to analyze the survey results to determine the correct benefits plan for each employee.

1. Open the file **Survey.xls**.
2. Select cell F5 and key the following information in cells F5 through I10 (some cells will be left blank):

FIGURE U4-1

	F	G	H	I
5	X	X	X	X
6		X		
7		X		X
8	X	X	X	X
9		X	X	X
10		X		

3. Select cell A12 and key **Count**. Apply bold formatting to cell A12.
4. Select cell E12 and write a formula using the COUNT function that counts the number of employees needing dependent coverage.
5. Select cell F12 and write a formula using the COUNTA function that counts the number of employees with co-insurance. Copy this formula to cells G12 through I12 to count the employees needing insurance in those categories.
6. Select cell J5. Write a formula using a nested IF function and multiple conditions to determine whether Plan A, B, C, or D is appropriate for the employee. If cells G5 and H5 and I5 equal "X," then "Plan A" should be assigned; if not, create another IF statement. If cells G5 and H5 equal "X," then "Plan B" should be assigned; if not, create another IF statement. If cells G5 and I5 equal "X," then "Plan C" should be assigned; if not, "Plan D" should be assigned.
7. Copy the formula from cell J5 to cells J6 through J10.
8. Select cell A13 and key **Maximum**. Apply bold formatting to cell A13.
9. Select cell D13 and write a formula using the MAX function that determines the maximum life insurance policy written.
10. Select cell A14 and key **Minimum**. Apply bold formatting to cell A14.
11. Select cell D14 and write a formula using the MIN function that determines the minimum life insurance policy written.

12. Add the standard header to the worksheet with your name, the filename, and the date.
13. Save the workbook as *[your initials]***u4-2.xls**.
14. Print the worksheet.
15. Create a formula printout in landscape orientation with grids and row and column headings. Use a Page 1 of ? footer.
16. Close the workbook without saving.

APPLICATION 4-3

Create a worksheet with a lookup function that uses date math to compute discounts; include a cell comment that describes appropriate data entry.

Dunkirk Canvas Company wants to use a worksheet to keep track of its accounts payable. Bills paid within 25 days of receipt receive a discount. The bills are date-stamped in the worksheet and a VLOOKUP function determines the appropriate discount. Calculations determine the date the invoice should be paid and the amount to be paid based on the discount.

1. Open the file **Payable.xls**.
2. Select cell C4. Create a cell comment that provides information about the dates to be entered in column C. Delete the default user name, key *[your initials]*: and press Enter.
3. Key the following text for the cell comment:

   Type the current date. Do not use the TODAY function.
4. Select cell A5 and key the following data (as the cell comment indicates, "current date" means type today's date in the format m/d/yy.):

FIGURE U4-2

	A	B	C	D	E
5	1250	Office, Inc.	*Current date*		250
6	1100	Materials, Inc.	*Current date*		575
7	1305	Regional Supply	*Current date*		990

5. Format the numbers in column E in Accounting format, with two decimal places. Left align the numbers in column A.
6. Select cell D5. Write a formula that displays the due date for the invoice by adding 25 days to the date in cell C5. Copy the formula from cell D5 to cells D6 through D7.
7. Insert a new worksheet, rename it from Sheet1 to **Table**, and cut and paste the lookup table in cells A23 through B26 in the Accounts Payable sheet to cells A1:B5 in the Table worksheet. Adjust the column widths appropriately. Select cells A2:B5 and name this range T_Discount.
8. Select cell F5 in the Accounts Payable sheet and determine the appropriate discount. Write a formula using the VLOOKUP function that looks up the company names and discounts in the table. (Make sure you use the range name when identifying the table_array so the formula can be copied.)
9. Copy the formula from cell F5 to cells F6 through F7.
10. Format the numbers in column F in Percent format, with no decimal places.
11. Select cell G5. Write a formula that calculates the dollar amount of the discount and subtracts it from "Amount of Invoice." The dollar amount due should be displayed in cell G5.
12. Copy the formula from cell G5 to cells G6 through G7.
13. Select cell A3. Key a formula that uses the computer clock to display the current date and time. Each time the worksheet is opened, the current date and time should be updated. Apply the date format of 3/4/97 1:30 PM to the cell.
14. Add the standard header to both worksheets with your name, the filename, and the date. Add a Page 1 of ? footer to both worksheets.
15. Save the workbook as *[your initials]***u4-3.xls**.
16. Print the entire workbook, including the comment at the end of the sheet.
17. Create a formula printout of the Accounts Payable worksheet in landscape orientation with grids and row and column headings. Do not include the Comments in this printout and use a Page 1 of ? footer.
18. Close the workbook without saving.

APPLICATION 4-4

Create worksheets using the NPER, PMT, and ROUND functions for analysis of a loan repayment schedule.

Dunkirk Canvas Company needs to buy several company cars and a local bank quoted an interest rate of 7% for a $20,000 loan for three years or an interest rate of 8% for a $20,000 loan for five years. Use the PMT and NPER financial functions to calculate the monthly payments and decide between the two loans.

1. Open the file **Carloan.xls**.
2. In the PMT worksheet, key the following data:

B5	**3**	D5	**5**
B6	**=B5*12**	D6	**=D5*12**
B7	**$20,000**	D7	**$20,000**
B8	**7%**	D8	**8%**

3. Select cell B10. Use the PMT function to determine the monthly payment due at the end of the month.
4. Select cell B11. Use the PMT function to determine the monthly payment due at the beginning of the month.
5. Select cell D10. Use the PMT function to determine the monthly payment due at the end of the month.
6. Select cell D11. Use the PMT function to determine the monthly payment due at the beginning of the month.
7. Edit the formulas in cells D10 and D11 only, adding the ROUND function so the answers are rounded to zero decimal places.
8. In the NPER worksheet, key the following data:

B3	6%
B4	**$200**
B5	**$20,000**

9. Select cell B6 and write a formula using the NPER function that determines the number of periods it will take to save enough money to reach the $20,000 goal. Remember to divide the rate by 12 to compute the monthly payment. Assume that payments will be made at the beginning of each month (type 1). The answer is displayed as a negative number.
10. Edit the formula in cell B6 to round the number to zero decimal places.
11. Key a new rate in cell B3, **7%,** and key a new payment amount in cell B4, **$500**.
12. Add the standard header to both worksheets with your name, the filename, and the date. Add a Page 1 of ? footer to both worksheets.
13. Save the workbook as *[your initials]***u4-4.xls**.
14. Print the entire workbook.
15. Create formula printouts of both worksheets with grids and row and column headings.
16. Close the workbook without saving.

APPLICATION 4-5

Create a worksheet that uses formulas with logical and statistical functions to compute operating expenses; convert the worksheet to a template; enter data in the new template.

Dunkirk Canvas Company needs a worksheet to track its actual annual operating expenses for use in budget analysis and planning. Create a worksheet sketch that includes worksheet titles, column and row headings, and a data area. There should be a column heading for expense categories, a heading for each month of the year, and a column heading for the average across the year for each expense. Under the expense heading are row labels for various company expenses, which are shown in Figure U4-3. The final row should show the totals for each month. Transfer the sketch into Excel, keying and formatting the labels.

Use formulas that include the SUM, IF, and AVERAGE functions in the worksheet. Once the worksheet is set up, including the formulas, create a template. Then use the template to start the 1997 operating expenses worksheet, entering January's data into the form.

The expense categories for the company are shown in Figure U4-3.

FIGURE U4-3

Expense Categories	January Expenses
Advertising	245
Depreciation - Equipment	800
Lease - Building	900
Insurance	500
Office Supplies	375
Salaries	45,250
Travel	400
Utilities	1,350

Total the expenses for each month with a SUM function. In the Average column, calculate the average spent for the year for each expense category. Use an IF function to make sure error messages are not displayed in the AVERAGE function because data is not filled in. The AVERAGE function is one result of the logical_test argument. (*Hint:* Have your logical_test in the IF function test for the presence of 0 in the Jan cell.) Format the headings attractively and format the numbers in comma style with no decimal places. Use landscape orientation, smaller margins, and smaller column widths to fit all the information on one printed sheet.

Rename Sheet1 appropriately and rename Sheet2 **User Information**. On the User Information worksheet, create documentation that includes the following: File Information (Created by, Date created, Date revised, Revised by, Contact for help); Purpose of spreadsheet (paragraph form); Instructions to User (special instructions needed by user to enter data correctly). Style the documentation for easy reading.

After completing the formulas, add the standard header to both worksheets with your name, the filename, and the date. Then save the worksheets as a template with the filename *[your initials]***u4-5.xlt**. Print the template and the User Information worksheet.

Once the template is developed, you can use it to enter the data for the January expenses as shown in Figure U4-3. Save the workbook with a new filename, *[your initials]***u4-5.xls,** so you do not save the changes in the template file. Print the worksheet. Create a formula printout with grids and row and column headings. Use a Page 1 of ? footer. Close the workbook without saving.

UNIT

5

Multiple Worksheets and Advanced Printing

Electronic Company Goes High-Tech

Feestone Electronics is a nationwide distributor of business machines. Its main products are cellular phones, fax machines, copy machines, and postage meters.

Feestone has four regional offices. Each office writes its own invoices and keeps track of its own sales and inventory. The regional offices send reports to the main office each quarter. Craig Herman, the company's bookkeeper, has requested that the information be delivered as Excel files via e-mail so that he can easily consolidate the figures.

Craig has discussed this project at length with the regional managers. They're enthusiastic, but a little unsure of the process, so Craig needs to make the transition as easy as possible. He needs to receive the sales information in a specific form for the consolidation reports.

Craig needs to create the following worksheets for both the regional managers and for his own use:

- ✔ A product list that contains descriptions and prices of all the items sold by Feestone, and an invoice form that can be used to copy product information and calculate totals, shipping costs, and sales tax. **(Lesson 14)**
- ✔ A worksheet for each region that is easy to use, and a consolidation sheet for the main office. **(Lesson 15)**
- ✔ A national sales report that is attractively formatted and can be printed in convenient sections. **(Lesson 16)**

Working with Multiple Worksheets and Files

OBJECTIVES

After completing this lesson, you will be able to:

1. **Manage worksheets.**
2. **Open multiple workbooks.**
3. **Arrange workbook windows.**
4. **Switch between open workbooks.**
5. **Copy and paste between open workbooks.**

Estimated Time: 1½ hours

As you know, Excel worksheets are contained in files called workbooks. A workbook can consist of 1 to 255 worksheets. Frequently, you may need to copy data from one worksheet to another in the same file. You may also need to work with information in multiple files. You already know how to navigate between worksheets. Now you learn how to manage worksheets and navigate between workbooks.

Managing Worksheets

You can add and delete worksheets, change the sequence of worksheets, copy data between worksheets, edit multiple worksheets, and print a range of worksheets.

EXERCISE 14-1 Add and Delete Worksheets

Each new workbook opens with three worksheets named Sheet1 through Sheet3. You can add and delete worksheets using the standard menu or the sheet tab shortcut menu.

FIGURE 14-1
Sheet tab shortcut menu

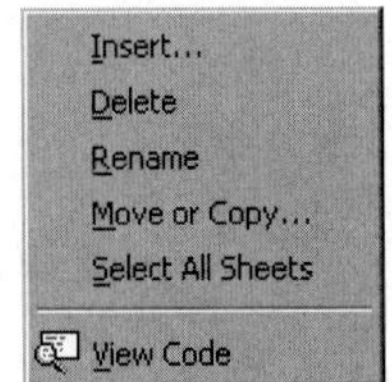

1. Open the file **Emplist.xls**. This workbook contains data on five worksheets. (Two worksheets were already added to this file.)
2. Right click the Sheet3 worksheet tab. The sheet tab shortcut menu appears.
3. Choose the Insert command from the shortcut menu. The Insert dialog box appears.

FIGURE 14-2
Insert dialog box

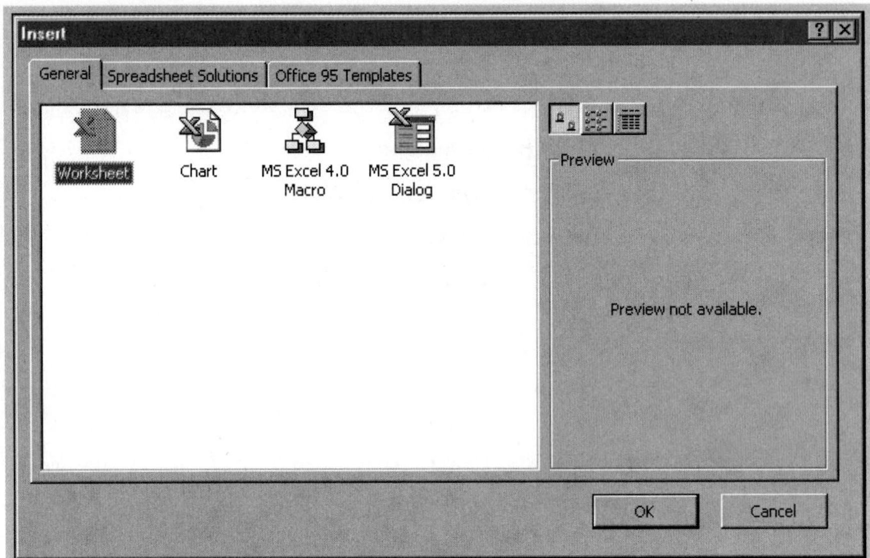

4. If necessary, click the General tab, click the Worksheet icon, and click OK. A new worksheet called Sheet6 is inserted to the left of Sheet3.
5. Choose Worksheet from the Insert menu. A new worksheet called Sheet7 is inserted to the left of Sheet6. Added sheets appear in front of the active sheet.
6. Right click the Sheet7 tab. The sheet tab shortcut menu appears.
7. Click Delete. An Excel Warning box appears, informing you that the selected sheets will be permanently deleted.
8. Click OK. Sheet7 is deleted.
9. With Sheet6 selected, choose Delete Sheet from the Edit menu and click OK in the warning box. Sheet6 is deleted.
10. With Sheet3 selected, press Shift+F11 and Sheet8 is inserted. Notice that Excel numbers the new sheet based on the last sheet inserted.

11. Delete Sheet8 using the Sheet shortcut menu.
12. To add multiple sheets, with Sheet3 selected press Ctrl and select Sheet4. Choose Insert from the shortcut menu and click OK. Sheet9 and Sheet10 are inserted.
13. Select Sheet9 and Sheet10 and delete them using the shortcut menu.

EXERCISE 14-2 Move a Worksheet

You can rearrange Worksheets in a workbook by dragging the sheet tabs. Giving descriptive names to worksheets also helps you manage them.

1. Double-click the Sheet5 tab, key **Total Staff**, and press Enter to rename the sheet.
2. Rename sheets 1 through 4 **NE**, **NW**, **SE**, and **SW**, respectively.

TIP: Using short names for worksheet tabs lets you see more tabs at one time. Be sure your worksheet names are clear, however. Use upper- and lowercase letters appropriately.

3. Position the mouse pointer on the tab named "Total Staff." Press and hold down the mouse button. A worksheet icon appears attached to the pointer and a black triangle indicates where the sheet will be inserted.
4. Drag to the left until the pointer is positioned on the NE tab—the first tab in the workbook—and the small triangle is in front of that tab.
5. Release the mouse button. The sheet that will contain the employee list for all four offices moves to the beginning of the workbook.
6. To make a copy of an existing sheet, select the Total Staff sheet. Press Ctrl, hold down the mouse button, and drag the icon to the right of the SW tab. Release the mouse button. A new sheet "Total Staff (2)" appears, which is a copy of the original sheet.
7. Delete the Total Staff (2) sheet.

EXERCISE 14-3 Copy and Paste Data Between Worksheets

You can use the Copy and Paste commands to build worksheets without rekeying information. For instance, you can copy the lists of sales staff in each region into the Total Staff sheet.

1. Click the NE tab.
2. Select cells A6 through C9.

3. Click the Copy button on the Standard toolbar. A moving border surrounds the selected range.

4. Click the "Total Staff" tab. The worksheet's full title is "Total Sales Staff."
5. Click cell A6 and click [Paste] on the Standard toolbar to paste the Northeast data into the Total Staff worksheet.
6. Click the NW tab and select cells A6 through C9.
7. Right click the selected range.
8. Choose Copy on the shortcut menu.
9. Click the Total Staff tab, right click cell A10, and click the Paste command on the shortcut menu. The data is copied to the Total Staff worksheet.

TIP: You can press Enter instead of choosing Paste. You can also use the Copy and Paste commands on the Edit menu and the shortcut key combinations Ctrl+C and Ctrl+V.

10. Copy the names from the SE sheet to cell A14 in the Total Staff sheet and from the SW sheet to cell A18 in the Total Staff sheet.

FIGURE 14-3 Total Staff worksheet after pasting data

A18 = LaConte

	A	B	C	D	E
5	Last Name	First Name	Employee ID Number		
6	Abbott	Martha	27641		
7	Conrad	Leon	48962		
8	Garcia	Ramone	88976		
9	Winkler	Brian	63947		
10	Santos	Julia	61577		
11	Tellman	Lowell	55409		
12	Underwood	Marc	84692		
13	Zimmer	Joseph	33448		
14	Edwards	Victor	33284		
15	O'Connor	Patrick	62390		
16	Wang	Thomas	22546		
17	Young	Emma	47899		
18	LaConte	Danielle	65347		
19	Northridge	Leroy	44739		
20	Panzer	Max	87642		
21	Williams	Celeste	59833		

Total Staff / NE / NW / SE / SW

Ready Sum=257561

EXERCISE 14-4 Edit Multiple Worksheets

You can select several worksheets and edit and format them all at once. This technique produces a uniform look. However, if you delete a row or column, it is deleted from all the selected worksheets.

1. Click the Total Staff tab, hold down Shift, and click the SW tab. The five worksheets are selected. The word "[Group]" appears in the title bar.

TIP: To select nonadjacent worksheets, click the first worksheet tab, hold down Ctrl, and click the other worksheet tabs.

2. In the Total Staff sheet, make the column labels in row 4 bold and italic.
3. Change the label in column C to wrap to two lines (line break after "Employee") and resize the column to better fit the label.
4. Add the standard header with your name, filename, and date to the same worksheet, and center the worksheet horizontally on the page.
5. Right click the Total Staff tab and choose Ungroup Sheets on the shortcut menu. Only the current sheet is selected.
6. Click the tabs for the rest of the selected worksheets to view the formatting changes, which are reflected in all selected worksheets. (Use Print Preview to see all the changes.)

TIP: You can also click any unselected sheet in the workbook to deselect the selected sheets.

EXERCISE 14-5 Print a Range of Worksheets

You can print all the worksheets in a workbook or only selected worksheets.

1. Click the Total Staff tab, hold down Ctrl, and click the SE tab.
2. Press Ctrl+P. The Print dialog box appears.
3. In the Print what section, make sure the Active Sheet(s) button is selected. If you wanted to print all five worksheets in the workbook, you would click Entire workbook in the Print what section.
4. Click OK. The Total Staff sheet and the SE worksheet are printed.

TIP: To print selected worksheets, you can also click the Print button on the Standard toolbar.

5. Click the NE tab to deselect the selected worksheets.
6. Click the Total Staff tab and save the workbook as *[your initials]***14-5.xls**.
7. Close the workbook.

Opening Multiple Workbooks

When you open a new or existing workbook, Excel opens a new workbook window. If you already have workbooks open, the new window covers the other windows, but they all remain open. As a result, you can easily move among them. You can also open multiple windows for one workbook if you need to view two different worksheets at the same time.

You can move to other windows by choosing them from the Window menu. You can also display the next window by pressing Ctrl+F6 or the previous window by pressing Ctrl+Shift+F6.

EXERCISE 14-6 Open Multiple Windows

FIGURE 14-4 Window menu listing open windows

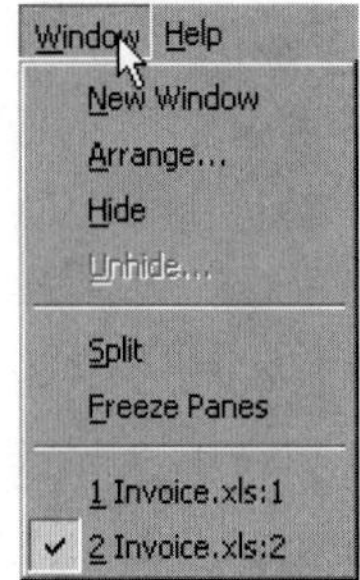

1. Close any open workbooks and open the file **Invoice.xls**.
2. Choose New Window from the Window menu. A new window is opened over the first window. The title bar displays **Invoice.xls:2**, indicating it is a second window containing that workbook.
3. Choose Window on the menu bar. The two open windows are listed at the bottom of the drop-down menu. The checkmark indicates the active window.

NOTE: Windows of the same workbook are just images of the same file. If you edit Invoice.xls:1, your changes appear in Invoice.xls:2 simultaneously.

4. Close the Window drop-down menu.
5. With **Invoice.xls:2** still displayed, open the file **Custlist.xls**.
6. Choose Window on the menu bar. The three open windows are listed at the bottom of the drop-down menu. The checkmark indicates **Custlist.xls** is the active window.
7. Choose **Invoice.xls:1** from the Window menu. The window containing the first version of **Invoice.xls** appears on top.
8. Open the Window menu again. The checkmark appears next to **Invoice.xls:1**.
9. Close the Window menu.

Arranging Workbook Windows

You usually work with three or fewer windows at a time. The number of windows that you can open, however, is limited only by your computer's memory.

You can arrange windows four ways: Tiled, Horizontal, Vertical, or Cascade. The best arrangement depends on the type of data and the layout of the worksheets. For example, if you are copying columns of data from one worksheet to another, use the vertical arrangement. If you are copying rows, use the horizontal arrangement.

EXERCISE 14-7 Arrange Windows Using the Arrange Command

1. Open the file **Shipping.xls**.
2. Choose Arrange from the Window menu. The Arrange Windows dialog box appears.
3. Click Cascade and click OK. The windows are arranged diagonally so you can see the workspace of the Shipping.xls workbook, but only the title bars and row selector buttons of the windows behind it.

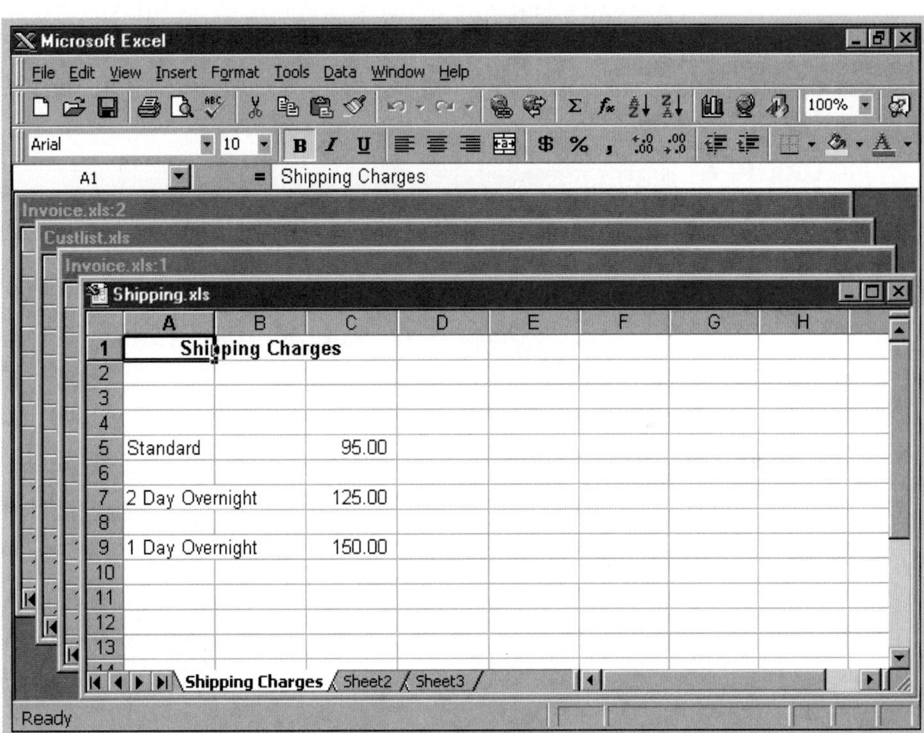

FIGURE 14-5 Cascading windows

4. Click the title bar of the Custlist.xls window. The workbook moves to the front of the display, like a card pulled from the bottom of the deck and placed on top. It also covers some of the other open window title bars.
5. Click the title bar of the window containing Invoice.xls:2. Only one window is active.
6. Choose Arrange from the Window menu.

7. Click the Windows of active workbook check box, which arranges the windows of only the active workbook. Click Vertical, and click OK. The two windows containing Invoice.xls are arranged side by side.
8. Click the Sheet2 tab in Invoice.xls:2. The Invoice sheet is still displayed in the window containing Invoice.xls:1.
9. Choose Arrange from the Window menu.
10. Clear the Windows of active workbook check box, click Tiled, and click OK. All windows are tiled. Notice that only the active workbook displays control buttons in its title bar.

EXERCISE 14-8 Maximize, Restore, and Minimize Windows

You can expand an active workbook to its full size by double-clicking the title bar or clicking the workbook Maximize button. This button then becomes a Restore button. Clicking displays the workbook in its previous, arranged size.

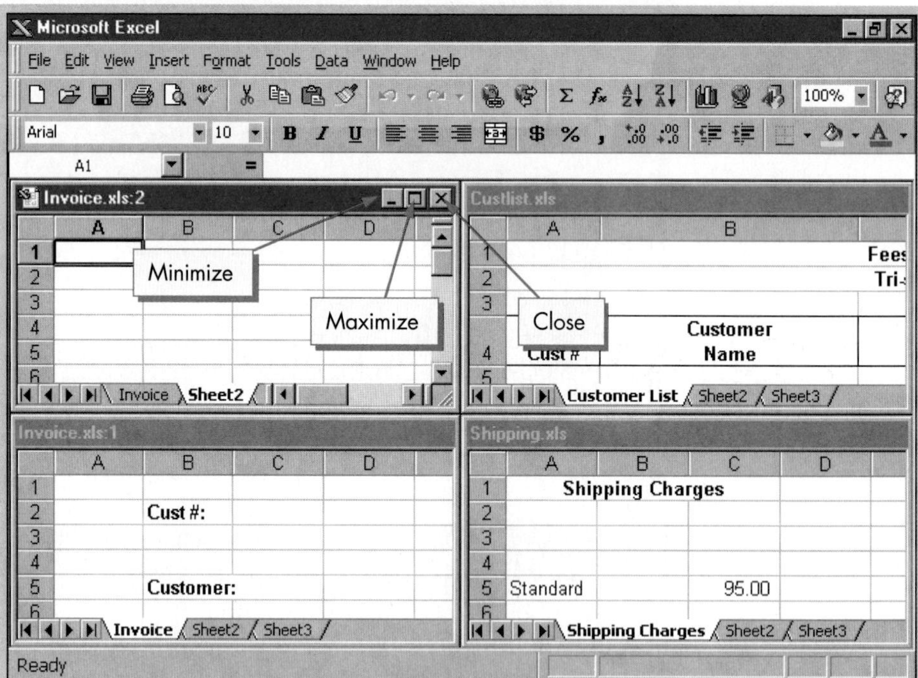

FIGURE 14-6
Tiled windows

The Minimize button reduces a workbook to a title bar in the lower part of the Excel window. You may need to drag windows out of the way to find and restore a minimized workbook. You also can choose a minimized workbook from the Window menu to restore it.

1. Click anywhere in the Custlist.xls window to activate it.
2. Click [Maximize]. The window is displayed at full size. The Restore button replaces the Maximize button.

FIGURE 14-7 Maximized window

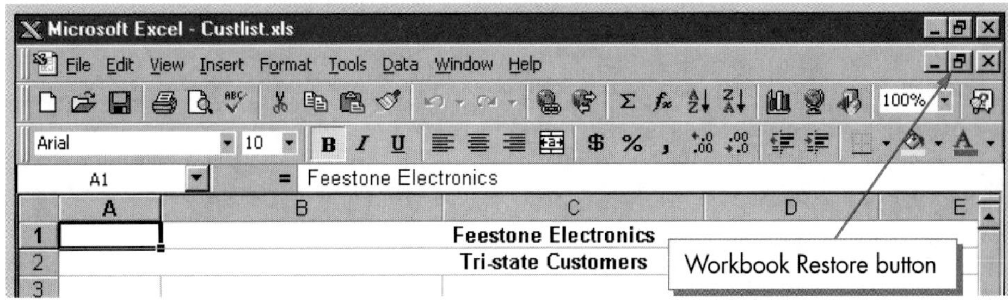

3. Choose Window from the menu bar and choose Invoice.xls:1 from the menu. The window containing this workbook is maximized (its previous size).
4. To restore all windows to their tiled size, click [Restore] in the workbook window.
5. Click anywhere in the window containing Shipping.xls and click [Minimize]. The worksheet changes to a title bar and moves to the lower left corner of the Excel window behind another window.
6. Drag the window in the lower left corner over to the right. The minimized title bar for the workbook Shipping.xl**s** becomes visible.
7. Minimize the window containing Custlist.xls (see step 5 and Figure 14-8).
8. To restore Shipping.xls to its previous size, click it and choose Restore from the shortcut menu.

FIGURE 14-8 Restoring a minimized workbook

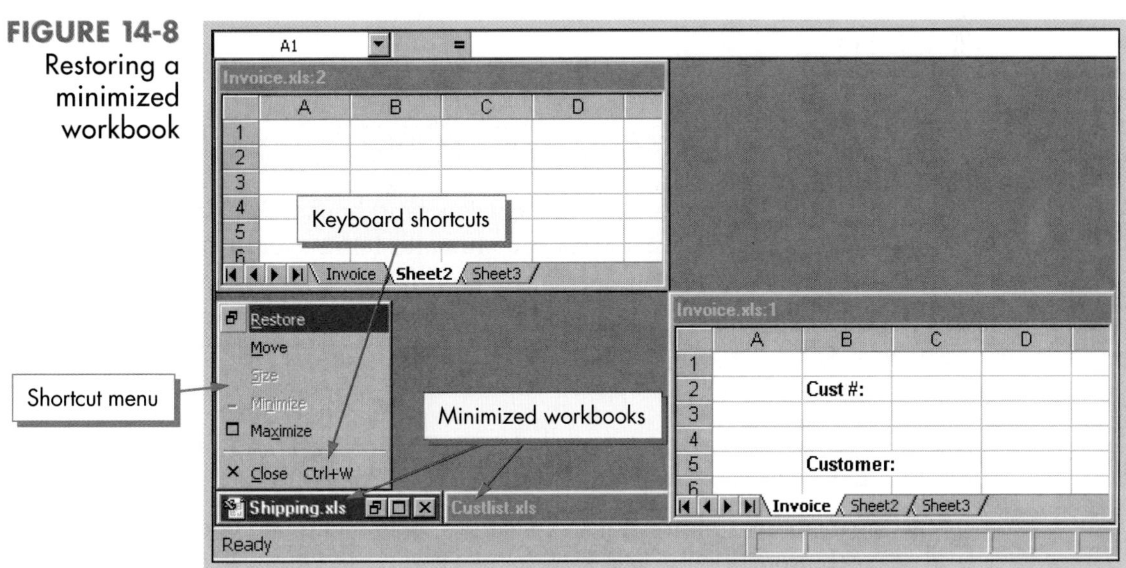

NOTE: In the active workbook, you can use the keyboard shortcuts Ctrl+F5 to restore, Ctrl+F10 to maximize, and Ctrl+W to close the window.

9. Restore the Custlist.xls window.
10. Arrange all windows horizontally.

Switching Between Open Workbooks

As you've seen, you can click a window to switch to it. You can also choose a window from the Window menu or use keyboard shortcuts. Ctrl+Tab or Ctrl+F6 moves to the next open window. Shift+Ctrl+Tab or Shift+Ctrl+F6 moves to the previous open window.

EXERCISE 14-9 Switch Between Open Windows

1. Double-click the title bar of the Shipping.xls window. The window becomes active and is maximized to fill the screen.
2. Choose Custlist.xls from the Window menu. The Custlist.xls window moves to the front.
3. Press Ctrl+Tab. The Shipping.xls window moves to the front.
4. Press Ctrl+Tab three more times to cycle through all open windows.
5. Choose Invoice.xls:2 from the Window menu.
6. Press Ctrl+W to close the Invoice.xls:2 window.

Copying and Pasting Between Workbooks

You can copy and paste between workbooks, just as you can between worksheets. You use the same commands to transfer data to another workbook window. After you cut or copy a section to the Clipboard, switch documents, position the pointer where you want the copied data to go, and paste it.

EXERCISE 14-10 Copy and Paste Between Workbooks

1. Choose Shipping.xls from the Window menu and click the Minimize button.

2. Choose Arrange from the Window menu, choose Vertical, and click OK. Custlist.xls and Invoice.xls are arranged vertically.
3. Right click cell A14 in Custlist.xls and choose Copy from the shortcut menu.
4. Click anywhere in the Invoice.xls window to activate it.
5. Right click cell D2 in Invoice.xls, choose Paste from the Shortcut menu, and press Esc to clear the moving border from the source cell.
6. Using the same method, copy cell B14 from Custlist.xls to cell D5 in Invoice.xls.
7. Select cells C14 and D14 in Custlist.xls and click [Copy] on the Standard toolbar.
8. Click cell I5 in Invoice.xls and click [Paste].
9. Move cell J5 in Invoice.xls to cell I6 by dragging it.
10. Close Custlist.xls and open the file **Products.xls**.
11. Arrange the windows vertically.
12. Select cells A8 through E10 in Products.xls. Press Ctrl+C to copy them to the Clipboard.
13. Activate Invoice.xls, click cell B13, and press Enter.
14. In Invoice.xls, select the Unit Prices in cells F13 through F15 and drag them to cells H13 through H15.
15. Close the Products.xls workbook.
16. Restore the file Shipping.xls and arrange the windows vertically.
17. Scroll to make cell J28 visible in Invoice.xls.
18. Using the drag-and-drop method, copy the charge for standard shipping from Shipping.xls to cell J28 in Invoice.xls. (Just drag the amount from one workbook to the other.)
19. Close the file Shipping.xls and click No when you are asked if you want to save the changes in the file. Maximize the file Invoice.xls.

EXERCISE 14-11 Complete the Invoice

1. Complete the invoice by keying the following data in the cells indicated:

I2	**20460**
I3	***[today's date]***
F13	**10**
F14	**2**
F15	**1**

2. Key the formula **=F13*H13** in cell J13 and copy the formula down two cells.
3. Enter the SUM function in cell J26 to total the three products and in cell J29 to add the total, tax, and shipping.
4. Format the amount due in currency style and leave the two decimal places.
5. Add the standard header including your name, filename, and date to the Invoice worksheet.
6. Delete any unnecessary blank columns and widen other columns to compensate for their removal and for column labels. (*Hint:* The invoice looks best if you leave the two outside blank columns because of the outline border.)
7. Center the worksheet horizontally on the page and turn off gridlines for viewing. Add formatting that enhances the appearance of the invoice aligning any data as you see fit.
8. Press Ctrl+Home, delete the blank worksheets in the workbook, and save the workbook as *[your initials]***14-11.xls**.
9. Print the Invoice worksheet and create a formula printout in landscape orientation with grids and row and column headings with a Page 1 of ? footer.
10. Close the workbook without saving it.

TIP: To close all workbooks with one menu command, press Shift and choose Close All from the File menu.

COMMAND SUMMARY

FEATURE	BUTTON	MENU	KEYBOARD
Arrange windows		Window, Arrange	
Close all workbooks		Shift+File, Close	
Delete a worksheet		Edit, Delete Sheet	
Insert a worksheet		Insert, Worksheet	Shift+F11
Maximize window	☐		Ctrl+F10
Minimize window	☐		Ctrl+F9
Open second workbook		Window, New window	
Restore a window	☐		Ctrl+F5
Switch to next window		Window, name	Ctrl+Tab or Ctrl+F6
Switch to previous window		Window, name	Shift+Ctrl+Tab or Shift+Ctrl+F6

USING HELP

If you often need to work with several windows open, you might get tired of constantly opening and arranging them. In Excel, you can save a workspace.

To find out more about workspaces, follow these steps to look up topics in Excel's Help:

1. Choose Microsoft Excel Help from the Help menu to open the Office Assistant.
2. Key **workspace** and click Search.
3. Select the topic "Save a group of workbooks in a customized workspace."
4. Go through the steps and try it with the Microsoft Excel dialog box open. Make sure you click .
5. When you finish, close the Help window and the Office Assistant.

Concepts Review

TRUE/FALSE QUESTIONS

Each of the following statements is either true or false. Indicate your choice by circling T or F.

T F 1. To delete a worksheet, you must first move it so it becomes the last worksheet in the workbook.

T F 2. To edit multiple worksheets, you select the worksheets to be modified and then make your changes to one of the selected sheets.

T F 3. You can print only selected sheets in a workbook, but they must be next to one another.

T F 4. If you are copying columns of data from one workbook window to another, the best window arrangement is horizontal.

T F 5. Tiling windows is a good option when you have many workbooks open and you need to see all of them at the same time.

T F 6. To minimize a workbook, click the Minimize button in the workbook window.

T F 7. After switching to an open window using the keyboard or menu commands, you must click in it to make the window active.

T F 8. You can use the same techniques to copy data between workbooks as you do to copy data between worksheets.

SHORT ANSWER QUESTIONS

Write the correct answer in the space provided.

1. What indicates the position of a worksheet tab while you are moving it?

____

2. Which key do you hold down while clicking worksheet tabs to select nonadjacent worksheets?

____

3. Which window arrangement displays open windows in a grid, both horizontally and vertically?

____

4. Which window arrangement displays the open windows diagonally, showing only the title bars and row selector buttons of the nonactive windows?

____

5. Which is the keyboard combination to switch to the next open workbook?

____

6. Which command do you choose to arrange open workbooks on the screen?

____

7. How many workbooks can you open at the same time?

____

8. When two workbooks are open, which window arrangement has the same effect as the tiling option?

____

CRITICAL THINKING

Answer these questions on a separate piece of paper. There are no right or wrong answers. Support your answers with examples from your own experience, if possible.

1. Excel provides several ways to arrange open workbook windows, including minimizing them. Discuss the advantage of each method. Why would you prefer one arrangement over another? Would you ever resize the windows manually? Why?
2. In Excel, you can rename worksheets and workbooks. In Windows, you can create folders to contain workbooks. Name and discuss situations in which good file management could be important.

Skills Review

EXERCISE 14-12

Add and delete worksheets, rename a worksheet, move a worksheet, copy and paste data between worksheets, edit multiple worksheets, and print a range of worksheets.

1. Open the file **Invoice2.xls**. (This workbook contains five worksheets. Two are already added.)

2. Add and delete worksheets by following these steps:

   a. Click the Shipping worksheet tab.

   b. Press [Shift]+[F11].

   c. Right click the Sheet1 worksheet tab.

   d. Choose the Insert command from the shortcut menu.

   e. If necessary, click the General tab, click the Worksheet icon, and click OK.

   f. Click the Sheet1 tab and choose Delete Sheet from the Edit menu.

   g. Click OK in the Warning box.

   h. Right click on the Sheet2 tab, choose the Delete command from the shortcut menu, and click OK.

3. Rename Sheet3 as **Invoice1**, Sheet4 as **Invoice2**, and Sheet5 as **Invoice3.**

4. Drag the Invoice3 sheet to the right of the Shipping sheet.

5. Copy data from the Customer List worksheet to the Invoice3 worksheet by following these steps:

   a. Click the Customer List sheet tab.

   b. Select cells A11 and B11 and click [Copy].

   c. Click the Invoice3 sheet.

   d. Click cell D2 and click [Paste].

   e. Drag cell E2 to cell D5 and left-align cell D2.

   f. Copy cells C11 through D11 on the Customer List sheet to the Clipboard.

   g. Paste the contents of the Clipboard to cell I5 in the Invoice3 sheet.

   h. In the Invoice3 sheet, drag cell J5 to cell I6.

6. Copy the standard shipping charge from cell C4 in the Shipping worksheet to cell J28 in the Invoice3 sheet.

7. In the Invoice3 sheet, enter **20478** in cell I2 and enter today's date in cell I3. Left-align both cells.

8. Edit a group of worksheets by following these steps:

   a. With the sheet named Invoice3 selected, press and hold [Shift] and click the sheet tab of the Invoice2 worksheet.

   b. Format cell J29 in currency style and keep the two decimal places.

   c. Widen column J to display the number.

   d. Add the standard header with your name, file name, and date.

   e. Horizontally center the worksheets on the page.

   f. Delete unnecessary blank columns and widen other columns to accommodate their removal and column labels. (*Hint:* The invoice looks best if the two outside columns remain blank due to the border outline.)

g. Turn off gridlines for viewing and add formatting to enhance the appearance of the worksheet.

h. Click the Invoice2 and Invoice1 sheet tabs to make sure columns are wide enough to accommodate their data and all formatting is uniform.

9. Click the Customer List tab to deselect the worksheets. Save the workbook as *[your initials]***14-12.xls**.

10. Select the three Invoice sheets again and choose Print from the File menu.

11. With the Active sheets option button selected, click OK.

12. Close the workbook without saving it.

EXERCISE 14-13

Open multiple workbooks, arrange workbook windows, arrange multiple windows of the same workbook, maximize a window, and restore a window.

1. Open the following files: **Allcity.xls**, **Automatn.xls**, **Stageup.xls**, and **Westcott.xls**.

TIP: In the Open dialog box, you can Ctrl+click to select multiple filenames and then click Open to open them all.

2. Choose Arrange from the Window menu, click the Horizontal option button, and click OK.

3. Arrange the windows using the Cascade option.

4. Arrange multiple windows of the same workbook by following these steps:

   a. Click the Automatn.xls title bar.

   b. Choose New Window from the Window menu.

   c. With Automatn.xls:2 active, choose New Window from the Window menu again.

   d. Choose Arrange from the Window menu and check the Windows of active workbook box.

   e. Click the Tiled option button and click OK.

5. Maximize a worksheet and enter data by following these steps:

   a. Click the Automatn.xls:3 window to activate it if necessary and click the worksheet Close button.

   b. Close the Automatn.xls:2 window.

   c. Choose Arrange from the Window menu and clear the Windows of active workbook check box.

   d. Make sure the Tiled option button is still selected and click OK.

e. Click [icon] in the Automatn.xls workbook.

f. Key **Feestone Electronics** in cell A1 in 12-point bold.

g. Click cell A2 and choose Insert, Rows on the menu bar.

h. Key **Invoice** in cell A2 in 12-point bold.

i. Center both titles across columns A through I.

j. Click cell A3 and choose Insert, Rows on the menu bar.

6. Click [icon] in the workbook Automatn.xls to display the tiled arrangement.
7. Copy data between open workbooks by following these steps:

a. Click in the Allcity.xls window to activate it, click cell A2, and insert two rows.

b. Insert two rows above row 2 in the Stageup.xls and Westcott.xls windows.

c. Select cells A1 and A2 in the Automatn.xls window and click [icon].

d. Click in the Allcity.xls window to activate it, click cell A1, and click [icon].

e. Click in the Stageup.xls window to activate it, click cell A1, and click [icon].

f. Paste the contents of the Clipboard to cell A1 in Westcott.xls and press Esc.

g. Center the pasted titles in all three worksheets across columns A through J.

8. Insert the standard header in all of the worksheets that contain data in each workbook.
9. Save the workbooks and print the active worksheets by following these steps:

a. Save Westcott.xls as *[your initials]***14-13a.xls** and click [icon].

b. Click in the Stageup.xls window, save it as *[your initials]***14-13b.xls**, and click [icon].

c. Click in the Allcity.xls window, save it as *[your initials]***14-13c.xls**, and click [icon].

d. Click in the Automatn.xls window, save it as *[your initials]***14-13d.xls**, and click [icon].

10. Close all open workbooks.

EXERCISE 14-14

Switch between open workbooks.

1. Open the following files: **Allcity2.xls**, **Automat2.xls**, **Stageup2.xls**, and **Westcot2.xls**.
2. Choose Allcity2.xls from the Window menu.

3. Press Ctrl+Tab three times to make Westcot2.xls active.
4. Format cells A1 and A2 by following these steps:
   a. In the Westcot2.xls window, format cells A1 and A2 as 12-point bold and center them across columns A through I.
   b. Press Ctrl+Tab.
   c. In the Allcity2.xls window, format cells A1 and A2 as 12-point bold and center them across columns A through I.
   d. Repeat steps b and c to activate the Stageup2.xls and Automat2.xls windows and format cells A1 and A2 in those workbooks.
5. Create the standard header for each worksheet that contains data in each workbook. Press Ctrl+F6 to move between workbooks.
6. Save the workbooks, print the active worksheets, and close the workbooks by following these steps:
   a. Press Ctrl+Tab until Automat2.xls is active.
   b. Choose Arrange from the Window menu, click the Cascade option button, and click OK.
   c. Save Automat2.xls as *[your initials]***14-14a.xls**, click the Print button, and click the worksheet Close button.
   d. Click in the Westcot2.xls window to activate it if necessary, save it as *[your initials]***14-14b.xls**, click the Print button, and click the worksheet Close button.
   e. Click in the Allcity2.xls window to activate it if necessary, save it as *[your initials]***14-14c.xls**, click the Print button, and close the worksheet.
   f. Click in the Stageup2.xls window to activate it if necessary, save it as *[your initials]***14-14d.xls**, click the Print button, and close the worksheet.

EXERCISE 14-15

Arrange windows, and copy and paste between open workbooks.

1. Open the files **Allcity3.xls** and **Stageup3.xls**.
2. In the Allcity3.xls worksheet, insert a row above row 31.
3. In cell F31, key **1 year service contract**.
4. In cell H31, key **150**. Format it in comma style with two decimal places.
5. Choose Window, Arrange from the menu bar, click the Vertical option button, and click OK.
6. Click in the Stageup3.xls window to activate it.
7. Insert a row above row 31 in the Stageup3.xls worksheet.
8. Click in the Allcity3.xls window to activate it.

9. Copy data from one workbook to another by following these steps:
   a. Copy cells F31 through H31 in the Allcity3.xls worksheet.
   b. Click the Stageup3.xls window to activate it.
   c. Right click cell F31 in Stageup3.xls.
   d. Choose Paste from the shortcut menu and press Esc.
10. Correct the formula in cell H32 in Stageup3.xls so it totals all the necessary cells to compute the amount due in the worksheet and copy the formula to Allcity3.xls.
11. Create the standard header in each worksheet containing data in both workbooks.
12. Save Stageup3.xls as *[your initials]***14-15a.xls**, click [Print], and close the workbook.
13. Save Allcity3.xls as *[your initials]***14-15b.xls**, click [Print], and close the workbook.

Lesson Applications

EXERCISE 14-16

Arrange windows, switch between windows, copy data from one worksheet to another, and format and print a group of worksheets.

Complete the invoice for Electronic Discount using information in several worksheets.

1. Open the file **Invoice3.xls**.
2. Open a second window of this workbook.
3. Arrange the two workbooks vertically.
4. In the Invoice sheet, complete the customer information for Electronic Discount by keying the data from Figure 14-9 and copying data from the Customer List sheet.

FIGURE 14-9

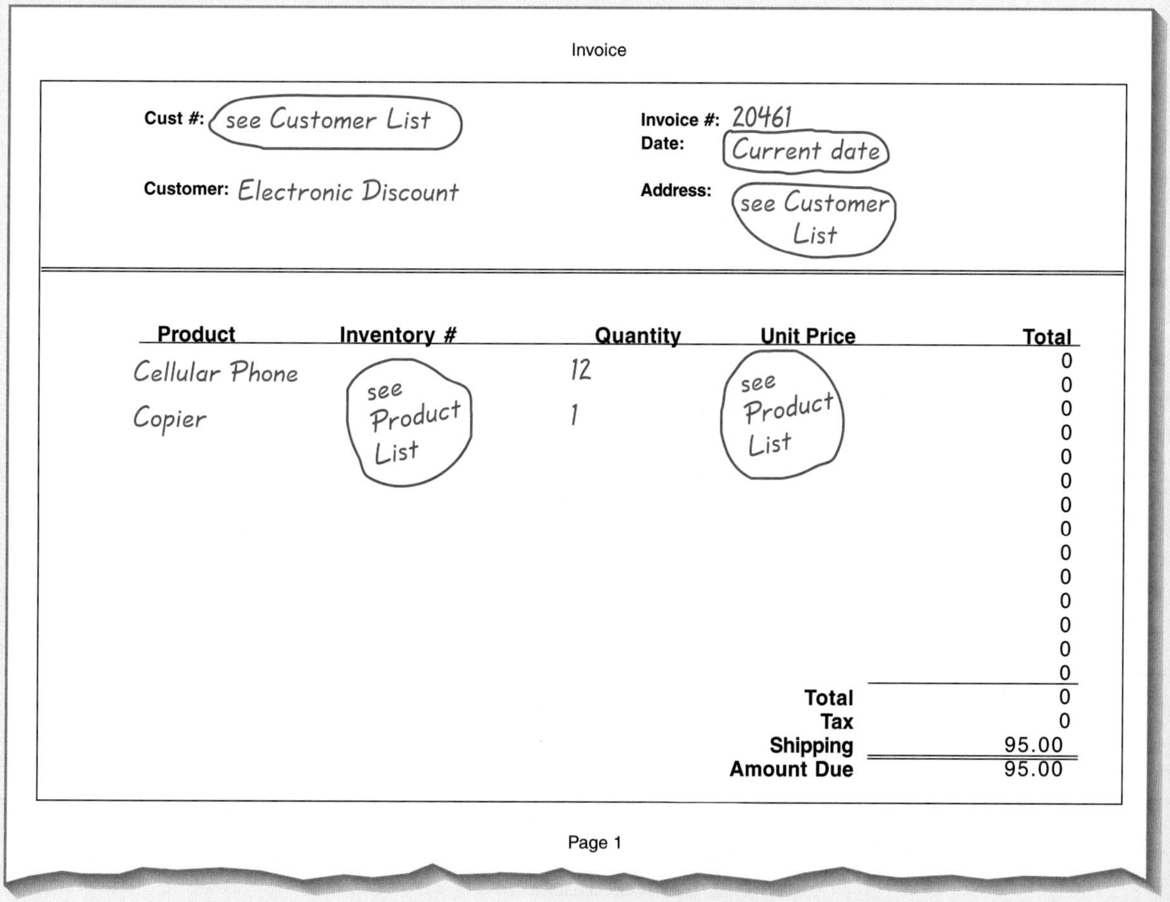

Invoice

Cust #: see Customer List

Invoice #: 20461

Date: Current date

Customer: Electronic Discount

Address: see Customer List

Product	Inventory #	Quantity	Unit Price	Total
Cellular Phone	see Product List	12	see Product List	0
Copier		1		0
				0
				0
				0
				0
				0
				0
				0
				0
				0
				0
				0
				0
			Total	0
			Tax	0
			Shipping	95.00
			Amount Due	95.00

Page 1

5. Complete the order information by keying data from Figure 14-9 and copying data from the Product List sheet.
6. Close the second window and maximize the remaining one.
7. In cell F12, convert the formula to an IF statement that displays a blank if there is no product in B12. Otherwise, it computes the total (the existing formula). Copy this formula from F12 to F13:F25 and format the column in Accounting Style with two decimal places and no dollar sign.
8. Check the formulas to verify "Amount Due."
9. Turn off grids for viewing and check all formatting including the borders.
10. Select the Invoice and Product List sheets. Center both horizontally on the page and add the standard header to both worksheets.
11. Save the workbook as *[your initials]***14-16.xls**.
12. Select the Invoice and the Product List sheets, if necessary, and print them only.
13. Create a formula printout for the Invoice worksheet with grids, row and column headings, and a Page 1 of ? footer.
14. Close the workbook without saving it.

EXERCISE 14-17

Open multiple workbooks, arrange windows, switch between windows, copy and paste data between workbooks, maximize a window, and delete blank worksheets.

Complete a worksheet that totals product sales by copying data from several workbooks.

1. Open the following files: **Allcity.xls**, **Automatn.xls**, **Totprods.xls**, and **Westcott.xls**.
2. Tile the windows.
3. Copy the quantities from the three invoice worksheets to the appropriate cells in the Totprods.xls workbook. For instance, copy cells D13 and D14 in Allcity.xls to cells B4 and B5 in Totprods.xls.
4. Maximize the Totprods.xls window.
5. Use [Σ] in cells E4 through E7 to sum the data in the four columns to the left of each cell. Center-align the totals.
6. Key **Total** in cell A9 and format it as bold and right-aligned.
7. Use [Σ] to create city totals and a grand total in the Total row. Center-align these amounts.
8. Format cells B4 through E9 as 12-point type.
9. Add the standard header to the worksheet and delete the two blank worksheets in the workbook.

10. Save the workbook as *[your initials]***14-17.xls** and print the worksheet.
11. Create a formula printout in landscape orientation with grids and row and column headings. Use a Page 1 of ? footer.
12. Close all workbooks without saving any of them.

EXERCISE 14-18

Open multiple workbooks, arrange workbook windows, switch between open workbooks, copy data from one workbook to another, and delete blank worksheets.

Feestone Electronics does not think that its analysis of total products is as useful as possible. Create a worksheet that lists not only the quantity of each product, but also the total sales for each product.

1. Open the files **Totprod2.xls** and **Products.xls**.
2. In Totprod2.xls, copy the three rows that are below "Cell phones" and insert them below each of the other products. Each product should be followed by a blank row, a "Quantity" row, and a "Total Dollars" row.
3. Move the quantities to the correct rows.
4. Copy the unit prices from Products.xls to the first cell directly below each product name (like cell A5) in Totprod2.xls.

TIP: Arrange windows vertically, and freeze panes in Products.xls to display column A beside column E.

5. Format the cells containing the unit prices in Totprod2.xls as 12-point type in currency style, keeping the two decimals.
6. Maximize the Totalprod2.xls window and in the "Total Dollars" rows, enter formulas to multiply the quantity of each product by its unit price.

TIP: Use an absolute or mixed reference for the unit price.

7. Format the "Total Dollars" rows in comma style keeping the two decimals.
8. Sum the values in the "Total Dollars" rows using the AutoSum function in the appropriate cells in column E.
9. Check the formula in cell E21 and edit it to sum only the dollar values in column E.
10. Format cell E21 in currency style keeping the two decimals and add a box border.

11. Create the standard header in the worksheet and delete the two blank worksheets in the workbook.
12. Save the workbook as *[your initials]***14-18.xls** and print the worksheet.
13. Create a formula printout in landscape orientation with grids and row and column headings. Use a Page 1 of ? footer.
14. Close all workbooks without saving any of them.

EXERCISE 14-19

Insert a new worksheet, rename a worksheet, open a new workbook, switch between open workbooks, copy and paste data between workbooks, and delete a blank worksheet.

For the month of December, Feestone Electronics hires extra sales staff to help meet the increased demand for its products. The payroll for the temporary staff has to be entered and calculated separately.

1. Create a sketch of a worksheet to compute the temporary staff's wages due. Include the temporary staff's names, number of hours worked, wages due, and total payroll for the temporary staff. Create an effective worksheet title and use F for formulas. You implement this worksheet later in the exercise.
2. Open the file **Emplist2.xls**.
3. Insert a new worksheet to the left of the Northeast worksheet.
4. Copy the worksheet title and column heads from one of the other sheets to the new worksheet. Resize the columns in the new worksheet to be the same size as in the other worksheets.
5. Edit the title in row 2 to **December Temporary Sales Staff**
6. Enter the names and ID numbers shown in Figure 14-10 (on the next page) into the new worksheet. Use the same format as the names in the other worksheets in the file.
7. Rename the worksheet tab **Temp Staff**, center the worksheet horizontally on the page, and add the standard header to the worksheet.
8. Save this file as *[your initials]***14-19a.xls**.
9. Open a new workbook and transfer your worksheet plan into the workbook. Format the title and labels attractively and increase column widths if necessary.
10. List each temporary staff member's last name, number of hours worked, and wages due. All temporary staff are paid at the rate of $9.50 per hour. Everyone except Maureen Daly and Waldo Franks worked 82 hours. Maureen Daly and Waldo Franks each worked 105 hours.

FIGURE 14-10

Last Name	First Name	Employee ID Number
Adams	Julia	90123
Bronfman	Harvey	90124
Castleman	Leonard	90125
Daly	Maureen	90126
Johns	Lisa	90127
Franks	Waldo	90128
Meth	Zena	90129
O'Reilly	Megan	90130
Petersen	Irene	90131
Wagner	Charlotte	90132

11. Calculate the wages due for each individual and format the numbers in comma style with two decimals.

12. Calculate the total payroll for the temporary staff and format this number in currency style with two decimals.

13. Create a standard header and center the worksheet horizontally on the page.

14. Turn off grids for viewing, format the entire worksheet attractively, including text or number alignment, and name the worksheet Temp Wages.

15. Create user documentation for the worksheet that includes the following: File Information (Created by, Date created, Date revised, Revised by, Contact for help); Purpose of spreadsheet (paragraph form); and Instructions to User (special instructions needed by user to enter data correctly). Format the documentation attractively and change column widths as needed. Spell-check your work.

16. Name the worksheet User Information and create a standard header.

17. Delete the blank worksheet and save this workbook as *[your initials]***14-19b.xls**.

18. Print the Temp Staff worksheet in *[your initials]***14-19a.xls** and the *[your initials]***14-19b.xls** workbook.

19. Create a formula printout of Temp Wages in landscape orientation with grids and row and column headings.

20. Close both workbooks without saving either of them. Submit the plan, worksheets, and the formula printout.

Consolidating Worksheets and Exchanging Data

OBJECTIVES

After completing this lesson, you will be able to:

1. **Link multiple files through formulas.**
2. **Design worksheets for consolidation.**
3. **Create the consolidated worksheet.**

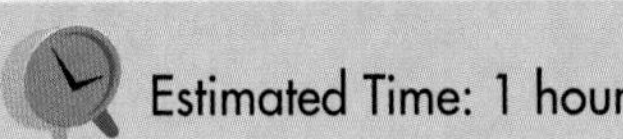

In Excel, you can link worksheets and workbooks so changes in one place are reflected in another place automatically. You can also create a consolidated worksheet—one that automatically summarizes data from other sources.

Linking Multiple Files through Formulas

You can include ranges from other worksheets or workbooks in a formula. References to such cells are called *dynamic links* (or "hot links"). Excel keeps track of the references for you. An *external reference* points to a different workbook. An *internal reference* points to a different worksheet within the same workbook.

A *dependent worksheet* uses data from another worksheet, known as the *source worksheet*. Source workbooks do not have to be opened after the links are created.

External references begin with the filename in brackets([]). Their cell references are absolute by default:

[external filename]worksheet name!absolute cell reference
[INVOICES.XLS]AUTOMATION!$A$1

Internal references begin with the worksheet name in single quotation marks. Notice that the exclamation point separates the worksheet name from the cell reference:

'internal worksheet name'!cell reference
'AUTOMATION'!A1

EXERCISE 15-1 Use Paste Link

Feestone Electronics wants an Invoice Analysis that shows the average unit price for each invoice. To perform this analysis, you must first link the customer names from the Invoices to the Invoice Analysis.

1. Open the files **Average.xls** and **Invoices.xls** and arrange them horizontally.
2. In Invoices.xls, select cell C5 in the Automation worksheet and click [Copy button].

TIP: To select a cell in another window quickly, double-click it. The first click activates the window and the second click selects the cell.

3. In Average.xls, select cell A4. Choose Paste Special from the Edit menu. The Paste Special dialog box appears.
4. Click the Paste Link button. The Formula Bar displays the external reference to cell C5 in the Automation worksheet of Invoices.xls.

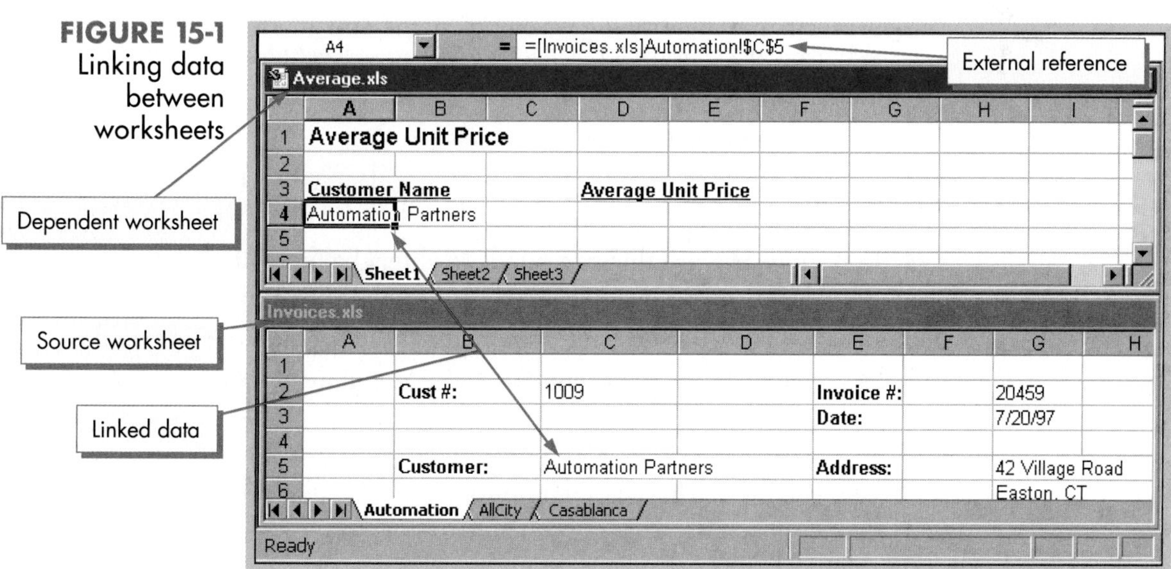

FIGURE 15-1 Linking data between worksheets

5. Press Esc to remove the moving border that surrounds cell C5.
6. In Invoices.xls, key **Westcott** in cell C5 and press Enter. Cell A4 in Average.xls is updated automatically.
7. Click the AllCity worksheet tab and copy the contents of cell C5 to the Clipboard.
8. In Average.xls, select cell A5, choose Paste Special from the Edit menu, and click Paste Link. The contents of cell C5 in the AllCity worksheet are linked to the Average.xls workbook. Press Esc to remove the moving border.
9. Paste Link the contents of cell C5 in the Casablanca worksheet in the Invoices.xls workbook to cell A6 in the Average.xls workbook.

TIP: You can right click the target cell and choose Paste Special from the shortcut menu.

EXERCISE 15-2 Create a Link with Formulas

A dynamic link can refer to a single label or to a range of cells within a formula. In this exercise, you average the unit prices for each invoice and then average the invoice totals.

1. In Average.xls, key **=average(** in cell D4.
2. In the Automation worksheet in the Invoices.xls workbook, select cells F13 through F15 and press Enter. Cell D4 is updated with the average unit price from the Automation invoice. Notice that the formula contains brackets that identify the workbook name and an exclamation point that separates the worksheet name from the range address. (See Figure 15-2 on the next page.)
3. In Average.xls, key **=average(** in cell D5.
4. In Invoices.xls in the AllCity worksheet, select cells F13 through F14 and press Enter.
5. In Average.xls, use the same steps to enter the following formula in cell D6: =**AVERAGE([Invoices.xls]Casablanca!$F$13:$F$15)**
6. In Average.xls, key **Average Invoice** in cell A8. Make the text bold.
7. In Invoices.xls, open a second and third window of the workbook (choose New Window from the Window menu twice).
8. Choose Arrange from the Window menu, select the Tiled option, and click OK. The three windows containing Invoices.xls and the window containing Average.xls appear tiled on the screen.

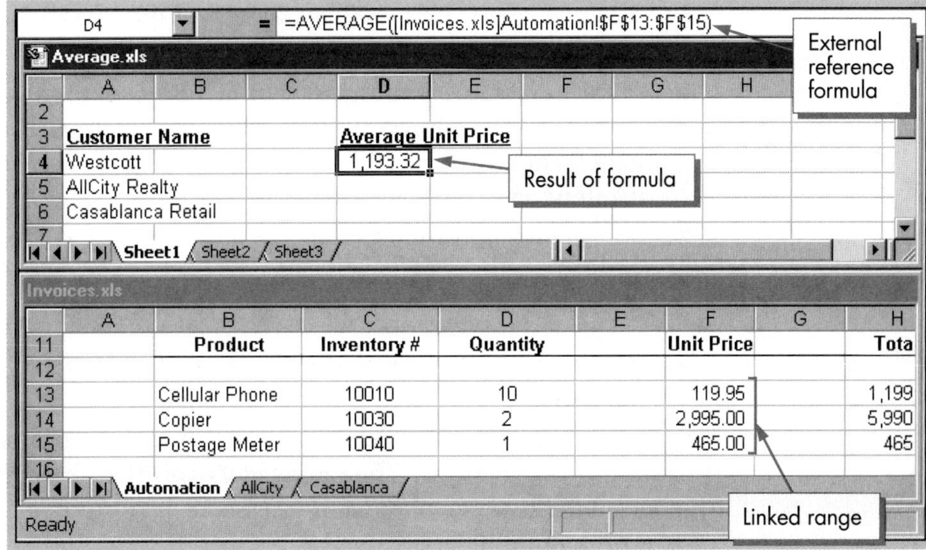

FIGURE 15-2
Linking worksheets with an external reference formula

9. In the first Invoices.xls window, click the Automation tab and scroll until you can see cell H29.

TIP: To move to another worksheet, use the worksheet tab scroll buttons at the bottom left corner of the worksheet. You can also choose a worksheet from the shortcut menu by right clicking a worksheet tab scroll button.

10. In the second Invoices.xls window, click the AllCity tab and scroll until you can see cell H29.
11. In the third Invoices.xls window, scroll until you can see cell H29 of the Casablanca worksheet.
12. In Average.xls, key **=average(** in cell D8.
13. Double-click cell H29 in the Automation worksheet.
14. Key a comma in the formula and double-click cell H29 in the AllCity worksheet.
15. Key a comma, double-click cell H29 in the Casablanca worksheet, and press Enter. The formula with references to three different worksheets is complete. The result is $9,755.49. Change the format of this average to comma style and keep the two decimals.
16. Maximize the Average.xls workbook window and press Ctrl+Home. The finished Invoice Analysis contains four formulas with external references.
17. Remove any blank columns, resize other columns to fit data, and make the worksheet attractive.
18. Create the standard header in the worksheet and delete the two blank worksheets.

19. Save the Average.xls workbook as *[your initials]***15-2.xls**, and print the worksheet.
20. Create a formula printout in landscape orientation with grids and row and column headings. Widen and reduce columns to see as much of the long formulas as possible and use Fit to if necessary to fit the formula printout on one page.
21. Close all workbooks. Do not save changes to Invoices.xls.

Designing Worksheets for Consolidation

You can design worksheets so people in different departments can record data in the same way. The worksheets can then be consolidated as long as common data items appear in the same positions or if they have common row or column labels.

EXERCISE 15-3 Copy the Base Form with Fill Across Worksheets

In general, the source worksheets and the consolidated worksheet should resemble one another. You can use the Fill Across Worksheets command from the Edit menu to keep content and formats consistent.

1. Open the file **Secndqtr.xls**.
2. Rename sheets 2, 3, 4, and 5 **Northwest**, **Southeast**, **Southwest**, and **Consolidated Report**, respectively.
3. Group all five sheets. (*Hint:* Activate the first sheet and Shift+click the last sheet tab.)
4. Select cells A1:E12 on the Northeast sheet.
5. Choose Fill from the Edit menu and choose Across Worksheets from the cascading menu. The Fill Across Worksheets dialog box appears.
6. Make sure the All option button is selected and click OK.
7. Examine the worksheets to review the copied material. (Note that you can fill across any number of worksheets. For instance, if the regional worksheets were already prepared, you could fill across the Southwest and Consolidated worksheet and get the same results.)

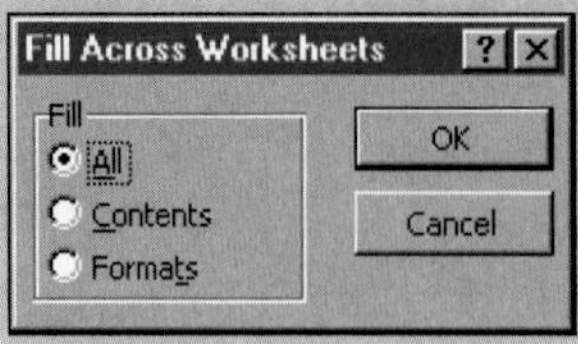

FIGURE 15-3 Fill Across Worksheets dialog box

8. Group the last four worksheets and widen column A to fit the labels. You only need to widen the column on one worksheet and all the worksheets are adjusted.
9. Format all five sheets to print centered horizontally. (Group all five worksheets to do this.)
10. Ungroup the sheets.
11. Change the title in cell A1 in the Northwest sheet to **Northwest Region** and change the name in cell A3 to **Adrian Needlehoffen**. The copied sheets still have the same data as the Northeast sheet.
12. Change the title in the Southeast sheet to **Southeast Region** and the name to **John Frisbee**.
13. Change the title in the Southwest sheet to **Southwest Region** and the name to **Jamaica Martin**.
14. Change the title in the Consolidated Report sheet to **Consolidated Report** and delete the name Holly Maplethorpe.

Creating the Consolidated Worksheet

A *consolidation table* summarizes the data from one or more source ranges. Placing your table in a separate worksheet—a *consolidated worksheet*--makes it easy to find. Source ranges can be on the same worksheet as the consolidation table or in different workbooks. You can also create dynamic links to ranges or cells in different worksheets or workbooks. When you consolidate the source data, you apply a summary function, such as Sum, to create the summary data.

You can consolidate data as long as common data items appear in identical positions or have common row or column labels.

EXERCISE 15-4 Consolidate Data Using Labels

In the last exercise, you created four regional worksheets and one worksheet for consolidating them. Because the row labels are identical, you can use these worksheets to create the consolidation table. The area for the consolidation table, however, must be blank.

1. Delete the row labels and data in the Consolidated Report worksheet. (Select cells A7 through E12 and press Delete to clear the cells.)
2. Leave the cells highlighted and choose Consolidate from the Data menu. The Consolidate dialog box appears with Sum as the default function for the Consolidate command.

3. Drag the Consolidate dialog box out of the way (to the top right of the screen).
4. With the insertion point in the Reference text box, click the Northeast tab and select the row labels and the data (cells A7 to E12). Notice that the dialog box disappears while items are selected so you can see what you are selecting.
5. Click Add in the dialog box. The absolute reference Northeast!$A$7:$E$12 is added to the All references text box.

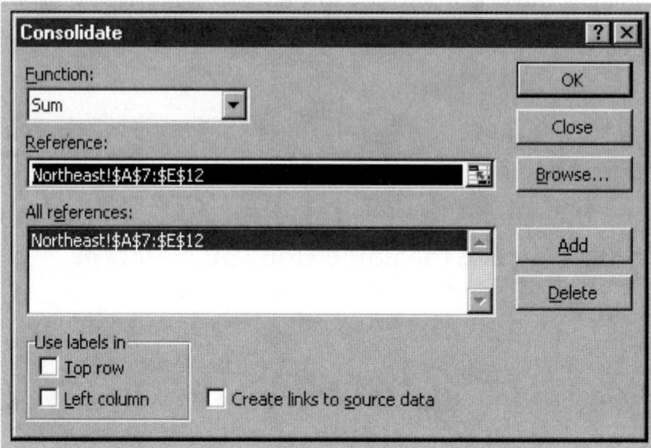

FIGURE 15-4
Consolidate dialog box

6. Add the same range for the Northwest, Southeast, and Southwest worksheets. Excel assumes you want to select the same range as in the Northeast worksheet and surrounds it with a moving border.
7. Check the Left Column box in the Consolidate dialog box and click OK. Excel consolidates the data. The Consolidate command correctly incorporated labels and data.
8. Click B7 in the Consolidated Report worksheet and notice that by default Excel places values—not formulas—in the consolidation table. (See data in row 12 and column E.)

NOTE: The data in the consolidation table is not dynamically linked to the other worksheets. Therefore, if you change the value in cell B7 in the Northeast worksheet, the consolidation table is not updated. In the next exercise, you create dynamic links.

EXERCISE 15-5 Consolidate Data by Position and Create Dynamic Links

Because the data elements in each worksheet appear in identical locations, you can also consolidate by position. You don't have to select labels, which allows you to protect those labels later. You can also create dynamic links in the consolidation table so if you change data in one of the worksheets, the consolidation table is updated. The consolidation range must be blank, as before.

1. In the Consolidated Report worksheet, select cells B7 through E12. Press Delete to clear the consolidation range.
2. With the cells still highlighted, choose Consolidate from the Data menu.
3. To define a new consolidation, select each of the previous cell references in the All References text box and click Delete.

NOTE: The Consolidate command uses previously defined references, so you must delete old references if your ranges change.

4. Click the Reference text box so you can select a range in a worksheet.
5. Click the Northeast tab, select cells B7 through E12, and click Add in the Consolidate dialog box.
6. Add the same range for the Northwest, Southeast, and Southwest worksheets.
7. Clear the Left Column check box, if necessary, and click Create links to source data. Click OK. The data from the four source worksheets are summed in the destination range of the Consolidated Report worksheet.
8. Select cell B11 in the Consolidated Report sheet. Excel places formulas in the consolidation table when Create links to source data is selected. Excel also creates an outline when data is consolidated and linked to its source. Notice the + and – buttons to the left of the row headings and that the row numbers have changed.

FIGURE 15-5
Consolidated data

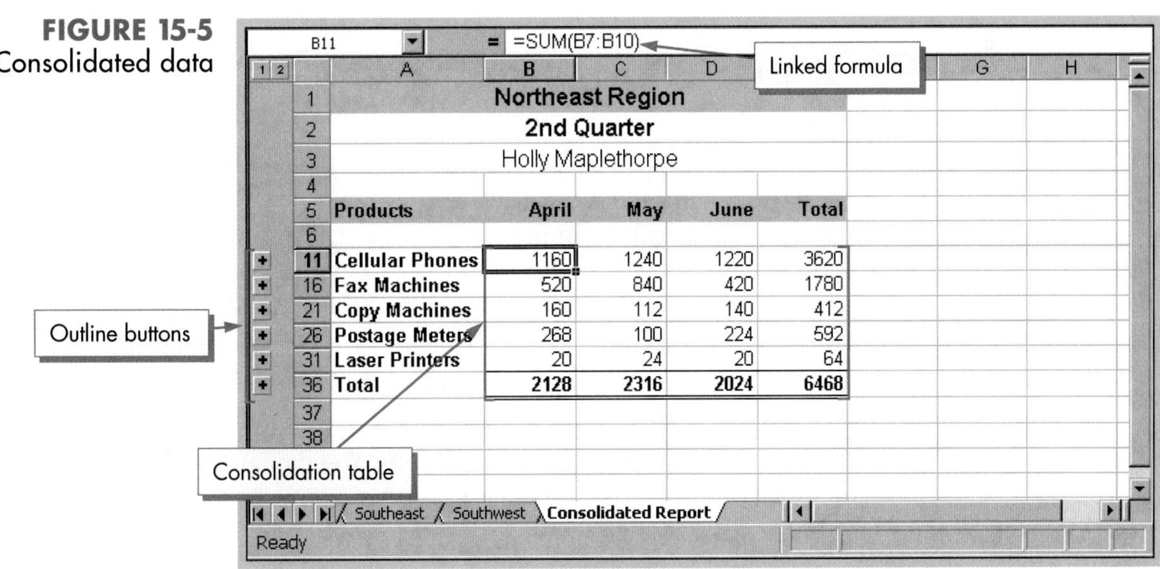

9. Click the first + button. Excel shows the makeup of the consolidated cell.
10. Click cell B7 and notice that the linked address appears in the Formula Bar.
11. Click the – button to go back up one level. Click other + and – buttons to see other cell makeups and linked addresses. Return to the first level for all rows when you finish.

NOTE: When you create a dynamic link in a consolidation table, none of the cells you select in the various worksheets you are consolidating from can be empty. (They can contain zeros.) The data is not included in the link.

EXERCISE 15-6 Update Source Data

When your source data changes, the consolidation table is updated because it is dynamically linked.

1. Key the data shown in Figure 15-6 in cells B7 to D11 of the Northwest, Southeast, and Southwest worksheets respectively.

FIGURE 15-6

Northwest			Southeast			Southwest		
240	300	250	200	300	400	150	250	350
140	240	300	210	320	450	400	200	300
260	160	180	320	450	500	150	250	350
340	240	250	180	290	390	250	350	400
15	20	10	10	20	15	5	10	20

2. Go to the Consolidation table and notice the new totals. Go down one level using the + buttons to see the data that was updated. Return to the first level.
3. Format all the numbers in the workbook as comma style with no decimals and add the standard header to all worksheets. (You can group the worksheets, open Page Setup, and add the standard header. Remember to ungroup the worksheets.)
4. Save the workbook as *[your initials]***15-6.xls** and print the entire workbook.
5. Create a formula printout of each worksheet in landscape orientation with grids and row and column headings. You can group the worksheets and format them for the formula printouts.
6. Close the workbook without saving it.

NOTE: If you want to add, delete, or change references to data in a consolidation table that has source links, you must delete the table and outline, then reconsolidate, or you can simply delete the sheet and start over. See the next section, "Using Help," to learn more about this.

USING HELP

Once you create a consolidation table, you may need to add, delete, or change the data in it. You do this differently depending on whether or not the table has source links in it.

To find out more about changing data in a consolidation table, follow these steps to look up topics in Excel's Help:

1. Choose Microsoft Excel Help from the Help menu to open the Office Assistant.
2. Key **consolidation** "What would you like to do?" and click Search.
3. Select the topic "Change a data consolidation" and click Search. The Microsoft Excel dialog box opens.

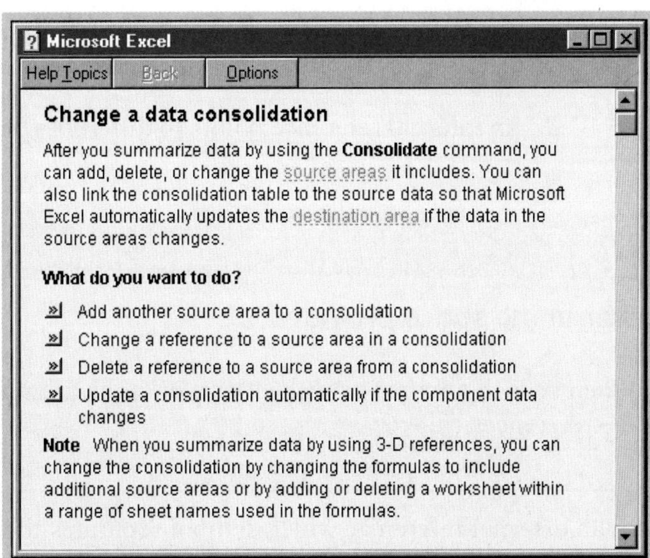

FIGURE 15-7
Microsoft Excel dialog box

4. Go through the topics on adding, changing, deleting, and updating data. Notice the instructions for adding, changing, deleting, or updating data in a source linked table with an outline.
5. When you finish, close the Help window and the Office Assistant.

Concepts Review

TRUE/FALSE QUESTIONS

Each of the following statements is either true or false. Indicate your choice by circling T or F.

T F *1.* When cells are linked, changing the value in the source cell causes the value in the dependent cell to change as well.

T F *2.* You can only link dependent worksheets to other worksheets or workbooks that are currently open.

T F *3.* Individual cells can be linked together, unlike cell ranges.

T F *4.* You must clear the cells in a consolidation table before consolidating data.

T F *5.* If you plan to consolidate worksheets, it's a good idea to plan them so common data items appear in identical locations.

T F *6.* If data elements do not appear in exactly the same location on each worksheet to be consolidated, then you cannot use the Data Consolidate feature.

T F *7.* Dynamic links are references to cells in other worksheets or workbooks.

T F *8.* An internal reference points to different worksheets in other files.

SHORT ANSWER QUESTIONS

Write the correct answer in the space provided.

1. When cells in another worksheet or workbook are referenced, what are the references called?

____

2. In an external reference, which symbol separates the name of a worksheet from the referenced cell range?

____

3. Which command duplicates a format to several worksheets?

____

4. When values from related worksheets in a workbook are consolidated in a summary worksheet, what is the summary worksheet called?

____

5. When rows and column headings are the same in a source worksheet, but the headings are not in the same location and the data elements are not identical, how does Excel consolidate?

____

6. Internal references begin with the worksheet name surrounded by what characters?

____

7. What is a worksheet called that contains a consolidation table?

____

8. What summarizes data from one or more source ranges?

____

CRITICAL THINKING

Answer these questions on a separate piece of paper. There are no right or wrong answers. Support your answer with examples from your own experience, if possible.

1. Would linking values be the best choice when creating a quarterly or annual report? Why or why not?
2. In what types of situations might you need to consolidate data from different workbooks?

Skills Review

EXERCISE 15-7

Link multiple files.

1. Open the files **Invoices.xls** and **Totdollr.xls** and arrange the workbooks horizontally.
2. Link the number of units of cellular phones sold on the three invoices in Invoices.xls to the Totdollr.xls workbook by following these steps:

   a. Scroll Totdollr.xls until you can see rows 4 through 7.

b. Click cell D4 and click the AutoSum button [Σ].

c. Click cell D13 in the Automation worksheet in the Invoices.xls workbook and key a comma.

d. Click the AllCity tab, click cell D14, and key a comma.

e. Click the Casablanca tab, click cell D13, and press [Enter].

3. Link the number of units of fax machines sold by following these steps:

a. Click cell D5 in Totdollr.xls and click [Σ].

b. Click cell D13 in the AllCity sheet in Invoices.xls and key a comma.

c. Click cell D14 in the Casablanca sheet and press [Enter].

4. Link the number of copiers sold by following these steps:

a. Click cell D6 in Totdollr.xls and click [Σ].

b. Click cell D14 in the Automation worksheet in Invoices.xls and key a comma.

c. Click cell D15 in the Casablanca worksheet in Invoices.xls and press [Enter].

5. Link the number of postage meters sold by following these steps:

a. Click cell D15 in the Automation worksheet of Invoices.xls.

b. Copy the cell's contents to the Clipboard.

c. Click cell D7 in Totdollr.xls and choose Edit, Paste Special.

d. Click Paste Link and press [Esc].

6. Maximize Totdollr.xls, press [Ctrl]+[Home], and create the standard header in the worksheet.

7. Delete unnecessary columns and resize others to accommodate column labels.

8. Delete the blank worksheets, save the Totdollr.xls workbook as *[your initials]***15-7.xls**, and print the worksheet.

9. Create a formula printout in landscape orientation with grids and row and column headings. Adjust column widths to fit long formulas and make sure the title prints (re-center the title across columns). Use a Page 1 of ? footer, if necessary.

10. Close all workbooks without saving any of them.

EXERCISE 15-8

Copy a base form, style worksheets, and copy formulas across worksheets.

1. Open the file **Regnpay.xls**.

2. Add a fourth worksheet after the first one and rename the sheets **NE**, **NW**, **SE**, and **SW**, respectively.

3. Copy the base form on the NE sheet to the other worksheets by following these steps:
   a. Click the NE tab and copy the cell range A1:F7 to the Clipboard.
   b. Click the NW tab, press and hold down Shift, and click the SW tab.
   c. Click cell A1 in the NW tab and paste the contents of the Clipboard to this location.
   d. Adjust columns A and B to accommodate about 15 characters. Adjust columns C, D, and E to accommodate about 10 characters.
   e. Right click the NW tab and choose Ungroup Sheets from the shortcut menu.
4. Change the title in cell A1 of the NW tab to **Northwest Region**
5. Change the titles in cell A1 of the SE and SW worksheets.
6. Edit the style of the worksheets by following these steps:
   a. Click the NE tab, press and hold down Shift, and click the SW tab.
   b. Turn off gridlines for viewing. (Choose Tools, Options, clear Gridlines and click OK.)
   c. Center the titles in cells A1 and A2 across columns A through F.
   d. Add light shading to the titles in cells A1 through F7.
   e. Make the labels in cells A6 through F7 bold and add a border below row 7.
   f. Format cells F8 through F12 in comma style with two decimal places.
   g. Set the worksheets to print centered horizontally on the page.
   h. Create the standard header in all worksheets.
7. Copy formulas across the worksheets by following these steps:
   a. With all four worksheets selected, select cells F8 through F12 in the Northeast worksheet.
   b. Choose Fill from the Edit menu and choose Across Worksheets from the cascading menu.
   c. Ensure the All option button is selected and click OK.
   d. Right click the Northeast tab and choose Ungroup Sheets from the shortcut menu. Check that formulas were copied to each worksheet. (Select individual cells in each worksheet and look at the formulas in the Formula Bar.)
8. Save the workbook as *[your initials]***15-8.xls** and print the entire workbook.
9. Create formula printouts of each worksheet in landscape orientation with grids and row and column headings. AutoFit all columns.
10. Close the workbook without saving it.

EXERCISE 15-9

Fill data across worksheets and consolidate data by location.

1. Open the workbook **Dllrsals.xls**.
2. Rename Sheet5 **Consolidated Report**
3. Copy labels to the Consolidated Report worksheet by following these steps:
   - *a.* Click the Southwest tab, press and hold down Shift, and click the Consolidated Report tab.
   - *b.* Select cells A1 through E1 in the Southwest worksheet.
   - *c.* Choose Fill from the Edit menu and choose Across Worksheets from the cascading menu.
   - *d.* Click the Formats option button and click OK.
   - *e.* Select cells A2 through E7 and choose Edit, Fill, Across Worksheets. Click the All option button and click OK.
   - *f.* Select cells A8 through A12 and fill across worksheets. Click the All option, if necessary.
   - *g.* Right click the Consolidated Report tab and choose Ungroup Sheets from the shortcut menu.
   - *h.* Key **Feestone Electronics** in cell A1 in the consolidated report.
4. Consolidate data by position by following these steps:
   - *a.* In the Consolidated Report worksheet, select cells B8 through E12.
   - *b.* Choose Consolidate from the Data menu.
   - *c.* Click the Northeast tab, select cells B8 through E12, and click Add in the Consolidate dialog box.
   - *d.* Repeat the previous step for the Northwest, Southeast, and Southwest worksheets and click OK.
   - *e.* Resize columns A through D to accommodate the data.
5. Format the consolidated worksheet by following these steps:
   - *a.* Turn off grids for viewing and add a single line border to the bottom of cells B11 through E11.
   - *b.* Add a double border below cells B12 through E12 and format the totals in these cells in bold.
   - *c.* Delete the title in cell A3.
6. Add the standard header to all the worksheets and format all worksheets to print centered horizontally on the page.
7. Save the workbook as *[your initials]***15-9.xls** and print the Consolidated Report worksheet.
8. Close the workbook.

EXERCISE 15-10

Fill data across worksheets, consolidate data by labels and position, dynamically link data, and use the outline feature.

1. Open the file **Dllrsal2.xls**. (These worksheets were designed for consolidation.)
2. Group the worksheets and edit the formatting. Add shading and borders and other formatting to enhance their appearance, including the values.
3. Ungroup the worksheets.
4. Insert a worksheet in front of the SW worksheet.
5. Move the new worksheet after the SW worksheet and rename it **Consolidated**
6. Copy the worksheet data to the Consolidated worksheet:
   - ***a.*** Group the SW and Consolidated worksheets.
   - ***b.*** Select cells A1:E11 in the SW worksheet.
   - ***c.*** Choose Fill from the Edit menu and choose Across Worksheets.
   - ***d.*** Make sure All is selected and click OK.
7. Ungroup the worksheets and edit the title to read **Consolidated Report**
8. Delete the contents of A3 and adjust the columns to fit the data.
9. Consolidate the data based on labels:
   - ***a.*** Clear the cells containing data you will consolidate (A7:E11).
   - ***b.*** With these cells selected, choose Consolidate from the Data menu.
   - ***c.*** Click the NE tab and select cells A7:E11.
   - ***d.*** Click Add and add the same cell addresses from the other three regional worksheets.
   - ***e.*** Select Left column and click OK.
   - ***f.*** Widen the columns to accommodate data.
10. Consolidate the data based on position:
   - ***a.*** Clear the cells containing data you will consolidate on the consolidation report (B7:E11).
   - ***b.*** With these cells selected, choose Consolidate from the Data menu.
   - ***c.*** Delete the references from the previous consolidation and place the cursor in the Reference text box.
   - ***d.*** Click the NE tab and select cells B7:E11.
   - ***e.*** Click Add and add the same cell addresses from the other three regional worksheets.

f. Clear the Left column check box and select Create links to source data and click OK.

11. Resize any columns that need it.
12. Use the + buttons to go to the second level of the outline created in the worksheet.

TIP: You can also click the 2 button above the + buttons to go to the second level of the outline. To return to the first level, click the 1 button.

13. Add the standard header to every worksheet and make sure they are set up to print centered horizontally on the page.
14. Save the workbook as *[your initials]***15-10.xls** and print the entire workbook. (The Consolidated Report should print with the second level of the outline showing.)
15. Create a formula printout of the Consolidated Report in landscape orientation with grids and row and column headings. AutoFit all the columns and make sure the titles print completely.
16. Close the workbook without saving it.

Lesson Applications

EXERCISE 15-11

Paste link values from one workbook to another.

Feestone Electronics does not think the analysis of average unit price is as useful as it might be. Create a worksheet that calculates averages which include not only the average unit price for each invoice, but also the average quantity ordered for each item.

1. Open the file **Average2.xls.** Click Yes to re-establish the links. If necessary, use the File Not Found dialog box to locate the file, Invoices.xls.
2. Make the changes indicated in Figure 15-8. When you finish, "Average Unit Price" appears in column G and column B is blank.

FIGURE 15-8

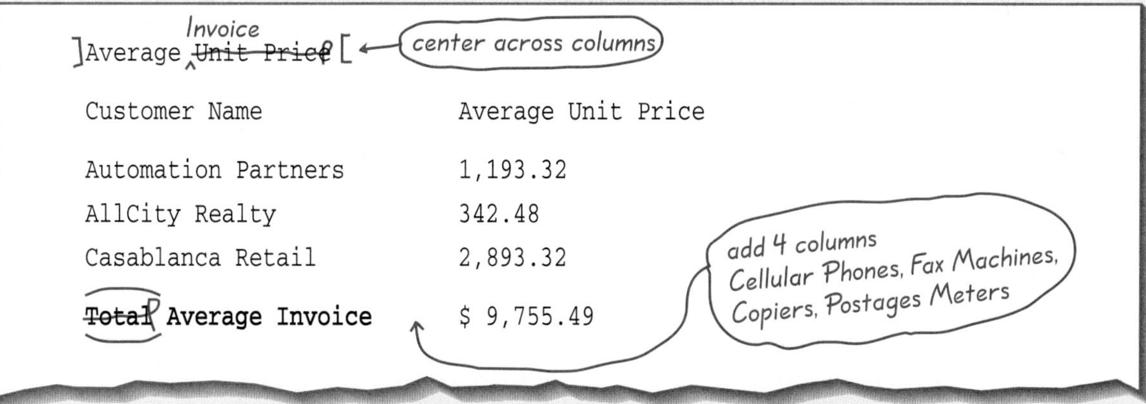

3. Format the headings in columns C through G as bold, centered with no underlines, and aligned to wrap text. Make the column width 10.
4. Open the file **Invoices.xls**, arrange the windows horizontally, and display the Automation sheet in the Invoices.xls window.
5. Paste Link the quantity ordered of each item from column D in each invoice in the Invoices.xls workbook to columns C, D, E, and F, respectively, in the Average Invoice worksheet. If an item was not ordered, key **0** in the cell in the Average Invoice worksheet.
6. Maximize the Average2.xls window.
7. Calculate the average quantity ordered of each item. If necessary, format the averages in normal type (not bold) with no decimals.

8. Delete the blank column B.
9. Add the standard header. Set up the worksheet to print centered horizontally on the page.
10. Delete the blank worksheets in the workbook.
11. Save the workbook as *[your initials]***15-11.xls** and print the worksheet.
12. Create a formula printout in landscape orientation with grids and row and column headings. AutoFit all the columns and left-align the title so it prints completely. Use a Page 1 of ? footer, if necessary.
13. Close all workbooks without saving them.

EXERCISE 15-12

Design worksheets for consolidation and consolidate worksheets.

Feestone Electronics needs to add unit prices and dollar-value sales revenues to its regional sales reports and to produce a consolidated report.

1. Open the file **Slsreprt.xls**.
2. In sheets 1 through 4, key **Unit Price** in cell H7 and key the following unit prices in cells H8:H12. (*Hint:* Group the sheets and work in sheet 4.)

Cellular phones	**119.95**
Fax machines	**565.00**
Copy machines	**7,995.00**
Postage meters	**465.00**

3. In all four sheets, copy the labels in cells A8:A12 to cells A17:A22. Key **Revenue** in cell A14 in bold.
4. In all four sheets, calculate revenues based on unit sales and unit price. (In cell C17, enter the formula **=$H8*C8** and copy this formula through cell E20.)
5. In all four sheets, calculate totals for the "Revenue" section (columns and rows).
6. In all four sheets, format the unit prices in currency style with two decimals, the individual product revenues in comma style with no decimal places, and the revenue totals in currency style with no decimal places.
7. AutoFit column widths to accommodate values. Remove column B and adjust column A.
8. Rename the worksheets as follows:

Sheet1	**Northeast**
Sheet2	**Northwest**
Sheet3	**Southeast**

Sheet4 **Southwest**
Sheet5 **Consolidated Report**

9. Copy the Southwest sheet to the Consolidated Report sheet, rename the sheet as **Consolidated Report**, and delete the regional manager's name.
10. In the Consolidated Report, delete the contents of the unit sales data (cells B8:E12) and consolidate the unit sales of the four regions by position. Link to source data.
11. Adjust column widths to accommodate data, check formulas, check title centering, and make formats consistent across all worksheets. (Add formatting to create a consistent display of values throughout.)
12. Format all sheets to print centered horizontally on the page and add the standard header.
13. Save the workbook as *[your initials]***15-12.xls** and print all worksheets.
14. Create a formula printout of each worksheet in landscape orientation with grids and row and column headings. AutoFit all columns and make sure the titles print completely. (Remove column F, if necessary, to get the formula printouts each on a single page.)
15. Close the workbook without saving it.

EXERCISE 15-13

Paste Link data from one workbook to another.

Feestone Electronics includes current prices in its product list. Recently, the vendor prices increased and the company decided to link its product list and its vendor price list, so the product list is automatically updated.

1. Open the files **Prodlist.xls** and **Vendpric.xls** and arrange the workbooks vertically.
2. Clear the prices in Prodlist.xls (cells B5:B8).
3. Paste Link the vendor prices in column B of Vendpric.xls to the appropriate cells in column B of Prodlist.xls.
4. Maximize Prodlist.xls and examine the newly inserted references.
5. Format the prices in 12-point type, if necessary.
6. In case someone else needs to use the worksheet, key in cell A10 **The vendor prices are linked to the workbook Vendpric.xls.**
7. Protect the worksheet from changes. No cells should be unlocked.
8. Set the worksheet to print centered horizontally on the page, add the standard header, and delete all blank worksheets.

9. Save the Prodlist.xls workbook as *[your initials]***15-13.xls** and print the worksheet.
10. Create a formula printout in landscape orientation with grids and row and column headings that fits on one page. Make sure the title prints. (You have to unprotect the sheet to manipulate data.)
11. Close all open workbooks without saving.

EXERCISE 15-14

Design worksheets for consolidation, consolidate worksheets, and Paste Link the consolidated worksheet into a word-processing document.

To decide how much inventory to keep on hand this year, Feestone Electronics is analyzing the quantity of product sold in 1995 and 1996 by quarter and on an annual basis. Construct a workbook containing a 1995 worksheet, a 1996 worksheet, and a consolidated worksheet averaging the quantity of product sold by quarter and for each year. Paste Link the averaged data into your word-processing application.

1. Create a sketch of the three worksheets. The labels are the four quarters and the products listed in Figure 15-9 (on the next page). Remember to design these for consolidation.
2. Open a new workbook to create the three worksheets. Create two worksheets using the data in Figure 15-9.
3. Create the consolidated worksheet with links to source data and format all three worksheets using group edit. Remember to use the Average function for consolidation. The consolidation worksheet should not contain any decimal places.
4. Rename all three sheet tabs and horizontally center them all on the page.
5. Create user documentation and name the sheet tab **User Information**. The sheet should include the following: File Information (Created by, Date created, Date revised, Revised by, Contact for help); Purpose of spreadsheet (paragraph form); and Instructions to User (special instructions needed by user to enter data correctly). Format the documentation attractively and change column widths as necessary. Spell-check your work.
6. Create the standard header in all worksheets and save the workbook as *[your initials]***15-14a.xls**. Print the entire workbook.
7. Create the memo shown in Figure 15-10 (on the next page) using your word-processing application. Paste Link the average sales data into the document.

FIGURE 15-9

	Qtr 1	Qtr 2	Qtr 3	Qtr 4
1995				
Cellular Phones	2,576	2,958	3,213	3,364
Fax Machines	2,287	2,189	2,608	2,367
Copy Machines	516	539	1,004	777
Postage Meters	536	589	1,323	656
Laser Printers	0	1,418	3,828	4,719
1996				
Cellular Phones	3,439	3,426	3,429	3,948
Fax Machines	2,904	1,986	2,578	3,255
Copy Machines	679	457	895	980
Postage Meters	543	498	783	486
Laser Printers	6,457	7,896	7,498	8,302

FIGURE 15-10

To: Regional Sales Managers/Feestone Electronics

From: Craig Herman

Date: *[today's date]*

Subject: 1995-1996 Average Sales

After consolidating 1995 and 1996, we have created the following average sales analysis:

8. Save the memo as *[your initials]***15-14b.***[your word processor's three-letter extension]*, print it, and close it.
9. Create a formula printout of the consolidated report in landscape orientation with grids and row and column headings. AutoFit all columns and make sure the titles print completely.
10. Close the workbook without saving it.

Advanced Printing

OBJECTIVES

After completing this lesson, you will be able to:

1. **Insert and remove page breaks.**
2. **Scale a worksheet.**
3. **Add print titles.**
4. **Change margins in Print Preview.**
5. **Change column widths in Print Preview.**
6. **Modify preset headers and footers.**
7. **Change page order and print page ranges.**
8. **Print named ranges.**

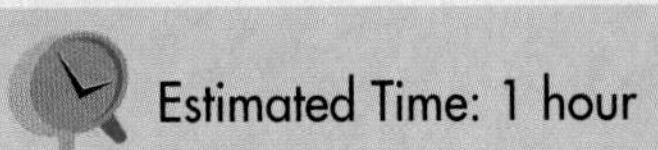

Excel provides many features that can make printed worksheets more readable. You can create a logical, attractive layout and automate repetitive data-entry tasks.

Inserting and Removing Page Breaks

You can insert page breaks to control what appears on each printed page. Onscreen, inserted page breaks appear as long dashed lines. Automatic page breaks appear as short dashed lines. You can also view page breaks in Page Break Preview mode.

In Lesson 4, you learned to split windows. Page breaks are inserted and removed in much the same way—above and to the left of the active cell.

You choose Page Break (or Remove Page Break) from the Insert menu.

EXERCISE 16-1 Insert and Remove Page Breaks

1. Open the file **Salesyr.xls** and zoom to 50% to see more of the worksheet.
2. Choose Options from the Tools menu, click the View tab, check Page breaks in the Windows options group, and click OK. An automatic page break is displayed between columns G and H.
3. View the worksheet in Print Preview, click Next or the scroll bar to see all three pages, and close Print Preview.

TIP: To navigate in Print Preview, you can also use PgUp, PgDn, ↑, ↓, Ctrl+↑, and Ctrl+↓.

4. Select cell F1 and choose Page Break from the Insert menu. Excel inserts a vertical page break to the left of the active cell. A new automatic page break appears between columns K and L. All the first quarter (Q1) information now appears on a separate page.

FIGURE 16-1
Page breaks

	A	B	C	D	E	F	G	H	I	J	K	L	M
1	NATIONAL SALES												
2	Full Year												
3	CONSOLIDATED REPORT												
4													
5	Unit Sales												
6	Produ	Jan	Feb	Mar	Q1	Apr	May	Jun	Q2	Jul	Aug	Sep	Q
7													
8	Cellular	980	978	988	2946	898	960	1100	2958	1056	1020	1102	31
9	Fax Ma	765	763	771	2299	701	749	858	2308	824	796	860	24
10	Copy M	229	229	231	689	210	225	258	693	247	239	258	7
11	Postage	251	251	253	755	230	246	282	758	271	261	282	8
12	Laser Pr	851	849	858	2558	780	833	955	2568	917	885	957	27
13	Total	3076	3070	3101	9247	2819	3013	3453	9285	3315	3201	3459	997
14													
15	Dollar Sales												
16	Produ	Jan	Feb	Mar	Q1	Apr	May	Jun	Q2	Jul	Aug	Sep	Q
17													
18	Cellular	117,551	117,311	118,511	353,373	107,715	115,152	131,945	354,812	126,667	122,349	132,185	381,20
19	Fax Ma	432,225	431,095	435,615	1,298,935	396,065	423,185	484,770	1,304,020	465,560	449,740	485,900	1,401,20
20	Copy M	1,830,855	1,830,855	1,846,845	5,508,555	1,678,950	1,798,875	2,062,710	5,540,535	1,974,765	1,910,805	2,062,710	5,948,28
21	Postage	116,715	116,715	117,645	351,075	106,950	114,390	131,130	352,470	126,015	121,365	131,130	378,51
22	Laser Pr	1,616,049	1,612,251	1,629,342	4,857,642	1,481,220	1,581,867	1,813,545	4,876,632	1,741,383	1,680,615	1,817,343	5,239,34
23	Total	#####	#####	#####	######	#####	#####	#####	######	#####	#####	#####	#####

Manual page break

Automatic page break

Year Sales

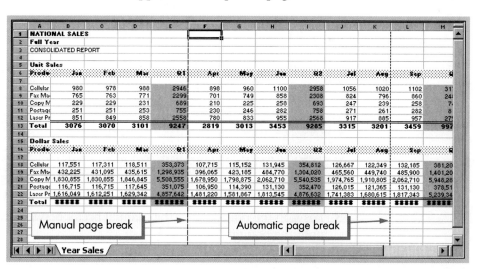

5. Select cell J1 and choose Page Break from the Insert menu. All the second quarter (Q2) information now appears on a separate page.

6. Insert a page break between columns K and L and between columns R and S.
7. Select cell A15 and insert a page break. This page break appears above the active cell.
8. View the worksheet in Print Preview. It now covers 12 pages (one is blank).
9. Close Print Preview.
10. Select cell F15. This cell is below one page break and to the right of another.
11. Choose Insert, Remove Page Break from the menu bar. The page breaks between columns E and F and above row 15 are removed.

EXERCISE 16-2 Adjust Page Breaks in Page Break Preview Mode

1. Choose Page Break Preview from the View menu. The Welcome to Page Break Preview dialog box appears.
2. Click OK. The automatic page break appears as a long dashed blue line. The manual breaks appear as solid blue lines.

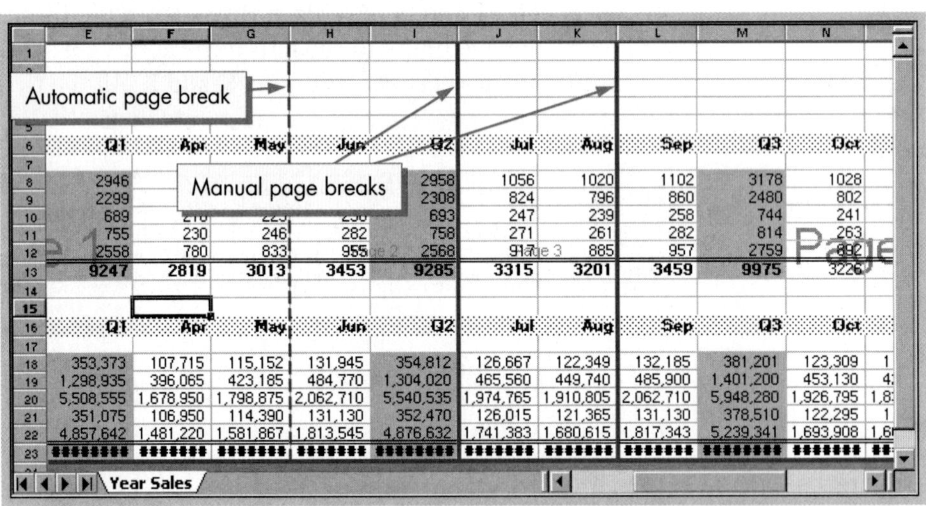

FIGURE 16-2 Page Break Preview mode

3. Position the pointer over the manual break between columns K and L until the pointer becomes ✛.
4. Drag the page break between columns M and N. Page 3 now contains all the third quarter data.
5. Choose Normal from the View menu to return to Normal view and remove the page break between columns M and N.

Scaling a Worksheet

Scaling is enlarging or reducing the size of a worksheet's contents. As you learned in Lesson 4, you can fit a worksheet onto a specified number of pages. You can also enlarge or reduce worksheet contents by a specified percentage. The Page tab of the Page Setup dialog box offers scaling options.

EXERCISE 16-3 Scale a Worksheet by a Percentage

1. Open the Print Preview window and click Setup.
2. Click the Page tab.

FIGURE 16-3 Page tab of the Page Setup dialog box

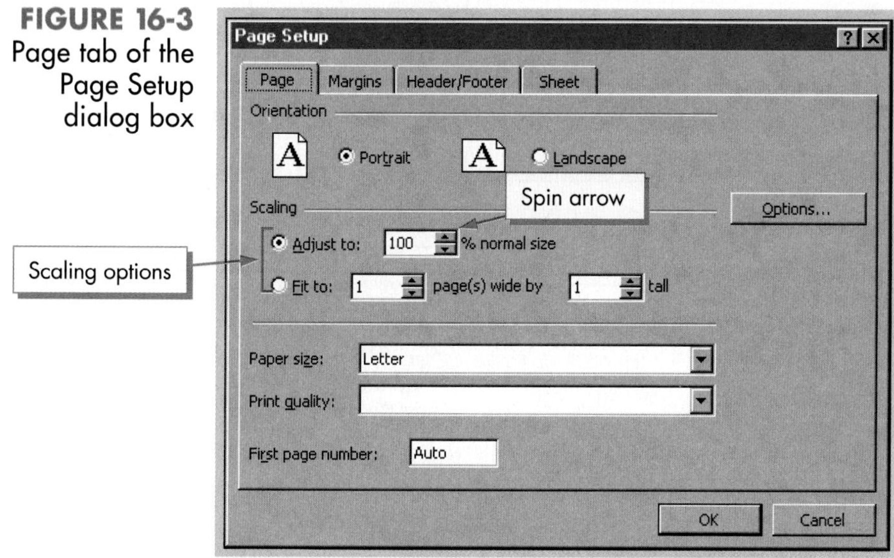

3. Click the Landscape option button.
4. Select the Adjust to option, if necessary, and key **80** in the % normal size box (or click the down spin arrow to change the value to 80).
5. Click OK. The worksheet now spans three pages.
6. Move to page 2 in Print Preview. The data on page 2 almost fills the landscape page.

Adding Print Titles

You can generate consistent titles and column or row headings across multiple pages. You specify which rows or columns to use in the Print Titles section of the Sheet tab in the Page Setup dialog box. Print titles can be in multiple rows or columns, but they must be adjacent.

EXERCISE 16-4 Set Print Titles for Each Printed Page

1. Click Previous to return to page 1. Only page 1 of the worksheet has the print title beginning "National Sales" and the labels in column A.
2. Close Print Preview.
3. Choose Page Setup from the File menu.

NOTE: You *cannot* set print titles by clicking Setup from the Print Preview window.

4. Click the Sheet tab.

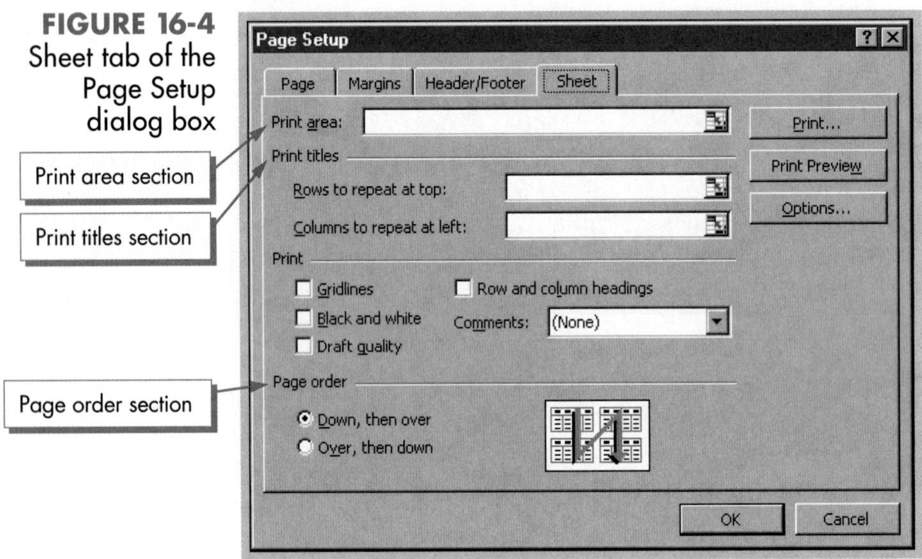

FIGURE 16-4
Sheet tab of the Page Setup dialog box

5. Key **A:A** in the Columns to repeat at left text box. You must key a range of columns (like A:A or B:D), even if you want to print titles from only one column.
6. Click Print Preview and page through the worksheet. All the pages now have the titles and labels from column A on page 1.

Changing Margins in Print Preview

You can change margins in the Page Setup dialog box or in Print Preview. To change margins in Print Preview, you drag margin lines to the desired position. An advantage of changing margins in Print Preview is that you see the results immediately.

EXERCISE 16-5 Change Margins in Print Preview

1. Return to page 1. If margin lines do not appear in Print Preview, click Margins at the top of the Print Preview window. Dotted lines delineate the header and footer areas and the margins and column handles appear at the top of the page.

FIGURE 16-5
Changing margins in Print Preview

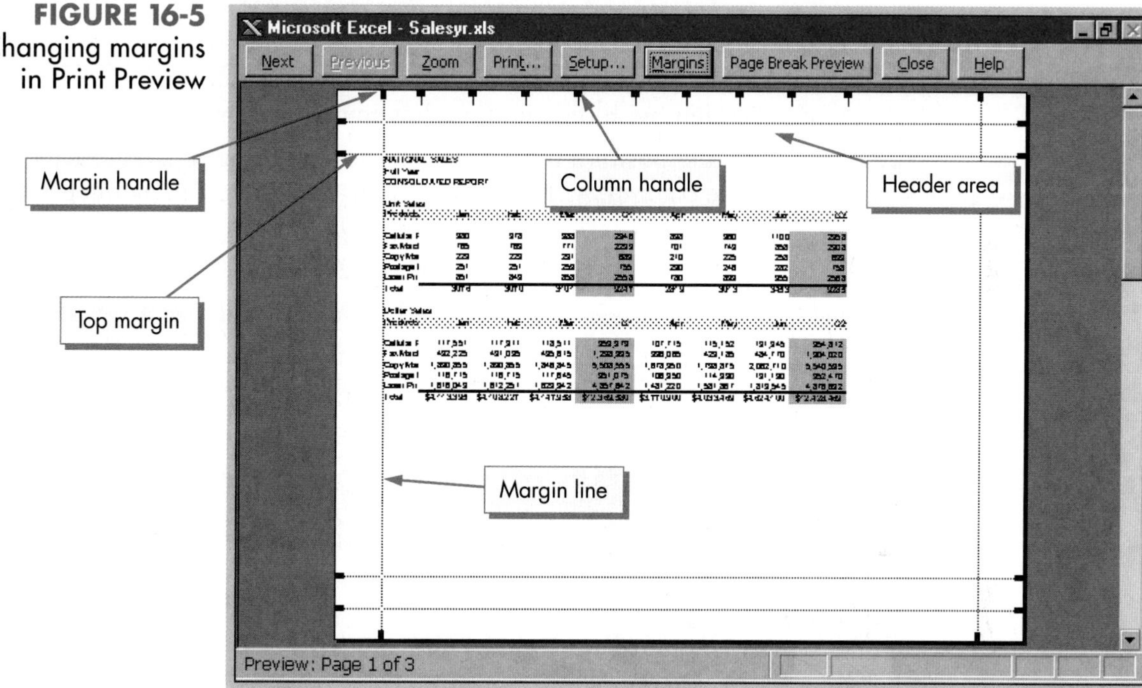

2. Click Setup and click the Margins tab.
3. Double-click in the Top text box and key **2** to set the top margin to 2 inches.
4. Click OK. Print Preview displays the new margin setting. View the other pages and notice that the margins changed on all three pages. Return to page 1.
5. Position the pointer on the top margin, either on the margin handle or on the dotted line itself. (It is the second dotted line from the top.) The pointer changes to the sizing pointer, like the one used to size rows in a worksheet.
6. Drag the line up to the one-inch line. Watch the indicator in the Status bar.

NOTE: You may not be able to move a margin to an exact position by dragging.

Changing Column Widths in Print Preview

You can change column widths in Print Preview by dragging the column handles (the square boxes at the top of the page).

EXERCISE 16-6 Change Column Widths in Print Preview

1. In Print Preview, with the Margins showing, display page 2.
2. Click Zoom and position the pointer on the first column handle. This is the Print title column, A. The pointer changes to the sizing pointer.
3. Drag the first column handle to the right until you see all the titles. The Status bar shows a measurement of about 27.
4. Click Zoom again, move to page 1, and notice that column A is widened there, too. Adjust the remaining column widths on page 1, so the data fills the page and columns B through I are evenly spaced (each about 15 characters wide).

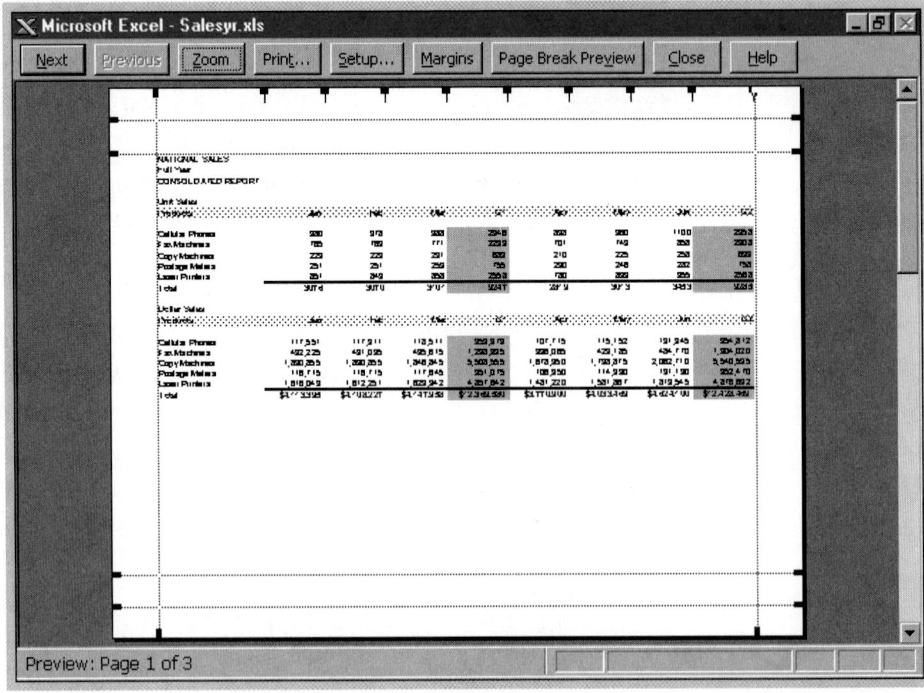

FIGURE 16-6
Page 1 in Print Preview after resizing columns

5. Click Next. The columns on page 2 already fill the page and need no adjustment.
6. Click Next. Only the Print titles and current prices appear on page 3.
7. Move to page 1.

Modifying Preset Headers and Footers

Headers print repetitive information about the worksheet across the top of the page. *Footers* print repetitive information across the bottom of the page. Headers and footers are positioned above and below the margins on the printed page.

You can key information in a header or footer; insert codes for the page number, total number of pages, date, time, filename, or sheet name; and format header and footer text. Excel also offers several preset headers and footers that you can use or edit.

FIGURE 16-7
Buttons in the Header dialog box

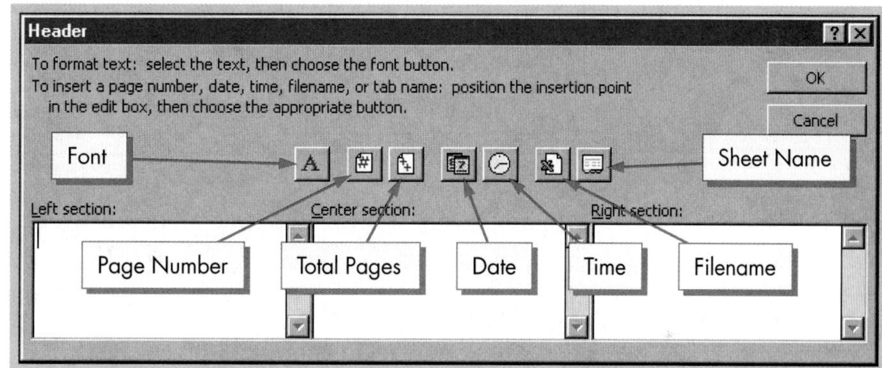

EXERCISE 16-7 Use and Customize Preset Headers and Footers

1. Click Setup in Print Preview and click the Header/Footer tab.
2. Click the Header drop-down arrow. The Header drop-down list displays preset headers. (See Figure 16-8 on the next page.)
3. Choose the preset header: Prepared by *[a name] [today's date]*, Page 1. The list closes.
4. Click Custom Header to edit the header.
5. In the Header dialog box, delete the name after "Prepared by," and key *[Your Name]*.

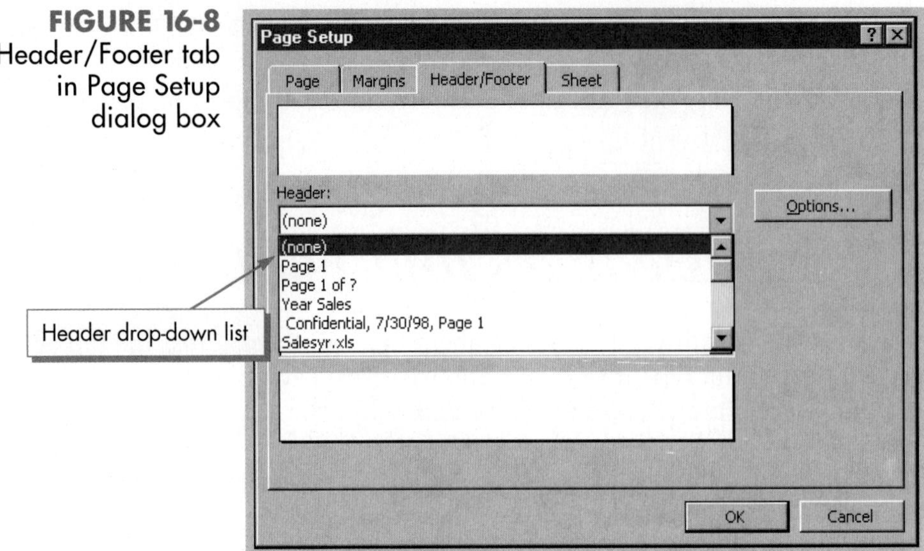

FIGURE 16-8 Header/Footer tab in Page Setup dialog box

6. Select the text excluding the date in the Center section (Prepared by *[Your Name]*) and click the Font button.
7. In the Font dialog box, choose Bold from the Font style list and click OK.
8. In the Right section delete all the page number information and click the Filename button to insert the filename.
9. Click OK to close the Header dialog box.
10. Click the Footer drop-down arrow and choose the preset footer: Year Sales, Confidential, Page 1.
11. Click Custom Footer to edit the footer.
12. Key **Feestone Electronics** before "Confidential."
13. Click OK to close the Footer dialog box and click OK to close Page Setup. Examine the headers and footers in Print Preview.
14. Close Print Preview.
15. Press Ctrl+Home.
16. Save the workbook as *[your initials]***16-7.xls**.
17. Print the worksheet and close the workbook.

Changing Page Order and Printing

When data is on more than one page, Excel prints by default from the first page down and then across. If you want the pages to print across and then down, you specify this in the Page Setup dialog box.

You can also print a specified range of pages. In the Print dialog box, choose Pages in the Page Range section and specify the beginning and ending pages in the from and to boxes.

EXERCISE 16-8 Print a Range of Pages Across and Then Down

1. Open the file **Salesyr2.xls**.
2. Move around the worksheet. The data for the first quarter is in the top left portion of the worksheet, the data for the second quarter is to the right of the first-quarter data, and the data for the third and fourth quarters is below the first and second quarters. It is clear that this worksheet is meant to be read across and then down, rather than down and then across.
3. Press Ctrl+Home to move to the top of the worksheet and open Print Preview. The data on page 1 is the first-quarter data.
4. Click Next to move to page 2. The third-quarter data is on page 2.
5. Click Next. Page 3 contains the prices used in the formulas that calculate Dollar Sales.
6. Page through the rest of the worksheet. The second-quarter data is on page 4 and the fourth-quarter data is on page 5. Excel is reading down the worksheet then across, which is not the intended order.

NOTE: Page 6 is blank because there is no data in the area to the right of the price data and below the fourth-quarter data.

7. Click the Previous button until you return to page 1.
8. Click the Setup button and click the Sheet tab.
9. In the Page order section, choose Over then down and click OK.
10. Page through the worksheet in Print Preview to see the corrected page order. The second-quarter data is on page 2, the third-quarter data is on page 3, and the fourth-quarter data is on page 4.
11. Insert the standard header with your name, filename, and date. Also insert a Page 1 of ? footer.
12. Close Print Preview.
13. Save the workbook as *[your initials]***16-8.xls**.
14. Press Ctrl+P, choose Pages in the Print dialog box, key **1** in the From box and **2** in the To box, and click OK.

Printing Named Ranges

As you know, you can select an area and print it or you can define the print area for a worksheet. You can also name ranges that you expect to print frequently so you can quickly select the named range and print it.

EXERCISE 16-9 Print a Named Range

1. Select cells A1 through G24.
2. Click in the Name Box, key **Qtr1**, and press Enter.

TIP: To name a range, you can also choose Name from the Insert menu and click Define.

3. Assign the name **Qtr2** to the range H1:N24, **Qtr3** to the range A26:G49, and **Qtr4** to the range H26:N49.
4. Press Ctrl+Home and save the workbook as *[your initials]***16-9.xls**.
5. Remove the footer and select Qtr3 from the Name drop-down list or the Go To dialog box.
6. Choose Print from the File menu, choose the Selection option, and click OK. Excel prints the selected cells.

TIP: You can also specify a named range to print in the Page Setup dialog box. Key the named range in the Print area text box in the Sheet options.

7. Close the workbook without saving it.

Concepts Review

TRUE/FALSE QUESTIONS

Each of the following statements is either true or false. Indicate your choice by circling T or F.

T F *1*. You can delete manual and automatic page breaks.

T F *2*. When you scale a worksheet, you change the size of the worksheet contents.

T F *3*. An advantage of changing the margins and column widths in Print Preview is that you can see the results immediately.

T F *4*. To change column widths in Print Preview, you double-click the column handles.

T F *5*. Although Excel has many preset headers and footers you can apply to your worksheets, you cannot change or add to any of the preset information.

T F *6*. Excel can only print going down the worksheet first, then across.

T F *7*. You must use the mouse to move around in Print Preview.

T F *8*. Printing a named range is like printing a selection.

SHORT ANSWER QUESTIONS

Write the correct answer in the space provided.

1. What do you call enlarging or reducing the size of data on a physical page?

____

2. Which option on the Page tab of the Page Setup dialog box do you use to make the worksheet automatically fit on a specific number of pages?

____

3. Which area on the Sheet tab of the Page Setup dialog box do you use to generate identical titles on each printed page?

____

4. What do you drag to adjust column widths in Print Preview?

____

5. What is the information positioned at the top of the page above the margin called?

____

6. If the preset headers and footers do not provide the information you need, what option can you use to modify them?

____

7. In what default direction does Excel begin to read a multiple page worksheet?

____

8. Which print option must you select to print a selected named range?

____

CRITICAL THINKING

Answer these questions on a separate piece of paper. There are no right or wrong answers. Support your answers with examples from your own experience, if possible.

1. You know how to adjust column widths several ways, in both the worksheet and in Print Preview. Which would you recommend to an inexperienced user? Why?
2. People are growing more conscious of the environmental impact of trash. The "paperless office" has long been a goal of the corporate world. Many people think, however, that the use of computers has actually caused people to use *more* paper than ever. Can you think of any alternatives to printing worksheets? What are some other ways to share relevant information without using paper?

Skills Review

EXERCISE 16-10

Add manual page breaks and scale the worksheet.

1. Open the file **Halfyr1.xls**.
2. Key the second-quarter information in the range F8:I13 as shown in Figure 16-9, entering SUM formulas in the "Q2" column and "Total" row.

FIGURE 16-9

Products	April	May	June	Q2
Cellular phones	341	365	418	
Fax Machines	266	285	326	
Copy Machines	80	86	98	
Postage Meters	87	93	107	
Laser Printers	296	317	363	
Total				

3. Apply formatting in the Quarter 1 and Quarter 2 data and AutoFit columns F through I.
4. Add and remove page breaks in the worksheet by following these steps:
   - *a.* Choose Options from the Tools menu and click the View tab, if necessary.
   - *b.* Check Page breaks and click OK.
   - *c.* Select cell F15.
   - *d.* Choose Page Break from the Insert menu.
   - *e.* Select cell A15.
   - *f.* Choose Remove Page Break from the Insert menu.
5. Use Page Break Preview mode to manipulate page breaks by following these steps:
   - *a.* Choose Page Break Preview from the View menu.
   - *b.* Click OK if the Welcome to Page Break Preview dialog box appears.
   - *c.* Move the pointer over the solid blue page break until it becomes ↔.
   - *d.* Drag the line between columns B and C to move the manual page break.
   - *e.* Drag the line back between columns E and F.
   - *f.* Choose Normal from the View menu.
6. Scale the data to fill the page by following these steps:
   - *a.* Click [Print Preview button].
   - *b.* Click Setup and click the Page tab.
   - *c.* Choose Adjust to and key **125** in the % normal size box (or use the spin arrow).
   - *d.* Select Landscape.

e. Click the Margins tab and center the pages horizontally.

f. Insert the standard header in the worksheet and a Page 1 of ? footer. Click OK.

g. Page through the worksheet and close Print Preview.

h. Press Ctrl + Home.

7. Save the workbook as *[your initials]***16-10.xls** and print the worksheet.
8. Create a formula printout with grids and row and column headings. Adjust to 100% in the Page tab options of the Page Setup dialog box. Remove the page break between columns E and F.
9. Close the workbook without saving it.

EXERCISE 16-11

Add print titles and change margins in Print Preview.

1. Open the file **Halfyr2.xls**.
2. Add print titles as indicated by following these steps:

a. Choose Page Setup from the File menu.

b. Click the Sheet tab.

c. Key **A:A** in the Columns to repeat at left text box.

TIP: Instead of keying a range, you can click in the Columns to repeat at left text box and select columns in the worksheet.

d. Click Print Preview. Make sure the small view is displayed.

3. If margin lines are not displayed, click Margins.
4. Drag the left margin line to the right, to the 2.0-inch mark.
5. Drag the right margin line to the left, to the 1.5-inch mark.
6. Add the standard header and a Page 1 of ? footer using the Setup button.
7. Close Print Preview.
8. Save the workbook as *[your initials]***16-11.xls** and print the worksheet.
9. Close the workbook.

EXERCISE 16-12

Change column widths in Print Preview and create headers and footers.

1. Open the file **Halfyr3.xls**.
2. Open Print Preview. If margin lines are not displayed, click Margins.
3. Adjust the column widths by following these steps:

   a. Drag the first column handle to the right until column A is about 22 characters wide.
   b. Drag the rest of the column handles to the right so each column is about 14 characters wide and the data roughly fills the page (margin to margin).
   c. Click Next.
   d. Starting with the second column handle, drag each column handle to the right so each column is about 14 characters wide and the last column moves onto page 3.
4. Choose a preset header and modify it by following these steps:
   a. Click Previous, click Setup, and click the Header/Footer tab.
   b. Open the Header drop-down list and choose Confidential, Northeast, Page 1.
   c. Click Custom Header and replace Confidential with **Feestone Electronics**.
   d. Select all the text in the Left Section, click the Font button, double-click Bold italic, and click OK.
5. Choose a preset footer and modify it by following these steps:
   a. Open the Footer drop-down list and choose Halfyr3.xls.
   b. Click Custom Footer.
   c. In the Left Section, key your name.
   d. In the Right Section, click the Date button.
   e. Click OK to close the Footer dialog box and click OK again to close the Page Setup dialog box.
6. View the header and footer in Print Preview and close the Print Preview window.
7. Save the workbook as *[your initials]***16-12.xls**.
8. Print the worksheet and close the workbook.

EXERCISE 16-13

Change page order and print named ranges.

1. Open the file **NESales.xls**.
2. Click [Print Preview button].
3. Page through the worksheet, then return to page 1.
4. Change the page order by following these steps:
   a. Click Setup and choose the Sheet tab.

b. Click Over, click down, and click OK.

c. Page through the worksheet to confirm it will print in the correct order. (You may want to Zoom in and out.)

d. Add the standard header with your name, the filename, and the date.

e. Close Print Preview.

5. Create named ranges for printing by following these steps:

a. Select cell B1 through cell E23.

b. Click the Name Box, key **First_Qtr**, and press Enter.

c. To the cell range F1:I23, assign the name **Second_Qtr**, and press Ctrl + Home.

d. Save the workbook as *[your initials]***16-13.xls**.

6. Print named ranges by following these steps:

a. Choose Page Setup from the File menu.

b. Click the Sheet tab.

c. Key **First_Qtr** in the Print area text box.

NOTE: Print titles are already set.

d. Click Print and click OK in the Print dialog box. The first-quarter data prints.

e. Click the arrow to open the Name Box drop-down list and click Second_Qtr.

f. Choose Print from the File menu.

g. Choose Selection in the Print dialog box and click OK

7. Press Ctrl + Home and add a Page 1 of ? footer.

8. Print pages 1 and 2 of the worksheet. (You have to clear the print area in the Sheet options of the Page Setup dialog box or choose File, Print Area, Clear Print Area.)

9. Close the workbook without saving it.

Lesson Applications

EXERCISE 16-14

Modify preset headers and footers, add print titles, insert and remove page breaks, scale the worksheet, adjust margins in Print Preview, and print a named range.

Feestone Electronics wants to print its quarterly sales data on two pages and print its price list separately, as needed.

1. Open the file **Salesyr3.xls**.
2. Widen column A to accommodate the longest title and set column A to print on each page.
3. Change the print header by moving "Year Sales" to the left section and adding the date to the right section. Change the footer by deleting the page number and entering the following information in the left and right sections:

   Prepared by *[your name]* **Filename, Page #**
4. Set the worksheet to print in landscape orientation centered horizontally on the page.
5. Remove the page break above the Dollar Sales row and insert a page break after the Q2 column.
6. In Print Preview, adjust the left and right margins to about 0.5 inches.
7. Scale the worksheet to approximately 88% or so quarters 1 and 2 fill page 1.
8. Adjust the top margin to 2 inches.
9. Name cells S16 through S22 **Prices**.
10. Press Ctrl+Home and save the workbook as *[your initials]***16-14.xls**.
11. Print the range Prices.
12. Print the worksheet and close the workbook.

EXERCISE 16-15

Insert and remove page breaks, add print titles, add a custom footer, and change margins and column widths in Print Preview.

Feestone Electronics' personnel manager needs to print the employee information worksheet for a meeting. The lookup data in the worksheet must be printed separately for the manager's use only.

1. Open the file **EmpInfo.xls** and key the date of birth and the hire date for the last 10 employees, as shown in Figure 16-10.

FIGURE 16-10

		Date of Birth	Hire Date
Rodriguez	Marta	6/29/67	4/6/90
Ross	Sarah	4/23/72	5/19/92
Slavitt	Robert	9/17/74	1/18/92
Smythe	Susan	3/25/73	12/12/95
Torrisi	Thomas	11/3/78	3/5/96
Troisi	Stephen	3/5/78	8/12/94
Tyler	Mary	10/14/69	5/15/96
Vu	Tri	8/16/70	12/15/95
Weinstein	David	2/27/75	12/8/93
Wysocki	Mark	6/6/75	6/10/92

2. Remove the page break to the left of column G.
3. Add a page break above the lookup table in row 49.
4. Add the worksheet title and labels in rows 1 through 4 as print titles (Rows to repeat at top).
5. Add columns A and B as print titles.
6. Modify the preset footer to include the department name (Personnel), the page number, and the sheet name, and add the standard header with your name, filename, and date.
7. Change the top margin to 1.5 inches.
8. In Print Preview, increase the width of column A to about 16 characters.
9. In Print Preview, increase the width of column B as much as possible without moving the column labeled "Wks Vactn" onto another page.
10. Save the workbook as *[your initials]***16-15.xls**.
11. Print pages 1 and 2 of the worksheet and close the workbook.

EXERCISE 16-16

Insert page breaks in Page Break Preview mode, set print titles, change the print order of the pages, adjust the margins and column widths in Print Preview, modify preset headers and footers, and create and print a named range.

A detailed financial statement of changes in net assets for the retirement accounts of the employees of Feestone Electronics needs to be reformatted for printing. It needs specific page breaks and headers and footers. Each year's data should fit on one page for a total of three pages with the same print title.

1. Open the file **Retracct.xls**.
2. Change the page orientation to landscape and examine the worksheet in Print Preview.
3. Close Print Preview and set page breaks to create three pages, one for each year's data. Use Page Break Preview mode and move the automatic page break if you need to.

NOTE: Insert page breaks the same way in Page Break Preview mode as you would in Normal view.

4. Set columns A, B, and C and rows 1 and 2 as print titles.
5. Change the page order so the worksheet reads over, then down.
6. Adjust the column widths to make the data fill the page and to have data fit in columns.
7. Select a header that includes "Prepared by," the date, and the page number. Modify the header to identify the accounting firm, Brown and Brown, that prepared the statement. Change the font to Arial.
8. Create a custom footer with your name and the filename. Change the font to Arial.
9. Lower the top margin to one inch, and horizontally center the worksheet on the page.
10. Re-center years over the figure columns.
11. Set up a named range **CapGrowth_97** for 1997's capital growth (the column D data), so you can print only this information for clients that request it, without giving them other confidential information.
12. Press Ctrl+Home and save the workbook as *[your initials]***16-16.xls**.
13. Print the range CapGrowth_97 and clear the Print Area, if necessary.
14. Print pages 2 and 3 of the worksheet and close the workbook.

EXERCISE 16-17

Insert and modify page breaks in Page Break Preview mode, scale the data, adjust column widths, modify headers, and print named ranges.

The Feestone Electronics company needs to create an attractive worksheet that shows the net investment returns of the retirement accounts of its employees.

1. Sketch a design of the worksheet on paper that includes the following:
   a. An appropriate title
   b. Three entry areas designated as **Monthly Dollar Averaged**, **Single Investment**, and **Variable Monthly Investments**. These should create three sections in the worksheet.
   c. Row labels that include **Capital Growth**, **Bond Income**, **Money Market**, and **Stock Index**
   d. Column labels for each entry area for the years **1990** through **1997**.
2. Key the title and all labels into Excel. Format them attractively and increase column width where necessary.
3. Key the data in Figure 16-11 (on the next page) into the worksheet as percentages. Format figures attractively keeping the decimal points. (*Hint:* You can key the percentage symbol after each number and Excel automatically considers it a percentage.)
4. Change the page orientation to landscape.
5. Insert and adjust pages breaks in Page Break Preview mode so each section prints on a separate page.
6. Scale the data, adjust columns, or adjust margins so the data fills each page and each page is centered horizontally.
7. Create print titles that include the title of the worksheet and row labels, if necessary, so these print on each page.
8. Add the standard header with your name, filename, and date in Arial bold italic.
9. Add formatting to further enhance the worksheet and delete extra worksheet tabs.
10. Create user documentation and name the sheet tab **User Information**. The sheet should contain the following: File Information (Created by, Date created, Date revised, Revised by, Contact for help); Purpose of spreadsheet (paragraph form); and Instructions to User (special instructions needed by user to enter data correctly). Format the documentation attractively and change column widths as necessary. Spell-check your work.
11. Add the standard header to the User Information sheet.
12. Save the workbook as *[your initials]***16-17.xls**.
13. Create a named range for each section and print each range separately. (Remember to clear the Print Area if you set it.) Print the User Information sheet.
14. Save the workbook again, close it, and submit the worksheet pages and your sketch.

FIGURE 16-11

Monthly Dollar Averaged

	1990	1991	1992	1993	1994	1995	1996	1997
Capital Growth	67.51	94.53	52.17	-9.11	30.30	-3.82	53.45	-6.38
Bond Income	18.34	14.43	1.91	7.99	11.91	7.71	17.55	7.80
Money Market	7.88	6.43	6.16	7.14	8.87	7.81	5.84	3.43
Stock Index	4.54	8.87	-12.40	15.93	29.70	-4.48	29.98	6.92

Single Investment

	1990	1991	1992	1993	1994	1995	1996	1997
Capital Growth	67.34	94.33	52.02	9.20	30.17	3.91	53.29	6.47
Bond Income	18.23	14.32	1.81	7.88	11.79	7.60	17.43	7.69
Money Market	7.78	6.32	6.05	7.03	8.77	7.71	5.74	3.33
Stock Index	6.65	11.21	-12.46	15.82	29.57	-4.58	29.85	6.81

Variable Monthly Investments

	1990	1991	1992	1993	1994	1995	1996	1997
Capital Growth	67.09	94.04	51.79	-9.34	29.57	-4.58	29.85	-6.61
Bond Income	18.05	14.15	1.65	7.72	11.63	7.44	17.25	7.53
Money Market	7.61	6.16	5.89	6.87	8.60	7.54	5.58	3.18
Stock Index	9.87	4.52	-12.55	15.65	29.37	4.72	29.65	6.65

Unit 5 Applications

APPLICATION 5-1

Open multiple workbooks, switch between workbook windows, copy and paste between workbooks and worksheets, modify headers, and scale the worksheets.

Feestone Electronics currently ships products through United Express. It wants to compare the costs of three other delivery companies. Since the costs might change, Feestone needs a summary worksheet linked to each company's rate card.

1. Open the files **Crntship.xls** and **Shipanls.xls**.
2. Copy the information from Crntship.xls to a new first worksheet in Shipanls.xls. Use the same formatting and positioning used in the other three worksheets and name the worksheet **United Express**.
3. Insert a worksheet in front of the United Express sheet, name it **Analysis**, and in cell A1 key the title **Shipping Costs Analysis** in bold.
4. Starting in column B, key the labels in bold as shown in Figure U5-1. Center the column labels.

FIGURE U5-1

	United Express	CPS Corp.	Packages R Us	Overnight Specialists
Standard				
2-Day				
Overnight				

5. Paste Link the shipping rates from each of the four delivery companies to the proper column in the Analysis sheet. (Right-align "N/A.")
6. In the CPS Corp. sheet, change both the 2-day and overnight rates to **125**.
7. In all worksheets create the standard header with your name, filename, and date in Arial bold italic.

TIP: Select all the sheets, then choose the Page Setup command on the File menu instead of setting up each page in Print Preview.

8. Center the worksheets horizontally on the page and scale the worksheets to 125% of their normal size.
9. Save the file as *[your initials]***u5-1.xls**.
10. Print the Analysis worksheet and then print the United Express and CPS Corp. worksheets.
11. Create a formula printout of the Analysis sheet in landscape orientation scaled at 100% with grids and row and column headings. Even though there are no formulas in the worksheets, the formula printout shows the linked cell references.
12. Close both workbooks without saving them.

APPLICATION 5-2

Copy and paste between worksheets, link workbooks, insert manual page breaks, set print titles, and modify headers and footers.

Employees at Feestone Electronics get paid vacation, sick, and personal time. All employees get 3 personal days and 12 sick days per year. The amount of vacation time each employee receives depends on how long the person has been employed. Employees who have worked at Feestone for 0 to 3 years receive 1 week (5 days) paid vacation. Employees who have worked at least 4 years receive 2 weeks vacation. Employees who have worked for the company 7 years or more receive 3 weeks per year. You need to link the employee list and hire dates to a worksheet that calculates the time off due each employee.

1. Open the files **Slryempl.xls** and **Timeoff.xls**.
2. Paste Link the Last Name, First Name, and Date Hired data from Slryempl.xls to Timeoff.xls.
3. Copy the formula in cell D10 down to calculate the vacation time due each employee.
4. Key the time off already used by each employee as shown in Figure U5-2. Key the vacation time used in column E, the sick time used in column G, and the personal time used in column I.
5. Create and copy formulas to calculate the vacation time left, sick time left, and personal time left. Remember, sick time and personal time are the same for each employee every year.
6. Set the worksheet heading as a print title and the "Last Name," "First Name," and "Date Hired" columns as print titles.

FIGURE U5-2

Last Name	First Name	Vacation Time Used	Sick Time Used	Personal Time Used
Abbott	Martha	3	5	0
Frisbee	John	5	1	0
Garcia	Ramone	10	9	1
LaConte	Danielle	10	12	0
Maplethorpe	Holly	5	0	3
Martin	Jamaica	5	0	0
Needlehoffen	Adrian	9	3	0
Northridge	Leroy	7	2	2
O'Connor	Patrick	12	0	0
Santos	Julia	5	1	0
Tellman	Lowell	5	0	3
Underwood	Marc	1	10	0
Young	Emma	15	11	1
Zimmer	Joseph	5	0	1

7. Insert page breaks so the worksheet prints on three pages, one for vacation time, one for sick time, and one for personal time.
8. Set up the worksheet to print in portrait orientation, centered horizontally.
9. Create the standard header with your name, filename, and date in Arial bold, italic. Modify the preset Page 1 of ? footer to be Arial bold, italic, and have the sheet tab print in the right section also in bold, italic.
10. Name the worksheet **Employee Time**.
11. Save the file as *[your initials]***u5-2.xls** and print all three pages.

12. Create a formula printout in landscape orientation with grids and row and column headings. AutoFit all columns, remove print titles, and remove manual page breaks, if necessary.

13. Close all workbooks without saving any of them.

APPLICATION 5-3

Link data between workbooks, create linked formulas, create custom headers and footers, and protect the worksheet.

Feestone Electronics gives bonuses to its sales managers if they exceed their sales goals for the year. Develop a new worksheet that calculates the bonuses for the managers for 1996. Create a worksheet sketch and use Figure U5-3 as a guide for row and column labels. Insert F for formulas based on the information following the figure. Key your sketch into Excel and include the managers and regions from Figure U5-3.

FIGURE U5-3

Manager	Region	Goal	Actual	Difference	Bonus
H. Maplethorpe	NE				
A. Needlehoffen	NW				
J. Frisbee	SE				
J. Martin	SW				
Total					

The goal for 1996 is a 10% increase over the 1995 total sales. In the "Goal" column, create linked formulas that multiply the regional sales in **95sales.xls** by 1.1. In the "Actual" column, link the regional sales in **96sales.xls**. In the "Difference" column, subtract the Goal from the Actual.

If a manager meets the goal (Difference >=0), he or she receives $10,000. Use an IF function to calculate the bonuses and total the bonuses. Format the worksheet attractively, name the worksheet tab, and center it horizontally.

Create user documentation and name the sheet tab **User Information**. The sheet should include the following: File Information (Created by, Date created, Date revised, Revised by, Contact for help); Purpose of spreadsheet (paragraph form); and Instructions to Users (special instructions needed by users to enter data correctly). Format the documentation attractively and change column widths if you think they need it. Spell-check your work.

Give both worksheets a standard header that includes your name, filename, and date, and a custom footer that identifies the purpose of the bonus worksheet.

Delete any blank worksheets in the workbook. Save the workbook as *[your initials]***u5-3.xls** and print both worksheets.

Create a formula printout in landscape orientation with grids and row and column headings. Insert the page numbers in the footer if the formula printout exceeds one page. Close all files without saving any of them and submit your sketch, worksheets, and formula printout.

UNIT

6

Graphics

Charting a Running Success

Harry Hascabar's Hand-Crafted Leather Goods has been in existence for over 20 years. The company makes briefcases, shoes, handbags, and laptop-computer cases and sells them in a five shops in the San Francisco area. But Harry Hascabar's real passion is running. He has often run in the Boston Marathon and is a nationally known sports figure.

For over a decade, the company has been quite successful making special running shoes for long-distance runners. Harry would like the company to continue moving into this market by selling sports drinks that enhance performance for long-distance runners. He's even thinking of creating a new subsidiary called "Marathon Products."

Harry wants to research all the competing sports drinks before he formulates his own. He will keep a detailed log of his distances, times, and the product he drinks before he runs. Harry will be collecting a considerable amount of detailed information, and he needs to summarize it in an attractive format to secure financing for his new company.

To present his results attractively and visually, he needs to:

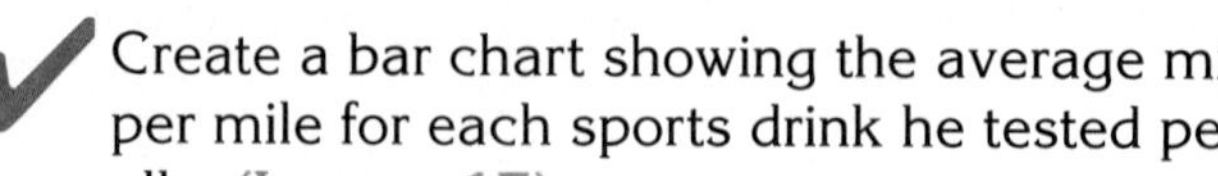

- ✔ Create a bar chart showing the average minutes per mile for each sports drink he tested personally. (Lesson 17)
- ✔ Create attractive charts that compare the various sports drinks he tested, with drawing objects and clip art. (Lesson 18)

Creating Charts and Maps

OBJECTIVES

After completing this lesson, you will be able to:

1. **Identify chart types and chart objects.**
2. **Use the Chart Wizard to create an embedded chart.**
3. **Size and move a chart.**
4. **Edit a chart.**
5. **Save and print a chart.**
6. **Create a chart on a chart sheet.**
7. **Create a data map.**
8. **Enhance a data map.**

Estimated Time: 1½ hours

A chart is a visual representation of worksheet data. You link charts to worksheet data through cell references so Excel can update the data in a chart automatically when you change the data in the linked worksheet.

Identifying Chart Types and Chart Objects

You can create many types of charts in Excel. Once you learn the different chart types, you can determine the purpose of the chart and match it to the data in the worksheet. Each Excel chart consists of various chart objects.

TABLE 17-1 Chart Types in Excel

TYPE	DEFINITION
Bar	Bar charts illustrate comparisons among items or show individual figures at a specific time. Also 3-D effects.
Column	Column charts show variation over a period of time or demonstrate a comparison among items. Also 3-D effects.
Line	Line charts show trends in data over a period of time at the same intervals, emphasizing the rate of change over time. Also 3-D effects.
Pie	Pie charts compare the sizes of pieces in a whole unit. Each chart shows only one data series. Also 3-D effects.
XY (Scatter)	XY (Scatter) charts compare trends over uneven time or measurement intervals plotted on the category axis. Scatter charts also display patterns from discrete x and y data measurements.
Area	Area charts show the relationship of parts to a whole and emphasize the magnitude of change. Also 3-D effects.
Doughnut	Doughnut charts compare the sizes of pieces in a whole unit. Each chart can show more than one data series.
Radar	Radar charts show changes or frequencies of data relative to a center point and to other data points. Each category has its own value axis radiating from the center point. Lines connect all values in the same series.
Surface	Surface charts are useful for finding optimum combinations between two sets of data. They can show relationships between large amounts of data that would otherwise be difficult to see. Also shown with 3-D effects.
Bubble	Bubble charts compare sets of three values. They are like scatter charts with the third value displayed as the size of the bubble marker. Also shown with 3-D effects.
Stock	Stock charts are called high-low-close charts and they require three series of values in this order They are frequently used to illustrate stock prices. Also shown with 3-D effects.
Cylinder	Cylinder charts have a cylindrical shape. They lend dramatic effect to 3-D column and bar charts.
Cone	Cone charts have a conical shape. They lend dramatic effect to 3-D column and bar charts.
Pyramid	Pyramid charts have a pyramid shape. They lend dramatic effect to 3-D column and bar charts.

Excel charts contain many objects that you can select and modify individually.

FIGURE 17-1
Excel chart objects

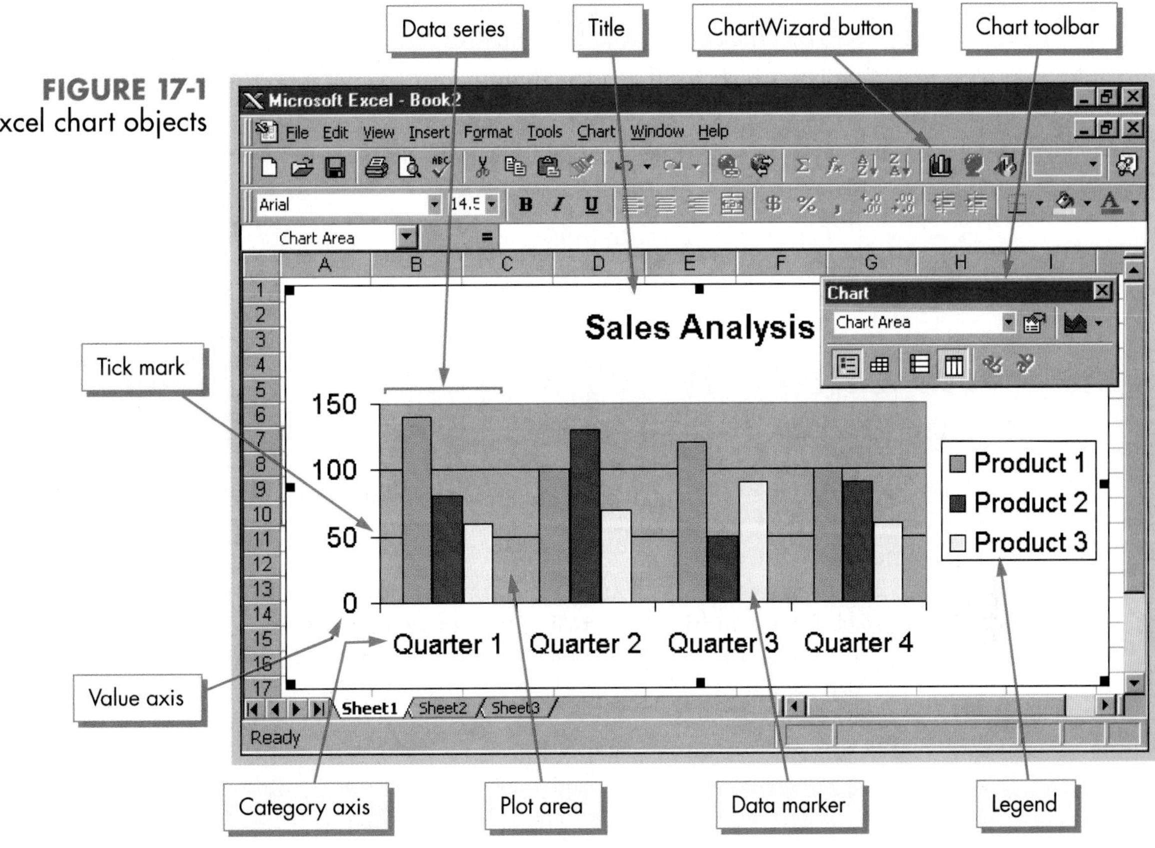

Each Excel chart object is described below:

- The *category axis* is the horizontal (or *x*) axis along the bottom of most charts; it frequently refers to time series.
- The *value axis* is the vertical (or *y*) axis against which data points are measured.
- The *plot area* is the rectangular area bounded by the two axes. It includes all axes and data points.
- A *data marker* is an object that represents individual data points. It can be a bar, area, dot, picture, or other symbol that marks a single data point or value.
- A *legend* is a guide that explains the symbols, patterns, or colors used to differentiate data series.
- A *tick mark* is a division mark along the category (x) and value (y) axes.
- A *data point* is a single piece of data.

- A *data series* is a collection of data points that are related. These values are usually found within the same column or row in the worksheet.
- The chart title gives the name of the chart.
- The Chart toolbar is available with special charting tools.
- The Chart Wizard button starts the Chart Wizard, which guides you step-by-step through the creation of a chart.
- The Chart menu replaces the Data menu in the menu bar. You use Chart menu commands to manipulate a chart.

Using the Chart Wizard

The Chart Wizard guides you through the process of creating an Excel chart using selected worksheet data. The completed chart is *embedded* in the worksheet. If you change data in the worksheet, Excel updates the chart automatically.

In the case study, Harry Hascabar wants to chart the effects of different sports drinks on his running speed. Before creating the chart, you need to develop a worksheet showing the sports drinks he used and the average minutes per mile recorded for each drink.

EXERCISE 17-1 Enter the Chart Data

1. Start a new workbook and key the following data in the cells indicated:

A1:	**Drink**	B1:	**Average Minutes**
A2:	**HydraPunch**	B2:	**7.63**
A3:	**SurgeQuench**	B3:	**7.77**
A4:	**AllSport**	B4:	**6.8**
A5:	**CynoMax**	B5:	**6.47**
A6:	**Endrun**	B6:	**7.2**
A7:	**Everlast**	B7:	**6.99**
A8:	**Innergize**	B8:	**7.57**

2. Modify the column widths as necessary.
3. Center the column headings and make them bold.

EXERCISE 17-2 Use the Chart Wizard

1. Select cells A1 through B8.
2. Click the Chart Wizard button on the Standard toolbar. The Chart Wizard Step 1 of 4 dialog box opens.

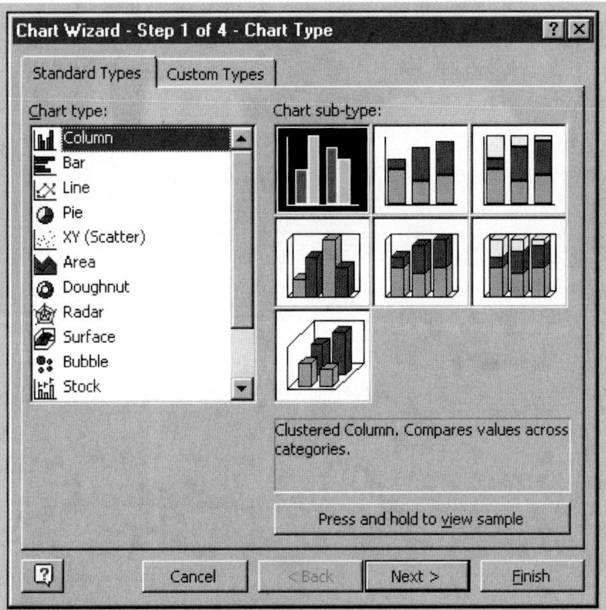

FIGURE 17-2 Chart Wizard - Step 1 of 4 dialog box

3. Click the Standard Types tab, if necessary.

TIP: There are many Custom charts available. Click the Custom Types tab to view the list.

EXERCISE 17-3 Choose the Chart Type

1. Click the Bar chart type. Six chart subtypes are displayed to the right.
2. Click the various subtypes and click the Press and hold to view sample button to see examples of the various subtypes.
3. When you finish viewing each subtype, choose the first subtype.

NOTE: Clicking Finish in the first step of the Chart Wizard creates the chart using the Excel 2-D column default chart format.

4. Click Next. The Chart Wizard - Step 2 of 4 dialog box appears.

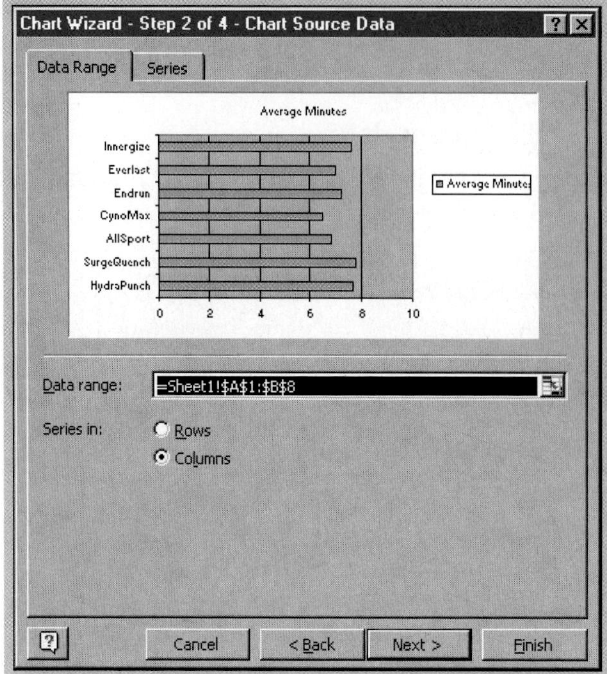

FIGURE 17-3 Chart Wizard - Step 2 of 4 dialog box

EXERCISE 17-4 Enter Additional Chart Information

In the Chart Wizard - Step 2 of 4 dialog box you specify plotting information to produce the desired chart.

1. Click the Data Range tab, if necessary. A moving border surrounds the data cells in the worksheet. (Move the dialog box if necessary.) Also notice the Data Range text box contains a formula with this cell range in it.
2. Select the Columns option, if necessary.
3. Click the Series tab and view the information for Name, Values (y-axis information), and Category. All these text boxes contain formulas with the cell addresses to plot the chart data and title it. You can edit these formulas here.
4. Click Next.

EXERCISE 17-5 Edit the Title, Add Labels and a Legend

1. Click the Titles tab, if necessary.
2. Key **Sports Drink Comparison** in the Chart title text box, overwriting "Average Minutes." The title appears in the Sample Chart.

3. Press Tab and key **Drinks** in the Category (X) axis text box.
4. Press Tab and key **Minutes** in the Value (Y) axis text box.
5. Click the Legend tab.
6. Make sure Show legend is selected and select Corner.
7. Click Next and the Chart Wizard Step 4 of 4 dialog box opens.

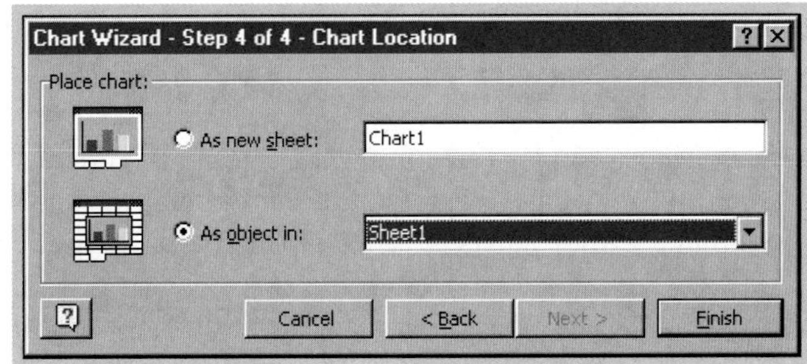

FIGURE 17-4 Chart Wizard - Step 4 of 4 dialog box

8. In the As object in text box, choose Sheet 1, if necessary.
9. Click Finish. A minimized chart is displayed in the worksheet. The Chart toolbar opens and the Chart menu appears in the menu bar replacing the Data menu.

NOTE: If the point size of some data in the chart is too big, some labels will not be visible and the entire chart will not appear. You learn to adjust the font size and resize the chart in the next two exercises.

Sizing and Moving a Chart

Once you create a chart, you can change its size, proportions, and position on the worksheet.

EXERCISE 17-6 Move and Size the Chart

1. Select the chart, if necessary, by clicking inside the chart. Small black squares, called *selection handles*, appear around the selected chart.
2. Point anywhere within the chart.
3. Click and drag the chart so the upper left corner is in cell A13. The pointer changes to a double-headed arrow.
4. Move the pointer over the bottom right selection handle until it changes to a double-headed arrow.

5. Using the double-headed arrow, enlarge the chart by dragging the bottom right corner to cell G31. Notice that the category axis labels are still not completely visible.
6. Click outside the chart to deactivate it. Notice that the Chart toolbar disappears and the Chart menu changes back to the Data menu.

Editing a Chart

After creating a chart, you may need to edit the chart font size so labels are readable and you may want to edit the chart's contents or change the chart type to make it more attractive or easier to understand. Before modifying an embedded chart, you must activate it by clicking it. Then you can use the Chart toolbar and Chart menu to make additional modifications.

EXERCISE 17-7 Activate the Chart and Display the Chart Toolbar

1. Move the mouse pointer inside the embedded chart and click it. The chart window is activated. A hatched border appears around the chart and the Chart toolbar is displayed again as well as the Chart menu.

FIGURE 17-5
Chart toolbar

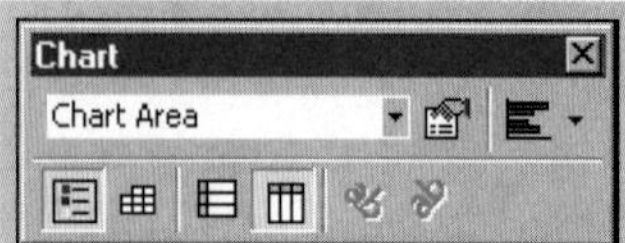

2. If the Chart toolbar is not displayed automatically, right-click any toolbar displayed on the screen and choose Chart from the shortcut menu.

TABLE 17-2 **Chart Toolbar**

BUTTON	NAME	DESCRIPTION
	Chart Objects	The drop-down list displays all the objects in the chart and allows you to select each of them.
	Format Object (varies)	Opens the corresponding dialog box for the object you selected in the chart.
	Chart Type	Displays the different chart types available.
	Legend	Removes and adds a legend.
	Data Table	Removes or adds a table containing the data series.
	By Rows	Plots a data series by rows.
	By Columns	Plots a data series by columns.

EXERCISE 17-8 Change the Chart Font Size

You can change the font size of any data in the chart using the Formatting toolbar.

1. Look in the Chart Objects text box to make sure "Chart Area" appears. If it doesn't, move the pointer around the white area of the chart until the Chart Area ScreenTip appears and click it.
2. From the Font Size drop-down list on the Formatting toolbar, choose 10 point. All the type in the chart is now 10 point and the labels are readable. This also enlarges the plot area.
3. Choose Chart Title from the Chart Objects drop-down list. (You can also click directly on the chart title.) Change the font size to 12 point in the Font drop-down list.

NOTE: You can also use these steps to change the font, but by accessing the font drop-down list on the Formatting toolbar. This is covered in detail in Lesson 18.

EXERCISE 17-9 Change the Chart Type

Viewing information arranged in a variety of chart types can provide different perspectives of your data. You can use the Chart toolbar or the menu bar to change the chart type.

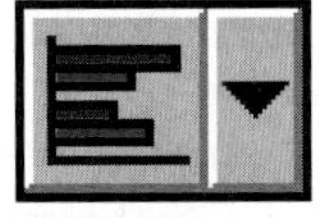

1. Click the down arrow to the right of the Chart Type button on the Chart toolbar. Excel displays a drop-down list of chart types.

FIGURE 17-6 Drop-down list of chart types

2. Click the Area Chart button in the top left corner. The chart is displayed as an area chart.
3. To view another perspective, re-open the drop-down list and click the Radar Chart button.
4. Choose Chart Type from the Chart menu.
5. Click the Standard Types tab, if necessary, select the Bar chart, and click OK. The first chart type you selected is restored.

TIP: Another way to change the chart type is to right-click the activated chart and choose Chart Type from the shortcut menu.

EXERCISE 17-10 Change Chart Subtype

Excel offers various formats, called subtypes, for each type of chart.

1. With the chart still activated, choose Chart Type from the Chart menu.
2. Click the Standard Types tab, if necessary.
3. Choose the fourth Subtype, clustered 3-D bar (the first subtype in the second row).
4. Click OK and the chart is 3-D.

NOTE: When you select different chart types, some labels may disappear. They need to have their point size edited to become visible again.

5. Press Ctrl+Z to revert to the previous chart type.

EXERCISE 17-11 Change Chart and Axis Titles

You may want to change titles, axes, or other items in your chart. You can select various chart items in an active chart by clicking the item.

1. Click the chart title "Sports Drink Comparison." The title is selected and "Chart Title" appears in the Name Box on the Formula Bar.
2. Type **Comparison for Weeks 1-5** and press Enter. The new text replaces the old title.
3. Click the category axis title "Drinks" and change it to **Sports Drinks**
4. Click the value axis title "Minutes" and change it to **Minutes Per Mile**

TIP: After selecting a chart text item, you can use the I-beam pointer to edit the text. Once a chart text item is selected, you can use the Formatting toolbar to change its font, style, or size.

EXERCISE 17-12 Use the Legend to Display Categories

In this chart, you can remove the category labels (the sports drink names) and list them in the legend instead.

1. Select the category axis in the active chart window. (To select the axis, you can click it directly, click a tick mark, or click one of the drink names.) "Category Axis" should appear in the Name Box on the Formula Bar.

2. Choose Selected Axis from the Format menu.
3. Click the Patterns tab, if necessary. In the Tick mark labels box, click None.

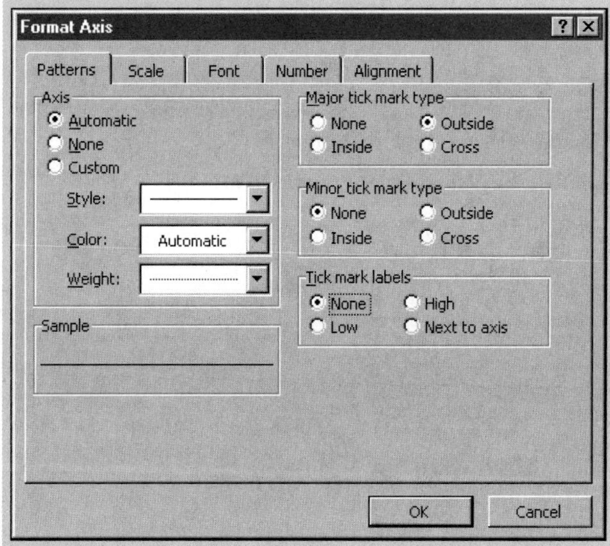

FIGURE 17-7 Patterns options in the Format Axis dialog box

4. Click OK. The sports drink names no longer appear next to the category axis.
5. Click one of the blue data series bars in the chart.

6. Click the button on the Chart toolbar to open the Format Data Series dialog box and click the Options tab.
7. Click the Vary colors by point check box to make each data point in the series a different color.

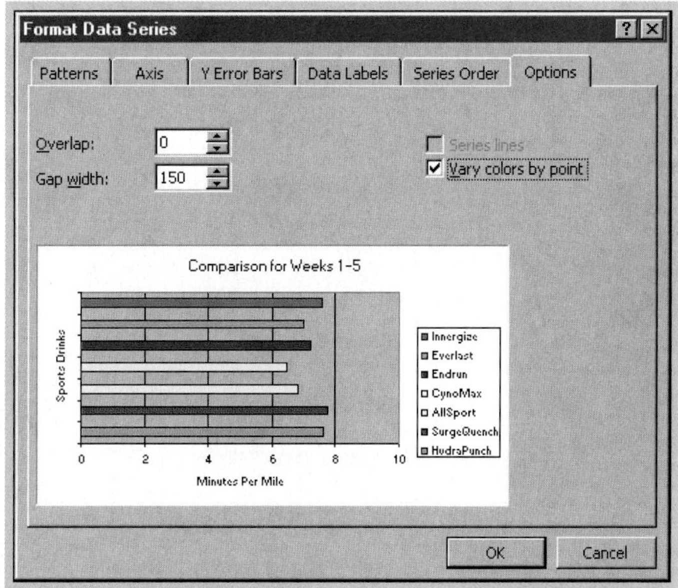

FIGURE 17-8 Options in the Format Data Series dialog box

8. Click OK. The legend displays the category labels and colors corresponding to the labels used in the chart.
9. Double-click the legend to open the Format Legend dialog box.
10. Click the Placement tab and click Right.
11. Click OK. Now you can see the complete chart again.

TIP: You can also resize the legend. Click on the legend to activate it and resize it by dragging one of its sizing handles.

EXERCISE 17-13 Add Data to a Chart

The easiest way to add data to an embedded chart is to enter it in the worksheet and extend the fill handles to include the new data.

1. In cell A9, key **PowerEase**
2. In cell B9, key **6.1**
3. Activate the Chart Area. (Look for "Chart Area" in the Chart Objects text box.)
4. Drag the fill handles in the lower right corners of cells A8 and B8 down to include the new data in row 9. The new data is incorporated in the chart. (See the chart legend.)

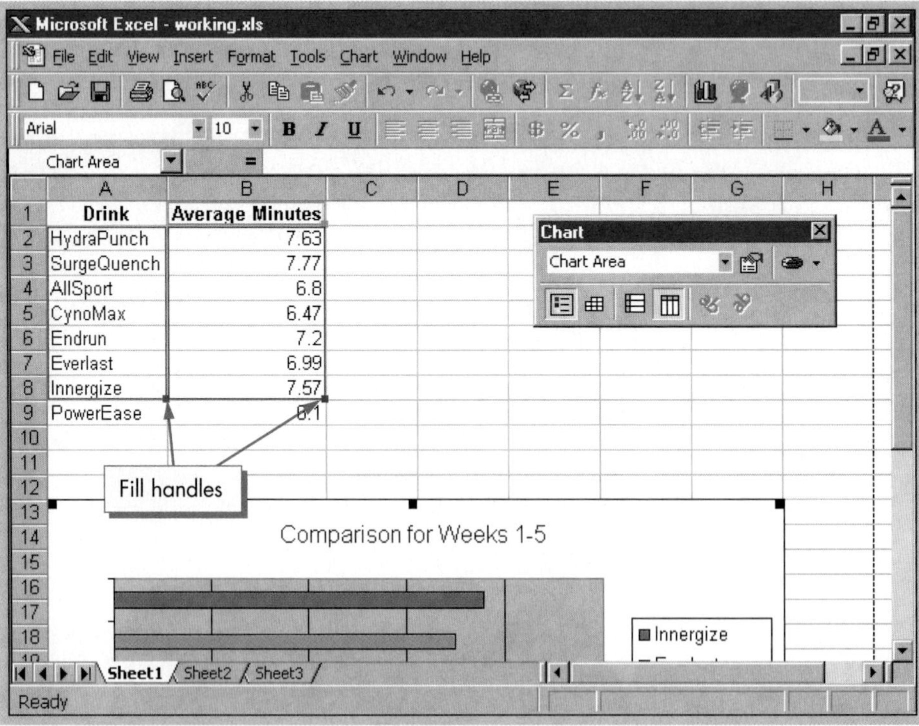

FIGURE 17-9 Activated chart and worksheet chart data

TIP: You can also drag the fill handles up to exclude data.

Saving and Printing a Chart

A chart is saved each time you save the workbook in which it is embedded. Once a chart is complete, you'll want to print it. Embedded charts print with the worksheet. You can preview the chart before printing to see how it looks on the worksheet. You can also print only the chart by activating it and then clicking [Print button].

EXERCISE 17-14 Saving and Printing

1. Click outside the chart to deselect it.
2. Move the data in columns A and B above the chart to columns C and D, so it is centered over the chart.
3. Adjust the widths of the columns appropriately.
4. Change the left margin in Print Preview so the chart is centered on the page horizontally. Make sure the chart does not move to the next page.
5. Add the standard header to the worksheet.
6. Save the workbook as *[your initials]***17-14.xls**.

Creating a Chart on a Chart Sheet

You can create a chart so it appears on a separate sheet in a workbook. If you need to print a chart to use in a presentation, for example, creating a chart on its own chart sheet is the best approach.

When you insert a chart in a sheet, you add the chart to the active workbook. Although you can print a chart sheet separately from the worksheet containing the chart data, it is saved with the other sheets in the workbook.

The charts are named Chart1, Chart2, Chart3, and so on by default. You can rename them by double-clicking the tab for the chart sheet and keying a new name.

EXERCISE 17-15 Create a Chart on a Chart Sheet

1. Select the same data you used for the embedded chart, plus the new row 9 data.

2. Choose Insert, Chart. (You can also click [Chart Wizard button].)
3. Click the Standard Types tab, if necessary, and select the Column chart type, subtype 1.
4. Click Next three times to accept the data, labels, title, and legend default settings.
5. In the Step 4 of 4 dialog box, click As new sheet and keep the default sheet name, "Chart1."
6. Click Finish. Chart1 appears as a new sheet in the workbook. Notice that the layout of the chart defaulted to landscape.
7. Open the Page Setup dialog box and click the Chart tab. (The Chart tab replaces the Sheet tab when a chart is activated.) Notice the three chart settings. Keep the activated setting.
8. Insert the standard header in the chart sheet.
9. Delete the unused worksheets in the workbook.
10. Save the workbook as *[your initials]***17-15.xls**.
11. Print the entire workbook and then close the workbook.

NOTE: You can also use F11 to insert a chart on a separate sheet. Just select the data you want to include in the chart and press F11. The default 2-D column chart is inserted.

FIGURE 17-10
New chart sheet

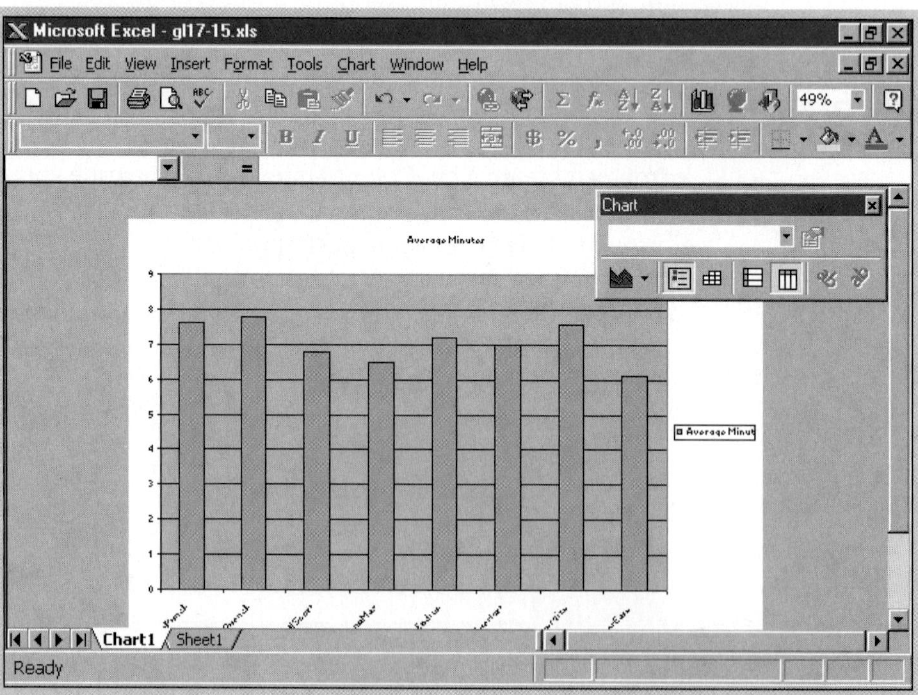

Creating a Data Map

Data Map is a feature in Excel that you can use to chart geographical data. Just as you created a chart based on worksheet data, you can display a map based on worksheet data to analyze information for a particular region.

Before you create a map, you need to organize the data so the Data Map Feature can read it. The first column must contain names or abbreviations of geographic regions, such as states or countries. The next column or columns contain numeric data related to each region.

When you select the data to create a map, include the column headings. These headings help Data Map automatically create legends and titles.

NOTE: You can use the Internet to locate other mapping data. For example, the Social Science Information Gateway Demographic page is a large source of information on census and demographics (http://www.esrc.bris.ac.uk).

EXERCISE 17-16 Create a Data Map

In this exercise, you create a map showing where in the United States Harry Hascabar competed in races and how many races he placed in in each state.

1. Start a new workbook.
2. Key the data as shown in Figure 17-11. Right-align the RACES label.

FIGURE17-11

	A	B
1	STATES	RACES
2	CA	5
3	FL	5
4	IL	10
5	NY	5
6	WA	3
7	TX	7
8	AZ	2

3. Select cells A1 through B8.

4. Click the Map button on the Standard toolbar.
5. With the crosshair pointer, click in cell D1 and drag down to cell G13.
6. Release the mouse button. Because the Data Map feature cannot determine which map to use when it analyzes the left column of data, it displays the Multiple Maps Available dialog box.
7. Choose United States in North America and click OK. The map is displayed in the worksheet. The Data Map toolbar replaces the Standard and Formatting toolbars and the Map menu appears. The Microsoft Map Control dialog box appears over your map.

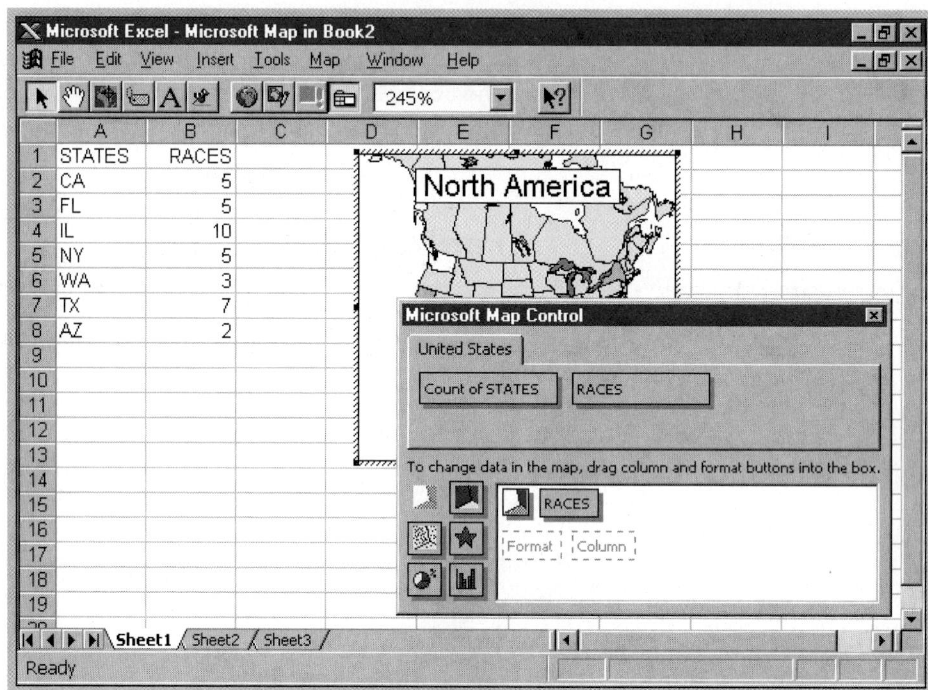

FIGURE 17-12 Using the Data Map feature

8. Move the Microsoft Map Control dialog box by dragging its title bar if it covers the map.

Enhancing a Data Map

When a data map is active, you can use the menu and toolbar designed to manipulate the data map object. Use the Data Map Control dialog box to change a map. You can also enhance a map by adding and formatting text and labels, changing fonts, and selecting a different color scheme.

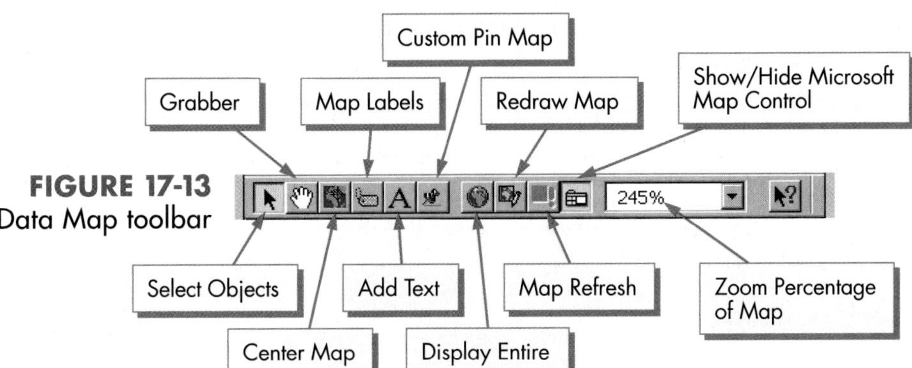

FIGURE 17-13
Data Map toolbar

EXERCISE 17-17 Insert Map Labels

1. Double-click the title on the map and highlight the text by dragging.
2. Key **UNITED STATES** as the new title and press Enter.
3. Click the Add Text button A on the Data Map toolbar.
4. Click the insertion point on California. Key **5** and press Enter.
5. Click the insertion point on Washington. Key **3** and press Enter.

TIP: After keying a number, you may want to move it for better positioning. Click the arrow button, point to the number, and click to select it. You can then use the four-headed arrow pointer to drag the number.

EXERCISE 17-18 Change Fonts

1. Point to the map title and right-click.
2. Choose Format Font from the shortcut menu to display the Font dialog box.
3. Choose Arial Black, bold, 14 point, and click OK.

EXERCISE 17-19 Change Map Features and Shading

1. Using the Microsoft Map Control dialog box, click the Category Shading button. The Microsoft Map dialog box opens saying the map data changed so the map needs to be refreshed. Click OK to refresh the map.

2. Drag the Category Shading button into the white box. Each category (state) is now specified by color.
3. Right-click anywhere within the activated map.
4. Choose Features from the shortcut menu to display the Map Features dialog box.

FIGURE 17-14
Map Features dialog box

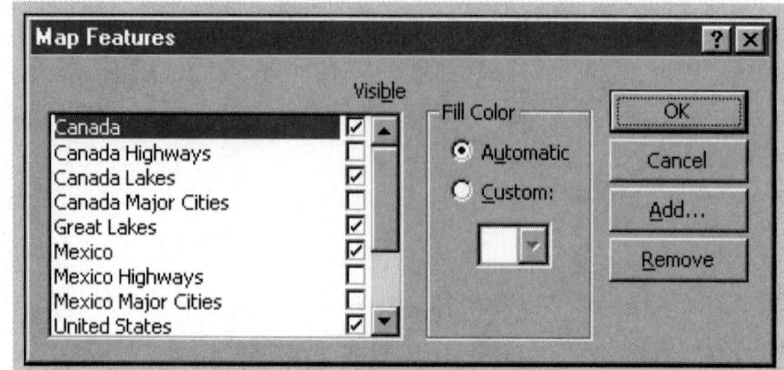

5. Because you want to show a map of the United States and not all of North America, click the following check boxes to deselect them: Canada, Canada Lakes, and Mexico.
6. Click OK. The map now includes just the United States.
7. Click the legend to select it and press Delete.
8. Drag the bottom left selection handle down and to the left to resize the map.

NOTE: You can move the map to any location in the worksheet. Activate the map by double-clicking on it and drag it to the desired location.

9. Click outside the map to deselect it and return to the worksheet.
10. Add the standard header to the worksheet and center the worksheet horizontally on the page.
11. Delete the blank worksheets in the workbook.
12. Save the workbook as *[your initials]***17-19.xls**.
13. Print and close the workbook.

COMMAND SUMMARY

FEATURE	BUTTON	MENU	KEYBOARD
Create a chart		Insert, Chart	F11
Create a map		Insert, Map	

USING HELP

Microsoft Excel Help offers extensive help on charts and maps. For example, you can refer to Help for a visual description of chart types and for information about creating and formatting data maps.

Use Help to view examples of charts and maps

1. Click the Office Assistant button.
2. Key **chart types** and click Search.
3. Display the topic "Examples of chart types."
4. Explore the Help window, viewing examples of the different chart types.
5. When you finish, click Help Topics.
6. Click the Contents tab and double-click "Displaying Data in a Map."
7. Display "About displaying data in a map."
8. Explore the Help window and close it when you finish. Close the Office Assistant.

Concepts Review

TRUE/FALSE QUESTIONS

Each of the following statements is either true or false. Indicate your choice by circling T or F.

T F *1*. Charts are linked to worksheet data through cell references.

T F *2*. A tick mark represents a single piece of data.

T F *3*. The Chart Wizard can create an embedded chart or a chart on its own chart sheet.

T F *4*. Once a chart is created, you cannot edit its contents.

T F *5*. The Chart toolbar is displayed when a chart is activated.

T F *6*. Embedded charts do not print with the worksheet.

T F *7*. Organizing your data is the first step in creating a map.

T F *8*. You activate a map by double-clicking it.

SHORT ANSWER QUESTIONS

Write the correct answer in the space provided.

1. Which type of chart shows trends in data over a period of time at the same intervals, emphasizing the rate of change over time?

____

2. Which chart element explains the symbols, patterns, or colors used to differentiate data series?

____

3. What appears around a chart after it is activated?

____

4. What are the various formats for each type of chart called?

____

5. Which axis is generally the horizontal axis?

____

6. If you create a chart on a chart sheet, what is the chart named by default?

____

7. What is the name of the area bounded by two axes on a chart?

____

8. Which dialog box do you use to select only the features you want to see on your map?

____

CRITICAL THINKING

Answer these questions on a separate piece of paper. There are no right or wrong answers. Support your answers with examples from your own experience, if possible.

1. Why would a business find the charting feature of Excel advantageous? What reasons could you give your boss for creating charts?

2. If you were working for a large retail store with many different outlets, would the mapping feature be an important tool for you? How many different ways could you use the Data Map feature to illustrate data from your company?

Skills Review

EXERCISE 17-20

Use the Chart Wizard to create an embedded chart.

1. Open the file **Times.xls**.

2. Use the Chart Wizard to create an embedded chart by following these steps:

a. Select cells A2:B6.

b. Click [Chart Wizard button] on the Standard toolbar.

c. Choose 3-D Column (the fourth subtype) and click Next.

d. Click Next in the second Chart Wizard dialog box to confirm the range and series.

e. In the third dialog box, key **Best Marathon Times** as the chart title, click the Legend tab, and deselect Show legend.

f. Click Finish.

3. Edit the font size of all data to be 9 point:
   a. Select Chart Area by clicking in the white chart area. (Look in the Chart Objects text box of the Chart toolbar to be sure it is selected.)
   b. Choose 9 points from the Font size drop-down list.
4. Resize chart.
5. Click outside the chart to deselect it.
6. Add the standard header in the worksheet.
7. Save the workbook as *[your initials]***17-20.xls**.
8. Print the worksheet and close the workbook.

EXERCISE 17-21

Add data to a chart, change the chart type, and size a chart.

1. Open the file **Drinks1.xls**.
2. Enter the following data in cells A9:B11:

Exceed	**6.11**
HydraFuel	**6.5**
PurePower	**6.89**

3. Incorporate the new data into the embedded chart by following these steps:
   a. Click the chart to activate the chart window.
   b. Drag the fill handles in cells A8 and B8 down to include the three new rows of data.
4. Change the chart type to Column by following these steps:
   a. Click the down arrow on [Chart Type button] on the Chart toolbar.
   b. Choose the Column chart.
5. Size the chart to fit the value labels by following these steps:
   a. Click the chart. Sizing handles appear around the chart border.
   b. Scroll to the bottom of the chart.
   c. Point to the right selection handle at the bottom of the chart.
   d. Using the two-headed arrow, drag the bottom border down until all the value text fits (1-9) which is about to row 33. Then drag the same selection handle over to the left between columns F and G. Make sure all the category labels are present. If they are not, resize the chart to see them all.
6. Deselect the chart.
7. Add the standard header to the worksheet.

8. Save the workbook as *[your initials]*17-21.xls.
9. Print and close the workbook.

EXERCISE 17-22

Create a separate chart sheet.

1. Open the file **Drinks2.xls**.
2. Create a separate chart sheet by following these steps:
   a. Select cells A1:B11.
   b. Select Insert, Chart.
   c. In the first Chart Wizard dialog box, choose the Pie chart subtype 1 and click Next.
   d. Click Next to accept the range and series.
   e. Click the Data Labels tab in the third dialog box and select Show value.
   f. Click Next and select As new sheet. Key **Pie Chart** in the text box beside it and click Finish.
3. Insert the standard header in the chart worksheet.
4. Save the workbook as *[your initials]*17-22.xls.
5. Print the chart sheet and close the workbook.

EXERCISE 17-23

Create a data map and enhance the map by adding map labels.

1. Start a new workbook.
2. Key the following data in cells A1:B7:

STATES	**NUMBER**
UT	**70**
FL	**86**
TX	**75**
NY	**35**
IL	**13**
CA	**96**

3. Create a data map by following these steps:
   a. Select cells A1:B7.
   b. Click the Map button on the Standard toolbar.
   c. Drag the crosshair pointer from cell A10 to cell G22.

d. In the Multiple Maps Available dialog box, choose United States (AK & HI Insets) and click OK.

4. Change the map title by following these steps:
   a. Double-click the map title.
   b. Drag to select the existing text.
   c. Key the new title **States Selling Most Drinks**
   d. Press Enter.
5. Move the title by following these steps:
   a. Click the title to select it.
   b. Using the four-headed arrow, drag the title to better center it across the top of the map. Resize the chart box if it overlays the map.
6. Move the legend:
   a. Click the legend to select it.
   b. Using the four-headed arrow, drag the legend to the bottom, left corner of the map.
7. Add labels to the map by following these steps:
   a. Click the Add Text button A on the Map toolbar.
   b. Click in each state and key in the number of drinks sold in that state.
   c. Adjust the position of the number labels, if necessary.
8. Click outside the map to deactivate it.
9. Add the standard header to the worksheet and delete the blank worksheets in the workbook.
10. Save the workbook as *[your initials]***17-23.xls**.
11. Print and close the workbook.

Lesson Applications

EXERCISE 17-24

Enter data and use the Chart Wizard to create a column chart and enter additional chart information.

Harry Hascabar tested eight different sports drinks over an eight-week period and recorded the number of miles he ran and his running times. Enter the data and create a chart to display it.

1. Start a new workbook.
2. Enter the data shown in Figure 17-15. Format all the times for two decimal places and increase column widths where necessary.

FIGURE 17-15

HASCABAR'S RACING RECORD

Weeks 1-8

DRINK	MILES	AVERAGE
HydraPunch	10	7.15
SuperQuench	15	7.77
AllSport	8	6.8
CynoMax	12	6.45
Endrun	10	7.2
Everlast	96	6.15
Innergize	107	7.35
PowerEase	10	6.10

3. Create an embedded column chart using the Chart Wizard. Include a legend, add the title **Hascabar's Racing Record**, and add the x-axis title **Sports Drink**

4. Size the chart to include all the data and move the legend if necessary. (*Hint:* You can click the legend to activate it and drag it to another location with the four-headed arrow.)
5. Rename the Sheet1 tab as **Column Chart**.
6. Add the standard header and center the worksheet data and chart horizontally on the page.
7. Delete the blank worksheets in the workbook.
8. Save the workbook as *[your initials]***17-24.xls**.
9. Print the chart with the worksheet and close the workbook.

EXERCISE 17-25

Create a new chart sheet, change the chart type, and add new chart information.

Harry Hascabar ran for another eight weeks and charted his speed and distance using a bar chart. He'd like a different perspective on his data by seeing it displayed in another type of chart.

1. Open the file **Wks9-16.xls**.
2. Create a Column chart as a new chart sheet. Use subtype 4, include a legend, and add the chart title **WEEKS 9-16**
3. Use the Chart toolbar to change the chart type to 3-D Bar.
4. Change the font size of the title to 14 point and the category and value axis labels to 12 point.
5. Add the standard header to the chart sheet.
6. Change the chart sheet tab to **Weeks 9-16**.
7. Save the workbook as *[your initials]***17-25.xls**.
8. Print the chart sheet and close the workbook.

EXERCISE 17-26

Create a data map with map labels and adjust the map features, font, and shading.

After competing in seven races over an eight-week period, Harry Hascabar wants to analyze how fast he ran in each state. He needs a map that shows where he ran and his running times.

1. Open the file **Map.xls**.
2. Reverse the position of the "Drink" and "Time" column headings and data. Insert a new column before column A. Adjust the column widths and alignment as necessary.

3. Add the following data to cells A3:A10:

   STATE

   AZ

   TX

   OR

   WY

   FL

   CA

   NY

4. Create a data map using the data in columns A and B.
5. Delete any features that don't belong on a map of the United States.
6. Change the map title to **RUNNING TIME PER STATE** and center it. (*Hint:* Resize the map if necessary.)
7. Use the Data Map Control dialog box to display the map with category shading.
8. Add map labels that show Harry's running time in each state. (*Hint:* If the map labels are hard to see over some of the colors, move them next to these states.)
9. Change the font of the running time labels to Arial Black.

TIP: Right-click each label and use the shortcut menu.

10. Make the map slightly larger.
11. Add the standard header to the worksheet and center the data and map on the page horizontally.
12. Save the workbook as *[your initials]***17-26.xls**.
13. Print and close the workbook.

EXERCISE 17-27

Choose the appropriate chart type, create a chart as a separate sheet, and add new chart information.

Harry Hascabar wants to see how his running times stack up against three of his colleagues. Using the data for all four runners, create a chart that compares the times and miles for each runner.

1. Sketch a worksheet to include a title and the labels in Figure 17-16. Plan the type of chart you will use and roughly sketch the chart type on the plan.
2. Start a new workbook and enter the data shown in Figure 17-16, using the alignment indicated.

FIGURE 17-16

NAME	MILES	TIME
Harry Hascabar	9.30	6.58
Jose Garcia	10.10	6.79
Mark Yingling	8.97	6.87
George Bunting	9.98	7.05

3. Create the chart as a new chart sheet, using the chart type that will best depict the information.
4. Use appropriate titles for the chart and the chart axes.
5. Enhance the chart using any method you learned in this lesson.
6. Rename the Chart tab, giving it an appropriate name.
7. Rename the Sheet tab, giving it an appropriate name.
8. Add the standard header to both worksheets and delete the blank worksheet.
9. Save the workbook as *[your initials]***17-27.xls**.
10. Print the entire workbook and close it.

Enhancing Charts and Worksheets

LESSON 18

OBJECTIVES

After completing this lesson, you will be able to:

1. Format chart text.
2. Enhance the legend.
3. Change data series colors and patterns.
4. Add backgrounds and borders.
5. Add drawing objects.
6. Format drawing objects.
7. Size, move, and copy drawing objects.
8. Import clip art.

Estimated Time: 1½ hours

To make your charts more attractive, you can enhance them by adding colors, patterns, borders, and new fonts. You can also add impact to charts and ordinary worksheet data by creating drawing objects (such as lines, arrows, or text boxes) or importing clip art.

Formatting Chart Text

Just as you can format the text in a worksheet, you can format chart text by changing its font, style, color, size, or alignment. Experimenting with formatting can create charts that have greater visual appeal.

EXERCISE 18-1 Change Font, Style, and Size

1. Open the file **Sports.xls**.
2. Activate the chart by clicking it.
3. Choose Chart Window from the View menu to open a separate chart window. This way you can view the entire chart as you work on it.
4. Click the chart title, "Sports Drink Comparison." The title is selected, and "Chart Title" appears in the Name Box on the Formula Bar.

NOTE: Each time you select a chart object, the Name Box on the Formula Bar displays its name, such as Chart Title, Value Axis, Legend, and so on. Refer to the Name Box to make sure you selected the desired object.

5. Use the Font drop-down list on the Formatting toolbar to change the font to Arial Black.
6. Right-click the value axis title, "Minutes Per Mile," to open the shortcut menu.
7. Choose Format Axis Title from the shortcut menu. Notice the various formatting options in the dialog box.

NOTE: Each element of the chart has its own dialog box, which enables you to change the appearance of that particular element.

8. Click the Font tab, if necessary. Change the font to bold italic and click OK.
9. Click the category axis title, "Sports Drinks," to select it. Click *I* on the Formatting toolbar to add italic formatting.

EXERCISE 18-2 Change Text Color

1. Double-click the chart title. The Format Chart Title dialog box opens.

NOTE: Double-clicking a chart element is another way to open the dialog box to format the element.

2. Click the Font tab, if necessary.
3. Under Color, click the down arrow to open the color palette.
4. Choose red from the third row of the palette.
5. Change the font size to 11 point in the Size text box and click OK.

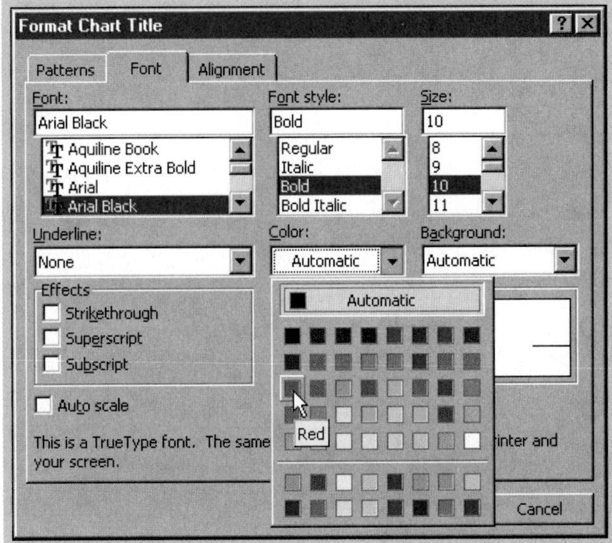

FIGURE 18-1 Formatting the chart title

Enhancing the Legend

Legends are a vital component of a chart. They focus the viewer on what the chart is trying to depict. For this reason, it's important to make the legend stand out. You can customize the legend in several different ways:

- Place it in a different area of the chart.
- Use colors and patterns.
- Customize the border.
- Change the font.

EXERCISE 18-3 Change Legend Color, Pattern, and Border

1. Double-click the legend. The Format Legend dialog box appears.
2. Click the Patterns tab. Check the Shadow box in the Border area to add a shadow to the legend.
3. Click Fill Effects to open the Fill Effects dialog box and click the Pattern tab if necessary. You use the Pattern options to choose a pattern and pattern color.
4. Click the Foreground down arrow and choose a color from the drop-down list, then click the Background down arrow and choose another color. (Avoid dark colors.) Notice that the foreground and background colors appear in the samples above.

5. Choose the fourth pattern in the second row.
6. Click OK twice. The legend now has a background color and pattern.
7. Deselect the legend.

NOTE: Because the legend is small, you may not be able to see the pattern in the chart window. When the legend is enlarged in Exercise 18-5, the pattern is more easily seen.

EXERCISE 18-4 Reposition the Legend

1. Double-click the legend.
2. Click the Placement tab in the Format Legend dialog box and choose Bottom.
3. Go back to the Font tab and change the font to Times New Roman, bold, 10 point.
4. Click OK. The legend appears at the bottom of the chart, below the category axis title.

FIGURE 18-2
Legend with a new format and position

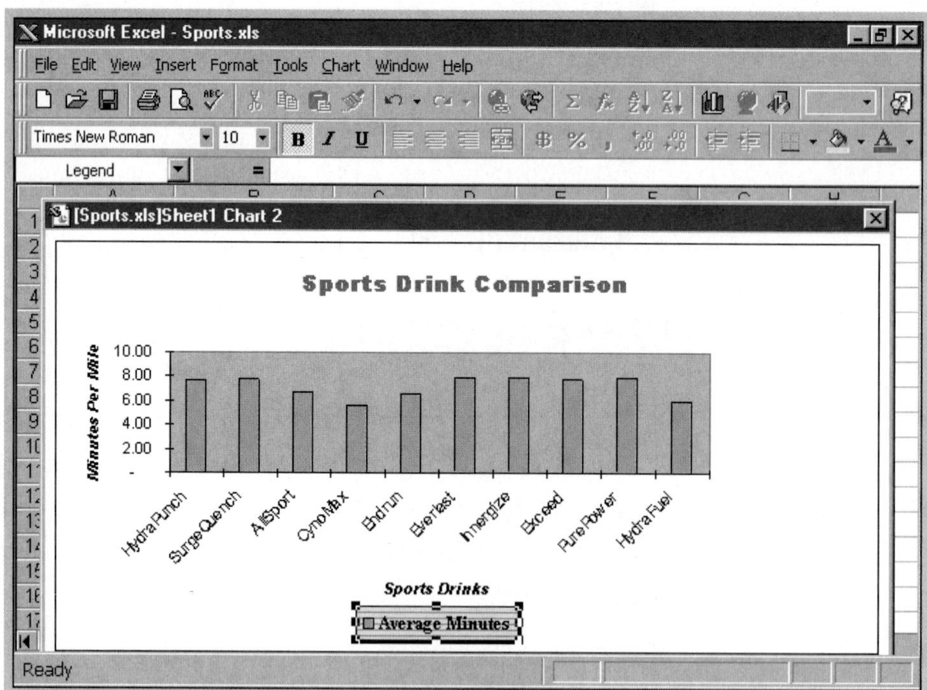

5. Close the chart window by clicking its Close button. Review the new position and formatting of the legend.

6. If the new formatting and placement now occupy space needed by the category labels (check the longest label, "SurgeQuench"), resize the chart. To do this, click the chart once to select it and drag the center selection handle at the bottom of the chart down one or two rows.

Changing Data Series Colors and Patterns

You can change data series colors and patterns for the entire chart or for individual data markers. When you change colors or patterns for individual markers, the legend reflects those changes by displaying the color key and data point labels.

EXERCISE 18-5 Change Color for a Data Series

1. Click the chart to activate it and choose Chart Window from the View menu.
2. Click a column in the chart to select the data series.
3. Choose Selected Data Series from the Format menu (or press Ctrl+1).

NOTE: You can also use the Format menu and Ctrl+1 to open the dialog box to format a selected chart item.

4. Choose another color from the color palette and click OK. The columns appear in the new color.
5. Click  to undo the color change.
6. Right-click one column in the chart and choose Format Data Series from the shortcut menu.
7. Click the Options tab.

NOTE: The Options tab in the Format dialog box varies according to the type of chart with which you are working. You may remember this dialog box and the one that follows from the previous lesson, in which you worked with a bar chart.

8. Click to select Vary colors by point and click OK. The data markers appear in different colors and the legend displays each color and label.
9. Close the chart window.

10. Resize the chart to accommodate the new legend, if necessary.

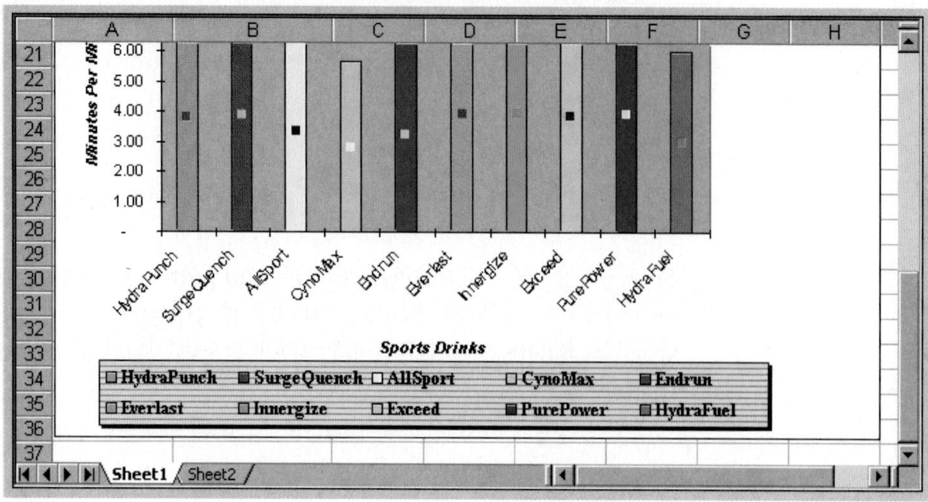

FIGURE 18-3
Legend reflecting color changes

Adding Backgrounds and Borders

To add variety to your chart, you can apply colored or patterned backgrounds and borders. Use the Format Chart Area dialog box, being careful not to make the chart look cluttered.

EXERCISE 18-6 Add Background Color and Borders

1. Activate the chart, if necessary, and open the chart window.
2. Right-click in the chart area (the white background) and choose Format Chart Area from the shortcut menu.
3. Click the Patterns tab, if necessary. Under Border, click Custom.
4. Open the Weight drop-down list and choose the last option (the heaviest line). (See Figure 18-4 on the next page.)
5. Choose a light color from the palette for the chart area and click OK. The chart area background changes to the color you choose and has a thicker border.
6. Click [Undo button] and double-click the chart area background to open the dialog box again.
7. Click Fill Effects and click the Texture tab.
8. Click the first texture and click OK twice to apply the background.

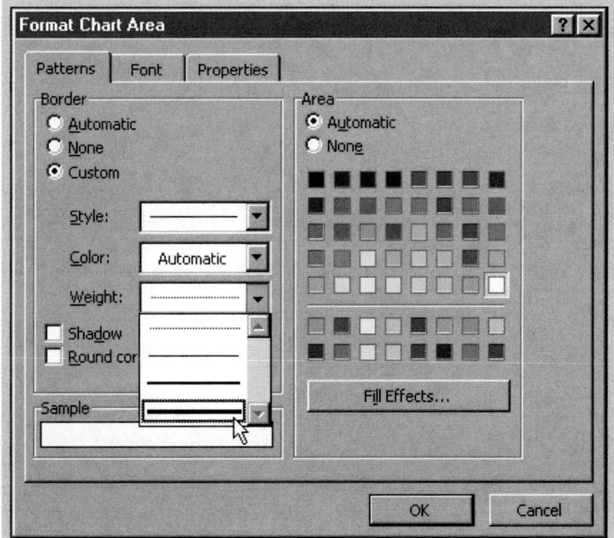

FIGURE 18-4 Formatting the chart area

9. Close the chart window.

NOTE: You cannot change the color of a texture. If you want a colored background, you must select a color in the Patterns option of the Format dialog box.

Adding Drawing Objects

An effective method for enhancing charts or highlighting important data is to create graphic objects with the Drawing toolbar. You can draw text boxes, arrows, rectangles, and other objects. You can then move, size, and format these items independent of the worksheet.

EXERCISE 18-7 Display and Position the Drawing Toolbar

Use the Drawing button on the Standard toolbar to display the Drawing toolbar. You can then position this toolbar anywhere you want for convenient access.

1. Click on the Standard toolbar. The toolbar appears in the same position in which it was previously placed.
2. Drag the toolbar to dock it under the Formatting toolbar, if necessary.
3. Examine each menu option and button on the Drawing toolbar by pointing to it. A ScreenTip identifies the button by name.

TABLE 18-1 Drawing Toolbar

BUTTON/MENUS	NAME	FUNCTION
Drawing menu		Offers various ways to manipulate a drawn object.
	Select Objects	Select drawn objects.
AutoShape menu		Offers a number of preset objects from which to choose.
	Free Rotate	Rotates an object.
	Line	Draws a line.
	Arrow	Draws an arrow.
	Rectangle	Draws a rectangle or square.
	Oval	Draws an oval or circle.
	Text Box	Draws a text box in worksheets and charts.
	Insert WordArt	Inserts WordArt.
	Fill Color	Adds a fill color to an object.
	Line Color	Adds a color to a line.
	Font Color	Changes the color of words.
	Line Style	Offers different line styles.
	Dash Style	Offers different dashed lines.
	Arrow Style	Offers different arrow styles.
	Shadow	Draws a shadow behind text boxes and most shapes.
	3-D	Adds a 3-D effect to objects.

EXERCISE 18-8 Add Text Boxes

You can position text boxes anywhere on a chart to provide labels or comments. Text boxes are frequently combined with arrows.

This exercise demonstrates two ways to create a text box: one involving keying text directly into the Formula Bar and a second that uses the Drawing toolbar.

1. Activate the chart if necessary and open the chart window.
2. Position the pointer in the Formula Bar. When the pointer changes to an I-beam, click the left mouse button.
3. Key **Best Tasting** and press Enter. The text box appears in the chart, surrounded by a dotted border with selection handles for sizing. You can move the text box to any position on the chart.
4. Point to the border of the text box. Use the four-headed arrow pointer to drag the text box so it's centered below the chart title. (You can only move it when the border is dotted, not hatched).
5. Click outside the text box to deselect it. By default, text boxes in charts do not have borders.
6. Close the chart window.

7. Click the Text Box button on the Drawing toolbar. The pointer changes to a crosshair (or cross).
8. Drag the crosshair pointer to draw a box that spans roughly from cell D2 through cell F3. Release the mouse button.
9. At the insertion point, key **The faster the time, the better the drink!**
10. Click outside the text box to deselect it. By default, text boxes in worksheets *do* have borders. If the box is not large enough to accommodate the text, select the box again and resize it using the sizing handles.

FIGURE 18-5
Creating text boxes

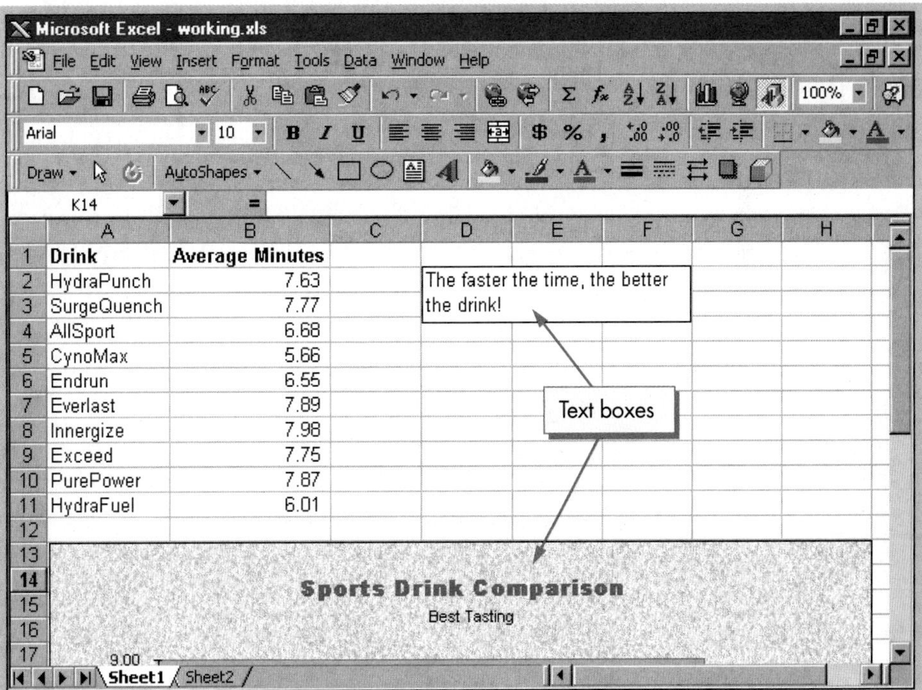

EXERCISE 18-9 Draw Lines, Arrows, and Shapes

Use the Drawing toolbar to create lines, arrows, rectangles, and ovals to highlight specific areas in a chart or worksheet.

Just as you created a text box, you can click the desired drawing button, position the crosshair where you want to start drawing, and drag the crosshair pointer to the desired size. When you release the mouse button, the drawing object is automatically selected and the object name appears in the Name Box on the Formula Bar.

NOTE: If you click a drawing button and decide not to draw, you can press Esc to cancel the drawing process and restore the normal pointer. In addition, if you draw an object and decide you don't like it, you can delete it immediately by pressing Delete.

1. Click the Rectangle button on the Drawing toolbar.
2. Position the crosshair pointer in the upper right corner of cell B2 in the worksheet. Drag down diagonally to the left to create a rectangle around the numbers 7.63 and 7.77. Release the mouse button. The rectangle is selected, as indicated by the selection handles, and the numbers are covered up by the opaque fill in the rectangle. (If you're not pleased with the shape of the rectangle, press Delete and try again.)
3. Click the drop-down list and select No Fill. The numbers reappear.
4. Click outside the rectangle to deselect it.
5. Click the Line button.
6. To connect the rectangle with the text box, position the crosshair at the right side of the rectangle you just drew. Drag straight across to the left side of the text box and release the mouse button.

FIGURE 18-6 Drawing a rectangle

Average Minutes	
7.63	
7.77	
6.68	
5.66	

TIP: Hold down Shift to keep lines vertical, horizontal, or at a 45-degree angle; to keep ovals circular; and to keep rectangles square. You can also hold down Alt to align the corner of the object with cell gridlines.

7. Click the Select Objects button and, using the arrow pointer, point to the rectangle around the two numbers until a four-headed arrow appears behind the arrow. Click the rectangle to select it and press Delete to delete the rectangle.

NOTE: You can select objects without using [arrow pointer]; however, this feature allows you to select only objects and not cells in the worksheet. This makes it easier to select the object you want. You can also use [arrow pointer] to deselect an object.

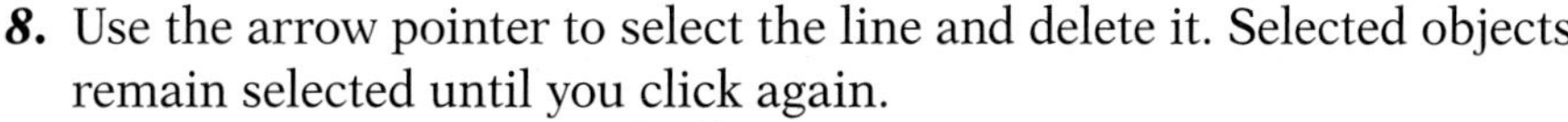

8. Use the arrow pointer to select the line and delete it. Selected objects remain selected until you click again.

9. Click the Oval button [Oval]. Position the crosshair just under the "M" in "Average Minutes." Drag down diagonally to the right until an oval surrounds numbers 7.63 and 7.77.
10. Click [Fill Color] (not the arrow beside it) to apply no fill to the oval.

NOTE: When you place the pointer on [Fill Color] and not the arrow beside it, it tells you what color fill is selected and you can apply that fill with the button.

11. Click the Arrow button [Arrow]. Position the crosshair at the left side of the text box in the worksheet. Drag to the left until the crosshair touches the right side of the oval. Release the mouse button.

FIGURE 18-7
Drawing an arrow

B	C	D	E
Average Minutes			
7.63		The faster the tim	
7.77		the drink!	
6.68			
5.66			

12. Scroll to the chart (but do not activate it).
13. Draw an arrow that begins just below the text "Best Tasting" that points to the top of the "Exceed" column (third from the right).
14. Save the workbook as *[your initials]* **18-9.xls**.

Formatting Drawing Objects

Once you create a drawing object, you can change its border style, line style, fill pattern, or color. You can also change the font, font style, and font size in text boxes.

EXERCISE 18-10 Format Drawing Objects

1. Click the oval in column B to select it. (Click [arrow pointer] to turn it on, if it is not activated.)
2. Choose AutoShape from the Format menu to open the Format AutoShape dialog box.

TIP: You can also open the Format AutoShape dialog box for a selected object by pressing Ctrl+1 or double-clicking the object.

3. Under Line, choose a bright color from the Color drop-down list. Apply a heavier weight using the arrows beside Weight. The higher the number the heavier the weight. Then click OK.
4. Click the worksheet text box (to the right of the oval) to select it. Using the Formatting toolbar, change the font style to bold italic.
5. Click the arrow beside Font Color button and select the color you just selected for the oval.
6. Click the Shadow button and select the first shadow in the last row. Deselect the text box to see it and click to turn the selection option off.

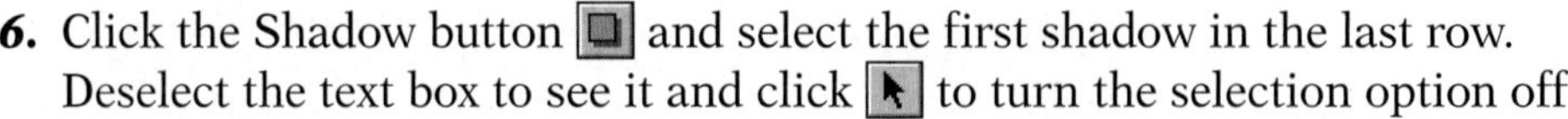

7. In the chart click "Best Tasting" to select it, right-click its hatched border with the selection pointer, and choose Format Text Box from the shortcut menu.
8. Click the Color and Lines tab in the Format Text Box dialog box. Under Fill click the arrow beside Color and select black.
9. Under Line, click the arrow beside Color and select any color you want for the line. Change the line weight to something heavier beside Weight.
10. Click the Font tab and choose Bold. Under Color, choose white from the color palette and click OK. Deselect the chart and notice that the text box now has a color border with white text against a black background.
11. Right-click the arrow in the chart and choose Format AutoShape.
12. Change the line to a dashed style in the Dashed drop-down list and change its weight to 1.5 using the arrows beside Weight. Click OK.

Sizing, Moving, and Copying Objects

Drawing objects are easy to reshape, size, and move. If you need multiple copies of the same object, you can draw it once and make as many copies as you need.

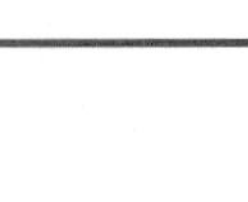

EXERCISE 18-11 Size and Move a Drawing Object

1. Click the text box in the worksheet (not the one in the chart) to select it.
2. Position the pointer on the middle selection handle on the right side of the text box. Using the double-headed arrow pointer, drag the handle to the left so it fits the text better.

NOTE: You may want to resize the text box more than once to get the perfect fit.

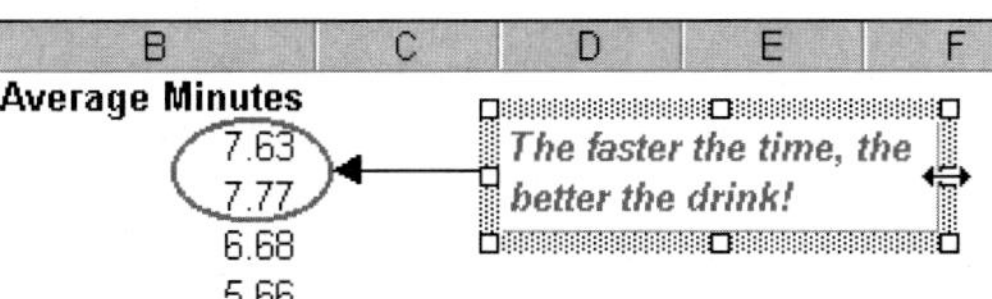

FIGURE 18-8 Resizing the text box

3. Select the oval in column B. Using the white arrow pointer, drag the object down to surround the values in rows 5 and 6.

NOTE: You do not have to activate [arrow button] to select an object. Use the white arrow pointer to select the arrow—not the crosshair pointer, which selects cells.

4. Select the arrow and text box together by first selecting the arrow, then pressing and holding down Shift and clicking on the text box.
5. Move the two objects down beside the oval.
6. Select the arrow in the chart. (If you activate the chart, the arrow isn't visible.)

NOTE: The arrow can be tricky to find. If you don't see it, try clicking in a cell beside the chart and see if it appears. If you still don't see it, click the area where the arrow was placed.

7. Position the crosshair pointer over the selection handle at the tip of the arrowhead until it becomes a double-headed arrow. Drag the handle so the arrow points to the second to last column (the data marker for "PurePower").

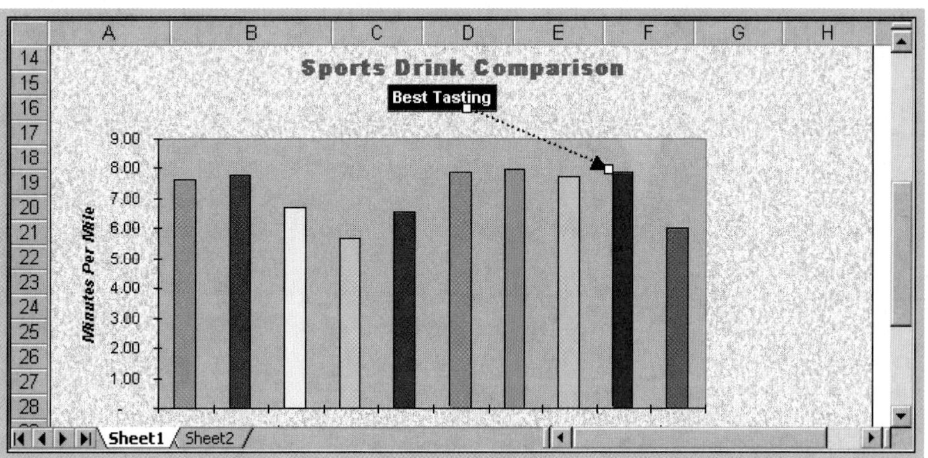

FIGURE 18-9 Repositioning the arrow

EXERCISE 18-12 Copy a Drawing Object

After selecting an object, you can Copy and Paste using the Formatting toolbar, keyboard shortcuts, the shortcut menu, or the Edit menu. You can also copy an object using drag and drop.

1. Draw an oval around the PurePower number in cell B10 of the worksheet. Use the same style and color you applied to the other oval. Reposition the object as necessary.
2. Select the text box above it. When you select the text box with the white arrow pointer not the crosshair pointer, make sure the border is dotted, and click [Copy] to copy it.
3. Select cell D10 and click [Paste] to paste the text box.
4. With the text box still selected, click in the box and use the I-beam pointer to highlight the text in the text box. Key as replacement text **Best tasting, but poor performance!** Resize the text box and reposition it to line up with the oval beside it.
5. Select the arrow at the top of the worksheet.
6. With the arrow pointer positioned over the arrow, hold down Ctrl and drag a copy of the arrow down to cell C10.

FIGURE 18-10 Copied drawing objects

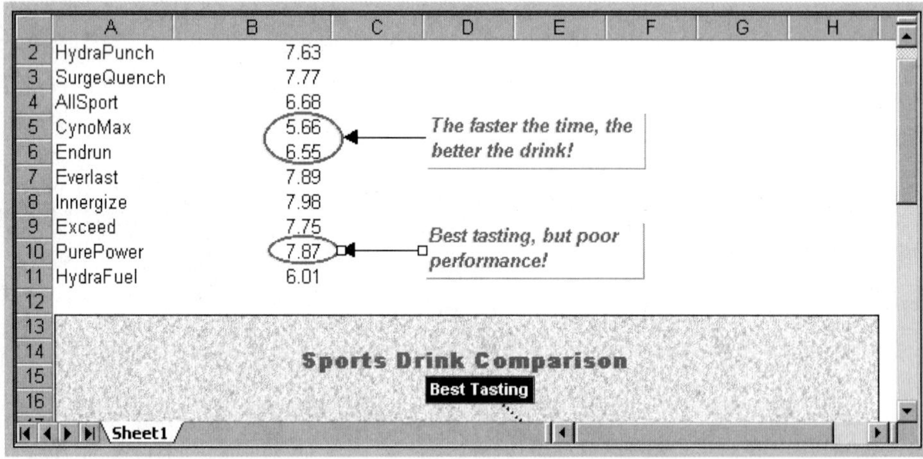

7. Deselect the arrow and click [Drawing] on the Standard toolbar to hide the Drawing toolbar.

Importing Clip Art

You can further enhance your worksheets by adding clip art. *Clip art* is a graphic image that is already created, which you can import into a worksheet or chart.

Some programs come with clip art collections. Microsoft Office, for example, includes images that you can use with Excel in the Msoffice\Clipart folder.

EXERCISE 18-13 Import Clip Art in a Worksheet

1. Select cell G2.
2. Choose Picture from the Insert menu.
3. From the cascading menu, choose Clip Art. The Microsoft Clip Gallery 3.0 dialog box opens.
4. Click the Clip Art tab, if necessary, and scroll down the display of images (not names) until you see a hand holding up one finger. Click it and click Insert. The picture appears selected with a border and the Picture toolbar opens. As with any object, you can move, size, copy, or format the picture.
5. Resize the picture as you would any object, but use the bottom right sizing handle and size to 20% x 20% (see the Name Box while resizing it for dimensions).
6. Drag the picture down and to the left until it is centered vertically between the two text boxes.

FIGURE 18-11
Inserting clip art

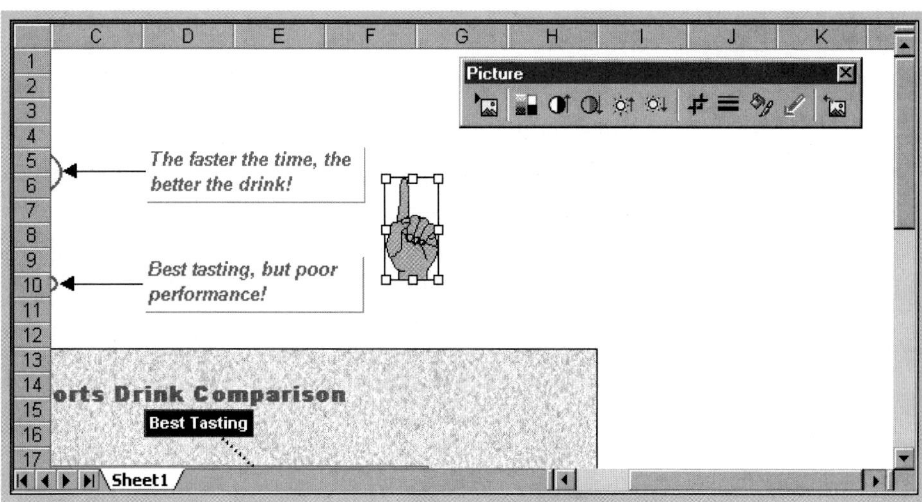

7. Deselect the picture and the Picture toolbar closes.

EXERCISE 18-14 Use Clip Art in a Chart

You can use clip art instead of ordinary data markers in a chart. For example, in a column chart, you can stretch a clip art image across the length of the column or stack images one on top of the other. Clip art can produce attention-getting results.

1. Select the chart. Copy it to cell A1 on Sheet2 of the workbook. (Click [Copy button], go to Sheet2, cell A1, and press [Paste button].)
2. Deselect the chart, use the Page Setup dialog box (Page tab) to change Sheet2 to landscape orientation, and return to the worksheet. Scroll over and notice that the dotted line in the worksheet indicates the next page now follows column M.
3. Make the chart wider by dragging the middle right sizing handle through column L.
4. Delete the "Best Tasting" text box, arrow, and the legend. (To delete an object, select it and press Delete or right-click and choose Clear from the shortcut menu. However, the text box border must be dotted and not hatched to delete the entire object.)
5. Click a data marker to select the data series and choose Picture from the Insert menu.
6. From the cascading menu, choose From file. From the Msoffice\Clipart folder, choose **1stplace.wmf** and click Insert. The data columns are replaced by stretched reproductions of the clip art image.

NOTE: Ask for help if you can't find the folder with the clip art.

7. Double-click the data series to open the Format Data Series dialog box. Click the Patterns tab, if necessary, and click Fill Effects.
8. Click the Picture tab and select Stack. Click OK twice and the images are stacked vertically.
9. Open the chart window and select the plot area of the chart by clicking the background behind the stacked images.

NOTE: When clip art is added, Excel may take longer to respond to your requests.

10. Resize the plot area so it fits in the chart better. Make sure you don't lose sight of the labels in doing so.

11. Choose Chart Options from the Chart menu and click the Gridlines tab.
12. Choose major gridlines for both axes and click OK
13. Change the chart colors, if you like, close the chart window, and preview the chart.
14. Center the chart vertically and horizontally. Make sure the chart is not selected when you use Page Setup.

FIGURE 18-12
Using clip art as data markers

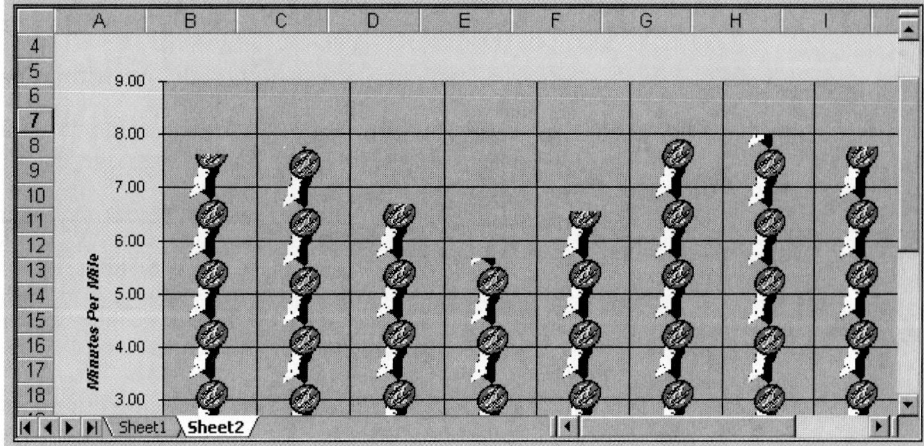

15. Add the standard header to both worksheets.
16. Save the workbook as *[your initials]***18-14.xls**.
17. Print the entire workbook and close it.

NOTE: When you print the worksheet, the labels in the legend may print with white backgrounds.

Concepts Review

TRUE/FALSE QUESTIONS

Each of the following statements is either true or false. Indicate your choice by circling T or F.

T F *1*. You use the Drawing toolbar to create an arrow in a chart.

T F *2*. You can drag a text box to any position on a chart.

T F *3*. You can change the font, style, and size of a chart element, but not its color.

T F *4*. When you finish drawing an object, it is automatically selected.

T F *5*. You cannot place legends in a different position on a chart.

T F *6*. You use the Format Chart Area dialog box to add chart borders and backgrounds.

T F *7*. You can use Delete to delete a chart element.

T F *8*. You cannot use the Formatting toolbar to change text objects in a chart.

SHORT ANSWER QUESTIONS

Write the correct answer in the space provided

1. After clicking the Text Box button on the Drawing toolbar, what shape is the pointer?

____

2. When drawing a line or an arrow, what key can you press to ensure your line is perfectly straight?

____

3. What appears when you double-click the legend in an activated chart?

____

4. How do you activate a chart?

____

5. Name two ways you can customize a legend.

____

6. How do you use the shortcut menu to delete a chart object?

____

7. Which shape must the mouse pointer be to select an object?

____

8. Which dialog box opens when you double-click a drawing object?

____

CRITICAL THINKING

Answer these questions on a separate piece of paper. There are no right or wrong answers. Support your answers with examples from your own experience, if possible.

1. What are the advantages of using the methods for enhancing charts you learned in this lesson? Are there any disadvantages? If so, what are they?

2. What are the advantages in adding drawing objects, such as lines, arrows, or text boxes, to a chart? Give some examples of how you might use these objects to present information.

Skills Review

EXERCISE 18-15

Format chart text and enhance the legend.

1. Open the file **MWMin1.xls**.

2. Format the chart text by following these steps:

a. Click the chart, choose Chart Window from the View menu, and double-click the chart title.

b. In the Format Chart Title dialog box, click the Font tab and choose Arial Black, italic, 14 point, and single underline. Click OK.

c. Click the categories title "Drinks" to select it and click *I* on the Formatting toolbar. Repeat the process for the values title.

d. Double-click a category axis label (a drink name) and change its font color to dark blue. Repeat this formatting for the value axis label.

3. Enhance the legend by following these steps:

a. Double-click the legend.

b. Click the Patterns tab.

c. Click the Shadow box.

d. Under Area, choose a background color.

e. Click the Placement tab and choose Bottom. Click OK.

4. Close the chart window.
5. Preview the chart. If necessary, resize it to accommodate the legend and category labels.
6. Add the standard header and center the worksheet horizontally on the page.

NOTE: When you center the worksheet horizontally, the chart shifts and the data above it appears to not move. The chart is centered and the data and blank columns above the chart are centered.

7. Save the workbook as *[your initials]***18-15.xls**.
8. Print and close the workbook.

EXERCISE 18-16

Change data series colors and add a background color and border to a chart.

1. Open the file **MWMin2.xls**.
2. Change the data series colors and pattern by following these steps:

   a. Activate the chart and open the chart window.

   b. Select the green data series (Men) by right-clicking one of the columns.

   c. Choose Format Data Series from the shortcut menu.

   d. Click the Patterns tab. Under Area, choose a color from the palette.

   e. Open the Fill Effects dialog box, click the Pattern tab, and choose a pattern from the third row. Click OK twice.

   f. Repeat the preceding steps for the second data series (Women), choosing a different color and pattern.
3. Add a border and background color to the chart by following these steps:

   a. Double-click the white background area of the chart.

   b. With the Patterns tab displayed, click the Custom option under Border.

   c. Click the arrow to the right of the Weight box and choose a thicker line for the border.

   d. Under Area, choose a light background color from the palette.

   e. Click OK.

4. Double-click the chart title. Under Border, click Shadow and click OK.
5. Double-click the legend. Choose white from the color palette to apply a white background and click OK.
6. Close the chart window and deselect the chart.
7. Add the standard header and center the worksheet.
8. Save the workbook as *[your initials]*18-16.xls.
9. Print and close the workbook.

EXERCISE 18-17

Add drawing objects to a worksheet and format the objects.

1. Open the file **Wks17-24.xls**.
2. Draw a text box in the worksheet by following these steps:
   - *a.* Click [button] on the Standard toolbar to display the Drawing toolbar, if necessary.
   - *b.* Click [button].
   - *c.* Using the crosshair pointer, draw a box that covers the cell range F5:G6.
   - *d.* Key **Same performance, different drinks!**
   - *e.* Click outside the text box. Resize the text box to fit the text, if necessary.
3. Draw arrows by following these steps:
   - *a.* Click [button].
   - *b.* Position the crosshair pointer in cell E5, at the left side of the text box. Drag the pointer through cell D5. (Hold down Shift as you drag to draw a straight line.) Release the mouse button. The arrow should point to 8.01 in cell C5.
   - *c.* Draw another arrow from the text box to cell C7. (Because you are drawing a diagonal line, do not hold down Shift.)
4. Format the text box by following these steps:
   - *a.* Click [button].
   - *b.* Click the text box to select it using the white pointer.
   - *c.* Use the Formatting toolbar to center the text and change the font style to italic.
   - *d.* Click [button].
5. Draw an oval around the PowerEase numbers by following these steps:
   - *a.* Click [button].
   - *b.* Position the crosshair in the upper left corner of cell D12 (diagonally below the number 6.21 in cell C11). Drag up and to the left until the

numbers 11 and 6.21 in row 11 are enclosed in the oval. Release the mouse button.

c. Click the arrow beside [button].

d. Choose No Fill. Reposition the oval around the numbers, if necessary.

6. Format the drawing object by following these steps:

a. Right-click the oval and choose Format AutoShape from the shortcut menu.

b. Under Line, choose a thicker weight and change the line color to red. Click OK.

7. To the right of the oval, draw a text box containing the text **Impressive!** Format the text as centered and italic. Resize the text box if necessary and add an arrow that points from the text box to the oval.
8. Add the standard header and center the worksheet horizontally.
9. Save the workbook as *[your initials]***18-17.xls**.
10. Print the worksheet and close the workbook.

EXERCISE 18-18

Size, move, and copy a drawing object and import clip art.

1. Open the file **Wks9-16.xls**.
2. Activate the chart window and reposition the legend at the bottom of the chart.
3. Create a text box by clicking the I-beam pointer in the Formula Bar and keying **Good timing but bad tasting!** Press Enter.
4. Move, size, and copy the text box by following these steps:

a. With the text box selected, use the arrow pointer to drag it to the bottom right-hand corner of the chart window.

b. Using the bottom right selection handle, drag the right side in and down so the text appears on two lines.

c. Drag the text box to the upper right corner of the chart window.

d. Format the text box with a blue border and pale yellow fill color. (*Hint:* Use the Colors and Lines options in the Format Text Box dialog box.).

e. With the text box selected, click [button] to copy it to the Clipboard.

5. Close the chart window.
6. Select cell F9 and click [button] to paste the text box.
7. Edit the new text box to read **Good tasting but bad timing!** Move the text box closer to the data in column C and draw an arrow from this text box to cell C6.

8. Without activating the chart, draw an arrow from the chart text box to the top of the "PowerEase Average Mile Time" data marker.
9. Insert clip art into the worksheet by following these steps:
   a. Select cell F1.
   b. Choose Picture from the Insert menu and choose Clip Art from the cascading menu.
   c. Scroll through the names list to the left and select Sports & Leisure, then select the top middle runner in the images to the right, and click Insert.
10. Resize the picture by following these steps:
    a. With the picture selected, hold down Shift and drag the bottom right selection handle toward the center of the picture until the picture is 35% x 35% (watch the Name Box as you resize it).
    b. Release the mouse button and Shift and move the picture to the right of the yellow text box on the left.
    c. Deselect the picture.
11. Add the standard header in the worksheet.
12. Save the workbook as *[your initials]***18-18.xls**.
13. Print the worksheet and close the workbook.

Lesson Applications

EXERCISE 18-19

Format chart text and add a background color and a border.

Harry Hascabar created a pie chart showing the breakdown of carbohydrates for one of the sports drinks he used. Enhance the chart to make it more appealing.

1. Open the file **Pie.xls**.
2. Format the chart title font as 14-point Arial bold underlined.
3. Format the legend text as bold.
4. In the upper right corner of the chart, below the chart title, add a text box with the text **Percentages are approximate**
5. Format the text in the text box as 10-point Times New Roman bold italic.
6. Add a line border to the text box.
7. Add an arrow that points from the text box to the pie.
8. Add a shadow border and a light background color to the chart. (*Hint:* Use the Patterns options in the Format Chart Area dialog box to add the shadow and color.)
9. Add a standard header to the worksheet. (Make sure the chart is deselected or a header is added to the chart only.)
10. Change the left margin to 1.0 and save the workbook as *[your initials]***18-19.xls**.
11. Print and close the workbook.

EXERCISE 18-20

Format chart text, enhance the legend, add a background color and border, and add and format drawing objects.

Harry Hascabar wants a separate chart sheet that uses a 3-D pie chart to show the carbohydrate breakdown of the sports drink Endrun.

1. Open the file **Pie.xls**.
2. Create a 3-D pie chart for only the drink Endrun as a separate chart sheet. Use subformat 2, show labels and percentages to show percentages, and include a legend.

TIP: Select the labels and information in rows 1 and 4 of the worksheet.

3. In the new chart sheet, format the chart title as 14-point Arial bold and format the legend text as 12-point Arial. (You may want to zoom in.)
4. Create an interesting pattern and border for the legend. Reposition the legend at the bottom of the chart.
5. Add a border and background color to the chart.
6. Draw an oval around the label "21%" (next to "Fructose"). Format the circle using a different weight and color.
7. Draw a text box containing **Comparable to PurePower**. Make the line around the text box match the oval.
8. Format the text box as 11-point Arial Black. Draw an arrow from the text box to the circled chart label.
9. Add the standard header to the chart sheet.
10. Save the workbook as *[your initials]***18-20.xls**.
11. Print the chart sheet and close the workbook.

EXERCISE 18-21

Format chart text, enhance the legend, add background colors, a texture, and borders, and add and format drawing objects.

Three new drinks were added to Harry Hascabar's study. Using a column chart, specify that the data series appear in rows instead of columns so the data markers for men and women are displayed as two groups.

1. Open the file **Drinks3.xls**.
2. Create a column chart as a new sheet. Include a legend and include the title **AVERAGE MINUTES**, but don't include axis titles.
3. Display the data series in rows. (*Hint:* Use on the Chart toolbar.)
4. Add a background texture and a border to the chart.
5. Reposition the legend at the bottom of the chart. Add a pattern and color to the legend, make the legend text bold, and resize it to fit all the legend text.
6. Make the category labels bold.
7. Below the chart title, create a text box that contains the name **SuperSport**. Draw two arrows that start at the text box and point to the SuperSport data markers for men and women.

TIP: Zoom in to approximately 75% to make the chart sheet easier to work with.

8. Format the SuperSport text box as bold italic with a border and a light fill color. Adjust the arrows, if needed.
9. Copy the chart text box and paste it to cell E14 on Sheet1. Change the new text box to read **New Drinks**
10. Draw arrows from the New Drinks text box to the three new drinks in rows 13 through 15.
11. Add the standard header to both worksheets and center Sheet 1 horizontally on the page.
12. Save the workbook as *[your initials]***18-21.xls**.
13. Print the entire workbook and close it.

EXERCISE 18-22

Format chart text, change data series colors, add background colors, add and format drawing objects, and import clip art.

Harry Hascabar and three of his running buddies are always trying to beat their best marathon times. Using the best times from their last marathon, Harry wants to depict the information in two column charts—one of which uses clip art instead of regular column markers.

1. Create a sketch that includes a worksheet title and the data in Figure 18-13. Roughly sketch where the chart will appear and the type of chart you will use (column in this case) including the title, Best Times, and the y-axis label, Hours, with no legend.
2. Transfer the sketch into a new workbook in Excel and key the data in Figure 8-13. Adjust column widths and add formatting.

FIGURE 18-13

	Times
Harry Hascabar	3:20
George Castle	3:38
Jerry Paglia	3:01
Sherry Raye	3:45

3. Create a column chart with the title **Best Times**, the y-axis label **Hours**, and no legend.

4. Size and position the chart so it extends from column A to column H and is approximately 20 rows high.
5. Format the chart title as 14-point Arial bold with a shadow border. Format all other text in the chart as 12-point bold, except format the value axis label as 10-point bold.
6. Format the chart columns as different colors.
7. Copy the chart onto Sheet2 of the workbook.
8. On Sheet2, insert the clip art file **Motorflg.wmf** to replace the colored data columns.
9. Change the orientation of Sheet2 to landscape.
10. Size the chart so it extends to the right margin.
11. Add a background color to the chart on Sheet2 and center the chart vertically on the page.
12. On Sheet1, turn off grids for viewing and draw an oval around the number 3:01 in cell B6. Change its fill to none.
13. Create a text box with an arrow pointing to cell B6. The text box should read **Still in the lead with best time!**
14. Size the text box to fit the text and add a red border.
15. Create user documentation and name the sheet tab **User Information**. The sheet should include the following: File Information (Created by, Date created, Date revised, Revised by, Contact for help); Purpose of spreadsheet (paragraph form); and Instructions to User (special instructions needed by user to enter data correctly). Format the documentation attractively and change any column widths you think might need it. Spell-check your work.
16. Add the standard header to all the worksheets and center Sheet 1 horizontally on the page.
17. Save the workbook as *[your initials]***18-22.xls**.
18. Print the entire workbook and close it.

Unit 6 Applications

APPLICATION 6-1

Add a border to a worksheet, create a 3-D bar chart, format chart text, format and resize the chart legend, and draw arrows.

After completing his experiment on sports drinks, Harry Hascabar is focusing on his leather goods business. He wants to chart the costs for each item he makes.

1. Open the file **Costs.xls**.
2. Format the first row as 10-point Arial Black, no bold.
3. Format the second row as the same font style but 9-point, no bold.
4. Center each column heading and resize the columns to fit the text. Format the column C heading as two lines.
5. Center the first two rows across columns A through E and apply light gray shading.
6. Place a blue border around the column headings.
7. Format cell ranges as follows:
   - Make cells A9 through A11 bold.
   - Format cells B4 through E10 in comma style, keeping the decimal places.
   - Format cells B11 through E11 in currency style.
8. Total the costs in row 9 and in column E including the Retail Price. Adjust column widths as needed.
9. Create a formula to determine the profit realized in each category.
10. Using the range A3:D8, create a 3-D bar chart with the subformat (#4) as a new sheet. Use **Mr. Hascabar's Costs** for the chart title, **ITEM** for the category axis title, and **COSTS** for the value axis title.
11. Format the chart title as 16-point Times New Roman bold with a shadow border.
12. Format the legend as follows:
    - Light blue shadow border using the second weight choice
    - 9-point Arial Narrow bold
    - Bottom placement

13. Resize the legend so all text is visible, if necessary, and center it at the bottom of the page horizontally.
14. Create a text box that contains the text **Highest Cost**. Format the text box as follows:
    - Black line border using a heavy weight and bright yellow fill color
    - 11-point Arial Narrow bold
15. Resize the text box, if necessary, and place it somewhere in the open plot area between the longest bar and the top of the chart.
16. Draw arrows from the text box to the bar in each category that represents the highest cost.
17. Format the numbers along the value axis in currency style with no decimal places. (Use the Formatting toolbar.)
18. Add the standard header to both worksheets.
19. Save the workbook as *[your initials]***u6-1.xls**.
20. Print the entire workbook and close it.

APPLICATION 6-2

Create a column chart, enhance the legend, add and resize a text box, change the color of the data series, and draw arrows.

To plan his future inventory, Harry Hascabar wants to chart the quantity of each item sold during the past eight months.

1. Open the file **Sold.xls**.
2. Key **August** in cell A4 and fill in the months down through March (A11).
3. Left-align the data in cells A4 through A11.
4. In cell A12, key **TOTAL**. Format the cell as right-aligned and bold.
5. Calculate the total number of each item sold at the bottom of each column.
6. Create a formula in cell E4 to show how many total items were sold and copy it through.
7. Format the data in cells B4:E12 in comma style with no decimals.
8. Rename the Sheet1 tab as **Months**
9. Create a column chart as a new sheet using the cell range A3:D11. Use the default settings for a column chart. Use **Number of Items Sold** for

the chart title, **MONTHS** for the category axis title, and **NUMBER SOLD** for the value axis title.

10. Place the legend at the bottom of the chart and resize the plot area to fill the area formerly occupied by the legend.
11. Resize the legend for text and drag the legend so it is centered under the category axis title "Months," if necessary.
12. Add a text box that contains the text **LAPTOP COMPUTER CASES ARE THE RAGE!** Move the text box to the top left corner of the plot area and format it as follows:
    - Line border and light background color
    - 12-point bold
    - Text wraps to two lines
13. Change the data series colors to your favorite colors, making sure they complement one another.
14. Copy the text box to the top right corner of the plot area. Modify the text box as follows:
    - Key **Highest Sales in December**
    - 11-point bold italic text
    - Resize text box to fit
15. Draw an arrow from the new text box to the "December Laptop Computer Case" column. Format the arrow to have a heavier weight.
16. Rename the Chart1 tab **No. Sold**.
17. Add the standard header to both worksheets.
18. Save the workbook as *[your initials]***u6-2.xls**.
19. Print the entire workbook and close it.

APPLICATION 6-3

Create three pie charts and add backgrounds to the charts.

Using the sales data for items sold, Harry Hascabar wants to see a pie chart comparison for the months of September, December, and February.

1. Open the file **Pie2.xls**.
2. Change the page orientation to landscape and make the top and bottom margins .75 inch.

3. Using the cell ranges A3:D3 and A5:D5, create a pie chart on the same sheet as the worksheet for the month of September, as follows:
   - Use the chart type Pie and the 3-D subformat (#2).
   - Enter the chart title **SEPTEMBER SALES**, have no legend, but show values.
   - Add a light background color to the chart.
   - Make the chart extend from cell A14 through cell C26.
4. Create a pie chart on the same sheet for the month of December, as follows:
   - Use the same chart type and subformat as the existing chart.
   - Enter the chart title **DECEMBER SALES**, have no legend, but show values.
   - Add a different background color to the chart.
   - Make the chart extend from cell D14 through cell H26. (Change the zoom to 75% so you can see more of the worksheet.)
   - Drag the December chart about one-half column to the right to separate the two charts.
5. Create another 3-D pie chart on the same sheet for February, as follows:
   - Create a chart that is approximately the same size as the existing charts and center it below the two charts.
   - Use the chart title **FEBRUARY SALES**, no legend, but show values.
   - Add a different background color to the chart.
6. Preview the worksheet. If all the charts do not fit on a single page, reposition the bottom chart so it overlaps the bottom edges of the other two charts.
7. Add the standard header to the worksheet.
8. Save the workbook as *[your initials]***u6-3.xls**.
9. Print the worksheet and close the workbook.

APPLICATION 6-4

Create and enhance a data map, draw and resize a text box, add a border, and draw arrows.

Harry Hascabar's business only services the Western states. He wants to see the sales distribution by state per item, and in particular, he wants a data map of laptop computer case sales so can plan his marketing strategy.

1. Start a new workbook.
2. Key the data shown in Figure U6-1. Use wide columns, so the worksheet extends almost to the right margin.

FIGURE U6-1

State	Laptop Computer Cases	Handbags	Briefcases
OR	315	175	205
WA	307	212	189
CA	579	343	297
AZ	437	313	278
NM	401	201	312
NV	579	234	277
UT	643	368	415
ID	247	156	217

3. At the top of the worksheet, add the title **Leather Goods Distribution by State**
4. Center the data under the column headings and center the title across the columns. Turn off grids for viewing and add additional formatting to make the worksheet attractive.
5. Using the column heads and data in columns A and B, create a data map that shows the distribution of laptop computer cases by state. Draw the map so it extends the width of the worksheet and use the United States map without the insets.
6. Use the Data Map Control dialog box to change the map to category shading and close the dialog box.
7. Use the Map Features dialog box to delete all parts of Canada and Mexico from the map.
8. Change the map title to **Distribution by State**. Right-click the title, change it to 14-point Arial bold, and center it above the map.
9. Drag the map legend to the bottom right corner of the map.

10. Deselect the map and draw a text box on top of the map as follows:
    - Placement: Bottom left corner of the map
    - Text: **Time to expand to the Midwest!**
    - Border and fill: Colored line and a shadow light background color
    - Font: 10-point Arial bold italic
    - Text alignment: Centered horizontally within the box
11. Resize the text box so the text appears on two lines and fits better inside the box.
12. Draw a rectangle around the laptop computer case data in the worksheet, including the column heading.
13. Format the rectangle with no fill and a blue shadow border and draw an arrow from the rectangle to the map. (If necessary, drag the map down to allow space for the arrow.)
14. Add the standard header to the worksheet.
15. Center the worksheet vertically and horizontally on the page.
16. Delete the blank worksheets and save the workbook as *[your initials]***u6-4.xls**.
17. Print the worksheet and close the workbook.

APPLICATION 6-5

Create a worksheet with drawing objects, borders, and clip art.

Harry Hascabar needs a new, professional-looking invoice for his leather goods business. He wants the invoice created in Excel and enhanced with clip art and drawing objects.

1. Create a sketch of an invoice for Harry Hascabar's Handcrafted Leather Goods. Include all the invoice components.
2. On a new worksheet, create the invoice. Use your creativity to format it with font, borders, colors, patterns, and drawing objects.
3. Import clip art to enhance the invoice.
4. Rename the sheet tab as **Invoice**.
5. Create user documentation and name the sheet tab **User Information**. The sheet should contain the following: File Information (Created by, Date created, Date revised, Revised by, Contact for help); Purpose of spreadsheet (paragraph form); and Instructions to User (special

instructions needed by user to enter data correctly). Format the documentation attractively and change any column widths you think might need it. Spell-check your work.

6. Add the standard header to both worksheets and center the invoice on the page horizontally.

7. Delete the blank worksheet and save the workbook as *[your initials]***u6-5.xls**.

8. Print and close the workbook, and submit your sketch, invoice, and documentation.

UNIT

7

Databases and Advanced Features

Indiana Iron Works

Indiana Iron Works

Out of the Frying Pan . . .

Indiana Iron Works was a small foundry started in 1854 by Dexter Peabody. The company produced cast iron frying pans and wrought-iron porch rails. In 1990, the business was taken over by Dexter's great-grandson, Dexter IV, who renamed the company "Indiana Iron Works" and set out to expand and improve production. Young Dexter's background is in art history, and while he was away at school, he became interested in the intricate iron work of the early Renaissance. He now travels worldwide in search of decorative works to reproduce in the foundry.

Dexter is in the process of selling off some of the properties his father acquired for the company over the years. He wants to use the profits to buy new equipment. He also wants to get a better handle on the company's overall profitability.

Dexter needs to do the following to keep track of Indiana Iron Works' customers and property holdings:

- ✔ Create a database of customer names, addresses, phone numbers, and amounts due, so he can sort by any of these categories as needed. **(Lesson 19)**
- ✔ Set up his customer database, so he can find specific data quickly and use database functions. **(Lesson 20)**
- ✔ Set up a database of the property owned by Indiana Iron Works. **(Lesson 21)**

Using Databases

OBJECTIVES

After completing this lesson, you will be able to:

1. **Set up a database in a worksheet.**
2. **Use the Data Form to enter and edit database records.**
3. **Sort data in the database.**

Estimated Time: 1 hour

A *database* is a collection of related information organized in a systematic way. Examples of databases include a company's list of client names, addresses, and phone numbers, or a library's card catalog that records book titles, authors, and publishers. Lessons 19 through 21 explain how to use Excel's database features. This lesson explains how to set up a database, enter and edit data, and sort information.

Setting Up a Database

A database begins in Excel with a *list*—a series of worksheet rows that contain data. You create databases by keying lists of data in a workbook. Once you set up a list of information, you can consult it and work with the data to support your business needs.

In a worksheet, each row corresponds to one database record and each column corresponds to one database field. A *field* is a category of information, while a *record* is a set of categories. For example, in a card-catalog database, the book title, author, and publisher are fields, while all the information entered for one particular book constitutes a record. Each field must be assigned a unique *field name,* which is a column label used to identify the contents of the field. In this example, "Title" or "Publisher" might be field names.

When you create a database in an Excel worksheet, you key the information you need into a list the same way you key it into a regular worksheet.

Keep these rules in mind as you set up your database:

- Field names must appear in the first row of the list.
- Field names must be unique.
- Field names can contain letters, spaces, and numbers, but the first character must be a letter.
- Do not skip any rows or columns within the list. Leave at least one blank row or column between the list and other data you enter in the same worksheet as the list, however—for example, between the field names and the title.
- Create only one list per worksheet.

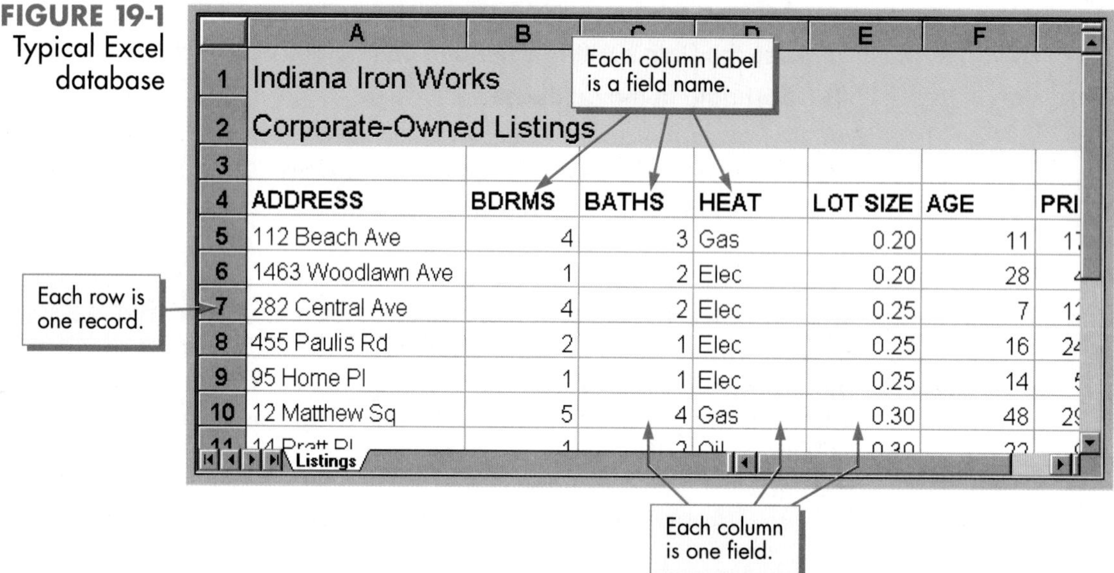

FIGURE 19-1 Typical Excel database

EXERCISE 19-1 Enter the Field Names and Data

Here are a few more points to keep in mind when you enter field names:

- If you are using multi-row names, Excel uses the last row.
- Format the field names to make them easier for Excel to differentiate between records.

- The maximum length of a field name is 255 characters.

1. Open the file **Iron1.xls**.
2. Starting in cell A3, key the following column labels in cells A3 through G3:

   Last First Address Suite/PO City State ZIP

3. Make all the column labels bold and center the labels in cells G3 through I3.
4. To display the leading zeros in the "ZIP" field, format the cells G4 and G5 with the Special Zip Code format, which you can find using Format, Cells, and selecting Number, Special.
5. Key the following information in cells A4 through G4, skipping the Suite/PO field:

   Brown Gail 97 Old Lyme Rd. Orange CT 06477

6. Add another record by keying the following information in cells A5 through G5, again skipping the Suite/PO field:

   Brawn Jean 194 Maplewood Rd. Essex VT 05452

NOTE: To visually differentiate between the first row containing the column labels and the first record containing data, use attributes, borders, and lines to format the column labels row. Do not enter dashed lines in a row or Excel will be unable to work with the data.

FIGURE 19-2 Database with bold column labels

	A	B	C	D	E	F	G	H
1	Indiana Iron Works Customer List							
2								
3	**Last**	**First**	**Address**	**Suite/PO**	**City**	**State**	**Zip**	**Pho**
4	Brown	Gail	97 Old Lymn Rd.		Orange	CT	06477	(203) 55
5	Brawn	Jean	194 Maplewood Rd.		Essex	VT	05452	(802) 55
6	Hailey	Linda	12 Garden St.	P.O. 542	Brooklyn	NY	11201	(718) 55
7	Marley	Luke	1028 College St.		Pittsburgh	PA	15206	(412) 55
8	Small	Cathy	11 Pomona Rd		Jersey City	NJ	07310	(201) 55
9	Small	Ray	455 Daniels Rd		Lakewood	CA	90715	(310) 55
10	Smith	Betty	12 Putman Ave.		Derby	MA	06484	(508) 55
11	Smith	Ed	1463 Woodlawn Ave.		Kent	OH	44240	(216) 55
12	Smith	Gary	287 Carmel Ave.	Suite 102	Hatfield	MA	01038	(413) 55
13	Wilcox	Wendy	690 Rice Ave.		Portage	MI	49008	(616) 55
14	Zepper	Ann	122 Stuyvesant Rd		New York	NY	10010	(212) 55

Customers

7. Widen columns where necessary.

EXERCISE 19-2 Enter a Series of Data Automatically

You can enter a series of data into a database field automatically using the Edit, Fill, Series command or the AutoFill feature. When you enter a series you can assign a number to each record in the database, which can help distinguish between similar records, such as customers with the same name.

1. Insert a new column to the left of column A.
2. Select cell A3 and key **No.**
3. Select cell A4 and key **1**
4. Adjust width of column A for AutoFit. (Hint: Double-click the right border of the column label.)
5. Select cells A4 through A15 and choose Fill from the Edit menu.
6. Choose Series from the cascading menu. The Series dialog box appears.

FIGURE 19-3
Series dialog box

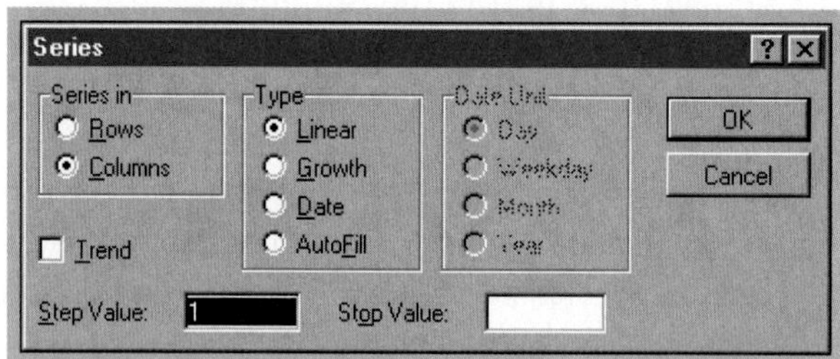

7. Select Columns in the Series in category, if necessary. Linear should be selected in the Type category.
8. Click OK. Excel enters numbers in the No. field for each record automatically.
9. Save the workbook as *[your initials]***19-2.xls**.

EXERCISE 19-3 Name the Database

It is good practice to assign a name to the range of cells that make up your database list. You can name the list using the Insert, Name command or using the Name Box on the Formula Bar.

1. Select cells A3:J15 (the entire list, including field names).
2. Click the Name Box on the Formula Bar.
3. Key **CustList**.
4. Press Enter.

NOTE: When you add records to the database, you must insert rows within the existing database, or redefine the range name for the database.

Using the Data Form

When you work with a list database, you see all the records in the worksheet simultaneously. If you want to work with one record at a time, you can use Excel's *data form*. The Data Form is a dialog box that displays the fields for one record in a vertical arrangement.

Even though the Data Form displays only one record at a time, you can scroll forward or backward, one record at a time, through all the records you entered in the database. You can add and delete records and search for a specific record using the data form. If a formula exists as part of a record, the Data Form copies it to the new record along with any formatting.

NOTE: If the database contains a large number of fields, all the fields may not fit on the data form. In this case, key the data directly into the rows.

EXERCISE 19-4 View Records with the Data Form

1. Select any cell in row 4 and choose Form from the Data menu. The Data Form dialog appears, displaying the first record.

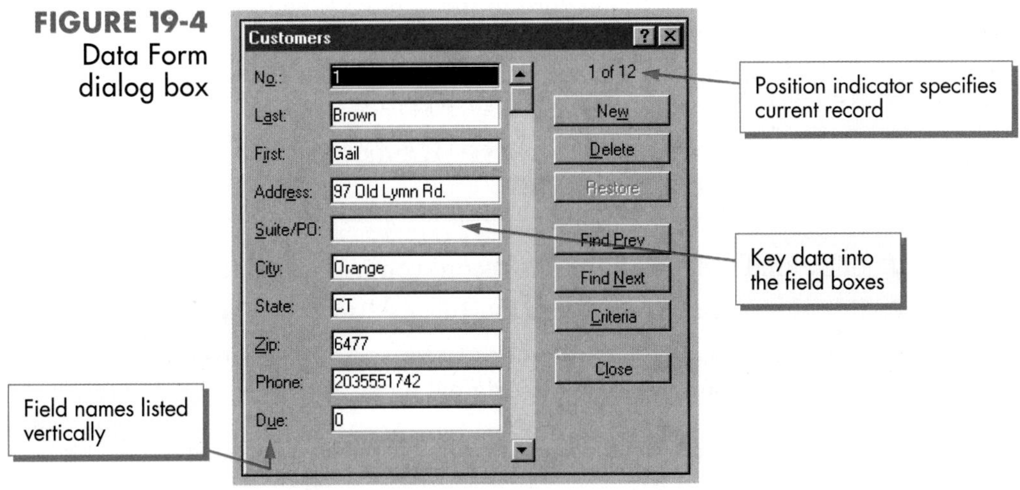

FIGURE 19-4 Data Form dialog box

2. To view the next record in the database, click Find Next.

3. Locate the position indicator in the top right corner of the Data Form dialog box. The position indicator tells you how many records are entered in the database and which record is currently displayed. In this instance, it tells you the current record is 2 out of a total 12.
4. Click Find Next again to scroll forward through several records.
5. Click the Find Prev button to scroll backward through the records.

NOTE: If you add records using Data Form, they are automatically included in the named range of the database. Any formulas in the list are automatically copied to the new record(s).

EXERCISE 19-5 Add Records with the Data Form

1. In the Data Form dialog box, click New.
2. In the No. field box, key **13**
3. Press Tab to move to the Last field box and key **Mercer**
4. Press Tab to move to the First field box and key **Donna**
5. Press Shift+Tab to move to the previous field.
6. Press Tab twice to move to the Address field box.
7. Key the remaining data for the record in the appropriate field boxes. Don't forget to skip the Suite/PO field:

   8 Windy Hills Rd. Dunwoody GA 30338 4045552552 100
8. Press Enter to add the record to the database. Excel displays a new blank data form.

EXERCISE 19-6 Edit and Delete Records with the Data Form

1. Click Find Prev to display the record you just added to the database.
2. Edit the address from "8 Windy Hills Rd." to **800 Windy Hills Rd.**
3. Click Restore. As long as you do not press Enter or scroll to a different record, you can revert to the original data.
4. Click Delete. Excel warns that you are about to delete the record permanently. You cannot use [Undo] to get it back.
5. Click OK. Excel deletes the record.

EXERCISE 19-7 Find Records with the Data Form

You can use the data form to search all records in the database to locate a specific record or group of records. Excel finds only records that match the *criteria,* the data you specify Excel must match when searching for a record.

1. To find records that have "Orange" in the City field, click Criteria in the Data Form dialog box and key **Orange** in the City field.
2. Click Find Prev. Excel searches backward through the database until it finds a record that includes "Orange" for the city. (You can also use Find Next to search forward through the database.)
3. Click Find Prev again. The record does not change because no other records match the specified criteria and the system beeps.
4. Click Criteria to display the Criteria Data Form.
5. Click Clear in the Criteria Data Form and key **MA** in the State field.
6. Click Find Next to scroll through the records of the customers in Massachusetts.
7. Click Criteria and click Clear. All the criteria keyed in the Criteria Data Form are cleared away.
8. Click Form.
9. Click Find Next or Find Prev several times to scroll through the records and verify that all records are shown.
10. Click Close to close the Data Form dialog box.

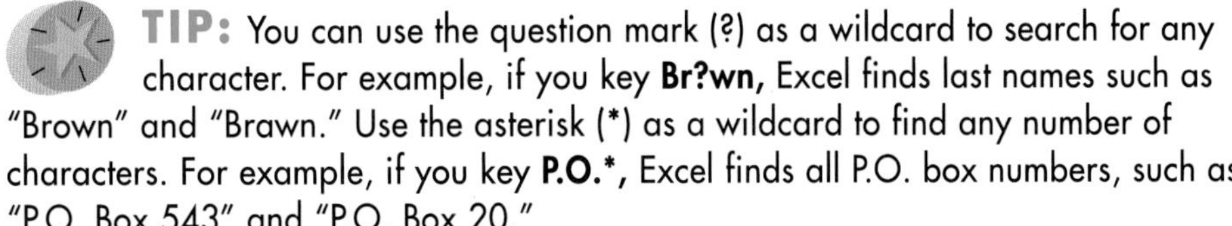

TIP: You can use the question mark (?) as a wildcard to search for any character. For example, if you key **Br?wn,** Excel finds last names such as "Brown" and "Brawn." Use the asterisk (*) as a wildcard to find any number of characters. For example, if you key **P.O.*,** Excel finds all P.O. box numbers, such as "P.O. Box 543" and "P.O. Box 20."

Sorting Data

You can sort data alphabetically or numerically, in ascending or descending *sort order*. You can sort any worksheet data using this feature—even data that is not set up as a database.

When you perform a sort, Excel rearranges rows according to the contents of the specified column. When sorting, you must indicate in the Sort dialog box if your list includes the field names. Excel includes these "Header rows" in a sort unless you indicate your list has them, in which case Excel excludes them.

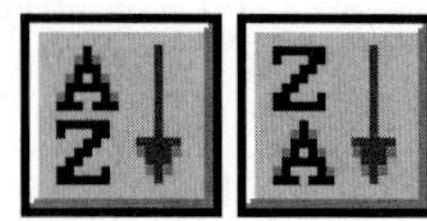

TIP: To sort a list in ascending order quickly, select a cell in the column you want to sort by and click [A↓Z] on the Standard toolbar. To sort in descending order, select a cell in the column you want to sort by and click [Z↓A]. If column headings are formatted differently, Excel excludes them from the sort.

EXERCISE 19-8 Sort Data

1. Select any cell in column J, the column for the Due amount.
2. Choose Sort from the Data menu. The Sort dialog box appears. Excel automatically places Due in the Sort by text box. The sort is also preset to perform an ascending sort. Header row is selected at the bottom of the dialog box, telling Excel to exclude the field names from the sort.

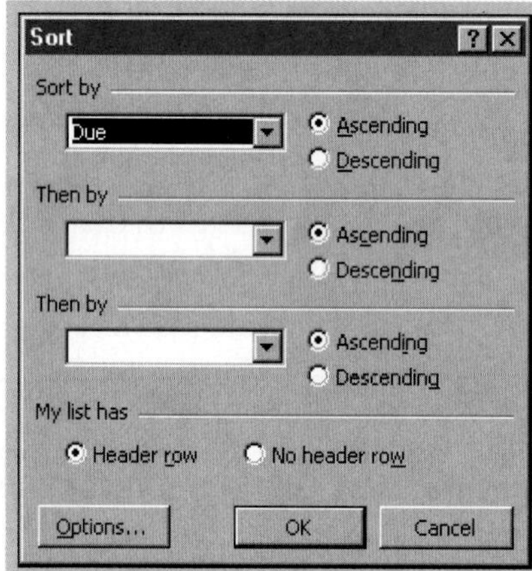

FIGURE 19-5
Sort dialog box

3. Click OK. Excel sorts the records numerically in ascending order by the amount due.
4. To change the sort to descending order, select any cell in the Due column and click [Z↓A].
5. Select any cell in the database and choose Sort from the Data menu. The Sort dialog box appears. Excel assumes you want to sort by the Due field.
6. Click the down arrow in the Sort by text box to open the drop-down list.
7. Select State in the list. Excel enters State into the Sort by text box.
8. Select Ascending next to the Sort by text box and click OK. Excel sorts the records in ascending order by state.

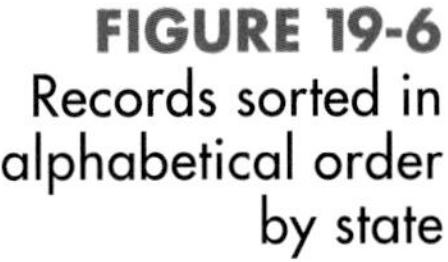

FIGURE 19-6
Records sorted in alphabetical order by state

	A	B	C	D	E	F	G	H	
3	No.	Last	First	Address	Suite/PO	City	State	Zip	
4	6	Small	Ray	455 Daniels Rd		Lakewood	CA	90715	(31
5	1	Brown	Gail	97 Old Lymn R		Orange	CT	06477	(20
6	12	Marley	Dave	20 Krammer		Bethany	CT	06524	(20
7	7	Smith	Betty	12 Putman Ave.		Derby	MA		
8	9	Smith	Gary	287 Carmel Ave.	Suite 102	Hatfield	MA		
9	10	Wilcox	Wendy	690 Rice Ave.		Portage	MI		
10	5	Small	Cathy	11 Pomona Rd		Jersey City	NJ	07310	(20
11	3	Hailey	Linda	12 Garden St.	P.O. 542	Brooklyn	NY	11201	(71
12	11	Zepper	Ann	122 Stuyvesant Rd.		New York	NY	10010	(21
13	8	Smith	Ed	1463 Woodlawn Ave.		Kent	OH	44240	(21
14	4	Marley	Luke	1028 College St.		Pittsburgh	PA	15206	(41
15	2	Brawn	Jean	194 Maplewood Rd.		Essex	VT	05452	(80
16									

NOTE: Excel's default for sorting is not case-sensitive, so it does not matter whether you key uppercase or lowercase letters when you specify criteria. If you want Excel to be case-sensitive, you can choose Options in the Sort dialog box.

EXERCISE 19-9 Sort by Multiple Columns

You can also sort within a sort. You can sort by up to three columns at one time.

1. Move to any cell in the database and choose Sort from the Data menu.
2. Click the down arrow in the Sort by text box and choose Last from the drop-down list.
3. Choose First from the Then by drop-down list and click OK. The records are sorted initially by last name and then by first name. (See Figure 19-7 on the next page.)
4. Add the standard header to the worksheet with your name, the filename, and the date.
5. Save the workbook as *[your initials]***19-9.xls** and print it.
6. To restore the database to its original order, select any cell in the database and choose Sort from the Data menu.
7. Choose No. from the Sort by drop-down list.
8. Choose [none] from the Then by drop-down list and click OK. Excel sorts the records by the numbers in the No. field, putting them back into the original order.

FIGURE 19-7
Records sorted by last name, then by first name

	A	B	C	D	E	F	G	H	
3	No.	Last	First	Address	Suite/PO	City	State	Zip	
4	2	Brawn	Jean	194 Maplewood Rd.		Essex	VT	05452	(80
5	1	Brown	Gail	97 Old Lymn Rd.		Orange	CT	06477	(20
6	3	Hailey	Linda	12 Garden St.	P.O. 542	Brooklyn	NY	11201	(71
7	12	Marley	Dave	20 Krammer Ct		Bethany	CT	06524	(20
8	4	Marley	Luke	1028 College St.		Pittsburgh	PA	15206	(41
9	5	Small	Cathy	11 Pomona Rd		Jersey Cit	NJ	07310	(20
10	6	Small	Ray	455 Daniels Rd		Lakewood	CA	90715	(31
11	7	Smith	Betty	12 Putman Ave.		Derby	MA	06484	(50
12	8	Smith	Ed	1463 Woodlawn Ave.		Kent	OH	44240	(21
13	9	Smith	Gary	287 Carmel Ave.	Suite 102	Hatfield	MA	01038	(41
14	10	Wilcox	Wendy	690 Rice Ave.		Portage	MI	49008	(61
15	11	Zepper	Ann	122 Stuyvesant Rd.		New York	NY	10010	(21
16									

Customers

9. Close the workbook without saving it.

COMMAND SUMMARY

FEATURE	BUTTON	MENU	KEYBOARD
Sort, ascending order	A↓Z	Data, Sort	
Sort, descending order	Z↓A	Data, Sort	

Concepts Review

TRUE/FALSE QUESTIONS

Each of the following statements is either true or false. Indicate your choice by circling T or F.

T F *1*. You can create a database in any Excel worksheet.

T F *2*. You must leave a blank row between the column labels and the first data record in a list.

T F *3*. You can use AutoFill to enter a series in a list automatically.

T F *4*. You can name a list in the same way that you name other cell ranges in a worksheet.

T F *5*. The only way to add new records to a list is by using a Data Form.

T F *6*. You can use a Data Form to view all the records in a database at the same time.

T F *7*. You can easily restore a deleted database record when it is deleted in the Data Form.

T F *8*. You can sort lists by as many as five fields.

SHORT ANSWER QUESTIONS

Write the correct answer in the space provided.

1. Which part of a worksheet corresponds to a database record?

____

2. Which part of a worksheet corresponds to a database field?

____

3. What is the name that Excel uses for a database in a worksheet?

____

4. Which key moves you between fields in a Data Form?

____

5. Which aspect of the data form tells you how many records are in the database and which one is displayed?

____

6. What kind of sort arranges records from A to Z?

____

7. What kind of sort arranges records from Z to A?

____

8. What must you specify if you want Excel to find and display a particular record?

____

CRITICAL THINKING

Answer these questions on a separate page. There are no right or wrong answers. Support your answers with examples from your own experience, if possible.

1. How can Excel's database features help a business?
2. Describe three different types of databases you could create with Excel.

Skills Review

EXERCISE 19-10

Set up a database of inventory parts by entering column labels, keying data in a list, and automatically numbering records.

1. Open the file **Iron2.xls**.
2. Beginning in cell A3, enter the three following column labels:

Description **Size** **Price**

3. Beginning in cell A4, key the following records into the worksheet to create the database:

Ornate Scrolls	**Large**	**55**
Ornate Scrolls	**Medium**	**45**
Ornate Scrolls	**Small**	**35**
Outlet Plates	**Standard**	**15**

4. Format the column labels using a larger font size and making them bold. Adjust the column widths accordingly.

5. Add a new column A and key **Part #** in the new cell A3. Apply the same formatting to cell A3 as the other field names and move the worksheet heading to start in column A.
6. Automatically number the records by following these steps:
   a. In cell A4, key **1**
   b. Select cells A4 through A7.
   c. Choose Edit, Fill, Series and click OK in the Fill Series dialog box.
7. Right-align cells A3 and D3.
8. Add the standard header to the worksheet with your name, the filename, and the date.
9. Save the workbook as *[your initials]***19-10.xls**.
10. Print the worksheet and close the workbook.

EXERCISE 19-11

Add records to a database by keying information directly into a list and by using a Data Form.

1. Open the file **Iron3.xls**.
2. Beginning in cell A8, add a record by keying the following data:

   5 Grates Large 45

3. To display the Data Form for the database, select any cell in the list and choose Data, Form.
4. Add a new record to the database by following these steps:
   a. Click New.
   b. Key **6** in the Part # field text box and press Tab.
   c. Key **Railing Cap** in the Description field text box.
   d. Key **Standard** in the Size field text box.
   e. Key **35** in the Price field text box.
   f. Press Enter to display a new record.
5. Add another record to the database by keying the following data:

   7 Door Knocker Medium 75

6. Click Close to close the Data Form.
7. Add the standard header to the worksheet with your name, the filename, and the date.
8. Save the workbook as *[your initials]***19-11.xls**.
9. Print the worksheet and close the workbook.

EXERCISE 19-12

Find, edit, and delete records using the data form.

1. Open the file **Iron4.xls**.
2. Display the Data Form.
3. Display Part #6 by clicking Find Next.
4. Change the price for Part #6 from 35 to **40**.
5. Restore the original price for Part #6.
6. Find and delete the record for Part #8.
7. Find all records for parts that are in stock by following these steps:
    a. Click Criteria.
    b. Key **Yes** in the In-Stock? field text box.
    c. Click Find Prev or Find Next to display each record.
8. To clear the criteria and display all records, click Criteria, Clear and click Form.
9. Click Close to close the Data Form dialog box.
10. Add the standard header to the worksheet with your name, the filename, and the date.
11. Save the workbook as *[your initials]***19-12.xls**.
12. Print the worksheet and close the workbook.

EXERCISE 19-13

Name a database, sort by a single field, and sort by multiple fields.

1. Open file **Iron5.xls**.
2. Name the database by selecting cells A3 through H15 and clicking the Name Box. Then key **Suppliers** and press Enter.
3. Sort the records alphabetically from A to Z by supplier name by following these steps:
    a. Select cell A3 and choose Data, Sort.
    b. Select Supplier Name in the Sort by drop-down list, if necessary. Make sure that the Ascending option button is selected.
    c. Select Ascending, if necessary, and click OK.
4. Sort the records alphabetically from Z to A by supplier name by clicking Z↓A.
5. Sort the records by State and then by City by following these steps:
    a. Choose Data, Sort.

b. Choose State from the Sort by drop-down list.

c. Select Ascending.

d. Choose City from the Then by drop-down list.

e. Select Ascending, if necessary, and click OK.

6. Add the standard header to the worksheet with your name, the filename, and the date.

7. Save the workbook as *[your initials]***19-13.xls**.

8. Print the worksheet and close the workbook.

Lesson Applications

EXERCISE 19-14

Create a database, add data series, use the Data Form to add a new record, and sort the database.

Indiana Iron Works wants to create a worksheet of delinquent invoices for its problem customers. They want to use the worksheet as a database that can be sorted by invoice number, customer name, invoice date, due date, or amount due.

1. Open the file **Iron6.xls**.
2. Key the data shown in Figure 19-8.

FIGURE 19-8

Customer	Invoice Date	Amount Due
Johnson Manufacturing	5/12/97	1,009.65
Anderson Metal Works	5/15/97	2,376.23
Acme Industries	3/30/97	34,987.22
Anderson Metal Works	4/15/97	203,979
Anderson Metal Works	6/15/97	542.18
Johnson Manufacturing	5/15/97	1,409.67

3. In the Due Date column, write a formula that calculates the dates in column C plus 30 days.
4. Format the values in column E in comma style with 2 decimal places.
5. Assign invoice numbers to the invoices, beginning with 1000.
6. Use the Data Form to add an invoice that contains the following information:

   1006 Metalware Design 2/10/97 311.98

7. Sort the database by Amount Due, from highest to lowest.
8. Sort the database by Customer and then by Invoice Date in ascending order.

9. Center the title across the worksheet and add the standard header to the worksheet with your name, the filename, and the date.
10. Save the workbook as *[your initials]***19-14a.xls** and print the worksheet with gridlines.
11. Return the records to their original order.
12. Save the workbook as *[your initials]***19-14b.xls**.
13. Print the worksheet and close the workbook.

EXERCISE 19-15

Add records to an existing database with the Data Form, find and delete records with the data form, and sort the database.

Indiana Iron Works has a database of corporate-owned homes that it wants to sell. The company needs to number the properties, search for specific records, and update the records to include five new properties.

1. Open the file **Iron7.xls**.
2. Key the data shown in Figure 19-9. Add the new records by keying them directly into the list or with the Data Form.

FIGURE 19-9

203 Narrow	4	2	Gas	0.60	12	95,000	08-Feb-97
14 Shaw Dr.	4	2	Oil	1.75	32	135,000	05-Apr-97
12 Franklin	2	2	Gas	0.75	15	12,000	30-Mar-97
690 Rice St.	1	2	Oil	0.60	25	92,000	01-Dec-96
194 Glenwood	1	1	Oil	0.80	35	76,000	23-Dec-96

3. Use the Criteria Data Form to view records with five bedrooms.
4. Clear this criterion and return to viewing all records.
5. Find and delete the record for 30 Lake.
6. Find 12 Franklin and change the Price to 75,000.
7. Sort the list by the number of bedrooms and then by the number of bathrooms. Use a descending sort.
8. Add a new field to the left of column A and key the column heading **ITEM #**. Make it bold, change the font size to 8 point, and right-align

the text. Move the worksheet heading to the left and add the appropriate shading and borders.

9. In the Item # field, number the properties in a series beginning with the number 1. Make sure the font size for the series is the same as for the rest of the data.
10. Adjust all column widths appropriately.
11. Sort in ascending order by price.
12. Add the standard header to the worksheet with your name, the filename, and the date.
13. Save the workbook as *[your initials]***19-15a.xls** and print the worksheet.
14. Restore the worksheet to its original sorting order, by item number.
15. Save the workbook as *[your initials]***19-15b.xls**.
16. Print the worksheet and close the workbook.

EXERCISE 19-16

Convert a worksheet into a database, use the Data Form to find and add records, name and add a data series, and sort the database.

To organize its checking-account transactions, Indiana Iron Works needs a worksheet set up as a database that serves as an electronic checkbook.

1. Open the file **Iron8.xls**.
2. Use the Data Form to add the checks shown in Figure 19-10.

FIGURE 19-10

Date	Check #	Description	Category	Amount
2/13/97	204	Pyramid Properties	Rent	(1,522.08)
2/19/97		Jacobson & Sons	Acct Rec	500.00
2/20/97	205	Clips Co.	Supplies	(54.86)
2/22/97		Arlington Industries	Acct Rec	652.99

3. Insert a column to the left of column A labeled **Trans #.** The format of the new cells should match the format of the existing cells. Format the new column so values display two leading zeros.

4. Number the records in the list, beginning with the transaction number 001.
5. At the right side of the worksheet, insert another column labeled **Balance** and enter formulas to calculate the daily balance. Assume an opening balance of $2,000. Format all the values in the Balance column in comma style with two decimal places.
6. Name the list **Checking**.
7. Sort the worksheet by Description. Notice the effect the formulas have on the balance column.
8. Use the Data Form to find out how much money was spent on office supplies.
9. Sort the worksheet by transaction number.
10. Add the standard header to the worksheet with your name, the filename, and the date.
11. Save the workbook as *[your initials]***19-16.xls**.
12. Print the workbook.
13. Create a formula printout in landscape orientation with grids and row and column headings.
14. Close the workbook without saving.

EXERCISE 19-17

Create a database, add a data series column and a field to compute percentage increases, and find and sort records in the database.

Indiana Iron Works needs a worksheet set up as an employee database that can help them keep track of employees and the payroll budget.

1. Create a sketch of the database that includes a worksheet title and a database with following fields: Last name, first name, position, hire date, 1997 salary, % increase, and 1998 salary. The entries for the last field should be computed with a formula.
2. Transfer the database sketch to Excel by keying and formatting the titles and headings. Key the records shown in Figure 19-11 (on the next page).
3. Sort the records by the date each employee began working for Indiana Iron Works.
4. Add a new column A labeled **Emp. #**. Format it to display two leading zeros. Format the new cells to match the formatting of the existing cells and center or right-align the values in the column.
5. Number the records consecutively beginning with 001.

FIGURE 19-11

Last	First	Position	Hire Date	1997 Salary	%
Davis	John	Manager	4/1/92	35,000	4%
Smith	Pat	Operator	6/15/93	28,000	3%
DeMarco	Tony	Smith	1/2/90	30,500	3%
Lee	Kathy	Assistant	5/5/95	25,000	4%
Kane	Sam	Operator	9/10/94	25,000	3%
Whittier	Chris	Designer	10/11/91	35,000	3%
Yang	Li	Designer	6/15/92	32,500	4%

6. In the 1998 Salary column, enter formulas that calculate the new salaries for each employee. Format the values in both salary columns in comma style with no decimals.
7. Sort the records by 1998 salaries from lowest to highest.
8. Locate the records for all employees who earned $35,000 in 1997.
9. Return to viewing all records.
10. Rename Sheet1 **Employees** and Sheet2 **User Information**.
11. In the User Information worksheet, create documentation that includes the following: File Information (Created by, Date created, Date revised, Revised by, Contact for help); Purpose of spreadsheet (paragraph form); and Instructions to User (special instructions needed by user to enter data correctly). Style the worksheet for easy viewing.
12. Apply gridlines to the Employees worksheet. Add the standard header with your name, the filename, and the date to both worksheets. Horizontally center both worksheets.
13. Save the workbook as *[your initials]***19-17a.xls**.
14. Print the entire workbook.
15. Sort the records by employee number.
16. Save the workbook as *[your initials]***19-17b.xls** and print the Employees worksheet.
17. Create a formula printout in landscape orientation with grids and row and column headings.
18. Close the workbook without saving.

Filtering Data

OBJECTIVES

After completing this lesson, you will be able to:

1. **Use AutoFilter.**
2. **Filter with Advanced Filter.**

Finding and selecting information in Excel is called *filtering*. After you set up a worksheet as a database, you can use Excel's filtering features to hide records you don't want and list only records you do want. For example, you can list only the records for customers who live in certain states. This option saves time and makes your work easier. Filtering is also convenient when you print, chart, delete, edit, format, or copy a subset of your database. When you print or copy as usual, only filtered data prints or copies.

Using AutoFilter

Use AutoFilter when your criteria for filtering are simple—for example, when you need to view all records with the last name "Small" or all amounts due over $50.

To use AutoFilter, select any cell in the database and choose Data, Filter and AutoFilter. Excel applies down arrows to field names in the list. Click a down arrow to choose the items you want to filter from a drop-down list. For example, you can click Smith to see only the records (rows) containing the last name "Smith." If you filter more than one field using AutoFilter, Excel displays only the records that meet all specified conditions.

Besides choosing a field like "Smith," you can use AutoFilter to choose the following options:

- (All)
  Shows all records in the database (this option removes the filter)
- (Top 10...)
  Shows records by number of items or by percent from the top or bottom of the database
- (Custom...)
  Shows records using a simple or two-field comparison
- (Blanks)
  Shows all records with blanks in the field
- (NonBlanks)
  Shows all records that contain data in the field

EXERCISE 20-1 Filter Directly with AutoFilter and Edit Records

1. Open the file **Iron9.xls**.
2. Select any cell in the 15-record list and choose Filter from the Data menu. A cascading menu appears.
3. Choose AutoFilter. The AutoFilter down arrows appear at the top of each column.

FIGURE 20-1 Fields with AutoFilter down arrows

	A	B	C	D	E	F	G	H	
1				Indiana Iron Works Customer List					
2									
3	N	Last	First	Address	Suite-PC	City	State	Z	
4	1	Brawn	Jean	194 Maplewood Rd.		Essex	VT	05452	(802)
5	2	Brown	Gail	97 Old Lyme Rd.		Orange	CT	06477	(203)
6	6	Marley	Dave	20 Krammer Court		Bethany	CT	06524	(203)

4. Click the AutoFilter down arrow for the Last field, which is located in cell B3. A drop-down list appears with all the unique entries in the field.
5. Scroll down the list and choose the name "Smith." Excel filters the list to show only records containing this last name. If you have a color monitor, the AutoFilter down arrow for Last becomes blue, indicating four records were filtered from this field. Row labels 8, 13, 14, and 18 are blue, indicating they are the result of a filter. The number of records found appears in the Status bar.

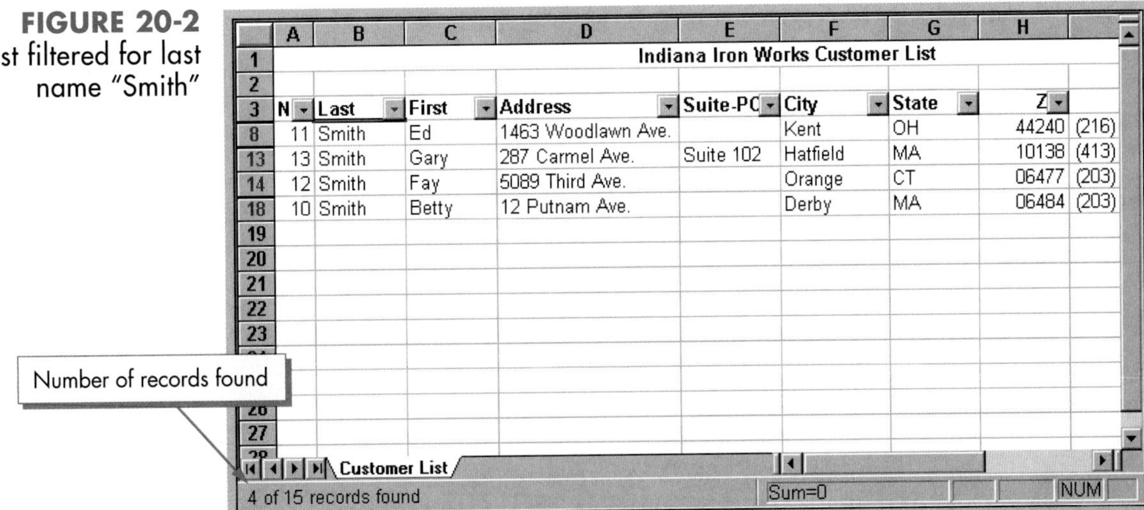

	A	B	C	D	E	F	G	H	
3	N	Last	First	Address	Suite-PC	City	State	Z	
8	11	Smith	Ed	1463 Woodlawn Ave.		Kent	OH	44240	(216)
13	13	Smith	Gary	287 Carmel Ave.	Suite 102	Hatfield	MA	10138	(413)
14	12	Smith	Fay	5089 Third Ave.		Orange	CT	06477	(203)
18	10	Smith	Betty	12 Putnam Ave.		Derby	MA	06484	(203)

FIGURE 20-2 List filtered for last name "Smith"

6. Click the AutoFilter down arrow for the State field and choose "MA" from the list. Only two records meeting both conditions (last name of Smith and state of Massachusetts) are displayed.
7. Click the AutoFilter down arrow for the Last field. Select (All) to show all records. The list is still filtered for the state, so only three records are seen.
8. Click the AutoFilter down arrow for the State field. Select (All) to show all records in the database.
9. Click the AutoFilter down arrow for the Phone field. Select (Blanks). Excel displays the record with a blank phone field.
10. To edit a field while filtering, select cell I17 and key **7185559874**
11. Click the AutoFilter down arrow for the Phone field again. Select (All) to show all records in the database.
12. Click the AutoFilter down arrow for the Suite-PO field and click (NonBlanks). Two records are displayed.
13. Double-click cell E13 and change the suite number to **105**
14. Click the AutoFilter down arrow for the Suite-PO field again. Select (All) to show all records in the database.
15. Choose Filter from the Data menu and click AutoFilter to turn it off.

EXERCISE 20-2 View Top or Bottom 10 with AutoFilter

You can use one AutoFilter option to select records from the top or bottom of the database. You can specify the top or bottom records by number of items or by percentage of items.

1. Select any cell in the database. Choose Data, Filter, AutoFilter.
2. Click the AutoFilter down arrow in the Due field located in cell J3. Select (Top 10...) from the drop-down list. The Top 10 AutoFilter dialog box appears.

FIGURE 20-3
Top 10 AutoFilter dialog box

3. Enter **2** in the middle box.
4. If necessary, select Items from the drop-down list on the right side of the dialog box and click OK. The two records listed have the highest balances in the customer database.
5. Add the standard header to the worksheet with your name, the filename, and the date.
6. Save the workbook as *[your initials]***20-2.xls** and print the worksheet.

EXERCISE 20-3 Customize AutoFilter

With AutoFilter, you can create custom criteria. You can then use a comparison operator, such as greater than (>) or less than (<), as well as the "and" and "or" operators. Comparison operators can be used to:

- Display the results of a single criterion, such as >500.
- Display either of two items in a field. For example, display all records with either "Smith" or "Jacobs" in the last-name field.
- Display records that fall within a range, such as >500 and <1000.

1. Click the AutoFilter down arrow for the Due field and click (All).
2. Click the AutoFilter down arrow for the Due field again and select (Custom...). The Custom AutoFilter dialog box appears.

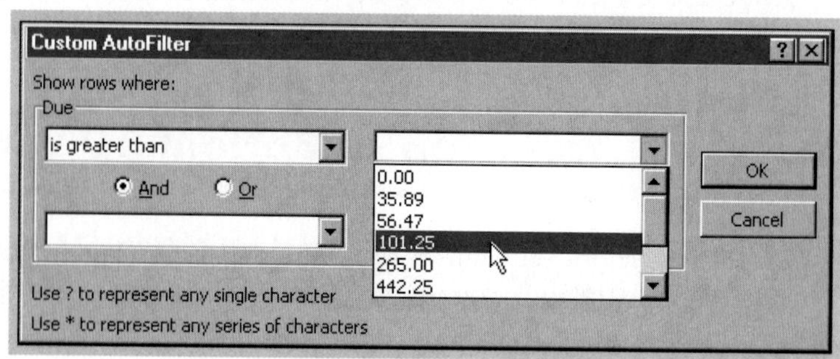

FIGURE 20-4
Custom AutoFilter dialog box

3. Click the down arrow in the top left text box to open the drop-down list for operators. Select "is greater than."
4. Click the down arrow in the top right text box to open the drop-down list for the values in the Due column. Select 101.25 and click OK. Excel displays five records for which the amount due is greater than $101.25.
5. Click the AutoFilter down arrow for the Due column and select (Custom...).
6. Key **300** in the top right text box and click OK. Excel displays four records where the amount due is greater than $300.
7. Click the AutoFilter down arrow for the Due field and select (Custom...). Click the down arrow in the bottom left text box and select "is less than" from the drop-down list.
8. Click the down arrow in the bottom right text box, select 2,100.00, and click OK. Excel displays two records where the amount due is greater than $300 but less than $2,100.
9. Click the AutoFilter down arrow for the Due field and select (All) to show all records.
10. Click the AutoFilter down arrow for the Last field and select (Custom...). Click the down arrow in the top right text box and select Smith from the drop-down list. Select Or.
11. Click the down arrow in the bottom left text box, and select "equals" from the drop-down list. Click the down arrow in the bottom right text box and select Small from the drop-down list.
12. Click OK. Six records containing the last names Smith or Small are displayed.

FIGURE 20-5 Filtering the database for Smith or Small

E17 = P.O. 542

Indiana Iron Works Customer List

	N	Last	First	Address	Suite-PC	City	State	Z	
8	11	Smith	Ed	1463 Woodlawn Ave.		Kent	OH	44240	(216)
10	9	Small	Ray	455 Daniels Rd.		Lakewood	CA	90715	(310)
12	8	Small	Cathy	11 Ponoma Rd.		Jersey City	NJ	07310	(201)
13	13	Smith	Gary	287 Carmel Ave.	Suite 105	Hatfield	MA	10138	(413)
14	12	Smith	Fay	5089 Third Ave.		Orange	CT	06477	(203)
18	10	Smith	Betty	12 Putnam Ave.		Derby	MA	06484	(203)

Customer List

6 of 15 records found

13. Select (All) from the drop-down list for the field Last to show all records.
14. Click the AutoFilter down arrow for the Suite-PO field and select (Custom...). In the top right text box, key **S***

NOTE: You can use Custom AutoFilter to search with wildcards. Remember, the question mark (?) is a wildcard for a single character and the asterisk (*) is a wildcard for a group of characters.

15. Click OK. Excel displays the single record containing a word that begins with "S" in the field for Suite-PO.
16. Click the AutoFilter down arrow for the Suite-PO field and select (All) to remove the filter.
17. Click the AutoFilter down arrow for the Last field and select (Custom...). In the top right text box, key **Br?wn**
18. Click OK. Excel displays three records with a last name that begins with "Br," ends with "wn," and has any one character in between.
19. Click the AutoFilter down arrow for the Last field and select (All) to remove the filter.
20. Choose Filter from the Data menu and click AutoFilter to turn it off.
21. Save the workbook as *[your initials]***20-3.xls**.

TIP: To redisplay all records at once, select Data, Filter, Show All.

Filtering with Advanced Filter

Using Advanced Filter requires more work than AutoFilter but you can filter data based on more complex or calculated criteria. You can also copy filtered data to another location on the worksheet and to display unique records.

Before you use Advanced Filter, you must:

- Set the list range.
- Set the criteria range.

EXERCISE 20-4 Set the List Range by Naming the Database

As you learned in Lesson 19, the *list range* is the area containing the database. It is easier to set the list range if the database is named. Setting the list range is the first step in using the Advanced Filter.

1. Select cell A3.
2. Click the Name Box on the Formula Bar, key **A3:J18**, and press Enter. The entire database is selected.
3. Click the Name Box again, key **Customers**, and press Enter. Click any cell to deselect the database, which is now named "Customers."

NOTE: Once the database is named, you can add records to it by simply inserting a row within existing records and keying the new record. This updates the defined range. You can also use Data, Form to add additional records and keep the defined name updated.

4. Press Ctrl+Home to make A1 the active cell.
5. Click the down arrow to open the Name Box drop-down list. The name "Customers" is listed. Select it and the database is again highlighted. Press an arrow key to remove highlighting.
6. Select cell D20 and choose Insert, Name, Paste or press F3. The Paste Name dialog box is displayed showing you a list of named cells in the worksheet.
7. Select Customers and click Paste List.

FIGURE 20-6 Pasting the list range

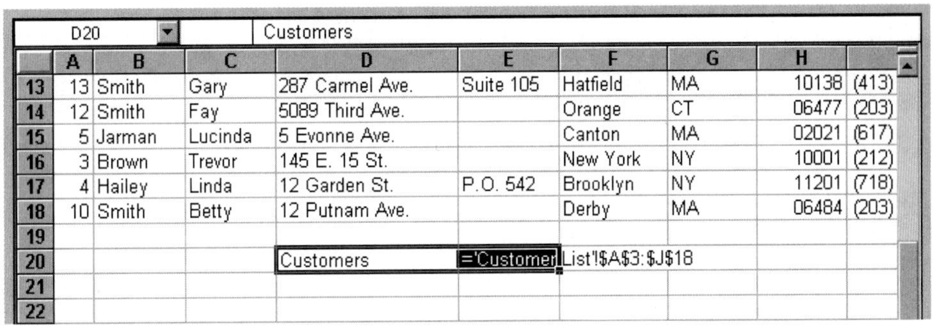

D20 | Customers

	A	B	C	D	E	F	G	H	
13	13	Smith	Gary	287 Carmel Ave.	Suite 105	Hatfield	MA	10138	(413)
14	12	Smith	Fay	5089 Third Ave.		Orange	CT	06477	(203)
15	5	Jarman	Lucinda	5 Evonne Ave.		Canton	MA	02021	(617)
16	3	Brown	Trevor	145 E. 15 St.		New York	NY	10001	(212)
17	4	Hailey	Linda	12 Garden St.	P.O. 542	Brooklyn	NY	11201	(718)
18	10	Smith	Betty	12 Putnam Ave.		Derby	MA	06484	(203)
19									
20				Customers	='Customer List'!$A$3:$J$18				
21									
22									

8. Save the workbook as *[your initials]***20-4.xls**.
9. Delete the list range in cells D20:E20.

EXERCISE 20-5 Set the Criteria Range

The *criteria range* is the area of the worksheet in which you specify the conditions that the filtered data must meet. The first row of the criteria range must contain the exact field name used in the database. The only exception to this is when you use calculated criteria. In that situation, you cannot use the field name if it exists in the database. Most users substitute the name "Calc" or

"Formula" to indicate a calculated—rather than a comparison—criterion. In the cell beneath the field name, you key the condition for each field. At a minimum, the criteria range contains two rows: one for field names and one for criteria. It is easier to work with the criteria range if it is named. Be sure to include all appropriate field names and conditions in the criteria range.

Two rules to remember when you enter criteria for more than one field are as follows:

- If you key criteria for more than one field in the same row, Excel treats them as if they are connected by "and."
- If you key criteria for more than one field on different rows, Excel treats them as if they are connected by "or."

Note that you may have multiple criteria ranges, but you can actually use only one at a time.

1. Choose Insert, Worksheet. A new sheet is added before the Customer sheet.
2. Right-click the worksheet tab labeled Sheet1.
3. Click Move or Copy and select (move to end). Click OK. The sheet is moved after the Customer sheet.
4. Rename the Sheet1 tab as **Criteria**

TIP: It is best to place criteria on a separate sheet from the database. If you then add or delete records or field names, it does not affect the criteria.

5. Click the Customer List tab and copy the Last field name in cell B3 to cell A2 in the Criteria worksheet.

NOTE: Always copy field names from the list range to the criteria range. The field names must be identical and copying them ensures that no typing errors or other differences occur between the two ranges, including the use of upper- and lowercase letters.

6. In cell A3 on the Criteria sheet, key **Smith**
7. Copy the field name in cell G3 from the Customer List worksheet (the State field name) to cell B2 on the Criteria worksheet.
8. In cell B3 on the Criteria worksheet, key **MA**
9. Click the Name Box on the Formula Bar, key **A2:B3**, and press Enter. The criteria range just entered is highlighted.
10. Click the Name Box again, key **Sm_ma**, and press Enter. The range for comparison criteria is named with an And condition.

NOTE: Be careful not to include blank rows when setting the criteria range. A blank row filters all records in the database.

11. Copy the field name in cell J3 from the Customer List worksheet (the Due field name) to cells D2:E2 on the Criteria sheet.
12. Key **>100** in cell D3 and **<2000** in cell E3.
13. Click the Name Box, key **D2:E3**, and press Enter. The criteria range you just entered is highlighted.
14. Click the Name Box again, key **Due_bet**, and press Enter. The second range for comparison criteria is named, using an And condition in the same field.
15. Copy the field name in cell B3 from the Customer List worksheet (the Last field name) to cell G2 on the Criteria worksheet.
16. Copy the field name in cell B2 of the Criteria worksheet (the State field name) to cell H2 on the same worksheet.

TIP: When you expect to use many different field names for your criteria, it is often helpful to just copy all the field names from the list to the first row of the Criteria sheet. This gives you easier access to the field names when copying.

17. Key **Smith** in cell G3 and **NY** in cell H4.
18. Click the Name Box, key **G2:H4**, and press Enter. The criteria range you just entered is highlighted.
19. Click the Name Box again, key **Sm_Ny**, and press Enter. The third range for comparison criteria is named using an Or condition.
20. On the Criteria sheet, copy cell G2 to cell A6 and copy cell D2 to cell B6.
21. Enter the following text in the cells indicated:

A7	**Smith**	B7	**>0**
A8	**Brown**	B8	**>50**

22. Click the Name Box, key **A6:B8**, and press Enter. The criteria range you just entered is highlighted.
23. Click the Name Box, key **SB_Due**, and press Enter. The fourth range for comparison criteria is named using an Or and And condition.
24. Add the standard header to the Criteria worksheet with your name, the filename, and the date, and the tab name as a footer.
25. Save the workbook as *[your initials]***20-5.xls**. Print the Criteria sheet only.

EXERCISE 20-6 Use Advanced Filter to Produce a Filtered List

After you set the list range and the criteria range, you are ready to run the Advanced Filter option. When you sum items on a filtered list, you are actually generating a subtotal.

1. Select cell A4 on the Customer List worksheet (not the Criteria worksheet). You can select any cell as long as it is located within the database.
2. Choose Data, Filter, Advanced Filter from the menu. The Advanced Filter dialog box is displayed.

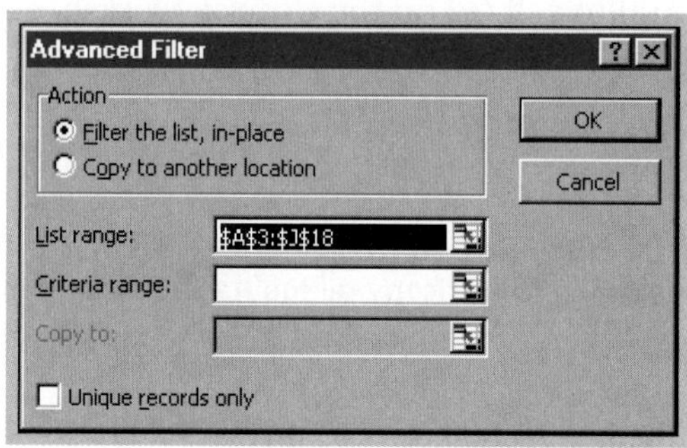

FIGURE 20-7 Advanced Filter dialog box

3. If necessary, select the Filter the list, in-place option. This option displays matching records in the database area of the worksheet.

NOTE: To place the filtered data in another area of the worksheet so the original data remain unaffected, choose Copy to another location in the Advanced Filter dialog box. If you use this option, the target area must contain the field names needed. Creating a range name makes the target area more accessible.

4. If necessary, click the List range text box. Key **Customers**, the name you assigned to the database. (It is easier to remember a name than a range address.)
5. Select the Criteria range text box and press F3. The Paste Name dialog box is displayed. Click the range name Sm_ma and click OK.
6. Click OK in the Advanced Filter dialog box. The database changes to display the only two records that match the criteria.
7. Save the workbook as *[your initials]***20-6a.xls**. Print the Customer List worksheet.

TIP: If your filtered list shows duplicate records, you can check Unique records only in the Advanced Filter dialog box. This option displays only the first record that meets the criteria and eliminates any duplicates.

8. Choose Data, Filter, Advanced Filter from the menu. Select the Criteria range text box and press F3. Select the range name Sm_Ny. Click OK twice. Seven records are shown in the database area. Print the Customer worksheet.
9. Choose Data, Filter, Advanced Filter from the menu. Select the Criteria range text box and press F3. Select the range name SB_Due. Click OK twice. Four records are shown in the database area.
10. Select cell J19 and click Σ. Review the formula in J19, noticing that the sum is actually a subtotal.
11. Save the workbook as *[your initials]***20-6b.xls**. Print the Customer worksheet.
12. Choose Data, Filter, Show All to remove the filter on the database and show all records.
13. Close the workbook.

Concepts Review

TRUE/FALSE QUESTIONS

Each of the following statements is either true or false. Indicate your choice by circling T or F.

T F *1*. AutoFilter is a quick way to search a list for a set of criteria.

T F *2*. The best method of filtering using complex criteria is AutoFilter.

T F *3*. One method of removing the filtered list in AutoFilter is to click the down arrow and select the option All.

T F *4*. A name for your database should not include the field names in the selected range.

T F *5*. When you set criteria for Advanced Filter, field names must appear in the first row.

T F *6*. Criteria located on the same row are treated as "or" conditions by Excel when using Advanced Filter.

T F *7*. Sums performed on filtered data are actually subtotals.

T F *8*. You can copy filtered data to another area of the worksheet.

SHORT ANSWER QUESTIONS

Write the correct answer in the space provided.

1. Which menu commands do you use to filter a list using simple criteria?

___

2. Which operator is used to indicate "less than"?

___

3. Which option is selected when you use AutoFilter to display the top 2 criteria?

___

4. Which menu commands do you use to filter a list using complex criteria?

___

5. Where should criteria be located when you use the Advanced Filter?

___

6. Which row arrangement should you use to have Excel read the criteria as an "or" situation when using Advanced Filter?

____

7. Which row arrangement should you use to have Excel read the criteria as an "and" situation when using Advanced Filter?

____

8. Which menu commands should you select to remove the filter when using Advanced Filter?

____

CRITICAL THINKING

Answer these questions on a separate piece of paper. There are no right or wrong answers. Support your answers with examples from your own experience, if possible.

1. Name three types of businesses that would find Excel's filtering options useful. Explain what types of information each company might filter.
2. More than one person is using your company's database for advanced filtering. Explain how you would organize the workbook containing the database for ease of use by all users.

Skills Review

EXERCISE 20-7

Use AutoFilter, filter a database using comparison criteria, and remove AutoFilter.

1. Open the file **Iron9.xls**.
2. Filter the database for all records with the last name "Small" by following these steps:
   a. Choose Data, Filter, AutoFilter from the menu.
   b. Click the down arrow in cell B3.
   c. Select Small from the drop-down list.
3. Add the standard header to the worksheet with your name, the filename, and the date.
4. Save the workbook as *[your initials]***20-7a.xls** and print the worksheet.

5. Remove AutoFilter by choosing Data, Filter from the menu and deselecting AutoFilter.
6. Save the workbook as *[your initials]***20-7b.xls**.
7. Print the worksheet and close the workbook.

EXERCISE 20-8

Use AutoFilter, filter a database using mathematical operators and the Top 10 option, and remove AutoFilter.

1. Open the file **Iron9.xls**.
2. Filter the database for all records with a balance of less than $500.00 by following these steps:
   a. Choose Data, Filter, AutoFilter.
   b. Click the down arrow in cell J3.
   c. Select (Custom...) from the drop-down list
   d. Click the down arrow in the top left text box.
   e. Select "is less than" from the drop-down list.
   f. Click the top right text box, key **500**, and click OK.
3. Add the standard header to the worksheet with your name, the filename, and the date.
4. Save the workbook as *[your initials]***20-8a.xls** and print the worksheet.
5. Filter the database for the four highest balances by following these steps:
   a. Click the down arrow in cell J3.
   b. Select (Top 10...) from the drop-down list.
   c. If necessary, select Top in the left box by clicking the down arrow and clicking Top.
   d. Click the down arrow in the center box until it displays 4.
   e. If necessary, select Items from the right box and click OK.
6. Save the workbook as *[your initials]***20-8b.xls** and print the worksheet.
7. Remove AutoFilter by choosing Data, Filter from the menu and deselecting AutoFilter.
8. Close the workbook without saving it.

EXERCISE 20-9

Name a list, add a criteria sheet, and set up a criteria sheet with an And criteria; use Advanced Filter and copy the results to another location.

1. Open the file **Iron9.xls**.

2. Name the database by following these steps:
   a. Click the Name Box, key **A3:J18**, and press Enter.
   b. Click the Name Box, key **Cust_List**, press Enter, and press an arrow key to deselect..
3. Insert a new worksheet, name the worksheet tab **Criteria**, and move it after the Customer List worksheet.
4. Set up an And criteria range by following these steps:
   a. Copy cell B3 in the Customer List worksheet (the Last field) to cell A2 in the Criteria worksheet.
   b. With the Criteria worksheet displayed, click the Name Box, key **A2:A4**, and press Enter.
   c. Click the Name Box, key **Names**, and press Enter.
   d. Key **Zepper** in cell A3 and **Brown** in cell A4.
5. Filter the records using the And criteria and copy the results to the Customer List worksheet by following these steps:
   a. Click the Customer List tab and select cell B4.
   b. Choose Date, Filter, Advanced Filter from the menu.
   c. If the List range does not show $A$3:$J$18, press F3 and select Cust_List.
   d. Select the Criteria range text box.
   e. Press F3 and select Names. Click OK.
   f. Select Copy to another location.
   g. Select the Copy to text box. Key **A22** and click OK.
6. Add the standard header to the worksheet with your name, the filename, and the date.
7. Save the workbook as *[your initials]***20-9.xls**.
8. Print the worksheet and close the workbook.

EXERCISE 20-10

Set up a criteria range using multiple criteria, use Advanced Filter, and remove Advanced Filter.

1. Open the file **Criteria.xls**.
2. Set the And criteria for records in which the last name begins with "S" and the customer lives in the state MA by following these steps:
   a. Copy cell B3 in the Customer List worksheet to cell A3 in the Criteria worksheet.

b. Select cell A4 and key **S***

c. Copy cell G3 in the Customer List worksheet (the State field) to cell B3 in the Criteria worksheet.

d. Select cell B4 and key **MA**

3. Use the Name Box to give the And criteria range A3:B4 the name **S_MA**
4. Set the Or criteria for customers who live in Massachusetts or Connecticut by following these steps:

a. Copy cell G3 in the Customer List worksheet (the State field) to cell D3 in the Criteria worksheet.

b. Key **CT** in cell D4 and **MA** in cell D5

5. Use the Name Box to give the Or criteria range D3:D5 the name **CT_MA**
6. Filter using the And criteria of S_MA by following these steps:

a. Click the Customer List worksheet tab and select cell B4.

b. Choose Data, Filter, Advanced Filter.

c. Click the Criteria range text box.

d. Press F3. Select S_MA from the drop-down list and click OK twice.

7. Add the standard header to the worksheet with your name, the filename, and the date.
8. Save the workbook as *[your initials]***20-10a.xls** and print the worksheet.
9. Filter for the Or criteria of CT_MA by following these steps:

a. Choose Data, Filter, Advanced Filter from the menu.

b. Select the Criteria range text box.

c. Press F3. Select CT_MA from the drop-down list and click OK twice.

10. Save the workbook as *[your initials]***20-10b.xls** and print the worksheet.
11. Remove the Advanced Filter by choosing Data, Filter, Show All.
12. Close the workbook without saving.

Lesson Applications

EXERCISE 20-11

Enter new records in a database, filter and edit a record with AutoFilter, and customize criteria with AutoFilter.

Indiana Iron Works needs to add records to its database of product sales. The company needs to filter the data by item number and company.

1. Open the file **Iron10.xls**.
2. Key the data as shown in Figure 20-8. Use the Data Form or insert six rows above row 13 and key the data directly.

FIGURE 20-8

Date	Company	Item	Price	Quantity
3/14/96	Items Unlimited	1-1111	475.00	10
10/14/96	Parts, Inc.	1-1122	453.21	9
3/14/96	Items Unlimited	1-1100	11.98	18
9/25/96	Parts, Inc.	2-1010	104.00	2
3/2/96	Items Unlimited	1-1100	11.98	1
11/1/96	NERS	1-1133	32.52	45

3. Filter the database using AutoFilter for the record dated 11/7/96. Edit the item number for this record to read 2-1010 and change the price to 563. Add a new row between rows 2 and 3. Add a subtitle to the report in cell A2, describing the record shown.
4. Add the standard header to the worksheet with your name, the filename, and the date.
5. Save the workbook as *[your initials]***20-11a.xls**. Print the worksheet.
6. Display all records.
7. Filter the records for the NERS company dated after 3/1/96. Add a subtitle to the report in cell A2 based on the records shown.
8. Save the workbook as *[your initials]***20-11b.xls**.
9. Print and close the workbook.

EXERCISE 20-12

Use AutoFilter with multiple conditions and custom criteria; generate reports for the top five records, sorting the outcome.

The management of Indiana Iron Works needs some reports showing sales by salesperson and sales amount.

1. Open the file **Sperson.xls**.
2. Filter the records for sales over $25,000 by Linda Brenner. Add a subtitle to the report describing the records shown.
3. Add the standard header to the worksheet with your name, the filename, and the date.
4. Save the workbook as *[your initials]***20-12a.xls** and print the worksheet.
5. Filter the records showing the top five sales amounts. Sort the records in descending order. Add a subtitle describing the records shown.
6. Save the workbook as *[your initials]***20-12b.xls**.
7. Print the worksheet and close the workbook.

EXERCISE 20-13

Set up a criteria worksheet for use with a database. Use the Advanced Filter to generate reports with multiple conditions, sorting the outcome.

Indiana Iron Works has two people who must filter the sales database. These two employees produce reports by salesperson and by sales amount. Create a criteria sheet that can be used repeatedly by both workers to filter the same database.

1. Open the file **Sperson.xls**.
2. Create a name for the database.
3. Insert a new worksheet for the criteria. Move the worksheet after the Salespersons worksheet and then name the worksheet tab **Criteria**.
4. On the Criteria worksheet, create and name criteria to be used to filter for a salesperson.
5. On the same worksheet, create and name criteria to be used to filter for a sales amount.
6. Produce a report for Michner using the appropriate criteria range. Add an appropriate subtitle to the report.

7. Add the standard header to the worksheet with your name, the filename, and the date.
8. Save the workbook as *[your initials]***20-13a.xls** and print the Salespersons worksheet.
9. Produce a report indicating all sales under $30,000 with records sorted in descending order. Subtitle the report appropriately.
10. Add the standard header to the Criteria worksheet with your name, the filename, and the date. Add a centered, tab name footer to both worksheets.
11. Save the workbook as *[your initials]***20-13b.xls**.
12. Print the entire workbook and close it.

EXERCISE 20-14

Set up a criteria worksheet using multiple criteria, generate different reports using the same criteria, and add formulas computing commissions and totals.

Indiana Iron Works needs reports that determine the commissions for each salesperson. Commissions are based on sales amounts. A 20% commission is given on the amount of sales exceeding $5,000.

1. Open the file **Sperson.xls**.
2. Create a name for the database.
3. Insert a new worksheet for the criteria. Move the new worksheet after the Salespersons worksheet and name the tab **Criteria**.
4. On the Criteria worksheet, create and name criteria to be used to filter for sales of more than $5,000 for any salesperson.
5. Filter the database for Victor's sales over $5,000. Add a column to the report that calculates the commission on each sale. (The commission is paid for sales above $5,000, so this amount must be subtracted before the commission is calculated.) Show a total for commissions and label the cell appropriately. Format cells in currency style with no dollar signs. Match the font size to existing data.
6. Add the standard header to the Salespersons worksheet with your name, the filename, and the date.
7. Add an appropriate subtitle to the report.
8. Save the workbook as *[your initials]***20-14a.xls** and print the worksheet.
9. Delete the formulas and repeat step 5 for Travis. Change the subtitle to reflect the new report.

10. On the Criteria worksheet, paste a list of the range names in cell A8 and widen the column appropriately.
11. Add the standard header to the Criteria worksheet with your name, the filename, and the date. Add a centered, tab name footer to both worksheets.
12. Save the workbook as *[your initials]***20-14b.xls** and print the entire workbook.
13. Create a formula printout in landscape orientation for the Salespersons worksheet with grids and row and column headings.
14. Close the workbook without saving.

Advanced Features

OBJECTIVES

After completing this lesson, you will be able to:

1. **Use database functions.**
2. **Work with data tables.**
3. **Get summary information with subtotals.**
4. **Create a pivot table using the PivotTable Wizard.**
5. **Convert a worksheet to HTML format.**
6. **Work with 3-D shapes.**

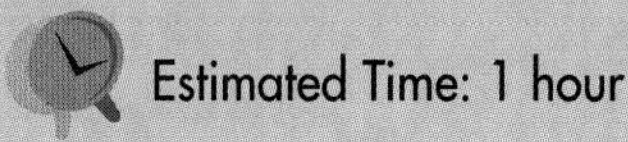

This lesson introduces four advanced Excel features that provide additional methods of computation and elementary database management: database functions, data tables, subtotals, and pivot tables.

Another advanced feature in this lesson teaches you how to convert a worksheet to HTML format so it can be read on the World Wide Web. Finally, you learn how to apply 3-D effects, so you can add depth to graphic elements in your worksheet.

Using Database Functions

You use database functions to perform calculations on the values in a specific field of a database. You can calculate the value for all records or just for records that meet specified criteria. All Excel database functions use the same format: FUNCTION(database,field,criteria)

The first argument, (database), refers to the database range. You can enter it as a cell range or as a name assigned to the database range.

The second argument, (field), is the field used in the calculation. You can enter the field name enclosed in quotation marks or the field's column number in the database. The first column in the database (starting at the left) is numbered 1, the second column is numbered 2, and so forth.

The third argument, (criteria), is the cell range that contains the criteria for the records to be included in the calculation. You can enter it by either cell address or range name.

TIP: It's good practice to assign range names to the database and criteria range when you work with database functions. You can then use the names in the function instead of the cell ranges.

TABLE 21-1 Database Functions

FUNCTION	RESULT
DAVERAGE()	Averages the numbers in a field.
DCOUNT()	Returns a count of the numbers in a field.
DCOUNTA()	Counts the nonblank cells in a field.
DMAX()	Returns the largest number in the field.
DMIN()	Returns the smallest number in the field.
DSUM()	Adds the numbers in the field.
DGET()	Returns a single record in a field.

EXERCISE 21-1 Produce Statistical Data Using Database Functions

1. Open the file **Property.xls**.
2. Select the Name Box on the Formula Bar and key **A5:I29**. The database is highlighted.
3. In the Name Box, key **Homes** to name the database. Click any cell to deselect the range.

4. Insert a new worksheet, position it after the Property worksheet, and name the new worksheet tab **Statistics**.
5. In cell A1 on the Statistics sheet, key **Statistics for Properties over 10 Years Old**
6. In cell A4, key **AGE**
7. In cell A5, key **>10**. The criteria specify homes over the age of 10.
8. Select cells A4 through A5 and name the range **AGE_10**
9. Select cell C6 and key **Average Price**. Widen column C to accommodate the entry.
10. In cell D6, key the following formula to calculate the average price of homes that meet the search criteria:
    =DAVERAGE(Homes,"PRICE",AGE_10)
    Excel calculates the average price of homes over 10 years old. Format cells D6 through D8 in comma style with no decimal places. Widen the column if necessary.
11. In cell C7, key **Highest Price**. Select D7 and key **=DMAX(HOMES,7, AGE_10)**. Notice that the field argument here is 7, which is the "Price" field. You can use either the field name in quotes (as in step 10) or the column number.
12. In cell C8, key **Lowest Price**. Select cell D8 and key **=DMIN(HOMES,"PRICE",AGE_10)**
13. In cell C9, key **Number of Homes**. Select cell D9 and key **=DCOUNT(HOMES,"PRICE",AGE_10)**
14. Select cell A5 and key **>5**. The database functions now show statistics for homes over five years old.
15. Key **>10** in cell A5. Format numbers and labels attractively and widen columns as necessary.
16. Add the standard header and a centered, tab name footer to both worksheets and horizontally center both worksheets.
17. Save the workbook as *[your initials]***21-1.xls** and print the Statistics worksheet.

Working with Data Tables

Data tables are useful for "what if" analyses. They illustrate how different values in a formula affect its results.

Excel offers two types of data tables. A *one-variable data table* calculates a formula containing one variable. A *two-variable data table* calculates a formula containing two variables.

EXERCISE 21-2 Create a Data Table with One Variable

When you create a one-variable data table, you must first designate a worksheet cell to be the input cell. An *input cell* is a cell referenced in the data table formula and varied to calculate the data table results. It can be any cell outside the table range. It is best if the cell is left blank. The data table is constructed so the input values are entered into consecutive cells of one column or one row.

One application of the data table might be to show the monthly payments on a loan with interest rates varying one-half percent above and below the current rate. The term is 15 years on a loan of $95,000.

1. Insert a new worksheet, position it after the Statistics sheet, and name the new worksheet tab **Mort. Payments**.
2. Key **Comparison Payments on Property Located at 203 Narrow Ave.** in cell A1.
3. Key the following percentages in cells B5 through B11:

   6.5%
   7.0%
   7.5%
   8.0%
   8.5%
   9.0%
   9.5%

   These percentages are the variables that the data table will use to calculate different monthly payments. They must be entered in consecutive cells.

TIP: These percentages form a series that is incremented by .5%. Use Edit, Fill, Series to create the percentages automatically. Or, key the first two percentages, select them, and use AutoFill and drag to cell B11.

4. In cell C4, key the following formula: **=PMT(A2/12,15*12,95000)**. It calculates the amount $527.78, which is shown in red. This result represents money going out of your pocket. Cell A2 is the blank input cell used by the formula to indicate the different interest rates.

NOTE: Notice that the formula is located one column to the right of the variables and one row up from the first variable. This setup is required for the one-variable data table.

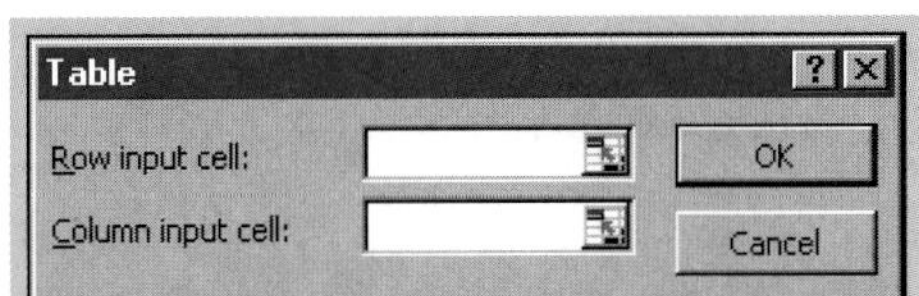

FIGURE 21-1
Table dialog box

5. Select cells B4 through C11 (the data table range) and choose Table from the Data menu. The Table dialog box appears.
6. In the Column input cell text box, key **A2** as your input cell and click OK. The formula located in cell C4 referenced the blank cell A2 for the interest rate variable. The monthly payments are calculated to the right of the corresponding interest rate. This method provides a quick way to compare different interest rates on the monthly payment amount.

TIP: You don't need to see the result of the formula in cell C4. To hide this result, you can change the font color to white. The cell still contains the formula, but the calculation isn't seen.

7. Format cells C5 through C11 in the same way as cell C4. Format the percentage values for one decimal place.
8. Add the standard header and a centered, tab name footer to the worksheet and horizontally center it.
9. Save the workbook as *[your initials]***21-2.xls** and print the Mort. Payments worksheet.

EXERCISE 21-3 Create a Data Table with Multiple Formulas

A data table can include more than one formula, as long as all formulas refer to the same input cell and are placed on the same row.

1. Display the Mort. Payment worksheet.
2. Select cell D4 and key **=PMT(A2/12,30*12,95000)**. The PMT function calculates the amount $263.89.
3. Select the data table range B4:D11.
4. Choose Data, Table from the menu. Key **A2** in the Column input cell text box in the Table dialog box and click OK. The mortgage amounts for a 30-year loan are calculated, along with the 15-year rates.
5. Format the data in column D in currency style using parentheses for negative values. Add column headings identifying the 15- and 30-year mortgages in cells C3 and D3 and format the title and column headings.
6. Add the standard header and a centered, tab name footer to the worksheet and horizontally center it.

7. Save the workbook as *[your initials]***21-3.xls**.
8. Print the Mort. Payment worksheet.

EXERCISE 21-4 Create a Data Table with Two Variables

You can use two input cells to calculate the result of a formula that depends on two varying input values. To construct a two-variable table, one set of variables must be arranged by row and the other set of variables must be arranged by column. The formula is located at the upper left corner of the table range.

1. Insert a new worksheet, position it after the Mort. Payment sheet, and name the new worksheet tab **Mort. Payments 2**. The worksheet will compare monthly payments using a different set of interest rates and a different set of terms.
2. In cell A1, key **Comparison of Monthly Mortgage Payments for Different Rates and Terms**
3. In cell B5, key **6.5%**, select cells B5 through B11, and use Edit, Fill, Series with a Step value of .5% to enter the following interest rates:

   6.5%
   7.0%
   7.5%
   8.0%
   8.5%
   9.0%
   9.5%
4. Key the following payment periods across row 4 in cells C4 through G4:

   10 15 20 25 30
5. Enter the following formula in cell B4: **=PMT(A2/12,A3*12,95000)**. This formula contains two input cells. Cell A2 is the input cell for the interest rates located in the column. Cell A3 is the input cell for terms located on the row. The formula results in the error message #DIV/0! Hide the result of this formula by formatting the font color as white.
6. Select the data table range B4:G11 and choose Data, Table. Key **A3** in the Row input cell text box. Key **A2** in the Column input cell text box and click OK. Calculations appear for interest rates and term.
7. In cell C3, key **Payment Periods** and center it across the table. Make the title and headings bold and format the values appropriately.
8. Add the standard header and a centered, tab name footer to the worksheet and horizontally center it.

9. Save the workbook as *[your initials]***21-4.xls** and print the Mort. Payment 2 worksheet.

EXERCISE 21-5 Edit, Copy, Move, and Clear Data Tables

1. If necessary, display the Mort. Payment 2 worksheet.
2. Beginning in cell C4, edit the term of years in row 4 to read as follows (notice that the table results are recalculated as the payment term changes):

   12 17 22 27 32

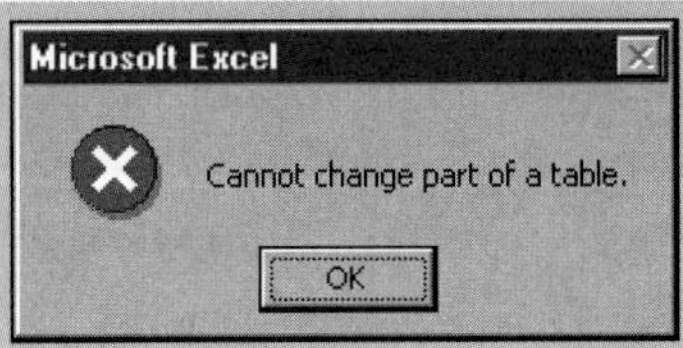

FIGURE 21-2 Cannot Change Part of Table message

3. Select cell E5. Press Delete. A dialog message box appears explaining the table cannot be changed. You cannot remove individual cells in a data table. To remove such cells, you must first clear all cells in the data table that contain the results.
4. Click OK.
5. Clear the results in the table by selecting cells C5 through G11 and pressing Delete.
6. Select cells E4 through G4 and press Delete. Recalculate the results by selecting the new table range B4:D11. Choose Data, Table from the menu. Key **A3** in the Row input cell text box and press Tab. Key **A2** in the Column input cell edit box and click OK. The table is recalculated.
7. To move the table, select cell C8 (or click any result cell). Press F5. Choose Special, select the Current array option, and click OK.
8. Click [Cut], select cell B14, and click [Paste].
9. Return the table to its original location by clicking [Undo]. Press Esc if the cut is still active.

NOTE: You copy using the same steps as moving, but you click [Copy] instead of [Cut]. The copy loses its underlying formulas and only the results are copied. The results do not change if new variables are entered.

10. Reposition the heading in row 3.
11. Save the workbook as *[your initials]***21-5.xls**.
12. Print the Mort. Payment 2 worksheet.

Getting Summary Information with Subtotals

Excel's subtotal function provides an easy way to produce subtotals and grand totals based on any specified group or groups. You don't create formulas with subtotals; Excel creates them automatically when you use this feature or when you use AutoSum [Σ].

To use the subtotal function, data must appear in a list or database using column labels or field names. The data in the list or database then must be sorted by the group to be subtotaled.

EXERCISE 21-6 Sort a Database List and Create Subtotals

1. Activate the Property worksheet by clicking the Property tab.
2. Select cell A6 and choose Data, Sort from the menu. Click the down arrow next to the Sort by text box. In the drop-down list, select BDRMS and then Ascending. Click the down arrow next to the Then by text box. In the drop-down list select BATHS and then Descending. Click OK.
3. Choose Data, Subtotals from the menu. The Subtotal dialog box appears.

FIGURE 21-3 Subtotal dialog box

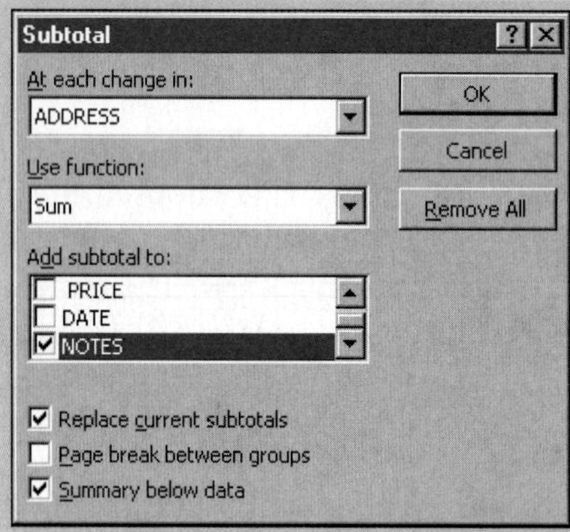

4. Click the down arrow next to the At each change in text box. In the drop-down list, select BDRMS (the group you want to subtotal by).
5. Click the down arrow next to the Use function text box. Select Sum from the drop-down list (the calculation you want to perform).
6. In the Add Subtotal to box, select PRICE (the data you want to calculate). Deselect NOTES.
7. Click OK. Excel inserts subtotal rows at the end of each group and a grand total row at the end of the database, performs the selected calculations, labels each row with appropriate titles, and outlines the data. Outline symbols appear at the far left of the worksheet.
8. Save the workbook as *[your initials]***21-6a.xls** and print the worksheet.

TIP: If you want the groups to print on separate pages, select the Page break between groups check box in the Subtotal dialog box.

9. Remove the subtotals by choosing Data, Subtotal and clicking Remove All. Then sort the database by heat.

10. With cell A6 or any other cell in the database selected, choose Data, Subtotals from the menu. Select HEAT from the At each change in drop-down list.
11. Make sure the Use function text box shows SUM and the Add subtotal to text box has PRICE selected. Click OK. New subtotals are calculated.
12. Choose Data, Subtotals from the menu. Click Remove All to remove all subtotals from the database and sort the database in descending order by bedrooms. If necessary, select BATHS in descending order in the Then by text box.
13. Choose Data, Subtotals from the menu. From the At each change in drop-down list, select BDRMS. Select Average from the Use function drop-down list. Make sure the Add subtotal to box shows PRICE. Click OK.
14. Choose Data, Subtotals from the menu. Make sure the At each change in text box reads BDRMS. Select Max from the Use function drop-down list. Make sure the Add subtotal to box shows PRICE.
15. Deselect Replace current subtotals. Click OK. The database includes subtotals for Average and Max.
16. Choose Data, Subtotals from the menu. Make sure the At each change in text box reads BDRMS. Select Min from the Use function drop-down list. Make sure the Add subtotal to box shows PRICE. Click OK.
17. Save the workbook as *[your initials]***21-6b.xls**.
18. Print the Property worksheet, making sure it fits on one page.

FIGURE 21-4
View of outline based on subtotals

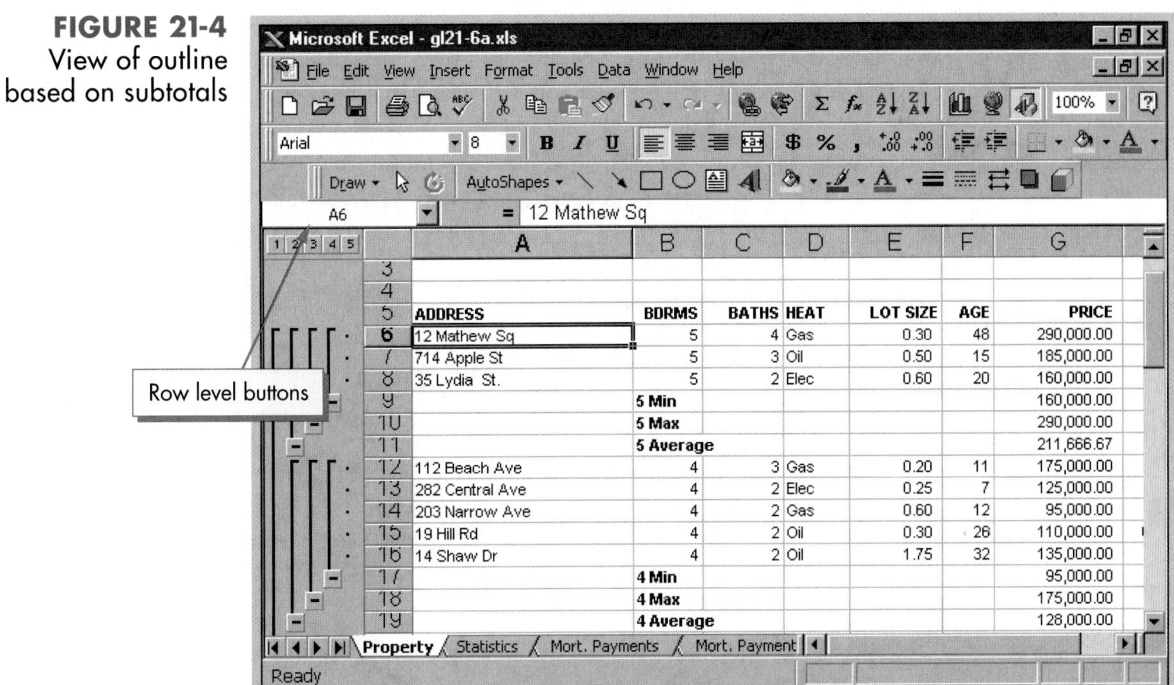

EXERCISE 21-7 Collapse and Expand a Subtotaled Database

Excel creates an outline of different levels based on subtotals you create. You can use the outline area to collapse and expand the data shown in the subtotaled database.

1. Click the row level 1 symbol (the button at the top of the outline that contains number 1). This selection displays grand totals and field names only.
2. Click the Display Detail button [+] in the gray outline area. The database is expanded.
3. Click the row level 2 button. This selection displays the subtotals and grand total only. For each subtotal group, a Display Detail button is created. Click the first Display Detail button under the row level 2 button area to expand only one subtotal area. The button becomes a Hide Detail button [-].
4. Remove all subtotals by clicking Data, Subtotals and Remove All.
5. Save the workbook as *[your initials]***21-7.xls.** Print the Property worksheet.

Using the PivotTable Wizard

In Lessons 19 through 21, you learned how to sort using Data Sort, how to filter using AutoFilter and Advanced Filter, and how to summarize data using subtotals. Pivot tables perform all three options—sorting, filtering, and summarizing—at once. You can use a *pivot table* to arrange the data in your database in different ways by rearranging rows and columns.

EXERCISE 21-8 Create a Pivot Table

1. If necessary, display the Property worksheet. Insert a worksheet and position it after the Property worksheet.
2. Name the new worksheet **Pivot Table**.
3. Choose Tools, Options from the menu and select the View tab. Deselect Gridlines under Window options and click OK. The grids are removed from the worksheet. Select cell A3.
4. Choose Data, PivotTable Report. The first PivotTable Wizard dialog box appears.

5. Click Next. The PivotTable Wizard - Step 2 of 4 dialog box appears. In the Range box, key **Homes**, which is the name of the Property database.

FIGURE 21-5
PivotTable Wizard - Step 2 of 4 dialog box

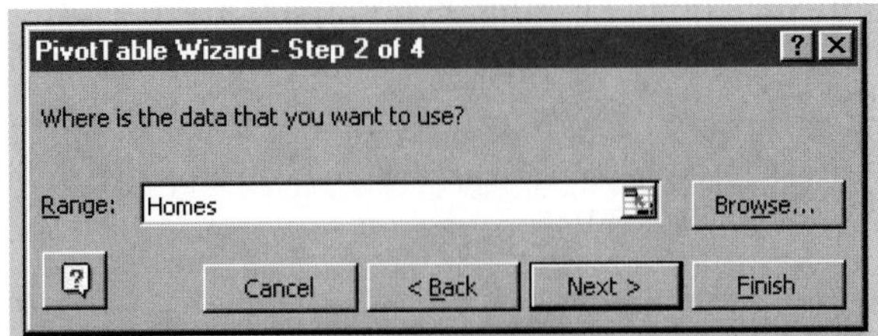

6. Click Next, and the PivotTable Wizard - Step 3 of 4 dialog box appears. Click and drag the field BDRMS to the area labeled ROW. Click and drag the field BATHS to the area labeled COLUMN. Click and drag the field ADDRESS to the area labeled DATA.

FIGURE 21-6
PivotTable Wizard - Step 3 of 4 dialog box

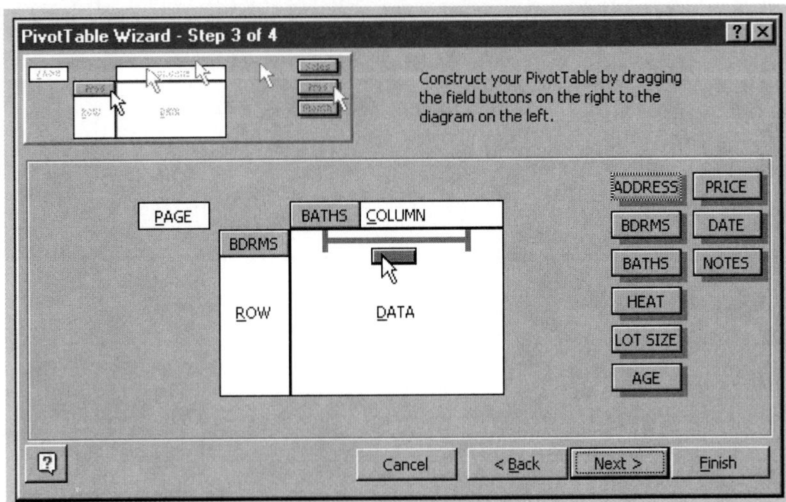

7. Double-click the Count of ADDRESS box located in the DATA area. The PivotTable Field dialog box appears. In the Name text box, change "Count of Address" to read **Count of Homes**.

FIGURE 21-7
PivotTable Field dialog box

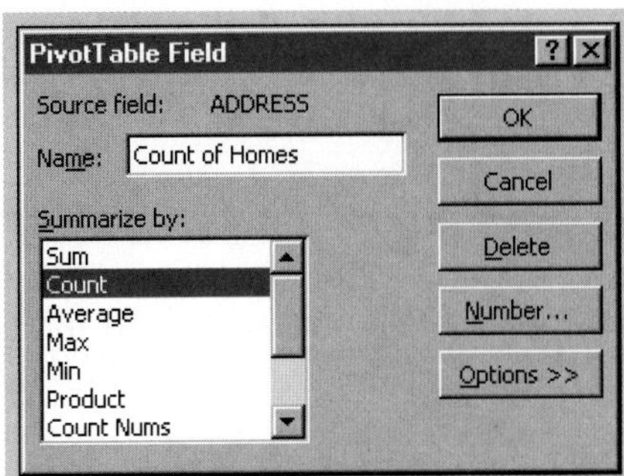

8. Click OK and click Next. The PivotTable Wizard - Step 4 of 4 dialog box appears.

9. Click Finish. The pivot table is created. (A PivotTable toolbar may be overlaid on the pivot table; if so, close the toolbar.) From the table, you can see that Indiana Iron Works owns three properties with one bath and one bedroom. The company owns a total of 24 properties, of which nine are two-bedroom homes.

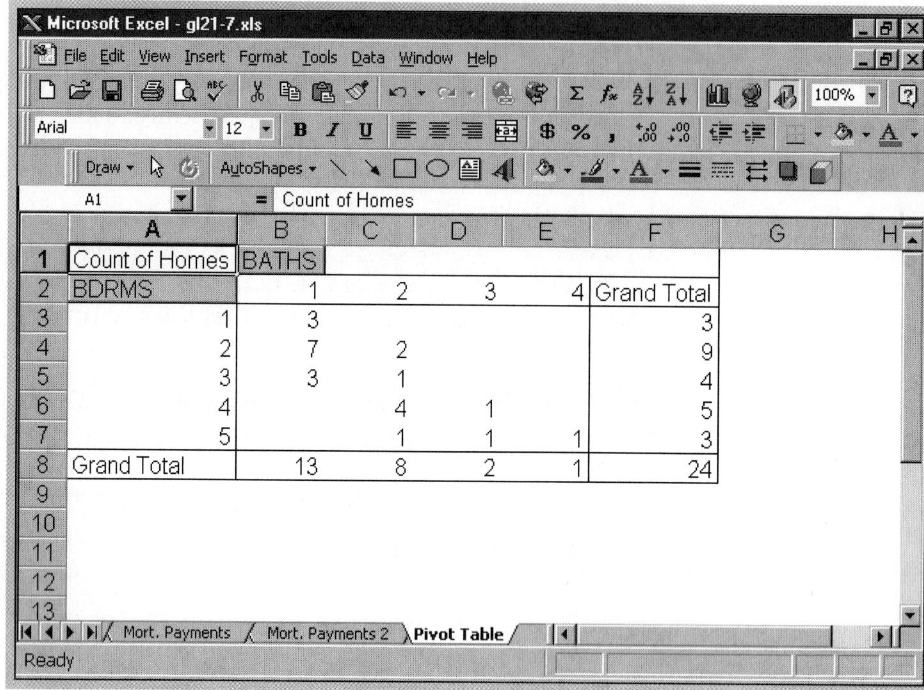

Count of Homes	BATHS				
BDRMS	1	2	3	4	Grand Total
1	3				3
2	7	2			9
3	3	1			4
4		4	1		5
5		1	1	1	3
Grand Total	13	8	2	1	24

FIGURE 21-8 Completed pivot table

10. Add the standard header and a centered, tab name footer to the worksheet and horizontally center it.

11. Save the workbook as *[your initials]***21-8.xls** and print the Pivot Table worksheet.

12. Close the workbook.

Converting a Worksheet to HTML Format

Documents on the World Wide Web are formatted in *Hypertext Markup Language (HTML)*. HTML is a system for tagging a document so it can be published on the Web. You can create your own Web page by converting an existing worksheet to HTML format. You can then share your Web page with others by publishing it on the Web.

EXERCISE 21-9 Convert a Worksheet to HTML Format

To convert a worksheet to HTML format, you use the Internet Assistant Wizard. Before doing this, it's a good idea to enhance the character formatting and increase the text size for easier reading as a Web publication.

1. Open the file **Property.xls**.
2. Delete column H (Date). Delete blank rows 1, 3, and 4.
3. Increase the title text to 18 point. Use  to merge and center the title across cells A1:H1. Change the title font to Arial Black. Change the title color to red.
4. Increase the font size for cells A2:H26 to 12 point. Adjust the column widths as needed and change the column headings to blue.
5. Select the worksheet area (A1:H26) and choose Save as HTML from the File menu. The first dialog box for the Internet Assistant Wizard appears, as shown in Figure 21-9. Check that the correct range appears in the dialog box.

NOTE: If the Save as HTML command is not available on the File menu, you need to install the Internet Assistant component. Ask your instructor for help.

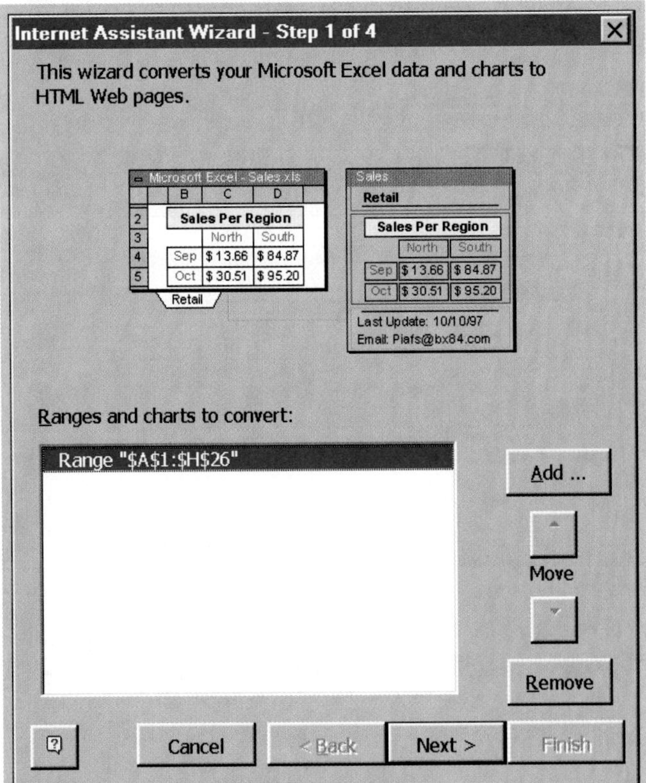

FIGURE 21-9 Internet Assistant Wizard - Step 1 of 4 dialog box

TIP: You can use the Internet Assistant Wizard to save only specific ranges or charts in HTML format. To do this, click the Add button, enter the range, and click OK. To delete a range that appears in the dialog box, use the Remove button.

6. Click Next. In the Step 2 dialog box you can create an independent HTML document from your data or insert your data into an existing HTML document. Make sure the first option is selected and click Next.
7. In the Step 3 dialog box, delete the text in the Title box. Edit the Header text to read **Property Listings**. Add your email address, if you want. Click Next.

FIGURE 21-10
Internet Assistant Wizard - Step 3 of 4 dialog box

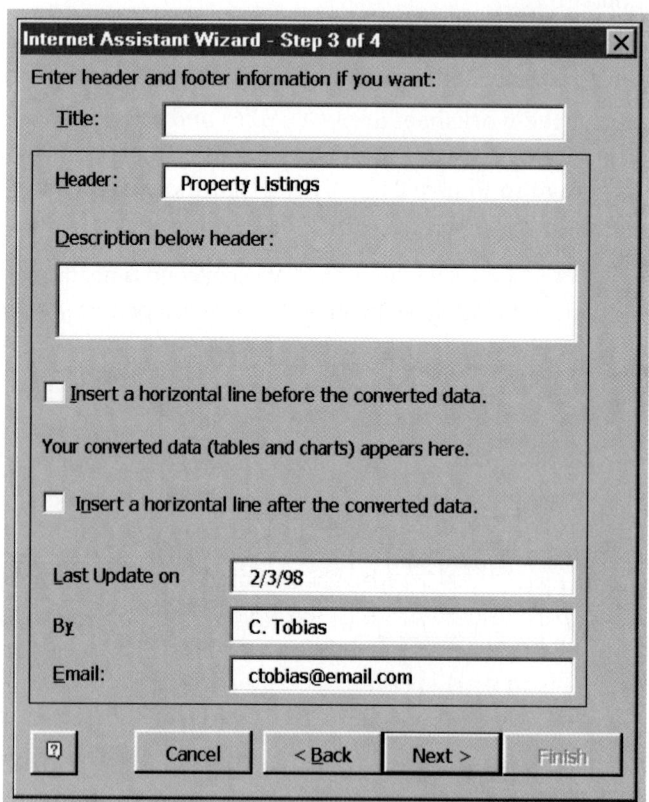

8. In the Step 4 of 4 dialog box (see Figure 21-11 on the next page), make sure the option to save the result as an HTML file is selected. In the File path text box, enter the correct path and the filename *[your initials]* **21-9.htm**. Click Finish.
9. To view the HTML file in Excel, click the Open button. In the Open dialog box, locate the file and click Open. (You can first choose HTML files from the Files of type drop-down list to display only HTML files.)

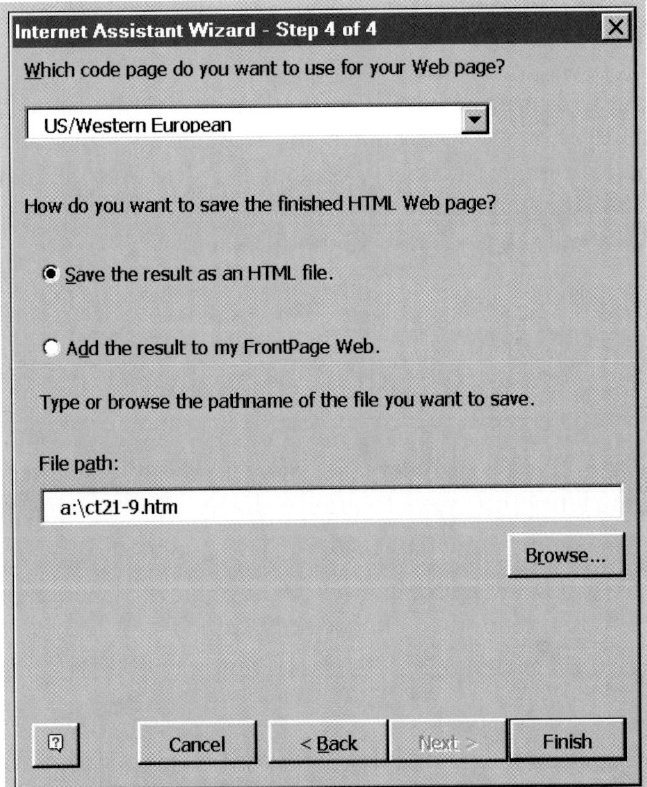

FIGURE 21-11
Internet Assistant Wizard - Step 4 of 4 dialog box

NOTE: If you receive an error message warning that some number formats were lost, click OK to continue.

10. Examine the HTML document, which now can be a Web page. Notice that if you included your email address, it appears at the end of the document and is formatted as a *hyperlink*. You click a hyperlink to link to another location, such as an Internet address or a Web site. A Web user reading this page could click the hyperlink to send you an email message.
11. Print and then close the HTML document. Close **Property.xls** without saving.

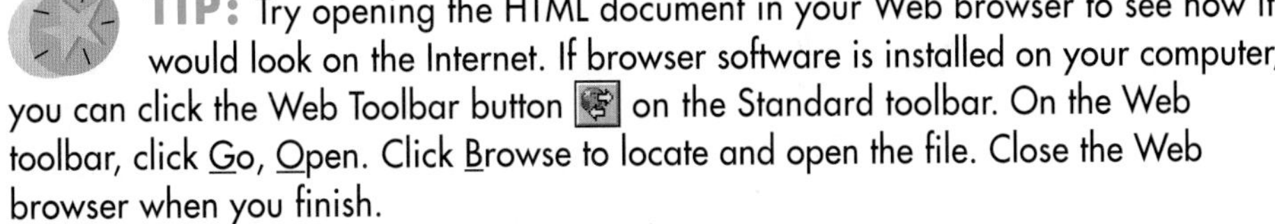

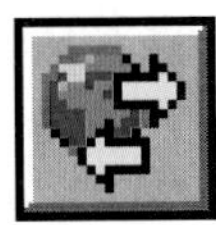

TIP: Try opening the HTML document in your Web browser to see how it would look on the Internet. If browser software is installed on your computer, you can click the Web Toolbar button on the Standard toolbar. On the Web toolbar, click Go, Open. Click Browse to locate and open the file. Close the Web browser when you finish.

Working with 3-D Shapes

Lesson 18 introduced you to the Drawing toolbar and the use of graphic objects to enhance your charts and worksheets. You can also use the Drawing toolbar to insert a variety of shapes called AutoShapes and then apply 3-D effects to add depth to these shapes. Once you create the shapes, Excel provides a full range of tools to modify them.

EXERCISE 21-10 Create and Modify 3-D Shapes

1. Open the file **Property.xls**. Increase the row height for row 1 to one inch. You'll use this space to draw a shape.
2. Display the Drawing toolbar (View, Toolbars, Drawing).
3. On the Drawing toolbar, click AutoShapes. Choose Basic Shapes from the pop-up menu, then choose the Plaque shape.

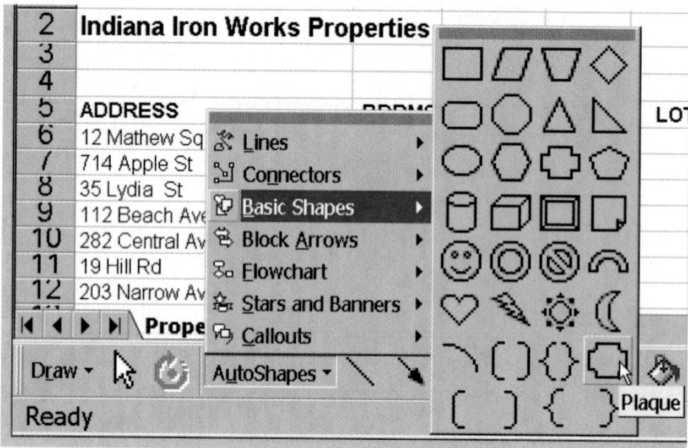

FIGURE 21-12 AutoShapes, Basic Shapes category

4. Using the cross-hair pointer, draw the plaque shape so it is about half the height of row one and as wide as columns B through F. The shape should sit at the bottom of row one.

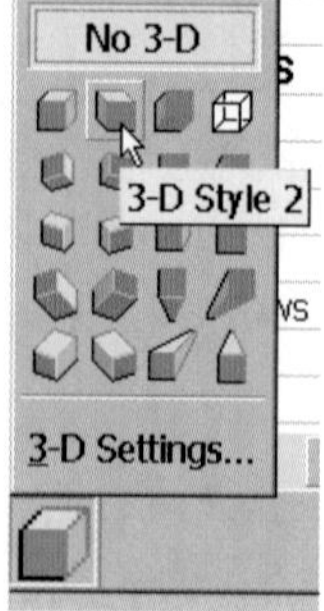

FIGURE 21-13 3-D effects

5. With the shape selected, click the 3-D button on the Drawing toolbar. A pop-up menu offers 20 different 3-D styles. Apply one of the styles to the shape. After experimenting with different styles, apply 3-D Style 2.
6. Click again. At the bottom of the pop-up menu, click 3-D Settings to display the 3-D Settings toolbar. You can use this toolbar to modify the depth, direction, surface, and color of the 3-D effect. (See Figure 21-14 on the next page.)

7. Click the Lighting button and change the effect so it is lit from the top (choose the second effect in the top row).
8. Click the Tilt Up button twice, then click Tilt Down twice. Click Tilt Right twice, then click Tilt Left twice.
9. Click the down arrow on the 3-D Color button and choose Turquoise from the fourth row of the color palette. Explore some of the other options on the 3-D Settings toolbar, and then close the toolbar.

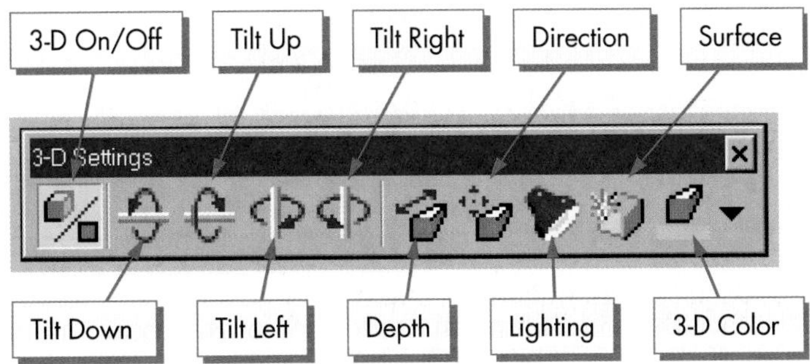

FIGURE 21-14 3-D Settings toolbar

10. Click the object to select it, if necessary. Key the text **Indiana Iron Works Properties**. A text box appears within the object as you key the text.
11. Select the text in the text box and make it bold. Click to center-align the text, then use the selection handles to fit the object size to the text and make the text fit on one line.

NOTE: Remember, you use the double-headed arrow to resize an object and the four-headed arrow to move an object.

FIGURE 21-15 Resized 3-D shape with text

EXERCISE 21-11 Change the Position of a 3-D Shape

In addition to modifying the 3-D effect of an object, there are several ways to alter the object's position on the worksheet. For example, you can rotate the object, align it to gridlines, drag it freely on the worksheet, or move it slightly using the Nudge feature.

1. Click the object to select it, if necessary. Click Draw on the Drawing menu to open the pop-up menu. Point to Rotate or Flip and click Rotate Left from the submenu. This rotates the object 90 degrees to the left. Notice, however, that the text is not rotated. Click [Undo button] or choose Rotate Right from the submenu to restore the object's position.

2. Click the Free Rotate button [Free Rotate button] on the Drawing menu (or choose it from the Rotate or Flip submenu). The selection handles become round rotation handles.

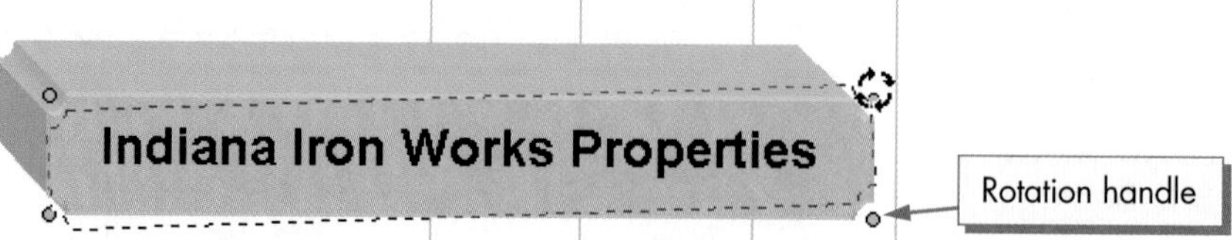

FIGURE 21-16
Rotating the 3-D shape

3. Move the rotation pointer over one of the round handles and drag up or down slightly. Click [Undo button] to restore the object's position. You can use the Free Rotate tool to rotate an object to any desired degree.

NOTE: It's best to rotate objects that do not contain text.

4. Click [Free Rotate button] again or press Esc to turn off the rotate tool.
5. With the object selected, use the four-headed arrow to drag the object freely to the right or left.
6. On the Drawing toolbar, choose Draw, Snap, To Grid. This turns the snap to grid feature on, which allows you to automatically align an object to the worksheet gridlines.
7. Drag the object to the left and then to the right. Notice that the object automatically aligns with the vertical gridlines. Drag the object up and down. The object aligns with the horizontal gridlines.
8. Align the object with the left edge of column A and the bottom of row 1.
9. Choose Draw, Snap, To Grid to turn snap to grid off.

NOTE: You can use the To Shape option on the Snap submenu to align an object with the vertical and horizontal edges of other objects.

10. On the Drawing toolbar, choose Draw, Nudge. Float the Nudge submenu by pointing to its top gray bar and dragging it onto the worksheet. (You can float any Drawing toolbar submenu that has this gray bar.) The Nudge submenu is now an easily accessible toolbar.

FIGURE 21-17
Nudge floating toolbar

11. Click the Nudge Right button several times to move the object by small increments to the right. Click the Nudge Up button several times to place the object slightly above the row gridline.

TIP: You can also use the Arrow buttons on the keyboard to nudge an object into position.

12. Close the Nudge toolbar.

13. Delete rows 2 through 4 and print the worksheet.

14. Save the workbook as *[your initials]***21-11.xls** and close it.

USING HELP

Excel Help offers a wide range of information about Web publishing and browsing.

Use Help to learn more about working with Excel and the Internet:

1. Choose Help, Contents and Index.
2. On the Contents tab, scroll to the topic "Using Microsoft Excel with the Internet, Your Intranet, or a Local Web." Double-click the topic.
3. Display the topic "About Microsoft Excel and the Internet" for an overview.

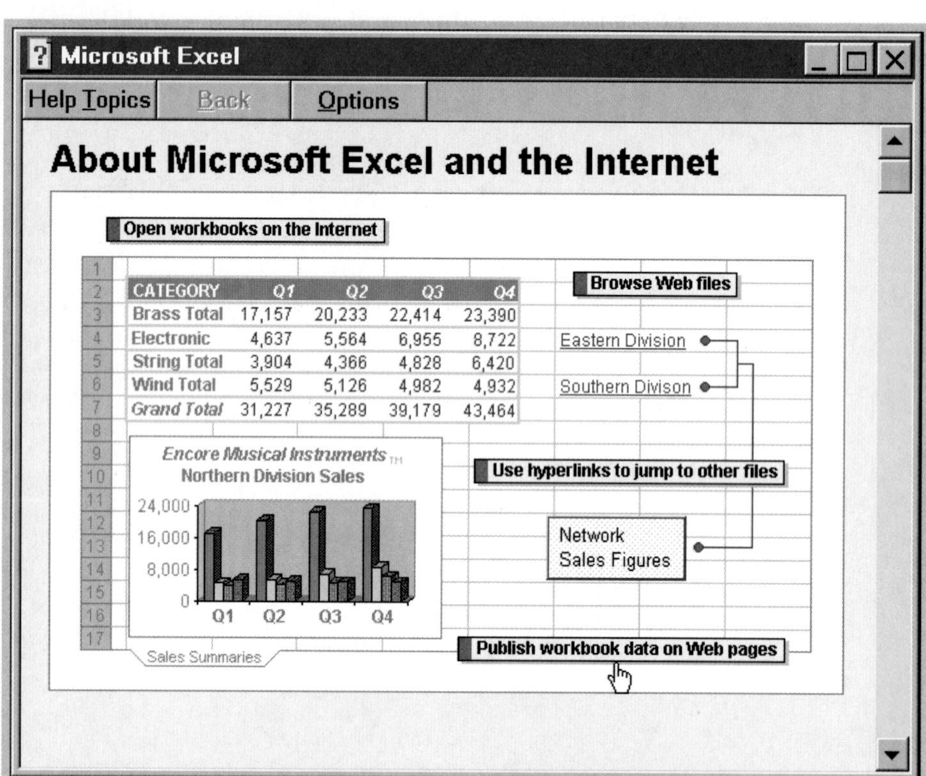

FIGURE 21-18 Help screen "About Microsoft Excel and the Internet"

4. Return to Help Topics, then explore the subtopics under "Working with Hyperlinks," "Working with Files on the Web," and "Navigating and Publishing on the Web."
5. Close Help when you finish browsing.

Concepts Review

TRUE/FALSE QUESTIONS

Each of the following statements is either true or false. Indicate your choice by circling T or F.

T F *1.* All database functions in Excel use the same argument format.

T F *2.* When using data tables, you must have an input cell located within the table range.

T F *3.* Variables used in the data table can be arranged in nonadjacent cells.

T F *4.* A data table can include more than one formula as long as each formula has its own input cell.

T F *5.* When using Excel's subtotals, you must create the formulas.

T F *6.* To create subtotals, the database must be sorted by the group to be subtotaled.

T F *7.* When you create a subtotal, Excel automatically provides an outline that is used to expand and collapse the data.

T F *8.* You can use pivot tables to rearrange the data in a database in different ways by choosing field names located in the database.

SHORT ANSWER QUESTIONS

Write the correct answer in the space provided.

1. Which database function would you use to calculate the average price of one-bedroom homes listed in a database?

____

2. Which database function would you use to calculate the number of homes listed in a database?

____

3. What kind of data table is needed to calculate a payment at varying interest rates and varying terms?

____

4. Where must the formula be positioned when using a one-variable data table?

____

5. Which menu commands do you use to create subtotals?

____

6. Which outline button is used to show grand totals and field names?

____

7. Which toolbar is used to change the color of an object's 3-D effect?

____

8. Which menu commands do you use to convert a worksheet so it can be read on the Web?

____

CRITICAL THINKING

Answer these questions on a separate piece of paper. There are no right or wrong answers. Support your answers with examples from your own experience, if possible.

1. List some examples of types of calculations that would be best performed with a data table. Remember that data tables provide "what if" analysis.
2. Imagine that you maintain an employee database. The database contains fields for years employed, gender, and pay. What types of data could be calculated and compared by using the database functions?

Skills Review

EXERCISE 21-12

Insert a worksheet, create criteria, and calculate basic statistics using database functions.

1. Open the file **Property.xls**.
2. Insert a new worksheet, position it after the Property sheet, and name it **Statistics**.
3. Name the database (cells A5 through I29) on the Property worksheet **HOMES**.

4. Create criteria on the Statistics worksheet to provide statistics on homes with five bedrooms by following these steps:
   a. In cell A3, key **BDRMS**
   b. In cell A4, key **5**
5. Name the criteria (cells A3 through A4) **FIVE** .
6. Calculate Statistical data for five-bedroom homes by following these steps:
   a. Key **Average Price** in cell C5. In cell D5, key the formula **=DAVERAGE(HOMES,"Price",FIVE)**
   b. Key **Highest Price** in cell C6. In cell D6, key the formula **=DMAX(HOMES,"Price",FIVE)**
   c. Key **Lowest Price** in cell C7. In cell D7, key the formula **=DMIN(HOMES,"Price",FIVE)**
   d. Key **Number of Homes** in cell C8. In cell D8, key the formula **=DCOUNT(HOMES,"Price",FIVE)**
7. Widen column C and format the cell range D5:D7 in currency style with no decimal places. Widen column D if necessary.
8. Key **Price Statistics for Five-Bedroom Homes** in cell A1 and make it bold.
9. Add the standard header to the worksheet and horizontally center the worksheet on the page.
10. Save the workbook as *[your initials]***21-12.xls** and print the Statistics worksheet.
11. Create a formula printout of the Statistics worksheet in landscape orientation with grids and row and column headings. Adjust the column width so that the printout fits on one page.
12. Close the workbook without saving.

EXERCISE 21-13

Create a one-variable data table.

1. Open the file **Property.xls**.
2. Insert a new worksheet, position it after the Property worksheet, and name it **Data Table**.
3. In cell A1 of the Data Table worksheet, key **Commission Comparison Table on a Sale of $125,000** and make it bold.
4. In cells B5:B9, key the following percentages:

   3%
   4%

5%
6%
7%

5. In cell C4, key the formula **=ROUND(125000*A2,2)**

NOTE: This formula calculates the commission on $125,000, rounding it to two decimals, and using the cell A2 for the commission percentage variables.

6. Select the table range B4:C9.
7. Perform the table calculations by following these steps:
   a. Choose Data, Table from the menu.
   b. Key **A2** in the Column input cell text box in the Table dialog box. Click OK.
8. Hide the "0" in cell C4 by changing the text font color from black to white. Format the numbers in column C in currency style with no decimal places. Widen the column if necessary.
9. Add the standard header to the worksheet and horizontally center the worksheet on the page
10. Save the workbook as *[your initials]***21-13.xls** and print the Data Table worksheet.
11. Change the text font color of cell C4 from white to black. Create a formula printout of the Data Table worksheet with grids and row and column headings. Adjust the column widths so that the printout fits on one page.
12. Close the workbook without saving.

EXERCISE 21-14

Create subtotals, collapse data to show grand totals, expand data to show subtotals, and create a 3-D shape.

1. Open the file **Property.xls**.
2. Sort the database in ascending order by type of heat.
3. Create subtotals showing the average price of a home based on type of heat by following these steps:
   a. Choose Data, Subtotals from the menu.
   b. Select Heat from the At each change in drop-down list.
   c. Select Average from the Use function drop-down list.

   d. Select Price from the Add subtotal to list. Deselect all other items, if necessary, and click OK.

4. Add the standard header to the worksheet and horizontally center the worksheet on the page.
5. Save the workbook as *[your initials]***21-14a.xls** and print the worksheet.
6. Collapse to show only the grand total average by clicking the row level 1 symbol.
7. Save the workbook as *[your initials]***21-14b.xls** and print the grand total average.
8. Expand to show the subtotals by clicking the row level 2 symbol.
9. Below the data, create and modify a 3-D shape by following these steps:
   a. From the Drawing toolbar, click AutoShapes, Basic Shapes, and choose the Sun shape from the sixth row.
   b. Using the cross-hair pointer, draw the shape approximately 12 rows high.
   c. Click the 3-D button and choose 3-D Style 12 from the third row.
   d. Click the 3-D button again and click 3-D Settings to display the 3-D Settings toolbar.
   e. Click the Tilt Right button to tilt the object slightly to the right. Close the 3-D Settings toolbar.
10. With the object selected, key the text **Solar home prices are the highest**. Drag to select the object text and change it to 8-point bold italic. Resize the object to fit the text.
11. Drag the object to move it below the column headings "ADDRESS" and "BDRMS."
12. Save the workbook as *[your initials]***21-14c.xls**, print it, and close it.

EXERCISE 21-15

Create a pivot table.

1. Open the file **Property.xls**.
2. Name the database (cells A5 through I29) on the Property worksheet **HOMES**.
3. Insert a new worksheet, position it after the Property worksheet, and name it **Pivot Table**.
4. Make the grids on the Pivot Table sheet invisible using Tools, Options, View.
5. Select cell A3 and create the pivot table by following these steps:

a. Choose Data, PivotTable Report from the menu.

b. In the PivotTable - Step 1 of 4 dialog box, click Next.

c. In the PivotTable - Step 2 of 4 dialog box, key **Homes** in the Range text box and click Next.

d. In the PivotTable - Step 3 of 4 dialog box, drag the field HEAT to the ROW area, drag the field BDRMS to the COLUMN area, and drag PRICE to the DATA area.

e. Double-click the Sum of Price box. Change "Sum of Price" to read **Total Value of Property**. Click OK and click Next.

f. In the PivotTable - Step 4 of 4 dialog box, click Finish.

6. Close the PivotTable toolbar, if necessary.
7. Center the data in columns B through G.
8. Format all price amounts in comma style with no decimal places.
9. Add the standard header, change the page orientation to landscape, and center the worksheet on the page.
10. Save the workbook as *[your initials]***21-15.xls**.
11. Print the Data Table worksheet and close the workbook.

Lesson Applications

EXERCISE 21-16

Name a database, create and name criteria, and calculate basic statistics.

Indiana Iron Works wants to extract some statistics from its database on its New York customers. The company wants to know the number of customers, and the highest, lowest, and average balances among amounts currently due.

1. Open the file **IndCust.xls**.
2. Name the database.
3. Insert a new worksheet, position it after the Customer List sheet, and name it **Statistics**.
4. Create and name criteria for those customers living in the state of New York.
5. Calculate the following statistics for New York customers: average balance owed, highest balance owed, lowest balance owed, and total number of customers.
6. Add an appropriate title and format the numbers.
7. Add the standard header to the worksheet.
8. Save the workbook as *[your initials]***21-16.xls** and print the Statistics worksheet.
9. Close the workbook.

EXERCISE 21-17

Create a one-variable data table.

Indiana Iron Works offers discounts to its customers. The discount rate ranges from a high of 6% to a low of 2%. Create a table that shows the amount owed after the discount is applied using the average balance due of $1,208.54. Use an increment of 1% for the discount rates.

1. Open the file **IndCust.xls**.
2. Insert a new worksheet, position it after the Customer List worksheet, and name it **Data Table**.
3. In cell C5, key a formula that computes the amount due after the discount, using a balance of $1,208.54 as a constant.

NOTE: Remember that a blank input cell is used in the formula as the variable for the discount rate.

4. Beginning in cell B6, set up the percentage variables to be used by the formula to compute the discounts in the table. Use Data, Table to create the table.
5. Hide the formula.
6. Provide appropriate titles for the table, widen columns if necessary, and format numbers.
7. Add the standard header to the worksheet.
8. Save the workbook as *[your initials]***21-17.xls** and print the Data Table worksheet.
9. Redisplay the hidden formula in cell C5 and create a formula printout with grids and row and column headings.
10. Close the workbook without saving.

EXERCISE 21-18

Create a pivot table.

Indiana Iron Works wants to generate a table from its database that shows total amounts due by state and product item.

1. Open the file **Orders.xls**.
2. Insert a worksheet for the pivot table, position it after the Customer List worksheet, and rename it **Pivot Table**.
3. Create a pivot table that displays the total amount due for each state and for each product item.
4. Format the amounts due in comma style with two decimal places and center the data in the columns. Format the Grand Total row in currency style with two decimal places.
5. Add the standard header to the worksheet and center it on the page.
6. Save the workbook as *[your initials]***21-18.xls**.
7. Print the Pivot Table worksheet and close the workbook.

EXERCISE 21-19

Produce statistics and summary reports, create a 3-D shape, and save a worksheet as an HTML file.

Indiana Iron Works needs a report generated from its Property database showing the price ranges and the number of homes over 20 years of age. The company also wants to see a report generated from the same database showing the properties categorized by heating type, with the highest-priced, lowest-priced, and the number of properties listed in each category. They also want to see how this categorized list would look as a Web page.

1. Create a sketch of the report generated from the database that includes a worksheet title and row labels for statistics on homes more than 20 years old. The row labels should describe the average price, the least expensive home, the most expensive home, and the total number of homes. In the cells adjacent to these labels should be formulas computing these values.
2. Open the file **Property.xls**.
3. Add a new worksheet, name it **Report**, and transfer the report sketch to the Reports worksheet. Format the titles, labels, and values attractively.
4. On the Report worksheet, draw a Left Arrow AutoShape from the Block Arrows category. The arrow should be pointing to the "Most Expensive" figure. Apply a 3-D style and then modify the shape using the 3-D Settings toolbar and the Drawing toolbar (for example, change the color of the 3-D effect and apply a fill color or texture to the shape).
5. In the Property worksheet, produce a summary report by type of heat showing the highest cost, lowest cost, and number of homes. Change the formatting where necessary.
6. Add the standard header and a centered, tab footer to both worksheets, and center them on the page.
7. Save the workbook as *[your initials]***21-19.xls** and print the entire workbook.
8. Create a formula printout in landscape orientation of the Report worksheet with grids and row and column headings. Adjust the column widths so that the printout fits on one page.
9. In the Property worksheet, increase the font size to 12 point, adjust the column widths, and then save only the range A2:G44 as the HTML file *[your initials]***21-19.htm**. Include an email address in the file, if desired. View the file in Excel or in your browser and print it. Close the HTML file.
10. Close the workbook without saving.

Unit 7 Applications

APPLICATION 7-1

Number records in a database, sort the database, and add a record using the data form.

Indiana Iron Works maintains an employee list. The Personnel Department converted the employees' salaried pay to an hourly rate as requested by the company president, Dexter Peabody. He requested reports from Personnel concerning the employee database. The information gathered will be used to assess the company's overall profitability.

1. Open the file **IndEmpl.xls**.
2. In column I of the database, create a field called "Record #." Number each record of the database. Format the heading to match and adjust the named range "Database."
3. Sort the list by male and female gender, and within the male and female classification by number of years employed using the ascending sort order.
4. Add the standard header to the worksheet and horizontally center the worksheet on the page.
5. Add an appropriate subtitle and center both the title and subtitle across the worksheet columns.
6. Save the workbook as *[your initials]***u7-1a.xls** and print the worksheet.
7. Using the data form, add the following employee record to the database:

   Jones Donna F 244-88-1228 Designer 1 1 $19.99 26
8. Re-sort the list using the same sort categories.
9. Save the workbook as *[your initials]***u7-1b.xls**.
10. Print the new report and close the workbook.

APPLICATION 7-2

Filter the database using AutoFilter.

The management of Indiana Iron Works needs several reports generated from its employee list. Managers want to see separate reports of male and female employees who have worked for the company over 10 years. They also need a report on the top five pay rates for employees.

1. Open the file **IndEmpl.xls**.
2. Using AutoFilter, produce a list of female employees who have worked for the company for more than 10 years. Sort by years employed using ascending sort order and add an appropriate subtitle.
3. Add the standard header to the worksheet and center it horizontally on the page.
4. Save the workbook as *[your initials]***u7-2a.xls** and print the worksheet.
5. Using AutoFilter, produce a list of male employees who have worked for the company for more than 10 years. Sort by years employed using ascending sort order and add an appropriate subtitle.
6. Save the workbook as *[your initials]***u7-2b.xls** and print the worksheet.
7. Produce a report showing the top five pay rates for employees.
8. Add an appropriate title to the report.
9. Save the workbook as *[your initials]***u7-2c.xls** and print the worksheet.
10. Close the workbook.

APPLICATION 7-3

Filter the database using Advanced Filter and multiple selection criteria, and copy the data to another location.

Using the employee list, managers of Indiana Iron Works want a report showing all designers and all engineers, as well as a report showing all clerks and secretaries earning more than $5.50 per hour.

1. Open the file **IndEmpl.xls**.
2. Insert a new worksheet, position it after the Database worksheet, and name it **Criteria**. Set up all criteria on the Criteria worksheet.
3. Using Advanced Filter, produce a report listing all designers using the option to copy the filter results to another location. Create the criteria used starting in cell A3 on the criteria sheet. Have the results copied to the bottom of the Database worksheet, beginning in cell A30.
4. Cut and paste the results to the Criteria worksheet, placing them under the criteria beginning in cell A10.

5. Produce a report listing all Engineers. Create the criteria used starting in cell D3 on the criteria sheet. Have the results copied to the bottom of the Database worksheet and cut and paste them to the Criteria worksheet, beginning in cell A16.

6. Filter the Database worksheet to list all clerks and secretaries whose pay exceeds $5.50 per hour. (*Hint:* Use the wildcard character ? to filter both Clerk 1 and Clerk 2.) Create the criteria used starting in cell F3 on the criteria sheet. You do not need to copy the results to another location for this filter.

7. Add the standard header to both worksheets and add centered, tab name footers to both worksheets. Center the worksheets horizontally on the page and adjust the column widths.

8. Save the workbook as *[your initials]***u7-3.xls**.

9. Print the entire workbook and close it.

APPLICATION 7-4

Create statistics with database functions and generate a summary report showing various database subtotals.

Indiana Iron Works needs some statistical information from the employee database concerning gender and pay. Specifically, managers want statistics for the number of female and male employees and their highest, lowest, and average pay. They also want a report generated from the database that summarizes the total pay, average pay, highest pay, and lowest pay by employee class.

1. Open the file **IndEmpl.xls**.

2. Insert a new worksheet, position it after the Database worksheet, and name it **Statistics**.

3. On the Statistics worksheet, use the top right area of the worksheet to set up the criteria. Use database functions to calculate the following statistics for all female employees: average pay, highest pay, lowest pay, and number of female employees. Format, label, and widen the columns appropriately.

4. On the same sheet, calculate the same statistics for men.

5. On the Database worksheet, produce a report that summarizes the total pay, average pay, highest pay, and lowest pay by class.

6. Add the standard header to both worksheets. Add a tab name and Page 1 of ? footer to the Database worksheet and a tab name footer to the Statistics worksheet. Center the worksheets horizontally on the page.

7. Save the workbook as *[your initials]***u7-4.xls** and print the entire workbook..

8. Create a formula printout in landscape orientation of the Statistics worksheet with grids and row and column headings. Change the footer to include Page 1 of ?

9. Close the workbook without saving.

APPLICATION 7-5

Create two pivot tables on a single page.

Indiana Iron Works needs two reports generated from its employee database: one showing average pay as a function of class and gender and one showing average years of employment as a function of class and gender. Management wants to see the data in tabular form on a single page.

1. Open the file **IndEmpl.xls**. Insert a new worksheet and rename the tab **Table**. Create a pivot table for the first report on the Table worksheet. The table should show average pay based on class and gender. Turn off the gridlines on the worksheet containing the pivot table. Format the pay in currency style with two decimal places. Align the labels and widen the columns where appropriate.

2. Position the cell pointer below the first table and produce a second pivot table that shows the average years employed based on class and gender.

NOTE: After step 2, the PivotTable Wizard displays a dialog box asking if you want to base your table on the same data as the first table in order to use less memory. Click No.

3. Format the years to show one decimal place. Widen the columns and align the labels appropriately. Add an appropriate title to the worksheet. Add the standard header to the worksheet and horizontally center the worksheet on the page.

4. Save the workbook as *[your initials]***u7-5.xls**. Print the Table worksheet and close the workbook.

Portfolio Builder

List of Files Produced in the Portfolio Builder

Filename	Document
*[Your initials]*Res1.doc	Résumé created using a Word Résumé Template
*[Your initials]*Res2.doc	Résumé created using the Word Résumé Wizard
*[Your initials]*Prospects.doc	List of prospective employers
*[Your initials]*Portfolio.doc	List of documents to include in your Portfolio
*[Your initials]*CvrLtr.doc	Cover letter (From scratch or using Word's Letter Wizard)
*[Your initials]*AppInfo.doc	Information for use in filling out Employment Applications
10-15 additional documents	The documents listed in your Portfolio List.

Optional Documents

Thank you letter

Contact Reference Sheet

Contact Reference Card

Portfolio Builder

OBJECTIVES

By using this Portfolio Builder, you will learn how to:

1. **Build a résumé.**
2. **Identify prospective employers.**
3. **Build a portfolio.**
4. **Target your résumé and portfolio.**
5. **Write a cover letter.**
6. **Fill out an employment application.**
7. **Prepare for a job interview.**
8. **Follow up an interview.**

Finding a job is difficult—especially today in the midst of downsizing. The number of applicants often exceeds the availability of jobs. So you need to distinguish yourself from other people interested in the same job. You need to show a prospective employer what you can do.

This *Portfolio Builder* helps you build a résumé that will tell prospective employers about your work background. It also assists you in building a "representational portfolio"—a collection of your best work that you can show as evidence of your skills. The documents in your portfolio will be geared to specific employers. Finally, the *Portfolio Builder* leads you though the job-search process: including contacting prospective employers, filling out an employment application, and following up after interviews.

FIGURE P-1
The job-search process

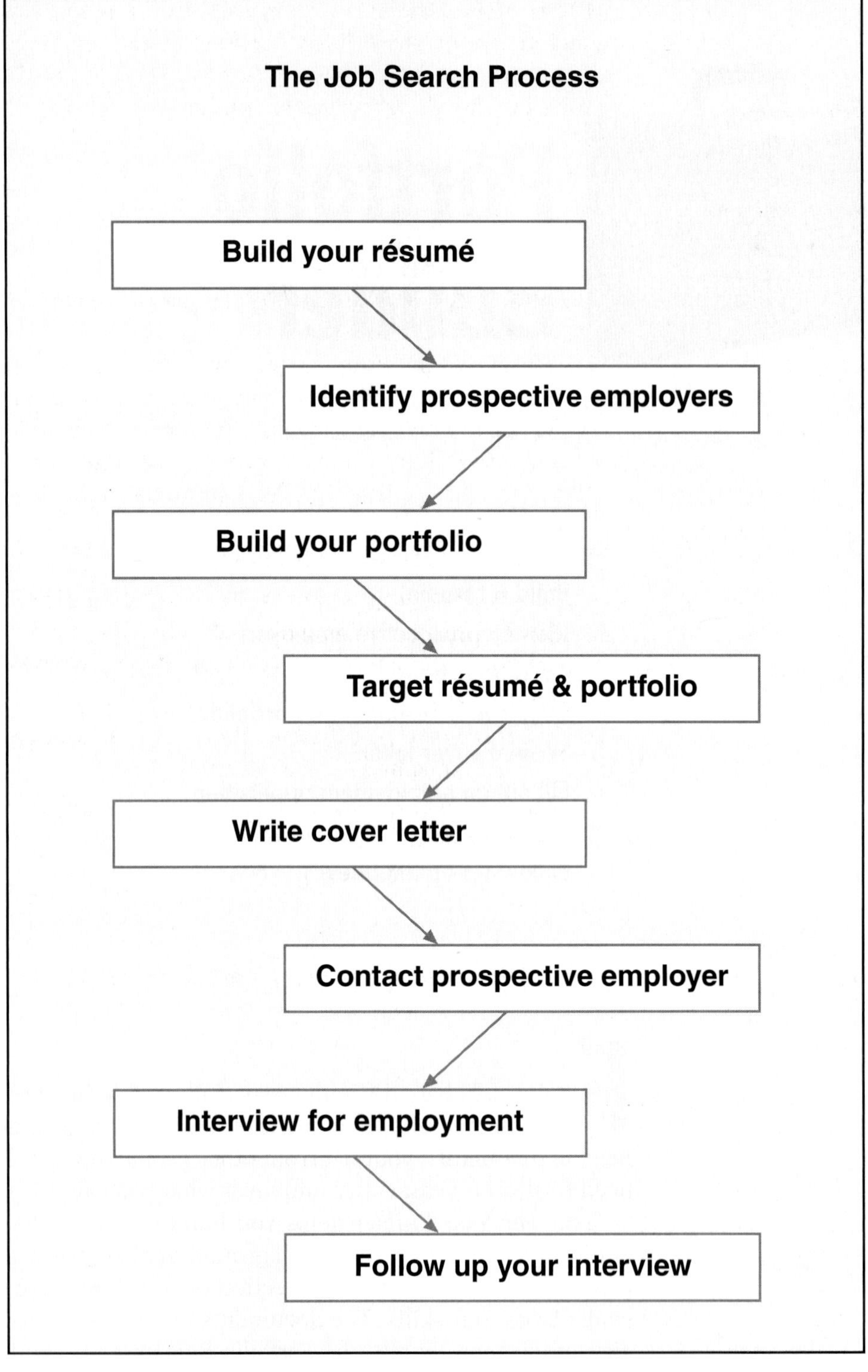

The *Portfolio Builder* will be helpful to you if you're planning to search for immediate employment. It is also a useful final project because it requires you to demonstrate skills you have gained from this course. Even if you're not looking for a job, it will help prepare you for an eventual job search.

Building a Résumé

A résumé is a representation of you on paper. It provides a first impression of you to a potential employer.

Building a résumé is an exercise in self-discovery. To create one, you must review your experience, identify your skills, and focus on a goal. Once you have created a résumé that states your strengths and objectives, you can begin the process of marketing yourself to prospective employers.

Although a good résumé will not guarantee a job, it is a primary tool in the job-search process.

There are three types of résumés:

- The *chronological* résumé is the traditional type of résumé. It lists your work history, starting with your most recent job. It includes a brief description of the position and your accomplishments. This is a "where you've been" type of résumé.
- The *functional* résumé highlights your skills or areas of expertise. It is a "what you can do" type of résumé.
- The *combination* résumé highlights your skill areas *and* lists the jobs you have held.

The following six pages illustrate these three kinds of résumés.

Chronological Résumé Description

Contact Information: Your name, address, and telephone number should appear at the top of the résumé. Spell out your address (do not abbreviate "Street" or "Avenue"). Include your ZIP code. Use a telephone number where you can be reached during the day or where a message can be left. Include other forms of contact, such as an e-mail address or fax number, if available. Don't use your current employer's telephone or fax number.

Job Objective: Your job objective represents the specific field or job title that you are pursuing. If you're targeting a specific job, tailor your objective to that position. Include the job type, the industry, and the geographical area in your objective (example: "Marketing position with a computer software vendor in the Chicago area"). To keep your options open, write a broader objective.

Work Experience: Describe the jobs that you have held, beginning with your most recent position. List the years of employment, company names and locations, and specific job titles. Include current and past jobs, part-time work, self-employment, volunteer work, and internships, as appropriate. The job description should focus on quantified achievements and specific skills.

Education: List the schools and training programs that you have attended. List your most recent education—school, degree or program, and date completed. Omit information about your high school if you have a college degree. Include any additional information, such as continuing education, seminars, or special course work that is related to your objective. This section can appear before **Work Experience** if you're a recent graduate, or if your education or training is your most important qualifying factor.

Additional Information: Your résumé can contain additional information that may be relevant to the job you are pursuing. For example, a section on computer proficiency can be included. You can also include **Activities**, **Professional Organizations**, or **Honors/Awards** as separate sections.

References: References are often not included on a résumé, but are provided separately if requested. Line up your references in advance, and list them on a sheet of paper. Include the name, address, telephone number, and title (if appropriate). You can ask a previous employer for a letter of recommendation, which you can then photocopy.

FIGURE P-2 Chronological résumé*

12 Juniper Drive
Any Town, State 00000
(000) 000-0000
E-mail: dmartin@xxx.xxx

Donald Martin

Objective

Seeking position as microcomputer salesperson in dynamic retail environment.

Work Experience

1996–1998 Electronics Depot Any Town, State

Sales Associate

- Specialized in sales of computer hardware and software in busy retail outlet.
- Selected Salesperson of the Year for Midwest region.
- Established customer training program for computer sales that produced $80,000 in its first year.

1994–1996 Video Time Any Town, State

Assistant Manager

- Managed video-rental store during most heavily-trafficked hours (evenings and weekends). Effectively handled as many as 250 customer contacts per day.
- Trained and supervised five sales assistants.
- Started "Old Time Cinema Club" that boosted sales of backlist videos by 50%.

1993–1994 Fairway Department Store Any Town, State

Sales Assistant

- Assisted customers in busy Electronics Department.
- Handled more than $2,000 per day in cash sales.
- Completed sales training program.

Education

1997 **Fargo Technical College** Any Town, State

- A.A., Microcomputer Systems Technology
- G.P.A. 3.93

Software/Hardware Training

- Proficiency in all Microsoft Office applications and PageMaker on both the PC and Macintosh computer.
- Can perform diagnostics on PCs and peripheral equipment, and can install/upgrade PC components such as network cards, memory chips, disk drives, and modems.

References

Available upon request.

*Created using a modified version of Word's Contemporary résumé style.

Functional Résumé Description

Contact Information: Your name, address, and telephone number should appear at the top of the résumé. Spell out your address (do not abbreviate "Street" or "Avenue"). Include your ZIP code. Use a telephone number where you can be reached during the day or where a message can be left. Include other forms of contact, such as an e-mail address or fax number, if available. Don't use your current employer's telephone or fax number.

Job Objective: Your job objective represents the specific field or job title that you are pursuing. If you're targeting a specific job, tailor your objective to that position. Include the job type, industry, and geographical area in your objective (example: "Marketing position with a computer software vendor in the Chicago area"). To keep your options open, write a broader objective.

Functional Sections: In a functional résumé, these sections provide the bulk of the information about you. Include two to four sections that describe a particular area of expertise or involvement. These areas should be directly related to the position you are pursuing. (In this résumé, the functional sections appear with the headings **Casework**, **Document Drafting**, and **Computer Skills**.) As an alternative to creating job-specific sections, create functional sections with the headings **Qualifications** and **Accomplishments**. Under these headings, list concise action statements that will catch the attention of a prospective employer.

Work Experience: A functional résumé lists your job history by date, company name and location, and title, beginning with the most recent position. Job descriptions are not included, as the résumé focuses on qualifications and skills, not work history.

Education: List the schools and training programs that you have attended. List your most recent education—school, degree or program, and date completed. Omit information about your high school if you have a college degree. Include any additional information, such as continuing education, seminars, or special course work that is related to your objective. This section can appear immediately below your **Objective** if you're a recent graduate, or if your education or training is your most important qualifying factor.

Additional Information: Your résumé can contain additional information that may be relevant to the job you are pursuing. For example, you can include sections with the following headings: **Activities**, **Professional Organizations**, **Honors/Awards**. The heading **References** may be listed at the bottom, followed by the text "Available on request" (see Chronological Résumé for more information).

FIGURE P-3 Functional résumé*

8809 Orange Terrace
Any Town, State 00000
Telephone (000) 000-0000
Fax (000) 000-0000

Lesley Brown

Objective Paralegal position in computer or patent law

Casework

- Researched state and federal computer and patent laws. Wrote briefs for attorneys.
- Prepared preliminary arguments and pleadings in computer law.
- Obtained affidavits.

Document Drafting

- Drafted contracts under the supervision of an attorney.
- Prepared tax returns, incorporations, patent filings, and trust agreements.
- Prepared reports and schematic diagrams.
- Assisted computer law specialists in preparing hardware and software patents, contracts, applications, shareholder agreements, and packaging agreements.

Computer Skills

- Word-processing software (Word for Windows and WordPerfect).
- Advanced use of database software (Access) and spreadsheet software (Excel).
- Researched on-line databases using Internet search engines.

Employment

1995–Present
Collimore & Hapke, Attorneys-at-Law — Any Town, State
Legal Assistant

Education

1998
York State Technical College — Any Town, State
Associate Degree, Paralegal Technology

Activities

Legal Eagles — Public Library
Volunteer coordinator of weekly youth discussion group that teaches basic law principles.

*Created using a modified version of Word's Professional résumé style.

Combination Résumé Description

Contact Information: Your name, address, and telephone number should appear at the top of the résumé. Spell out your address (do not abbreviate "Street" or "Avenue"). Include your ZIP code. Use a telephone number where you can be reached during the day or where a message can be left. Include other forms of contact, such as an e-mail address or fax number, if available. Don't use your current employer's telephone or fax number.

Job Objective: Your job objective represents the specific field or job title that you are pursuing. If you're targeting a specific job, tailor your objective to that position. Include the job type, the industry, and the geographical area in your objective (example: "Marketing position with a computer software vendor in the Chicago area"). To keep your options open, write a broader objective.

Functional Sections: Include two or three sections that describe a particular area of expertise or involvement, or that summarize your qualifications and accomplishments. Use concise statements that are easy to read.

Work Experience: As in the chronological résumé, list and describe the jobs that you have held, beginning with your most recent position. Include the years of employment, the company names and locations, and the specific job titles. You can include current and past jobs, part-time work, self-employment, volunteer work, internships, and so on, as appropriate. The job description should focus on quantified achievements and specific skills. Be careful not to repeat the same information here that you have listed in the Functional Sections.

Education: List the schools and training programs that you have attended. List your most recent education—school, degree or program, and date completed. Omit information about your high school if you have a college degree. Include any additional information that might be relevant, such as continuing education, seminars, or special course work. This section can appear above **Work Experience** if you're a recent graduate, or if your education or training is your most important qualifying factor.

Additional Information: Your résumé can contain additional information that may be relevant to the job you are pursuing. For example, you can include sections with the following headings: **Activities**, **Professional Organizations**, **Honors/Awards**. The heading **References** may be listed at the bottom, followed by the text "Available on request" (see Chronological Résumé for more information).

FIGURE P-4 Combination résumé*

ANNA LUPONE
1002 LOOKOUT POINT
ANY TOWN , STATE 00000
TELEPHONE (000) 000-0000
E-MAIL 00000@AOL.COM

OBJECTIVE

Corporate Word Processing Administrative Assistant

SUMMARY OF QUALIFICATIONS

- ◊ Four years experience in administrative/clerical support positions.
- ◊ Easily establish rapport with managers, staff, and customers.
- ◊ Proficient at analyzing statistics and market trends to develop accurate forecasts and effective sales presentations.
- ◊ Excellent problem-solving, project management, decision-making, and time management skills.
- ◊ Proven ability to prioritize and complete multiple tasks, independently and with little supervision.
- ◊ Bilingual: English/Spanish.

COMPUTER SKILLS

Operating Systems:	DOS and Microsoft Windows 95
Word Processing:	Word for Windows, WordPerfect
Graphics:	PageMaker, PowerPoint
Database and Spreadsheets:	Access, Excel, Lotus 1-2-3
Keyboard Speed:	85 wpm

PROFESSIONAL EXPERIENCE

1994–Present COCA COLA COMPANY Atlanta, Georgia
Administrative Assistant

- ◊ Analyze sales volume and profit.
- ◊ Finalize and package forecasting reports for annual sales of $100 million.
- ◊ Monitor monthly spending and reconciliation for $8 million budget.
- ◊ Manage $200,000 in advertising and promotional materials.

EDUCATION

1998 Blake Business Institute Any Town, State
A. S., Administrative Office Technology

- ◊ Dean's List, 4.0 GPA

REFERENCES

Available on request.

*Created using a modified version of Word's Elegant résumé style.

Choosing a Résumé Format

What type of résumé is right for you? Consider the following:

TABLE P-1 Choosing a Résumé Type

RÉSUMÉ TYPE	PREFERABLE IF:
Chronological	You have a history of steady work that reflects growth, and you are looking for a job in the same field or a related field.
Functional	You are new to the workforce, have gaps in your work history, or are changing careers.
Combination	You have some work history that is worth showcasing *and* want to highlight your marketable skills.

Be aware that the chronological résumé is the most traditional and conservative type of résumé. It is also the easiest to prepare. The functional and combination résumés, which use more innovative approaches, require greater thought, planning, and creativity.

Tips on Résumé Writing

When preparing your résumé, give yourself plenty of time, and keep in mind the following basics:

Content

- Everything in your résumé should support your job objective. Omit anything that doesn't.
- Be clear about what your skills are, both in your own mind and on paper. Your résumé should answer the question, "Why should I hire you?"
- Your résumé should convey the impression that you're focused. It should be targeted to a specific occupation or career field.
- Don't shortchange yourself. Emphasize any accomplishments, awards, and recognition you've received that supports your job objective.
- Mention promotions, raises, and bonuses, if appropriate, to prove your track record.
- Don't misrepresent yourself. Lying or exaggerating can only hurt—not help—you.

- Stress the positive—never include negative information about yourself. Your résumé should reflect what you *can* do, not what you can't.

Writing Style

- Strive for crisp, concise writing. Use short, easy-to-understand sentences.
- Use action words and phrases in your job and skill descriptions. For example, begin each description with words such as "Analyzed," "Administered," "Developed," "Initiated," "Organized," and so on.
- Use buzzwords and terminology that relate to the job you are pursuing.
- Proofread your résumé thoroughly for typographical, grammatical, or punctuation errors.

Appearance

- Your résumé should look professional. It should have an attractive layout, an easy-to-read format, and enough "white space" so that it is not too text-heavy.
- Use a good-quality printer to print your résumé. Avoid sending out photocopies, if possible.
- Limit your résumé to one page, unless you have substantial work experience that is relevant to your current job objective.

Getting Help

- Attend résumé and career workshops offered at your school or in your community.
- Read books about résumé writing to learn how to identify your skills, document your experience, and deal with special problems. Review résumé samples in such books.
- Ask someone whose judgment you trust to read your résumé before you send it out.

Résumé Templates and the Résumé Wizard

Word provides three résumé templates and a Résumé Wizard to help you create a résumé.

NOTE: This Portfolio Builder assumes that you're using Word as your word-processing application. If you aren't, check your word processor for help on preparing résumés.

Before using a résumé template or the Résumé Wizard, check the New dialog box to see if they are available. (The templates may have to be installed separately. Refer to "Installation Checklist" in the Preface.)

NOTE: Use the Résumé Wizard or résumé templates as a basis upon which to build your résumé. Modify the layout and formatting of the résumé to make it unique. Remember, you don't want your résumé to look exactly like everyone else's.

EXERCISE P-1 Use a Résumé Template

The résumé templates allow you to create a chronological résumé based on one of three styles: Elegant, Contemporary, and Professional.

1. Choose New from the File menu, choose the Other Documents tab, and then double-click one of the résumé template icons.

NOTE: To preview the template before choosing it, click the résumé template icon, and then view it in the Preview box.

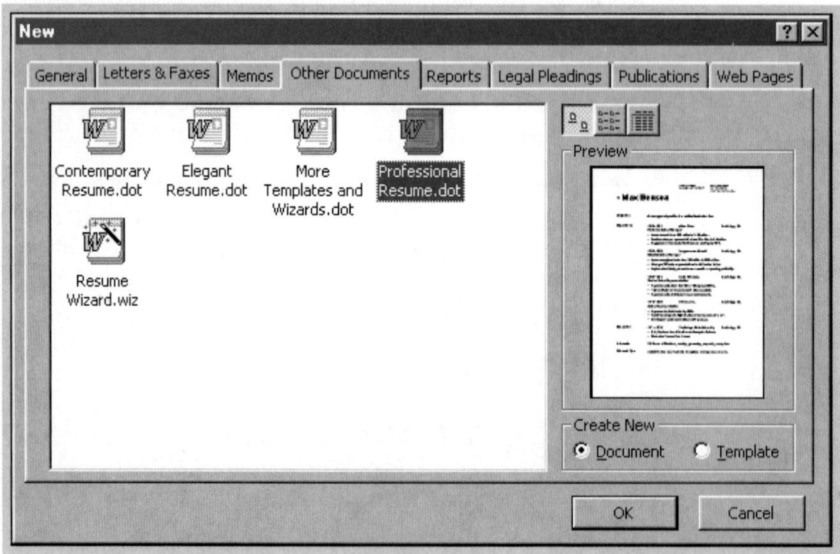

FIGURE P-5 Résumé templates in the New dialog box

2. Replace all of the placeholder text in the document with your own information.
3. Make any formatting modifications. Save the document as *[your initials]***Res1.doc** and print it.

EXERCISE P-2 Use the Résumé Wizard

The Résumé Wizard guides you through the steps needed to create a chronological or functional résumé using one of the three résumé styles.

1. Choose New from the File menu, choose the Other Documents tab, and then double-click the Résumé Wizard icon. Click Next to start.
2. In the next dialog box, choose a résumé style. Click Next to display the next dialog box.

FIGURE P-6
Choosing a résumé style

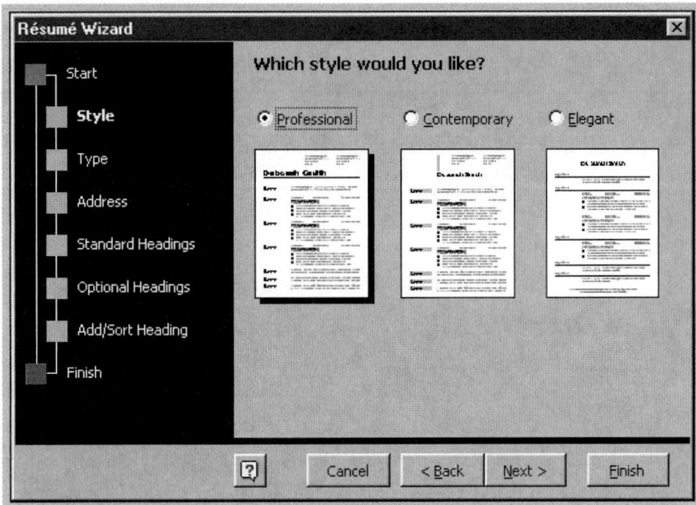

3. Choose the résumé type, and then click Next.
4. Enter your name and mailing address, and then click Next.

FIGURE P-7
Choosing headings for your résumé

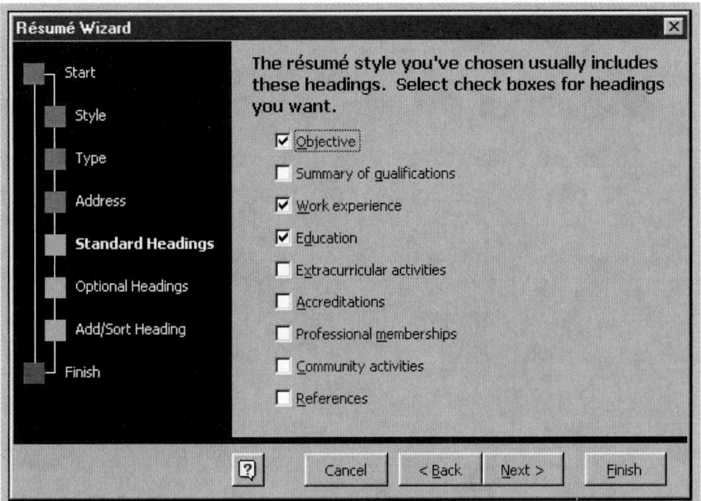

5. Choose the résumé headings you want, and then click Next.
6. Choose any additional headings you desire, and then click Next.
7. Key any additional headings you want to add to the résumé, and then click Next.
8. Reorder any of the résumé headings you've chosen, and then click Next.
9. Click Finish to view the résumé.
10. At the Office Assistant prompt, choose an option or click Cancel.

TIP: You can click the Office Assistant option to create a quick cover letter at this point. The letter will contain sample text for you to replace with your own information. See the section "Writing a Cover Letter" in this Portfolio Builder to learn about cover-letter basics.

11. Replace the placeholder text in the résumé with your own information.
12. Make any modifications. Save the document as *[your initials]***Res2.doc**.

Identifying Prospective Employers

Now that you've prepared a résumé, it's time to think about who will view it. Your next step is to identify the companies in your area—and the people within those companies—who may be hiring people with your skills.

Always try to identify the manager in each company or organization who heads up the division, department, or group in which you hope to work. Avoid applying through a Human Resources staff member, if at all possible. In the Human Resources Department, it's easy to become just another applicant who receives no special attention.

Help Wanted Ads

Help-wanted ads can represent a useful way to research the hiring trends of a local company. Help-wanted ads are, however, less useful as a source of real employment opportunities. They should never be used as the primary focus of your job search. In fact, some experts believe that only 10 percent of all available jobs are listed in the newspaper.

Use the back issues of your local newspapers to find out whether a company has been hiring recently, what kinds of jobs have recently been advertised, and if a particular contact person was listed in the ad.

Networking

Talk to people who are in a position to provide information about job leads and the hiring process at particular companies. They can be friends, relatives, acquaintances—anyone who can put you in touch with a job contact. Try to identify the people within a company who have the power to hire you. Get the correct spelling of each person's name, official correct job title, department, company, and, if possible, a telephone number.

Company Research

An easy way to begin your company research is with the *Yellow Pages*. Use it to locate businesses in the field in which you're interested. (You may need to use the "Business-to-Business" section for some types of businesses.)

The business section of your local library contains reference books that can give you even more information about local companies. Some of the best sources are:

- *Standard & Poor's Register of Corporations, Directors, and Executives.* McGraw-Hill. (Volume 2 lists companies by location.)
- *The National Directory of Addresses and Phone Numbers.* Gale Research, Inc.
- *Million Dollar Directory*. Dun & Bradstreet.
- *Job Seeker's Guide to Private and Public Companies*. Gale Research, Inc.
- *Job Opportunities for Business and Liberal Arts Graduates*. Peterson's Guides, Inc.
- *Job Opportunities for Engineering, Science, and Computer Graduates.* Peterson's Guides, Inc.

Some of these sources are also available in easy-to-use software versions that allow you to search for particular companies based on specific criteria. Your local librarian can often provide help in locating information about specific companies as well.

Using the Internet

Many sources of company and career information are available on the Internet. Many companies operate their own Web site or home page, and some even list their job openings there. If a prospective employer is a large company, search the Internet based on the company's name. Often, promotional materials from the company (and available in a local public library) will indicate its Internet or Web site address.

Microsoft Network, America Online, CompuServe, and Prodigy offer many career-oriented services as well. Search for such general keywords as "career," "employment," or "job." A targeted search using more specific keywords may produce results that prove more immediately useful to your job search.

You can also use your Internet browser to search for locations with a appropriate keywords. For example, one recent search showed 600,000 matches for the keyword "career." Obviously, the more targeted your search of the Internet, the more useful it may be.

Specialized employment search engines on the Internet may prove useful. Because these services list jobs from across the nation (and around the world), they may be less useful for a local job search. A list of places to look for jobs on the Internet follows (remember that Internet options change rapidly, so this list may need to be updated and new options may be available):

- E-Span Employment Database
  Search by keyword and company name.
  http://www.espan.com
- On-Line Career Center
  Search by keyword.
  http://www.occ.com
- The Monster Board
  Search by location and job discipline.
  http://www.monster.com
- CareerPath
  Searches classified ads in U.S. newspapers by category.
  http://www.careeerpath.com

EXERCISE P-3 Identify Prospective Employers

1. Identify at least five prospective employers. They may be located anywhere, but should represent the type of company for which you could imagine working.
2. For each prospective employer, obtain the name of a job contact. (This person would typically be a manager of the department, division, or group in which you would like to work.)
3. Key the list of prospective employers in a document. Include the contact's name, department, company name, address, city, state, ZIP code, telephone number, and fax number. Save the document as *[your initials]***Prospects.doc** and then print it. You'll use this list throughout this *Portfolio Builder*.

Building Your Portfolio

Your résumé *describes* your experience and your skills. Your portfolio *demonstrates* your skills. It represents the best work that you can do. It also should be work with which a prospective employer can identify–that is, documents that the employer will understand.

The first step in building your portfolio is to decide what types of documents belong in it. Use the following checklist as a starting point to create a list of possible documents for your portfolio.

TABLE P-2 **Possible Documents for Portfolio**

DOCUMENT	COMMENTS
Worksheets and Tables	Create attractive stand-alone worksheets and tables. Include charts and maps.
Invoices	Check Excel's invoice template.
Purchase Orders	Check Excel's purchase order template.
Expense Statements	Check Excel's expense statement template.
Budget Sheets	Check Excel's personal budgeter template.
Loan Statements	Check Excel's loan manager template.
Profit & Loss Statements	Obtain information from annual reports available at public library. Possibly include charts.
Balance Sheets	Obtain information from annual reports available at public library.
Databases	Create an Excel database. Show data filtered in multiple ways.
Letters	Create business letters with the appropriate letter formatting. Attach or embed related worksheet, chart, or map.
Memos	Create business memos with the appropriate memo formatting. Attach or embed related worksheet, chart, or map.
Reports	Include graphics, index, table of contents, footnotes or endnotes, and embedded worksheet, chart, or map.
Brochures	Check Word's brochure template. Possibly show worksheets and charts.

continues

TABLE P-2 Possible Documents for Portfolio (continued)

DOCUMENT	COMMENTS
Newsletters	Check Word's Newsletter Wizard. Include graphics, special effects, and embedded worksheet, chart, or map.
Press Releases	Check Word's press release templates. Include an attached worksheet or chart.

NOTE: If any of these Wizards or templates are not installed on your computer, refer to your installation disks. You can also go to the Microsoft Office Web site (http://www.microsoft.com) and download templates and wizards.

EXERCISE P-4 Develop a Plan for Your Portfolio

1. Develop a list of 10 to 15 documents for inclusion in your portfolio. Use Table P-2 as a checklist, but also consider documents that you may have prepared in other courses related to your field of work. If you have work experience, list actual documents that you have created. Use the following headings for your list (see Figure P-9 on the next page):

   Number **Type of Document** **Description**

2. Save the list as *[your initials]***Portfolio.doc** and then print it.
3. Finalize your list by reviewing it with someone who is familiar with your job search area. Adjust the list as needed. Save and print it.

EXERCISE P-5 Build Your Portfolio

It isn't necessary to create every document from scratch. In fact, it may not even be a good idea. Use material from your other courses, key material from brochures and newsletters you might receive from a professional association, or recreate sample documents from people in positions similar to the one in which you are interested.

1. Create each of the documents in your portfolio list.
2. Adjust every document to give it as professional an appearance as it can possibly have. Focus on formatting. Demonstrate the skills that you have learned in this course.

3. Consult the appropriate style reference for your profession to check that your formatting is acceptable.
4. Spell-check, save, and print your documents.
5. Ask someone familiar with your future profession to review your documents and then modify them as necessary.
6. Save and print your documents again.

FIGURE P-8 Sample portfolio list for student seeking accounting clerk position

No.	Type of Document	Description
1.	Invoice	For bookkeeping or accounting services
2.	Database	Client database, filtered in various ways
3.	Accounts Payable	Client's Accounts Payable statement
4.	Account Receivable	Client's Accounts Receivable statement
5.	Employee List	Records of employees including date hired, years employed (with calculations)
6.	Purchase Order	For office supplies
7.	Loan Statement	Showing principal, annual percentage rate, and so on
8.	Check Register	Showing checks, deposits, and balance
9.	Cash Flow Statement	Showing cash receipts and cash disbursements
10.	Amortization Schedule	Showing various interest rates and payment periods
11.	Income Statement	Showing cash, accruals, and net income
12.	Balance Sheet	Showing assets and liabilities
13.	Chart	Showing sales over a 12-month period, for a presentation or handout
14.	Map	Showing states shaded to reflect sales, for a presentation or handout
15.	Report	Report with accompanying worksheet, including charts and maps

Targeting Your Résumé and Portfolio

So far you've created a résumé and a portfolio of documents that reflect something about you. Now it's time to *target* a specific company and tailor your portfolio, including your résumé, to that company.

EXERCISE P-6 Target Your Résumé to an Employer

1. From your list of five prospective employers, choose one as your target. Review the information you've gathered about the company. If you feel you don't have enough information, collect additional material. Ultimately, you should be very familiar with the company—and the position—you've targeted.

2. Review Table P-3.

TABLE P-3 Targeting your résumé

TARGETING SUGGESTIONS
Objectives
☐ Change the job type to one that more closely resembles a job type available at the targeted company.
☐ Change the description of the industry or geographical area to one that more closely resembles those for the target company.
Chronological Résumé
☐ Reorder the bullets under a previous job in "Work experience" to emphasize skills that apply to the targeted position.
☐ Reorder or modify "Additional information" areas to emphasize skills that apply to the targeted position.
Functional Résumé
☐ Reorder or modify the "Functional sections" to emphasize skills that apply to the targeted position.
☐ Reorder or modify "Additional information" areas to emphasize skills that apply to the targeted position.

continues

TABLE P-3 Targeting your résumé (continued)

☑	TARGETING SUGGESTIONS
	Combination Résumé
☐	Reorder or modify the "Functional sections" to emphasize skills that apply to the targeted position.
☐	Reorder the bullets under a previous job in "Work experience" to emphasize skills that apply to the targeted position.
☐	Reorder or modify "Additional information" areas to emphasize skills that apply to the targeted position.

3. Based on the checklist shown in Table P-3, modify your résumé to increase its appeal to your targeted company.

NOTE: Modifying a résumé does not mean fabricating work experience. You can, however, increase your appeal to a specific employer by highlighting certain skills. You can also minimize potential problem areas through the design and format selected for your résumé (for example, by deciding to use a functional résumé rather than a chronological one).

4. Spell-check and save your résumé.
5. Print the final copy of your résumé on appropriate paper stock.

Choosing Paper

The most commonly used résumé papers are 20-pound bond or 50-pound offset (both weigh the same) in a linen (textured) or laid (flat) finish. A 24-pound paper is thicker, has more texture, and is usually more expensive than 20-pound bond or 50-pound offset papers. You might consider using 24-pound Nekoosa, Classic Linen, or Becket Cambric for higher-level positions.

Let your résumé speak for itself. Don't go overboard in selecting a paper that will make your résumé stand out. Such a strategy could backfire. Don't use colored stock, for example. Neutral stock in different shades of white, gray, or beige is recommended.

If you're uncertain about paper choices, visit a stationery store, an office supplies store, a printer, or a local copy shop. Buy enough paper to use for your résumés, cover letters, and follow-up letters. Your envelopes should match the stationery. Your portfolio documents shouldn't be printed on the same stock as your résumé, however.

EXERCISE P-7 Target Your Portfolio to an Employer

The job contact at your targeted company is likely to respond more favorably to your portfolio if you take the time to tailor it to the company. It shows that you made an effort to learn about your prospective employer. It may also provide more conversational opportunities in a job interview.

1. Review Table P-4.

TABLE P-4 Targeting your portfolio

☑	TARGETING SUGGESTIONS
☐	Use the targeted company's name in document titles and its address where appropriate.
☐	Modify the contents of portfolio documents so that they apply specifically to the targeted company.
☐	Do not change a report from one of your classes (other than to make any corrections your instructor may have recommended). It's a good idea to let the targeted company know that the report was submitted as a class assignment, especially if it relates to your chosen field.

2. Based on the checklist shown in Table P-4, modify the documents in your portfolio to increase their appeal to the targeted company.

3. Spell-check and save the portfolio documents.

4. Print the final copies of your portfolio documents. Use standard printer paper.

Writing a Cover Letter

It's been said that sending a résumé without a cover letter is like giving a gift without a card. It's incomplete and confusing, and it only decreases the value of the résumé that you've spent so much time preparing and fine-tuning.

The Cover Letter Recipient A cover letter should be addressed to the job contact at a targeted company—never to Human Resources or Personnel.

First Paragraph The first paragraph should explain what job you are applying for and why you are interested in it. Be as specific as you can. Describe how you heard about the job opening. If someone told you about the company or the job opening, mention the person's name (but make sure to get his or her permission first). Describe why the work of the department or company holds particular interest for you, but don't go overboard with superlatives or hype.

Second Paragraph Describe your credentials in the second paragraph. Don't repeat your résumé. Focus, instead, on the skills, experiences, or accomplishments that are most likely to appear relevant to the employer. If you're responding to an ad, incorporate language from the ad. If you've previously read a job description or had a discussion with the employer, try to use the language the employer used in describing the position. Mention two or three key credentials.

Third Paragraph Use the third paragraph to describe what you can do for the company. You need to show that you understand the employer's needs and that you have something to offer. In this paragraph (or as a separate paragraph), you should request a personal meeting. You could then indicate the time when it's easiest to reach you, whether the employer can contact you at work, and if you'll be following up with a phone call.

General Tips

- Your cover letter should be printed on the same paper as your résumé and should be printed in the same way.
- Do not use the letterhead of your current employer.
- Use the same typeface for both your cover letter and your résumé.
- Use the standard business letter format.
- Don't send your portfolio with your résumé and cover letter. The portfolio is generally shown in an interview, but it can be sent to a prospective employer who expresses an interest in viewing it.

FIGURE P-9 Sample cover letter

Donald Martin
12 Juniper Drive
Any Town, State 00000
(000) 000-0000

January 22, 1998

Ward T. Cleaver, Manager
The Computer Warehouse, Inc.
6 Old King's Highway
Any Town, State 00000

Dear Mr. Cleaver:

I am seeking a position as a microcomputer salesperson, and read in the *Any Town News* that The Computer Warehouse was opening a new store on Old King's Highway. I have visited The Computer Warehouse in Lincoln and was impressed with the variety of hardware and software carried by the store. The store's focus on customer service was also exceptional, both through its "Trouble-Free Technical Support" program and its wide range of software training courses.

As my enclosed résumé indicates, I specialized in the sales of computer hardware and software at the Electronics Depot on Main Street. Although the sale of computers and software constitutes only a small portion of the overall sales of the Electronics Depot, computer and software sales increased by 42 percent in the past year. Part of this increase was due to the Customer Training Program that I developed. In its first year, the program produced revenues of $80,000.

Opening a new store and training a new sales staff is a difficult prospect. With my proven background in sales and customer training, I feel I would be an asset to your sales staff and would welcome the opportunity to meet with you personally to discuss your staff needs. I will contact you in the next week to schedule an appointment at your convenience. Thank you for your consideration.

Sincerely,

Donald Martin

Enclosure

EXERCISE P-8 Write a Cover Letter

Using your word-processor application, write a cover letter to accompany your résumé.

1. Using the standard business letter style (if necessary, check the *Gregg Reference Manual*), write a cover letter for your résumé. Use the three-paragraph format described earlier.
2. Ask someone familiar with your résumé and with jobs in your chosen field to review your letter. Make any necessary modifications.
3. Spell-check the cover letter and save it as *[Your initials]***CvrLtr.doc**.
4. Print your cover letter using the same stationery as your résumé.
5. Print an envelope for your cover letter and résumé. If possible, use the same stationery for the envelope, cover letter, and résumé.

NOTE: Some people believe that you should use a large envelope so you don't have to fold your résumé. Others recommend a standard business envelope.

TIP: You can use Word's Letter Wizard to write a cover letter for your résumé. Choose New from the File menu, choose the Letters & Faxes tab, and double-click the Letter Wizard icon. Follow the steps to create the letter. Remember to choose the page design that matches your résumé, specify whether you're using preprinted letterhead, include "Mr." or "Ms." in the recipient's name area, and include an enclosure notation. After creating the letter, you can add, remove, or change letter elements by choosing Letter Wizard from the Tools menu.

Filling Out an Employment Application

Some companies require that every applicant, at every level, fill out an employment application. Other companies don't even use one. Generally, however, companies do use some form of an employment application. Whether you need to fill out such a form will depend on the company's internal personnel policies.

Often applicants are asked to fill out an employment application when they arrive at the company for an interview. To minimize stress in an already stressful situation, prepare for the employment application beforehand by creating a reference sheet that contains any information that might be included in the application and isn't found on your résumé. (Of course, you should refer to your résumé in filling out your employment application. Make sure to bring an extra copy for reference.)

Tips for Employment Applications

- Be as specific as possible when describing the position that you are seeking.
- Be careful when listing a required salary. A salary that is too high may eliminate you for some acceptable jobs, while a figure that is too low might weaken your negotiating position. Sometimes it is better to leave this line blank.
- Be prepared to list dates (month and year) for the schools you have attended. Some applications may also ask for your grade-point average and your class rank.
- Be prepared to list the following information for your previous employers: address, telephone number, name and title of supervisor, start date and end date (month and year), and a description of your duties.
- If some questions are not applicable to the job you are seeking, it is usually acceptable to write "Not Applicable" next to the question.

EXERCISE  P-9 Create a Reference Sheet for an Employment Application

1. Review the "Tips for Employment Applications." Note any information that isn't covered by your résumé.
2. Key all information that you will need to fill out an employment application. Use any format that makes sense to you.
3. Save the file as *[Your initials]***AppInfo.doc** and then print it.

Employment Interviews

Once you have contacted a potential employer and scheduled an appointment to meet, you'll need to prepare yourself to make a good impression in person. No matter how good your résumé or credentials may be, only the interview can, ultimately, land you the job.

The more interviews you go on, the better your interviewing skills will be.

NOTE: If possible, avoid scheduling an interview on a Monday, which is often the most hectic day in a business environment.

Preparing Yourself

- Confirm your appointment the day before, and make sure you arrive at the interview on time.
- Become as familiar with the company as possible. Read articles about the company, if they are available, or talk to people who are, or have been, employed by the company. It's always flattering to a prospective employer when an applicant appears knowledgeable about the company in an interview.
- Approach the interview with a clear mental picture of your capabilities and your job objective. Review your résumé immediately before meeting the prospective employer. Think positively.

Presenting Yourself

- Come to the interview equipped with copies of your résumé, your references, and any recommendation letters you have gathered. Have your portfolio on hand, as well as a notepad and a pen.
- Look your best. Your attire and grooming are critical to making a good impression. Dress neatly and professionally, in a manner that is appropriate to the company you are visiting. If necessary, get help in selecting an interview outfit from someone who dresses well.
- Be yourself. Act as relaxed as you possibly can, sit in a comfortable position, and focus on the interviewer.
- Ask questions. Learn what you can about the job, the company, to whom (or to how many people) you'd report, and so on. If no job is available, or the job opening is not appropriate for you, ask for recommendations about other people in the company that you might contact.
- At the end of the interview, if you want the job, express your interest in it, and be ready to explain why the company should hire you.

Frequently Asked Interview Questions

The following are frequently asked interview questions. You may want to rehearse your answers before the interview. Never offer negative or unnecessary information to an interview question.

- Can you tell me about yourself?
- Why should I hire you?
- What are your major strengths? Weaknesses?
- What are your short-term goals? Long-term goals?
- Why do you want to leave your present job? (if employed)
- Why did you leave your previous job?
- What do you enjoy most (or least) about your current (or previous) job?
- Why do you want to work here?
- What salary do you expect to receive?

Following Up the Interview

To be successful in the interview process, you should take two important follow-up steps:

- Send a "thank you" letter.
- Keep track of your contacts.

"Thank You" Letters

Always send a "thank you" letter within 24 hours after you've interviewed with someone. It creates a positive impression, shows that you have good follow-up skills and good social skills, and reminds the person of your meeting.

The letter should be short and friendly, thanking the person for his or her time and for any information he or she may have provided. You may want to mention something that reminds the person of who you are, in case many people have interviewed for the position.

Even if you know that the interview will not lead to a specific job offer, a "thank you" letter demonstrates your professionalism.

FIGURE P-10 Sample "thank you" letter #1

Dear Ms. Jones:

Thank you for the opportunity of interviewing for the sales position. I enjoyed meeting you and appreciate the information that you shared with me.

I am very interested in the position and believe I could quickly become a productive member of your sales team.

Thanks again for the interview, and I look forward to hearing from you.

Sincerely,

FIGURE P-11 Sample "thank you" letter #2

Dear Ms. Jones:

Thank you for the interview and the information you gave me yesterday. I really appreciate your recommendation that I meet with John Doe in the Marketing Department.

I have scheduled an interview with Mr. Doe and look forward to meeting him. If this contact eventually leads to a job offer, I will be most grateful.

Thanks again for your time and help.

Sincerely,

Keeping Track of Contacts

Be organized in your job search. Keep track of everyone who has received your résumé by creating a contact log.

FIGURE P-12
Sample format for contact log

Date Sent	Contact Name	Company	Telephone	Comments

In addition, develop a system for organizing your contacts so that you can follow up with telephone calls as appropriate. You can use a computer application of your choice or simple index cards to create the system.

If you use index cards, enter all pertinent reference information for each contact on the card. Place the cards in a box, and then sort them in the order that you want to contact the individuals. You can use tabs as date markers.

FIGURE P-13
Sample format for contact reference card

Company: ______________________________

Contact Person: ______________________________

Position: ______________ Department: ______________

Address: ______________________________

Phone: ______________ Fax: ______________

Notes: ______________________________

____

____

____

Appendices

APPENDIX A

Windows Tutorial

If you're unfamiliar with Windows, we suggest that you review this Windows tutorial.

If you've never used Windows before, you may need additional help with some basic Windows actions. At appropriate points in this Tutorial, a Note will guide you to one of the two Appendixes covering basic Windows actions (Appendix B: "Using the Mouse," and Appendix C: "Using Menus and Dialog Boxes").

Starting Windows

Individual computers may be set up differently. In most cases, however, when you turn on your computer, Windows will load and the Windows desktop will appear.

The desktop contains *icons*, or symbols representing windows. If you double-click an icon, the window represented by that icon opens. Two icons are especially important:

- My Computer
  Opens a window that contains icons representing each input and output device on your printer or in your network.
- Recycle Bin
  Opens a window listing files you have deleted. Until you empty the Recycle Bin, these files can be undeleted.

TIP: If you don't know how to use the mouse to point, click, double-click, or drag and drop, see Appendix B: "Using the Mouse."

Using the Start Menu

The Start button on the taskbar at the bottom of the desktop is probably the most important button in Windows. Clicking displays the Start menu from which you can perform any Windows task.

NOTE: If Microsoft Office is installed on your computer, additional options may appear on your Start menu.

1. Turn on the computer. Windows will load, and the Windows desktop will appear.

NOTE: When you start Windows, you may be prompted to log on to Windows or, if your computer is attached to a network, to log on to the network. If you are asked to key a user name and a password, ask your instructor for help.

2. Click Start on the Windows taskbar. The Start menu appears.

TIP: If you don't know how to choose a command from a menu, see Appendix C: "Using Menus and Dialog Boxes."

FIGURE A-1
Windows desktop

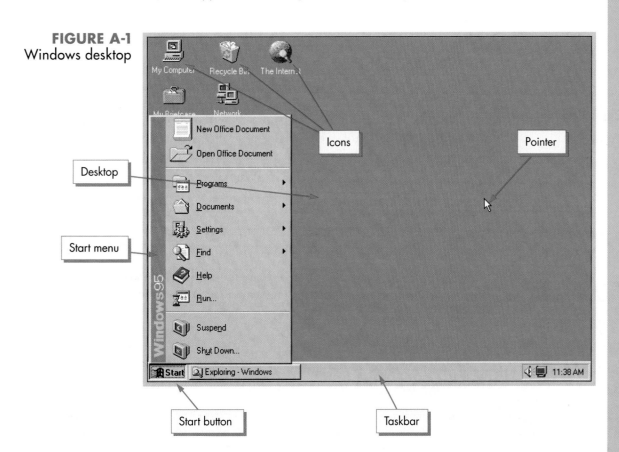

TABLE A-1 Start Menu

COMMAND	USE
Programs	Displays a list of programs you can start.
Documents	Displays a list of documents that you've opened previously.
Settings	Displays a list of system components for which you can change settings.
Find	Helps you find a folder or a file.
Help	Starts Help. You can then use Help to find out how to perform a task in Windows.
Run	Starts a program or opens a folder when you type an command.
Shut Down	Shuts down or restarts your computer, or logs you off (if you are on a network).

Using the Programs Command

The Programs command is the easiest way to open a program.

1. Click Start.
2. Point to Programs. The Programs submenu appears, listing the programs present on your computer. Every computer will have a different list of programs.

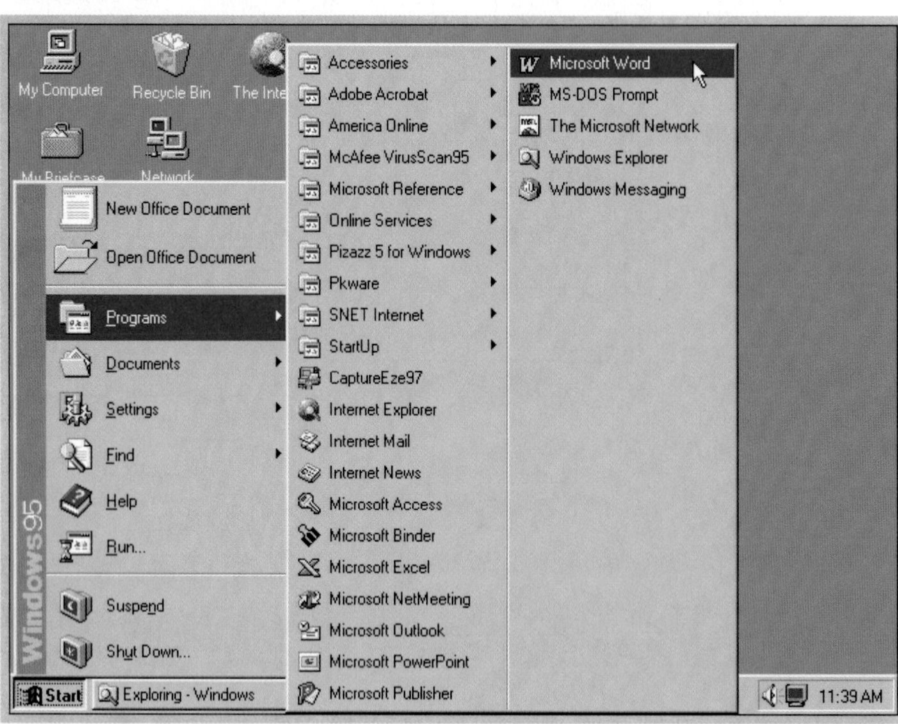

FIGURE A-2
Programs submenu

3. Point to a program that you want to open and then click. In a few seconds, the program will load and its first screen will appear. Notice that a button for the program appears in the taskbar. Keep the program open.

NOTE: Many items on the Program menu represent names for groups of programs. These group names have an arrow ▶ across from them on the right side of the menu. When you point to the group name, a submenu will appear listing programs that you can click to select.

Using the Taskbar

One of the major features of Windows is that it enables you to work with more than one program at a time. The taskbar makes it easy to switch between open programs.

The window in which you are working is called the *active* window. The title bar for the active window is highlighted, as is its taskbar button.

1. The program you opened in the preceding procedure should still be open. (If it's not, open a program now.) Open a second program using the Program command. Notice how the second program covers the first. The window containing the second program is now active. Its title bar is highlighted and its button on the taskbar is highlighted.

FIGURE A-3
Active window

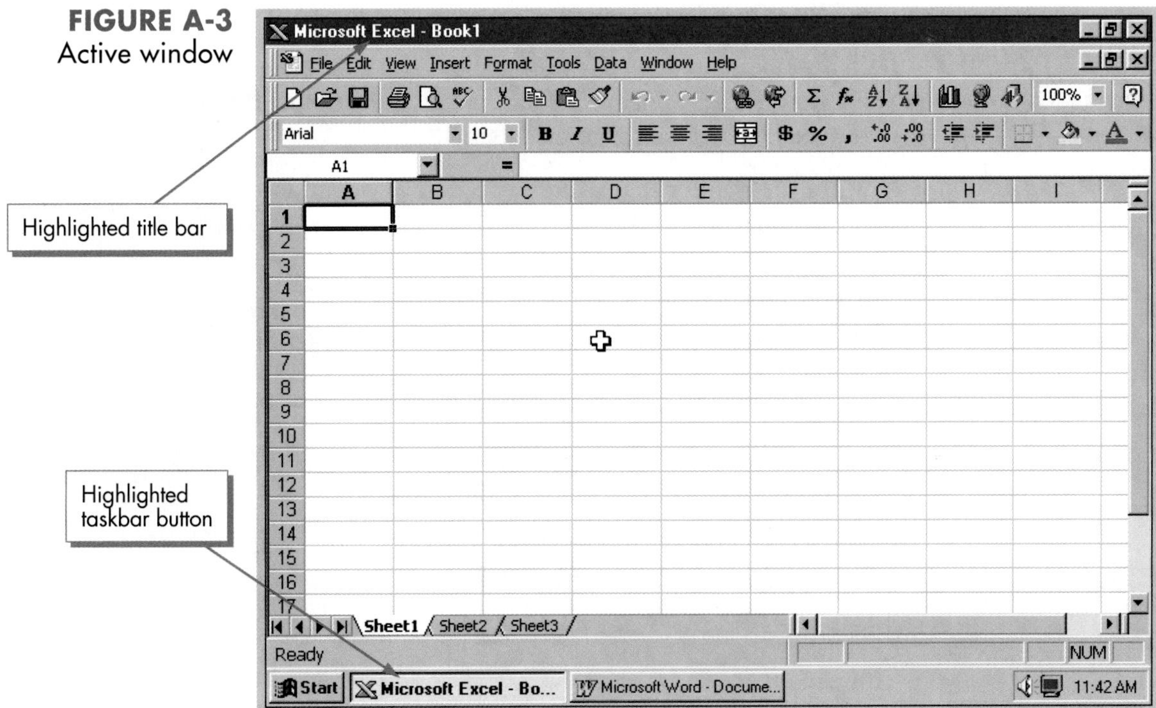

2. Click the button on the taskbar for the first program you opened. The program appears again.
3. Click the button on the taskbar for the second program to switch back to it.

Changing the Size of Windows

In Windows it's easy to adjust the size of your windows using the pointer.

You can also use the Minimize button, the Maximize button, and the Restore button to adjust the size of windows.

TABLE A-2 **Sizing Buttons**

NAME	BUTTON	USE
Minimize button		Reduces the window to a button on the taskbar.
Maximize button		Enlarges the window to fill the desktop.
Restore button		Returns the window to its previous size. (Appears when you maximize a window.)

1. In the open window, click at the right side of the title bar of the window. (If appears instead of, the window has already been reduced. In that case, go on to step 2.)
2. Move the pointer to a window border. The pointer changes to a double-headed arrow ↔.

TIP: Sometimes the borders of a window can move off the computer screen. If you're having trouble with one border of a window, try another border.

3. When the pointer changes shape, you can drag the border to enlarge, reduce, or change the shape of the window.
4. Make the window smaller. Notice that the other open program appears behind the currently active window.

5. Click the window that had been behind the first window. It now appears in front of the first window because it has become the active window.

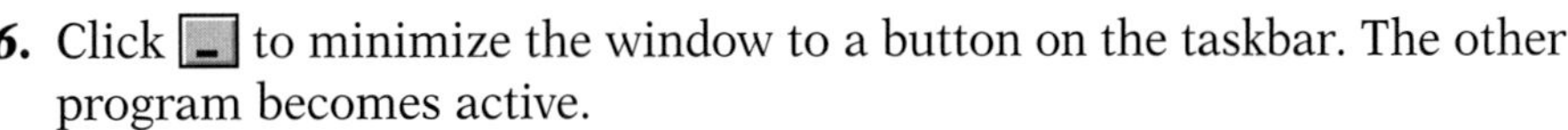

6. Click [minimize] to minimize the window to a button on the taskbar. The other program becomes active.

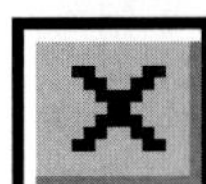

7. Click the Close button [X] at the top right corner of the window to close the current program. The desktop should now be clean.

8. Click the button on the taskbar for the other program you have open. Close the program by clicking [X]. You have a clean desktop again.

Using the Documents Command

You can open an existing document by using the Documents command on the Start menu. This command allows you to open one of the last 15 documents previously opened on your computer.

1. In the Start menu, point to Documents. The Documents submenu appears, showing documents that have been previously opened.

2. Click on a document. The document opens, along with the program in which the document was written (for example, if the document were a Word document, it would open within Word). A button for the document appears on the taskbar. You could now work on the document, if you wanted.

3. To close the document, click [X] on the document window. Click [X] to close the program window that contained the document.

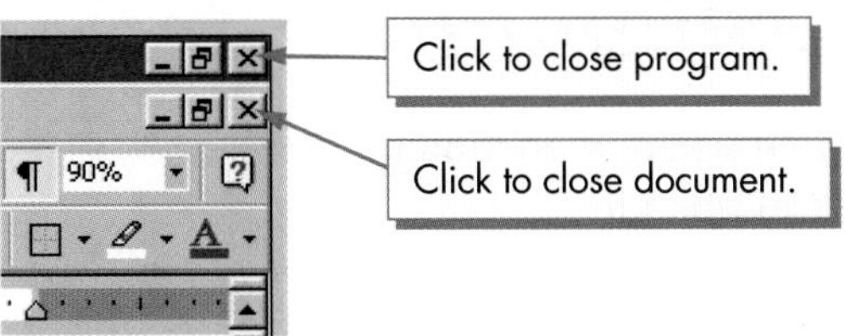

FIGURE A-4
Close buttons

Using the Settings Command

You can change the way Windows looks and works by using the Settings command. Be very careful when changing settings. Don't change them unless it's really necessary.

NOTE: Before changing any settings, talk to your instructor.

1. Open the Start menu, and point to Settings. The Settings submenu appears.

FIGURE A-5
Settings submenu

2. Click the option that relates to the settings you want to change. Close any open windows and clear your desktop.

TABLE A-3 Settings options

OPTION	USE
Control Panel	Displays the Control Panel, which allows you to change screen colors, add or remove programs, change the date or time, and change other settings for your hardware and software.
Printers	Displays the Printer window, which allows you to add, remove, and modify your printer settings.
Taskbar	Displays the Taskbar Properties dialog box, which allows you to change the appearance of the taskbar and the way it works.

Using the Find Command

If you don't know where a document or folder is, you can use the Find command to find and open it.

1. On the Start menu, point to Find. The Find submenu appears.

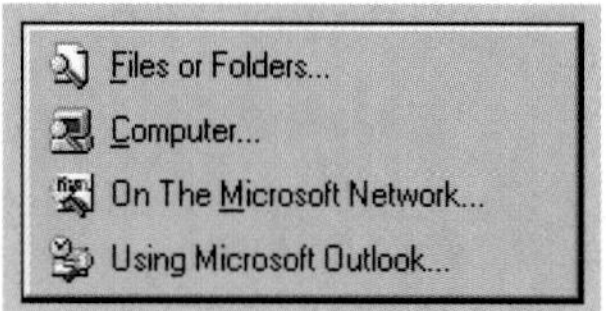

FIGURE A-6
Find Submenu

2. Click Files or Folders. The Find: All Files dialog box appears. (See Figure A-7 on the next page.)
3. In the Named box, key the name of the file or folder you want to find.

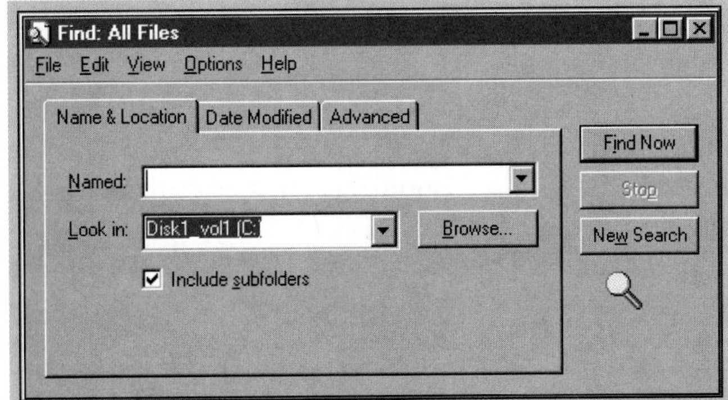

FIGURE A-7 Find: All Files dialog box

4. Click the arrow next to the Look In box to specify where to search. (You could also check Browse.)

TIP: You can use the Advanced tab to search files for specific text.

5. Click Find Now to start the search. Any matches for the file will be shown at the bottom of the dialog box.
6. To open a file that was found, double-click on the filename.
7. When you have finished viewing the file, close all open windows and clear your desktop.

Using the Run Command

If you know the name of the program you want to use, you can use the Run command to start it easily. This command is often employed to run a "setup" or "install" program that installs a new program on your computer.

1. In the Start menu, click Run. The Run dialog box appears.

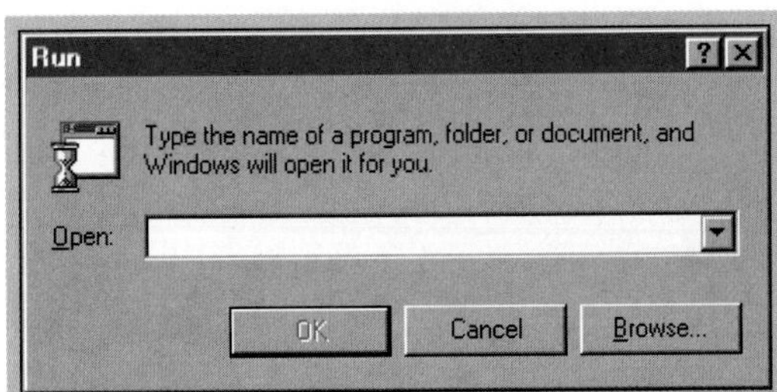

FIGURE A-8 Run dialog box

2. If you know the name of a program you want to run, key the name and click OK. The program you specified will start. Otherwise, you can click Browse to look for the program.
3. When you're finished, close the program.

Using the Right Mouse Button

When the pointer is on an object in Windows and you click the right mouse button, a shortcut menu will typically appear. This menu provides you with the commands that would be most useful in working with the object to which you were pointing.

A shortcut menu is available for Start. The shortcut menu options for Start are described in Table A-4.

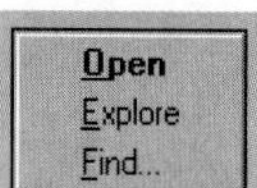

FIGURE A-9
Shortcut menu for the Start button

1. Click Start with the right mouse button. The right mouse button Start menu appears.
2. Investigate the options on the right mouse button menu, and then close any open programs.

TABLE A-4

Shortcut menu for the start button

OPTION	USE
Open	Opens the Start Menu window. Double-click the Programs icon to open the Program window. Then, double-click the icon for the program you want to open.
Explore	Opens Windows Explorer (see Appendix E: "File Management").
Find	Opens the Find: All Files dialog box.

Using the Shut Down Command

You should always shut down Windows before you turn off or restart your computer. You can then be sure that your work will be saved and no files will be damaged.

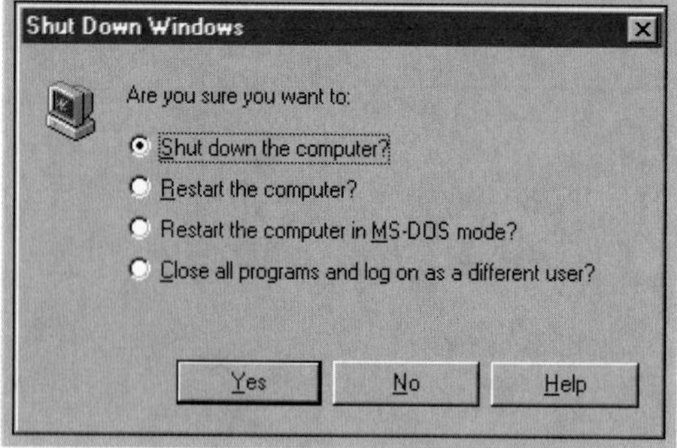

FIGURE A-10
Shut Down Windows dialog box

1. In the Start menu, click Shut Down. The Shut Down Windows dialog box appears.
2. Click Yes. Windows will prompt you to save changes to any open documents, and will then shut down your computer.

APPENDIX B

Using the Mouse

Although you can use a keyboard with Windows, you'll probably find yourself using the mouse. Typically, you roll the mouse on a *mouse pad* (or any flat surface). A *pointer* shows your on-screen location as the mouse moves.

To select items on the computer screen using a mouse, you usually press the left button on the mouse. (Whenever you're told to "click" or "double-click" the mouse button, use the left mouse button. In those cases where you should use the right button, you'll be told to do so.)

When using a mouse, you'll need to become familiar with these terms.

TABLE B-1 Mouse Terms

TERM	DESCRIPTION
Point	Move the mouse until the tip of the on-screen pointer is touching an item on the computer screen.
Click	Press the mouse button and then quickly release it.
Double-click	Press and quickly release the mouse button twice.
Triple-click	Press and quickly release the mouse button three times.
Drag (or drag-and-drop)	Point to an object, hold down the mouse, and move the mouse to a new position (dragging the object to the new position). Then release the mouse button (and drop the object in the new position).

The mouse pointer changes appearance depending on where it's located and what you're doing. Table B-2 shows the most common types of pointers.

TABLE B-2 Frequently Used Mouse Pointers

POINTER NAME	POINTER	DESCRIPTION
Pointer		Used to point to objects.
I-beam		Used when keying, inserting, and selecting text.
2-headed arrow		Used to change the size of objects or windows.
4-headed arrow		Used to move objects.
Hourglass		Indicates the computer is processing a command.
Hand		Used in Help to display additional information.

APPENDIX C

Using Menus and Dialog Boxes

Menus

Menus throughout Windows applications use common features. To open a menu, click the menu name. An alternative method for opening a menu is to hold down Alt and key the underlined letter in the menu name.

TIP: If you open a menu by mistake, click the menu name to close it.

FIGURE C-1
Edit menu (Excel)

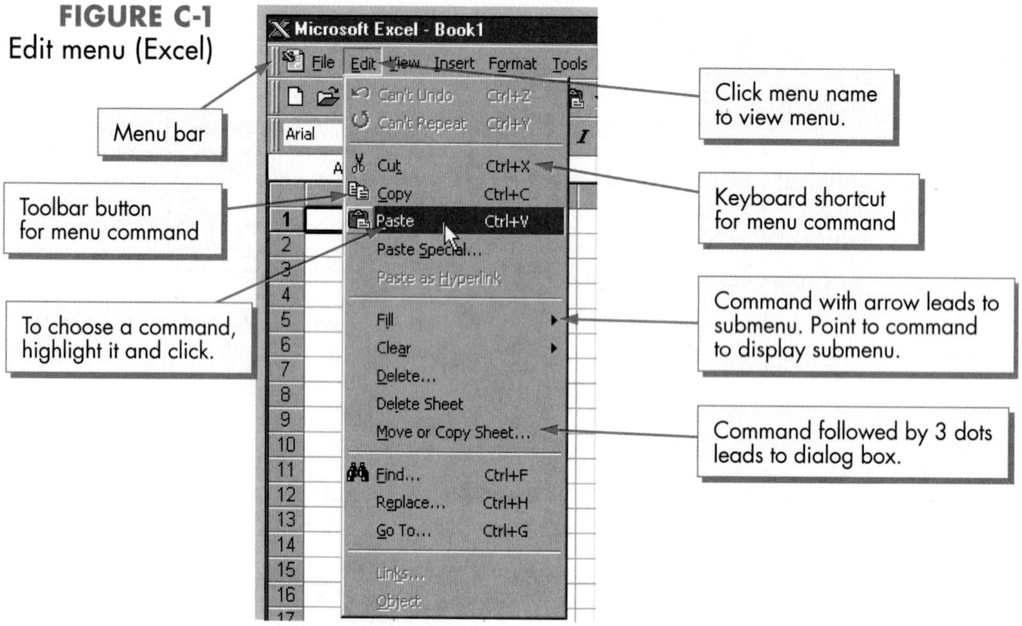

Menu bar

Toolbar button for menu command

To choose a command, highlight it and click.

Click menu name to view menu.

Keyboard shortcut for menu command

Command with arrow leads to submenu. Point to command to display submenu.

Command followed by 3 dots leads to dialog box.

FIGURE C-2
View menu (Word)

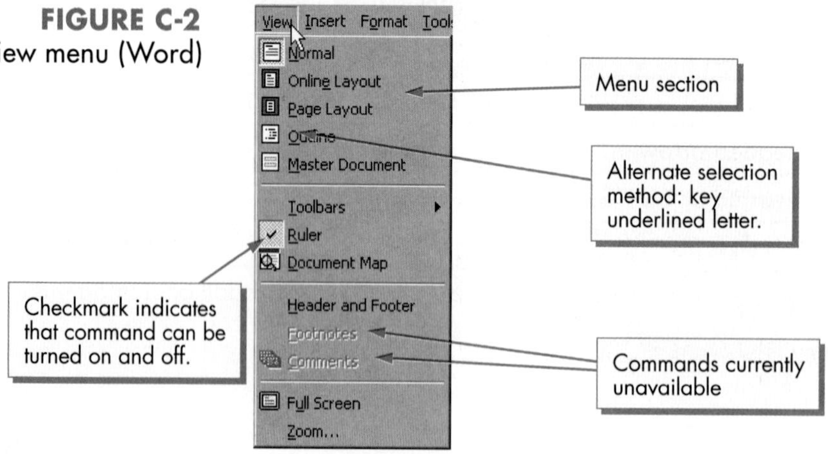

Menu section

Alternate selection method: key underlined letter.

Checkmark indicates that command can be turned on and off.

Commands currently unavailable

Dialog Boxes

Dialog boxes enable you to view all of the current settings for a command, as well as change them. Like menus in Windows, dialog boxes share common features. The following examples show the most frequently seen features.

FIGURE C-3
Print dialog box (Word)

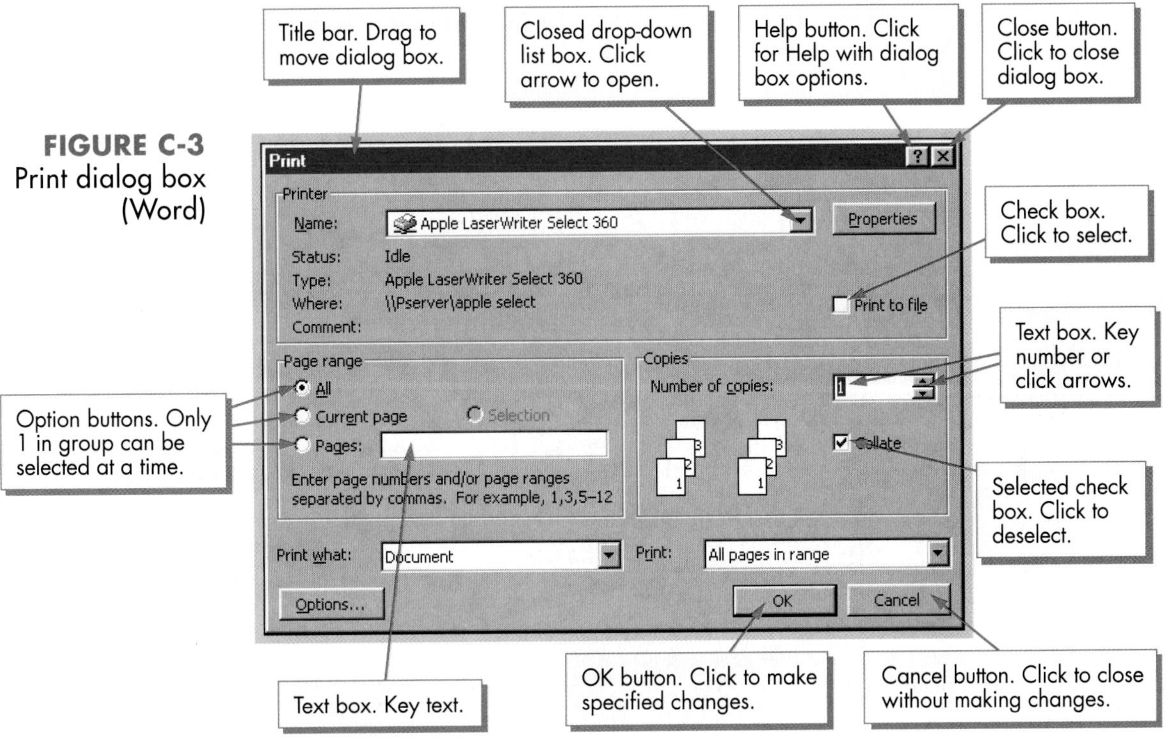

FIGURE C-4
Format Cells dialog box, Font tab (Excel)

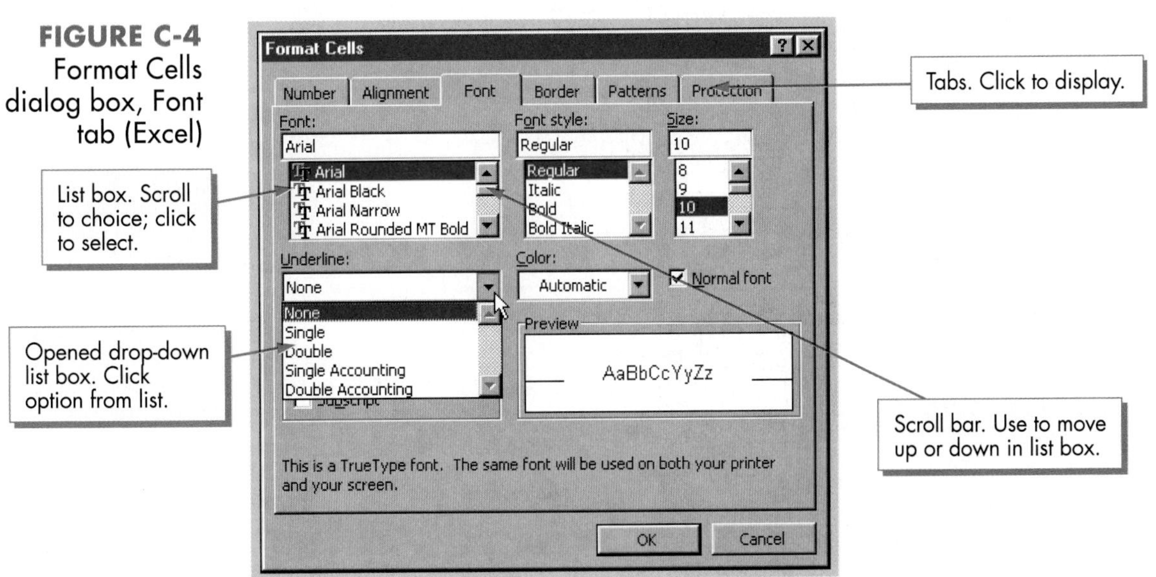

APPENDIX D
Excel Toolbars

The following toolbars are most commonly used in Excel:

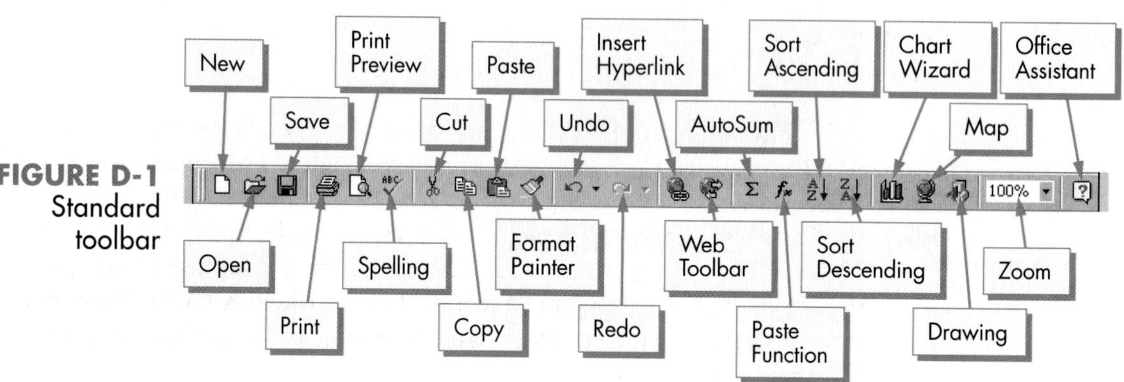

FIGURE D-1 Standard toolbar

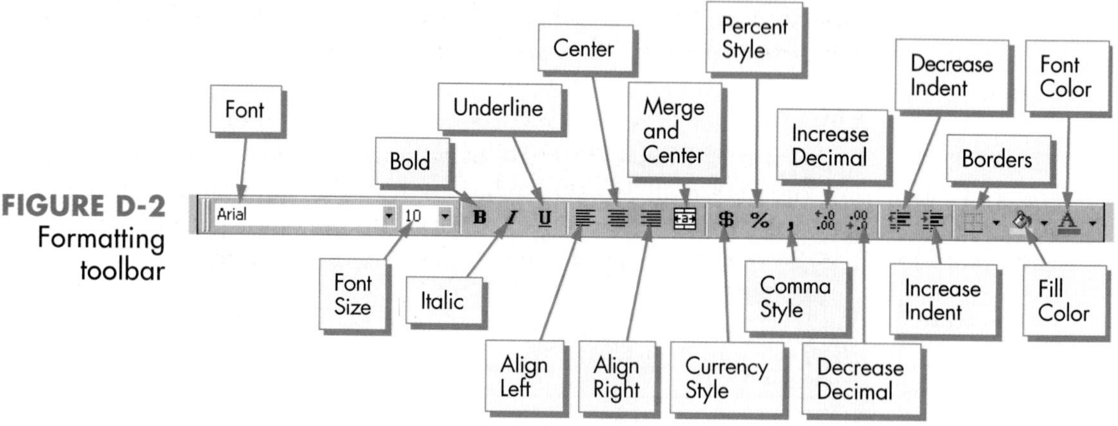

FIGURE D-2 Formatting toolbar

APPENDIX E

File Management

This Appendix briefly explains how information is stored in Windows. It also introduces one of the most useful tools for managing information in Windows—the Windows Explorer.

Files, Folders, and Paths

In Windows, the basic unit of storage is a *file*. The documents you create and use are files, as are the programs you use. These files are stored in *folders*, which can also contain other folders.

Windows supports filenames that can contain up to 250 characters. A filename also has a three-letter extension, which identifies the type of file. For example, the extension "doc" identifies a file as a Word document. The extension is separated from the filename by a period. For example: "Birthdays.doc."

NOTE: In this course, we assume that your machine displays file extensions. If it doesn't, open Windows Explorer, select Option from the View menu, and make sure that the following option is *not* selected: "Hide MS-DOS file extensions for file types that are registered."

A file's *path* is its specific location on your computer or network. A file's path begins with the drive letter, followed by a colon and a backslash (example: c:\). The path then lists the folders in the order you would open them. Folders are separated by backslashes. The last item in the path is the filename.

For example: c:\My Documents\Letters\Reservations.doc

Windows Explorer

One of the most useful tools in Windows for managing files is the *Windows Explorer*, which gives you a view of your computer's components as a hierarchy, or "tree." Using Windows Explorer, you can easily see the contents of each drive and folder on your computer or network.

To open Windows Explorer, click the Start button Start with the right mouse button. Then click Explore in the Start button shortcut menu.

Table E-1 describes how to accomplish common file management tasks using Windows Explorer and shortcut menus.

FIGURE E-1
Windows Explorer

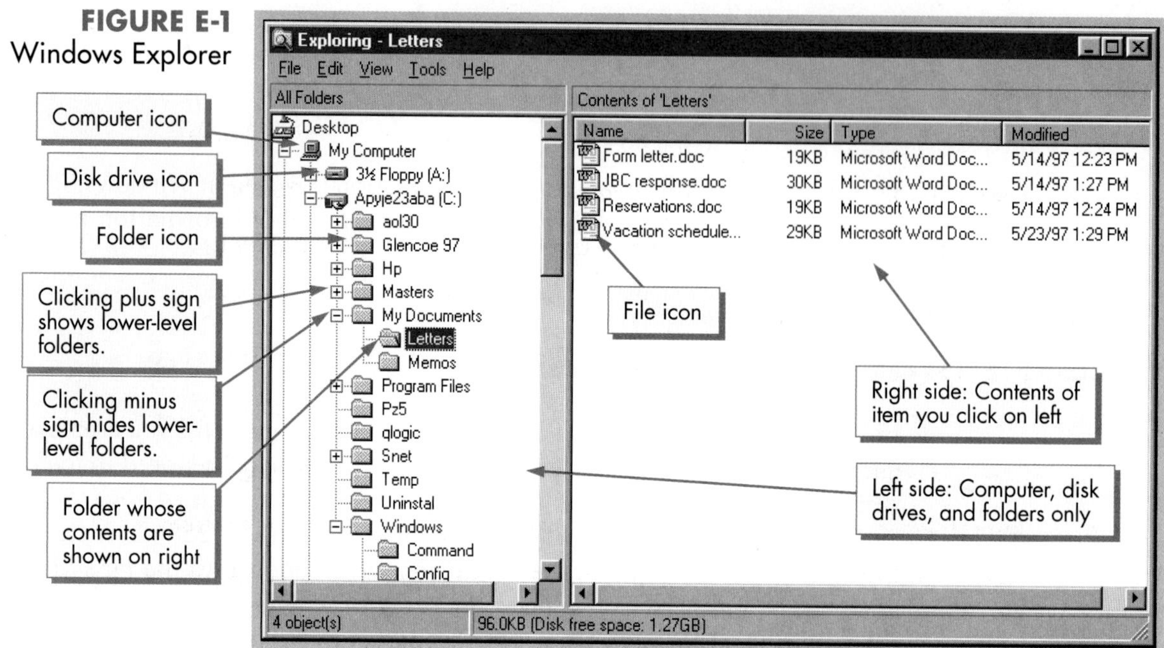

TABLE E-1 Common File Management Tasks

TASK	HOW TO DO
Copy file or folder	Right-click file or folder to be copied and click Copy, then right-click folder in which you want to copy file and click Paste. (Alternative: Drag and drop a file from one folder to another.)
Move file or folder	Same method as above, but using Cut and Paste.
Delete a file or folder	Point to icon for file to be deleted and press Delete.
Create a new folder	Choose New from File menu, and then choose Folder. Creates new folder at current position.
Copy file to floppy disk	Point to icon for file to be copied and press right mouse button. Point to Send To and click floppy disk drive in submenu.
Edit/rename file	Point to icon for file you want to rename, press right mouse button, and click Rename.
Open file	Double-click icon for file.

APPENDIX F

Proofreader's Marks

PROOFREADER'S MARK		DRAFT	FINAL COPY
⁀‿	Delete space	to gether	together
# ^	Insert space	Itmay be	It may be
∩∪	Transpose	beleivable	believable
○	Spell out	(2) years ago	two years ago
^	Insert a word	How much ^is it?	How much is it?
OR	Delete a word	it may ~~not~~ be true	it may be true
^ OR	Insert a letter	temperture (a)	temperature
OR	Delete a letter and close up	committment to buyy	commitment to buy
OR	Change a word	~~and~~ but if you ~~won't~~ can't	but if you can't
stet	Stet (don't delete)	stet I was very glad	I was very glad
/	Make letter lowercase	Federal Government	federal government
≡	Capitalize	Janet L. greyston	Janet L. Greyston
⊙	Insert a period	Mr Henry Grenada	Mr. Henry Grenada
^	Insert a comma	a large old house	a large, old house
∨	Insert an apostrophe	my childrens car	my children's car
∨	Insert quotation marks	he wants a loan	he wants a "loan"
=	Insert a hyphen	a first rate job	a first-rate job
___	Insert underscore	an issue of Time	an issue of <u>Time</u>
ital ___	Set in italic	ital The New York Times	*The New York Times*
bf ~~~	Set in boldface	bf the Enter key	the **Enter** key
rom ___	Set in roman	rom the *most* likely	the most likely
{ }	Insert parentheses	left today May 3	left today (May 3)
⊐	Move to the right	$38,367,000 ⊐	$38,367,000
⊏	Move to the left	⊏ Anyone can win!	Anyone can win!

APPENDIX G

Excel Operators, Formulas, and Functions

Mathematical Operators

OPERATOR	DESCRIPTION
+	Add
-	Subtract
*	Multiply
/	Divide
%	Percent
^	Exponentiation
( )	Parentheses—used to control the hierarchy of mathematical operations

Formula Construction

Basic Formulas

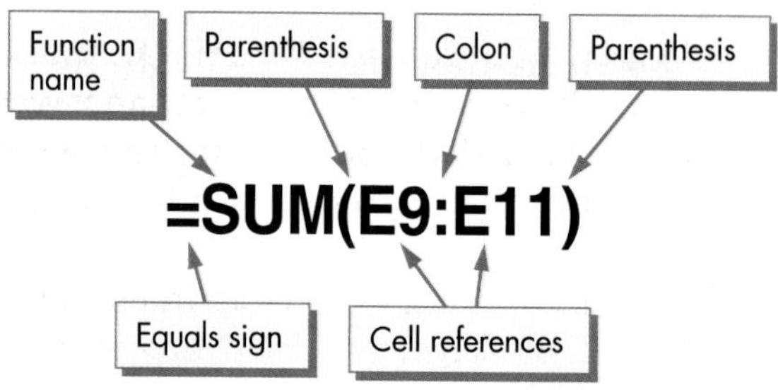

Formula with Nested Functions

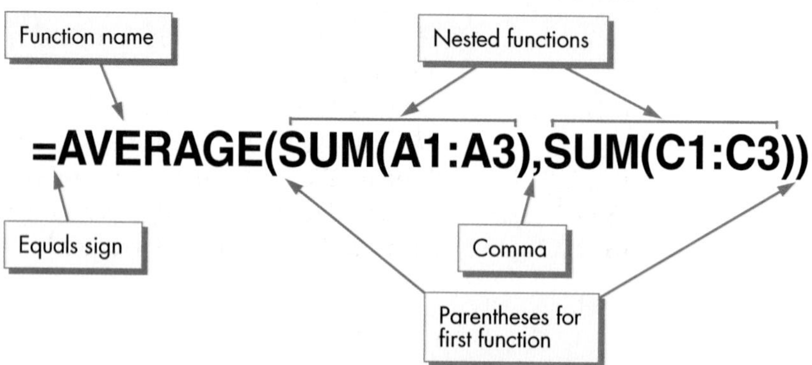

Common Excel Functions

Date & Time Functions

Function	Description
DATE	Returns the serial number of a particular date
NOW	Returns the serial number of the current date and time
TIME	Returns the serial number of a particular time
TODAY	Returns the serial number of today's date
WEEKDAY	Converts a serial number to a day of the week

Database & List Management Functions

Function	Description
DAVERAGE	Returns the average of selected database entries
DCOUNT	Counts the cells containing numbers from a specified database and criteria
DCOUNTA	Counts nonblank cells from a specified database and criteria
DGET	Extracts from a database a single record that matches the specified criteria
DMAX	Returns the maximum value from selected database entries
DMIN	Returns the minimum value from selected database entries
DSUM	Adds the numbers in the field column of records in the database that match the criteria

Financial Functions

Function	Description
FV	Returns the future value of an investment
NPER	Returns the number of periods for an investment
PMT	Returns the periodic payment for an annuity
PPMT	Returns the payment on the principal for an investment for a given period
PV	Returns the present value of an investment
RATE	Returns the interest rate per period of an annuity

Information Functions

Function	Description
CELL	Returns information about the formatting, location, or contents of a cell
ISBLANK	Returns TRUE if the value is blank
ISERR	Returns TRUE if the value is any error value except #N/A
ISERROR	Returns TRUE if the value is any error value
ISNUMBER	Returns TRUE if the value is a number
ISTEXT	Returns TRUE if the value is text

Logical Functions

Function	Description
AND	Returns TRUE if all its arguments are TRUE
FALSE	Returns the logical value FALSE
IF	Specifies a logical test to perform
NOT	Reverses the logic of its argument
OR	Returns TRUE if any argument is TRUE
TRUE	Returns the logical value TRUE

Lookup & Reference Functions

Function	Description
HLOOKUP	Looks in the top row of an array and returns the value of the indicated cell
VLOOKUP	Looks in the first column of an array and moves across the row to return the value of a cell

Math & Trigonometry Functions

Function	Description
ABS	Returns the absolute value of a number
INT	Rounds a number down to the nearest integer
ROUND	Rounds a number to a specified number of digits
SQRT	Returns a positive square root
SUM	Adds its arguments
TRUNC	Truncates a number to an integer

Statistical Functions

Function	Description
AVERAGE	Returns the average of its arguments
COUNT	Counts how many numbers are in the list of arguments
COUNTA	Counts how many values are in the list of arguments
MAX	Returns the maximum value in a list of arguments
MIN	Returns the minimum value in a list of arguments

Text Functions

Function	Description
LOWER	Converts text to lowercase
PROPER	Capitalizes the first letter in each word of a text value
TRIM	Removes spaces from text
UPPER	Converts text to uppercase

Glossary

Absolute cell reference A formula cell address that specifies the exact address of a cell, regardless of the position of the cell containing the formula. Example: $A$1. (11)

Active cell The cell that is current—that is, ready to receive information. (1)

Annuity A constant periodic payment paid over a fixed period of time. (12)

Argument A value or other data operated on by a function. (10)

Block A group of adjacent cells. (2)

Category axis The horizontal (or x) axis along the bottom of most charts; it frequently refers to time series. (17)

Cell The rectangle that is formed by the intersection of a row and a column, which can contain text, numeric values, or formulas. (1)

Cell address The location of a cell in a worksheet, indicated by its column letter and row number. (1)

Character string A sequence of characters in a formula or text. (7)

Circular reference An error condition in a formula in which a cell is both operated on by the formula and serves as the location of the formula. (11)

Clip art Any ready-to-use graphic image that can be imported into a worksheet or chart. (18)

Clipboard Temporary storage in the computer's memory. (3)

Consolidation table A table that summarizes the data from one or more source ranges. (15)

Consolidation worksheet A worksheet that contains a consolidation table. (15)

Constants Unchanging values that are used in formulas. (6)

Criteria range The area of the worksheet where you specify the conditions the filtered data must meet. (20)

Criterion The specified information that Excel must match when searching for a record. (19)

Data form A dialog box that displays the fields for one record in a vertical arrangement. (19)

Data marker An object that represents individual data points. It can be a bar, area, dot, picture, or other symbol that marks a single data point or value. (17)

Data point A single piece of data. (17)

Data series A collection of data points that are related to one another. These values are usually within the same columns or row in the worksheet. (17)

Database A collection of related information organized in a systematic way. (13)

Database A collection of related information organized in a systematic way. (19)

Dependent worksheet A worksheet that uses data from another worksheet. (15)

Docked toolbar A toolbar that appears in a fixed position outside the work area. (5)

Dynamic link A formula reference to a different worksheet that is automatically updated when data changes. (15)

Embedded chart A chart that is part of a worksheet. (17)

External reference A reference to a cell, cell range, or defined name in another workbook. (15)

Field A category of information in a database, arranged as a single column of data. (19)

Field name A column label used to identify the content of a field. (19)

Fill handle The small box in the lower right corner of an active cell. (5)

Filtering The process of finding and selecting information from a database. (20)

Floating toolbar A toolbar positioned over the work area. (5)

Font A type design applied to an entire set of characters, including all letters of the alphabet, numerals, punctuation marks, and other keyboard symbols. (9)

Footer Repetitive information about a worksheet that is printed across the bottom of the page. (16)

Format Attributes of text or numbers, such as font style, underlining, bold, number of decimal places, or alignment. (8)

Full precision Numbers stored and used in calculations, regardless of how the number is formatted on the screen. (8)

Header Repetitive information about a worksheet that is printed across the top of the page. (16)

Hyperlink Text or graphic in a file that you click to link to another location, such as an Internet address or a Web site. (21)

Hypertext Markup Language (HTML) A system for tagging a document so it can be published on the World Wide Web. (21)

Input cell A cell referenced in the data table formula and varied to calculate the data table results. (21)

Interest The amount paid to the lender as profit at a set rate. (12)

Internal reference A reference to a cell, cell range, or defined name in another worksheet within the same workbook. (15)

Label Text that is excluded from calculations and that can include any character. (2)

Landscape orientation Horizontal page orientation, which is represented by 11″ x 8½″. (4)

Legend A guide that explains the symbols, patterns, or colors used to differentiate data series. (17)

Line break A method to force the insertion point to the next line down within a cell. (8)

List A series of worksheet rows that contain data. (19)

List range The area containing the database, which includes the field names and all records. (20)

Logical values The values TRUE and FALSE, which are the results of formulas that use comparison operators such as = or >. (10)

Mixed cell reference A formula cell address in which part of the address has an absolute cell reference and the other part of the address remains relative. Examples: $A1 and B$1. (11)

Nested functions A function that contains another function as an argument. (10)

Normal style The default style for a workbook.(9)

One-variable data table A table that calculates a formula containing one variable. (21)

Order of precedence The preset order in which mathematical operations in a formula are performed. (2)

Page orientation The vertical or horizontal direction in which you can print worksheets. (4)

Panes Multiple sections that you split worksheets into so you can see row and column labels as you enter data or formulas. (4)

Pivot table A table that you use to arrange the data in a database in different ways by rearranging rows and columns. (21)

Plot area The rectangular area bounded by the two axes; it includes all axes and data points. (17)

Point size A measure of type size, with 72 points equaling one inch. (9)

Portrait orientation Vertical page orientation, which is represented by 8½″ x 11″. (4)

Precision as displayed An option that stores numbers as the rounded values that appear on the screen. (8)

Principal The portion of a loan that represents the amount borrowed or the present value. (12)

Print area The specific range of cells you want to print. (4)

Range Any group of cells specified to be acted upon by a command. (2)

Range name The name you give a cell or range of cells. (6)

Record A group of fields that comprise one complete set of data in a database, arranged in a single row. (19)

Relative cell reference A cell address characteristic in which the cell reference adjusts to its new position when you copy it. (5)

Relative cell reference A formula cell address that specifies the address of the cell relative to the cell containing the formula. Example: A1. (11)

Result The value returned by a function. (10)

Scaling Enlarging or reducing the size of a worksheet's contents. (16)

ScreenTip Identifies elements on the screen. ScreenTips are available for dialog boxes, menu commands, and button names. (1)

Selection handles Small black squares appearing around a selected object that are used to resize the object. (17)

Serial number Numbers arranged in order by rank. In Excel, dates are stored as serial numbers, ranging from 1 (for January 1, 1900) to 2,958,525 (December 31, 9999). (12)

Sort order The order in which Excel arranges records during a sort. (19)

Source range The area of the worksheet from which you copy or remove data. (5)

Source worksheet A worksheet that contains the data being used by other, dependent worksheets. (15)

Split bar The bar that splits the screen into panes. (4)

Split boxes The gray rectangular boxes that appear in the upper right corner of the document window above the vertical scroll arrow and at the far right of the horizontal scroll bar at the bottom of the document window. You use split bars to split a screen into multiple panes. (4)

Style A set of formatting instructions that you can apply to the cells of a worksheet. (9)

Target range The new location for data that you copy or move. (5)

Template Formatted model of a worksheet. (13)

Test data Simple numbers that are easy to calculate in your head which you enter into worksheets to test formula calculations. (4)

Tick mark A division mark along the category (x) and value (y) axes. (17)

Two-variable data table A table that calculates a formula containing two variables. (21)

Value axis The vertical (or y) axis against which data points are measured. (17)

Wildcard A symbol that stands for any combination of letters or numbers. (7)

Workbook An Excel worksheet or group of worksheets saved as a file. (1)

Worksheet The area in which text, numeric values, and formulas are entered. Worksheets contain a series of rows and columns. Worksheets are collected into workbooks, which can contain up to 255 worksheets. (1)

Zoom The option that changes the magnification of the display. (4)

Index

E

F

S

T

Photo Credits

Pages 4 & 9: Telegraph Color Library/FPG; Pages 5 & 231: Buss/FPG; Pages 6 & 393: Laird/FPG; Pages 7 & 469: Weber/FPG; Pages 7 & 533: Kahn/FPG